CRUSADE TEXTS
IN TRANSLATION

About the volume:

The 'Book of Deeds' is the first known autobiography by a Christian king. Its author was James I of Aragon (1213–76), known as 'The Conqueror', one of the great political figures of 13th-century Europe and a successful crusader. In his 'Deeds', James describes the turbulent years of his minority, the thrilling capture of Majorca, the methodical conquest of the kingdom of Valencia, the reconquest of the kingdom of Murcia after Castile had failed to hold it, and many of the important events of his reign. While crusade and conquest of Spanish territory from the Muslims and Christian–Muslim relations on the frontier are central features of the account, the 'Deeds' are also a treasure trove of information on the image, power and purpose of monarchy, loyalty and bad faith in the feudal order, the growth of national sentiment, and medieval military tactics. At the same time, the book presents a unique insight into the mind of a medieval ruler, the supreme example we possess of the fears and ambitions of a man at the very centre of events.

About the authors:

Dr Damian Smith is Batista i Roca fellow at the Universitat Pompeu Fabra in Barcelona, Spain, and currently writing a second book for Ashgate on Innocent III and the kingdom of Aragon.

Dr Helena Buffery is lecturer in Catalan and Spanish in the Department of Hispanic studies at University of Birmingham, UK.

The Book of Deeds of James I of Aragon

Titles in this series include:

Peter W. Edbury
The Conquest of Jerusalem and the Third Crusade
Sources in Translation
in paperback

Janet Shirley
The Song of the Cathar Wars
A History of the Albigensian Crusade
in paperback

Helen J. Nicholson
The Chronicle of the Third Crusade
The Itinerarium Peregrinorum et Gesta Regis Ricardi
in paperback

Thomas S. Asbridge and Susan B. Edgington
Walter the Chancellor's *The Antiochene Wars*
A Translation and Commentary

Janet Shirley
Crusader Syria in the Thirteenth Century
The *Rothelin* Continuation of the *History* of William of Tyre
with Part of the *Eracles* or *Acre* Text

Janet Shirley and Peter W. Edbury
Guillaume de Machaut
The Capture of Alexandria

D.S. Richards
The Rare and Excellent History of Saladin or
al-Nawadir al-Sultaniyya wa'l-Mahasin al-Yusufiyya
by Baha' al-Din Ibn Shaddad
in hardback and paperback

Thomas A. Fudge
The Crusade against Heretics in Bohemia, 1418–1437
Sources and Documents for the Hussite Crusades

and forthcoming

Paul Crawford
The 'Templar of Tyre'
Part III of the 'Deeds of the Cypriots'

The Book of Deeds
of James I of Aragon

A Translation of the Medieval Catalan *Llibre dels Fets*

DAMIAN SMITH
Universitat Pompeu Fabra, Barcelona, Spain
University of Birmingham, UK

HELENA BUFFERY
University of Birmingham, UK

ASHGATE

Published by
Ashgate Publishing Limited
Gower House
Croft Road
Aldershot
Hampshire GU11 3HR
England

Ashgate Publishing Company
Suite 420
101 Cherry Street
Burlington, VT 05401-4405
USA

Ashgate website: http://www.ashgate.com

British Library Cataloguing in Publication Data
James, I, King of Aragon, 1208-1276
  The book of deeds of James I of Aragon. - (Crusade
  texts in translation)
  1. James, I, King of Aragon, 1208-1276 2. Aragon (Spain) -
  History - James I, 1213-1276 - Early works to 1800
  I. Title II. Smith, Damian III. Buffery, Helena
  946.5'502'092

Library of Congress Cataloging-in-Publication Data
James I, King of Aragon, 1208-1276.
  [Llibre dels fets. English]
  The Book of deeds of James I of Aragon : a translation of the medieval Catalan Llibre dels fets / Damian J. Smith, Helena Buffery.
       p. cm. -- (Crusade texts in translation ; 10)
  Includes bibliographical references and index.
  ISBN 0-7546-0359-8 (alk. paper)
     1. Aragon (Spain)--History--James I, 1213-1276. I. Smith, Damian. II. Buffery, Helena. III. Title. IV. Series.

DP129 .J3513 2002
946.5502'092--dc21

l005034768

2002027916

ISBN 0 7546 0359 8

Printed and bound in Great Britain by MPG Books Ltd, Bodmin, Cornwall

Contents

Acknowledgements

The translation of the *Llibre* was undertaken very much as a collaborative venture. We were conscious of the superhuman effort of John Forster in preparing the first English translation, without the support on which we were able to count. In preparing this edition, we have had recourse to numerous libraries and archives, although, in particular, we would like to dedicate this text to the memory of Professor Derek Lomax, whose legacy to the University of Birmingham has made its library an excellent resource for research into Medieval Iberia. We must also thank Father Robert Ignatius Burns for his encouragement of the project. We only hope that our version will reflect at least some of the value of his extensive research into the reign of King James I.

Part of the research that went into this book was undertaken with funding from the Batista i Roca scholarships of the Generalitat de Catalunya. We would also like to thank all the Department of Hispanic Studies at the University of Birmingham for their support, and especially the University of Vic, at which we were able to run workshops on parts of the text in the early stages of the translation process. We must also thank Dr Victor Farias at the Universitat Pompeu Fabra in Barcelona, Dr Francisco Núñez, of the same university, who prepared the maps that illustrate the text, and Daniel Figuerola who kindly transported many books from Birmingham to Barcelona.

James's Book is packed with references to the culture, beliefs, geography and history of Medieval Europe, and specialist knowledge was required for the translation of many sections. We are indebted to Dr Aengus Ward and Dr Patrick Quinn for advice on the references to thirteenth-century Castile and Navarre which appear in the text; to Dr Julian Whicker and Wilf Buffery for their insights into military and nautical references; and to Dr Andrew Dowling and Graham Pollock for their thoughts on translation problems and long discussions about the Book. We especially acknowledge Dr Josep Maria Pujol Sanmartin, for his wide-ranging suggestions about the structure and layout of our edition.

Dr Buffery would especially like to thank Dr Liam O'Toole for his invaluable help in the construction of this text, and Dr Smith thanks Professor Bernard Hamilton for his advice after reading through the various drafts and Dr John Smedley and his team at Ashgate, who have patiently directed the final stages of the work.

List of Abbreviations

Alicante   *Alicante y su territorio en la época de Jaime I de Aragón*, ed. José Martínez Ortiz, Alicante, 1993.

CDCZ   *Colección diplomática del Concejo de Zaragoza I. 1119– 1276; II, 1276–1285*, ed. Ángel Canellas López, Zaragoza, 1972–5.

CDI   *Colección de documentos inéditos del archivo general de la Corona de Aragón*, ed. P. de Bofarull y Mascaró et al., 42 vols., Barcelona, 1847–1973.

CHCA   *Congreso de Historia de la Corona de Aragón.*

Desclot   *Crònica de Bernat Desclot*, ed. Miquel Coll i Alentorn, Barcelona: Edicions 62, 1999.

Diplomatarium   *Diplomatarium of the Crusader-Kingdom of Valencia: The Registered Charters of Its Conqueror, Jaume I, 1257–1276*, ed. Robert Burns, 2 vols. to date, Princeton: Princeton University Press, 1985.

DPI   *La documentación pontificia de Inocencio IV (1243–1254)*, ed. A. Quintana Prieto, 2 vols., Rome, 1987.

G   *The Chronicle of James I, King of Aragon, surnamed the Conqueror*, translated by John Forster, with an historical introduction, notes, appendix, glossary, and general index by Pascual de Gayangos, 2 vols., London: Chapman and Hall, 1883.

H   *Documentos de Jaime I de Aragón*, ed. Ambrosio Huici and Maria Cabanes, 5 vols., Valencia-Zaragoza, 1976–82.

M   Miret, Joaquim, *Itinerari de Jaume I "El Conqueridor"*, Barcelona, 1918.

Marichalar   *Colección diplomática del rey Don Sancho VII (el fuerte) de Navarra*, ed. Carlos Marichalar, Pamplona, 1934.

MDH   *La documentación pontificia de Honorio III (1216–1227)*, ed. Demetrio Mansilla, Rome, 1965.

MDI   *La documentación pontificia hasta Inocencio III (965–1216)*, ed. Demetrio Mansilla, Rome, 1955.

Muntaner   *Crònica de Ramon Muntaner*, ed. Vicent Josep Escartí, 2 vols., Valencia: Institució Alfons el Magnànim, 1999.

P   *Llibre dels Fets*, trans. Josep Pujol, Barcelona: Teide, 1994.

RHGF   *Recueil des historiens des Gaules et de la France*, eds. M. Bouquet and L. Delisle, 25 vols., Paris, 1869–1904.

S   *Les quatre grans cròniques*, ed. Ferran Soldevila, Barcelona: Editorial Selecta, 1971.

Map 1   Aragon

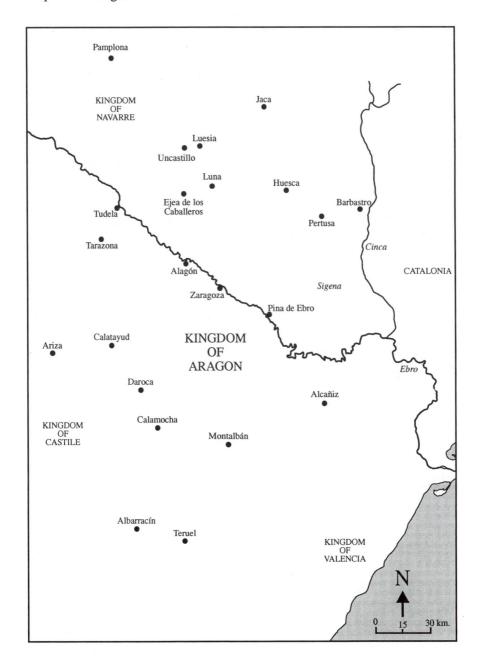

Pamplona

KINGDOM
OF
NAVARRE

Jaca

Luesia
Uncastillo

Luna

Huesca

Ejea de los
Caballeros

Barbastro

Tudela

Pertusa

Tarazona

Cinca

CATALONIA

Alagón

Sigena

Zaragoza

Pina de Ebro

Calatayud

KINGDOM
OF
ARAGON

Ariza

Ebro

Daroca

Alcañiz

Calamocha

KINGDOM
OF
CASTILE

Montalbán

Albarracín

Teruel

KINGDOM
OF
VALENCIA

N

0   15   30 km.

Map 2   Catalonia

Montpellier

Béziers

Carcassonne

Narbonne

Perpignan

KINGDOM
OF
ARAGON

La Seu
d'Urgell

Solsona

Vic

Girona

Tamarite
de Litera

Segre

Monzón

Agramunt

Balaguer

CATALONIA

Cervera

Cinca

Lleida

Montblanc

Villafranca
del Penedés

Barcelona

Ebro

Salou

Cambrils

Tarragona

Tortosa

N

Amposta

0   15   30 km.

VALENCIA

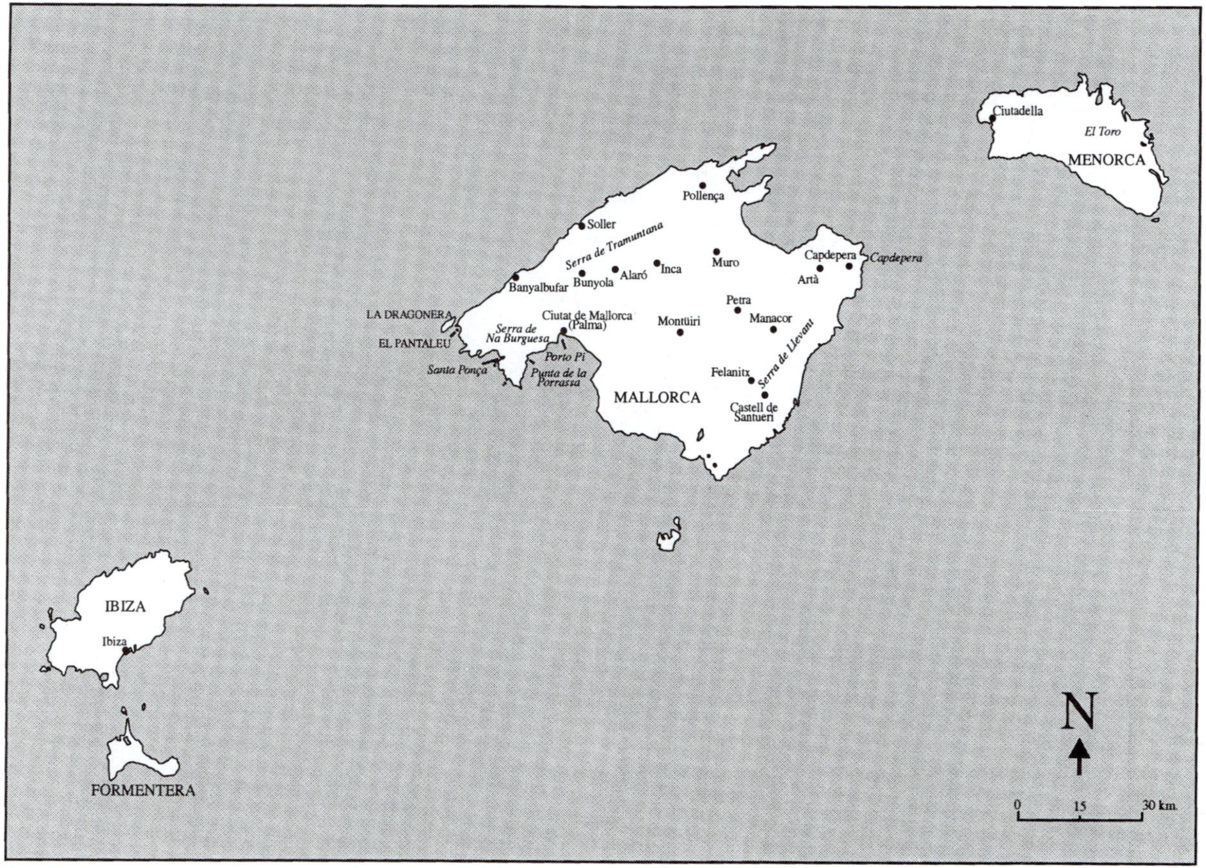

Map 3   The Balearics

Map 4   Valencia

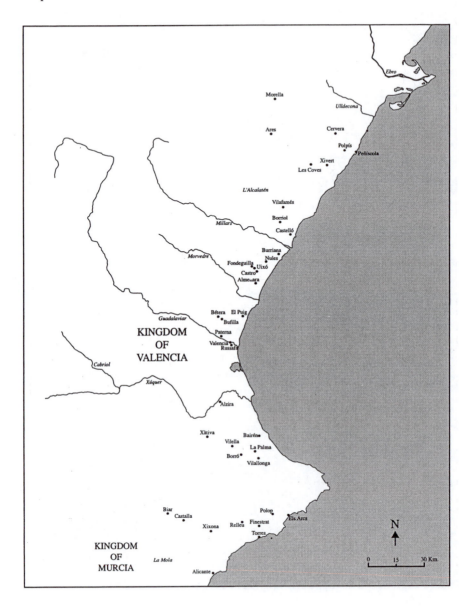

Map 5   Murcia

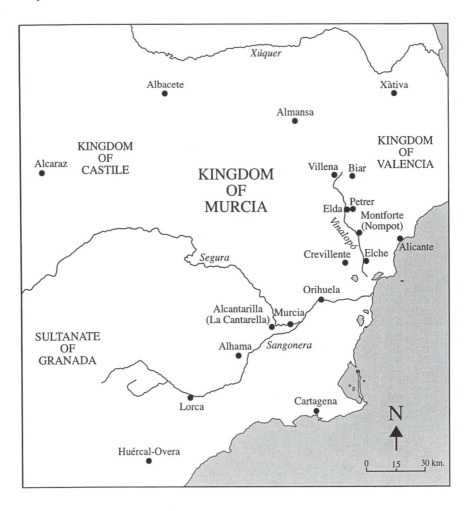

Xúquer

Albacete

Xàtiva

Almansa

KINGDOM
OF
CASTILE

Alcaraz

KINGDOM
OF
MURCIA

KINGDOM
OF
VALENCIA

Villena   Biar

Petrer

Elda   Montforte
(Nompot)

Vinalopó

Segura

Crevillente   Elche   Alicante

Orihuela

Alcantarilla
(La Cantarella)   Murcia

SULTANATE
OF
GRANADA

Alhama   *Sangonera*

Lorca

Cartagena

Huércal-Overa

N

0   15   30 km.

Introduction

In 1134,[1] a few weeks after being defeated at the battle of Fraga, Alfonso I of Aragon and Navarre died. Alfonso, known as "the Battler", had been a formidable Christian warrior, imbued with the crusading spirit. He had greatly expanded his kingdom by conquests against the Moors. His exploits had helped ensure that the Church would view the conquest of Spain as little less pressing a task than the conquest of the Holy Land.

But Alfonso had left no heir. In a will of 1131, he had taken the unusual step of bequeathing his kingdom to the military orders of the Temple and the Hospital and the canons of the order of the Holy Sepulchre. The move was certainly that of a crusading king but it was also almost certainly calculated to prevent the ruler of Castile, Alfonso VII, from obtaining his kingdom. The papacy wished to uphold the will, while for the nobles of Aragon that was wholly unacceptable. They demanded a king and the continuation of the dynasty. Alfonso had a brother, Ramiro, and Ramiro was a monk, but, in spite of this, they made him their king. Ramiro took as his wife Agnes of Aquitaine, while Navarre seceded from the union and elected its own ruler. Ramiro and Agnes then produced a child, Petronilla, the name of St Peter's disciple perhaps being chosen by way of apology to the papacy for the whole extraordinarily uncanonical business. Ramiro happily returned to his monastery, while Petronilla was betrothed to Ramon Berenguer IV, Count of Barcelona,[2] who ruled over a loose confederation of counties in Catalonia. The military orders were richly compensated for their lost inheritance and the papacy accepted the done deed. In 1148–9, Ramon Berenguer undertook the important conquests of Tortosa and Lleida, opening up the path to the kingdom of Valencia. (The conquests were a part of the Second Crusade, which, in spite of these very notable successes, is generally viewed as a failure.) It was the prelude to Ramon's marriage in 1150 to Petronilla, who was then of canonical

---

[1]Detailed accounts of the general history of this period are provided by Thomas Bisson, *The Medieval Crown of Aragon*, Oxford: Clarendon Press, 1986; David Abulafia, *The Western Mediterranean Kingdoms 1200–1500*, Longman, 1997; Josep Salrach, *El procés de feudalització (segles III–XII)*, Barcelona: Edicions 62, 1998; Carme Batlle, *L'expansió baixmedieval (segles XIII–XV)*, Barcelona: Edicions 62, 1999; Ángel Canellas López, *Aragón en su historia,* Zaragoza: Caja de Ahorros de la Inmaculada, 1980.

[2]The best account of Ramon's reign remains Ferran Soldevila, *Ramon Berenguer IV el Sant*, Barcelona: Barcino, 1955.

age to marry. Thus was born the union that we tend to call the Crown of Aragon.

Aragonese and Catalans, two peoples with different landscapes and languages, different laws, customs, and institutions, different economic prospects and political ambitions, were tied together in political union. Ramon Berenguer, who never took the title king, was careful to preserve that union. The careful balancing act he performed with regard to Aragonese and Catalonian interests was the policy to be adopted by his successors. Ramon died in 1162, when his heir, Alfonso, was just five years old. For many years Alfonso was supervised by advisers from both his realms and his centre of government was at Lleida, which acted as a bridge between his two lands. Alfonso,[3] a noted troubadour, proved himself a fine administrator (it was during his reign that the *Liber Feudorum Maior*[4] was compiled to secure the ruler's rights to castles in Catalonia and other lands). Alfonso greatly increased the influence of the crown in the south of France but he was frustrated in his attempts at conquest in Valencia and Murcia by the strength of the Almohads, who had invaded the Peninsula in 1157. Such was Alfonso's inability to make any real headway that in the 1170s a pretender arose, claiming to be Alfonso the Battler. The incident of the pseudo-Alfonso reflected widespread baronial discontent with the lack of military action and territorial gain. To strengthen his sacral authority, Alfonso drew himself into an ever closer alliance with the church in Aragon and the papacy. In his last days, with the encouragement of Pope Celestine III, a great expert in the affairs of the Iberian Peninsula, he desperately sought to unite Christian Spain in a crusade against the Almohads, after the king of Castile, Alfonso VIII, had been humiliated at the battle of Alarcos in 1195.

Alfonso's son, Peter II of Aragon,[5] was perhaps the most charismatic ruler of the dynasty. Persuasive, energetic and headstrong, often Peter's ambitions outweighed his means. When, in 1204, a projected crusade to the Balearics proved impractical, the king then planned an expedition to the Holy Land and a marriage to the heiress of Jerusalem, Marie de Montferrat (although he was already married to Marie of Montpellier). Yet Peter did have considerable success in his Valencian campaign of 1210, and, most importantly of all, in 1212, participated in the Christian coalition that defeated the Almohads at Las

---

[3] For his reign, see Jordi Ventura, *Alfons el cast, el primer comte-rei*, Barcelona: Aedos, 1961.

[4] *Liber Feudorum Maior*, ed. Francisco Miquel Rosell, 2 vols, Barcelona, 1945–7.

[5] There is no general history of Peter's reign. Jordi Ventura, *Pere el Catòlic i Simó de Montfort*, Barcelona: Aedos, 1960, deals with the Albigensian crusade and Martín Alvira, *El Jueves de Muret: 12 de septiembre 1213*, Barcelona: Universitat de Barcelona, 2002, with the events surrounding his death. Enric Bagué's study 'Pere el Catòlic' in *Els primers comtes-reis: Ramon Berenguer IV, Alfons el Cast, Pere el Catòlic*, ed. Percy Schramm, Barcelona: Vicens Vives, 1960, is a rigorous synthesis.

Navas de Tolosa and then led the assault that saw the Christians take the city of Úbeda, a psychological blow from which the Almohads never recovered. At home, prior to Las Navas, Peter struggled to appease his barons and the church. He was profligate; the expenses of his court coupled with costly ventures such as his coronation by Pope Innocent III at Rome in 1204 left his kingdom in a parlous financial state. Though himself a persecutor of heretics, he was drawn into the Albigensian crusade on the side of the southern French lords against the crusade and, in September 1213, was defeated and killed in the battle of Muret when he underestimated his opponent, Simon de Montfort, and perhaps overestimated the loyalty of his Languedocian vassals.

After Muret, Peter's heir, James,[6] five years old and an orphan, was in the hands of Montfort. His kingdom was facing financial collapse. Factions were formed throughout his lands as his relatives contended for power or the throne itself. James survived through the loyalty of many of the nobles, the efforts of Pope Innocent III and his legate, Cardinal Peter of Benevento, and through sound administration and fiscal management, where Templars and Jews played a notable role. Brought up at the forbidding Templar fortress at Monzón, the years of his minority saw almost constant squabbles between the higher nobles who jockeyed for position and influence. James's first attempt to establish his own authority, a campaign against the Muslim castle at Peníscola in 1225 ended in humiliating failure. His next campaigns were against the nobles in Aragon, with whom he came to terms in 1227, and the count of Urgell, whose power he diminished in 1228. By then James already had his heart set on the conquest of Majorca.[7] Backed by papal support, in 1229, between September and December, the king led a dramatic campaign that captured the capital. Militarily, the attack contained many errors of judgement, and two of Catalonia's great lords, Guillem and Ramon de Montcada, fell at the battle of Porto Pí when there was a lack of coordination between the vanguard and the rest of the men. But the brilliance of the venture is without question. In the following years the rest of the island was reduced, while Minorca submitted to a tribute-paying status in 1231 and Ibiza was conquered in 1235, with forces led by the archbishop-elect of Tarragona. Opportunities in León and Navarre failed to capture James's attention since he focused himself on the conquest of the kingdom of Valencia. This was a campaign of a very different nature to that

---

[6]James's early reign is covered in Ferran Soldevila, *Els primers temps de Jaume I*, Barcelona: Institut d'Estudis Catalans, 1968, and much of the later part by the same author's *Pere el Gran*, 2 vols, Barcelona: Institut d'Estudis Catalans, 1995. He has been the subject of two congresses of the history of the crown of Aragon, the first in 1908 (I *CHCA*, 2 vols, (1909–13)) and the second in 1976 (X *CHCA*, 3 vols, (1978–82)).

[7]See Àlvar Santamaria, 'La expansión político-militar de la Corona de Aragón bajo la dirección de Jaime I', X *CHCA* (1979), 3, pp. 91–146.

in the Balearics.[8] In Valencia, there was not simply a central Muslim authority to defeat. The disintegration of Almohad power meant there were many rulers of many castles and James had to proceed slowly and patiently, often by tactful negotiation, sometimes by simple bribery, taking major castles and thus forcing the lesser to surrender, often ravaging crops and taking cattle in order to starve the Muslim population or executing the defenders of one captured fortress as an example to the others. The conquest can be divided into four essential stages. In the first stage (1231–5), the northern zone of the kingdom was conquered, the king following in the wake of independent action by the Aragonese barons. James's determined capture of Borriana was the key to the continuation of the conquest. In the second stage (1236–8), backed by strong support from Pope Gregory IX, the region of Valencia and then Valencia itself were taken after help for the Muslim population from the sultan of Tunis proved to no avail. In the third stage (1239–46) the lands to the south of the River Xúquer were captured and, once the formidable castle of Xàtiva (1244) was conditionally surrendered, it was almost inevitable that the entire kingdom would soon be in James's hands. But there was much spirited resistance from individual Muslim rulers. In a fourth stage (1247–58), James was forced to spend much time subduing serious rebellions. The most notable of the Muslim leaders was al-Azraq.

The victories in Majorca and Valencia offset the king's failure to halt the advance of Capetian influence in the south of France. Though the king, born in Montpellier, took a deep interest in the affairs of the region and at least three times broke off from the campaign against the Moors to lend his support to the southern French lords, the 1240s saw Toulouse pass to Alphonse of Poitiers and Provence to Charles of Anjou. Béarn fell to Foix, and James's lack of desire to take decisive action meant that Navarre remained with the counts of Champagne. In May 1258, at the treaty of Corbeil, James renounced almost all his rights and claims in the Midi while Louis IX did little more than renounce rights in Catalonia which had long been a dead letter. Only with the marriage in 1262 of James's son, Prince Peter, to Constance of Hohenstaufen, heiress of Sicily, did the king inflict a blow.

James failed to cut off France's path to the Mediterranean, whereas in spite of differences over Navarre and the definition of their respective conquest zones in the south, he generally supported Castile and especially his son-in-law Alfonso X. In 1264 the Castilians were seriously troubled by a North African

---

[8]Though many aspects of the chronology of the Valencian campaigns remain very confused, useful accounts are provided by Pedro López Elum, *La conquista y repoblación Valenciana durante el reinado de Jaime I*, Valencia 1995, and Antonio Ubieto Arteta, *Orígenes del reino de Valencia. Cuestiones cronológicas sobre su reconquista*, Valencia: Anubar 1975. An excellent study of post-conquest Valencia is Robert I. Burns, *The Crusader Kingdom of Valencia: Reconstruction of a Thirteenth-Century Frontier*, 2 vols, Cambridge Mass: Harvard University Press, 1967.

invasion supported by much of Muslim Spain, which encouraged an uprising in the kingdom of Murcia, tributary of Castile. James took prompt and decisive action to quash that revolt,[9] though only receiving hesitant support from the Catalans and practically none at all from the Aragonese nobles who remained in a permanent state of disgruntlement because of their perceived secondary status. War with the nobles preceded the victory over Murcia, which came with the taking of the capital in January 1266 (though Prince Peter had paved the way in the previous year with damaging raids).

There were few glories after Murcia. An expedition to the Holy Land in 1269 was a failure even for the section of the fleet that arrived, and more so for the king who turned back due to bad weather and, it was rumoured, because he could not bear to be parted from his mistress. Similarly, in 1274, at the council of Lyons, the king's enthusiasm for another crusade to the East did not amount to giving any practical help. Continued support for Castile and tax demands led to further baronial revolts in the 1270s. These were put down by Prince Peter who was thus reconciled with his father after many squabbles, which had first arisen over James's desire to divide his realms between his different sons (though by this time only Princes Peter and James were left of the legitimate ones). In James's final days a renewed Muslim attack, led by al-Azraq, occupied his attentions and those of his sons, and when he died in July 1276 the kingdom of Valencia, which he had laboured so long to conquer, appeared as insecure as ever.

James's reign is notable for (among other things) advances in administrative practice, the influx of Roman law, the increasing sophistication in methods of taxation, the rise (and decline) of parliament, the expansion of Mediterranean trade and shipbuilding, and the beginnings of the Dominicans, Franciscans and Mercedarians. Of course, not all progress was due to James (indeed, the reduction in the number of parliamentary assemblies was his own doing) but in the field of literature we are especially indebted to him. His reign saw the production of the remarkable work that we now usually call the *Llibre dels Fets* or "Book of Deeds", an account in the first person plural (with occasional lapses into the first person singular, usually during direct speech) of James's major military campaigns and some selected political events of his reign. The work that is translated here was produced in Catalan (and only later translated into Latin)[10] and is one of the great works of medieval Catalan literature. It is also an historical record without parallel. For the author of the book was the king.

---

[9]Two good accounts are Juan Torres Fontes, *La Reconquista de Murcia en 1266 por Jaime I de Aragón*, Murcia 1966, and Josep-David Garrido, *Jaume I i el regne de Múrcia*, Barcelona: Rafael Dalmau, 1997.

[10]In 1313, by the Dominican friar Pere Marsili. The best edition is *La crónica latina de Jaime I: edición crítica, estudio preliminar e índices*, ed. Maria de los Desamparados Martínez San Pedro, Almería: Gráficas Ortiz, 1984.

Nobody but James himself could be the author of this work. The arguments against another possible author are strong[11] (Who else could the author be? Why would they have written it? Why would they have written as if they were the king himself? Who would have had sufficient knowledge of the details of James's life? Who would have had the imagination?), but the arguments in favour of James are equally strong. There is the detailed knowledge of all the king's campaigns and the political events of the king's adult life 'dovetailing exactly with the mentality in much of the king's independent documentation'.[12] Events are seen almost entirely from what would have been James's perspective. So, in the Majorca campaign we read of the death of the Montcadas at the battle of Porto Pí only after the battle is over, when James receives news of their deaths, and there is no account of their heroic performance in the battle, since James did not see it.[13] There is a justification of the actions of the king, which nobody but the king need justify.[14] Thus, James labours much on the embarrassing failure of his expedition to the Holy Land in 1269–70, which another author would have passed over quickly as uneventful and irrelevant.[15] The *Llibre* reveals feelings that only the king could have felt. There is an adoration of James's mother, Marie of Montpellier, and an ambivalent attitude to his father, Peter II (hero of Las Navas, villain at Muret, and bad husband to Marie) which another author, even one trained in psychology, would not capture.[16] There are many intimate memories of events (for instance, the indignation of his first wife at James's adopted plan for her escape from the Aragonese nobles; a mother swallow who had nested on James's tent; a night spent sweating at Puig when his knights were ready to abandon him and the Valencia campaign).[17] Throughout the text there is an easy familiarity with the rulers and major figures of James's reign.

The purpose of the king in composing the *Llibre* was, as he says,[18] so that other kings would see what he had been able to achieve with God's help. The kings in question were most likely to be James's successors (and were – the

---

[11]The argument is well made by Ferran Soldevila in his preface to the *Llibre* (*Les quatre grans cròniques*, Barcelona: Selecta, 1971, pp. 36–7).

[12]Robert Burns, 'The Spiritual Life of James I the Conqueror, King of Aragon-Catalonia, 1208–1276: Portrait and self-portrait', X *CHCA*, 1, p. 328.

[13]Chs. 63–5; Stefano Asperti, 'Il re e la storia: Proposte per una nuova lettura del "Libre dels feyts" di Jaume I', *Romanistische Zeitschrift für Literaturgeschichte*, 3 (1984), p. 276.

[14]Martí de Riquer, *Història de la literatura catalana*, 3 vols, Barcelona: Ariel, 1964, 1, p. 402.

[15]Chs. 476–93.

[16]Chs. 6–7.

[17]Chs. 23 (wife), 215 (swallow) , 237 (Puig).

[18]Ch. 1.

book had no wide distribution outside the family circle).[19] The work is, then, something of a guidebook for how to rule,[20] and no doubt inserts some political events (such as agreements with Navarre and disputes with Urgell) because they were problems James expected his successors would have to deal with and where the crown had claims to defend. The *Llibre* then functions as propaganda, education, and legitimization. The work was probably undertaken at various times in the king's reign. The initial impetus was perhaps provided in the 1230s by demands for the king's personal account of the conquest of Majorca,[21] of which the troubadours sang, and no doubt stories were already being told with additions by those who had taken part in it. The stories of the Valencian campaign were probably told in the 1240s and early 1250s and then, after a long gap, James returned to his stories towards the very end of his life. There is a long gap between 1245 and 1264 when James relates nothing except the campaign against al-Azraq and then only briefly.

The format the king chose owed something to the troubadours, something to Christian *Gestes*, and perhaps a little to a consciousness of the Arab world where rulers customarily set down what they had been able to achieve thanks to divine assistance. The majority of the participants in the Majorca campaign were Catalans and James chose Catalan as the language for his work. On some occasions James inserts words from other languages to indicate that the speaker is talking a language other than Catalan.[22] James most probably narrated his stories[23] (for the *Llibre* is a succession of stories rather than a chronicle) in diverse sessions to knights of his household[24] while a scribe wrote everything down in shorthand. James expected the work to be read out loud.[25] As James's court was itinerant, it is quite possible that sometimes he had many documents to hand which could aid his memory, and at other times very few.

James's work, while a narrative treasure in a land that had possessed few,[26] can only be used with extreme caution for the reconstruction of the history of his reign. The accounts of the king's military campaigns are invaluable but

---

[19]Josep Pujol, 'The *Llibre del rei En Jaume*: A matter of style', *Historical Literature in Medieval Iberia*, ed. Alan Deyermond, London: Department of Hispanic studies, Queen Mary and Westfield college, 1996, pp. 35–7.

[20]Lola Badia, 'Llegir el Libre del Rei Jaume', *Serra d'Or*, 385 (1992), p. 55; *Llibre dels Fets de Jaume I*, trans. Antoni Ferrando and Vicent Josep Escartí, Barcelona: Editorial Afers, 1995, pp. 9–10.

[21]Miquel Coll, 'Llibre dels Feits', *Gran Enciclopèdia Catalana*, 14 (1987), p. 71.

[22]Antonio Badia, *Coherència i arbitrarietat de la substitució lingüística dins la "Crònica" de Jaume I*, Barcelona: Institut d'Estudis Catalans, 1987.

[23]Pujol, 'Llibre del Rei', pp. 44–7; Joaquim Molas, *Diccionari de la literatura catalana*, Barcelona: Edicions 62, 1979, pp. 339–40.

[24]Ch. 16; Stefano Asperti, 'Indagini sull' "Llibre dels Feyts" di Jaume I: Dall'originale all'archetipo', *Romanistisches Jahrbuch*, 33 (1982), p. 271.

[25]Ch. 69.

[26]Thomas Bisson, 'Unheroed Pasts: History and Commemoration in South Frankland before the Albigensian Crusades', *Speculum*, 65 (1990), pp. 281–308.

James sometimes wrote of things of which he had little knowledge. For instance, his account of the time before he was born and of his earliest years is, at times, not surprisingly, wildly inaccurate.[27] His grandfather Alfonso had not attempted to marry a Byzantine princess; his father, Peter II, had not given James for Simon de Montfort to raise because he trusted Montfort so much; his great-uncle Count Sancho made little or no attempt to snatch the throne after Peter II's death.[28] At times, James's account is subject to paranoia. He sees all the troubles of his minority in terms of the treachery of the nobles towards him, whereas, in reality, they had little occasion for grievance against him but rather tended to fight against each other. James also leaves out events with which he was uncomfortable. So the failed siege of Peníscola passes without a mention, as does the treaty of Corbeil. Indeed, the king's interventions in the Midi receive barely any mention throughout. James rarely mentions his wives and children (though there was plenty of scope) or matrimonial politics, and rarely any events that had caused scandal, such as when he had been excommunicated for chopping out part of the bishop of Girona's tongue (he had revealed the king's secrets). There was, of course, reason to omit all this since none of it demonstrated how God had successfully guided James in his deeds, but that is of little help to the historian. James often gives us a partial perspective of events. Actions in the Majorcan, Valencian, and Murcian campaigns when James was not present tend to receive much less attention than those where he was present. On some occasions the king is downright deceitful. The impression he leaves of having gained victory over the Aragonese nobles in the 1220s and in the 1260s leaves little trace of the important concessions he was forced to make to them on both occasions. When James tells his story it can be pure propaganda. His accounts of his dealings with Sancho of Navarre and in Urgell are surely designed to help strengthen future claims there.[29] He places all the blame on Sancho for having failed to fulfil a treaty of mutual adoption, which would eventually have given James Navarre, when it was as much the hesitancy of James himself that spoilt the deal. This is not to say that we should ignore James. An account from one great king of his negotiations with another great king cannot be tossed aside lightly. It is to say that while James often tells the truth, as he sees it, he cannot tell us the whole truth and, at times, tells us anything but the truth. The *Llibre* must be read alongside other accounts of the period, where they survive, and, above all, with reference to the rich archival sources.[30]

---

[27]Donald Kagay, 'The Line between Memoir and History: James I of Aragon and the *Llibre del Feyts*', *Mediterranean Historical Review*, 11 (1996), pp. 169–70.

[28]Chs. 2 (Alfonso), 8 (Montfort), 11 (Sancho).

[29]Chs. 138–52 (Navarre), 34–46 (Urgell).

[30]On which, see Lawrence McCrank, 'Documenting Reconquest and reform: the growth of archives in the Medieval Crown of Aragon', *The American Archivist*, 56 (1993), pp. 256–318.

While the king is a partial commentator, he tells us much of his times and of himself. 'No king in history ever revealed himself better to prosperity'.[31] Though we know the king was a serial adulterer, vindictive to his children, often cruel to his enemies, and generally not overly endowed with the virtue of humility, there is little doubt that James believed that he was guided by God in his actions. It was the world of Augustine. History was a plan conceived by God and James was a part of that plan.[32] It is through God's will that James is born, protected in the cradle, and defeats the opponents of his youth. It is with God's guidance that James reaches Majorca though storm clouds gather against him and it is God who gives James that kingdom. It is God who prevents the arrow that strikes James at the siege of Valencia penetrating more deeply into the king's forehead, and it is God who wills that James conquers the city. At the siege of Murcia, James is so confident that God will forgive him if he takes the city that he forgoes absolution from his confessor for the adulterous, incestuous relationship he had entered into with one of the noblewomen.[33] The king was sacralized by divine power and his was a divine commission in which he considered he was aided by Our Lady (to whom he clearly had a special devotion), and which most certainly was supported by churchmen whose military and economic backing pervades the text.

In the *Llibre*, James wishes to give to his successors his vision of the power and purpose of monarchy. James is a military leader involved in epic knightly deeds, leading his people in military conflict and defending the land against encroachments from outside (hence the harsh treatment given to the Castilians when they encroached on James's conquest zone) or internal foes (so the almost constant battles against the nobles). It is also for the king to dispense justice, especially when a person has no other recourse (as with Aurembiaix of Urgell) or when there is a serious threat to the stability of the realm (the forging of coins at Tarazona). It is for the king to persuade the nobles and the church to give taxes for military enterprises (a matter in which James's efforts were rarely outweighed by his success) and not to give away land wastefully (as James's father had done).[34] It is the king's role to conduct political negotiations, as with Sancho of Navarre or Alfonso X of Castile. Most importantly, the king must maintain the divinely ordained order of society. As

---

[31]Bisson, *Medieval Crown*, p. 84.

[32]Joan Pau Rubiés and Josep Salrach, 'Entorn de la mentalitat i la ideologia del bloc de poder feudal a través de la historiografia medieval fins a les quatre grans cròniques', *La formació i expansió del feudalisme català. Actes del col·loqui organitzat pel Col·legi Universitari de Girona (8–11 de gener de 1985)*, ed. Jaume Portella, Girona: Estudi General, 1985–6.

[33]Chs. 48 (wills James's birth), 5 (protects cradle), 29 (nobles), 56–58 (storm), 105 (gives Majorca), 266 (arrow), 282 (Valencia), 426 (confessor).

[34]Chs. 339–42 (Castilians), 34–7 (Aurembiaix), 466–71 (Tarazona coins), 11 (wasteful father).

James advises Alfonso, the king must keep the loyalty of all his subjects.[35]
Above all, the king should keep the Church, the poor and the cities on his side
because the knights are treacherous. The towns, he comments in his later years,
know just as much of war as the knights do.[36]

James loved his lands. He was struck by the beauty of Palma and Xàtiva.
When he captured Valencia and Murcia, he wept and kissed the ground.
"Aragon!" was the king's rallying cry when he pursued the rebel Pedro
Ahones. James spared the houses of some of those who had plotted against his
lordship in Montpellier, so as not to uglify the town. He is conscious of Spain.
Before the Murcian campaign, he calls on the Aragonese nobles to save Spain.
He left one session of the council of Lyons of 1274, triumphant, confident that
all Spain had been honoured by his performance. However, his greatest love
appears to have been reserved for Catalonia, which he considered the best
kingdom in Spain.[37] Catalan was the language he chose for his *Llibre* and this
Catalonian partiality, like that of the Latin chronicle the *Gesta Comitum
Barcinonensium*,[38] could have done little to unify so many different peoples.

There are, no doubt, a thousand and one other things that the reader will
find of interest in the king's book. It is a unique historical record. As much as it
can be categorized, it is an autobiography, and it is by a king who was a
formidable ruler by the standards of any age.

Damian Smith

---

[35]Ch. 498.

[36]Ch. 397.

[37]Chs. 67 (Palma), 318 (Xàtiva), 282 (Valencia), 443 (Murcia), 26 (Aragon), 304
(Montpellier), 392 (Spain and Murcia), 535 (Spain honoured), 392 (Catalonia).

[38]*Gesta Comitum Barcinonensium*, ed. Louis Barrau Dihigo and Jaume Massó Torrents,
Barcelona, 1925; Paul Freedman, 'Cowardice, Heroism and the Legendary Origins of
Catalonia', *Past and Present*, 121 (1988), pp. 3–28; Thomas Bisson, 'L'essor de la Catalogne:
identité, pouvoir et idéologie dans une société du xii siècle', *Annales*, 39 (1984), pp. 459–64.

Notes on the Translation

The importance of James's Book can be observed in the range of different manuscripts based upon his narrative account of his reign.[1] Whilst there is evidence that the text as he dictated it became an important reference work and heirloom for his descendants, the original manuscript has been lost. This gap has led to the development of numerous hypotheses about the nature of the original version, including attempts to argue for the existence of an epic poem based on the events recounted.[2] Marsili's Latin translation of 1313 is certainly the earliest surviving manuscript version of James's Book, and was commissioned by James II of Aragon as a way of bringing some order to his grandfather's accounts.[3] For a time it was thought that the earliest Catalan manuscripts derived from the Latin version. However, the many errors which were once thought to be mistranslations from the Latin, as well as the shifts in register that occur in the Marsili's text, and his occasional lapses from a third person narrative into the first person narrative that marks out the history as the memoirs of the king, are now considered to be certain indicators of the priority of a Catalan version, as copied in the manuscripts of 1343 and 1380.[4]

The six later manuscripts are all thought to derive from those of the fourteenth century, and are evidence of the continued relevance of the Book of the King. In particular, there is a strong tradition of transmission of the text in Valencia, and some experts argue for the priority of the Valencian and Occidental Catalan family of manuscripts.[5] However, the majority of philologists and historiographers continue to consider the 1343 manuscript of the monastery of Poblet to be the most closely related to a lost original, and nearly all printed editions of James's book of deeds or conquests have been based on Celestí Destorrents's copy.

---

[1] On the manuscript tradition, see, Stefano Asperti, 'La tradizione manoscritta del Libre dels Feyts', *Romanica Vulgaria*, 7 (1984), pp. 107-67.

[2] This view, held by Manel de Montoliu (*Les Quatre Grans Cròniques*, Barcelona: Alpha 1959) and Soldevila (S) has been convincingly refuted in recent years by *Josep* Pujol (*Sens i Cojuntures del llibre delRei en Jaume*, PHD thesis: University of Barcelona, Divisió dels Centres Universitaris del camp de Tarragona, 1991).

[3] Pujol, 'The Llibre del Rei', pp. 35-7.

[4] Asperti, 'Indagini', pp. 276-9.

[5] *Llibre dels fets de Jaume I*, trans. Antoni Ferrando and Vicent Josep Escartí, Barcelona 1995, pp. 18-26.

For our own translation we have referred mainly to Jordi Bruguera's transcription of the Poblet manuscript,[6] although we have consulted the Latin version and variant readings from other manuscripts in order to make our version as coherent and intelligible as possible. We have also consulted other modern editions of James's chronicle. In particular, the edition of Casacuberta,[7] which is accompanied by a parallel translation into modern Catalan, and Pujol's (P) edition of selected passages have proved invaluable in the production of a coherent translation. Furthermore, we have been able to consult the modern translation of the Valencia manuscript,[8] and Forster's nineteenth-century English translation[9].

Our first concern in translating the text has been to facilitate comprehension of a work that has for a long time remained inaccessible to any but the specialist reader. Notwithstanding the importance of James I for the history of the Catalan-speaking regions, and for the construction and projection of concepts of Catalan cultural identity and nationhood, the *Llibre dels Fets* has rarely been published in forms accessible to the majority of the Catalan-speaking population. Although the editions of Casacuberta and Soldevila (S), alongside the studies of Nicolau d'Olwer, Manel de Montoliu and later Riquer, recovered the text as a sign of the richness and variety of the Catalan linguistic heritage, it has remained a text that is rarely read except in fragments in the classroom. Where its relevance cannot be avoided is in Medieval Catalan Philology and in studies of the history of the Crown of Aragon, though even here its legacy has been a contested one, with questions raised over its origins, authorship, authenticity and chronology.

The version we have produced here is marked by the knowledge that the most of our readers are likely to be historians. Hence, where possible, we have sought to resolve textual ambiguities, even when they are the result of the deictic nature of oral narrative, or even evidence of the story-telling prowess of the king. Awareness of our target audience has also influenced other translation choices: the title of the book, the choice of register, the organization of the text, and the translation of names.

Our version is called The Book of Deeds by James I, not because this was the title chosen by the king, but because it is the name by which it is most widely known. Equally, where there are English versions of proper nouns, as in the case of kings, but also certain place-names, we have used them. In other cases, when we have been able to identify the name, we have generally translated all names whose origins lie in Catalonia, Valencia or the Balearic

---

[6]*Llibre dels Fets del rei en Jaume*, ed. Jordi Bruguera, Barcelona 1991, vol. 2.

[7]*Crònica de Jaume I*, ed. Josep Maria Casacuberta, 2 vols, Barcelona, 1926-64.

[8]*Llibre dels fets de Jaume I*, trans. Ferrando and Escartí (n. 6).

[9]*The Chronicle of James I, King of Aragon (1208-1276), surnamed the Conqueror*, London: Chapman and Hall, 1883.

Islands into the modern Catalan version, and all other names into the language of their region. Hence, for instance, the names of Aragonese nobles are given their Spanish spelling. Throughout the Catalan text the words En and Don are used interchangeably to refer to nobles. However, usage is not consistent, and for this reason, as well as to avoid confusion with modern Catalan use of 'en' as interchangeable with 'el' with any masculine proper name, we have removed all the ens from the English version. James often uses non-Catalan words to indicate when somebody is speaking a language other than Catalan but this is not an artistic device. Notes indicate the major occasions when this occurs.

Most problematically, we have kept the chapter divisions used in most editions because they are widely used for references by historians. However, we have made every effort to indicate in the layout of the text that these chapter divisions do not coincide with narrative units, and to organize the text into coherent narrative blocks.[10] Our overall division of the text into seven sections is intended to maximize the readability of the text and, at least until the end of part VI, responds to clearly demarked sequences in James's narrative. The final part is made up of a number of miscellaneous episodes, although these all reflect the aims and spirit of the early sections of the text.

It would have been impossible for us to produce a "Medieval English" version of James I's memoirs, thus this is, in the main, a target-oriented translation. Nonetheless, as far as possible we have tried to remain true to the flavour of the king's narrative. His use of the royal 'we' has been maintained as a sign of distinction in the text, as well as allowing us to reproduce the effect of the switches to first person singular which mark the *Llibre* out as being a text dictated by the king. We have also endeavoured to preserve the oral nature of the text, the constant shifts between direct and indirect speech, the asides and the references to its mode of composition.

As a transcription of a number of oral narratives, the Book of Deeds has many features that make it an engaging and enjoyable read. Its directness and simplicity of style lend an immediate and authentic quality to the dramatization of events and dialogues, and we are able to witness the king as a competent and chameleonic communicator in a range of different languages and contexts. However, there are features of his narrative that have had to be modified to aid readability and comprehension. The almost exclusive use of the conjunction 'e' to introduce sentences has been reduced in our version, as we felt that the constant repetition of 'and' or 'and then', notwithstanding its suggestion of speech, would have become rebarbative. More importantly, where James's recourse to deixis – to the 'thats' and 'theses' and 'theys' that indicate the circumstances of the Book's creation, in the presence of others who knew of

---

[10]See Josep Pujol (*Sens i conjuntures*, 1991) for a detailed reading of the narrative construction of the *Llibre*.

the events and people involved and could see the face and gestures of the king as he told of them – might lead to confusion, we have added information to disambiguate the text.

The Catalan language is the only language in which medieval kings (and two of them) have written their memoirs,[11] leaving the reader with a strong sense of their character, culture and concerns. Although we are well aware that the main interest of this version is in the picture of the conflicts of the Crown of Aragon it provides, we hope to have allowed some of its literary quality to show through: to allow the voice of king, conqueror and storyteller to be heard.

Helena Buffery

---

[11]See Pere III of Catalonia (IV of Aragon), *Chronicle*, ed. J. Hillgarth and trans. M. Hillgarth, 2 vols., Toronto 1980.

1

The Early Years

[1]¹ My lord Saint James relates that faith without good works is dead.² Our Lord wished this saying to be confirmed in our deeds; for though it is true that faith without works is worthless, when the two are combined they bear fruit, a fruit that God wishes to receive in His mansion. So, although the circumstances of our birth were good, there was need for improvement in our actions. This was not because we did not have the faith in us to believe in Our Creator and His works, nor through lack of prayers to His mother to intercede for us to her Beloved Son that He might pardon the wrongs we had done Him. Rather it was that through that very faith, He might lead us to the true salvation.

Our Lord Jesus Christ, Who knows all things, knew that our life would be so very long that we would be able to do a great deal of good works with the faith we had within us. Because of this, He showed us such grace and mercy that despite our many sins, both mortal and venial, He did not wish that we should receive any dishonour or harm which could shame us in the court or in any other place. Neither did He wish that we should die before we had completed these works.

So great was the mercy that He conceded to us, that at all times He has granted us the respect of our enemies, both in word and in deed, and He has kept our person in good health throughout our life. If sometimes He has given us illnesses, He has done so by way of warning to us, like a father who corrects his son; for as Solomon says, he who spares his son the rods of chastisement, does him ill and in no way appears to wish him well.³ Moreover, Our Lord never punished us so greatly that he did us harm. And for this we thanked Him each time He punished us, for the very punishment He gave us. Now we thank Him more than ever, since we know that He did it for our good.

---

¹While this prologue was probably written after the body of the text and it has been suggested (Asperti, 'Indagini sull' "Llibre dels feyts"') that the second half of the prologue may be the work of a second hand (possibly that of Bishop Jaume Sarroca, who may also have influenced the king in the final chapters of the work), nothing in the prologue conflicts with the sentiments expressed by James throughout his work, with the emphasis on God's guidance and the king's sense of mission, and it can reasonably be argued that the prologue too is the work of James (Pujol, 'Cultura eclesiàstica').

²James 2: 17, 20, 26.

³Proverbs 13:24 (cf. Eccl, 30: 1).

For we remember well a passage of Holy Scripture, which says: *Omnis laus in fine canitur*,[4] and means that the best thing a man can have, he shall have at the end of his days. And the mercy of the Lord of glory has worked in such a manner with us, so fulfilling the words of Saint James: for in our last years He has willed that our works should accord with our faith. And we, contemplating and reflecting on the nature of this world, in which men live their worldly lives, and how petty the times are, how frivolous and full of scandal, and how the other world brings glory everlasting, which Our Lord gives to those who desire and seek it, and contemplating, moreover, how great His power is and how feeble our weakness, we recognized and understood the truth of this phrase from scripture: *Omnia pretereunt preter amare Deum*,[5] which comes to mean that all the things of the world are fleeting and pass away, save only the love of God.

Knowing this to be the truth, and all else lies, we wished to offer our works and our thoughts, and to direct and shape them to the commandments of Our Saviour. Thus, we abandoned the vanities of this world in order to obtain His kingdom. For as He tells us in the Gospel: *Qui vult venire post me, abneget semetipsum et tollat crucem suam, et sequatur me*,[6] which means, in romance,[7] that he who wishes to follow Him, should abandon his own will for that of the Lord.

Recalling, moreover, the great mercies that He has done us many times in our life and, above all, towards the end of our days, we have decided to submit our will to His.[8] And so that all men may recognize and know, when we have passed from this mortal life, the deeds that we have done with the help of the powerful Lord, in Whom is true Trinity, we leave this book as a record for those who might wish to hear of the mercies that Our Lord has shown us, and to give an example to all the other men of this world so that they should do as we have done and place their faith in this Lord Who is so powerful.

---

[4]Not a direct biblical quotation, but an oft-used medieval proverb (cf. Isaiah, 42: 10; Psalms 48:10). The usual meaning of the proverb (that the result of an undertaking cannot be securely known until it has been completed) has been adapted here to suit the theme of the prologue.

[5]Probably derived from a poem of Venantius Fortunatus (c. 530–600) (Pujol, 'Cultura eclesiàstica', p. 154) but based on a Pauline theme (I Cor, 7:31; 13: 8; cf. Psalms 144: 4). The phrase is also used in the final will of James of 26 August 1272 and in a donation of James to the hospital of Sant Vicenç de València on 13 June 1276. Riera argues for the influence of Jaume Sarroca (Riera, 'Personalitat eclesiàstica', p. 589).

[6]Matthew, 16:24 ("If any man would come after me, let him deny himself and take up his cross and follow me") (cf. Luke, 9:23).

[7]Catalan.

[8]This is a reference to James's decision to retire to the monastery of Poblet (Tarragona), the most powerful Cistercian house in Catalonia, and end his days there as a monk.

[2] It is certainly true that our grandfather, King Don Alfonso,[9] negotiated marriage terms with the emperor of Constantinople,[10] asking for his daughter as a wife. However, although both parties, that is to say our grandfather and the emperor, negotiated and agreed the terms, our grandfather then married Queen Doña Sancha, who was the daughter of the emperor of Castile.[11]

The emperor of Constantinople, unaware that the marriage had taken place, sent his daughter to King Don Alfonso of Aragon, who was the count of Barcelona and marquis of Provence. And, on arriving at Montpellier, a bishop and two nobles,[12] who had come with her, discovered that King Don Alfonso, our grandfather, had married Queen Doña Sancha, daughter of the emperor of Castile. And they were greatly perplexed and worried as to what they should do, since Alfonso had taken another wife.

Now, William of Montpellier was lord of Montpellier and of all that pertains to Montpellier. And those nobles who had accompanied the daughter of the emperor asked him what they should do about the deceit and the insult that they had received. For they had come with the daughter of the Emperor Manuel to the court of King Don Alfonso so that he would marry her, yet the king had married another. And they asked him to advise them in what manner they should proceed. And he replied to them that he would take it before his council.

When William of Montpellier had assembled all his council, he was advised by his nobles, his knights, and all the notables of the city of Montpellier, to take her as his wife. For they said that since God had granted him so great a mercy that the daughter of the Emperor Manuel, who was at that time the most important man in Christendom, had come to his town and the place where he was, and had been abandoned by the husband she should have had, he should take her as his wife and not allow her to return home on any account. On that advice, he gave his response to the bishop and the nobles who had come with

---

[9]Alfonso II of Aragon, the first count-king (1162–96).

[10]Manuel Comnenos (1143–80).

[11]James's account is inaccurate here. Alfonso II married Sancha of Castile (d. 1208), daughter of Alfonso VII of Castile-León (1126–57), on 18 January 1174. Later, to cement an alliance against the Emperor Frederick Barbarossa (1152–90), a marriage was arranged between Alfonso's brother, Raymond Berenguer, the count of Provence, and Eudoxia, daughter of a nephew of the Emperor Manuel. But when Eudoxia arrived (1179), Raymond refused her, possibly due to an alteration in Aragon's relationship with Barbarossa after his reconciliation with Pope Alexander III in 1177. In Spring 1179, Eudoxia was nevertheless married to William VIII (1172–1202) of Montpellier, a key ally of Alfonso II (Vajay, 'Eudoquía', pp. 628–30; Aurell, *Noces*, p. 405). James may have genuinely confused Eudoxia's parentage because, while Manuel would be 'autocrator' and his nephew a 'basileus', both would translate as 'emperador'.

[12]The presence of three envoys is confirmed by the *Annales Pisani* (VI, 2, p. 68). These envoys did, however, obtain success in their main mission in successfully negotiating, in Paris, the marriage of Agnes, daughter of King Louis VII of France (1137–80), to Alexis, son and heir of Manuel, in the winter of 1178–9 (Vajay, 'Eudoquía', pp. 629–30).

her. And this was the response that he sent through his messengers: that since God had granted him such grace that she was unable to have the husband whom she ought to have had, he wished to take her for his wife.

When the envoys of the emperor heard these words the confusion that they had felt at first was doubled, for the daughter of the emperor could not take as a husband any but a king or an emperor, because no other matched her status. And they entreated him most insistently that, for the sake of his own honour and in God's name, he should allow the daughter of the emperor to leave. For they had promised to the emperor that if the marriage did not take place, they would return her to her father by land or sea. And they said that he should not impede them, as there was no reason for him to do so, for she had not come to marry him. But William of Montpellier and his council responded that it could not be otherwise. Thus, when the messengers of the emperor understood their intent and that things could not be otherwise, they asked for time to deliberate, and he gave them until the next day.

Now, the bishop and the nobles who had come with her saw that William of Montpellier and his council would have their way, and they decided to agree to the marriage on one condition: that any son or daughter born to William of Montpellier and the daughter of the emperor, if he or she survived, was to be lord of Montpellier.

So they returned to give their response. And they said to William of Montpellier and to his council that they could attack them, imprison them, or snatch her from them, but that the marriage would not take place with their consent or hers unless it was done in the manner they proposed. He had to promise to them, upon his honour, and make all of the men of Montpellier of ten years and upwards swear, that any son or daughter born of them both would be lord of Montpellier if it was a man, and likewise if it was a woman.[13] And these words were put in writing.

In this manner, William of Montpellier, on the advice of his nobles and his council, agreed the terms and contracted the marriage. And that lady bore William of Montpellier a daughter called Maria.[14]

[3] Much later, a marriage was negotiated between King Don Peter,[15] our father, and the daughter of William of Montpellier (who was lady of Montpellier and of all its territories). And she agreed that she would give her

---

[13]James is here primarily concerned with his own claims in Montpellier (where, particularly in the 1240s and 1250s, and again in the 1270s, he faced considerable difficulties from many in the town who were prepared to ally against him and in favour of France).

[14]Marie of Montpellier, Queen of Aragon (1204–1213).

[15]King Peter II of Aragon (1196–1213).

body and Montpellier with all its appurtenances. So the marriage took place and so increased her renown, for now she had the name Queen Doña Maria.[16]

[4] Afterwards William of Montpellier, with his wife still living, married another lady, who was from Castile (the name of whose father we do not recall, but her name was Doña Agnes).[17] By her he had these sons: one by the name of William of Montpellier[18] who held Paulhan until the hour of his death, and another, Bergunyó; and Bernat Guillem, to whom we gave patrimony and a wife named Juliana, who was, through her mother, of the lineage of Entença and was daughter of Ponç Hug, brother of Count Hug d'Empúries;[19] and another brother, called Tortoseta, who was raised by our father.

Now this William of Montpellier, who was the eldest son of William of Montpellier, fought to be lord of Montpellier, because he was the male heir. And because the dispute came before the pope, our mother, Queen Doña Maria, went to the court of Rome to defend her rights, so that we, who were her heir, would be lord of Montpellier.[20] And they so defended their cause before the pope that he gave them a sentence (and there was a decretal written of the sentence of the pope), judging that the children of William of Montpellier and Agnes were not children of a legal marriage (for they were begotten in adultery, William already having another wife). And the pope judged that Montpellier belonged to the Queen Doña Maria and to us, as we were her son.

---

[16]The marriage took place on 15 June 1204 (Miret, 'Itinerario del Rey Pedro', 3, pp. 278–9). Marie had previously been married in 1191 to Viscount Barral of Marseilles (d.1192) and, in 1197, to Count Bernard IV of Comminges (1176–1225), who repudiated her in 1201. Peter II ceded to Bernard the prize of the Val d'Aran in 1201. Bernard may have been 'holding' Marie until a suitable time when she could be given to Peter, who could then marry her and take control of Montpellier after the death of William VIII (1202) (Higounet, *Comté de Comminges*, pp. 79–87).

[17]Eudoxia was politically useless after 1182 when the violently anti-Western Andronicus Comnenus seized power (and she did not provide a male heir). In April 1187, William VIII married Agnes, a distant relation of Alfonso I of Aragon (1104–34), and probably a dame of honour to Queen Sancha of Castile (Peter II's mother) at the court of Barcelona (Aurell, *Noces*, pp. 406–7)

[18]William IX of Montpellier. In fact, Agnes gave William VIII six sons and two daughters.

[19]Juliana appears to be daughter of Count Hug III of Empúries (1154–73) and Jusiana d'Entença and thus sister to Ponç Hug II (1173–1200), while Count Hug IV (1200–30) was Ponç Hug II's son (Sobrequés, *Barons*, p. 74; Aurell, *Noces*, p. 456). Bernat Guillem appears often in James's narrative particularly in relation to the Valencia campaign.

[20]Marie of Montpellier went to Rome for two reasons: to defend herself in the divorce case brought by Peter II (a case that had been running since 1206 (Vincke, 'Eheprozess'), and to defend her own and her son's rights in Montpellier. In January 1213, Pope Innocent III pronounced in favour of the validity of her marriage (*MDI*, no. 497. James does not mention this), and in April 1213 decreed that the marriage between William VIII and Agnes was not a legal one and therefore Marie and not William IX was rightfully ruler in Montpellier (Aurell, *Noces*, p. 434).

[5] Now we will relate the manner of our conception[21] and our birth. Firstly, the manner of our conception: Our father, King Don Peter, did not wish to see the queen, our mother. And it happened that one time the king, our father, was at Lattes, and the queen, our mother, was at Mireval.[22] But a noble by the name of Guillermo de Alcalá came to the king and besought him so insistently that he persuaded him to go to Mireval, where the queen, our mother, was staying. That night when they were both at Mireval, Our Lord willed that we should be conceived.

When the queen, our mother, found out that she was pregnant, she went to Montpellier. And here Our Lord willed us to be born in the house of the Tornamira,[23] on the eve of Our Lady Saint Mary of Candlemas.[24]

As soon as we were born, our mother sent us to Santa Maria, and they carried us there in their arms. In the church of Our Lady[25] they were saying matins, and at the very moment they brought us through the porch, those inside began to sing *Te Deum laudamus.* And the clergy did not know that we were to enter there, but we entered while they sang that canticle. And afterwards they carried us to Saint Firmin, and when those who carried us entered the church of Saint Firmin, those inside were singing *Benedictus Dominus Deus Israel.*[26] When they returned us to the house of our mother, she rejoiced at all the good signs that had befallen us. And she ordered twelve candles to be made, all of equal size and measure, and had them all lit at the same time. On each one she placed the name of an apostle, and she promised Our Lord that whichever candle burned longest would be the name we would receive. And that of Saint James lasted a full three fingers breadth longer than the others. Thus, for this reason, and through the grace of God, we have the name James.[27]

And that is how we descend from our mother's side and from King Peter, our father. Moreover, it would seem to be God's work, in that the agreement that our grandfather had made to marry was fulfilled. A woman of the line of

---

[21]The theme is a commonplace of Catalan literature, imaginatively developed by the chroniclers *Muntaner* (chs. 3–5) and *Desclot* (ch. 4) who have Marie being surreptitiously substituted into Peter's bed in place of one of his mistresses.

[22]South of Montpellier above Setes.

[23]The temporary residence of Peter II after his palace had been destroyed in an uprising of the Montpellierans in October 1206 against his financially burdensome rule.

[24]1 February 1208 [The eve of the Purification of the Blessed Virgin Mary (Candlemas Day)].

[25]Notre-Dame-des-Tables.

[26]This is all less miraculous than James makes out. Had the clergy not been singing the *Te Deum* at matins and the *Benedictus Dominus Deus Israel* (Luke 1:68–79) at lauds, it would have been more noteworthy. These hymns are part of the ordinary of the divine office.

[27]Marie's practice reflects a normal popular devotion. The name also suggests the popularity of pilgrimage to Santiago de Compostela. Peter II, in his documents, referred to his son as Peter.

the Emperor Manuel married our father King Peter, and, through that marriage, the wrong that had taken place concerning the other marriage was undone.

And later, while we were lying in the cradle, someone threw a rock down on us through a trapdoor, and it fell near the cradle, but God wished to protect us so that we should not die.[28]

[6] Our father, King Peter, was the most generous king there ever was in Spain, and the most courteous, and the most affable. In fact, his generosity was such that his revenues and lands decreased.[29] Moreover, he was a good knight-at-arms, if ever there was a good one in the world.[30] Of the other good qualities that he had we do not wish to speak, so as not to lengthen this work.

[7] Of the Queen Doña Maria, our mother, we wish to say the following: that if ever there was a good woman in the world, it was she, in fearing and honouring God, and in the other good qualities that she had. We could say many good things about her but we will say just one thing that is worth all the rest: that she is loved by all the men of the world who know of her conduct. And Our Lord loved her so much and gave her such grace, that she is called the Holy queen by those who are in Rome and throughout the world. And many sick people are cured when they drink, with wine or water, the stone scraped from her tomb. She lies buried in Rome, in the church of Saint Peter, near Saint Petronilla, who was the daughter of Saint Peter.[31]

And consider, those of you who read this text, if this is not a miraculous thing. Our grandfather, King Don Alfonso, promised that the daughter of the emperor would be his wife but then he married Queen Doña Sancha. Yet, Our Lord wished that the original promise, to take the daughter of the Emperor Manuel as his wife, should be fulfilled. And that would seem to be the case, since the granddaughter of the Emperor Manuel was afterwards wife of our father from whom we descend. For that reason, it is a work of God that the agreement that was not fulfilled in those times should be fulfilled later, when our father took as his wife the granddaughter of the emperor.

---

[28]*Desclot* (ch. 4) also reports this and says the force of the blow was such as to break the cradle. *Desclot* comments that the identity of the perpetrators of the crime was uncertain but he believed it to be the work of James's relatives, who hoped to have his lands for themselves.

[29]The study of the financial aspects of Peter's reign by Thomas Bisson (*Fiscal Accounts*, 1, pp. 122–50), bears witness to the king's profligacy and mismanagement.

[30]Peter II was a victor at the decisive battle of Las Navas de Tolosa (16 July 1212) at which the Almohad power in Spain was crushed.

[31]Marie made her final will at Rome on 20 April 1213 and died soon afterwards (Aurell, *Noces*, pp. 435–6). Petronilla was also the name of one of her daughters by Bernard IV of Comminges. The *Gesta Comitum Barcinonensium* (ch. 35) also fostered Marie's cult, commenting that after she had been honourably buried in the church of Saint Peter by the altar of Saint Petronilla, the Lord had worked many miracles at her tomb.

[8] Some time after our birth, Simon de Montfort,[32] who held the lands of Carcassonne and Béziers and, in Toulouse, the land that the king of France had won, wished to be friends with our father. So, he asked him to deliver us to him, that he might raise us. And our father trusted so much in him and in his love that he delivered us to be raised by him.[33]

While we were in his power, the people of those lands that we have mentioned came to our father, and they said to him that he could be lord of those lands if he wished to take them and protect them.[34] Now, King Peter, our father, was sincere and compassionate, and because of the compassion that he felt for them, he said that he would protect them.

However, they tricked him with pretty phrases. And with the one hand they gave their word, and with the other they took it away by their deeds. For we have heard Guillem de Cervera[35] and Arnau de Castellbò[36] and Dalmau de

---

[32]Simon de Montfort (d. 1218) was lord of Montfort l'Amaury, near Paris, and also titular earl of Leicester. In 1209 he was chosen as military leader of the Albigensian Crusade, a task he fulfilled with ruthless efficiency. He was made viscount of Béziers-Carcassonne in 1209 without consultation of Peter II, the overlord. One of Simon's sons, also Simon, became earl of Leicester in 1231. The king of France to whom James refers is Philip II Augustus (1180–1223).

[33]This appears to be self-deception. The Albigensian Crusade (to destroy heresy) had proved successful in increasing the power of the Northern Franks in southern France. Peter II's own ambitions in the region were under threat but his prime concern was the battle against the Muslims in southern Spain. Peter sought compromises between the crusaders and the nobles of southern France. In January 1211, Peter accepted Montfort's homage for Béziers-Carcassonne, and sought a reconciliation between Montfort and the count of Foix. Then he agreed to a marriage between James (who was still not three) and Montfort's daughter, handing James over to be brought up by Montfort (Miret, 'Itinerario del Rey Pedro', 4, pp. 16–17). In April 1211, Peter arranged a marriage between his sister Sancha and the future Raymond VII of Toulouse (Vaux-de-Cernay, *Histoire Albigeoise*, ch. 211; Ventura, *Pere el Catòlic*, p. 147). Peter was seeking a divorce from Marie of Montpellier, James's mother. In fact, James was an expendable pawn in a larger political game.

[34]By the beginning of 1213, many of the major southern French lords, as well as the consuls of Toulouse, already felt that they had no other option in combatting the crusade than placing themselves under the lordship of Peter II, who had gained great prestige by his victory at Las Navas. Peter, from late January 1213, acted as a virtual 'emperor of the Pyrenees' (Roquebert, *L'Épopée Cathare 1213–1216*, pp. 105–11).

[35]Guillem IV de Cervera (d. 1245), a faithful ally of Peter II, had fought at Las Navas. His second wife was Countess Elvira de Subirats of Urgell, and he was step-father and chief adviser to Countess Aurembiaix of Urgell. In 1230 he entered Poblet (Gonzalvo, 'Guillem IV de Cervera', p. 417). He was a key figure in the politics of James's minority and a member of the regency council appointed by Innocent III in 1216 to support the procurator Sancho in managing the king's affairs (*MDI*, no. 537).

[36]Viscount Arnau de Castellbò (1185–1226), a fixture at the courts of Peter II and James, he was a powerful figure in the Pyrenean world, who constantly battled against the counts and bishops of Urgell. His daughter, Ermessenda (d. 1230), married Count Roger Bernard of Foix, uniting the two houses. Both Arnau and Ermessenda were very sympathetic to Catharism and, in 1269, both were posthumously condemned as heretics by the Inquisition (Miret, *Investigación Histórica*, pp. 164–5).

Creixell,[37] and others who were with him, say that those people said to him: "Lord, see our castles and our towns: take them under your protection and place your bailiffs in them." Yet when he wished to occupy them they said to him: "Lord, what are you doing turning our wives out of our houses? Both we and they are yours and will do your will." And in this way, they did not do any of the things they had promised to him. And they presented to him their wives and their daughters and their kinswomen, the most beautiful they could find, and, as they knew he was a ladies' man,[38] they took away his better judgement and bent him to their will. But as the details would take a long time to relate, however serious and important, we do not wish to speak on them further.

[9] Simon de Montfort was at Muret with a good eight hundred to a thousand knights, and our father came upon him near the place where he was.[39] With him from Aragon, there were Don Miguel de Luésia, and Don Blasco de Alagón, Don Rodrigo Lizana, Don Ladrón, Don Gómez de Luna, Don Miguel de Rada, Don Guillermo de Pueyo, Don Aznar Pardo, and many others of his household.[40] There were others whom we cannot remember, but we remember very well that those who were there and knew the facts said that except for Don Gómez, Don Miguel de Rada, Don Aznar Pardo, and some of his household who died there, the others abandoned the battle, and fled. From Catalonia, there were Dalmau de Creixell, Hug de Mataplana, Guillem d'Horta, and Bernat de Castellbisbal, and they fled with the others.[41]

---

[37]One of the principal advisers of Peter II, he also held many interests in the south of France. He took part in the defence of Toulouse in 1217 and 1218. He was brother of Arnau de Creixell, Bishop of Girona (1199–1214). He made his will on 27 November 1220 (Marquès, *Pergamins*, no. 108).

[38]Peter II left a reputation as a notorious womanizer (as did James). According to the chronicler Puylaurens (*RHGF*, 19, ch. 21, p. 208), a letter from Peter to a noble lady of Toulouse, declaring that he came to fight the French for love of her, was intercepted by Montfort, who declared "I shall not fear a king who comes against the business of God for a courtesan."

[39]The battle of Muret (12 September 1213).

[40]Of the nobles who are mentioned here, the most important are Miguel de Luesia, Blasco de Alagón, and Rodrigo Lizana. Miguel, a hero of Las Navas, was the closest noble adviser of Peter II throughout his reign and led the party who called for a battle against Montfort rather than a siege of Muret (*Chanson de la Croisade*, 2, ch. 139, p. 24). Blasco was a key supporter of James in his minority (Arroyo, 'Blasco de Alagón', pp. 80–1) but fell into disfavour. He encouraged the Valencian campaign and took Morella, which he delivered to the king. Roderigo Lizana was an Aragonese noble, who often opposed James during the minority but later greatly distinguished himself in the conquest of Valencia. Guillermo de Pueyo died in 1220 at the siege of Albarracín (ch. 16). Aznar Pardo was a key adviser of Peter II and had distinguished himself at Las Navas (Huici, *Las Grandes Batallas*, pp. 255, 263).

[41]After the battle Dalmau threw himself into the River Louge, crying out, "God help us! A great misfortune has befallen us: the good king of Aragon is dead and defeated, and many others besides, dead and defeated. Never has there been so great a loss!" (*Chanson de la Croisade*, 2, ch. 140, p. 30).

But we do know for certain that Don Nunó Sanxes[42] and Guillem de Montcada,[43] who was the son of Guillem Ramon and Guillema de Castellví, were not at the battle, but sent word to the king saying that he should wait for them. However, the king did not wish to wait for them and waged the battle with those who were with him.

And the day that he went into battle he had lain with a lady. For we later heard his steward, who was called Gil, and was to become a brother of the Hospital, and was present there, along with others, who saw it with their own eyes, say that even at the Gospel he was unable to stand on his feet, so he sat in his seat while it was read. And before the battle Simon de Montfort wished to place himself in the king's power to do his will, and wished to be reconciled with him. But our father did not wish to accept the offer.[44] On seeing that, Count Simon and those who were inside the town confessed themselves and received the body of Jesus Christ, saying they would rather die on the battlefield than inside the town. And, with that resolve, all as one, they went out to fight.

However, those on the king's side knew neither how to place order in the lines nor how to move in formation, and each noble fought for himself, and broke with the rules of arms. And because of their disorder and the sin that was in them, and because they had not shown mercy to those who were inside, the battle had to be lost.[45]

---

[42]Count Nunó I of Rousillon and Cerdagne (1212–1241/2). One of the most important figures in James's narrative. He was son of Count Sancho of Provence (d. 1223) and grandson of Count Ramon Berenguer IV of Barcelona (1131–62). In 1209, he gave military aid to King Frederick of Sicily [the Emperor Frederick II (1212–50)]. In 1212, he was made count of Rousillon and Cerdagne by Peter II. He participated in the battle of Las Navas. After the death of Peter II (1213), he led a defensive alliance against Montfort. He fought with the Montcada family for control during James's minority, but then allied with them, leaving James in a difficult position. He participated in the conquest of Majorca (1229–30) where he played a decisive role. Jointly with Peter of Portugal and archbishop-elect Guillem of Tarragona, he conquered Ibiza in 1235. He was present at the siege and capture of Valencia in 1238.

[43]Guillem de Montcada, Viscount of Béarn (1223–9). Together with Nunó, he continued the battle against the crusaders after Muret. During the minority, in a power struggle, he fell out with both Nunó and the king. But he accompanied James in the siege of Peníscola (1225) and later formed part of his council in the campaign against the Cabrera (1228). He was the most powerful magnate in the Majorca campaign, where he died at the battle of Porto Pí (1229). His father, Viscount Guillem Ramon I (1215–23), left a good reputation as an administrator, although as a youth he had notoriously killed Archbishop Berenguer of Tarragona after a bitter dispute (1194) (Shideler, *Montcadas*, pp. 123–8).

[44]The legates with the crusading army attempted to negotiate a peace with Peter several times in the days leading up to the battle but Peter's terms were unacceptable (Ventura, *Pere el Catòlic*, p. 212). Montfort was not personally involved in these negotiations.

[45]It is difficult to establish what happened in the battle. James's work is one of the few which attempts to define the reasons for the defeat of Peter's superior forces, but his view of the battle both reflects his own military outlook and perhaps also his own failure to halt the Capetian advance to the south. There certainly appears to have been dissension in Peter's camp over the battle plan, but most chroniclers concentrated on the king's sinfulness in defending

And our father died there, since it has always been the custom of our line, in the battles they have fought and in which we shall fight, that either we must win or die.

Meanwhile, we remained in Carcassonne in the power of the count, since he was raising us and was lord of that place.

[10] Later on, after that had happened, our subjects, that is to say, Don Nunó Sanxes, Guillem de Montcada, and Guillem de Cardona,[46] father of Ramon Folc, demanded our return and they went to war against the Franks and against the lands held by them. As well as the war that they waged at Narbonne and other places, they sent envoys to the pope, Innocent III, asking him to resolve to threaten Simon de Montfort, through excommunication or by other means, so that they might recover us.[47] For we were their natural lord, since our father had left no legitimate son except us.[48]

And this holy father, Innocent III, was the best pope, so much so that from the time that we compose this book going back a hundred years there has not been so good a pope in the church of Rome. For he was very learned in the matters that it pertains for a pope to know, and he had a natural wisdom, and knew a great amount about the secular sciences.[49] And he sent such forceful letters and such forceful envoys to Count Simon that he had to agree to return us to our people.[50] And so, the Franks took us as far as Narbonne, where a great party of the nobles and the citizens of Catalonia came out to receive us. And we must then have been six years and three months old.[51] On our arrival

---

heretics, his impetuous folly on the battlefield, or more favourably, his righteous motives in defending his vassals (Alvira, 'La cruzada Albigense', pp. 947–75).

[46]Viscount Guillem de Cardona (1177–1226), a member of the regency council appointed by Innocent III in 1216, he was also one of James's most important creditors. He had fought at Las Navas.

[47]After Muret, attempts to recover James from Montfort proved unsuccessful, and an embassy was sent to Rome, led by Bishop Hispan of Segorbe-Albarracín (d. 1215) (Rodrigo, *Historia de Rebus Hispanie*, Bk 6, ch. 5).

[48]James emphasizes that he was the only legitimate heir. Peter II certainly had two other children by a lady of the house of Sarroca: Pere (d. 1254), who became sacristan of Lleida, and sometimes acted as an adviser to his half-brother; and Constança, who, in 1212, married the Seneschal Guillem Ramon V (d. 1228), and later became the prioress of the Trinitarian house at Avinganya (Lleida).

[49]Pope Innocent III (1198–1216). He had been educated in Rome, Paris and Bologna. His training was primarily as a theologian.

[50]On 23 January 1214, Innocent III warned Montfort that it would be unseemly for him to hold James and that he should be handed over to the papal legate. The letter was accompanied by a thinly veiled threat of excommunication if he did not do so (*MDI*, no. 516). The pope sent Cardinal Peter of Benevento, a close confidant (Maleczek, *Kardinalskolleg*, pp. 172–4), to recover James and organize the government of the minority. Cardinal Peter played a crucial role in restoring order in Aragon and Catalonia.

[51]James was taken to Capestang and there handed over to Cardinal Peter who took him to the Catalan nobles at Narbonne (Vaux-de-Cernay, ch. 506). This was in April 1214.

in Catalonia, they decided who would raise us. And all agreed that the master of the Templars at Monzón should raise us. The name of that master was Guillem de Mont-rodon,[52] and he was from the region of Osona, and was master of the Temple in Aragon and Catalonia.

[11] And they took another decision: that in our name and with the new seal that they had had minted for us, we should convoke the *Cort* of the Catalans and the Aragonese at Lleida.[53] The archbishop, the bishops, the abbots, and the nobles[54] of each of the kingdoms would attend the *Cort*, and from each city, there would be ten men, with the authority of the other men, who would fulfil whatever was decided there.

All of them came on the day of the *Cort*, except Don Ferdinand and Count Don Sancho, because both of these hoped to be king.[55] And there they all swore to us that they would defend our body and our members and our land, and that they would defend us in all things and above all things. The place where we were at that time was where Archbishop Aspàreg,[56] who was of the

---

[52]Guillem de Mont-rodon entered the Temple in 1203 and was commander of Gardeny (1206–12) and then master of the Temple in Provence, Catalonia, and Aragon (1214–18) (Pladevall, *Guillem de Mont-rodon*, pp. 30–5; Forey, *Templars*, passim). He was a member of the regency council appointed in 1216.

[53]The *Cort* at Lleida in August 1214 (*Cortes*, 1, pp. 90–1; Gonzalvo, *Constitucions*, no. 23) overseen by Cardinal Peter, imposed the Peace in Catalonia and enacted legislation that was to have lasting influence in the financial and administrative government of the Crown. James does not appear to have had a seal until 1217 (Kagay, 'Line between Memoir', p. 170). The decision to summon the *Cort* was most probably that of the cardinal, advised both by James's great uncle, Count Sancho, and the Montcada family.

[54]The 'rics hòmens' or, in Castilian, 'ricos hombres'. In Aragon, they were the highest rank of the feudal nobility and part of the king's council. In Catalonia, the term was more widely applied, but still only to those who were above the knights.

[55]Prince Ferdinand of Aragon (d. 1245) was Peter II's youngest brother. As a child he was given to the abbey of Poblet but in 1205 became abbot of the powerful Augustinian house of Montearagón (Huesca). He was ill-suited to a contemplative life. He nurtured anarchy in Aragon during the minority and aimed for the throne himself. He later sided with James in the conquest of Valencia, which he had initially opposed. Count Sancho of Provence (d. 1223) was the youngest son of Raymond Berenguer IV and hence James's great uncle. He was appointed procurator both for Raymond Berenguer V in Provence (1209) and for James (1214). He sought to continue the war against Montfort and avenge Peter II's death, but there was much opposition to him. He resigned in 1218. He does not appear to have aimed for the throne (Sanpere, 'Minoría de Jaime I') and lacked a power base in Aragon to do so. He is also referred to as count of Rousillon, even when his son Nunó held the county. Almost certainly, both Ferdinand and Sancho attended the *Cort* at Lleida in 1214 (Soldevila, *PrimersTemps*, pp. 71–5, 82–4).

[56]Aspàreg de la Barca, Bishop of Pamplona (1212–15), Archbishop of Tarragona (1215–31). Thus he was still bishop of Pamplona when this assembly took place. James sometimes refers to him in documents as his uncle. He is probably uncle to the husband of one of the two daughters of Marie of Montpellier by Bernard IV of Comminges. Being a relation to James was a factor in his election as archbishop (Linehan, *Spanish Church*, pp. 35–6). He was a

house of the Barca and was our relation, held us in the crook of his arm; in a room that is now vaulted but then was made of wood. It was next to the window where the kitchen is now, and through which they now give food to those who dine in the palace.

After the oath was sworn, the *Cort* dissolved. And the master took us to Monzón[57] and we remained there, in the care of a lieutenant, for two and a half years.

By that time, all the rents that our father held in Aragon and Catalonia had been pledged to Jews and to Saracens. Even the *honors*, some seven hundred knights' fees at that time, had been given or sold by our father, King Don Peter, with only one hundred and thirty remaining.[58] Thus, when we entered Monzón, we had not even enough food for one day, so wasted and pledged was the land![59]

[12] While we were at Monzón, the nobles of Aragon formed themselves into gangs and factions. Don Pedro Ahones,[60] Don Atorella, Don Jimeno de Urrea, Don Arnaldo Palazín, Don Berenguer de Benavent, Don Blasco Maza, and others, both nobles and knights, whom we do not remember, made pacts and alliances with the Count of Rousillon, Sancho, who was their leader, and they followed his path. Whereas Don Pedro Fernández de Albarracín,[61] Don Rodrigo Lizana, and Don Blasco de Alagón went with Don Ferdinand, and they made him their leader. Don Pedro Cornel[62] and Don Vallés de Antillón did

---

permanent member of the regency council. At Lleida, he appears to have lifted James up so that the nobles could see the young king in order to swear the oath to him.

[57]The Templar fortress of Monzón (Huesca). James was there from August 1214 until June 1217.

[58]The *honors* were the estates given by the king in benefice in return for service. The knights' fees (cavallerias) were the sum fixed for the maintenance of a knight and in Aragon it was equal to five hundred Jacan solidi. James says that of a possible revenue of three hundred and fifty thousand solidi, only sixty-five thousand solidi remained to him.

[59]The studies of Bisson bear witness to the fact that Aragon had suffered badly from the mortgage of Peter II's domain and Catalonia far worse ('Finances of the Young James').

[60]Of the nobles mentioned here Pedro Ahones was the most important. He was a member of the regency council but he later battled against James and was killed by the king's forces (ch. 27). Atorella was an Aragonese knight often in James's company in the early years. He opposed James after Pedro Ahones's death but later took part in James's third voyage to Majorca in 1232 and the early Valencian campaigns. Blasco Maza took part in the negotiations between James and King Sancho VII of Navarre in 1231 and was at the surrender of Valencia in 1238 (*S*, p. 196).

[61]Pedro Fernández de Azagra, a Castilian knight, lord of Albarracín, and major-domo in Aragon (1218). From an immensely powerful and influential family, he often sided against the king in the minority but played a long and significant role in the Valencian conquests (Martínez, 'Turolenses', pp. 102–9).

[62]Pedro Cornel was an important Aragonese noble who took part both in the expedition to Majorca and the Valencia campaigns. Much later he rebelled against James and in 1263 fled to Navarre (*H*, 5, no. 1345) but was reconciled to the king.

not yet possess land or *honors*, because they were so very young, and at times they would follow one faction, and at other times the other.

Now, Don Jimeno Cornel[63] was then already old, and the great evils that he saw in Aragon grieved him, since he was the wisest man there was in Aragon at that time and the one whose advice was most respected.

Every so often they would come to Monzón, and entreat us to leave the castle of Monzón to join one of the factions, so that by placing ourselves on the side of one faction we might destroy the other.

[13] When we were nine years old, neither we nor the count of Provence[64] could be held any longer at Monzón, so greatly did we desire to leave there. And since it was necessary for the land, the master and the others took the decision that they would allow us to depart from that place.

About seven months before we left there,[65] a message came for the count of Provence from the nobles of his land, saying that on a fixed day they would come with a galley to Salou. They would take him secretly from the castle of Monzón, and they would go with him to Provence. And it was carried out just as was planned.

When he was about to leave, he said that he wished to speak with us, and he revealed his secret to us. Then, weeping, he said farewell to us, as did those who had come for him. And we wept with him for our sadness at his parting, but were greatly pleased for him that he was able to leave. And the next day, near to twilight, he left the castle with Pierre Auger, who raised him, and with two squires, travelling by night, they got beyond Lleida pretending to be other men and in disguise. The following night they arrived at Salou, boarded the galley, and went to Provence.

(And so that you may know how old we both were, he was two and a half years older than us).[66]

[14] When the brothers saw that the count of Provence had gone, and that he had not let them know of it, they realized that our continued presence there would not be in their interests. And when Count Don Sancho heard of the departure of the count of Provence, he was very angry. On finding out that the

---

[63]Jimeno Cornel was a constant companion of Peter II and fought at Las Navas. He was uncle of Pedro Cornel and one of the regency council named by Innocent III.

[64]Count Raymond Berenguer V of Provence (1209–45) was James's cousin. His father, Count Alfonso II (1196–1209), brother of Peter II, had died in Palermo, while accompanying his sister Constance to marry Frederick II (Benoit, *Recueil*, no. 66). In 1209, Count Sancho was appointed procurator of Provence by Peter II. Raymond was probably taken to Monzón at the same time as James.

[65]November 1216.

[66]James was eight years and nine months old.

count had gone, he, with those who were of his faction in Aragon, wished to take over Aragon.

We then sent word to Don Pedro Fernández, Don Rodrigo Lizana, and their faction, and to Guillem de Cervera, that they should come to us at Monzón, because we wished to leave by whatever means possible. And they assured us they would help us and defend us with all their power.

But when Count Don Sancho learnt of it, he assembled the men of his faction and he said that he would cover with a scarlet cloth all the land of Aragon that we and those who were with us crossed on the other side of the Cinca.[67]

We left Monzón at dawn, and on arrival at the bridge, our people received us and told us that Count Don Sancho was at Selgua with all his forces, and that he would fight us.

We were then no more than nine years old, and fearing the battle that we expected to wage, a knight, whose name we do not recall, gave us a light coat of mail[68] to wear. And so began the first deed of arms that we undertook.

That day we went to Berbegal, finding no resistance on the road, and the next day we entered Huesca. Then we went to Zaragoza. And that was the first time we were in Aragon,[69] and the people were very happy at our arrival.

[15] While we were at Zaragoza, we were with the faction of Don Pedro Fernández and those whom we have mentioned above. And a message arrived telling us that Don Rodrigo Lizana had taken prisoner Don Lope de Albero, who was a relative of Don Rodrigo Lizana.[70] Don Pelegrín de Atrosillo had

---

[67]James is confusing events here. Count Sancho was with him at Monzón on 19 June 1217 (*H*, 1, no. 2) just prior to his departure and was still with him (24 June 1217) when he went to visit his father's remains recently returned to Sixena (Huesca) from the Hospitaller house at Toulouse (*M*, p. 23). In 1217, Sancho continued the support of attacks on Simon de Montfort. Toulouse was liberated in September 1217 and then Simon's brother Guy was killed. Pope Honorius III (1216–27) threatened Sancho and the nobles of the Crown with excommunication if they gave further help against the crusade and, in December 1217, in a letter to James, he threatened Aragon with invasion (*MDH*, nos. 94, 106, 107). It would appear that in the first months of 1218, when James had returned to Monzón (*M*, p. 25) some members of the regency council, together with Ferdinand of Aragon and his followers, took the resolve, in Sancho's absence, to abandon the cause of the south of France. Then Sancho made his threats. But soon afterwards he resigned the procuratorship, perhaps when news of the death of Montfort (25 June 1218) reached Aragon, though probably before. On 8 September 1218, James and Sancho arrived at an accord, and Sancho was conceded lands in Aragon and a pension *(H*, 1, no. 14).
[68]A hauberk. A tunic of mail, sometimes with sleeves and a hood, which protects the body. Throughout the *Llibre* the term 'gonió' is used rather than 'ausberg', as appears in *Desclot*, suggesting there was some difference between the two types of tunic.
[69]Monzón was not then considered part of Aragon.
[70]These chapters relate further power struggles during the minority in 1220. The resignation of Count Sancho only led to new conflicts. Both Rodrigo Lizana and Pedro Fernández were supporters of Ferdinand of Aragon (ch. 12). In July 1219, Honorius III had named a new regency council (*MDH*, no. 234: Archbishop Aspàreg, Jimeno Cornel, Guillem de Cervera and

married the daughter[71] of Don Lope de Albero. This Pelegrín and his brother Don Gil begged us and called on our love and mercy that we should give advice and help in the matter of the imprisonment of Don Lope de Albero. For when Don Rodrigo had taken him prisoner, he had given no warning to Don Lope de Albero, nor had he defied him.[72] What is more, he had seized the castle and the town of Albero, and ten thousand *cafizes* of grain, which belonged to Don Lope, as well as doing harm to the Christians and Saracens of Albero.

Everyone with us held it to be an evil deed, as did all the people in Aragon who knew about it. And it was agreed by our council (since we did not possess the good prudence then to decide for ourselves, let alone for others) that we should attack him, and rescue Don Lope de Albero and repair the damage that had been done to him, and that we should deliver him from imprisonment.[73]

So, we went to Albero with a *fenèvol*, which we had ordered to be made at Huesca. And those men that Don Rodrigo had placed inside as a garrison surrendered immediately, having seen the *fenèvol* firing for two days.

When we departed from there we went to Lizana, where Don Rodrigo had imprisoned Don Lope de Albero, and we besieged it. Inside, as a garrison, were Don Pedro Gómez and another knight, whose name we do not recall, and squires and other men-at-arms. But Don Pedro Gómez, the most noble and the best of them, was in charge of them and of the castle.

And we set up the *fenèvol* there, in the month of May, and when it was prepared, the *fenèvol* fired five hundred stones per night, and a thousand per day. When the hour of vespers arrived, the *fenèvol* had demolished so large a part of the wall that a great breach had appeared. And the cry went up amidst the army that they should go to fight, and they armed themselves and commenced the battle.

And the men of the army fought with shield and lance, alongside all the crossbowmen of the army that were there.

Throughout the battle the *fenèvol* did not once cease firing, and so ferocious was the battle and so accurate the *fenèvol* that a great number of those inside the town were wounded, both squires and other men-at-arms.

Pedro Ahones), while Guillem de Montcada acted as procurator in Old Catalonia. Ferdinand and his supporters had military but not political power. The council appears now to have attempted to reduce the military power of Ferdinand's supporters.

[71] The daughter was Sancha López. Don Pelegrín was an Aragonese noble from the province of Huesca, he was a prominent member of the king's entourage during the first part of his reign and later took part in the conquest of Majorca and the siege of Valencia.

[72] That is to say, he had acted illegally, because if Lope was his enemy, he would first have to make a formal declaration to indicate the fact, then wait some days before hostilities were allowed to commence.

[73] These events are of May–June 1220.

Seeing that the castle that he had held for his lord was soon to be lost, Don Pedro Gómez, in full armour, with his shield on his arm, his iron helmet on his head, and his sword in his hand, placed himself at the breach, as one who awaits death rather than life. And the *fenèvol* had made great inroads, so that because of the great amount of dust from the earth it had displaced, he was almost buried up to his knees. And the battle continued without anybody climbing to the top of the wall.

But there was a good climber in the army, and one with a mind to climb it. There was a squire, whose name we do not remember, though we believe it was Don Pedro Garcés de Alfaro, and he was wearing a coat of light mail and an iron cap, and had his sword in his hand. Seeing that the battle was waning, he started to run as quickly as his feet could carry him, and began to climb, in such a manner that Don Pedro Gómez was unable to stop him from climbing (for Don Pedro Gómez was unable to move, so deeply was he buried in the earth from the wall). So the men of the army climbed, and the castle was taken. And we recovered Don Lope de Albero, who had been imprisoned there.

Now Don Rodrigo Lizana was a friend of Don Pedro Fernández de Azagra, and negotiated with Don Pedro Fernández for help in the war, asking him to renounce his obedience to us and saying that in return he would give him Santa María de Albarracín. And although Don Pedro Fernández was with us when we made our entry into Aragon, he joined Don Rodrigo, and they both broke from us, and from that moment forth they did us wrong.

And Don Pedro Ahones and his followers joined us and were with us at the capture of these two castles, and afterwards Don Jimeno Cornel did so as well, for he was wiser than the others, and was the greatest noble of Aragon, except for our uncle Don Ferdinand. And this faction was on our side.

[16] And the marriage of the niece of Don Jimeno Cornel, sister of Don Pedro Cornel, was arranged, so that Don Pedro Ahones should take her for his wife.[74]

After that, we summoned our army for the summer months and we went against Albarracín,[75] pitching camp near the tower of the Andador, on a hill that overlooks the tower. We think we must have been at that siege for around two months, and there we set up an *almajanech* that fired against the tower of the Andador, and built hurdles in front of the *fenèvol*.[76]

---

[74]Indication of a firm alliance between Jimeno Cornel and Pedro Ahones, the two Aragonese members of the regency council. The marriage would draw Pedro Cornel into an alliance against the king after Pedro Ahones's death (ch. 28).

[75]July 1220.

[76]James here uses the terms *almajanech* and *fenèvol* interchangeably. The use of the Arabic term, *almajanech*, to designate this siege-engine perhaps indicates it was of Islamic design. All types of trebuchet, being made of wood, were vulnerable to fire if the defenders of a town sallied forth. Therefore it was often the practice to protect the machines from attack (Chevedden, 'Artillery', pp. 70, 79).

Inside the town there were some one hundred and fifty Castilian, Aragonese, and Navarrese knights,[77] having as their leaders Don Pedro Fernández, who was lord of that place, and Don Rodrigo Lizana. Meanwhile, with us were Don Jimeno Cornel, Don Pedro Cornel, Guillem de Cervera, Don Vallés, Don Pedro Ahones, Don Pelegrín (his brother), and Don Guillermo de Pueyo, father of the Guillermo de Pueyo who was with us when we were making this book.[78] And there were men from the cities of Lleida, Zaragoza, Calatayud, Daroca, and Teruel. Yet, among all these nobles that served us, there were not even one hundred and fifty knights.

Because we were a child, still less than eleven years old,[79] all that we did, we did on the advice of the nobles who were with us. And this was fitting, for we did not know then how to govern our lands nor take decisions, so we needed others to advise us.

The relatives and friends of Don Pedro Fernández who were with us would inform the townspeople, night and day, of all the army's actions. Indeed, there were even some knights and squires who would go, in full view of everybody, and enter inside at all hours, letting them know all the army's business, and giving crossbows and provisions to them.

Thus, apart from Don Pedro Ahones and his brother Don Pelegrín, and Don Guillermo de Pueyo, the others served us as badly and as falsely as they could do, to such an extent that our men let those inside the town know on which night Don Pelegrín would guard the *almajanech*.

That night he and Don Guillermo de Pueyo were on guard. And at midnight, the men inside the town lit their torches, and went straight to the pallisades with their entire force of knights, squires, and footmen. And they went there to the *fenèvol* with burning torches, and attacked Don Pelegrín and Don Guillermo de Pueyo, who had the watch. On seeing so great a multitude coming towards them, all those who were with Don Pelegrín and Don Guillermo de Pueyo abandoned them. And Don Pelegrín de Ahones and Don Guillermo de Pueyo died there, because they had more honour than the others and did not wish to fly. And the *fenèvol* was razed to the ground, and not one of the army would go to their aid.

---

[77]Albarracín is close to the Castilian border. Pedro Fernández was born in Castile but married into a Navarrese family and held territory in Aragon. During the minority both Pedro Fernández and Ferdinand of Aragon strongly allied themselves to the wealthy King Sancho VII of Navarre (1194–1234) who took the opportunity to increase his long-held interests in the area (*Marichalar*, nos. 61, 69, 144, 145, 180).

[78]This is one of the comments in the *Llibre* which reminds us of the circumstances of its creation as an oral text.

[79]James is twelve years and five months old.

Afterwards, when our council saw that we had been tricked and badly served by our men, they advised us to lift the siege.[80] And so we had to leave because there were as many knights or more inside as we had outside. And we were unable to take decisions nor did we have anybody with us whom we could consult, since we were only eleven years old.[81]

[17] A year and a half after we had gone from that place,[82] Queen Doña Berenguela,[83] mother of King Don Ferdinand, proposed a marriage between us and her sister who was called Doña Eleanor.[84] Both of them were children of Don Alfonso. And these were the sons and daughters of King Don Alfonso: Queen Doña Blanca,[85] who was the wife of King Louis of France, son of King Philip; and another daughter was Doña Berenguela, the wife of the king of León, who was called Alfonso, and was the father of King Ferdinand; and another was Doña Urraca,[86] who was queen of Portugal, and the other was Doña Eleanor, whom we took as our wife. Of the sons that King Don Alfonso had, one was called Prince Don Ferdinand[87] and the other was called Henry,[88] who was afterwards king of Castile. And Prince Don Ferdinand died before his father, King Don Alfonso. Later on, when King Don Alfonso died, Henry was made king. Yet, whilst playing a game with some youths, whom he himself had divided into two teams, one of those playing in that game threw a tile at his head. And he had positioned himself with his team against their opponents on a hill, which represented a castle, and he was wounded there, and he died from that blow. So the kingdom remained in the hands of Doña Berenguela, whose son was Don Ferdinand, King of Castile.

[18] We married Queen Eleanor on the advice of our men, who told us that, since our father had left no son except us, we should take a wife while young, because they greatly feared for our life, because of illnesses or poisons that might be given us. Yet, above all else, they desired that we should leave an

---

[80]Even with full support, Albarracín was a difficult town to capture. In 1284, during the war between France and Aragon, it took James's son, Peter III (1276–85), five months to force the surrender of the rebel town (*Desclot*, chs. 117, 118, 130).

[81]James was twelve and a half.

[82]There are only seven months between these events.

[83]Berenguela (d. 1246), daughter of Alfonso VIII of Castile (1158–1214), wife of Alfonso IX of León (1188–1230), mother of King Saint Ferdinand III of Castile-León (1217/1230–1252). Peace between Castile and Aragon was generally seen as beneficial by both kingdoms so they could pursue their objectives elsewhere.

[84]Eleanor, youngest daughter of Alfonso VIII. Her marriage to James was annulled in 1229.

[85]Blanche, second daughter of Alfonso VIII, wife of Louis VIII of France (1223–6), son of King Philip Augustus (1180–1223).

[86]Urraca, third daughter of Alfonso VIII, she married King Afonso II of Portugal (1211–23).

[87]Prince Ferdinand, eldest son of Alfonso VIII (d. 1211).

[88]King Henry I of Castile (1214–17).

heir, so that the kingdom should not pass from our line, because Count Don Sancho, son of the count of Barcelona, and Don Ferdinand, who was our uncle and was the son of King Don Alfonso, both aimed to be king. Indeed, they had already fought for the kingdom in our youth when we were at Monzón. Fearing that, they advised us that we should take as a wife the daughter of King Alfonso of Castile. And we were given that advice by Jimeno Cornel and Guillem de Cervera, who were our senior advisers, and Guillem de Montcada who died at Majorca, and by others, whom we do not remember. Thus, we married her at Ágreda.[89]

[19] We were armed as a knight at the church of Santa Maria de la Huerta in Tarazona,[90] and after hearing the Mass of the Holy Spirit we girt on our sword, which we took from upon the altar. We must then have been at least twelve and were entering upon our thirteenth year, so we were a full year with her without being able to do what men should do with their wives, because we were not old enough.[91]

[20] After the marriage, we and our wife the queen entered into Aragon and into Catalonia; and all of the nobles strove to be our favourites, so that we would do everything we did on their advice. Now Don Nunó Sanxes, son of Count Don Sancho, to whom our father had given Rousillon, Conflent and Cerdagne, for his lifetime, was a great friend of Guillem de Montcada. However, because of a quarrel that Don Nunó Sanxes had with Guillem de Cervelló over a male goshawk that Guillem de Cervelló did not wish to give him, they spoke ill of each other and insulted one another.[92] Guillem de Montcada said to Don Nunó that from then on he did not wish to be friends with him, and Don Nunó replied that if he did not desire his friendship, he did not want his either. He told him that he should no longer trust in him, for he

---

[89]6 February 1221 (*M*, p. 37).

[90]The cathedral church of Tarazona. It was customary to take the two rites of passage of marriage and knighthood together.

[91]Much has been made of these lines but it is unlikely that James would have mentioned this if it had caused him any serious psychological problems.

[92]James suggests they fought over a goshawk (that is to say, not even a falcon) and a male one at that (the female of the species being deadlier). James, who generally held his nobles in the highest disregard, deliberately here trivializes one of the most important conflicts of the minority. This round of disputes probably begun in late 1222. Nunó (the son of the formally retired Count Sancho) jostled for position with Guillem de Montcada, who had briefly acted as procurator (at least in Old Catalonia) and was one of James's chief creditors. In 1223, Guillem became viscount of Béarn, increasing his power. The incident with Guillem de Cervelló, a relative of Guillem de Montcada, lies only at the surface of a deeper conflict, first to control the king and then, as he was growing rapidly, to win his favour. The factions within the kingdom were now redefined as the Montcada family allied with Pedro Fernández (who had reconciled himself to the king) and Nunó with Ferdinand of Aragon, now in alliance with Pedro Ahones.

would not be his friend from that moment on. Then Guillem de Montcada established pacts of friendship with Don Pedro Fernández and with his faction, whereas Don Nunó wished to ally himself, and did so, with Don Ferdinand and Don Pedro Ahones and their faction.

Now Guillem de Montcada and Don Pedro Fernández joined forces at a *Cort* that we had convoked at Monzón, of all those on whom we could count. All together there were more than three hundred knights, and they went to a town of the Templars that is called Vallcarca.[93] Meanwhile, Don Ferdinand and Don Pedro Ahones assembled their factions, and they went to Castejón del Puente.[94] As we were coming from Lleida to celebrate the *Cort* at Monzón, Don Nunó met us on the road and said to us that we should give him help and advice. If not, he would receive grave dishonour or death. So we asked him what dishonour that would be, and he said: "Lord, you see that Guillem de Montcada and Don Pedro Fernández are coming; and as you know, Don Guillem and I are at odds, and tomorrow they will be at Vallcarca, and they are coming with more than three hundred knights, and they desire to provoke me to combat. If they defy me and dishonour me I will have no choice but to answer them. And if I respond, I fear that they will kill me or bring me to such shame that it would be the same as death."

(And at that time we were no more than fourteen years old.)

So, we said to him that what he told us grieved us very much, because his shame would be ours, so close was the kinship between the two of us.[95] As regards what he had told us, we answered him that we knew a way in which he would not receive any harm or dishonour. And that we would do the following: as soon as we had entered Monzón, we would send for the dignitaries of the town so that they should come to our presence and that we would speak to them in the following manner: "We beseech you and we order you to guard the town, and close all the gates, and place gatekeepers and armed men there, so as not to allow any noble or any knight to enter there, neither by day nor by night, without letting us know about it; and if they are to enter, each noble must not be allowed to enter with more than two knights, and no more than that should be admitted."

And so it was.

When Don Nunó heard that we had arranged that so well, to our honour and his, he said that he could not be more grateful, for he could see very well how much we loved him, as the decision we had taken had spared him from dishonour and death.

---

[93]To the south-west of Monzón.

[94]To the west of Monzón, on the other side of the River Cinca.

[95]Nunó was the grandson and James the great-grandson of Count Ramon Berenguer IV of Barcelona.

After that, Guillem de Montcada and Don Pedro Fernández arrived with all their forces, and they were unable to enter except with the men we had stipulated. And Don Ferdinand and Don Pedro Ahones entered with the same number. When Guillem de Montcada and Don Pedro Fernández saw that they were unable to carry out what they intended, they left from there. Even so, they began to provoke an argument, but we stopped them, saying that if they said anything to Don Nunó they would pay dearly for it. In this way, Don Nunó left with his honour intact, and they were disappointed in what they had wished to do.

[21] After that had happened, we entered Aragon. And Guillem de Montcada assembled his men in Catalonia, and Don Nunó learnt of it. We and the queen were at Huesca,[96] and Count Don Sancho and Don Nunó came to see us, and they explained to us, in front of the queen, that Guillem de Montcada wanted to enter into Rousillon to attack Don Nunó and blight a land that our father had given to him and that afterwards was to return to our power.[97] Don Nunó besought us and called on our friendship and our favour so that we should help him in the matter, as they wished to harm him and dishonour him and neither he nor his father had any other relatives in Aragon or in Catalonia except us. He said that he was ready to give satisfaction to anybody who had a case against him; and that if he did that, we should help him and protect him, for such was the hope and faith he held in us. And whereas Guillem de Montcada had relations and friends who could harm him, he did not have any relatives or friends to protect him, except us. Immediately afterwards, he placed as security Don Ató Foces[98] and Don Blasco Maza and all that he had in Rousillon, which our father had given him for his lifetime, promising that he would give satisfaction to Guillem de Montcada or any other man who held a claim against him.

After that, we sent letters to Guillem de Montcada saying that he should not harm Don Nunó, as the latter had bound his lands over to us in order to submit to our judgement. But he took little notice, nor did he abandon his proposal, and he entered Rousillon with his lineage and took, with shield and lance, a

---

[96]Between April and June 1223.

[97]Nunó was married to Countess Peronella de Bigorre in 1215 but the marriage was annulled by Pope Honorius III in the following year. He then married Teresa López, daughter of the Lord of Vizcaya, but they had no issue. Through an extramarital union he appears to have had two daughters, Sancha and Maria, and a son, known as the Bastard of Rousillon, who participated in the defence of Elne in 1285 but later collaborated with the French (Coll, 'Nunó', p. 259).

[98]Ató de Foces was one of James's most faithful companions during the early part of his reign and supported him in all his struggles with the nobles. He was major-domo in Aragon in 1224 (*S*, p. 201).

castle named Valric, which belonged to Ramon Castell-Rosselló.[99] Then he went to Perpignan, where Jaspert de Barberà[100] was inside in the service of Don Nunó. And Guillem charged against those of the town so that they were forced outside. And the men of Perpignan came to be defeated, and he took Jaspert de Barberà prisoner in that attack.

As we had sent letters to Guillem de Montcada, and he did not wish to obey our orders, instead attacking Don Nunó and entering Rousillon, we convoked our army in Aragon. Then we attacked him, taking from him, from his kin, and from his followers, one hundred and thirty fortresses, among them towers and castles. We took Cervelló in thirteen days. And after that we went to besiege Montcada.[101]

Now Guillem de Montcada, Don Pedro Cornel, Don Rodrigo Lizana, Don Vallés, and Bernat de Santaeugènia,[102] brother of Ponç Guillem de Torroella, had shut themselves inside there. And we were not more than fourteen years old when we besieged it.[103] With us were Count Don Sancho, and Don Nunó, and Don Ferdinand, and Don Pedro Ahones, and Don Ató Foces, and Don Artal de Luna,[104] and the people of our Aragonese household. All told we must have had about four hundred knights, and inside there must have been some one hundred and thirty knights.

We ordered Guillem de Montcada to give us power over Montcada. And he responded to us that he would have given it to us willingly, if we had asked it of him in a different fashion. But since we had done him a great wrong in coming with an army against him, he said that for that reason he would not give it to us; and he did not give it to us. So, we conducted the campaign against him from one of the hills that overlooks the town, where the market was, and we were there a good three months.[105] And if it had not been for the provisions that they were taking from our camp with the consent of the

---

[99]He is found among the following of James in spring and summer 1223, presumably seeking justice (*M*, pp. 45–6; *S*, p. 201).

[100]Jaspert de Barberà (d. 1274/5). A vassal of Nunó, he was admired by James for his abilities as a military engineer, and played a vital part at the battle of Porto Pí and the siege of Majorca (1229). Much involved in southern French politics over many years (Costa, *Xacbert*), he was sympathetic to Catharism and protected its adherents, which drew him into conflict with the Inquisition but he was himself protected by James and Saint Ramon de Penyafort (d. 1275).

[101]The Montcada family held many castles and fortresses over a widespread territory. In June 1223, we find James at Lleida and Huesca; in July, Barbastro; in August, Tarragona and Cervelló; in September, Barcelona (*M*, p. 46; *H*, 1, nos. 45–7; *S*, pp. 201–2). The siege of Montcada must have taken place after mid-September 1223.

[102]Bernat de Santaeugènia, a knight of Empúries, was to play a lead role in the conquest of Majorca and was left there by James as his lieutenant (ch. 105).

[103]James was at least fifteen years and seven months old when the siege began.

[104]Artal de Luna was major-domo of Aragon in 1222 and later took part in the conquest of Valencia (*S*, p. 202).

[105]September–December 1223.

38 *The Book of Deeds of James I of Aragon*

Aragonese who were with us, (as the Catalans gave them food, which they transported from Barcelona, in exchange for the money of the Aragonese people who were in Montcada) after three days they would not have had anything left to eat.

(But because we were still very young, we did not know how to proceed.)

And because, except for Count Don Sancho, Don Nunó, and Don Pedro Ahones, those who were with us would not have been pleased at any harm being inflicted on those inside, and since the fortress is one of the best in Spain, we had to abandon that place.

For the castle of Montcada is such that, if they have good provisions there, no army is able to take it, except through hunger, because they have plenty of water there on the side of the castle, from a spring that rises on the side of the north wind, and nobody is able to take the water without first taking the castle.

After that we went to Aragon,[106] and Guillem de Montcada went against Terrassa with his forces, and took the entire town except the castle. He took L'Arboç and sacked the whole town, and then went to Piera but was unable to take it. Then he made an alliance with Don Ferdinand and Don Pedro Ahones. And Guillem de Montcada entered Aragon and went to Tauste,[107] which Don Pedro Ahones held from us as an *honor*. And Zaragoza, Huesca, and Jaca entered into this alliance. Meanwhile, we were at Alagón[108] and on our side we had Don Nunó, Don Pedro Fernández, Don Blasco de Alagón, Don Artal, and Don Rodrigo Lizana; but in Alagón there were none with us except Don Nunó, Don Pedro Fernández and Don Ató. And Don Ferdinand, Guillem de Montcada, and Don Pedro Ahones made an alliance to join with Don Nunó and Don Pedro Fernández against all men.[109] And Don Lope Ximenéz de Luesia, vassal of Don Nunó and brother of Ruy Ximenéz,[110] negotiated it.

Then they sent a message to us, saying that they would come to us and do our will, even though they had already made pacts amongst themselves with oaths and in writing. And Don Nunó and Don Pedro Fernández spoke for them on that matter to us. After that they asked us to go out and receive Don Ferdinand, who was our uncle, and Guillem de Montcada, who was a respected man, and Don Pedro Ahones. So we went out to them and we said to them that it was a winter's day and that it was already late, and that they should enter

---

[106]James was in Huesca in April 1224 and in Zaragoza in June 1224 (*H*, 1, nos. 52, 56).

[107]In the province of Zaragoza.

[108]James may here be moving forward in time a little, making the stay at Alagón of winter 1224–25 since James indicates later in this chapter that it was winter.

[109]At times, there are bewildering shifts in alliance. Ferdinand of Aragon and Pedro Ahones, who supported Nunó at the outset, moved to the side of Guillem de Montcada. Pedro Fernández, who had supported Guillem, moved to the side of Nunó and the king. All five nobles then ally, leaving James stranded.

[110]Both Rodrigo (chs. 64, 218) and Lope Ximénez de Luesia (chs. 83, 258) took part in the conquests of Majorca and Valencia.

with four or five knights, and send the other men to the farmhouses outside. Thus, when the hour arrived, we went to our house, and they remained at the gates of the town, which we had ordered closed. However, Don Nunó and Don Pedro Fernández, to whom we had entrusted the guard of the gate, allowed all who wished to enter in, without our knowledge. And some two hundred knights who came with them entered Alagón.

And we were a child and were no more than fifteen years old.[111] And they said to Queen Doña Eleaonor: "You should know that all the knights who came with Don Ferdinand and with Guillem de Montcada and Don Pedro Ahones have entered and they are here, inside Alagón."

Now we were greatly surprised by that. So we asked those who guarded the gate for us why they had allowed them to enter and who had let them in. They said to us that Don Nunó and Don Pedro Fernández had let them enter. And we said to ourselves, "Holy mother, great treason is this, for those in whom we trusted have betrayed us and have allowed our enemies to pass."

[22] And afterwards, when it was morning, we went to hear Mass at the major church of Alagón. In the chancel, where the priests sing, were Don Ferdinand, Guillem de Montcada, Don Pedro Ahones, as well as Don Pedro Fernández and Don Nunó (whom we had thought were on our side, but they were all in it together). Then Don Ferdinand got to his feet and said: "Lord, already you know how closely related I am to you, as the brother of your father, and I do not wish to do anything to displease you. For that reason, we have come here, with Guillem de Montcada and Don Pedro Ahones, to obey you as our lord; and we do not have any quarrel with you nor do we wish for one."

After that Guillem de Montcada got up and said:

"Lord, the rumour alone that you wish us ill grieves us. Prepare yourself to come to Zaragoza to enter your city and to take your rightful place, and there you will be able to deal with your affairs as you wish. And we are disposed to do what you order."

And Don Pedro Ahones said: "Enter Zaragoza, as we are determined to obey you as our lord."

After that they flattered us so much with pretty phrases and arguments, that we entered there the next day.

And when we were there, at the lodgings that we have in front of the Toledo gate, and which used to be called the Zuda, after night fell, they told us that there were a hundred armed men between our gate and a small gate through which one could go out to the wall of the town. Then they sent Guillem Boí and Pere Sanç de Martel, who came to our chamber and made their beds where the women usually sleep. And the queen, on hearing the armed men who were

---

[111]The events are of winter 1224–25. James was almost seventeen.

outside and those who entered the chambers to sleep in our presence, broke down in tears and we, being with her, comforted her. Then Guillem Boí and Pere Sanç Martell entered into our presence and Guillem Boí said to the queen: "Lady," he said, "Do not weep,[112] except as much as may comfort you. For through the tears that a man sheds he loses the rancour that he holds and these tears will all be turned into joy, and your anger will pass."

All this lasted for some three weeks, with the guard and those men sleeping in our presence. And they did not allow Don Ató Foces,[113] who had entered the town, to come before us to advise us nor to be alone with us even for a little time. And he said that as it dishonoured him to be here when he was not called to give counsel, he hoped it would not grieve us if he returned home.

And we said to him, "Go, as your presence brings honour neither to you nor to us."

And he returned to the lands of Huesca.

After that, we took Don Pedro Ahones to one side and we said to him, "Don Pedro Ahones, we have shown you much love and we have made Don Artal de Luna honour you, and yet you are a party to this great dishonour we have received? From this time forth we abandon your friendship, and as long as we live we shall not be friends with you."

And he said, "For what reason?"

"Because you have seen our dishonour and the harm done to us, and if you had not been involved they would not have been able to do it. You could have prevented it and you did not prevent it."

He argued with us about that, and said that what he had done had in no way been to our dishonour or harm, and he took little note of our words.

[23] After this dispute we went to see the queen and we said to her: "Well do we recognize and observe the harm and shame that you and we have received, and although we may be a child, we will avenge us both, if you wish."

And we continued: "In this chamber there is a trap door. We shall take two ropes and we will set you on a board and we will lower you down from there. And on the night we are going to do it we shall send word to Don Artal that he should come here with his men, and when we know that he is here, you will go out through the gate and Don Artal will go with you, and I will remain here at Zaragoza. For I dare do nothing now in case they mistreat you, but as soon you have left from here, I will seek to have words with Don Ferdinand, or Guillem de Montcada, or Don Pedro Ahones, and I will say to them that what they have

---

[112]From here on, his words are in a mix of Catalan and Castilian, perhaps for the queen's benefit.

[113]The major-domo in Aragon. On 14 March 1225, while still held at the Zuda, James confirmed the law-codes of Zaragoza and Jaca (González Anton, 'Revuelta', p. 150).

done against us was treason; and I will mount a horse and take up arms;[114] and I will do it in such a manner that they will be unable to avoid me killing one of them. And we do not believe that they will catch us; since we reckon we shall have such a good horse that we need have no fear of them pursuing us for long."

Yet she replied to us: "You must know that not for anything in the world would I be lowered from here with a rope and a board."

And although we pleaded with her a great deal, she would not do it. And then we calmed things down and, because we feared for her safety, we did not carry out the plan.

[24] Afterwards, Guillem de Montcada arrived and, through Don Ferdinand, asked us to recompense him for the damage we had caused him in Catalonia. And we replied, "All we have done, we have done legally", and that we would give him no compensation.

However, they said that we should do it, because the compensation that we would give would represent much for him and little for us, and that we should give him twenty thousand *morabetins*.

We insisted that we ought not to give it to him, but we allowed ourselves to be convinced by their threats and persuasion, in order to sure that they would thus abandon the treacherous conduct they had pursued. And we promised him twenty thousand *morabetins*.[115] A short time afterwards, we went to Tortosa,[116] while the queen went to Burbáguena.

And Don Ferdinand and Guillem de Montcada and Don Nunó divided the *honors* of Aragon; and they deceived us by asking our advice on the matter, whilst really they were dividing them up as they pleased.

---

[114]This contains one of the most notorious instances of lexical obscurity in the text, which has 'E cavalcaré l. caval e hauré l. guilando'. There is little agreement about the meaning of 'guilando'. Here we have followed a reading from the Alcover-Moll *Diccionari*, where it is read as the name of a weapon. Bruguera (*Vocabulari*, pp. 43–4) relates it to the Castilian form 'aguinaldo' or 'aguilando', suggesting the meaning might be related to prize or prowess. As James then suggests the horse will be good enough to outrun all others, perhaps 'guilando' refers to the quality of his steed rather than his own expertise.

[115]This is exactly the case and it is confirmed by a document of 1 June 1225 that James had conceded to Guillem de Montcada the half of the king's revenues in the dioceses of Barcelona, Vic, and Girona, and the half of the *monedatge*, *bovatge*, and *paria* of Spain (Soldevila, *Primers Temps*, p. 218). This was not only compensation for damage done to Guillem in their disputes but for unpaid debts throughout the minority. The *morabetin* was a gold coin, originally of the Almoravids.

[116]April 1225. The king convoked a general court here (*H*, 1, no. 67) and as well as reconfirming the statutes of Peace and Truce, he asked for help in a campaign against the Moors. It marks the end of the regency.

[25] After that had happened, we left Tortosa, without their knowledge, and we went to Horta de Sant Joan,[117] which belongs to the Templars. There we ordered that the nobles, in virtue of the *honors* that they enjoyed in our name, should attend us at Teruel,[118] because we wished to enter the kingdom of Valencia to attack the Moors, and that they should do service according to the *honors* that we had conceded to them. And we fixed a day for them to be there. After that we went to raise provisions. And Don Pascual Muñoz,[119] who was a close friend of our father, and one of the best townsmen we had in our land at that time, said to us that he and all his friends would give willingly and very gladly all that they could. So he lent us all that we would need for three weeks.

When the day arrived for the nobles of Aragon to join us, nobody came except for Don Blasco de Alagón, Don Artal de Luna and Don Ató Foces. And we saw that they were not coming on the day that we had indicated. Because of their absence we had to consume the supplies that we had reserved for going into the lands of the Moors. So we took the decision to make a truce with Zeit Abuzeit, who was then king of Valencia, in exchange for a fifth part of his rents in Valencia and Murcia, without counting our peatges.[120] And he agreed with letters and pacts that he made with us; and we made the truce with him.[121]

After the aforementioned three weeks, we, having eaten the provisions we had intended for the raid, left the territory of Teruel and entered into Aragon.

---

[117]In the diocese of Tortosa, to the north-west of Tortosa itsef and on the other side ot the Ebro.

[118]James now jumps forward, missing out an important event which he did not wish to recall. Both out of political and financial necessity, the seventeen-year-old king took the cross in April 1225 at Tortosa and launched his first campaign against the Moors besieging Peníscola in August–September 1225 (Gual, *Precedentes*, nos. 61–5), but it was strong and well-provisioned and the siege had to be abandoned (*Desclot*, ch. 13). The events here appear to relate to a new offensive (López Elum, *Conquista y repoblación*, pp. 29–30; González Anton, 'Notas', pp. 418–19), perhaps in the early summer of 1226.

[119]He was one of the representatives from Teruel in the *Cort* at Lleida in 1214, and founder of a noble line (Martínez Ortiz, 'Turolenses', pp. 110–11).

[120]A charge on merchandise in transit.

[121]Abū Zayd governed Valencia as *wālī* in the name of the crumbling Almohad empire. He was great nephew of 'Abd al-Mu'min, founder of the Almohad caliphate. While he had harried James sufficiently in his youth for Pope Honorius III, in June 1222, to call for a crusade, with the usual indulgences, to aid James (Burns, 'Many crusades', p. 172) his position weakened rapidly. As Ibn Khaldūn later wrote concerning this period 'Every *qā'id* and man of influence, who could command a score of followers or who possessed a castle to retire to in case of need, styled himself sultan and assumed the insignia of royalty' (*Muqaddimah*, 1, pp. 315–16). Abū Zayd came under intense pressure from both Castile (in the shape of Ferdinand III) and Aragon, but worse still as representative of the Almohads he was unpopular with Peninsular Muslims and was opposed by two powerful commanders, Zayyān and Ibn Hūd. In January 1229, he was overthrown by Zayyān and fled to Segorbe, allied himself to Aragon (20 April 1229), and converted to Christianity, taking the name Vincent. James long continued to place value in the alliance and in the Valencian campaigns made best use of the following and power that remained to Abū Zayd.

And when we arrived at the second town after Calamocha[122] we came across Don Pedro Ahones, in the company of fifty or sixty knights, and we asked him what he was doing there and where he was going. And he said that he was going to enter the lands of the Moors, together with his brother, the bishop of Zaragoza.[123] And we said to him that he should turn back with us as we wished to speak to him on that matter. But he urged us not to delay his journey. So we said to him: "Don Pedro Ahones, we will not be delaying you much if you accompany us one league, for we would like some nobles of Aragon to be present when we say to you what we want to say."

And he said that he agreed.

Then we went to Burbáguena, to a house of the Templars that is on the road from Daroca to Teruel, and is at the entrance of the village, coming from Daroca. And Don Blasco de Alagón was there, along with Don Artal de Alagón,[124] Don Ató Foces, Don Ladrón, Don Assalit de Gúdar,[125] and Don Pelegrín de Bolas, who was vested in his purpoint[126] and his girted sword and wore a hood of iron mail on his head.[127] And we were then entering our seventeenth year.

There we said to him: "Don Pedro Ahones, we have waited for you at Teruel three whole weeks since the day we indicated to you that you should be there, because we thought to carry out, with you and with the nobles of Aragon, an excellent raid. We say an excellent raid for this reason: because we have not yet seen the Moors in combat and it would please us much to see it and to have seen it. Given that you, and especially you, have let us down, we decided not to enter into the land of the Moors, because, with the very few knights that we had at Teruel, if God did not wish to help us, we might have received dishonour or death. Afterwards, Zeit Abuzeit indicated to us that he would give us the fifths of Valencia and Murcia if we made a truce with him: and we accepted it. For that reason we ask you, Don Pedro Ahones, and we command you, that you respect these truces and you do not break them."

But he said that the preparations that he and his brother the bishop had made had cost them a lot of money, and that we should not desire that he lose what had cost him so dearly.

---

[122]In the province of Teruel. It is half way between Teruel and Calatayud.

[123]Bishop Sancho Ahones of Zaragoza (1216–35).

[124]Brother of Blasco de Alagón, he later fought on the side of the Moors (ch. 227) but then took part in the siege of Valencia and died in a raid on Murcia (ch. 291).

[125]A knight of Teruel, a jurist and man of letters, he was to be one of James's envoys for the surrender of Menorca (chs. 120–1), envoy to Hungary to arrange James's marriage to Violante (along with Pelegrín de Bolas mentioned here, who was a major-domo of the royal court), and was chosen by the king to oversee the division of lands after the conquest of Valencia (ch.295).

[126]A padded tunic that is worn over the hauberk.

[127]It was a 'batut', which protected the head, part of the face, the neck, and the upper part of the chest.

And on that we said to him: "Don Pedro Ahones, you have spoken a great deal of nonsense, because if we have made a truce, it is through your fault, since you did not come on the day that we ordered you to… and now you say that you will not leave off this raid despite our orders! Watch what you do, because you are affronting our lordship, something that we would not have expected of you. And we wish to know if you will renounce your intentions if we ask it and we command it."

He responded that he would do everything we asked of him and everything we commanded him to do, but that in this matter he was unable to comply, because it had cost so much money. Therefore he asked us that we should allow him to enter into the lands of the Moors, together with his brother, and that he would give us good service.

And we said to him that he would serve us ill, "if you break the truce that we have conceded. And we wish to know if you will do it or not."

And he said that he had no other choice.

And after that we said to him: "Since you intend to disobey us in so important a matter, we must inform you that you will be taken prisoner."

[26] And after that no more was said.

Then he stood up. And those who were with us, that is, those whom we have listed above, leftus with him and went to the other end of the room, and holding their hands to their knives, with their shields on their arms, and vested in their purpoints, they left us alone with him. Now, he was a great knight and very good with weapons, and he attempted to place his hand on his sword. But we held his sword with our hand so that he was unable to draw it.

The knights of Don Pedro Ahones had not dismounted from their horses and were outside. And when they heard the noise that arose in the house, some thirty or forty knights dismounted all at once. And while his men came, he tried to draw his knife but we prevented him and he was unable to draw it.

At that moment his men entered the house (and ours were on the way to their lodgings) and they took him from our hands by force, since he alone would have been unable to escape us. And those of our men who were there in the house did not help us, but remained looking on while we fought with him.

Then they put him on his horse and placed him in front, whilst they with their weapons rode behind. And they rode off from there with him.

And we said to a knight of Alagón, called Miguel de Aguas, who had a horse outside the gate, that he should deliver it to us, and as soon as we mounted it, and were vested in our purpoint, they brought our weapons, and we set off in pursuit.

But before we could be ready, Don Ató left with four more knights and a little after Ató, Don Blasco and Don Artal followed with their knights.

And Don Ató caught up with them at the end of the road flanked by the walls of the vineyard of Burbáguena, and a knight said to Don Pedro Ahones: "Look there! Don Ató is pursuing us."

Then Don Pedro Ahones said: "Let us turn towards him so that he cannot escape, the villain!" (even though he was not a villain nor in any way uncourtly).

And those who were with Don Ató broke away from him rather than staying close to him, as they should have done, so opening up a path to his adversaries, through which they were able to wound him.

Two knights wounded him, one giving him a blow under the left side of the mouth and the other wounding him through the side of his shield, and he, realizing that the blow would not be of the same force if he was not upright in the saddle, allowed himself to fall to the right side of the horse and sheltered beneath his shield, so that they would not kill him. Meanwhile Don Blasco de Alagón and Don Artal de Alagón arrived by road, and we passed Don Ató and we asked him why he was seated and what had happened. And he said: "I am wounded," and, "Look, over there! There they go!"

And there was nobody with us except Don Assalit de Gúdar and Don Domingo López de Pomar. Then we saw Don Pedro Ahones with twenty knights who had not left his side, riding up a hill on the left-hand side, in order to escape to a castle that belonged to the bishop of Zaragoza, and was called Cutanda.[128] And Don Blasco de Alagón and Don Artal de Alagón rode after him at the distance of a crossbow shot.[129]

Don Pedro Ahones took refuge on a hill, with those who were with him, and halted there. Then Don Jimeno López de Riglos dismounted. And he said to Don Pedro Ahones that he should mount his horse instead, because his own was tired, and that he should seek to escape. While they were doing that, his men threw great and small stones at those below, so that they could not go up. And Don Pedro Ahones changed horse. And we, on seeing the place where this was going on, said to Don Assalit and Don Domingo López de Pomar, that we could arrive there by means of a slope to the right of that place. And we went in front of those two because our horse could run faster than theirs. As we went up there, Don Pedro Ahones' men threw stones against the men of Don Ató and Don Blasco, so that they were unable to go up the hill that the others occupied. And as we rode up, we cried out: "Aragon! Aragon!"

Then we and our company went up the hill together; and all the knights that guarded Don Pedro Ahones abandoned him, except one who was called Martín Perez de Mezquita, and came after us following his lord. Meanwhile Sancho Martínez de Luna, the elder brother of Martín López, arrived and wounded him

---

[128]Cutanda, in the diocese of Zaragoza and the province of Teruel, and just to the east of Calamocha.

[129]275 metres.

through the right side with his lance, and he sank his spear half a foot into Don Pedro's right side through the opening of the purpoint, beneath his arm.

And he, who rode before us (so that there was nobody between us and him, so close were we), realizing he was wounded, stopped, and clung to the neck of his horse.

We went immediately to his side as he allowed himself to fall to the left side of his horse. As he began to slide, we dismounted, and we protected him with our arms. Supporting him, we said to him: "Ah, Don Pedro Ahones, you were born in evil hour! Why did you not wish to believe what we advised you?"

And he was unable to speak but looked us in the face.

[27] While we were there Don Blasco arrived and said: "Ah, lord, leave this lion to us, so that we may avenge what he has done to you."

And we said to Don Blasco: "God confound you for the words that you have just spoken. I tell you that if you harm Don Pedro Ahones it will be as if you harmed me and you will have to wound me first. We most strongly forbid you to do this."

Then we mounted him on a beast, with a squire to support his body. But he died on the road before we reached Burbáguena.

Then we went to Daroca.[130] And we took Don Pedro Ahones in a coffin to Daroca, and we placed him in the church of Santa Maria de Daroca.

As we were leaving, the men of Daroca insulted our men (those who had arrived after us), striking a squire of ours, a relative of Don Pelegrín de Bolas, on the jaw with a stone, when he dared to answer them.[131]

Now Don Pedro Ahones held in pledge Bolea and Loarre, which our father had pawned to him, and he had held the pledges for such a long time that by now he should have been able to recoup the debt.

When we went there, we found Don Ferdinand and Don Pedro Cornel holed up there, and with them some seventy or eighty knights. Yet we had gone there thinking we would not find anybody there and that we could enter there, since the men that guarded those places were our men. However, the people of the town were on their side and against us, and they gave us as much trouble as they could, as if we were not their lord. And we saw that a large garrison of knights and footmen protected the castle and that with what they had in the town alone they easily had provisions for a year. So we decided that we should move on and leave there.

---

[130] These events are of June 1226.

[131] The death of Pedro Ahones caused great resentment in Aragon, which was nurtured by Ferdinand of Aragon. This incident at Daroca was the first stirring of what was to become a general revolt.

[28] As we were leaving, the cities of Aragon rose up against us, together with Don Ferdinand, Don Pedro Cornel, and the followers of Don Pedro Ahones. Then they sent for Guillem de Montcada so that he should come, and he came with all his forces. And all the cities of Aragon were against us, with the single exception of Calatayud.[132]

We left for Almudévar and remained there some three weeks.[133] Then we moved on to Pertusa[134] and we sent for Ramon Folc de Cardona,[135] who came to our aid a month later with his brother Guillem de Cardona[136] and some sixty knights. We sent the detachments of Don Blasco and Don Artal de Luna against the men of Zaragoza and only Don Ató, Don Rodrigo Lizana, and Don Ladrón remained with us. And the bishop of Zaragoza, brother of Don Pedro Ahones, sent his men in ambush. Moving by night they arrived at Alcubierre, and took it and sacked it completely. All this took place during Lent. Yet he absolved them all of the evil that they had done, and gave license to eat meat to all that wanted it.

Another time, the men of Zaragoza went to Castellar, and Don Blasco and Don Artal were at Alagón and crossed the river Ebro and fought with them on the hill that is outside Castellar, before Zaragoza. And all the men of Zaragoza were defeated, and some three hundred men were either killed or captured.[137] And when Ramon Folc arrived at Pertusa we took bread from the men of Zaragoza and Huesca and the knights who had come to their aid, for at Monzón we had only bought some two thousand pounds according to the Aragonese measure.[138] Then we built an *almajanech* and went to Ponzano,[139] and we took the place.

---

[132]This was the case. At Jaca, on 13 November 1226, three leagues were formed: between Zaragoza, Huesca, and Jaca; between these cities and Ferdinand, Bishop Sancho of Zaragoza, Pedro Fernández, Pedro Cornel, and others; between these cities and Guillem de Montcada, the viscount of Béarn (*CDCZ*, 1, nos. 54–56; Soldevila, *Vida de Jaume I*, pp. 87–90).

[133]December–January 1227. The town is a little to the south-west of Huesca.

[134]Huesca province. Half-way between Huesca and Monzón. February 1227.

[135]Viscount Raymond Folc III of Cardona (1226–33). He had allied with the Cabrera on the side of James in his struggles with the Montcada until a truce in May 1226, but not when they later disputed with the king over Urgell. He did not participate in the conquest of Majorca, possibly because of the strong Montcada presence. Here at Pertusa, on 8 February 1227, James gave him 25,000 Barcelonan sous in return for service against the king's enemies (*H*, 1, no. 88).

[136]Guillem de Cardona later took the side of the Cabrera against the king over Urgell (chs. 35–6). He was master of the Temple in Catalonia, and he later participated in the Valencia campaigns. He participated in the crusade of King St Louis IX (1226–70) of France to Egypt in 1253 (*M*, p. 232; S, p. 208).

[137]This victory of February or March 1227 marked a turn in the king's fortunes.

[138]The king was at Monzón on 14 February 1227 (*M*, p. 69). The Aragonese measure for a pound was 350. 8 grams, whereas the Catalan measure was 400 grams (*P*, p. 70, n. 32). Thus James had bought 701.6 kilograms of bread, insufficient for a sizeable army.

[139]Just to the west of Barbastro.

[29] From there we moved on to Lascellas,[140] and we set up the *almajanech*. After it had been firing for three days, a squire who had command of the castle offered terms, saying that we should fix a day and if at the end of that day nobody had come to his aid, he would surrender the castle. And Ramon Folc, Don Rodrigo Lizana, Don Ató, Don Ladrón, and Don Pedro Pomar considered that we should agree a day, providing it was soon. The squire asked us for fifteen days, and we said that we would give him only five days; but finally we agreed on eight. And Don Ató said that he would cross to the other side of the river, and that if he saw somebody coming against us he would return immediately and let us know of it.

On the eighth day we went to Pertusa and held our council early in the morning. Invoking the lordship that we had over them, we ordered them that the next day, first thing in the morning, they should be at Lascellas with their weapons, and that anybody who was not there would lose all the possessions that he held in our lands; and we sent letters in the same terms to Berbegal and Barbastro saying that all should be with us the next day.

After we had eaten (for it was a fast day),[141] Don Pelegrín and Don Gil Atrosillo arrived by the Huesca road. They came alone, with lance and shield, galloping as fast as they were able. And our men pointed them out to us and we did not recognize them until they were at the bridge of Pertusa. We awaited them there, at the church of Santa Maria, in the graveyard, and they came and they said: "God save you. Don Ferdinand and Don Pedro Cornel, and the men of Zaragoza and Huesca are coming to help Lascellas. We have left them at Velilla and they are coming as quickly as they can."

We ordered them to saddle, and there were no more than four knights with us. And we ordered the men of the council[142] to follow behind us, under penalty of treason, and we also sent notice to the men of Berbegal and Barbastro.

Then we set out at once for Lascellas and there we found Ramon Folc, Guillem Cardona, Don Rodrigo Lizana, and our household, and in all there were not more than seventy or eighty knights. And we said that they should arm their horses, as Don Ferdinand was coming and the men of Zaragoza and of Huesca were accompanying him. Thus, all hurried to arm themselves.

As we were saying these words, Don Pedro Pomar, who was an experienced knight of our household, said to us: "Lord, I will give you some good advice: here outside there is a hill that is very secure, go up there, and the towns will learn of it and will all come to your aid."

And we responded to him: "Don Pedro Pomar, we are the king of Aragon and the kingdom is ours by right, and those who come against us are our

---

[140] Just to the north of Ponzano and to the right of the River Alcanadre. Province of Huesca.
[141] It was Lent. March 1227.
[142] The council of the town or perhaps here, specifically, the militia.

subjects, and in coming to fight us they do what they ought not to do, since we defend what is right and they do wrong; and so God must help us. And while we live, we shall not abandon this town and we shall defeat them. Thus, on this occasion we will not follow your advice."

And we awaited them. But they did not come, so we took the castle.

[30] Afterwards we returned to Pertusa, where we were joined by the archbishop of Tarragona, Aspàreg by name, who was our relative. When he heard that the lands of Aragon were in chaos and that they were doing us all manner of wrong, he urgently besought us, in the name of God and for the love that we had for him, that we would reach an agreement with our people, allowing him to act as an intermediary. And we conceded that to him. Thus, after having obtained our agreement, the archbishop spoke with them. However, he was unable to find a solution since they asked us to make concessions that would prejudice our lordship. And with that he had to leave.

And when they saw that we had taken Lascellas, the men of Huesca sent word to us, through Don Martín de Perixolo, who was our merino,[143] and through other friends that we had there, that we should come to Huesca, as they could guarantee that we would be able to do as we pleased there. And we went to Huesca, but we did not allow our knights to bear arms, so the townsmen would not change their minds because of us. Before we arrived there, some twenty of the leading men of the town came out to receive us at Santa María de Salas.[144] So we spoke with them, saying that we considered what had happened very surprising, because we desired them nothing but good; and that if previously those of our line had done them good and had loved them, we would love them even more. On hearing this, they thanked us very much, and said that we were welcome to enter the town, for they would treat us just as a man ought to treat his natural lord. And when we made our entry, the children and the people of the town were very glad at our arrival.

We entered the town at the hour of vespers (and with us also Don Rodrigo Lizana, Don Blasco Maza, and of our household Don Assalit, Don Pelegrín de Bolas and many others), but the townspeople did not tend to us in any way. And after we had eaten, we said, in good humour, that we could see very well that they would do our will, so well had they received us.

[31] Later, when we and all those who slept in our presence had already gone to bed, one of our gatekeepers came, and he said that there were some hundred armed men at the gate, and we said to him: "Go away. We have just taken off our armour and you want us to put it on again? Perhaps they are guarding the town..."

---

[143]Essentially, in Aragon, the king's bailiff.
[144]A town just to the north of Huesca.

And he said: "Lord, give us one of your squires and we will show it to him."
And we said: "Let us sleep. God's will shall be done."

When morning came, and after having risen and heard Mass, we had the council[145] called to come to the yard between our houses and the monastery of Montearagón. And we were on horseback and they were on foot before us, and we made a great speech, saying to them: "Worthy men, we do believe that you know, and so you ought, that we are your natural lord, and have been so for a long long time, for, with us, there have been fourteen kings of Aragon,[146] and the older the natural bond between us, the closer we should be, because with the dispersal of relations of kinship, the natural bond becomes stronger.[147]

"And we have never treated you badly nor have we spoken ill of you, rather on the contrary, our intention is to love you and to treat you honourably; and we will continue to respect all the legal rights that you have been accustomed to enjoy under our lineage, and we will concede to you still more important things if what you have is insufficient.

"For it seems very strange to us that we have had to be on our guard against you and that we do not dare enter the cities that God has given us, which our father has left to us; and it grieves us greatly that there has been conflict between us and you. And we beseech you and we order you that it should be at an end, since it grieves us so much. And of this much you may be sure, that as I have come among you and trust in your love, I intend to pardon you and be your friend."

With that we brought our speech to an end; and they responded saying that that they thanked us for what we had said and that the council would deliberate and give us a response. Then they went to reach a decision at the monastery of Montearagón, and their deliberations lasted a long time.

[32] Afterwards, while we were waiting for them, a messenger arrived at the council saying that Ramon Folc and his men were outside and were attacking the town. And we, seeing that the council was afraid, said to them: "Be calm and listen to what we have to say."

And we sent for those who had gone to deliberate, that they should come; and some of them came, but they did not respond to what we had said to them. And we said to them: "Worthy men, it is very strange that you are afraid for no reason, because it is impossible that while I am with you anybody would dare

---

[145]The council of the town.

[146]With James there had been eight kings of Aragon if one includes Ramiro I (1035–63). James may be referring to fourteen generations of his family stretching back to Count Aznar Galíndez of Aragon (809–39) or possibly to the fourteen counts of Barcelona, stretching back to Wilfred the Hairy (878–97).

[147]"E on pus luyn és la naturalea entre nós e vós, més acostament hi deu haver, que parentesch s'alonga, e naturalea per longuea s'estreyn". Interpretation of *P*, p. 75.

do you any harm. Moreover, for every penny that you lose (a thing that cannot happen) we will give you ten."

And they said: "What you say is all very well... but you ought to forbid it."

And we said: "So it is forbidden."

And immediately we sent someone to see what was happening and we discovered that nothing had happened.

Yet, even after that they did not give us any response at all, and everybody stood up. So we returned to our house with Don Rodrigo Lizana and Don Blasco Maza, and those of our household (that is, Don Assalit) and Rabassa,[148] our notary; and we were told that chains were being put out and the gates of the town locked.[149] And we said to Rabassa: "Do you know any law that might favour you and us?"

And he replied: "Lord, I do not believe that any law or any right can help us."

And we said to him: "Do you have anything more to say on the matter?"

And he responded: "No, but you ought to ask the opinion of the nobles."

So we asked their opinion, and they said that great treason was being done to us but that they were unable to give us any solution.

Then we said that we would take a decision: "The best decision possible: we will send for mutton to be bought from the butcher's, and they will think we are preparing to dine.[150] Meanwhile, you saddle up and leave; and do it right now. And I will send for my horse, my hauberk, my purpoint, and my weapons, and you all be ready and prepared in the square."

And so it was done. Don Rodrigo Lizana and Don Blasco Maza came with us, and we were no more than five knights.

We dismounted at the gate that gives on to the Isuela[151] and the road to Bolea. As I found the gate closed, I asked who had closed it, and I found a woman who said that the councillors had shut it. And we said to a squire: "Where is the gatekeeper?"

And he said: "He is usually up there."

And I sent two of my squires to find him. All pale he came, and we asked him: "Who has the key to the gate?"

And he said: "The councillors of the town have it."

---

[148]Guillem Rabassa, a royal notary and later a canon of Lleida (*S*, p. 210).

[149]The councillors of Huesca deliberately delayed giving the king any response since they had already sent word to Ferdinand of Aragon and the men of Zaragoza that they should come and capture the king. Meanwhile, they quietly closed all the exits of the town, so James could not escape.

[150]James wished to give the Huescans the impression that he was unaware of their intentions.

[151]A river to the right of Huesca which joins with the Alcanadre.

And we said: "Give it to us now,[152] or I will give you such a blow on the head with my sword that I shall leave you dead."

Then we ordered the squires to accompany him, and they brought the keys and bound him over to us a second time with the key, and we ordered him to open the gate with my men. We then remained at the gate until the knights came, and when they arrived we went outside.

And they said to us that the beasts and the squires had been held inside, and we said to some twenty or thirty men of Huesca who were outside with us that one of them should go to the town to tell them to hand over to us all that was ours there, because we would take prisoner any of their people who were with us. Then they sent us all that we had inside the town.

And we went down to the Isuela and we found Ramon Folc and Guillem de Cardona with all the other knights and our household and Don Ató, weeping, because they thought we had been captured. And the townsmen of Huesca had already sent word to Don Ferdinand and to the men of Zaragoza that they should come as we had been captured us at Huesca.

[33] After that had happened, we went to Pertusa. And while we were there, Don Ferdinand, Guillem de Montcada, and Don Pedro Cornel went to Huesca and there they discussed the possibility of arriving at terms with us, since they considered that they had behaved foolishly.

Both our council and we were very pleased with the message that they sent us and we asked them how they wished to arrive at terms with us.

They said they would go to the mountain that is near Alcalá del Obispo,[153] and that we should go there with seven men of our council. They would come with six or seven men, without the rest (indeed, they even said they would have come to Pertusa had they not feared that someone might be wicked enough to try to start a quarrel with them), for they wished to speak with us as vassals speak to their natural lord, and before we had left them they would do what was necessary to satisfy us.

And all took place just as had been agreed.[154]

We went to the meeting vested in our purpoints and with swords girt, and with us were Ramon Folc, Guillem de Cardona, Don Ató Foces, Don Rodrigo Lizana, Don Ladrón (the son of Don Ladrón, who was noble and of great lineage),[155] Don Assalit de Gúdar, one of our knights, whose name we do not recall, and Don Pelegrín de Bolas. And on their side came Don Ferdinand, who was our uncle, Guillem de Montcada, father of Gastó,[156] Don Pedro Cornel,

---

[152]James realized the gatekeeper was stalling.
[153]A town of the province of Huesca, to the south-east of Huesca.
[154]31 March 1227.
[155]The son of the Ladrón in chapter 9 and perhaps the Ladrón in chapter 25. He participated in the conquests of Majorca, Menorca, and Valencia.
[156]Viscount Gastó VII of Béarn (1229–90).

Don Fernando Pérez de Pina,[157] and others of their party whom we do not recall.

And Don Ferdinand began the negotiations and said: "Lord, we have come here before you, and we are very sorry for the war that there has been between you and us, and we have come to put an end to it. And we ask you that you pardon us, for we intend to serve you – I, Guillem de Montcada, Don Pedro Cornel and all those on our side; since we have received harm from you and we have done harm, a thing that grieves us greatly. And if we had to make good the damage, we would be unable to do so, and the compensation would represent little for you and much for us. For that reason, it is necessary that you show us clemency.

"And we beseech you, moreover, that, if we serve you well, you will treat us well. For my part, you are obliged by the kinship that unites me to you, and for Guillem de Montcada, because no king of Spain has any vassal as honoured as you have in his person nor any that can serve him so well."

And with that, he ended his speech. And afterwards Guillem de Montcada said: "Lord, the debt that I owe you, nobody in the world knows better than you yourself, since your line, and especially the count of Barcelona,[158] has made ours what it is. And, by the grace of God, I am more powerful than the others are, since I have the riches of the line of Béarn, in Gascony, such that none of the other lineages has obtained. Yet, all that I have, or might ever have, I place at your service. And what I have done, God, Who knows all things, knows I have done for your honour and your benefit; but as I see that it does not please you neither does it please me, and I consider that I have behaved wrongly. And so I ask your clemency, that you pardon me and pardon all those who have participated in this affair. For I tell you truthfully that never more will I go to war with you, because I hold you in such regard that I do not believe that you would do wrong to me or my friends or my relatives; and if you were to do so, with prayers and with love I would win you over, and with the service I will loyally show you. And this is all I can do to prove to you my worth."

Thus he finished his speech. And when he had finished we told them that we would deliberate, and they withdrew from our presence.

And the nobles who were with us said that they had expressed themselves nobly and correctly and with great devotion, and that the terms were acceptable.

---

[157] A knight of the king's household. He was the fourth man to enter the city of Majorca at its capture (ch. 84) and participated in the early Valencian campaigns.

[158] A reference to Count Ramon Berenguer IV (1131–62) who dramatically increased the power of Seneschal Guillem Ramon II, lord of Montcada for more than sixty years, in return for his generally loyal and devoted service.

After that we called them back and we said to them: "What you have declared with so much devotion is acceptable to us. We are satisfied and we accept as compensation your good intentions and we wish to preserve you as friends in our grace."

And the knights of each of the sides, who had been at a distance, came and learned of the cessation of hostilities and the agreement that we had established, and all were happy and satisfied.[159]

And once this was done we left for Lleida.

[34] About a year and a half later,[160] when we were at Lleida, the countess of Urgell[161] came, who was the daughter of Count Ermengol and the countess of Subirats. She had been married to Álvaro Pérez,[162] but they had parted because they were closely related, and she had borne him no children. (And her name was Aurembiaix.) We made her welcome and, after she had been there for two days, we went to see her. Guillem de Cervera,[163] Lord of Juneda, was of her council, and she was guided by him more than by any other person in the world. He was able to advise her in her affairs because he had taken her mother as his wife. Furthermore, as he was an old man and one of the wisest in Spain,

---

[159]The disputes were placed before three arbitrators (the archbishop of Tarragona, the bishop of Lleida, and the master of the Temple) who dictated their sentence on 31 March 1227 (*CDI*, 6, no. 15). All the leagues entered into were dissolved. James pardoned the rebels in return for homage and oaths of fealty. James was forced to make considerable financial concessions, particularly to Ferdinand of Aragon, the bishop of Zaragoza, Pedro Cornel, and Atorella. It was perhaps more a victory for the Aragonese nobles than for the king (González, 'Revuelta', p. 161). On 1 April 1227, the league between the Aragonese cities was dissolved and James ordered them to satisfy the damages done to him, in return for which James pardoned them and confirmed their law-codes (*H*, 1, no. 91; *CDCZ*, no. 57).

[160]Late July–August 1228 (*M*, p. 71). So, about a year and four months later.

[161]Aurembiaix was named as heiress of the important county of Urgell in her father's will in 1208. Ermengol VIII died in 1209. Guerau de Cabrera sought the county through the rights of his mother, Marquesa, sister of Ermengol VIII. James's father, Peter II, also sought power over the county and, with the consent of Ermengol's widow, Elvira, Aurembiaix was promised to James in October 1209. Elvira ceded to Peter her rights in the county but without prejudice to Aurembiaix's rights. Peter II then waged war on the Cabrera family to obtain the county. But in January 1211, Peter was forced by the problems in the Languedoc to betroth James (then nearly three) to the daughter of Simon de Montfort. While Guerau was defeated and captured in 1211, after Peter's death at Muret in 1213, the chaos in Aragon and Catalonia allowed Guerau to take control of the county from Elvira (Sobrequés, *Barons*, pp. 65–6).

[162]After Guerau had obtained the county, Aurembiaix was promised and later married to Álvaro who was of the powerful Castro family. Aurembiaix left Urgell and went to Toledo with her husband. But Álvaro was descended from a daughter of Count Ermengol VI of Urgell who had married an ancestor of his called Pedro Fernández (*S*, p. 213). They were thus related within the prohibited degrees. The marriage was annulled in 1228.

[163]After Ermengol's death in 1209, the Countess Elvira had married Guillem de Cervera (also widowed), who took Aurembiaix under his protection. Guillem had been a close ally of Ermengol VIII and continued to press the rights of Aurembiaix against the Cabrera in her long absence.

she did by his advice all that she put before us and the others who were there. And he took care of her business and all of her affairs.

She said to Guillem de Cervera that he should explain her thoughts to us on her behalf. But Guillem de Cervera said to her: "Lady, you should say it, as you know better than I how to explain it and say it."

So she was made to speak for herself, and she said that she had come for our help. For, she said that from what she knew, and from what people said, she would find justice and mercy in us. She said she had come to us because a grave injustice had occurred in our land. All the world knew that she was the daughter of the count of Urgell, Ermengol, and that therefore that county belonged more to her than to any other person. For she was his daughter, and he had no son or daughter except her. Hence, she called on our love and mercy to defend her right, since there was nobody else in the world who could help her, except us. Afterwards, Guillem de Cervera and Ramon de Peralta supported her reasons for speaking. This Ramon de Peralta had not wished to surrender Montmagastre until the countess came.[164] But when she had come, he gave her Montmagastre and the rights that the count had held there, retaining for himself the power over four castles.[165] And they turned to us and they said: "Lord, such is the duty of the king, to give justice to all those who are unable to obtain it elsewhere. For God has set you in His place to maintain just law. As you know, this lady who has come before you is of great lineage on the part of both her mother and her father, and she has been disinherited of the possessions of her father in your kingdom and under your rule. Hence, she comes to ask that through your mercy all that is hers and all that her father left her be returned to her. And she is a person of such good breeding that that must mean something to you. And for that reason we ask your mercy, joining our voice to hers in what she has expressed better than any of us."

Ramon de Peralta spoke in a similar manner. And we said to them that their entreaties were just, and that we would take counsel and do what it was necessary to do in this matter.

So we asked the advice of the bishop, whose name was Berenguer d'Erill,[166] and of Guillem de Montcada, Ramon Folc,[167] and Guillem Ramon,[168] brother of Ramon de Montcada and father of Pere,[169] and of Don Assalit, and Don

---

[164]Montmagastre is a town of the county of Urgell. Aurembiaix, when still in Toledo, had ceded the castle to Ramon de Peralta on 1 May 1226 in return for his good service towards her.

[165]Purroy, Gavàs, Rocafort, and Pelegrí (*S*, p. 213).

[166]Berenguer d'Erill, bishop of Lleida (1205–35)

[167]Ramon Folc III, viscount of Cardona (1226–33).

[168]The seneschal Guillem Ramon V de Montcada (c. 1198–1228), also called Guillem Dapifer. He was married in 1212 to Constança, natural daughter of Peter II, who gave him Aitona, Serós, Mequinenza and Albalate. He was one of the Montcadas who battled against James in 1224.

[169]Pere I de Montcada (1228–67), sixth seneschal, grandson of Peter II of Aragon.

García Pérez de Mediano,[170] and the notables of the city of Lleida. And they encouraged us to give her Guillem Sasala[171] as her advocate. She then gave him the right of the Caldera[172] of Lleida, to be held for the rest of his life; and it was not then worth more than two hundred sous in rent but afterwards rose to three thousand sous.

[35] The decision of the bishop and the nobles was to call upon the count of Urgell, Guerau de Cabrera,[173] to come to our court to do right by the countess, and that all the citations should be made, all three, as the law required. After the first citation had been made, he did not appear. But before we could pass sentence against him or take further action (since this was the manner of the law), we returned to her and we said we could only proceed according to the order dictated by law, and that so should she and her counsel.

Thus, we agreed to cite Guerau de Cabrera, who then possessed the county of Urgell.[174] But when we had called upon him, and the day arrived, Guillem de Cardona (brother of Ramon Folc), who was the master of the Temple,[175] came as the procurator of Guerau, who held the county of Urgell. He said to our court, in the presence of everyone, that Guerau, Count of Urgell, and all who had heard of the matter were greatly perplexed. For he had held that county for twenty or thirty years[176] without any claim being made upon it, even though the countess was alive all that time. And as no previous claim had been

---

[170]An Aragonese knight of the king's household who took part in the conquest of Majorca and died there in 1230 (ch. 92).

[171]A very important figure in thirteenth century Lleida, he was a royal notary, lawyer, and creditor of James, who accompanied the king to Majorca (*S*, p. 214).

[172]The Cauldron fee. A tax collected by the Crown on each vat used by any class of citizen (Burns, *Medieval Colonialism*, p. 39). It seems that towards the end of James's reign, when Guillem Sasala had died (c.1267) the figure had risen to seven thousand sous but the figure has been put as high as fifteen thousand sous in 1257 and fourteen thousand sous in 1268 (Soldevila, *Primers Temps*, p. 276). The figure of three thousand sous is one of the indications that James dictated these passages much earlier in his reign.

[173]Guerau, viscount of Àger and Cabrera, de facto count of Urgell (1213–27). The son of Ponç de Cabrera and Marquesa, daughter of Ermengol VII of Urgell. Guerau was the cousin of Aurembiaix. After being captured by Peter II at Llorenç, he was imprisoned at Jaca, but afterwards participated in the battle of Las Navas de Tolosa (16 July 1212). The minority council accepted Guerau's possession of Urgell as a fact and in 1217, 1222, and 1223 (*H*, 1, nos. 2, 39, 43) his position as count of Urgell was strengthened by a series of agreements with James, which, however, reserved the rights of Aurembiaix should she wish to reclaim them.

[174]Guerau had entered the order of the Temple by 1227. There is a slight confusion in the passages that follow as to when James is dealing with Guerau and when with his son Ponç I, Count of Urgell (1236–43), who was vigorously to pursue his claims in the county both at this time and after the death of Aurembiaix in 1231.

[175]Guillem de Cardona was provincial master of the Templars (1244–52). He had been commander of Gardeny (1239–43) and lieutenant of the provincial master (1238–41).

[176]He had held it for eleven years since the agreement with James at Monzón of June 1217, almost fifteen since the death of Peter II at Muret in September 1213, and had claimed the county for nineteen years since the death of Ermengol VIII.

made, even though the matter was now placed in question and a plea made, he was not obliged to answer to it. And secondly he asked us not to bring this plaint against him, for he was not a man to whom such strange and unworthy claims should be made.

Then Guillem Sasala spoke these words on behalf of the countess: "Lord, how can Guillem de Cardona, who is a noble man and of great and honoured lineage, consider this demand strange? Surely it would be far stranger not to grant justice to so good a lady as the countess. And if she demands justice in your court and he says he will not give it to her he speaks against all reason. For God, my lord, has put you in His place so that you may give justice and reason to those who cannot find either; and the countess requests that you defend her rights."

But Guillem de Cardona said: "I have not come here for any other reason, not even to plead with you, but only to say what I have been charged to say."

Then Guillem de Montcada said: "Do you have anything to advocate on behalf of Guerau?"

And he said: "No. What they have charged me to say, I have already said, and I have not come here for anything else; and, now I have said it, I will go."

Yet Ramon de Montcada said: "Wait, while the king takes counsel, and he will respond to what you have said."

So, they left our presence and we deliberated. And when the decision had been made, they asked us that we ourselves should give the reply, and we said: "Guillem de Cardona, you have not brought here any procuration from Guerau; and, what is more, you do not wish to respond according to the law. However, we will ask you again if you will respond to the petition that Guillem Sasala has made of you."

Then he replied and said that he would not say anything more. And we said to him: "Then we shall do what we must. We will cite him again, and that will make three citations. And if he wishes justice to be done, we will receive him, but if not, we will take further action, as the law decrees."

And with that he left, and we made another citation; and Guillem de Cardona came on the appointed day.

[36] And we were at the house of Ramon,[177] our steward, and all the court and the nobles came to listen. And Guillem Sasala stood up and said: "Lord, I beseech you that you will allow me to be heard. It was God's will that in these times there would be kings, and that their office should be to give justice to those who might need it, especially to widows and orphans. Thus, when the

---

[177]On 1 August 1228, he was witness to the agreement between James and Aurembiaix at Lleida concerning this dispute (*H*, 1, no. 102). He witnesses as Raymundus Reposter rather than Raymundus repositarius suggesting this was actually his name, though a name which would have proceeded from the office.

countess did not have anybody to turn to but us, she came before you for two reasons: firstly, because the plaint she has is in your land, and, secondly, because you are the only person in the world who can help. Because of this she asks your mercy, just as one should of a just lord, that you might demand a response of Guerau, or of Guillem de Cardona, who appears here in his name. For, in this matter you have already signaled two days and, because of his failure to appear, you and your court were unable to resolve the matter. Now this is the last day, so the countess entreats you, as to a lord from whom she awaits all that is good and just, that she might receive justice from you as follows. If Guillem de Cardona does not appear disposed to do what is right, you should proceed against Guerau and his goods, so that the countess might see justice done in the petition she makes."[178]

Then Guillem de Cardona said: "Listen, Guillem. Do you really think that the count will lose his county through the art of pleading you have learnt in Bologna?"[179]

And Guillem Sasala replied: "I only demand that justice be done for the countess. And if we are in the right, we trust that the lord king will recognize it, for I'll not leave off defending her right because of you."

Then Guillem de Cervera asked: "And how, Guillem de Cardona, could you have it otherwise?"

To which he replied: "Be assured, Guillem de Cervera, that the count will not lose his county through a plea alone. Something more will be necessary."

So Guillem de Cervera said: "And so it shall be."

Then, Guillem de Cardona said: "Lord, give me safe conduct, and I will go from here."

And we said: "Will you have it no other way?"

And he said not. So, Guillem de Cervera responded: "By my faith, you shall do something else."[180]

"Now," said Guillem de Cardona, "It will be as God wills." And he commended us to God.

---

[178]At Lleida, Aurembiaix agreed to cede her rights in Lleida and to receive the county of Urgell in fief from James, in exchange for which James would help her to recover Agramunt, Linyola, Balaguer, and other places in the county of Urgell which were in the power of Viscount Ponç de Cabrera (*H*, 1, no. 102).

[179]In the first half of the thirteenth century there was a great increase in the number of scholars from Catalonia who went to study law at Bologna. Catalonia produced a number of exceptional lawyers in this period and many were in the service of the king. Roman Law tended to strengthen the position of the king opposite to the nobility. Guillem de Cardona is not merely objecting to Guillem Sasala's art but to a system which clashed with the customs and usages of the nobility.

[180]This exchange is rather obscure, and there are numerous variants in the different manuscripts of the *Llibre*. Bruguera's reading (*Llibre*, 2, p. 47) has been followed. The function of the passage would seem mainly to be to show that tempers are fraying.

[37] We immediately sent a letter to Tamarite[181] saying that on an appointed day they should go to Albesa[182] with their weapons and with three days of provisions, and that we would be there. And we said to Guillem and Gastó de Montcada, and to Ramon and Guillem de Cervera, that they and those of their lineage should come with us "And we will attack Ponç."[183]

While the letters were on their way, Don Pedro Cornel was with us, and all together we were thirteen knights. When we got to Albesa[184] we did not find the men of Tamarite or the others there, but only Bernardo de Calasanz and Raimundo de Calasanz, with sixty or seventy footmen. And we were very disappointed that the men of Tamarite were not there. Meanwhile, the men of Albesa held the fortified town with their shields and crossbows and other weapons. And we said: "How can it be that they are holding the town?"

At once we left the horses with the squires, we dismounted and then we took up our weapons and went to fight them, and we took the town. And only when we had taken the town, after a little time, did some of the men of Tamarite begin to arrive. The Albesans had us negotiate at sundown, saying that if we protected them they would surrender the castle to us and it would remain in our power. And when morning came they surrendered the castle.

[38] Then we moved on from there, saying: "Let us go to Menàrguens,[185] for before they know it we will have taken much of it from them." By then, the knights of our company had come to us, so that we were some thirty knights who went to Menàrguens. And we said to the company: "Halt here, and we will go forward with three or four knights of our company."

Rocafort[186] was there with three other knights whom we cannot recall. And already the men had all gone up to the castle with their weapons and with all the provisions that they had been able to bring from the town. We were at the gate of the castle, and we said to them: "Worthy men, you know very well that

---

[181]Tamarite de Litera, in the diocese of Lleida and the province of Huesca.

[182]In the Pla d'Urgell, sixteen kilometres from Lleida. Bruguera (*Vocabulari*, p. 84) suggests it may in fact be Albelda, on the border between La Litera and La Noguera and Segrià. Either is possible. Albesa was one of the places that had to be taken by James according to the agreement at Lleida. Moreover, Albesa is very near Menarguens and at the beginning of the next chapter James says they will be able to take Menarguens virtually before anybody can know about it. On the other hand, Albelda is very near to Tamarite so James would have had reason to be disappointed that the men of Tamarite did not turn up. Moreover, Calasanz is nearer Albelda than Albesa so Raimundo and Bernardo could have got there very quickly.

[183]It is Ponç, rather than his father Guerau, who holds the places that have to be recovered.

[184]August–September 1228.

[185]Menàrguens, a town of the county of Urgell, to the right of the Segre, between Lleida and Balaguer. Another of the towns that James was obliged to recapture by the agreement at Lleida.

[186]Bernat de Rocafort, "majordomus curie" according to two documents of this year (*M*, pp. 73, 547; *S*, p. 217). He later took part in the conquest of Majorca (ch. 63).

the countess is your natural lady, and she does not wish your destruction nor that you should die here, nor that you lose anything of yours. Go back to your houses and we shall protect you, in her name and ours, and we will do you no harm but rather defend you against all men."

Then one of them said: "And what, lord, should we do with the castle that Guerau de Cabrera has entrusted to us?"

And we said: "You know well that our lordship is worth more than that of anyone in the world, and so we shall protect you, that you do nothing against your word. Come down in peace, and, on our honour, we will protect you."

And one of them said: "Let us do as the king tells us, as it is he who says so."

But before they opened the gate they said to us: "Are you sure that we may come down protected by your word?"

"Aye," we said. So they came down with their weapons and with their possessions.

Then we sent for the knights and they came, and when the men of the town saw that there were so few knights, they considered themselves rather unfortunate. And we had no meat, nor did we wish to take it from them. Because of that, we sent some twenty knights to make a raid into Balaguer.[187] And they brought us sixteen cows and calves, and we bought bread and wine, and so we had meat for three days.

[39] Meanwhile, companies from Catalonia and Aragon arrived, and we were some two hundred knights, and we had around a thousand footmen. Three days later we were at Linyola.[188] Whilst we were at Linyola, Ramon de Montcada arrived the next morning, and the whole army armed itself for combat and they surrounded the whole town. And Ramon de Cardona came and said: "We would advise you, lord, not to fight, as there are faithful servants here, and it is not worth the effort you and the army will have to make to take the town. Let me speak with them, and I will see if I can gain good terms for you."

But we did not wish to listen to him. So we went to the town and we fought them. And on foot, with those soldiers, we took the town. The men of the town had locked themselves in a fortress where there was a very fine tower and an *albacar*,[189] but that same day they surrendered. One day after they surrendered, we established our garrison in the castle.

---

[187]Menàrguens is eight kilometres from Balaguer.

[188]A town of the Pla d'Urgell, twelve kilometres from Balaguer. It was another of the towns James was obliged to capture by the agreement at Lleida.

[189]The part of the castle between the tower and the outer wall.

[40] Afterwards we went to Balaguer to besiege it;[190] and we crossed the river by a place called Almata,[191] setting up two *fenèvols* there. Guillem de Montcada, Guillem de Cervera, and the nobles of Aragon were present;[192] and there were some four hundred knights with us.

When we had spent eight days in that place, a message came to us from Menàrguens and Pere Palau, who were among the best men of the town, saying that if we wished to complete the occupation of Balaguer, we should send for the countess, who was at Lleida. She should ask them to surrender the town as she was their natural lady, and because her father had been lord of it. Yet we understood that the words they sent were significant and carefully weighted, and that they could not send us the message they wished to for fear that they would lose their lives. We answered them saying that we thanked them very much, and that we would reward them for the love they had shown us, in a manner that would profit both them and their lineage.

A few days later, the messenger, who was a young student (so we took little notice of him),[193] returned to our presence and persevered on their behalf saying the same words that they had spoken before. And we said two things to them: "Do they say that for themselves or by the counsel of others? This we must know, for this matter is very very important, and, if anyone is against them, they are not powerful enough to be able to prevent what they do from being undone."

Then we asked them: "When do they wish that the countess should come to the army?"

To which he said: "I will send to them and ask them that."

They sent word to us that she should come on an appointed day. And on that day the countess came.

After four or five days they returned their response to us and they said that we should have squires and armed men to go before her, and that they should go close enough for those on the wall to hear her words; and that with God's will they would be true to their word and to all that they had said to us. So we did this, in the manner that we had agreed with them. And the count saw that there had been negotiations between us and those inside the town.

[41] One day, between nones and vespers, Ramon de Montcada had the guard of the *fenèvols* all day and night. While he was on guard, he had with him

---

[190]October 1228 (*M*, p. 72)

[191]On the plain that leads to the Segre and from where the king could best besiege the town.

[192]The most notable Aragonese were Ató de Foces, Rodrigo Lizana, and Pedro Cornel (*M*, p. 72).

[193]From his first days, James was trained as a soldier, but as a ruler he made full use of university men and in the 1240s attempted to establish a university at Valencia (Burns, *Crusader Kingdom*, 1, p. 108), an enterprise that had the backing of Pope Innocent IV (*DPI*, nos. 132–4).

Sancho Pérez de Pomar,[194] son of Pedro de Pomar, and Bardell, who was his bailiff at Castellserà,[195] and Arnau de Rubió, a knight. Now, when the men of Balaguer and Guillem de Cardona, who was inside with them, saw how few of them there were, they went out with armoured horses through a breach they had made in the wall, and entered into the moat unobserved, with dry torches soaked in grease. We were in Guillem de Cervera's tent, as we had gone to see him, and we were speaking with him. And they cried out: "To arms! To arms! They have come to burn the *fenèvols*. They are carrying lighted torches."

And Guillem de Cardona had some twenty-five armed knights and two hundred footmen with him, amongst those who carried the torches and the others. And Sire Guilleumes,[196] a son that the king of Navarre had had by a lady, rode out with him. Now, Don Sancho Pérez de Pomar did not have enough courage to stay there, and he fled back to the army. So only Arnau Rubió and Guillem Bardell remained with Ramon de Montcada. And Guillem de Cardona went, lance in hand, to attack Ramon de Montcada, and said: "Surrender! Ramon, Surrender!"

And Ramon said: "To whom should I surrender, you foul-smelling minion? To whom should I surrender?"

Meanwhile they started a small fire on the hurdles, because they could not stay much longer as we were running to help with the rest of the army. And we went up to the *fenèvol*. And Blasco de Estada had armed his horse in order to test out his armour. He quickly took up his weapons and rode out and attacked with those of the army, helmet on head and lance in hand. Meanwhile, Juan Martínez de Eslava[197] went on foot, armed with his shield and with his sword in his hand. And, like this, he overtook many of those of the town who went on horseback, and he wounded a horse when they were retreating after having tried to burn the *fenèvol*. And Blasco de Estada went a good stone's throw into the moat, and with lance in hand, he wounded a knight, and returned without receiving any blow, either from them or from the stones that were being thrown from the wall above.

[42] On the third day the countess arrived, and in the presence of Guillem de Cervera we explained to her the conversations we had held with those inside. She said that she would do all that we ordered, and that she would say those words willingly, as long as we preserved her from the arrows. And we said that we would do that. At once we ordered fifty knights to arm, clothed with

---

[194]Probably, like his father, a knight of the king's household (*S*, p. 218).

[195]A town of the Pla d'Urgell, fifteen kilometres from Balaguer. The bailiff is Guillem Bardell.

[196]A natural son of Sancho VII of Navarre (1194–1234). He took part in the conquest of Majorca (chs. 64, 84).

[197]A knight of the king's household who was to be the first to enter the city of Majorca during the assault (ch. 84).

purpoints, and with shields, so that they might go with her and protect her. Riding out there on her horse, she dismounted and went close to the wall, so that she was little more than a small stone's throw away from it. And one of the knights said in her name: "Are the men of Balaguer here?"

However, they remained silent and did not respond the first time. And he said to them: "The countess is here. Are the notables there?"

And one said: "Aye. What do you want? And what do you want to say?"

A knight said: "The countess requests that you listen to her a little, for she is a woman and is unable to shout."

Then she said: "Worthy men, well you know that you were the natural subjects of my father; and as you were his subjects, so you are mine, for I am his daughter. For that reason, I beseech you and I order you, for the lordship I hold over you, that you surrender Balaguer to me, just as you ought to surrender it to your natural lady."

They replied: "We have heard your message. Now we will discuss the matter and we will do what we ought to do, and nothing besides."

Then a knight responded on behalf of the countess and said: "Worthy men, the countess thanks you very much for saying you will do what you ought to do, and she hopes this will be so."

In the meantime the countess returned to the army.

At vespers, they sent word to us, through the student that came and went between them and us, that we had proceeded very well. Then they told us that we and she should come to an agreement, and that they would arrange things so that a noble would hold Balaguer in the name of Ponç and in the name of the countess. They did not dare oppose him, because he had great power and held the castle, and they would be unable to accomplish everything. But as soon as the count were to leave the castle for any motive, they would arrange for the castle and the town to surrender to the countess.

[43] One morning the notables of the town were speaking on a flat roof and Ponç ordered a crossbowman to take up his crossbow and fire an arrow to where the council was taking place. But he did not hit anybody.

"How now?" they said. "Why are they firing arrows at us? Shall we bring the place to destruction and do what we ought not to do for his sake?"

Then they sent word to him through two notables, saying that they were very surprised that he shot at them, what with them being in fear of their lives because of the king, who was wasting the countryside and was upon them. And that if he was going to behave in that manner, they would have to take another course.

Thus, Guerau[198] and Guillem de Cardona and those of their council saw that the men wished to take heed of the words of the countess, and that they had taken decisions without them, and that they did not know anything of what had been decided. So they said that they would negotiate with us and that they would place the castle in the power of Ramon Berenguer d'Àger[199] and that, in our presence, it should be seen who had the better claim, them or the countess. And the men of the town sent a message to us saying that we should agree to that, as we would be able to gain everything if the count came out.

We spoke with Guillem de Montcada, and told him of the deal they wished to make, by which they would entrust the castle to Ramon Berenguer d'Àger, for him to hold it in fealty and surrender it to whoever won in the dispute between Guerau and the countess.

Yet Guillem de Montcada replied and said: "That is not a thing I think you should do, because now you are here, you ought to carry out all that you agreed, and not to go from here until this place is yours."

For we had then still not revealed to him the words the townsmen had spoken to us. And we said to him: "Guillem, guile is worth more than force here, even though you have said just what you ought. I wish to reveal to you why I must do what I am going to tell you. The best men of the town have spoken with us, and they have said that they will hand over the town and the castle, and that is why the countess has come here. And let me tell you, if this castle goes into the hands of Ramon Berenguer d'Àger, as soon as Guerau is outside, the castle and the town will be ours. There is no need to fear that through their fealty it shall pass into his hands, as the opposite is true, and soon he will lose everything."

And he said: "And you promise it will be as you say?"

"Yes," we said, "Exactly as we say, you shall soon see it come to pass."

[44] Meanwhile, we sent a messenger to Guerau de Cabrera and to the townsmen, saying that we authorized that, from that moment, Ramon Berenguer d'Àger should hold fealty over the castle. And Guerau, who did not possess the wisdom of Solomon, became afraid of the townsmen. He had a moulted falcon, which was very fine and very beautiful; and he took his falcon in his hand, and went to the bridge, and immediately sent a messenger, Berenguer Finestres,[200] to us, saying that he was disposed to deliver the castle to Ramon Berenguer.

---

[198]Either both Guerau and Ponç are present or James is vacillating between the two.

[199]He took part in the first siege of Peníscola, the conquest of Majorca, and the siege of Valencia. He became a knight of the Temple. He had been of the party of the Cabrera and Cardona.

[200]In 1242, he was a witness when James conceded in fief to Ponç the castle and town of Balaguer (*M*, p. 159).

Then the townsmen sent us another message, saying that we should send our standard and that they would put it on the castle. And we sent a knight and five squires, who went with the standard, which they covered up to carry, and they took a lance upon which to place it when they were in the castle. Meanwhile, Berenguer de Finestres spoke to us and said that we should send Ramon Berenguer d'Àger to receive the homage, and that he would receive the castle into his power. But, as we had already sent our standard to the castle, we detained him with words, though he urged that we allow him to return, as the count wished to leave from there. All the while we kept watch to see if our standard was on the castle; and on seeing it, we said to him: "Berenguer de Finestres, you can go now, since Balaguer is ours."[201]

"How, yours?", he said.

And we said to him: "Look, can you not see our standard on the castle?"

And he was greatly ashamed and saddened, and he went from there without saying anything. And the count went from there to Montmagastre.

[45] Then the decision was taken to send Guillem de Cardona to Agramunt; and they went there with some fifteen knights. When the men of Agramunt heard it said that there were agreements between Balaguer and us, they said to Ramon Jafa of Agramunt and to other men of the town, that if the countess went to Agramunt they would surrender. So the matter was negotiated even before Balaguer was taken. And Ramon de Montcada spoke with Berenguer de Peraixens. And Ramon de Montcada said to us, and to the countess, and to Guillem de Montcada, Guillem de Cervera and our council, that if Balaguer was taken, we should go afterwards to Agramunt, since Berenguer de Peraixens had come to see him and had agreed that they would surrender it to us.

After having delivered the castle of Balaguer to the countess, we went with her to Agramunt,[202] and we camped on the side of the mountains of Almenara, in sight of Agramunt. When Guillem de Cardona saw that we were camped in that place, he left there by night, and travelled throughout the night. And when, the next morning, we heard it said that he had left there, we got up. Then the

---

[201] Sometime between 11 and 20 October 1228.

[202] James was at Agramunt on 20 October (*M*, p. 72). It was another of the places James was obliged to take. On 23 October, Aurembiaix gave James the county of Urgell as his own frank allod, the main conditions being that she would hold the county during her lifetime and that James would promise to recover the remaining castles after he had returned from the attack on Majorca (which was already uppermost in James's mind). It was also agreed that, if Aurembiaix died first, the county would fall to James or to any child they might have together (Soldevila, *Primers Temps*, pp. 298–300). James was already seeking the annulment of his marriage to Eleanor of Castile on grounds of consanguinity and a marriage between James and Aurembiaix, who had been betrothed as children in 1209, was evidently under consideration.

men of Agramunt came to receive us, and we entered Agramunt and we placed the countess inside the castle.

[46] And the men of Ponts[203] sent a message saying that the countess should go there, and we agreed that she should go there. However, we did not wish to go there because we had not defied Ramon Folc, who held the place, since we had not broken our friendship with him nor he with us. The countess went there and found the town had been abandoned; and Guillem de Montcada and Ramon de Montcada[204] and all the company, except us, went with her there, and we remained with five knights. And the townsmen went out with men on horseback, with their horses armed as if for a tournament. And the castellan, too, went on horseback, with his men. Then the men who went with the countess armed their horses and rode against them until they cut off the pass near to the castle. And according to what they told us, the man who fought best was Bernat Desllor, brother of the sacristan of Barcelona.

That same day, in the evening, Guillem de Montcada and Ramon de Montcada sent us a message saying that we should go there immediately, because, if we went there, the countess would have the castle, and that there was no other way that she would be able to have it.

And we said: "How can we go there, when we have no quarrel with Ramon Folc? For it is he who holds the castle."

But they said: "You should know that if you do not go there, the countess will not have the castle, whereas if you do go there, the countess will have it."

And we said: "What should we do when we are there?"

And they said: "If only you speak to them and advise them to surrender the castle to the countess, then they will surrender it."

And we said: "We shall do so, saving the right of Ramon Folc, if he has any right there."

And, then we went there,[205] and we ordered all those who came with us to leave their horses and weapons behind.

And on the morning we arrived there, some twenty of the townsmen came down to us, and the castellan with them. And we asked them why they had sent for us. And they said: "We wish to ask your advice about the castle: what it is necessary to do and what not to do."

And we said: "We advise you in this manner: that I and the countess promise to the castellan and to you that the rights that Ramon Folc has in this

---

[203] A small town in the valley of the Segre. By 23 October, all the places which James had to recapture had been taken except two (Ponts and either Calasanz or, more probably, Oliana (Soldevila, *Primers Temps,* p. 289).

[204] They were with the king at Agramunt on 20 October 1228, as were Guillem de Cervera, Ramon Alemany, Ferrer de Sant Martí, Pedro Cornel, Assalit de Gúdar and García Pérez de Meitats (*M*, p. 72).

[205] Sometime between 23 October and 10 November (*M*, p. 72).

castle will be respected. But, you must formally assure us, since she has recovered the rest of the county by the judgement of our court, and by right and reason, and the others have recognized it, that you also shall recognize it and you will surrender your castle to her." And immediately they surrendered it.

Then we sent a message to Oliana,[206] and when they found out that the castle of Ponts had surrendered, immediately they also surrendered to the countess. And we did not wish to ask anything in our name, by reason of the right she held there.

---

[206] A town further up from Ponts on the Segre, in Alt Urgell. It was one of the towns James had been obliged to recapture.

2

The Conquest of Majorca

[47] Half a year later, we were at Tarragona.[1] And Our Lord willed it that, although we had not convoked the *Cort*, the majority of the nobles of Catalonia were there with us. And these were their names: Don Nunó Sanxes, who was the son of Count Don Sancho, Guillem de Montcada, the count of Empúries,[2] Ramon de Montcada, Guerau de Cervelló, Ramon Alemany, Guillem de Claramunt,[3] and Bernat de Santaeugènia, lord of Torroella.

And Pere Martell,[4] a citizen of Barcelona, who understood a great deal about seafaring, invited us and all the nobles who were with us to be his guests. And when we had almost finished eating, they began to talk among themselves. And we asked what land was Majorca and how great its kingdom.[5] And they asked Pere Martell because he was master of the galleys. And Pere Martell said that he would tell them all about it because he had already been there once or twice,[6] and that he reckoned that the island of Majorca was three hundred miles round; and that Menorca was towards Sardinia, facing the north-

---

[1]The king was at Tarragona on 16 November 1228 (*M*, p. 73), less than one month after the events he has just described.

[2]Hug IV (1200–1230), son of Ponç Hug II and Adelaida de Montcada. He participated in the Third Crusade, the Las Navas campaign and was probably at Muret. He was consistently loyal to the young James and one of the most enthusiastic collaborators in the Majorca crusade where he died in 1230.

[3]Another member of the Montcada family who died at Majorca (ch. 92).

[4]The merchant Pere Martell clearly gave great service to the king since he receives a generous portion in the *Repartiment de Mallorca* (*Còdex*, 3r, 30v, 55r, 55v). But little is known of his life. Salvat, following Marsili (*Crónica latina*, II, 1, p. 155), vigorously argues for his Tarragonan origins (*Tarragona*, p. 44). His house appears to have been in the sector between the walls of the Rambla Vieja and the sea, and would most probably have looked out to the sea (Salvat, *Tarragona*, pp. 26–8). Pere's presence here is a reminder that commercial as well as dynastic interests were at play in the expedition. For the burghers of Barcelona the Balearics were essentially a market and a base for commercial expansion on the route to North Africa.

[5]The capture of the Balearics, not only valuable in themselves but also a means of controlling the seas in the Western Mediterranean, was, in fact, a long-established ambition of the Catalan rulers and others (Barceló, 'Expedicións militars'). Ramon Berenguer III, in alliance with Pisa, had taken Ibiza and Majorca briefly (1114–15), and both Alfonso II and Peter II had planned expeditions to the islands. James was certainly planning the expedition before he ever arrived at Tarragona and it had beem mentioned in the pact with Aurembiaix in October 1228 (Soldevila, *Primers Temps,* pp. 298–300).

[6]One of a number of indications of Christian trade with Muslim Majorca before the conquest (Abulafia, *A Mediterranean Emporium*, pp. 107–112).

eastern island, and that Ibiza was towards the south-west wind. In addition, he said that Majorca was more powerful than the other islands, and the men of those islands did what the lord of Majorca ordered them to do. And there was yet another island inhabited by the Saracens called Formentera, and it was near Ibiza,[7] and between Ibiza and Formentera there was a stretch of sea a mile long.

When we had eaten, they came before us and they said to us: "Lord, we have asked Pere Martell something that we think will please you, about an island that is called Majorca. And in this island there is a king, and under this kingdom there are other islands: Menorca and Ibiza, and these are subject to the king of Majorca. Now, what God wills nobody can avoid or impede; therefore it should please you, and we hold it for a good thing, that you should conquer that island, for two reasons: the first, because you and we will increase our worth; the second, because it will seem a marvellous thing to all who hear about this conquest, for you will have taken a land and kingdom in the sea, there where God wished to fashion it."

And we listened to their words and we were greatly pleased by them. And we replied to them: "We are very happy at this idea of yours and as we are moved to do it, it shall not remain unaccomplished."

And in that very place we immediately agreed and planned to celebrate the general *Cort* at Barcelona, stipulating that it should be the general *Cort*[8] of the archbishop of Tarragona, the bishops, the abbots and the nobles we have mentioned above, together with the citizens of Catalonia; and on the appointed day they were at Barcelona with us.

[48] On the day we had ordered for the celebration of the *Cort*, we were at Barcelona,[9] with the archbishop, the bishops and the nobles as well. And when the *Cort* met the next day,[10] everybody was at our ancient palace,[11] which had been built by the count of Barcelona.

---

[7] The distance between Ibiza and Formentera is almost ten kilometres.

[8] In the lawsuits (1255–71) involving the question of the bigamous Count Àlvar of Urgell and his wives, when claims to lands given at the conquest of Majorca were being disputed, six witnesses were called to give evidence concerning the Barcelonan *Cort* of 1228 where the land divisions had been arranged. One witness, G. Berenguer de Salano, recalled that in Tarragona the king had ordered one of his scribes (Berenguer, a nephew of Rabassa) to write letters of summons for the Christian assembly (Kagay, 'Emergence of "Parliament"', pp. 226, 235).

[9] 19 December 1228.

[10] *H*, 1, no. 111.

[11] The Palau Major.

Then, when all were there before us, we began our speech in this manner: "*Illumina cor meum, Domine, et verba mea de Spiritu Sancto.*[12] We ask the Lord God and the holy virgin Mary His mother, that we may say words that will be to our honour, and to the honour of those who hear them,[13] and that they will be pleasing to God and His mother, Our Lady Saint Mary. For we wish to speak of good works, and good works proceed from and belong to Him. These words that we say will concern good works. And may it please Him that we bring these good works to fruition. It is certainly true that our birth came about through God's grace, since our father and our mother did not care greatly for each other, and it was rather by the will of God that we were born into this world. (And if we spoke of the happenings and good signs that accompanied our birth, they would be great, but we refrain from speaking of it because we have done so already at the beginning of this book.[14]) Moreover, we know full well that you know we are your natural lord, and that we are an only child, our father having left us no brother or sister born of our mother. We came among you when very young, only six and a half years old,[15] and we found Aragon and Catalonia in turmoil, with everyone taking up arms against each other. Indeed, there was no agreement on anything, since what some wanted the others did not want; and you had an evil reputation throughout the world for the things that happened. We can give no remedy for this evil except in two ways: first, through the will of God guiding us in our business; and second, because you and we may undertake such enterprises as will be pleasing to God, and that the enterprise may be so important and good that the bad reputation that you have may be erased, since the light of good works overcomes the dark.

"So, we strongly beseech you for two reasons, that is to say for God and the natural lordship we hold over you, that you give advice and help in three things: first, that we may establish peace in our land; second, that we may be able to serve Our Lord in this voyage that we wish to make to the kingdom of Majorca and the other islands that pertain to it; and third, that we may accomplish this action to the honour of God."

And having said that, we ended our speech.[16]

---

[12]This invocation, asking for God to bring light into the king's heart and for the Holy Spirit to guide his words, is not a biblical quotation, but perhaps in imitation of a prayer often used by preachers before beginning a sermon (Pujol, 'Cultura eclesiàstica', p. 155).

[13]Recollecting the assembly, G. Berenguer de Salano said that neither he nor the nobles about him could understand what the king was saying. This may have been a matter of acoustics or, if, as seems possible, James were directing the speech in Latin, simple ignorance, or possibly a combination of both. However, the fact that not everybody could hear and understand made little difference, since, when James had finished his speech, there was a general clamour for the invasion of Majorca (Kagay, 'Emergence of "Parliament"', pp. 235–6).

[14]James here addresses the scribe or the reader rather than his men.

[15]He had been six years and two months old.

[16]There is another report of the speeches in *Desclot* (chs. 14–28).

[49] Then Archbishop Aspàreg of Tarragona[17] arose, because the nobles called for him to speak first, and he responded in this manner: "Lord, well we know that you were young when you came among us, and that you need great counsel from us for words as great as those which you have set before us today. So then, we shall deliberate, that we may respond to you in a way that will be to the honour of God, and to your honour and ours."

And Guillem de Montcada responded for the nobles and for himself, and said that he greatly thanked Our Lord for the good purpose he had given us, but, as the matter was important and of great nobility, they were unable to respond without deep consultation: "But we can say this before all present, that the advice will be as is fitting for you to accept and for us to give."

Afterwards the men of the cities spoke. Berenguer Girard,[18] who was from Barcelona, and spoke for them, stood up and said: "Our Lord, Who is lord of you and us, has given you the will to pronounce these good words. And it would please Him for us to respond in such a way that you might fulfil your will to the honour of God and yourself. Hence, we will take a decision together with the others, and we will reply to you."

Then the archbishop said: "The clergy shall assemble in one part, and the nobles in another, and the citizens will deliberate amongst themselves."

And all found the proposal to be sound. And in this manner that day the *Cort* broke up, in order to discuss the matter; and on the third day they responded to us.

Meanwhile, we had a secret council to one side; and the nobles took part in it, and they spoke with us before the archbishop and the bishops did. And the count of Empúries stood up and said: "Lord, I will tell you the response that your nobles must give to you before they do so. Though there be men in the world who have an evil reputation, we, in contrast, have a good one, that is to say, we did have once; and having come among us as our natural lord, it is necessary that you perform works such as this, with our help, so that we may recover the good name we have lost. And recover it we will, by doing this, if you, with our help, take a kingdom of the Saracens that is in the sea. Indeed, we will lose all the evil reputation that we have had to bear, and it will be the best deed that Christians have carried out in a hundred years. Better it is to die and recover the good name we used to hold, and the good fortune of our lineages, and of our men, than to live with the evil reputation that we have. For which reason I say to you that, to my mind, this deed should be accomplished above all else."

---

[17]The archbishop of Tarragona was spiritual head of the province of Tarragona, which included the Aragonese dioceses (Huesca, Tarazona, Zaragoza), the Catalonian dioceses (Barcelona, Girona, Lleida, Tarragona, Tortosa, Urgell, Vic) except Elne, and the dioceses of Calahorra (Castile) and Pamplona (Navarre). In the history of the early Crown, the ecclesiastical province was one of the key focuses of unity.

[18]From one of the most prosperous patrician families in the city.

All were in agreement with the words the count of Empúries had spoken. And each spoke as well as they could in favour of the fulfilment of this deed.

That evening it was decided that the general *Cort* should be held there in the morning, and that they the nobles would respond first, in order to encourage the clergy and the citizens. And we sent word, through the nobles, to the archbishop, abbots and bishops, that they should come before us in the morning, to give us their response.

[50] When it was morning and the morning Masses had been celebrated, all came to the *Cort*,[19] and they called on Guillem de Montcada to speak, and they said to him that he should set out what they had agreed. And he got up and said: "Lord, it is true that God made you to rule over us, that we might serve you well and loyally; and we will not serve you well or loyally unless we exalt your good name and your honour as much as is possible, because your good reputation is an honour for us and your good benefits us. So then, it is reasonable that if these two goods accord, we should desire them. And it seems that this good deed of which you have spoken to us, to conquer the kingdom of Majorca that is in the sea, will be of more glory than if you were to conquer three kingdoms on land; and, lord, we must strive for your honour above everything else in the world. Hence, regarding the three pieces of advice you ask of us, that you may pacify your land, and we may help you in a manner that fulfils your glory and ours, we say to you firstly, you should establish a peace and truces[20] throughout Catalonia and that you should note down in a document those who wish to take part. And Don Nunó, who is here, and is the grandson of the count of Barcelona,[21] will take part in this peace jointly with us, and for two reasons. One, because of the close kinship he has with us, and the other, because of the good works that you wish to do. And if there is anyone in Catalonia who does not wish to participate, we will make him participate whether he likes it or not. Moreover, we wish you to levy the *bovatge*[22] upon our men, for we shall grant it to you as a donation, even though you have already taken it once by your right – as is the custom of kings, who may levy it once. On this occasion, we give it to you through grace and love, so that you may carry out your deeds successfully. For myself, I give my word to you that I and those of my lineage will serve you there with four hundred

---

[19]21 December 1228.

[20]Before undertaking military action, order had to be imposed on the interior of the country with the promulgation of a constitution of Peace and Truce, and the *bovatge* levied to finance the campaign.

[21]Count Ramon Berenguer IV (1131–62).

[22]The *bovatge* had already been levied soon after James had left Monzón and Guillem insists it could only be levied once by a king by right.

armed knights,[23] who will remain with you until God has given you the island of Majorca, along with the rule of the other islands that are around it, Menorca and Ibiza. And we shall not leave you until the conquest is complete.[24] And Don Nunó and the others will say, each for himself, what help they will give you. All we ask of you is that, as we will do these three things for you, you may give us a share of the conquest that you make with us, both in moveable and immoveable goods. Because we will serve you well there, and we wish to have a share that will always be a record of the service we give to you."

And with that he brought his speech to an end.

[51] Next, Don Nunó Sanxes, son of Count Don Sancho and grandson of the count of Barcelona[25] arose and said: "Lord, the speech that Guillem de Montcada has made is a very fine one, and he speaks well for himself and his line. I, however, will respond to you for myself. Our Lord, Who made you, wished that you should be our lord and our king, and as it pleases Him, so should it please us (and me, above all, because of the kinship I have with you and for the lordship you have over me). For, if you obtain fame and glory, I will have a share of it, because God willed that I should be of your lineage. The deed is good for this reason: because it is a work of God, and he who carries out his actions in God's name cannot do them badly. As regards the peaces and the truces, I grant them for me and for the land that your father gave me,[26] that is to say, Rousillon, Conflent and Cerdagne, which I have for as long as I live; and I, too, concede to you that you may levy the *bovatge*. Furthermore, I will go with you with one hundred knights armed at my expense,[27] if you will give me a part of the land and of the moveable goods in exchange for the footmen and horses I will bring, as well as for the ships and galleys armed by me; and I will serve you in that land until God may allow you to gain it."

Once Don Nunó had finished his speech, the count of Empúries arose and said: "Lord, nobody can praise too highly this deed that you wish to undertake,

---

[23]On 23 December 1228, Guillem, along with Ferrer de Sant Martí and Guillem de Cervelló, swore to cross to Majorca with one hundred knights and servants (*H*, 1, no. 113; *M*, p. 75). On 28 August 1229, Guillem again swore to this (*H*, 1, no. 124). Even adding the knights offered by the other Montcada (seventy by the count of Empúries, fifty by Ramon de Montcada, thirty jointly by Ramon Alemany de Cervelló and Guillem de Claramunt) the figure does not arrive at four hundred.

[24]In *Desclot*, many of the speeches at the *Cort* (chs. 15–17, 21, 23–8 (ch. 25 is the speech of Guillem de Montcada) end with this guarantee.

[25]Again the renewed mention of Ramon Berenguer IV demonstrates how Nunó's prestige derived from his relation to the count.

[26]The lands that Peter II gave to Nunó in 1212.

[27]On 23 December 1228 and 28 August 1229, Nunó swore to go to Majorca with one hundred knights and squires. He gained very substantially in the *Repartiment* (*Còdex*, 25r, 26v, 27r, 27v, 29r, 34v/35v, 45v, 48r, 48v, 83v, 86r, 86v/87r, 88v/89r; Soto i Company, 'Porció de Nunó').

as its excellence shows through in the good that can come of it. So, I promise you I will go there with sixty knights[28] with armoured horses. And although God made me count of Empúries, Guillem de Montcada is the best man of our lineage, and the most noble, because he is lord of Béarn and of Montcada, which he holds in your name, and of Castellví,[29] which is his allod, and I approve the words he has spoken. Thus, on top of the four hundred knights he has promised, I put my sixty, so that you will take all of our line with you. And of that share that has been promised to him and the others, give also to me for the horsemen and foot soldiers I will bring, for all the knights that I and the others will take there will go with armoured horses."

[52] After that the archbishop of Tarragona arose and said: "*Viderunt occuli mei salutare tuum.*[30] This phrase is from Simeon, when he received Our Lord in his arms and said, 'My eyes have seen your salvation,' and my eyes likewise have seen yours. And I will add something else, even though scripture does not say it; that in seeing your salvation we see our own. And in this is found your salvation: when you begin to apply your heart to good works. And so is it ours: when you gain in reputation, honour and worth. For if your courage and your renown are works of God, we have you for our own valour and renown. This idea that you and these nobles who are here with you have formed and wish to undertake is to the honour of God and all the celestial court, and is and will be to the profit of you and your men in this world and in the next, which has no end. And so Our Lord, Who it so pleased to assemble this *Cort*, wishes that it may be to His service and to your profit and to that of all the nobles who are found here, that each one of your nobles makes such an offering to you that you cannot help but show your gratitude. Hence, when God gives you this kingdom, which you, and those who are with you, desire to conquer, you should repay them, and divide the lands and the moveable goods with all those who wish to help and serve you in the enterprise. And I say to you, as much for myself as for the church of Tarragona, that I have never taken part in deeds of arms, and I am already so old[31] that I would not be able to do anybody any harm. But, as regards my goods and men, I give them into your power that they may serve you as your own men do.[32] And if any bishop or abbot wishes to

---

[28]In these same agreements Hug swore to go to Majorca with sixty knights (*H*, 1, nos. 113, 124).

[29]Guillem de Montcada held the seigneurie of Castellví through his mother Guillelma (*S*, p. 224).

[30]Luke 2:30. Archbishop Aspàreg appropriately takes up the words of Simeon who took the child Jesus in his arms (Luke 2:28), just as he himself had taken up James in his arms at the *Cort* at Lleida in 1214 (ch. 11).

[31]He was archbishop of Tarragona from 1215 until 1236. He had previously been bishop of Pamplona (1212–15).

[32]There does not seem to be any concrete offer of military help from the archbishop in the surviving documents (many of the documents from the Tarragonan archives were destroyed

serve you and go there in person, it would satisfy us a great deal, and we give licence on behalf of God and ourselves, as, in so good an enterprise as this, everybody must help, in word and deed. And may God, Who came to earth to save us, allow you and the others to accomplish this deed, in accordance with your will and ours."

[53] Then the bishop of Barcelona, Berenguer de Palou,[33] arose and said: "Of you it is possible to say the same thing as did the Father when He sent Our Lord Jesus Christ, Son of God, to a mountain called 'Excelsis'.[34] Because Our Lord, Son of God, and Moses and Elias and St Peter were there. And St Peter said: "It would be very fitting that we made here three places for tabernacles, the first for our Lord Jesus Christ, the other for Moses, the other for Elias." And immediately a great clap of thunder came from heaven and all fell to the ground. And, when they had all fallen, they then arose full of fear. And a cloud came from heaven and came down to them, and said: *Ecce, Filius Meus dilectus, qui in corde Meo placuit.*[35] And the same may be said of you, that you are a son of Our Lord, at such a time as you wish to pursue the enemies of the Faith and of the cross. And I have faith in Him that, for this good proposal that you have, you will come into the celestial kingdom. And I offer to you in my

---

during the Napoleonic wars), but on 28 August 1229 James recognized having received from the archbishop free barley for the crossing to Majorca (*H*, 1, no. 123), and the provost of Tarragona, Ferrer, played a leading part in the campaign in return for ample rewards from the king (*H*, 1, no. 126). *Desclot* (ch. 15), as well as the barley, has the archbishop offer one thousand silver marks and one hundred knights.

[33]Nephew of another Bishop Berenguer de Palou of Barcelona (1200–1206), he was himself bishop of the see from 1212 until 1241. He participated in the Las Navas campaign, was ambassador at Paris to Philip Augustus in 1213 to halt the Albigensian Crusade, took part in the Fifth Crusade to the East, played a major role in the Majorca campaign (where, it appears, his foot was mutilated) and participated in the siege of Valencia. He was chancellor to James. He supported the foundation of the Dominican, Franciscan, and Mercedarian orders in his city. A statesman and scholar, his tomb is conserved in the cathedral of Barcelona at the chapel of Saint Michael.

[34]Based on the reading of Pujol ('Cultura eclesiàstica', pp. 156–7) of this difficult passage concerning the Transfiguration. Matthew (17:1) and Mark (9:2) refer to a high mountain, while Luke (9:28) simply refers to a mountain. 2 Peter 1:17–18 refers to the holy mountain. The confusion appears to arise from Matthew and Mark who both have 'et ducit illos in montem excelsum seorsum'. Hence the high mountain of the Transfiguration (usually Mount Thabor) has here been given the name 'Excelsis'. It is not entirely clear why Berenguer chooses the theme of the Transfiguration (then the theme of the Gospel of 9 November), or, indeed, if James interpreted what Berenguer said accurately (this seems unlikely). Nor is it clear why Saints James and John make no appearance. Pere Marsili (*Crónica latina*, II, 10, p. 167) discreetly corrected the passage when translating the text into Latin.

[35]Based on Matthew 17: 5 [Et ecce vox de nube, dicens: Hic est Filius meus dilectus, in quo mihi bene complacui (Lo, a voice from the cloud said, 'This is my beloved Son, with whom I am well pleased')]. The thunder may have arrived from John 12:29. Pere Marsili (*Crónica latina*, II, ch. 10, p. 167) again amends the passage in the Latin edition.

name, and that of the church of Barcelona, one hundred knights or more,[36] to be maintained by me until God concedes to you the conquest of the isles of Majorca, if you will give me a share for the men that I take there,[37] both for the sailors and for the knights."

After him the bishop of Girona[38] said: "To our Lord I give thanks for the good will that God has shown to you and to your *Cort*, and I could say much in praise of this good work, if I wished to, but our archbishop, and the bishop of Barcelona, and Guillem de Montcada, Don Nunó, and the count of Empúries have already said all that I wished to say. But I make you an offering, for me and for the church of Girona, to go with you with thirty knights; if you will give me my share in accordance with what you give the others."

[54] And the abbot of St Feliu de Guíxols[39] arose, and said that he would go with us with five well-equipped knights. And afterwards the provost of Tarragona[40] arose and said: "I do not have as many knights as them, but I will follow you accompanied by four knights and with an armed galley."

When these speeches had finished, Pere Grony[41] arose and said: "Lord, all the citizens of Barcelona thank God for the good intent that He has given you, and we trust in Our Lord that you will accomplish it according to your design. And we offer you, firstly, all the persons, and ships, and the boats that are at Barcelona, to serve you in this glorious expedition for the honour of God. And we shall act in such a manner that, for the service we will now do for you, we will have your thanks for all time."[42]

And we will say no more of the cities for this reason, because none of them are greater than Barcelona.[43] And Tarragona and Tortosa agreed with the words that were spoken by the notables of Barcelona.

---

[36]In the cited documents Berenguer swears to pass personally to Majorca with one hundred knights.

[37]On 30 December 1228, James conceded to the church of Barcelona all of the churches of the Balearics, Oriola and Dénia (*H*, 1, no. 115).

[38]Guillem de Cabanelles, Bishop of Girona (1227–45).

[39]Bernat, who gained in the *Repartiment* (*Còdex*, 19r, 25v) and who was also with the king in his second stay at Majorca in 1231 (*M*, p. 95).

[40]Ferrer de Pallarès. Having played a significant part in the campaign, he gained substantially in the *Repartiment*, for which reason his house was attacked (ch. 91). An able administrator and loyal servant of the crown, he was elected bishop of Valencia in 1240 but was killed in a Muslim ambush in April 1243.

[41]The Grony were one of the city of Barcelona's most illustrious patrician houses. It is slightly uncertain which member of the house is speaking here, and it has been suggested that James simply chooses the name of a prominent citizen, who had actually died in 1227 (Bensch, *Barcelona and Its Rulers*, p. 277).

[42]On 10 January 1230, James conceded to Barcelona the free commerce of the Balearic islands and their waters [*H*, 1, no. 146 (dated 1231)].

[43]This passage is difficult to interpret but this appears to be the most likely meaning [cf. *Muntaner* (ch. 23) 'Barcelona és la pus noble ciutat e la mellor que el senyor rei d'Aragó haja'].

[55] Thus, when the speeches had been heard, they said that we should prepare a charter,[44] according to which the division of the lands and moveable goods that we gained with them would be agreed. And the form of the document was as follows: according to the knights, armed men, ships, galleys, vessels and the armament that would go in them, we, when Our Lord had conceded the victory to us, would give them a share, for those who went with us, on foot and on horseback, and for the munitions that they carried. This division would be decided on the basis of the gains that were made, by whatever means, in that voyage, as soon as the army had returned. And we promised this there, in God's name and ours, to abide by the agreement without trickery, as long as they served me loyally and did not declare more men than would make the crossing with us.

And that was the beginning of the crossing that we made to Majorca. We then signalled a day in mid-May[45] for all to be at Salou, and with that we dissolved the *Cort* and all went away to prepare themselves. And all the nobles had taken an oath there, that on the first day of May[46] they would all be at Salou without fail, with all their equipment, to embark for Majorca.

And on that signalled day, we were there. And we were there until the beginning of September,[47] organizing the crossing and awaiting the ships and vessels and galleys that were coming to us. We waited so long because we wanted the fleet to be complete. And one portion of the ships was situated at Cambrils, and the greater part, in which we found ourselves, was in the port of Salou and on the beach, and the remainder of the ships were at Tarragona, because they were from there. The fleet was made up of twenty-five full ships, eighteen *tarides* and twelve galleys, and one hundred buzas[48] and galliots.[49] And so there were one hundred and fifty big vessels, without counting the small barques.[50]

---

[44]The charter of 23 December 1228.

[45]The charter indicates that the crossing will take place 'in hac proxima estate, ultima scilicet septimana mensis madii'.

[46]As was usual in these expeditions, there was a considerable delay.

[47]James was at Salou on 27 August 1229, at Tarragona on 28 August, and at Salou again on 1 September (*M*, pp. 80–1) but he had not been there continuously from May. He was at Lleida in June, at Valls in July, and at Barcelona during July and August (*M*, pp. 78–9).

[48]Rounded, full-bodied, single-masted sailing ships. Normally identified with coastal trade and fishing.

[49]Small single-masted, single-sailed galley type vessels usually with twenty oars. The army probably consisted of about six hundred and eighty knights and six to eight thousand infantry (Santamaria, 'Expansión político-militar', pp. 122–3).

[50]Mediterranean, principally Iberian, craft mounting three lateen-rigged masts, and noted for speed.

[56] Before setting sail, we ordered in what manner the fleet should proceed. At the front, Bovet's ship,[51] in which Guillem de Montcada sailed, was to serve as a guide, and had to carry a lantern as a light; whilst Carròs's[52] ship had the rearguard and carried another lantern as a light. And the galleys had to go around the outside of the fleet, in such a manner that if another galley came it would encounter our galleys.[53]

We set sail on Wednesday,[54] in the morning, from Salou, with a land breeze, for, after the long stay we had made there, any wind was acceptable that could carry us from the land. And when those of Tarragona and of Cambrils saw that the ships were setting sail from Salou, they made sail. And it was a wonderful sight to behold, both for those who remained on the land and for us, because the whole sea appeared white with sails, so large was our fleet.

Now, we set sail at the rear of the fleet, in the galley of Montpellier; and we ordered a good thousand men who wished to go with us to do so in smaller boats, so that no one missed the crossing. And when we had sailed twenty miles to sea, the wind changed to a warm south-west wind;[55] and the commanders of the galleys came before us, on the advice of the sailors, and they said: "Lord, we are your subjects and we are obliged to guard your body and members, and to give you good advice on all those things that we understand." Then they added: "This weather, with the south-west wind that we have, is unfavourable to us and to your ships, and is so much against you that you will be unable to gain land on any part of the island of Majorca. And we advise you to turn back and return to land, for God will soon give you weather that permits your crossing."

Yet we, when we had heard their words and advice, said to them that we would do no such thing, because there were many there, being already in their ships, who, for the evil that the sea had already done them, would flee and not dare to embark again with us, and that if we returned, they would leave us, if they were not men of valour: "And we set out on this voyage in the faith of God and for those who do not believe in Him, going against them for two reasons: to convert them or to destroy them, and to return that kingdom to the Faith of Our Lord. As we go in the name of God, we are confident that he will guide us."

---

[51]Nicolau Bovet, a merchant and seaman (Danus, 'Notas sobre Nicolau Bovet').

[52]On 1 April 1230, James named him admiral of Catalonia and Majorca (*H*, 1, no. 128). He appears as admiral of the kingdom of Majorca and Catalonia in a document of 11 April 1231 (*M*, p. 93). Possibly of German origin (Zurita, *Anales*, 3, ch. 7), he remained a key military figure for the next three decades and as lord of Dénia assumed a position of considerable political power.

[53]The galleys could manouevre more rapidly to encounter enemy ships.

[54]5 September 1229.

[55]The 'Lebeg' – the wind from the southwestern coast of Africa.

On that, when the masters of the galleys saw that this was our will, they said to us that they would do all that was in their power, and that the same faith that we had would guide us all.

The hour of vespers came. And near the first watch, we overtook the ship of Guillem de Montcada, which carried the guide. And we climbed up to the lantern and we hailed them and we asked them what ship that was. And they asked us which was our galley. And those of the galley responded that it was the galley of the king, and they said that we were welcome one hundred thousand times, and said that their ship was that of Guillem de Montcada. But then the sails took us away from them. And so, although we had been last to set sail from Salou, at the first watch we found ourselves ahead of all the others; and we sailed all that night with the south-west wind.

And we and all the others sailed with the wind, as fast as we were able. And sailing as we were, by night and in front of the fleet, we did not lower sail and change course, and we allowed the galley to go as quickly as it could go. And when it was between the hour of nones and vespers, the sea became rough with the rising wind, and it was so rough a sea that a third of the galley, to prow, was washed by the waves of the sea.

And when we had passed this rough sea, near vespers, before the sun had set, the wind calmed; and as the wind ceased, we saw the island of Majorca, and we could make out La Palomera, Sóller and Almeruig.

[57] They then said that, as we could see the island, it would be sensible to lower sail, if we wished to, because if we did not they would see us from the land. We said that it seemed a good idea to us, and we lowered sail. And when we had done so, the sea was calm, and they said that they would light a lantern, but they feared that the watchmen on the island would see it. And we said that they could take a word of advice on that: they could build a small shelter on the side facing the island, and put the lantern near there to poop and cover it with a cloth to hide it from the view of the mountain, but so that the fleet could see it from the sea. They told us it seemed a good idea to them, and we did it. And having done that, we saw lanterns on the ships and some of the galleys; and we realized that they had seen us and we knew by that that the fleet was coming.

And when it was near the first watch, two galleys caught up with us, and we asked them for news of the fleet. And they said that they were coming as fast as they could. And when it was midnight, we saw thirty or forty ships there, galleys and *tarides*. And there was a beautiful moon, and a breeze came in from the south-west; and we said that with that wind we would be able to go to Pollença, for it had been agreed that the fleet would arrive there. And we raised the sail and so did those who were able to see it, and were in the same part of the sea as us.

And as we sailed with that good sea and with that good weather that we had, a cloud came against the wind from the side of Provence; and one of the officers of the galley, named Berenguer Gairan, who was a sailsmaster said: "I don't like the look of that cloud that I can see coming from the region of the Provençal wind."

And he ordered the sailors to be prepared, some at the climb, some at the poop, and some others at the prow. And just as he had got the galley ready, so that everyone was prepared, the wind came upon a part of the sail, and when the wind came, the sailsmaster cried: "Lower sail! Lower sail!"

And the ships and galleys that went around us found themselves in great travail and in great difficulties trying to lower. And there was a great clamour, for the cloud had appeared to be of good aspect. All the others and we lowered sail, because it was a terrible sea, as this Provençal wind went against the south-west wind that had been blowing. And all the ships, the galleys, and the surrounding vessels, were down to the bare wood.[56] For, because of that wind from Provence, there was a rough sea; and nobody in the galley where we were said a word, and all were quiet; and all the other vessels went around us.

And we, when we were aware of the peril, were greatly discouraged, but we addressed Our Lord and His mother and we made the following prayer: "Lord God, well we know that You have made us king of the land and the goods that our father had through Your mercy, and we have never undertaken any great or perilous deed before this present adventure. And just as we have felt Your help from our birth, and You have made us prevail against the bad men who have come against us, now, Lord, my Creator, help me, if You please, in this very great peril, so that this very important deed which I have begun is not lost. Since not only would the loss be mine but Yours would be the greater loss, as I have undertaken this voyage to exalt the Faith that You have given me, and to subdue and to destroy those who do not believe in You. Therefore, true and powerful God, may You guard me in this peril, and help me to bring to fulfillment the desire I have to serve You. And You should remember us, as nobody has ever pleaded for mercy from You and not found it, above all those who seek to serve You and suffer adversities for Your sake: and I am one of these. Also, Lord, think on all the people that go with me to serve You. And you, mother of God,[57] you who are a bridge and pathway for sinners, I beseech you, for the seven joys and for the seven sorrows that you underwent for your Beloved Son, that you remember to pray for me to your dear Son that He should save me, and those who go with me, from this danger and difficulty in which I find myself."

---

[56] That is, without sails.
[57] Here James shows his special devotion to Our Lady.

[58] Having said this prayer, a thought occurred to us: that although it was agreed by the noble barons and those who understood seafaring that we had to land at Pollença, we should ask if, in the galley we were in, there was anybody who had been to Majorca and to the island. And when we had asked this, Berenguer Gairan, seamaster of the galley, responded to us that he had been in that land. And we asked him what harbours there were near the city, on the side that faces Catalonia. And he said to us that there was a hill at three leagues distance from the city by land, and twenty miles by sea, that had the name Dragonera,[58] and it was not joined with the mainland of Majorca. There was a well of fresh water there, so that the time when he had been there, his sailors brought water from there. Near the land there was, separated from the mainland, a little hill, which was called Pantaleu;[59] and it was a crossbow shot from the land to that hill. And we said to him: "Then why should we seek any other place to land than this, if we have fresh water, and we have a good port, and the horses will be able to rest in spite of the Saracens? And our entire fleet can go there, and once there we can decide to go wherever suits us."

And we said to them that they should raise sail with the Provençal wind, so that with that wind we would be able to enter there. And we made sail, and said to the galley that it should communicate to the ships that they should do the same as us, and that it was we who had made sail, and that they should all follow us to the port of Palomera. All raised their sails at once on seeing that we had done so.

And see how great must be the virtue of God: that with that wind with which we sailed to Majorca, we could not arrive at Pollença, as had been decided. And that wind which we thought was against us, ended up helping us, because even the vessels that were rudderless, with that wind, all arrived at Palomera, where we were, and no vessel or boat was lost, nor any missing. And we entered on the first Friday of September[60] to the port of Palomera, and by Saturday night we had all our vessels with us.

[59] When Saturday came we sent for our nobles, that is to say, Don Nunó, the count of Empúries, Guillem de Montcada, and for all the others who were with the army; and we convoked those of highest authority amongst the shipmasters. And this was what was decided: to send Don Nunó in a galley that was his, and Ramon de Montcada in the galley of Tortosa, to go along the coastline towards the city of Majorca and land where they thought the fleet should land. And they

---

[58]La Dragonera is a small island off the west coast of Majorca, some thirty kilometres from Ciutat de Mallorca.

[59]Pantaleu is another island, much smaller than La Dragonera, very close to the west coast of Majorca.

[60]7 September 1229. Despite James's dramatic account of the voyage, they had crossed to Majorca in normal time (Santamaria, 'Expansión político-militar', p. 125).

found a place called Santa Ponça,[61] which it seemed was a good place to land because there was a hill near the sea, and, with five hundred men, we could put up there, we would not fear losing it before the rest of the fleet arrived. So it was decided that on that Sunday they should take that hill of Pantaleu.

After that, on Sunday,[62] at Midday, a Saracen who was called Alí,[63] from La Palomera, came swimming towards us, and brought us news of the island, the king and the city.

And we ordered that, when it was midnight, the galleys and *tarides* should weigh anchor, but that when they weighed them, nobody should make a sound, not even "Anchors away",[64] but rather that instead, each should, on weighing the anchor (for it was a good harbour and only one anchor had been necessary), hit with a stick the prows of the *tarides* and galleys. And this was done, because, before us, on the seashore, there were some five thousand Saracens, and there were some two hundred on horseback, and they had already pitched their tents.

And when it was Midnight you would have said that in our entire fleet not a sound was heard. And each of the twelve galleys left, towing its *tarida*, and they continued towing the *tarides* from the port little by little. But the Saracens heard it and roused themselves. And our men who towed the *tarides* stopped rowing and remained in silence, and the Saracens kept listening; but our men were able to continue towing the *tarides* little by little. And a little time afterwards, the Saracens began to shout out with great cries for a little time; and we recognized that they had heard everything. And they shouted, and we cried out as we left: "God speed!"

And the Saracens went by land, on foot and by horse. And we looked out for where we should go to land; and our twelve galleys and the twelve *tarides* sped so fast that they arrived at land before them.

[60] The men who went on to the land were Don Nunó, Don Ramon de Montcada, the master of the Temple,[65] Bernat de Santaeugènia and Gilabert de Cruïlles.[66] And before they could arrive at that hill which was near the sea with some seven hundred Christian footmen (and our men on horseback must have

---

[61] An inlet to the southeast of La Dragonera.

[62] 9 September 1229

[63] ʿAlī. According to *Desclot* this ʿAlī was major-domo of the king of Majorca. ʿAlī had been informed by his astronomer mother that James would conquer the island (ch. 35).

[64] 'Ayoç' can also be translated as 'Heave', which is appropriate in ch. 161.

[65] Bernat de Campanes, commander of La Ribera and Miravet, and lieutenant of the master of the Temple. He had promised to go on the expedition with all the knights he could muster (*H*, 1, no. 124).

[66] Gilabert was a knight from Empúries. Together with Bernat de Santaeugènia he swore to take part in the conquest with thirty knights (*H*, 1, no. 124). He is one of the witnesses to the document of concession of the liberties and law-codes at Majorca (*H*, 1, no. 150).

been some one hundred and fifty) the Saracens were ranged before them, with some five thousand footmen and two hundred horsemen.

And Ramon de Montcada came and said that he would go to survey them. And he went all alone and said: "Let nobody come with me."

And when he got near to them, he called for our men; and when they arrived there, he said: "Let us attack them, for they are nothing!"

And he was the first to attack them. And when the Christians were so near the Moors as four lances length away at the most, the Moors turned tail and fled; but they were pursued with such speed that more than one thousand five hundred Saracens died, as there was no desire to take any prisoners. And when that was done our men returned to the seashore.

And we left the sea, and we found our horse saddled, and the knights of Aragon,[67] who had disembarked from our *tarida*, and we said: "Know that it grieves us that the first battle of Majorca has been won without our presence. Are there knights who wish to go on with us?"

And those who were ready went with us, and there were around twenty-five of us. And we went trotting and at the gallop to where the battle had taken place. And we saw some three hundred to four hundred Saracen foot soldiers above on a hill. But they also saw us, and they went down from that hill to climb another that was there. And a knight of those of Ahé,[68] who are originally from Tauste, said: "Lord, if you want to overtake them, we should hurry."

And we made haste; and at the first engagement we killed four or five of them. And in the meantime our men kept coming; and they killed and overthrew the Moors they found there.

Meanwhile, with three knights that went with us, we encountered a knight who went on foot; and he had his shield on his arm, and a lance in his hand, and his sword girt; and he had a Zaragozan helmet on his head, and wore a coat of mail. And we said to him that he should surrender, and he turned to us, with his lance ready, and in no manner wished to speak with us. And we said: "Barons, our horses are very valuable to us in this land, and each of us has but one and a horse is worth more than twenty Saracens. I will show you how it is necessary to kill him: let us place ourselves all around him, and when he thrusts his lance at someone, let another come and strike him in the back and we will put him to the earth and in this manner he will not do harm to anybody."

---

[67]Though most of the leading nobles in the campaign came from Catalonia, nevertheless many Aragonese knights participated and played a significant part in the conquests of Majorca and Menorca (Santamaria, 'Expansión político-miltar', p. 123). The *Llibre* mentions sixty-eight participants of whom thirty-five are Catalan, twenty-five Aragonese, and eight from other places. This is in marked contrast to *Desclot* who mentions forty-four Catalans, four Aragonese, and three from other places (Cateura, 'Sobre la aportación Aragonesa', pp. 29–36).

[68]Ahé is the name of the Aragonese lineage. Tauste is in the province of Zaragoza.

And while we were preparing to do that, Don Pedro Lobera[69] came, and charged against the Saracen, who saw him coming, thrust his lance at him, and gave him such a blow on the breast of his horse with the lance that he drove it an arm's length in. But Don Pedro gave him such a blow with the breast of the horse that he fell. He wished to get up and put his hand to his sword. Meanwhile we attacked him, but in no manner did he wish to surrender before he died; rather, when anyone said, "Surrender," just "Le" came out, which means "No." And some eighty others died there. And we returned from there to the camp.

[61] When we entered into the camp, it must have been near sunset, and Guillem de Montcada and Ramon de Montcada, with the knights that were with them, came out to receive us. And we dismounted and we walked towards them. And Guillem de Montcada was smiling and we were very glad, because we feared that he would rebuke us; and we thought that things would not go so badly as we had feared.

Then Ramon de Montcada said to us: "What have you done? Do you wish to get yourself and us killed? What if by chance you had been lost – and you did run the risk of being lost – the army and all the rest of the expedition would also be lost and this great deed would not afterwards be done by anybody in the world."

And Guillem de Montcada added: "Ramon, the king has been foolish; but we have to take into account the fact it was in deeds of arms and in so good an act, because he was very annoyed at not having been in the battle. But, lord, correct yourself, for in you lies our life and our death. And console yourself thinking that, from the moment you have set foot in this land, you are king of Majorca. And if you die, you would die as the best man in the world, and although you might be ill in bed, you can hold this land as your own, for it is yours."

Then Ramon de Montcada said: "Lord, now we must decide how to go about guarding you well this night, as this is the most dangerous night we shall pass in this land, because if we do not hurry to fortify our position before they come to confront us, all this deed will be completely destroyed."

And we said: "Speak, as you know more than I do, so that we may do what you suggest."

And they said: "Then, lord, set up a watch as far afield as possible, so that the army is able to arm before they are upon us."

And we said that he had spoken exceedingly well.

And we still had not eaten, and we said that when we had eaten dinner we would send a message to the nobles, saying that each should arm the third part

---

[69]An Aragonese knight of the royal household (*S*, p. 227). He also took part in the siege of Xàtiva in 1244 (*M*, p. 165).

of his company, and that they should send scouts out to listen out and, if they heard something, they should let us know. And having eaten, we sent our officers to each of the nobles, but they were unable to send anybody, because they, the companies, and the horses were so tired, because of the disembarkation and the battle that they had waged. And we thought that they would send them when they could, and went to sleep.

And our ships, with some three hundred knights who were inside (and the horses also) found themselves at the Cape of Porrassa[70] and, at vespers, they saw the army of the king of Majorca, which had gone to the mountain of the harbour of Porto Pí. And Don Ladrón, a nobleman of Aragon, who was with us, arranged, with the knights of the ship, to send us a boat by sea, to let us know that the king of Majorca, with his army, was on the mountain of the port of Porto Pí, and that he had pitched his tents, for which reason it was necessary that we make ourselves ready. And this message arrived to us at Midnight, which was the night of Tuesday to Wednesday.[71] And we sent word to Guillem de Montcada, Don Nunó and the nobles of the army. Yet, in spite of that, we did not rise until dawn. And at dawn we all got up, and we heard Mass in our tent. And the bishop of Barcelona[72] delivered this sermon:

[62] "Barons, now is not the time to deliver a long sermon, as the occasion does not permit it, because this deed in which our lord the king and we find ourselves is the work of God and not our work. And it is necessary for you to take heed of this: those who die in this deed will do so in the name of Our Lord and they will receive paradise, where they will have everlasting glory for all time, and those who live will have honour and renown for all their lives and a good end in their deaths. Therefore, Barons, console yourselves in the name of God, because the king our lord, and we and you wish to destroy those who deny the name of Jesus Christ. And all must remember that God and His mother will not abandon us today, but that they will give us victory; so you must have good heart that we will defeat all today, because it is today the battle must be fought. And console yourselves well and rejoice, because we go with a good and legitimate lord, and God, Who is above him and us, will help us." And with that he ended his speech.

---

[70]Punta de la Porrassa.

[71]11–12 September 1229.

[72]Berenguer de Palou. According to Francisco Diago (*Historia de la Provincia*, f. 103v) Berenguer lost half a foot during the Majorcan expedition. Diago adds that in spite of this Berenguer did not faint away or put up his sword and, moreover, with his foot and a half, he later led his knights and footsoldiers in the attack upon Valencia city. Diago aside, the crusading spirit of the short sermon here is noteworthy.

[63] And when Mass had finished,[73] Guillem de Montcada received communion,[74] as we and the majority had done before going to sea; and, kneeling, crying, and with tears running down his face, he received his Creator. After that they talked about who should lead the vanguard. And Guillem de Montcada said: "You take it, Don Nunó."

And Don Nunó said: "No, you can both have it today."

And Ramon de Montcada said: "Nunó, we know well that you say and do that for the sake of being wounded in the battle that we have to wage at La Porrassa."[75]

And Guillem de Montcada said: "Be it as it will. It should not concern us."

And Guillem and Ramon de Montcada had already decided between them that they would not stop until they found themselves in battle with the Saracens.

Meanwhile one of our men came and said: "Look at all those soldiers who are about to leave the host and go forward."

And they were at the point of advancing. And we climbed onto a rouncy,[76] and Rocafort, who went with us, found a mare and rode her bareback, because his horse was not there as it was still on the ship. And we ordered that they should bring our horse out; and then, when we found ourselves with our soldiers, who were between four and five thousand men, we said to them: "You evil traitors![77] How can you go there? If they find you without knights they will kill you all."

They understood that we were right and they halted and said: "The king speaks the truth; we were mad to be going."

And we kept them there until Guillem de Montcada, Ramon, the count of Empúries, and those of their lineage had arrived. And we said to them: "Here you have the infantry; I have stopped them as they were about to leave."

---

[73]Dawn, 12 September 1229.

[74]According to *Desclot* (ch. 36) the whole army heard Mass and confessed, while Marsili (*Crónica latina*, II, ch. 21, p. 181) says that Guillem had waited until that day on which he was to receive the crown of martyrdom to receive communion.

[75]It is not clear here whether Ramon was suggesting that Nunó was frightened of leading the vanguard or, as perhaps seems much more likely, Ramon thought that a major battle lay ahead and that Nunó wished to lead the forces then, when the glory (and the booty) would be greater.

[76]A 'rossí'. It was a war-horse but generally not of very high quality (though perhaps of a little higher quality than 'rouncy' can faithfully convey) and was more usually for a squire (*P*, p. 85, n. 1). The circumstances did not permit the king or Bernat de Rocafort to wait for more adequate horses.

[77]James does not call them traitors because they are running away but rather because they are advancing without the protection of cavalry. In these passages we have some indications of the mistakes made by James in the campaign: the young king divides his army through choosing two disembarkation points; he risks himself unnecessarily; he lacks authority before both his knights and the infantry; he is taken unawares by the Muslim advance; he fails to keep the vanguard and the rearguard sufficiently close together.

And they said: "You have done very well."

And we delivered them over to them and they left with them.

And a little after they had gone, we heard a great noise,[78] and we said to a messenger[79] that he should go to Don Nunó to tell him to hurry, as we had heard a great clamour and we feared very much that our men had encountered the Saracens. But the messenger did not return and, on seeing that they were taking too long, we said: "Rocafort! Go there and make haste, and tell Don Nunó that we look unfavourably on his delay here today, as it may happen that the evil that could happen is so great that his money would not make up for it, and that it is not right that the vanguard and the rearguard are so far separated that one cannot see the other."

And he said: "You are all alone here, and there is no way I would separate myself from you."

And speaking with him, we said: "Holy Mother! And still Don Nunó and his knights do not come. How long will Don Nunó and his knights dither? They are truly doing us great wrong."

And then Don Nunó came, and with him were Bertran de Naia, Lope Ximénez de Luésia, Don Pedro Pomar and all his company, and Dalmau and Jaspert de Barberà.[80] And they said to us: "Why are you here?"

And we said: "We are here because of the footmen that I had to stop. Now it seems that they are engaging with the Saracens. And for the love of God, we must hurry."

And Bertran de Naia said: "Do you have your body mail?"

And we said: "No."

"Lord," he said, "Then take this."

And we dismounted and put on body mail,[81] and our purpoint, and we had our iron helmet tied on our head.

Then we sent a message to Don Pedro Cornel, Don Jimeno de Urrea and Oliver,[82] to hurry them up, as there was a battle.

---

[78]The beginning of the battle of Porto Pí (12 September 1229).

[79]A 'troter'. A servant who was accustomed to bring or carry letters or messages (*P*, p. 86, n. 2).

[80]These knights all appear to have been vassals of Nunó and presumably Dalmau was, like Jaspert, from Barberà. They were probably brothers.

[81]The passage indicates that James was not expecting an attack since he was not wearing his armour.

[82]Oliver de Termes (1197–1275), the son of the notorious Cathar lord of Termes, Raymond, who was dispossessed by Simon de Montfort in 1210. Oliver passed some of his youth in Catalonia at James's court. In 1228 he was reconciled to the Church. His sympathies were with the South and he took part in the attack on Carcassonne in 1240. He was excommunicated in 1242 and reconciled again in 1247. He fought in the crusades with King Louis IX of France and received back his father's lordships and territories of the Termenès and Aguilar. He conducted the siege of Queribus in 1255, where his opponent was his ancient companion at Majorca, Jaspert de Barberà, whose surrender he received. He continued crusading in his later

[64] And, in that place where they had encountered the Saracens, we found a knight and we said to him: "How has it gone? And what have our men done?"

And he said: "The count of Empúries, and the Templars went to attack those in the tents, and Guillem de Montcada and Ramon went to surround those on the left."

And we said: "And do you know anything more?"

"Yes. That the Christians have overcome the Saracens three times, and that the Saracens have overcome the Christians three times."

And afterwards we said: "Where are they?"

And he said: "On this mountain."

And we came across Guillem de Mediona, of whom they used to say that in all Catalonia nobody tilted better, and that he was a good knight. He was leaving the battle, and blood came from his top lip. And we said to him: "Guillem de Mediona, why are you leaving the battle?"

And he said: "Because I am wounded."

And we thought that he had been wounded by some mortal blow that they had given him on his body.

And we said to him: "And how were you wounded?"

"A stone with which they have struck me on the mouth has wounded me."

And we took him by the reins and we said to him: "Return to the battle, for a good knight should be spurred on by such a blow as this, and not leave the battle."

And, after watching him for a while, we were unable to see him anymore.[83]

When we got up to the top of the hill, there were not more than twelve knights with us, along with the banner of Don Nunó, carried by Rotlan Laí, and also Sire Guilleumes,[84] son of the king of Navarre; and there may have been all together seventy knights who went ahead of us. High on the hill where the Saracens were, there was a large company of foot soldiers, who held a red and white banner divided lengthways,[85] with the head of a man, or of wood, on the spike. And we said to Don Nunó, "Let us go up against the company that retreats there, as they are defeated, and all disorganized, and when a company is in such a state in battle, no one can fail to beat them soundly, if they attack them."

---

years, was at Tunis in 1270 and set out for the Middle East for the last time in 1273 (Peal, 'Oliver de Termes', pp. 109–130; Adroer, *Càtars i Catarisme*, p. 75).

[83] James is not suggesting that was the last that was seen of Guillem de Mediona as Marsili implies in his text (*Crónica latina*, II, ch. 21, p. 182). Guillem appears as witness to a document of James at Piera of 9 October 1231 (*S*, p. 230).

[84] After siding with the Cabrera (ch. 41) clearly Guilleumes was reconciled with the king and he was with James at Valls on 15 July 1229 (*M*, p. 79).

[85] It was the banner of Guillem de Montcada, the viscount of Béarn, and the suggestion is that he was already defeated and dead. The head was possibly that of one of his company.

Yet, together with Don Pedro Pomar and Ruy Ximénez de Luésia, he took me by the reins and said to me: "Today you would have us all die, and your impetuosity will kill us."

And they tugged on our reins insistently, until we said to them: "There is no need for you do that, as I am not a lion or a leopard, and, since you desire it so much, I will stop. But may God save us from regretting this delay."

[65] Meanwhile, Jaspert de Barberà came and said to Don Nunó that he should go forward. And he said: "I shall do it."

And we said: "If Jaspert is going forward, so shall I."

"What do you mean, you?" said Don Nunó, "Have they already made you a lion of combat here? Surely you can see that you can find plenty of knights as good as or better than you."

Yet before Jaspert de Barberà could reach those seventy knights, the Moors let out a cry and were able to make a small advance by throwing stones. And the banner of Don Nunó and those who were with it turned tail. And in such a grand act, they came down a stone's throw towards us. And some cried: "For shame!" However, as the Saracens did not follow them, these men of ours stopped. And in the meantime our banner arrived and our household, with some one hundred knights, or more, who guarded it; and they said: "Here you have the banner of the king."

We went down the hill and we joined with the men of the banner, and we all went up together. Then the Saracens fled. And we came upon some two thousand Saracens, who were fleeing on foot before us; but we could not pursue them, because our horse and those of the knights were so tired.

When the battle had been won and we were back on the hill, Don Nunó came to our side and said: "You and we have had a good day, for all is ours, as you have won this battle."

[66] Upon this, we said to Don Nunó: "Let us go to the town, as the king of Majorca is on the mountain and will not be able to arrive there as quickly as our men. And you can see him amidst that crowd, as he is dressed in white; and by doing this we will cut off his return to the town."

As we were beginning to go down the hill and to go to the plain on the road to the town, Ramon Alemany came to us and said: "Lord, what do you want to do?"

And we said: "We want to go to the town, to cut off the passage of the king, so that the enemy cannot enter there with his army."

"Ah, lord, you do something that no king has ever done having won a battle, if you do not pass the night in the place where you have won, to find out what you have gained and what you have lost."

And we said to him: "Know, Ramon Alemany, that it is better so."

Then we continued down the slope, going gradually down to the road that leads to the town. And when we had ridden a mile, the bishop of Barcelona came to us and said: "Lord, for the love of God, do not hurry so."

"Why not, bishop, if it is better so?"

And he said: "I wish to speak to you."

So we left the road, and he said: "Ah, my Lord. You have lost more than you realize, as Guillem de Montcada and Ramon are dead."

"What! Dead?" we said, and we began to cry. Afterwards we said to the bishop: "Let us not cry, as now is not the time for weeping, but let us take their bodies from the field, since they are dead."

"Let us do so," he said.

"Go and wait for us, for we shall do it," we said.

[67] Then we went little by little to the hill of Porto Pí.[86] From there we saw the city of Majorca, which seemed to us and to those who were with us, the most beautiful we had ever seen. Whilst there, we came across Don Pelegrín de Atrosillo, and we asked him if there was water nearby where we could camp that night. And he said yes, that he had seen a sheikh[87] with twenty horsemen enter, and they had watered their horses there. However, as there had been only four of them, they did not dare attack them. So, we continued onwards and we found that stream of water[88] and we camped there for the night. And we said to Don Nunó: "By the Faith I owe to God, I am very hungry as I have not eaten all day."

Then he said: "Lord, Oliver has pitched his tent and has prepared a meal, and you can eat there."

"Let us go, then," we said, "To where you suggest."

And we went there and we ate.

When we had eaten, one could see the stars in the sky.

And Don Nunó said: "Lord, it would be a good idea, if you have finished eating, to go to see Don Guillem de Montcada and Don Ramon."

And we said that he spoke well and we went there, taking torches and candles. There we found Don Guillem de Montcada lying upon mattresses, and he had a cover over him. And we stayed there a little while crying and afterwards we did the same over Ramon.

When we had done that, we returned to the tent of Oliver, and we slept there all night, until it was almost day. And when it was morning, they said: "Let us change camp."

---

[86]The hill of Bendinat.

[87]James here and elsewhere uses the word 'vell' which in this context can be translated sheikh rather than elder.

[88]The spring of L'Ermita.

And we said not, but that instead we should reinforce the camp. Then, putting on our body mail and our purpoint, we placed the Aragonese on one side and the Catalans on the other,[89] with the irrigation channel dividing them. Indeed, we made the camp so narrow, that it did not appear there could be more than a hundred knights camped there. So closely were the cords tied to one another that for eight whole days it was impossible to ride through the camp.

[68] When it was morning,[90] and the camp was secure, the bishops[91] and the nobles assembled and came to our tent. And the bishop of Barcelona, Berenguer de Palou, said: "Lord, it would be fitting to bury the dead bodies."

And we said: "Aye, good. When do you want to bury them?"

And they said: "In a while now, either in the morning, or when we have eaten."

And we said: "It would be best to do it in the morning[92] when nobody will see it, not even the Saracens."

And the nobles said that we were right. Thus, at sunset we collected wide and long cloths, and we had them put up facing the town, so that the Saracens would not see the candles when we buried them. Yet, when the moment arrived to bury them, all started to weep in earnest and to lament and cry out. But we told them to be quiet and listen to what we had to say to them, and this is what we said: "Worthy men, these nobles died in the service of God and in our service. If we were able to redeem them, so that they could return from death to life, and God would grant us such a grace, we would give so much of our land that it would seem madness to those who heard how much we would give. But as God has brought us here, you and us, in so great a service to Him, it is not fitting that we should mourn and weep. Hence, though our sorrow may be great, we should not show it. Thus, I order you, by the lordship I hold over you, that nobody should cry nor weep, for we will take their place as your lord, and whatever good they owed to you, we will give you. And if anybody loses a horse or anything else, we will give you recompense and fully cover your needs; so that you neither miss the presence of your lords nor notice their absence in anything, such good care will we take of you. Moreover, whatever grief you show would be a discouragement for the army, and you would not profit from it. So I order you, on pain of losing my protection, that nobody shall weep. But, do you know what form your grief should take? That we with you, and you with us, make the Saracens pay dearly for their deaths, serving

---

[89] Possibly to avoid trouble between the two sets of knights and a further indication of the strong Aragonese presence in the campaign (Ribas, *Conquista de Mallorca*, p. 47).

[90] 14 September 1229.

[91] The bishops of Barcelona and Girona.

[92] Presumably meaning very early in the morning.

Our Lord in that which has brought us here, so that His name may be blessed forever."

After we had said those words, they left off their weeping, and they buried them.

[69] The next day in the morning, we convoked our council, with the bishops and with the nobles of the army, so that they would order the unloading of the vessels that were in the sea. And there was a *trebuchet* and an *almajanech*. And the Saracens, on seeing that we carried the timber from the sea, hurried to prepare two *trebuchets* and *algarrades*.

And the seamasters and the sailors of the four or five ships from Marseilles[93] came to us and they said: "Lord, we have come here to serve God and you, and we propose to you, in the name of the men of Marseilles that are here, to make a *trebuchet*, at our expense, from the masts and wood of the ship, for the honour of God and for your honour."

We prepared our *trebuchets* and the *fenèvol* before the Saracens had prepared theirs. And the war machines, when they were prepared, were, counting those inside and outside the town, our two *trebuchets*, a *fenèvol*, and a Turkish *manganell*. And the Saracens made two *trebuchets* and fourteen *algarrades*. One of these *algarrades*, the best that has ever been seen, was able to fire over five or six tents, and penetrate into the army; but one of our *trebuchets* that we brought by sea fired further than any of theirs.

Then our men began to fire on those of the town, and they hurried to get their weapons ready as fast as they could. Jaspert de Barberà[94] said that he would show them how to make a mantelet that could go up to the edge of the moat, inspite of the machines and of the crossbows. And he had made a mantelet that went upon wheels, and the hurdles were in three double rows, and it was of good wood and strong inside. It went upon wheels, beginning near the *trebuchets*. As it went forward it was reinforced with forked poles and beams, so making something like a house covered with hurdles and with branches on top; and on top of these branches, there was earth. It was built in such a manner that if any of the stones of the *algarrades* hit there, it would suffer no damage. Then the count of Empúries made a mantelet and, bringing it to the side of the moat, he placed men of arms and sappers there so that they could enter underground and come out at the bottom of the moat. And we, with those of our company, made another, in that same manner. And so we began to

---

[93]The men of Marseilles, as well as those of Montpellier, played a very important part in the conquest and received substantial rewards when the land was divided (Santamaria, 'Comunidades Occitanas'; Baumel, *Histoire d'une Seigneurie*, 2, pp. 75–6). On 23 October 1230, James gave to the commune of Marseilles three hundred houses in the city of Majorca and a sixth part of the town of Inca (*H*, 1, no. 139).

[94]Ribas (*Conquista de Majorca*, p. 63) suggests that James had placed Jaspert in charge of all siege operations.

dig our tunnels. And when the tunnels were begun, that of Jaspert went above ground, and the others underground. And the army was very happy, because they saw that it was a great opportunity.

And nobody ever saw an army that fulfilled its duties so well; just as was preached by a Dominican friar who was called Friar Michael.[95] He was in the army and was a reader in theology, and his companion was brother Berenguer de Castellbisbal.[96] And when he gave absolution (which he had permission to do from the bishops), everybody would bring everything that he told them they should, whether it was wood or stone. Even the knights did not wait for the foot soldiers to bring things, but helped in every way they could. In front of them in their saddles they would bring by horse the stones[97] for the *fenèvols*. And the men of their houses did the same to supply the *trebuchets*, delivering the stones on frames that they had tied with cords round their necks. Indeed, when we ordered them to go with armoured horses to guard the war machines by night, or by day to guard those digging the tunnels, or to do whatever else that was necessary for the army, if it was ordered fifty should go, a hundred would go.

And so that those who hear this book may know what happened at Majorca was a singular deed of arms, we will tell you yet another example. In the space of three weeks, no footman, sailor or any other dared to sleep in the camp with us, but only ourselves, the knights and the squires that served there. The other foot soldiers and the sailors would come early in the morning, from the vessels where they slept at night. And the provost of Tarragona was one of these. So they would spend all the day with us, and in the evening they returned to the sea. And we had the camp fortified with a palisade and with moats; and there were two gates, so that nobody was able to leave without our order.

---

[95]Marsili says that he was the first 'lector' of the Order of Preachers, which office he received from St Dominic himself at Toulouse. He was much loved by the army, while the Saracens for many years afterwards said that Mary and Michael captured Majorca. He was with the king at Valencia and remained in the Dominican house which he founded there. He was buried there and there were many miracles surrounding his tomb (Marsili, *Crónica latina*, II, ch. 24, p. 187). He was the first of Dominic's followers to become a professor of theology at Paris and was for a time confessor to James (Burns, *Crusader Kingdom*, pp. 203–4).

[96]He was caretaker bishop of Valencia after the conquest, a candidate at Barcelona in 1241, and bishop of Girona (1245–54) where his preaching role was limited. In 1246, James, seemingly believing that Berenguer had disclosed his secrets and plotted against him, cut out part of his tongue. The incident was notorious. James was excommunicated by Pope Innocent IV, who was stunned by the enormity of the crime, and the king had to undergo a heavy penance to atone for his actions (*DPI*, 1, no. 304; *H*, 2, nos. 432–3, 443–4).

[97]Great quantities of stone were needed for the siege-engines, more than could be simply procured at the site of the siege. Pre-cut stone missiles were brought by ship from the major arsenals of the realm and then unloaded from the ships and carried forward to the engines (Chevedden, 'Artillery', p. 77).

[70] While we were there, our troubles returned.[98] A Saracen of that island, named Ifantilla,[99] brought together all the men of the mountain, that were a good five thousand, with more than one hundred horsemen, and he went to a strong hill that was above the fountain of the city of Majorca, and there he pitched his tents; and there were thirty or thirty-five or perhaps even forty of them. Then the Saracens went out with hoes and diverted the water that flowed from the spring to the town, making it go downwards in a torrent, in such a manner that we lost that water and we could not use it.

Now, we realized that the army would be unable to bear that. So we decided that one captain or two[100] should go with some three hundred knights, and that they should fight and recover the water. Then we told Don Nunó to go there, and he prepared himself and we made him the leader of that company. And what with his knights and those who were loaned to him, there were some three hundred knights who went with him.

The Saracens aimed to defend that hill, but our men went against them, and they defeated them on top of the hill, trapping Ifantilla, who was their leader, and killing him and more than five hundred who died with him. The rest took flight to the mountain, and our men captured their tents and sacked the camp. They then brought the head of Ifantilla to the army, and we ordered it placed in the sling of the *almajanech* and thrown into the town. Then our men redirected the water to the camp; and that night, understandably, given the great obstacle we had overcome, the army was happy.

[71] After that, a Saracen of that island named Ben Aabet[101] sent a message to us, through a Saracen who carried his letter, saying that he would come to us, and would arrange for the people of one[102] of the twelve parts of the island to bring supplies and all that they could to the army. In fact, he was certain that, if we treated him well, he could get all the other Saracens on our side. When we explained this to the nobles of the army, they all said that it was good that it should be done. Then the Saracen said that we should send knights to a place that was only a league away from the army and that was of easy access, and that he would go there protected by our word, and that he would make an agreement with us to serve us in good faith and without trickery, as long as we recognized the great service that he would do for us. So, we sent twenty

---

[98]'tornà nostre frau'. This seems to be the most likely meaning of another particularly obscure phrase. Bruguera suggests it may mean the plan turned against them (*Vocabulari*, p. 42).

[99]Most probably Ifant Allāh (Burns, *Islam under the Crusaders*, p. 307, n. 24).

[100]*Desclot* (ch. 40) says the leaders of the expedition were Guerau de Cervelló and Ferrer de Sant Martí and gives them an unspecified number of knights and 200 men-at-arms.

[101]Ibn 'Abīd.

[102]The district under his authority was that of Pollença and the districts to which his influence extended were Canarrosa and Inca (*S*, p. 235).

knights there, and they found him in that place. He came with his present, bringing some twenty beasts laden with barley, kids, fowl, as well as grapes, which were so good that though we carried them in sacks they were neither broken nor bad. And we shared that present that he brought among the nobles of the army. So acted that angel that God had sent us; and when I say angel I mean the Saracen, who was so good to us that we took him for an angel, and for that reason we say he was like an angel.

He asked us for our pennant, so that if his messengers came to the army, our men would not do them harm. And we gave it to him willingly. Later he sent us messengers saying that two or three other parties wished to follow his example, and that he would not let any week pass without sending provisions of barley, flour, fowl, kids and grapes, so that the army would be refreshed and remain content. In this manner, at the end of fifteen days, we had in our service all the districts of Majorca between the city and the part that faces Menorca; and they served us obediently. And we trusted him because we found nothing but truth in him.

Afterwards he came to see us and asked us for two Christian bailiffs to hold those districts in our name, and, with his advice, we named the two bailiffs of the land that he had placed under our command. We appointed as our bailiffs Berenguer Durfort[103] of Barcelona, and Jacques Sanz,[104] who were of our household and were men who were well prepared for the role.

[72] And so that those who see this book may know how many regions there are in Majorca, there are fifteen. The first is Andraig, and afterwards there is Santa Ponça, Bunyola, Sóller, Almeruig and Pollença, these being in the biggest mountains of Majorca, that face Catalonia. And the regions that are found on the plain are these: Montüiri, Canarossa, Inca, Petra, Muro, Felanitx, where the castle of Santueri is, Manacor and Artà. And in the district of the city there are fifteen markets; but in the time of the Saracens there were only twelve.

Our men hurried to continue the tunnels on three sides, the one above and the others below, until they could enter the moat. And their men came into the tunnels whilst ours defended them; some going through the tunnels and others from above, so much so that they drove them from the moat once and many times. Armed and with picks, the sappers got as far as the towers, and they began to dig, inspite of the Saracens, who could not prevent them. First they undermined the foundations of one tower; and when that tower was

---

[103] He had already been lieutenant to the bailiff in Barcelona, his brother Bernat Durfort (*M*, p. 67). Both had taken part against Guerau de Cabrera in the siege of Balaguer (*S*, p. 235). In 1249, Berenguer was named 'paer' (peaceman) of Barcelona by James (*M*, p. 195).

[104] Probably of French origin and perhaps from Montpellier. In 1242, he succeeded Berenguer Durfort as the chief bailiff of Majorca (*S*, p. 235). His presence is confirmed by the *Repartiment* (*Còdex*, 9v).

undermined they started a fire at the foundations, until the tower sank. And when the Saracens saw that things were going badly, they came down from the tower. Afterwards, we used the same procedure to demolish three at once.

Yet before we had demolished the first, the provost of Tarragona said: "Lord, would you like us to play a good trick?"

"Yes," we said.

"I," he said, "will place a cable at the foot of the tower, and the men will pull upwards from the tunnel so that, when the tower has been undermined, the foundations will fail and it will come down."

And it was done just as was said. And, when it was destroyed, three Saracens fell and the men in the tunnels went out and brought them inside.

[73] Afterwards two men from Lleida, called Proet and Joan Xico,[105] and another companion of theirs, came to see us, and they said: "Lord, if you give us reason to, we will level the moat, and armoured horses will be able to enter there."

And we said: "And you are sure that you can do it?"

"Yes," they replied, "With the will of God and if you protect us."

We said that it pleased us very much and that we thanked them for it, and that if they began it, we would provide those who would guard them. Then they began to level the moat as follows: they laid a bed of timber in the moat and then another of earth. Throughout the fifteen days that they did that the Saracens were unable to stop them, as they had the men of the army so close at hand.

And on Sunday, we dressed ourselves well and we prepared ourselves. We then conducted our affairs and had our food prepared for us and, alongside the bishop of Barcelona, Carròs and other knights, we watched the war-machines firing. Then we all saw smoke coming from the moat because of a tunnel that the Saracens had made underneath it, leading in the direction of the supplies. And when we saw it, it grieved us greatly, because we feared we would lose all the time and effort we had put into the mission. For we had trusted that by this deed the town would be taken, and to see it lost in so short a space of time weighed heavily on us. Everyone fell silent, and we reflected a while. Then God gave us the idea of filling the moat with water in this manner: by ordering one hundred men to arm, with shields and lances and all their equipment, and to go out with hoes, without the Saracens seeing them, and to go to the highest part, and to direct the water there where the provisions were, to water that place and so put out the fire. And just as we devised it so was it done. And the Moors did not try that again.

---

[105] A number of participants from Lleida took part in the conquest though Lleidatan help was far more important in the Valencia campaigns (Lladonosa, 'Jaime el conquistador', pp. 454–5). Joan Xico's presence is confirmed in the *Repartiment* (*Còdex*, 7r).

But later they came to the tunnels that we made underground, and they made one against ours, and they made it so low that they met with our men in the tunnel. And the Saracens forced our men out of the tunnel. A message came to us telling us this, and that they had occupied it. But we sent one of our shift crossbow[106] there, and he fired at two shielded Saracens who were the first in the tunnel with such force that both were killed at a single blow, notwithstanding their shields. When those inside saw this blow, they abandoned the cave, and this was how the underground tunnels were made, almost touching the moat.

[74] After that the Saracens understood that they could not defend the city, and they sent a message to us saying that if we sent messengers to them, they were willing to speak to them; and they asked that these be persons whom we trusted. So we discussed it with the bishops and with the nobles who were in the army agreeing that as they wished to speak with us we ought not to impede it, rather that it was good that somebody should go there. Then we sent Don Nunó with ten of his knights, and, to interpret, a Jew from Zaragoza, who was called Don Bahiel[107] and knew Arabic.

When they were there, the Saracens asked Don Nunó what he wanted and if he wished to say anything.

And Don Nunó said: "I have not come here because I wish to say anything, but because you sent a message to my lord the king, saying that he should send a messenger to you in whom he had much confidence. He chose me for this, for, what is more, I am his relative. And for that reason, and out of respect for you, he has sent me, in order to hear what you wish to say to him."

But the king of Majorca replied to him telling him to go back, as he did not wish to say anything. So Don Nunó came back to us.

At once we ordered all our council to assemble, the bishops and the nobles. Before beginning to speak, Don Nunó started to laugh. So we asked him why he was laughing. And he said that he had good reason to, since the king of Majorca had said nothing but had only asked him what he wanted.

"And I said to him that it seemed very strange to me that a man as wise as he had sent a message for you to send him a man who you trusted very much, and that he should then ask me what I wanted to say. We then replied that he ought to say what he had to say to us, for since he had been the one who had sent for us, we would not say anything unless he told us why he had done so."

---

[106]It is more commonly known as an 'arbalest a tour', or a crossbow drawn by a windlass.

[107]A Jewish savant of a distinguished family, he also played a prominent role in negotiations at Xàtiva and Murcia, as his brother Salomó was to do at the surrender of Menorca (*G*, 1, p. 151, n. 1; Burns-Chevedden, *Negotiating Cultures*, p. 138; Burns, 'Jaume I and the Jews', pp. 278–9).

And all our council said: "The time will come when he will willingly speak."

And after that the council broke up.

[75] A while after they had gone from there, Don Pedro Cornel, who had attended the council, said to us: "Gil de Alagón,[108] who has the name Mahomet, has twice sent me word that he wishes to speak with me, and, if it pleases you, I will speak with him, as perhaps he wishes to reveal something important that will be to your profit."

We said that it seemed a good idea to us, and he went. And the next day, early in the morning, as soon as he had returned, he told us all that Gil de Alagón (who originally, had been a Christian and a knight, and afterwards had become a Saracen) had said. And what he had said was that he could arrange for the king of Majorca and all the Saracens and the sheikhs of the island and of the land, to pay all the expenses that we and the nobles had incurred on our passage, and that they would allow us to leave safely and surely; and that he would guarantee it to us in such a manner that we would be very safe.

When we heard what he said, we said to him: "Don Pedro Cornel, it is very surprising to us that you should negotiate such a treaty with that Saracen, because we have promised to God, for the faith that He has entrusted and given to us, that, even if somebody were to give us as much gold as would fit between that mountain and the army, we would not accept it; nor can they make a treaty with us about Majorca, if we do not take the town and the kingdom. For never will we return to Catalonia without passing through Majorca first. Thus we order you, upon our love, that you will never again speak to us of such a thing."

[76] Later, the king of Majorca sent us another message saying that we should send Don Nunó and he would speak with him. So we sent him to him. The king of Majorca came out through the gate of Porto Pí, and ordered a tent to be prepared and seats so that he and Don Nunó could sit there. And Don Nunó went to him. The entire army stopped fighting, while those negotiations took place, and they did no evil to those inside nor did those inside attack those who were outside. And when they were close to one another, the king of Majorca and Don Nunó dismounted and they went straight into the tent. And only the king and two of his sheikhs, Don Nunó and the *alfaquim*,[109] who had gone to interpret, spoke. Meanwhile, the knights who had gone with Don Nunó remained outside with some Saracens who were there with them.

---

[108] Of one of the most noble Aragonese families, but a renegade. He was among the Christians after the conquest of the city (ch. 90) and received great booty.

[109] 'Alfaquim' from Arabic Ḥakīm, meaning master, teacher.

Don Nunó said to the king of Majorca that he should tell him why he had sent for him. And he said to him that it was for this reason: "Because I do not remember ever doing your king wrong; so it seems strange to me that he should be so angry with me that he should wish to take the kingdom which God has given me. Hence, I would entreat him, and ask you to advise him, that he should not desire to take my land; and whatever it has cost him or you that have come here, I and the people of the land will cover it. And if he and all those who are with him depart in peace and good will, nobody will show you anything but good treatment and friendship. So, let the king go back, for however great the amount we and the people of this land will have to give you, we will do it inside five days. Moreover, through the mercy of God, we have here sufficient weaponry and provisions and all the things necessary for the defence of the city. And so that you may better believe what I have said to you, let your lord the king send two or three men of his confidence, and I swear to you on my own head that they can come and go unharmed, and we will show them the provisions and the weapons. And if it is not as we have said, then let him not agree to the treaties of which I have spoken. For you must know that it is not of great importance to us that you have destroyed the towers that you have undermined, as we are not afraid that through there anyone may enter the city."

[77] On hearing those words, Don Nunó responded to him and said: "Regarding what you say, that you have not done any great offence against our king, we have to say that yes you did so, in taking a *tarida* of his kingdom with a great quantity of merchandise that the merchants carried.[110] And he then sent you a message and asked you very kindly about it through a man of his household called Jacques,[111] and you replied with great insolence and harshness, and you asked him who was the king who asked for the *tarida*, and he responded that he was the son of him who had defeated the army in the

---

[110]The *Llibre* has previously said nothing of this incident. It was developed by *Desclot* (ch. 14) and Marsili (*Crónica latina,* II, ch. 29, p. 194) though Marsili characteristically prefaces this passage by saying the first reason for the conquest is one of faith. al-Maqqarī wrote that the Muslim governor of Majorca captured three ships (Tortosan, Barcelonan, and Genoese) in response to a Catalan attack on the Muslim fleet bringing supplies from Ibiza (Miravall, *Ponç de Torrella*, p. 28). Most importantly, a witness of the Barcelonan assembly of December 1228 remembered that James had delivered a speech saying that the king of Majorca had captured a ship belonging to his men and that James had sent his scribe 'Jasquius' to the king to demand its restitution. The king refused and James said he had called the *Cort* together to decide upon the manner in which he should respond, and ultimately it was decided that James should go with his army to capture the city and land of Majorca (Kagay, 'Emergence of "Parliament"', p. 237). The recollections of this witness (P. de Castronolo, a citizen of Barcelona) contrast sharply with the king's account of his own speech (ch. 48) but coincide with *Desclot*.

[111]Most probably the same Jacques who appeared in ch. 71.

battle of Úbeda.[112] And you were offended and angered against him, and you said to him that if it had not been that he was the messenger, it would have cost him dear to have pronounced these words. And he responded that he had come on your assurance, but that you could do with him as you saw fit, for it was very necessary that you should know the name of his lord, as all the men of the world knew it, and they know how powerful and revered he is among Christians, for which reason you ought not to be indifferent to knowing his name. For that reason I have said these words to you, for the evil response you gave to him. And as regards the other question, we respond that our king is young, as he is only twenty-one,[113] and this is the first great enterprise he has undertaken; and you must know he has the desire and it is his will not to go from here for anything in the world until he has taken the kingdom and land of Majorca. And even if we advised him otherwise when we spoke to him, we know for certain that he would not do anything else. But it would be better to speak of other things, because these things are of no account, as he would not do it nor would we advise him so."

[78] After that the king of Majorca said: "Since you do not wish to accept the terms I have proposed to you, I will do this: I will give him five *bezants* for each man, woman, and child; and we will abandon the town, if he gives us some of the ships and vessels that he has, so we can go to Barbary; and as for those that wish to remain, let them remain here."

Then, Don Nunó, hearing the words that the king had said, came to us very happy. And nobody knew about it except him and the *alfaquim*, and he whispered in my ear that he had good news. And we said that we would send for the bishops and for the nobles, so that they were present when he spoke those words, for as they would have to be made public, it was better that he spoke them in front of everybody. And he agreed, and we sent for them. But while they came he told us everything that had happened. And when they came he told us what he had discussed with the king of Majorca and how he had replied to him; and this was what he said, in short: that he would surrender the town, and that he would give five *bezants* for each person who was in the town, and that it would be paid inside five days, and that we should allow him, his lineage and all his household, male and female, passage to Barbary, and that those ships and vessels in which they made the crossing should leave them on the land, and that that would be sufficient for them if it was done.

---

[112]In the Middle Ages, the battle of Las Navas de Tolosa (16 July 1212) was often referred to as the battle of Úbeda, the formidable castle which the Christians, led by Peter II, successfully besieged after the battle (a psychological blow from which the Almohads never recovered).

[113]Having been born in February 1208.

Now the count of Empúries, who was in the army, did not wish to take part in the councils that we convoked with the other nobles; rather, he was in a tunnel,[114] and said that he would not leave it until the town was taken; and for that reason we were unable to have him in that council. Gathered there together of the relatives of Guillem de Montcada,[115] there were Ramon Alemany, Guerau de Cervelló, son of Guillem de Cervelló and nephew of Ramon Alemany, and Guillem de Claramunt, and the bishop of Barcelona, who took part in the council, and the bishop of Girona, and the provost of Tarragona, and the Abbot of Sant Feliu; and all said to the bishop of Barcelona that he should give his opinion.

So the bishop responded, and said that great harm had been received in that island, with the deaths of so many nobles and good men, and that if anyone was able to avenge them by serving God, then the vengeance would be good; but that the nobles and the knights understood more of questions of arms than he did, because they were more accustomed to it. Then he said that they should speak, at which they said that Don Nunó should give his opinion.

And Don Nunó spoke in this manner: "Barons, we have all come here to serve God and our lord the king, who is here before us; and we came here to take Majorca. And it seems to me that if our lord the king accepts the treaties that the king of Majorca proposes, we will fulfill that for which we came. And I do not wish to say anything more, since I am the bearer of the message, so you can give him your counsel."

Then Ramon Alemany began to speak, and said: "Lord, you came here, and we with you, to serve God, and you have lost here, for they died in your service, such vassals that no king could have better, and God has given you the opportunity to avenge them, and avenging them, you will have all the land. Moreover, the king of Majorca has such wisdom and knows the land of Majorca so well that if he passes to Barbary, with what he would be able to say and with the knowledge that he has, he would bring so many people of the Saracens to this land, that even what you have won with God's help and ours, could still be taken from us by him, because you will not be able to stay here. And since you have the opportunity, you should avenge them and win the land, for then afterwards it will not be necessary to fear Barbary."

And Guerau de Cervelló and Guillem de Claramunt said with one voice: "Lord, for God we entreat you to remember Guillem de Montcada, who loved you and served you so well, and Ramon, and the other nobles who have died with them on the battlefield."

---

[114] *Desclot* (ch. 40) also indicates that Hug remained in the tunnel he had constructed.

[115] Santamaria ('Expansión político-militar', pp. 128–9) identifies these men as the 'hawks' who are determined to seek an unconditional surrender, desiring to avenge the deaths of the Montcada lords.

[79] When we had heard their advice, we said to them: "Regarding the death of the nobles, there is nothing we can do about it, because what God ordains must be accepted. However, our intention in coming to this land was to conquer it and serve God. Thus as Our Lord has wished to fulfil our will, so that, with this treaty, the conquest of the land might be accomplished and we might gain great riches, it seems to me that we should accept this agreement. Because those who have already died, in having the glory of God, have more land than we do. Nevertheless, the counsel that I give here, although it runs counter to that which you have given, is that which I must give."

And that entire lineage, and the bishops with one voice, said that it was better to take the town by force and that we should not accept the peace. And we sent a message to the king of Majorca saying that he should do what he must do, and we would do what we must do. And when these discussions were finished and the Saracens knew the decision that we had communicated to them, they became very alarmed.

When the king of Majorca saw how frightened they were, he convoked a general council and said to them in his Arabic: "Worthy men, you know well that Miramolino[116] has held this land for more than one hundred years,[117] and he wished that I should be your lord, and it has been held in spite of the Christians, who have never, until now, dared to attack this land; and we have our wives and our daughters and our relatives here. Now they tell us that we should leave the land, and in such a manner that we would become their captives. And furthermore they talk of something even worse than captivity; that they will take our women and all that they can take there, and once we are in their power, they will be able to rape them and do what they want to them. And I, who have come here among you, would rather lose my head than accept something so cruel against our law. But I wish to know from you what you think, and that you give me your advice."

And all the people cried out with a single voice, and they said that they would rather die than suffer so great a shame as that would be. And the king said: "Then, since I see you are of such a good disposition, let us prepare to defend ourselves so well that every man will be worth two."

And after that, they dispersed and returned to the wall, and each Saracen was worth more than two had been before.

[80] A few days later, we said to Don Nunó: "Don Nunó, I think that our nobles wish they had not given the advice they gave the other day; as now they would wish to accept the treaties, even though they did not want to at first."

---

[116]A Christian corruption of Amīr al-Mu'minīn, 'Commander of the believers'.
[117]Since the Catalano-Pisan expedition of 1114–15, Muslim powers had held the Balearics for one hundred and fourteen years continuously.

And we said to those who had given advice upon the treaty: "What do you think of it now? Would it not have been better to accept that treaty that they proposed to us than it is now with them defending themselves so well?"

And they were silent and ashamed of what they had said.

When it was evening, two of those who had advised that course of action, the bishop of Barcelona and Ramon Alemany, came and said to us: "Why do you not go back to the treaties that we spoke about the other day?"

And we said to them: "Would it not have been better that you had agreed to it then rather than now telling me what to do?"

"And I say to you that it would not seem to me a good deed, because if we now introduce them again, it would be a sign of weakness. However, if they propose a second time the deal that they proposed the other day, do you think that we should accept it?"

And they said that they thought it would be a good thing and they would arrange that those who had not wished it would accept it. And we said: "Now if they send a message to us, since you are in agreement, we will do it, since we will be accepting it with your counsel."

And immediately we left. Yet Our Lord, who guides those who follow His path, did not wish it to happen in the manner that the Saracens had proposed, and gave a better remedy to it, which was as follows. Just as the Saracens had been encouraged by the speech of the king of Majorca, God willed that the Christians also would be strengthened and that the Saracens would be weakened. And though we continued with the tunnels,[118] in the end they all had to be abandoned, except for the one that went above land, into which we put so much effort that it was finished, in spite of them.

[81] Meanwhile, four days before invading the city,[119] we, the nobles and the bishops, agreed to convoke a general council, and that in that council all should swear upon the Holy Gospels and upon the cross of God that, on entering Majorca, when it was invaded, no noble, knight or footman, should turn back, since, having been moved to enter the city, he should not stop unless he had received a mortal blow; and if any received a mortal wound and at his side there was any relative of his or any man of the army, that they should pick him up and leave him in a sheltered place, and they should continue to advance; and they should enter the town by force, without turning head or body, and that

---

[118]We know from *Desclot* (chs. 43–4) that the mining operations continued apace in late November and early December with three assaults on the city repelled and with strong Muslim counterattacks. Bad weather hampered the siege operations throughout November and early December (Santamaria, 'Expansión político-militar', pp. 129–30). Meantime, Pope Gregory IX, fearing a waning of enthusiasm, ordered the preaching of the crusade in the provinces of Narbonne and Arles in support of James (Villanueva, *Viage*, 21, p. 252; Goñi, *Historia de la Bula*, p. 161).

[119]27 December 1229.

he would be held for a traitor who did otherwise, like those that kill their lord. And we wished to swear to that oath just as they had sworn it, and the nobles stopped us from doing so; but we said to them that they should take it as if we had sworn it. And when the oaths had been taken, the bishops and the nobles assembled apart with us, and one of our company, whose name we do not recall, spoke to us in this fashion: "Lord, if we do not do this one thing, nothing we have done will be worth anything, because if the Saracens of the island break the agreements that they have made with our lord the king, and two, three, four, or five thousand of them enter the city, it would not be so easy to take Majorca, since they have enough to eat, and, if they are reinforced by more people, they will defend the city well. For which reason, I would advise that we remain near the city, so that nobody can enter it."

And all said with one voice that the advice he had given was good, and that it was necessary to follow it.

[82] The next day the bailiffs, by the names of Jacques and Berenguer Durfort, whom we had sent to the districts of Majorca, came from there, because they did not dare to remain there for fear that the Saracens would do them harm. And as we saw them coming, they said to each other: "Now the plan that we agreed must seem better than it did at first."

And we decided to establish three watches. One watch was at the war machines and at the hurdles; the other was before the gate of Barbelec,[120] near the castle that we afterwards gave to the Temple; and the third was in front of the gate of Porto Pí. And each guard contained one hundred armed knights.

And it was then between Christmas and New Year, and it was so very cold that the guards, when they were outside and had walked a league or two, returned to the tents and the barracks, because they were so cold, and sent scouts to see if they were able to come to the camp. And we, at night, would send a messenger to where we had placed the guards to see if they were there, and they would tell us that they were not there. And we got up at night, and we reprimanded them for the evil they had done, and we replaced them with fresh men from the people of the nobles and of our household.

And that lasted five days. And the last three days of those five, we did not sleep by night or day, because everybody called on us to give advice upon all that it was necessary to do, as much regarding the tunnels, as regarding the breach through which we had to enter the town, so much so that nobody in the army would do anything worth twelve diners[121] if he had not first consulted us about it.

---

[120]Bāb al-balad, later to be known as the 'Porta dels Camps', both meaning 'the gate of the fields'.

[121]That is, one sous (a very small amount).

And we obtained sixty thousand pounds from the merchants who were in the army,[122] to be repaid to them when we had taken the town, so that we could do all that was necessary for the benefit of the army, because the town was about to be taken. And we stayed awake three days and three nights, as whenever we were on the verge of going to sleep messengers would come on behalf of those who needed our advice, and when we wished to sleep we were unable to do so, as we slept so lightly that when anyone came close to the tent, we immediately heard it.

[83] So it was that the night before New Year's Eve came, and it was decided in the army that, at dawn, having heard Mass, we should all receive the Body of Jesus Christ, and everybody should prepare themselves as for a battle. And that night, after the first watch, Lope Ximénez de Luésia[123] came to our bed and called us and said: "Lord, I come from the tunnels, and I have ordered two of my squires to enter into the town and they have entered there, and they have seen that many people are lying dead in the squares, and that from the fifth to the sixth tower there was no Saracen on watch."

And he advised us that we should order the army to arm itself, so that we could take the town, since there was nobody to defend it, and a thousand, or even more than a thousand, could enter without them even knowing.

"Ah, you old fool![124] And this is how you would advise me, to enter the city by night, and on a dark night at that? Even in the day, the men are quick to draw their weapons. Yet you want me to order them to enter by night, when nobody can see who anybody else is? If ever the men of the army enter the town and are expelled by them, we shall never take Majorca afterwards."

And he understood that what we were saying was true, and he acknowledged it.

[84] When dawn broke, it was decided we would hear Mass and receive the Body of Jesus Christ.[125] And when we had heard Mass, and received the Body of Jesus Christ, we said that everybody should arm themselves with the weapons they had to carry. And we all went out before the town, into the plain that was between them and us. And that was at the hour when the day was becoming clear.

And we went to the men on foot who were in front of the knights, and we said to them: "Go, worthy men, begin to march in the name of Our Lord God."

However, even with these words, nobody moved, though they had all easily heard them, the knights and the others. And when we saw that they did not

---

[122]Marsili (*Crónica latina,* II, ch. 32, p. 200) provides information on the merchants.
[123]His presence is confirmed by the *Repartiment* (*Còdex,* 71v).
[124]'A, Don veyl!' (*P*, p. 82, n. 3).
[125]Dawn, 31 December 1229.

move, we were filled with anguish, because they did not obey our order. And we called upon the mother of God, and we said: "Oh, mother of our Lord God, we come here that the sacrifice of your Son might be celebrated: entreat Him that we should not receive this dishonour, neither I nor those who serve me in your name and that of your Beloved Son."

And we shouted to them another time: "Go, worthy men, in the name of God! Do you fear them?"

And we said it three times. And after that, our men gradually began to march.

When all had begun to march, the knights and the men-at-arms, they approached the moat where the breach was, and all the army began to shout: "Santa Maria! Santa Maria!"

And this invocation had hardly left their mouths when they said it again and then again, and the more they said it, the stronger were their cries. And they said it a good thirty times or more; yet when the armoured horses began to enter, they fell silent. When the pass opened through which the armoured horses had to enter, there were already some five hundred footmen there inside. And the king of Majorca, with all the people of the Saracens of the city, had already come to the breach; and they attacked those on foot who had entered there with such force that, if the armoured horses had not arrived, all would have been killed. And according to what the Saracens themselves told us, they saw a white knight with white weapons enter first, on horseback; and our belief is that it was Saint George,[126] as we have found it written in histories that in other battles between the Christians and the Saracens he has been seen many times.

And of the knights, the first who entered there was Juan Martínez de Eslava, who was of our household, and afterwards Bernat de Gurp, and near Bernat de Gurp, a knight who went with Sire Guilleumes, who was called Soyrot[127] – and this name had been given him as a joke. And after those three, there went Don Fernando Pérez de Pina.[128] And we cannot remember the others. But each of them entered as quickly as he could. And there were one hundred men or more in the army, who, if they could have entered first, would have done what the first man did.

---

[126]James was little given to talk of miracles (Burns, 'Spiritual Life', p. 336). Here he relies on the report of the Saracens themselves.

[127]Possibly a term of endearment derived from French 'sor', an adjective applied to young goshawks that had not yet moulted (*P*, p. 104, n. 6).

[128]*Desclot* (ch. 47) has Fernando enter the city third, after Martín Pérez and Bernat de Gurp.

[85] Meanwhile, the King of Majorca, Xech Abohehie,[129] rode over on a white horse, and cried to his men: "Roddo!",[130] which means "Hold." And of the Christian footmen there were twenty or thirty armed with shields, and also there were men-at-arms mixed in with them; and on the other side there were Saracens with small shields. And on both sides they had drawn their swords, but they did not dare attack each other. Yet when the knights entered with their armoured horses, they went to attack them. And so great was the multitude of the Saracens, that they stopped them with their lances; and the horses reared up, unable to pass because of the density of the lances, which was so great that they were forced to turn round. And as they turned round the others pushed back, and the knights were able to continue to enter, until there were some forty or fifty of them there. And the knights and the foot soldiers carrying shields were so near the Saracens that they could attack them with their swords, so close in fact that nobody dared to put out his arm, for fear that some sword of the other side would wound him on the hand. And, a little after, when there were already some forty or fifty knights there, they turned to face the Saracens, with their armoured horses, and they all cried with one voice: "Help us, Mary, mother of Our Lord!"

And we shouted: "For shame, knights!"

Then we attacked the Saracens and put them to flight.

[86] When the Saracens of the town saw that the city was being invaded, some thirty thousand men and women[131] left by two gates, that of Berbelec and that of Porto Pí; and they fled to the mountain. And so great were the riches and booty that the knights and the footmen found in the city, that they were unconcerned about those who fled. And the last Saracen to go from that place was the king of Majorca. And the other Saracens, when they saw that the knights with their armoured horses and the footmen had overcome that place, went to hide themselves in the houses, each as best he was able. But they did not hide themselves so well that some twenty thousand did not die on our entry into the city; to such an extent that, when we were at the Almudaina[132] gate, we found some three hundred dead there; for when they tried to retreat into the Almudaina, the others had closed the gate, and our Christians then arrived and killed them. And when we went there, they did not defend themselves, but instead a Saracen who knew our Latin[133] said to us that if we gave them a guard to protect them from death, they would surrender the Almudaina.

---

[129] Abū Yaḥyā. He was *wālī* from soon after the Almohad capture of the islands (from the Almoravids in 1203) and was almost independent of outside authority.

[130] 'radd' means to resist, repel or reject.

[131] Yet the entire population of the city was probably not much more than half this figure.

[132] L'Almudaina (that is 'the citadel') was essentially the walled area equivalent to the old Roman city and contained the principal mosque and the alcazar.

[133] 'nostre llatí', meaning Catalan.

[87] While we were negotiating that, two men of Tortosa came and said to us that they wished to speak with us on an affair that would be very profitable to us. And we withdrew to one side and we listened to them; and they said that if we conceded them a reward, they would deliver to us the king of Majorca. And we asked them what they wanted; and they said that they wanted some two thousand pounds. And we replied to them that they asked too much, for as the king was to be found in the town, we would take him in the long run, but, even so we said that on the condition he was not harmed, we would give them a thousand pounds. And they said that they agreed.

Then we left a noble in our place, and we ordered that nobody should attack the Almudaina until we had returned. And we had Don Nunó called and we said to him that we had found the king of Majorca, and that he should come with us. And he said that it pleased him greatly, and we went there. And they brought us to the house where he was, and Don Nunó and we dismounted, armed as we were, and we entered the house. And there were three bodyguards[134] there defending him with their spears.[135] And when we were near him, he got up. And he was wearing his white cloak, but he wore body mail under his coat, and under that a robe of white samite. And we ordered it to be said to him in Arabic, by one of the men of Tortosa, that we would allow him two knights and some of our men, and that he need not fear death now, because he was in our power. And we left him some of our men there to prevent him from being attacked.[136]

Then we returned to the gate of the Almudaina, and we told them that they should give us hostages and should come out onto the old wall in order to speak to us. And they brought to us the son[137] of the king of Majorca, who would have been about thirteen years old, and they said that he was the hostage they gave us; and that they would open the gate, but we should take good care over whom we allowed to enter there. And we ordered two Dominican brothers[138] to enter, in order to guard the king's chambers and treasure, and two knights with them, good and prudent men, so that with their squires they

---

[134]'aixurtiquins' which is from an Arabic word simply meaning soldiers.

[135]An 'atzagaia', which was a short spear used by the Moors.

[136]*Muntaner* (chs. 7–8) has James take the Saracen king by the beard as revenge for that king having fired Christian captives into James's camp from *trebuchets*. *The Chronicle of San Juan de la Peña* (ch. 35) relates that James, finding the king in a dead-end street, seized him by the beard.

[137]According to Zurita (*Anales*, bk 3, ch. 8), James had him brought up at his court, under the tutorship of a Dominican Friar, who converted him to Christianity, the king himself acting as godfather at the baptism. Later on James married him to a lady of the house of Alagón and made him lord of Illueca and Gotor (*G*, 1, p. 175, n. 1).

[138]Probably as Marsili says (*Crónica latina*, II, ch. 34, p. 204) these two Dominicans were Miguel de Fabra and Berenguer de Castellbisbal. The only illustration of the codex of the Comte d'Aiamans depicts the two Dominicans in front of the fortress (*P*, p. 108).

should help to protect and watch over the Almudaina, as we were very tired and wished to rest, as the sun had already set.

[88] In the morning,[139] we examined our affairs to put them in order. And look how Our Lord had arranged it, that all the men of the army found so much to take that it was unnecessary to fight among themselves, for each thought himself richer than the other. And Don Ladrón, a noble who was with us, called on us, and said to us that one of his men had come to see him and had said there was a good house and that he had prepared a good cow to eat, and that we would be able to sleep there. And we said to him that we thanked him very much and we would go there. And when it was morning no man of our house came to us, nor did they come back for eight days; because each had that which he had taken, and was so much pleased with it that he did not wish to come to us.

[89] Once the city was taken, the bishops and nobles assembled, and they said that they wanted to speak with us. And they said it was necessary to auction the Moors and the booty that was there, and everything else. And we said we did not think it a good idea, for this reason: that if we held an auction, it would take a long time; and that it would be more fitting that, profiting from the fear the Saracens then felt, we should conquer the mountains, and that the booty should be divided. And they asked us: "And how shall we divide the booty?"

And we said by gangs: "And if we promptly divide the Saracens and the booty, the people will be happy. And it is necessary that we do it in eight days, and afterwards we shall go against the Saracens who are outside, and we shall conquer them. And we shall reserve the assets for the galleys. And that is the wisest thing we can do."

Yet Nunó, Bernat de Santaeugènia, and the bishop[140] and sacristan of Barcelona wished to auction absolutely everything. And they were all agreed on this since they planned to trick all the others with their cunning, believing that, as they knew more than the men of the army, these would be unaware of their plans. And we said to them: "I think that this would not be an auction but a trick.[141] And we fear that we might take so long over this that the Saracens will become stronger, so that afterwards we will be unable to conquer them so easily. So it would be better that we conquer now while they are afraid, than afterwards, when they have regrouped."

---

[139]1 January 1230.

[140]Berenguer de Palou gained substantially in the *Repartiment* (*Còdex*, 25r, 27r/29v, 30r, 36v, 83v, 87r, 89r), but Bernat de Santaeugènia did not (25r) and in chapter 105, James indicates that Bernat was more concerned with reputation than financial gain.

[141]A play on words by James: 'aquest encant no sera encant, que engan sera'.

And they asked why we were against them, insisting that their plan was better.

And we said: "God's will be done, then. But I fear we will regret it."

[90] Then we began to conduct the auction, which began at Carnival[142] and lasted until Easter.[143] And when it was finished the knights and the people thought each would be given a share,[144] and each awaited a share, since they did not want to pay for their share. And the knights came together with the people and said all over the town:

"This is wrong! This is evil!"

And with that, they rioted, and cried with one voice: "Let us go and sack the house of Gil de Alagón."

And they went there, and they sacked it.

And when we went outside to go to them, they had already sacked it; and we said to them: "Who has ordered you to sack anybody's house, with us here, and without you having presented any complaint to us?"

And to that they responded: "Lord, each of us deserves to have a share of the things that have been taken, just as the others have them; and we do not have our share, and we will die of hunger, here, and we would like to go back to our lands. And for this reason the people are doing what they are doing."

"Men,"[145] we said, "You have done wrong, and you will regret it. And do not do it again, as you should know I would not tolerate it; and it would be worse if we had to punish you, as you would grieve much for the evil you received and we would regret deeply having to do you harm."

[91] And two days later, they revolted again, and they began to cry out: "Let us go to the house of the provost of Tarragona!"[146]

And they went to the house of the provost of Tarragona, and they sacked the entire house and they took all the booty that was there and, except for the two horses that he rode, which were at our quarters, they left him with nothing.

After that, the nobles and the bishops came to our presence, and we said to them: "Barons, this cannot be tolerated, as if we continue to appease them, there would not be one amongst you who had not been killed or had all that you possessed plundered. But we will suggest to you a good way forward. When they begin again, let us be prepared to arm ourselves and to arm our horses, and let us go to the square, where there is no barrier nor chain to stop us, and of those whom we find who do evil, let us hang twenty of them in all.

---

[142]17 February 1230.

[143]7 April 1230.

[144]They appear to be harking back to the *Corts* at Barcelona in 1228.

[145]The Catalan 'Barons' here, as often, is used simply to address the men.

[146]Ferrer de Pallarès. His house is attacked because he had gained very substantially in the *Repartiment* (*Còdex*, 27r, 34v, 48v, 50v, 54r, 71r, 76v, 78v, 80v, 82r, 85v).

And if we do not find them, let us take the first that we find, and let us hang them, to teach the others a lesson. And if we do not do that, all will be in great danger. And our share, which we have at the Almudaina, we shall transport it to the Temple. And we in person shall protect it until it gets there, so that those there may guard it for us."

And, after that, we spoke with the people of the town and we said to them: "Men, you have begun to do the most unusual thing that has ever been seen, in sacking these houses, and, above all, of those who have done you neither little nor great harm. And I shall let you know that hereafter it will not be tolerated, but we shall hang so many in the streets that the town will stink. And I and the nobles here with me wish you to have your share, both of the goods and of the lands."

And when they heard these fine words that I spoke to them, they quietened down and left off the evil that they had begun. But we were unable to reassure the bishops or the provost sufficiently for them to risk leaving the Almudaina all that day, until the town was calmed, as we said to them that we would make a reckoning of things and afterwards we would give them their share. And that night, when the people were becalmed, each went away to his house.

[92] After Easter, Don Nunó armed a ship and two galleys to go as a privateer to the Barbary coast.[147] However, while he was arming the ship, Guillem de Claramunt fell ill, and eight days after the onset of his illness, he died. And at his burial, Ramon Alemany and Don García Pérez de Mediano (who was from Aragon, and a man of good lineage and of our household) fell ill, and eight days later both died. And after these two died, Guerau de Cervelló, son of Guillem de Cervelló, elder brother of Ramon Alemany, fell ill, and he died eight days later. And the count of Empúries, when he saw the death of these three, said that all those of the lineage of Montcada would die there, and he immediately fell ill, and he had only been ill for eight days when at the end of those eight days, he died.[148] And these four nobles and great men of Catalonia died in the space of one month.

And seeing that this mortality had affected such important members of the army, we were greatly troubled. And Don Pedro Cornel let us know that he would go to Aragon, and he said to us that if we gave him one hundred thousand sous, he would return there with one hundred and fifty knights, that is

---

[147]Nunó's voyage, if it took place, was, one expects, in part to see whether a relief force was going to arrive from North Africa (the Majorcan governor's own fleet, whose actions were the pretext for the invasion, is entirely absent from the campaign) and possibly also to harry Genoese ships trading with the Saracens.

[148]The necrology of Girona indicates that the count of Empúries died on 23 February (*S*, p. 244). His son Ponç Hug already witnessed a document as count on the 1 April (*H*, 1, no. 128), six days before Easter, making these events slightly earlier than James implies, perhaps beginning in mid-January.

to say, one hundred for the money and fifty for the *honor* that he held in our name. And we gave it to him, and we ordered him to go to Aragon.[149]

[93] And then we agreed with Don Nunó, who had remained with us, and with the bishop of Barcelona, that as the knights Guillem and Ramon de Montcada, and those nobles whom we have mentioned above, had died, it was necessary to send letters to Don Ató Foces and Don Rodrigo Lizana, who were from Aragon, saying that they should come to serve us for the *honor* that they held in our name. And we did so, and they sent letters saying that they would come most willingly.

While they were preparing to come, we agreed to make a raid, because the Saracens had gone up into the mountains of Sóller, Almeruig and Banyalbufar, and occupied all these mountains and defended them against the Christians, who could only attack them as far as Pollença. And with the knights and footmen we could find (for the majority had already gone, some to Catalonia, and others to Aragon), we went from the town and we went through a valley that has the name Bunyola. And with those we could assemble we began to make that raid. And we left behind us a castle that is there in that mountain, called Alaró,[150] and is the strongest castle on the right side of the kingdom of Majorca. When we were on top of the mountain, the leader of the vanguard sent word to us that the soldiers did not wish to camp in that place where he had ordered them to, but rather had continued towards Inca. And we left the rearguard under Guillem de Montcada,[151] son of Ramon de Montcada, and went to look for them, thinking that we would find them and that we would make them remain there. And when we were there, we saw them at the foot of the slope, already on their way to a village called Inca. On seeing that, we did not dare abandon the company.

Now, two or three beasts of burden[152] had been seized from the company. And we returned as quickly as we could to the rearguard, with three knights who were with us. And when we arrived there, our rearguard had already charged and had driven them back up a gentle slope there and had recovered the beasts.

---

[149]James probably requested this in January since Pedro had returned by the beginning of March 1230 (Santamaria, 'Expansión político-militar', p. 132).

[150]Alaró is an inland town a small way from Inca, at the foot of a hill and surrounded by mountains. The castle was considered the strongest on the island.

[151]Guillem I de Tortosa (1229–c. 1278). He took part in the sieges of Borriana, Valencia, and Xàtiva.

[152]Mules played a vital part in James's campaigns. They were suited to rough terrain, could travel twenty-five miles a day bearing loads in excess of two hundred pounds, and required less food and water than horses. James repeatedly placed muleteers and their mules under his special protection to ensure the flow of goods in his realms (Kagay, 'Army Mobilization', p. 110).

[94] And when we arrived, we found our men who had returned to the road, and saw some six hundred Saracens, or more, who were on the hill, watching them, to see if they could attack them. And this was why they had attacked the company, because they saw that the vanguard was leaving. And we, all together once more, went to that place where we had chosen to camp and we agreed there what it was necessary to do. And Guillem de Montcada, son of Ramon, Don Nunó, and Don Pedro Cornel,[153] who had already returned, and other knights who understood deeds of arms, said it would be imprudent for us to camp so close to their forces, because there were some three thousand of them, and as the beasts of burden, the majority of the provisions and the footmen had all gone, it would not be a good idea to remain in that place.

So we agreed to go that very night to Inca.[154] And we placed our beasts in front of those men who remained with us. And when we saw that they had reached the foot of the slope, we went down little by little and in silence. And there were not forty knights in the entire rearguard. And when the Saracens saw that we had been so wise in our movements, they did not dare to come against us. And we went to camp at Inca, which is the largest village there is in Majorca. And afterwards we returned to the town.

[95] When we returned to the city of Majorca, the master of the Hospital, who was called Hugh de Forcalquier,[155] came, with his brothers and around fifteen knights. And he came to us, with the fifteen knights, when he heard news that Majorca was taken, because he had not taken part in the conquest of Majorca.[156] Now, we had made Hugh de Forcalquier master in our land, which we had asked of the grandmaster of Ultramar, and he was a man whom we loved very much, and he us.

On arriving, he said that he wished to speak with us only in the company of his brothers. And he besought us with much insistence that, for the love that we had for him and for the faith that he had in us, we might wish that the Hospital should have a share in that island, and that we would arrange it with the bishops and with the nobles; as the Hospital would forever be dishonoured if it

---

[153]Pedro Cornel had returned by 1 March (Santamaria, 'Expansión político-militar', p. 132) and these events are probably to be dated to around that time. On 28 June 1230 he witnessed a treaty between James and the Genoese (*H*, 1, no. 133).

[154]29 kilometres north-east of Palma (Majorca).

[155]Hugh of Forcalquier (a town east of Avignon and north of Aix). The commander of Amposta from at least 1224 until 1245 (Burns, *Crusader Kingdom*, p. 184) was a close friend of the king who conceded many privileges to the order while Hug was master (Bonet, *La Orden del Hospital*, p. 48). He was at Majorca certainly from 1 March 1230. It is Hugh who in 1232 at Alcañiz proposes to the king the conquest of Valencia.

[156]The initial absence of the Hospitallers is not to be taken as any indication of the non-military character of the order in Aragon at this time. Hugh participated in the subjugation of Majorca, the siege of Borriana, and the taking of Valencia in 1238 (Bonet, *La Orden del Hospital*, pp. 48–9).

did not take part in so good a deed as the conquest of Majorca: "And with you being our lord, and God having given it unto you to take it, and that the Hospital should have no part in it, people will say: 'The Hospital and the master took no part in so great a deed as that of Majorca,' which God has allowed you to bring to a good conclusion. And we shall be dead and shamed forever more."

And we replied to them that he knew well that we had always loved him and honoured him, both him and the Hospital, and that we would do what they asked of us, willingly and gladly, and that it greatly pleased us. But the greatest difficulty that we found was this: that the lands and goods had already been divided, and that there were many of those who had taken part who had already gone; otherwise it would have been easy to do: "But in spite of everything, you will not lack my help, so that you may go from my presence satisfied."

[96] And we assembled with the bishop of Barcelona, Don Nunó, Guillem de Montcada, and with those we could find of those who were in the land, and entreated them very insistently that we should give to the master a share of what we had won.

But we found them very ill-disposed to do that, because they asked how could it be so, that after everything had already been divided, a share should be given to them. And that it was a thing that could not be done, especially as the nobles were not there, and had gone.

And we said to them: "Barons, we know a solution. And, as there is a solution, we would do well to retain the master and the Hospital."

And they asked us what that solution was. And we said: "We have half of the land; and from our share we will give him one of our villages, a good and honoured one. And let us go to see Ramon d'Empúries, who knows your shares. You, however, cannot give any village except that it be taken from one or other of you; but if we take lands according to the shares that you have taken, with those lands and that village that we give him, he will have his full share. And it should please you, because it is not a good idea to get on the wrong side of a man such as this and an order such as this, but rather it is fitting to fulfil their will. And as regards us, it does not matter to us."

And with what we said to them, we convinced them that they should accept our will, and they said that they would do it, since we desired it so much.

[97] Then we sent for the master, and the nobles said to us that we should give the response in the name of them all. And when he came we said to him: "Master, you have come here to serve God first of all, and afterwards to serve us, in this conquest that we have made. Now, know that we and the nobles have the intention and the will to do what you have asked, but that the difficulty that we find is this: that the shares have already been divided, and the majority of

those who captured the land have gone home; but, that notwithstanding, we will not fail to give you the share corresponding to thirty knights, and we shall order it noted in the book,[157] along with the others. And we shall give you a village of ours, a good and honoured one; but, as the others are unable to give you any village, they shall give you so great a share of the lands that they possess, according to the share that they themselves have here, that it will be enough for you to divide among thirty knights. And we do you great honour, because we give you the same share as the Temple,[158] who participated here."

And the master and the brothers who were present got up and they wished to kiss our hand, but we did not give it to the master to kiss, but only to the brothers. And afterwards they said: "Lord, since you have granted so great a mercy to the master and the Hospital, we ask you to give us a share of the moveable goods, and houses where we are able to live."

And we turned to the nobles and we said to them, laughing: "What do you think of what the master and the other brothers ask us?"

"Lord," they said, "That cannot be done, as those who already have their money and their booty will not return it. As for the houses, it is acceptable to us that we send in search of some, or for some place where we can build them."

And we said: "And if somebody gives you a solution to all that, and it costs you nothing, would you accept it?"

And all said that it seemed good to them. "Let us give them, then, the shipyard building, as the walls are already there, and there they can build good houses; and, as for the moveable goods, let us give them four galleys that are here, as a moveable good which we found, that had belonged to the king of Majorca. And so they will have a share of everything." And the master and the brothers were very happy and they kissed my hands, and the brothers wept while kissing them. And the bishops and barons were pleased, for the good solution we had hit upon.

[98] And Nunó, and the bishop of Barcelona, and Don Jimeno de Urrea, were still with us on the island when we went to go up into the mountain against the Saracens. And when we arrived at Inca,[159] the master of the Hospital came there; and we sent for the nobles, so that we could agree with them what to do and what not to do, with the guides[160] who guided us and knew the roads of the territory. The advice of Don Nunó, and Jimeno de Urrea and the master of the

---

[157]After the conquest, a minute inventory was made by a group of experts, an exhaustive division of the city and the rural zone according to the agreement reached at the *Corts* in Barcelona in December 1228.

[158]This was not the case. Though the Hospital gained a reasonable share (*Còdex*, 1r, 2r, 3r, 8v, 22r, 25v, 26r), it was far less substantial than the share of the Templars (3r/3v, 5r, 8v, 24v, 27r, 28r/28v, 50r/50v, 56v/57r, 62r/62v, 65v/66r, 68r/68v, 76r/76v, 78v, 80v/81v).

[159]20 March 1230.

[160]'Aldalils'.

Hospital was that, as we had so few people in the company, it did not seem opportune that we should go up into the mountain, because there were three thousand armed Moors who were in those mountains of Sóller, Almeruig and Banyalbufar, where we had to go. And their leader was Xuaip,[161] who was a native of Xurert, and he had twenty or thirty horsemen there. And they advised us that we should not enter there, as we would place ourselves in great danger of losing our company and ourselves. We recognized that they gave good advice and we followed it, but it grieved us much that we should be unable to undertake that adventure.

[99] When they had left us and returned to their shelter, we called for the guides to come to us and we spoke to them in private, we and they alone. And we said to them: "We order you that, for the natural lordship we hold over you, you should tell us the truth about what we ask, that is, if any of you know of any other Saracens in another place in the island of Majorca than in this mountain range, for it seems to us that the other mountain we see over there is very high, and we wish to know if any of you have been there."

And one of them said: "I have been there on a raid no more than eight days ago, and we almost caught some Saracens in a cave, in that range that you see; and when we thought we had them, sixty armed Saracens appeared from inside and shielded them back into the cave."

When we had heard this news we were very pleased, and we called again for Don Nunó and the master of the Temple and Don Jimeno de Urrea, and for those knights who were with us on the raid and understood matters of arms, and said: "We have found a way not to have to return to the city of Majorca in such an unfortunate manner, so that nobody can say that, having come to this mountain, we have done nothing, and so return in shame."

And they asked us what solution we had found. And we said: "Behold, this guide will show us a good raid against the Saracens. For it is not eight days since he left them, and they are in this part of this mountain that I will show you, and it is the mountain of the lands of Artana."

And they said, "With God's help, it is good that we should do it." And the guide came and told us how he had found them there.

[100] And we agreed that, early in the morning, we should pack up our tents and our effects, and that we should go straight there, and that we should designate runners to cut off their[162] escape so that they should not be able to go out until we had arrived. And just as we had decided it, so it was done. And we arrived at the hour of vespers, and our runners came and they said to us: "You

---

[161]Ibn Shu'ayb. Here he is 'natural de Xurert', while in ch. 113 'era estat de Xiver'. Both perhaps refer to Xivert.

[162]The men of Ibn Shu'ayb.

don't have to look far for them, as they have already crossed spears with us, and here you have them."

And at that very moment the Saracens lit their beacons towards the mountain where the greater part of the Saracens were.

Now, our mules were tired by the heat, so we camped by a river that was down there at the foot of the slope. And we agreed that, when it was dawn, we should prepare our knights and ourselves. And there were perhaps thirty-five who went with armoured horses. And so it was agreed that the men-at-arms should go and attack the rock and trap them inside, and that in the meantime we would decide what to do. And so it was done: our men fought them at the entrance to the cave. And the mountain was so steep and so high, that it finished in a point, and the rock jutted out; and in the middle of that rock, the caves had been made, in such a manner that any stone that came from on high could not do harm to the caves where the Moors were, but stones could be thrown at some of the huts that they had made. And when our men fought them and they in turn tried to come out to prevent the attack, some of the stones that our men threw harmed them. And that went on for a long time (as well any man would know who saw how they fought).

[101] And, with that, Don Nunó said: "Lord, why are you and we here? All that we are doing serves no purpose; because the stones that we throw can do them no harm, and neither can they be disturbed from below. It is already midday.[163] Would it not be a good idea to go down, as we have gone a day without eating food, and you should eat? Afterwards you can take a decision regarding what we have to do."

And we said to Don Nunó: "Do what you must! Do not get so worked up and anxious, for, in good faith, we will have them."

And the master of the Hospital said: "Don Nunó, I think that the king speaks the truth and that he is right, but do as you say: you and the king go and eat, and, having eaten, send the company here, and we will agree what we must do."

And we said: "The master speaks very well."

And we and Don Nunó followed the advice that he had given us, and went down.

[102] While we were eating, the master made a chain of his beasts, and tied one to the other; and with a strong rope he ordered a man lowered, and at the head of the chain he had a fire burning with dry wood in a pot; and they lowered this man gently and carefully with the fire burning. And when he saw that he was level with the huts, he set fire to one of them; and as it was very

---

[163]21 March 1230.

windy, they caught fire one after another, and with that, some twenty huts were burnt. And we, whilst we were eating, when we learned of that fire, were very happy.

And then the master sent them a message to say that they should surrender, and if they did not, they would all die. And they said that they would do this deal: that from the morning of the next day, which was the day of St Lazarus in Lent,[164] until eight days later, if those of the mountain had not come to help them, they would leave, and they would surrender, but not as prisoners. And they would surrender the fortification and all that was there. And the master came to us to tell us of this pact, and he said to us before we could respond to him: "Do not accept the pact if they do not surrender to you as prisoners, as they are suffocating and are dead, the villains."

And all agreed that it should be done in the manner he had said. And the master returned up there, and they conceded that they would surrender to us as captives, if those of the mountain had not helped them at the end of eight days.

And the eighth day was Palm Sunday, and by agreement they gave us as hostages the sons of the ten best men who were in the caves. And we rested there awaiting that day, but in the meantime, apart from two days when we were able to get by on the little bread that we had, we and Don Nunó got to the last day with a good hundred men who dined with us, on only seven pieces of bread. And those of the army did not have bread but went to seek wheat in the villages of the Saracens, and they roasted it and ate it.

And they came to us to ask if they could eat meat and we gave them licence to eat it.

[103] And Don Pedro Maza[165] made a raid with knights and with men of the army, and with *almogàvers.* And they found a cave where there were Saracens, and he sent us a message saying that we should send crossbows, arrows, and picks. And we saw to it that it was done. And they fought them for two days and captured five hundred Saracens.

And when Palm Sunday arrived,[166] at sunrise, we sent a message to the Saracens of the caves saying to them that they should fulfil the agreement that they had made. And they said that it was not yet terce and we would have to wait. And we said to them that they were right, but that they should prepare to come down. And they equipped themselves and gathered up their clothes and left a lot of wheat and barley up there. And when it was half-terce they began

---

[164]The Friday of the fourth week of Lent (22 March 1230), the Gospel read that day being the raising of Lazarus (John 11:1–45).

[165]An Aragonese noble who participated in the conquest, stayed at Majorca after James's departure with his retainers, led military operations against the Muslim rebels, sought out the king before James's second crossing to Majorca, and was at the king's side during the surrender of Menorca. He was later to take part in the sieges of Xàtiva and Biar (*S*, p. 247).

[166]31 March 1230.

to come down, and one thousand five hundred left from there. And we took two thousand Saracens, for that rock was a good league in length; and the raid had taken some two thousand cows and thirty thousand sheep. Then we entered the city of Majorca, joyful and contented.

[104] Then a message arrived from Aragon, saying that Don Ató Foces and Don Rodrigo Lizana were coming to us; and we were very glad that they were coming because we were in urgent need of reinforcements. And Don Rodrigo Lizana chartered one of the *tarides* that had taken part in the crossing to Majorca and two other vessels to carry provisions. And the *tarida* was good for carrying the horses, and the other vessels carried the provisions. And he arrived at Pollença; and he came with thirty knights well prepared with all that was necessary for them, both in weapons and provisions.

And Don Ató Foces hired one of those Bayonne cocas;[167] but when they were at sea, it took on so much water that in two or three places they had to catch the water in little pots and pans, and they tried to caulk with tow what they could, in order to arrive at land in the first place they could find, whether in Catalonia or Majorca. And the coca in which Don Ató Foces and Don Blasco Maza came, with the company of knights that came with them, had to return to Tarragona because of the storm (for that was where the wind took it). And they thought that they would all die together, because the ship took on much water and was old, so much so that they were hardly able to bring out the provisions and the horses; and when they had brought them to land, the ship split in two and broke up on the sea.

[105] After having spent all that summer in Majorca, Bernat de Santaeugènia, Lord of Torroella, came to us. And we asked him that, since we had been in Majorca for a long time from when it had been taken,[168] and we wished to go to Catalonia, he would remain in our place at Majorca. And we said that we would order the knights and all the other men that they should do for him what they would do for us. And he said to us that he would do so, but he asked us, so that the people would see that he was loved by us, that we should give him, for his lifetime, Pals,[169] a castle that was near Torroella and Palafrugell, so that the people would understand that we loved him. And we conceded it to him; and he thought more of the love that we showed him than of the gift, because that place was not worth much in revenue.

---

[167]A cog. Bayonne cogs usually sailed these waters quite happily. Bayonne was one of the major ports that linked the Mediterranean trading world to that of Flanders and England.

[168]From September 1229 until October 1230. James probably chose this time to return because he was confident that a Muslim fleet would not sail to help Majorca with winter approaching.

[169]In the province of Girona.

And, when we had done that, we drew up a charter recognizing that we would repay him all that he spent on his mission in Majorca. And we convoked the general council, that is to say, all the knights and all the settlers who were at Majorca, and we spoke to them in this manner: "Worthy men, we have been here fourteen months, and in no circumstance have we wished to separate ourselves from you. But now the winter is coming, and I think the land has nothing to fear, by the mercy of God. And we wish to go from here, because we will be able to give you more help from there than being here with you, whether sending you companies so that the island can be defended, or by coming in person if it is necessary. And you must believe in good faith that there will not be any moment, day or night, in which the greater part of our thoughts are not with you. And since God has done such grace to us that He has given us a kingdom inside the sea, a thing that no king of Spain has ever achieved before, and as we have built here a church dedicated to Our Lady Saint Mary,[170] (and so many others that will be here), know that I will never abandon you, but that through my help or in person, often and at each moment you will see us and you will have us with you."

And we began to cry, and they made their farewells. And when we had been there a while, we and they, unable to speak for the sadness we felt, we said to them that we would leave them Bernat de Santaeugènia as their leader,[171] and that they should do for him just as they would do for us; and that, if any news reached us, from whatever part, referring to any fleet coming to attack them, then immediately we would come in person.

[106] After that, we left them, and they had to bear our departure, which was for the best, both for them and for us. And there were two galleys: one belonging to Ramon de Canet, and the other, from Tarragona. And we left the horses and the weapons to those that remained there and needed them. And we went to Palomera, and we embarked on the galleys: we in that of Ramon de Canet,[172] which was one of the best galleys there was in the entire world, and one part of those who went with us in the other. And on the day of Saints Simon and Jude[173] we put out to sea, and we were there all that day, the night,

---

[170]Either a reference to the commencement of the building of the cathedral or to the conversion of a mosque which was then dedicated to Our Lady.

[171]Bernat was left as lieutenant on the island. Essentially, Bernat was in charge of the administration of the island, while Pedro Maza was in charge of public order and attacks against Muslim guerillas (Santamaria, 'Expansión político-militar', p. 135).

[172]Ramon appears among the witnesses of the first document (31 October, at Tarragona) James is known to have issued after his return (*M*, p. 248).

[173]28 October 1230. The last documents issued by James in Majorca were dated 23 October 1230 (*H*, 1, nos. 138–9).

and another day. And on the third day,[174] at Midnight, we arrived, with a very good sea, at Porrassa, which is between Tamarit[175] and Tarragona.

Here we found Ramon de Plegamans,[176] and he came to salute us and kiss our hand; and in greeting us he begun to cry because of the great joy he felt on seeing us. And he knew of the treaties that there were between me and the king of León,[177] who was supposed to give us his kingdom and his daughter as a wife; and he told us that the king of León had died.[178] And we asked him if he knew it for certain. And he said that men of Castile had arrived at Barcelona and reported it.

When we heard that news it grieved us greatly, but, although we were very sad, we consoled ourselves, because the conquest that we had made by taking Majorca was worth more to our honour than the gain we would have made possessing that kingdom. And if God did not will it, we ought not to interfere in what God does not will. And we slept until it was day.

[107] When it was clear day, we went on board the galleys, and we entered by oarpower to the port that is at the beach[179] at Tarragona. And the people of the town, men and women, received us gladly and with flags. And when we had eaten and we had brought from the galleys all the booty that our men and the sailors had, a warm south-west wind arose. And it was so strong that in those galleys that were moored by the port (in front of the church of Saint Michael that Archbishop Aspàreg had ordered built), and where three men had remained in each, four of them drowned and the other two saved themselves. And in that Our Lord showed us a great miracle.

---

[175]Roman quarry with a castle and farmhouses nearby. It now forms part of Tarragona. La Porrassa must have been a bay in between, perhaps named after the local vegetation.

[176]The same rich citizen of Barcelona who contracted to provision the fleet for the conquest of Mallorca. He was vicar and bailiff of Catalonia during the absence of the king in the Majorca campaign and remained as lieutenant. His career had started under Peter II when he had served as vicar of Barcelona and then as vicar and bailiff of Roussillon-Cerdagne, and he had remained active as vicar of Barcelona and a creditor under James (Bisson, 'Finances', passim). The Plegamans family was influential both in urban government and at the royal court throughout the Thirteenth Century (Bensch, *Barcelona and its Rulers*, pp. 321–2).

[177]Alfonso IX was unhappy that after his death the kingdom of León would fall into the hands of his son Ferdinand III of Castile. After the annulment of James's marriage to Eleanor in 1229, one of his prospects was a marriage with Alfonso's daughter Sancha and a claim to the succession in León. But the prospect of holding a faraway kingdom in the face of Castilian opposition was never a realistic one and León was united to Castile under Ferdinand in 1230.

[178]24 September 1230 (González, *Alfonso IX*, 1, p. 212).

[179]The Miracle beach. On 31 October 1230, James was at Tarragona dealing with matters concerning the debts left by Guillem de Montcada, Viscount of Béarn (*H*, 1, no. 140; *M*, p. 89).

And after staying in Tarragona, we went to Montblanc and to Lleida and to Aragon.[180] And everybody, wherever we went, received us with processions and joy and great gladness, as great as that which anyone in the world had ever received their lord; and they thanked God for all the good that He had done us.

[108] And after having passed that winter in Aragon, we returned to Catalonia. And while we were in Barcelona, news reached us to say that the king of Tunis[181] wished to cross to Majorca and was preparing himself, and that he was capturing the ships of the Pisans and Genoese and all the Christians were being taken.[182] And concerning that we asked counsel of the nobles who were with us and the notables of Barcelona, to see how they would respond before the news that had reached us. And they said that it would be a good idea that we should know the thing with more certainty than we did know it, because much news that is told of far off lands is untrue.

And because of some disputes Guillem de Montcada had with the men of Vic, we had to go there.[183] And when I had been at Vic for one day, and it was near the hour of half-terce, a messenger arrived, after having travelled all night, who was sent to us by Ramon Plegamans; and he said to us that definite news had arrived at Barcelona that said the king of Tunis was already at Majorca. And when we heard these words, we hurried ourselves as much as was possible, lest any misfortune should befall us. And we ate very little and did no more than ride, and at the hour of vespers we arrived at Barcelona. Because we had undertaken an arduous journey, that night we rested.

And when the morning came we rode right down to the sea in search of news. And we saw a ship with sail coming in, and we awaited it; and they, as they had fair weather, arrived very quickly. And it was a vessel from Majorca,

---

[180]James was at Barcelona from 22 November until 5 December (*M*, p. 90). Probably James was at Montblanc in November before going to Barcelona and then at Lleida in December before going to Monzón where he was on 4 January 1231 (*M*, p. 91).

[181]Abū Zakarīyā' Yaḥyā (1228–49), the first of the Ḥafṣid dynasty. He governed in traditional Almohad style, but brought relative peace and economic prosperity and much of North Africa accepted his sovereignty. His rather too tentative interventions against Aragon (perhaps here, certainly later) were partly the result of a desire not to upset trading relations which during his reign were strongly established with Barcelona and the ports of southern France and Italy.

[182]The passages concerning the king's second and third visits to Majorca are not in chronological order. This passage refer to events of April 1232 when the king is known to have been in Barcelona (*H*, 1, no. 165).

[183]The dispute perhaps related to rights on the market called the Quintana, an old bone of contention between the Montcada and the church in Vic. Guillem (who had died at Majorca) had pledged the Quintana to his wife Garsenda without regard to the rights of the church. In his will, Guillem had ordered the rights of the church to be respected but Garsenda and her son Gastó had refused to comply (Gudiol, 'Les bregues sobre lo senyoriu', pp. 196–8; Freedman, *The Diocese of Vic*, passim). On 26 March 1232, Gregory IX set up a commission to judge the quarrels between the Montcada and the Church (Junyent, *Jurisdiccions*, no. 89, p. 141).

and a man of that vessel left in a boat prior to the others; and we asked him what news he carried from Majorca. And he arrived to our presence, all pale, and said: "Lord, we believe that the king of Tunis must already be there."

And we said: "You bring bad news! But we have confidence in God that we will be there before him."

And on the day that we had decided we arrived at Tarragona; and concerning what they had advised us at Barcelona, we said: "It does not seem to me to be good advice for us or for the land. Because the best thing that has been done, for one hundred years, Our Lord has wished that we should do it in taking Majorca; and if God has given it to us we will not lose it through laziness or cowardice, but rather we wish to go there to help. And this is our decision: We will signal a day to those who were with us at the conquest of Majorca, and we shall send letters to Aragon, saying that those who hold *honors* in our name and those that are of our household should come to help us with all that they have and can obtain; and at the end of three weeks, they should join with us at the port of Salou. Because it is worth more to us to receive death in Majorca, than to lose Majorca through our fault. And know that we will not lose it, without God and men knowing it not to be our fault."

And just as we said these words, so we accomplished the deed.

[109] And that day, and even before that day, we were at Tarragona. And we had chartered ships and *tarides* and a galley in which we went to get news of whether the Saracens were at Majorca. And the ships and the *tarides* were prepared for three hundred men, and two hundred and fifty came there; and with fifty that we found on the land, we were three hundred knights when we got there. And before we made the crossing, the archbishop of Tarragona, who was of the lineage of Barca and was our relative, and Guillem de Cervera,[184] who was the confessor we had at Poblet, came to us and besought us that for God and for the fealty that they held from us and for the counsel they were accustomed to give us, that we should not risk our person, but that we should send knights who had assembled there for the crossing, and that Don Nunó should be their leader. And they began to weep as fervently as they could, but at no moment did we take compassion on their weeping. And we responded to them in this way, saying that not for anything in the world would we leave off from undertaking that crossing. And they strongly strove to embrace us, in order to keep us there, but we broke away from them, and left them and went

---

[184]The same Guillem de Cervera who was stepfather to Aurembiaix of Urgell, being husband to the Countess Alvira. On 6 May 1232, at Tarragona, James made his first will, naming his son Alfonso as his heir and wishing for Guillem de Cervera to leave the Cistercian monastery of Poblet to educate his son at Monzón. (One might speculate whether Guillem had fulfilled a similar role for James when he was a boy at Monzón.) Guillem continued to act as a royal adviser throughout the 1230s and was one of the king's most trusted advisers (*H*, 1, no. 168; Gonzalvo, 'Guillem', p. 412).

to Salou. And we had exchanged the land of Majorca with Prince Don Peter of Portugal[185] and we had sent word to him once or twice that he should hurry to go and help the island of Majorca. And he gave us good response, but did nothing in deed.

[110] Around midnight, as we ordered the galley and the other vessels to weigh anchor, in order to cross to the aforementioned land, Don Nunó came to the seashore and cried in a loud voice: "Hey you, on the galley."

And they responded: "What?"

And they said: "Don Nunó says to you and beseeches you that you wait a little, as the prince of Portugal is here, who wishes to speak with you."

And we wished to set sail, but, then we decided that, since he was there, we ought to see him, though we would not leave off from setting sail because of him. And we saw him, as he came in a boat, with Don Nunó; and he climbed onto the galley and we asked him what he wanted. And the prince said that he had come to cross to Majorca.

"And how many knights do you have with you here?"

And he said: "Well, there are a good four or five, and the others are coming."

And we said: "God help us, but you do not come well prepared for the crossing! None the less here you have our ships and *tarides* which will set sail in the morning; and if you wish to embark, you are welcome to do so, as we will not delay in going from here, because, in all events the king of Tunis and his army are already there at Majorca."

And he said that he would remain in the galley with one knight and one squire, and that Don Nunó should order the others to cross. And they were easily able to bring them across, as except for the four knights that came with

---

[185]The son of King Sancho I of Portugal and brother of Afonso II of Portugal. His mother was Dolça, daughter of Count Ramon Berenguer IV and Petronilla, who were James's great-grandparents. His reputation as a man completely deprived of scruple in political affairs (Martínez Ferrando, *Tragica storia*, p. 34). On bad terms with his brother Afonso, he had attacked Portugal in 1212 with the aid of Alfonso IX of León and later passed to Morocco (*G*, 1, p. 202, n. 1). His kindred with James procured him a marriage with Aurembiaix of Urgell in 1229 and on her death (September 1231) he was left lord of her great possessions. James, wishing to incorporate her estates to those of the Crown, immediately agreed an exchange whereby James enfeoffed the kingdoms of Majorca and Menorca to Pedro and received the county of Urgell in return (*H*, 1, no. 159). After Pedro's death, his successors were to hold on the same terms one third of them and the king was presently to hold three key fortresses of the island (L'Almudaina, Pollença, and Alaró). In 1244, Pedro returned this grant to the king in exchange for many important towns and castles in Valencia (*H*, 2, no. 394) which led to his involvement in the early stages of the war against al-Azraq. Ten years later, he gave these up for 39,000 sueldos annually and some dominion again in Majorca. He returned to Portugal where he was still living in 1256. Though generally viewed as a shameless condottiere, Peter did at least negotiate with the sultan of Tunis for the liberation of Christian captives (Dufourq, 'Vers la Méditerranée', no. 13, p. 29).

him, there were no more nor did more come.[186] And Don Nunó left the galley and he remained with us.

[111] And we ordered the anchor weighed, and we put hands to the oars, and we went out to sea.[187] And, sometimes sailing and at other times rowing we arrived on the second day at midday at Sóller; and there we found a small Genoese ship, and when they saw us coming in they were exceedingly afraid; but afterwards, when they saw our banner, they understood that the galley was ours, and, free from fear, they piled into the boat, calm once more. And immediately they came to our presence, and we asked them: "Worthy men, what news do you carry from Majorca?"

And they said: "Good news."

And we asked them if the fleet of the king of Tunis had arrived, and they said that there was not a single foreign Saracen on the island. And we were very happy at the good news that they had for us. And they brought us two fowls. And we sent two men of the ship to Majorca, to let them know we were at Sóller. And they came to receive us with great joy, and they carried a good fifty saddled beasts for us to ride on into the town of Majorca.

[112] Then we entered the town and the galley entered by oarpower to the port of the town. And those whom we had left there said to us that it certainly seemed that we had not forgotten them and remembered the honour God had given us in conquering that kingdom, and they could not refrain from weeping for the happiness that they felt at our arrival. And three days after we had arrived at Majorca, our ships and our *tarides* came with the knights, who arrived well and calmly without any harm.

And we came to a decision as to what we would have to do if the Saracens came. What we planned was to establish our watchtowers, so that, before they arrived, we would know the Saracens were coming, while we were in the town. And we said to them that we would show them a way in which we could defeat the invaders. In the place where they directed their sails, neither we, nor the knights, nor those who were good in battle, would go down to the seashore, but instead we would prepare an ambush on the route through which the Saracens had to pass. And to the others we would give horsemen, of the sort who did not have armoured horses, and some two thousand footmen would go with them. And these would pretend to be there to prevent the invaders from landing but

---

[186]From the *Repartiment*, it can be gleaned that the size of Peter's contingent was slightly larger than James suggests (Cateura, 'Aportación Aragonesa', pp. 29–30). It is clear that James had no higher opinion of Peter than he has obtained subsequently.

[187]This voyage must have taken place between 15 May 1232 when the king was still in Tarragona (*M*, p. 98) and 7 July 1232 when James issued a document at Majorca (*H*, 1, no.169).

when most of them had disembarked they should begin to flee in the direction of our ambush.

("And the Saracens will have to hurry to try to catch them and they will think there is nobody else there but those men on horseback and those on foot.")

And then as they passed our ambush, we would give the Saracens assault with the armoured horses and the men who had remained with us, except for the other two thousand; and the two thousand and the others on horseback who had led them to the ambush would return to us, and we would do nothing else but attack them until they reached the sea. And when those of the ships saw that the first were dead or defeated, they would not dare to put to shore because of the damage we would have done to their men.

And for full fifteen days watches were placed throughout the whole island, so that they could make beacons if they saw the fleet of the king of Tunis coming.

[113] And on the fifteenth day, we knew that neither the king of Tunis nor that fleet would come against the island of Majorca.[188] Then we undertook the conquest of the mountains and the castles that they held, named Alaró, Pollença, and Santueri.[189] And the Saracens were perhaps some three thousand men at arms, and of the others there were some fifteen thousand, with woman and children. And he whom they had made their leader and lord, who was called Xuaip and had been of Xiver, spoke of a treaty with us regarding all the Saracens of the mountains and of the castles, saying that if we had mercy on him and did well by him, in a manner that he could live honourably, he would surrender the castles and mountains to us. And as this treaty was good for us and for all the Christians that lived there or would live there, and as the island could not be secure while there was so great a war going on, the nobles who were with us, the knights and all the others, agreed to accept that pact.

And the conditions were these: that we should give estates to him and to four others who were of his lineage, and that we should give horses and weapons, and to each a rouncy or mule or mare that was good and fitting; and that those Saracens who wished to live with us could remain in the land, and with those that did not wish to be obedient or to include themselves in the peace, we could do what we pleased. And that was written in documents and was fulfilled as had been undertaken. But still there remained some two

---

[188]It is not clear to what extent this was a false alarm. Possibly the fleet was prepared at Tunis but, because Abū Zakarīyā' Yaḥyā's grip on power was still then not firm (and also perhaps because Tunis was already doing trade with the Catalans and did not want to sacrifice economic benefits in a lost cause) and since James was swift to act, the expedition was abandoned (Santamaria, 'Expansión político-militar', p. 136).

[189]The first two in the Serra de Tramuntana, the other in the Serra de Llevant.

thousand Saracens in the mountains who did not wish to surrender to our mercy.

[114] When we were sure that that fleet would not come, we returned from there and we left there Bernat de Santaeugènia and Don Pedro Maza, who was lord of Seguereny and was of our household, along with around twelve to fifteen companies of knights and squires who wished to remain there with Don Pedro Maza. And we went back to Catalonia and they began to wage war with those of the mountain; and that war lasted all winter until May.[190] And the Saracens had some strong fortifications in the mountains so that they could not attack them in their persons. But they did do them harm, for they could not collect wheat except from some unproductive places, so that they did not have enough, to an extent that there need became so great that they ate the grass on the mountains, in the manner of beasts.

And Bernat de Santaeugènia and Don Pedro Maza agreed to send people to the mountains, so that they should surrender to them; and they sent word to them through letters and through a Saracen who carried them. And the Saracens responded by letter that they would never surrender to them, but only to the king who had gained the land. And when Bernat de Santaeugènia and Don Pedro Maza and the knights of the land saw that, they decided that the two of them should come to our presence, and that we should cross there, so that we could conquer all the land.

[115] They came to us at Barcelona, and said they wished to speak with us, to give us good news. And we said to them that it was good that they had come and that we would listen to them and hear their good news. They said to us that we should hurry to Majorca, because the Saracens would only surrender in our presence, since that is what they had arranged with them. And we said to them that they were welcome, that they carried good news, and that we would go there. And those that came from there agreed that it was unnecessary for the knights or other men to go there, but only our person together with some men who served us; because with our person and with those that were there, they had as many to conquer the mountains as if they had a thousand knights. And Bernat de Santaeugènia said: "Lord, order two or three galleys to arm, and embark on them, and we shall go with you. And the Saracens on seeing you will surrender to you."

[116] Then, just as he had suggested, we ordered three galleys armed between Barcelona and Tarragona. And on the fifteenth day they were with us at

---

[190]Winter 1230–May 1231. James is now relating the events that preceded his second voyage to Majorca.

Salou.[191] And it was a dark and stormy night, but we set sail in spite of the sailors. And when we had sailed ten miles with a little breeze behind us, a beautiful night and a good sea and a beautiful moon came to us; so much so that Berenguer Sesposes[192] said that God loved us so much that we could cross the sea in wooden clogs: "For we thought that we would have bad weather and you have such weather as armed galleys require, and it seems that God acts in your favour."

And we said to him that we served such a Lord that we thought we could not fail in anything that we did in His Name, and we thanked Him as much as we could and knew how to. And on the third day, early in the morning, between the rising of the sun and the hour of terce, we arrived at Porto Pí, and we hoisted our flags on each of the galleys and ordered our horns to be sounded as we entered the port of the city of Majorca.

[117] And when the men of the city saw us coming, they recognized that it was us, and that those whom they had sent had gained a good response to their message. And all of them, men, women, and children, went out to the port with much happiness and with very great pleasure because we had come, as did those of the Temple and those of the Hospital, with the knights who were in the city.

And when we had arrived at our quarters at the Almudaina, Ramon de Serra the younger, (who was then commander of the Templar brothers on the island, and was so named because there was another Ramon de Serra,[193] commander of Monzón), said to us: "Lord, I would like to speak to you a little in private."

And we listened to him and he said: "Do you wish to deliver a good stroke of war? If you send the galleys to Menorca, armed as they are, and you make it known to them that you have come to Majorca, they will be afraid. And you should let them know that if they wish to surrender to you, you would accept it, and that their death would grieve you much, and is a thing that you do not wish, if they do not wish it. And as they will be very afraid, I believe you will gain a great prize to your honour."

And we called for Bernat de Santaeugènia,[194] Don Assalit de Gúdar, and Don Pedro Maza, and we related to them the advice that the commander had

---

[191]May 1231. On 21 May 1231, James was already at Majorca (Santamaria, 'Expansión político-militar', p. 135).

[192]On 30 March 1232, James recognized a debt of two hundred maravedís to Berenguer Sesposes, who here provides us with this beautiful image, for the use he had made of his galley on his return to Majorca in 1231 (*H*, 1, no. 164).

[193]Ramon de Serra was certainly commander at Majorca (June 1231–November 1232), while his older namesake was certainly commander at Monzón (August 1231–April 1234) (Forey, *Templars*, app. 2).

[194]In the treaty of submission of Menorca that takes place during this stay of James at Majorca, these three appear as witnesses (Barceló, 'Tractat de Capdepera', pp. 82–4; *S*, p. 252) and likewise in two documents dated at Majorca on 8 July 1231 (*M*, pp. 94–5). The presence

given us, in his presence. And all said that they were agreed and that it was a good idea for us to do what the commander had said.

[118] Then we ordered Bernat de Santaeugènia, Don Assalit de Gúdar and the commander who had spoken those words, that each of them should go in one of the galleys and they should say that we had arrived with our army and that we did not wish their deaths; and that already they had seen and heard what had become of those of Majorca who had not wished to surrender to us, when they were captured. And that, if they wished to surrender to us and to behave towards us as they would towards the king of Majorca, we would receive them into our mercy. But if they preferred death and prison to coming to our mercy, we could not deliver them, and death is what they would have to undergo.

And through our *alfaquim* of Zaragoza, named Don Salomó, brother of Don Bahiel, we ordered letters of credence to be made, in Arabic, so that they would trust the three who gave the message in our name. Furthermore, we said to them that we would go to Capdepera, which is thirty nautical miles from Menorca, and that when we knew of their decision they would find us there.

[119] And we ordered the galleys to sail with the messengers by night; and the next day they arrived at Menorca, between the hour of nones and vespers. And the *alcaid* and all the sheikhs and the people of that land came out against the galleys at the port of Ciutadella,[195] and they asked: "To whom do the galleys belong?"

And they said they belonged to the king of Aragon, Majorca, and Catalonia, and that they were his messengers that were coming. And the Saracens, when they heard that, ordered all the other Saracens to leave their weapons and place them on the ground. And they said to them that they were welcome and that they could disembark safely and securely upon the guarantee of their leaders, and that they would treat them with favours, honour and friendship.

And the galleys backed on to the land. And they had sent for mattresses, mats and cushions, so that they could sit down and assemble. And all three went from the galley, with a Jew whom we had given them as interpreter. And the *alcaid*,[196] his brother[197] and the *almoixerif*[198] – whom we afterwards made *rais* of Menorca and who was a native of Seville – and all the sheikhs, listened

---

of Assalit and Pedro is further testimony to the very notable participation of Aragonese in the conquest of the Balearics.

[195]The capital, in the north-west of the island, and where the governor resided.

[196]Abū 'Abd Allāh Muḥammad.

[197]'Alī ibn Hishām. He was the first after his brother the *qā'id* to sign the treaty of submission (Barceló, 'Tractat de Capdepera', p. 84).

[198]The *almoixerif* (the Christian form of *mushrif*) was in charge of the collection of taxes. He was Abū 'Uthmān Sa'īd, who governed the island from 1232.

very carefully to the letter and the message that we had sent them, and they said that they would consider what to do.

[120] And this is what the sheikhs decided: to ask them to wait until the next day, in order to send for other sheikhs of the island to come, as they were not found in that place, and all wished to consult more fully. And Bernat, Don Assalit de Gúdar, and the commander,[199] responded that if they desired it they could do it. And immediately the sheikhs invited them to enter, if they wished to, the town of Ciutadella, in order to do them great honour, for the love of the lord king whose subjects they were. And our men said that they would not enter there until response was given to them, as they had not been ordered to do so by us. And the others said that it should be as they wished. After a little time there, ten cows were brought to them, along with a hundred sheep and two thousand fowl, and as much bread and wine as they wanted; and the Saracens stayed with them until the hour of vespers to keep them company. And at vespers, when the Saracens entered into the town, our messengers entered into the galleys.

And that day, at the hour of vespers, we were at Capdepera, which can be seen from Menorca. And behold how vast was the army of the king that we had with us, as there were only with us six knights and four horses, a shield, five squires to serve us, ten manservants and the scouts. And when it became dusk, before eating, we made a fire, and we said to our men that they should all come with us, and we lit fires at more than three hundred places in the bushes, from here to there, so that it seemed there was a large army camped there. And when the Saracens saw that, they sent two sheikhs to ask our messengers how was it that there were fires there on Capdepera. And they said to them that that was the king, who was there with his armies; for we had instructed them to say so. "And he wishes soon to hear your response one way or the other."

And when the Saracens heard that, a great fear grew amongst them.[200] And when the morning came, they said that our representatives should wait a little, and shortly they would have the response. And they said that they would do it.

[121] When morning came,[201] and the Saracens had said their prayer, the *alcaid*, his brother, the *almoixerif*, the old men, and some three hundred Moors,

---

[199]Ramon de Serra. All appear in the treaty of the submission of Menorca.

[200]The Menorcans may have been duped and it had certainly been 'James's most brilliant use of effrontery' (Burns, *Islam under the Crusaders*, p. 167), but it is unlikely they would have offered strong resistance. With Majorca taken, help from Africa unlikely, and Christians settling on former Muslim lands, they appear to have taken the sensible option and allowed themselves a degree of security and autonomy they had not previously possessed (Abulafia, *A Mediterranean Emporium*, p. 65). While the Muslim ruler in Majorca had been close at hand, they could count on the Christian ruler to spend most of his time in other lands.

[201]13 June 1231.

of the best men of the island, came out and they said that they greatly thanked God and us for the good words that we had sent them, as they understood well that they could not defend themselves for any length of time against us; and that they would have written, in agreement with us, the pact that they would make.[202] And the treaties were these: they said that the island was very poor and in that island there was no place where they could grow corn which could satisfy a tenth of the population that was there; but that they would have us for their lord, and they would divide what they had with us, since it was right that a lord received a share of what his men had. And so each year they would give us three thousand quarteres[203] of wheat and one hundred cows and five hundred head of goats and sheep; and we should make a charter to guarantee to them that we would guard them and defend them as our men and vassals; and this pact they would fulfil to us and to our men for ever more.

Then our messengers said that they would still have to do another thing, that is to say that it was necessary that they should give us the power over Ciutadella and the hill[204] where the biggest castle of the island is, and that, if there were other fortresses, that they should give us the power over all of them. And they agreed this under duress and unwillingly, but finally it was agreed; and they said that, if we wished it, they would do it, because they had heard it said that we were a good lord to our people, and they hoped we would also be so with them.

And in completing this pact, that is, in drawing up the documents and making all the principal and best men of the island swear upon the Koran, it took three days there before they could finish it.[205] And Don Assalit had it written in the documents that each year we would have two quintars[206] of butter and two hundred barques to transport the cattle.

And all the while we were at Capdepera, waiting for the galleys with the messengers whom we had sent, each day we lit those fires that we had lit on the first night.

---

[202]*H*, 1, no. 153; Barceló, 'El tractat de Capdepera', pp. 82–4.

[203]'The quartera, not to be confused with the quarter, was a variable dry weight of nearly 70 liters of cereal, the total here amounting to 210,000 liters of wheat; a liter today is .906 of a dry quart' (Burns, *Medieval Colonialism*, p. 117).

[204]The mountain of Toro, at the centre of the island.

[205]14–16 June 1231. The treaty required the oaths of all the notables of the island. Since in Islamic law the individual alone was endowed with a legal personality, theoretically only the individual Muslim could be obligated to fulfil the terms of a treaty by an oath sworn before the other party to the treaty. The men of the notables were not legally bound by the oaths taken by their leaders but would be expected to co-operate out of loyalty (Burns-Chevedden, *Negotiating Cultures*, p. 185).

[206]'The butter was measured at 2 quintars, each about 42 kilograms (a kilogram being over two pounds); this was not the metric quintar of 100 kilograms' (Burns, *Medieval Colonialism*, p. 117).

[122] At the end of four days,[207] very early in the morning, when the sun had risen and we had heard our Mass, a messenger came to us saying that the galleys had arrived. And our messengers sent word to us that we should prepare the dwellings which we were in fittingly. And we ordered them to be decorated and adorned with much fennel, because we had no other type of reed, and we placed our bedcovers and those of all who were with us on the walls of the house, in the part where we would receive them. Then we and those who accompanied us dressed ourselves in the best clothes that we had.

And these were the messengers who came from Menorca: the brother of the *alcaid*, the *almoixerif*, and five of the most honoured sheikhs of the island. And we sent horses and other beasts of burden for them to come to us. And when they were in our presence, they greeted us with great reverence and went down on their knees, and they said that they greeted us on behalf of the *alcaid* one hundred thousand times, as to a lord in whom he had all his hope. Then we replied to them that God might give them good fortune and that their coming pleased us greatly. And so that those of the army should not disturb us or put pressure on the conversations that we had to have with them, we moved from there, so as better to be able to speak with them. And they gave much thanks to God and to us for the words that we spoke to them.

[123] And the messengers began to explain their message and their response. And they showed us the documents that they had agreed with them to see if they were pleasing to us. And we said we would discuss it, and they went outside. And we said to our men: "We have good reason to give thanks to Our Lord, because that which we do not have He gives us, without sin and to our great honour. The only decision possible is to accept what you have done and thank the Lord for the mercy he has shown us."

And we said to them that the pact that our men had made with them greatly pleased us; and we ordered charters to be drawn up with our seal, and gave them to them, saying that they would be ours and of our people for all time, as long as they always gave that tribute to us and to our people.

[124] Ever since we made this pact with them, we have obtained as much again or more than was then agreed, for they, when we ask it of them as is fitting, give us all that we ask. And every year we receive from them, without needing to ask for it, such things as they collect for us.

Concerning the Saracens of the island who had gone up into the hills, we enslaved them to do with them what we wished, and we gave them to whomsoever wanted them, so that they could live on the territory as slaves.

---

[207] 17 June 1231.

And in this voyage, made with only three galleys, we brought to a conclusion these two deeds, in such a way as was pleasing to that Lord Who made us.

And afterwards we returned to Catalonia[208] and to Aragon; and from then on, by the grace of God, the island of Majorca did not need our help, but God has made it prosper so that it is worth double now what it was in the time of the Saracens.

[125] When two years had passed, the sacristan of Girona, called Guillem de Montgrí,[209] who was archbishop-elect of Tarragona, came with Berenguer de Santaeugènia and his brother to Alcañiz. (And we were very glad at his election.) When he was before us, he asked that we should be pleased that he had come and said that if we wished to give him Ibiza, he would conquer it, with his lineage. Furthermore, he said that as we did not possess it and we had other things to do, we should certainly wish him to conquer it, so that men would say that the archbishop of Tarragona had conquered Ibiza and that he would hold it for us. And we deliberated, and, as we understood that he would do us great honour in conquering the land and possessing it in our name, we agreed to it.[210]

Then he prepared himself, with his lineage, and arranged the things necessary for his crossing, and had a *trebuchet* and a *fenèvol* made. And when the prince of Portugal[211] and Don Nunó saw that, they met with the archbishop and said they would go to help him if he would give them a share corresponding to the horsemen and footmen that they brought to his help. And the archbishop agreed to it, and all formed part of that company.

---

[208] James was at Lleida on 22 July and then at Huesca on 10 August 1231 (*S*, p. 254).

[209] Archbishop Aspàreg de la Barca had died on 3 March 1233. Gregory IX rejected the Tarragonan chapter's election of Bishop Berenguer de Palou of Barcelona, and both Saint Ramon de Penyafort and Cardinal Gil de Torres turned the post down. Guillem was archbishop-elect certainly from September 1234, but he preferred the Ibizan crusade and Girona, and the pope relieved him of Tarragona in April 1236, though he remained as procurator until February 1237 when Ramon de Penyafort replaced him in order to oversee the election of a new archbishop. In February 1238, the chapter elected Pere d'Albalat, then bishop of Lleida, who proved highly competent in his charge. Guillem lived on for over two decades more (Linehan, *Spanish Church,* p. 60, n. 1).

[210] At Lleida, 7 December 1234, James enfeoffed to Guillem de Montgrí, archbishop-elect of Tarragona, the islands of Ibiza and Formentera (*M*, p. 113; Macabich, 'Feudalisme a Ivissa', p. 466), perpetually and with all their revenues, with the condition that Guillem would realize the conquest with his own fleet before the next Feast of Saint Michael in September (29 September 1235). Pope Gregory IX conceded the crusade indulgence for the enterprise (Goñi, *Historia de la Bula,* p. 163).

[211] On 29 September 1231, James had enfeoffed Ibiza and Formentera to Peter of Portugal and Nunó Sanxes on the condition that they conquered the islands within two years (*H*, 1, no. 160). Both had been in Majorca during May–July 1233, probably with an eye to these conquests (*M*, pp. 103–4).

[126] Then they crossed to Ibiza,[212] and they disembarked without the men of the island opposing them. And they went with armoured horses, with the ships and with the vessels, to the port of Ibiza, and they camped there and attacked the town. And when they had set up the machines of war, the *fenèvol*, which could not fire as much, targeted the town, and the *trebuchet* fired at the castle. And when they saw that the town wall was collapsing under the blows from the *fenèvol*, they began to dig. And when those of the army saw that it was the time to attack, firstly they began with small incursions; and when they saw that it was the time for them to fight, the whole host armed, and took the first enclosure of the town entirely. And when the Saracens saw that they had lost it, they became disheartened and parleyed saying that they would surrender.

And Joan Xico,[213] who was from Lleida, was the first man who entered the breach of the wall of the town. And so they won, in this manner, the town, and the castle, and the *trebuchet* did not even fire ten stones. And after Ibiza was taken, Saracen galleys went there many times, but, by the grace of God, each time they received more harm than they could do.

---

[212]The conquest took place in 1235.
[213]He had already participated in the conquest of Majorca and is mentioned in ch. 73 as one of the two citizens of Lleida who had levelled the moat so that the armoured horses could cross.

3

Valencia – The Northern Campaign

[127] Now, we were hunting small game in our own kingdom, in Aragon, relaxing and at leisure. We were at Alcañiz,[1] and with us were the master of the Hospital and Don Blasco de Alagón. Both came to us, on the roof of the building. While we were sunning ourselves and chatting, Hugh de Forcalquier, Master of the Hospital, began to speak, and said: "Lord, since God has guided you so well in the conquest of Majorca and those islands, might you and we not begin something over here, in this kingdom of Valencia, which has always stood before you as a frontier to your lineage,[2] and which they have always struggled to conquer and never been able to gain? This is why, with God's help, I think it would be a good idea to consider it, now that we are in your presence; for Don Blasco knows more about it than any other man in the world. So he ought to tell you which place in that land seems to him best fitted for you to begin your invasion, and we shall capture it."

Then Don Blasco de Alagón responded: "I will say clearly to the king all that I know of Valencia that might profit him. Since you wish, master, that I speak of it, so I shall."

And we besought him that he should say where he thought we might first enter into the kingdom of Valencia.

[128] Don Blasco turned to us and said: "Lord, the master of the Hospital speaks the truth. Now that God has allowed you to conquer by sea, you should also conquer that which is at the gate of your kingdom. And it is the best and most beautiful land in the world. For I, lord, spent a good two years or more in Valencia, when you expelled me from your land.[3] There is not today, under

---

[1] Either on 15 January 1232 or 1233, James was at Alcañiz, where he made a donation of Torrent and Silla to Hugh de Forcalquier, Master of the Hospital, while Don Blasco acted as a witness (*H*, 1, no. 173 (14/1/1233); *S*, pp. 254–5; *M*, p. 101 (dated to January 1233), López, *Conquista y Repoblación*, pp. 41–5; Ubieto, *Orígenes*, p. 51 (dated to 1233)).

[2] Both Alfonso II and Peter II enjoyed some success in their Valencian campaigns and in 1210 Peter incorporated the castles of Ademuz, Castielfabib, El Cuervo and Serrella (Gual, *Precedentes*, passim).

[3] The reasons for Blasco's exile (if real exile it was) remain unclear. But Blasco is absent from James's documents from 20 April 1229 until 15 January 1232 or 1233. One suggestion is that he had attacked the escort of Queen Eleanor when she returned to Castile after the annulment of her marriage with James, but this seems very uncertain (*S*, p. 255). Possibly Blasco had lost out in the power struggles of James's minority years. Possibly, with James's

God, a place so delightful as the city of Valencia and all that kingdom;[4] and the land is a full seven days' journey in length. And if God wishes you to conquer it – and He must wish it – you will have conquered the best of all the beautiful places and strong castles that there are in the world. So I will tell you what I think. If I were to advise you to go and besiege a strong castle, it would be bad advice, because there are a good forty or fifty there that, for as long as they have provisions, neither you nor all your forces can take.[5] But from what I know and understand, I advise you to go to Borriana, and for this reason: Borriana is a flat place, and it is near your land, and it will go better for you there, both by sea and by land, than it would if you were further inland. And I trust in God that, at the worst, you will have it inside of a month, and you will find many provisions there. This is the best place that I know of for you to commence the conquest of the kingdom of Valencia."

Then the master of the Hospital said: "Lord, Blasco speaks the truth, for in all the world there is not so good a place as that to take; and all those who have been to the kingdom of Valencia confirm it, and it is a well known thing."

[129] And we said: "Now, we have listened to your advice and that of Don Blasco, and we hold it to be good and loyal advice; so let it be done, in the name of God, as we have agreed it. For what you have advised me is the best course. And now I will tell you another thing; that it seems that God wills this. We were at Majorca, at Capdepera, when Menorca surrendered,[6] and with us were Don Sanç d'Horta,[7] Don García d'Horta, his brother, and Pedro López de Pomar, who had been on our embassy to the *alcaid* of Xàtiva; and we were singing the praises of the land of Majorca before them. Yet while we were praising it, Don Sanç d'Horta said: "Lord, you can sing the praises of Majorca and the kingdom of Majorca all day long, but were you to conquer Valencia

---

tacit consent, Blasco was working alongside Abū Zayd in Valencia against Zayyān (Pallarés, 'Don Blasco', p. 222), both protecting the frontier during the Majorcan campaign and helping James's ally to recover his position.

[4]The beauty of the city and the kingdom of Valencia was often remarked upon by Christian and Muslim authors alike. A contemporary poet of the city, Ibn Ḥarīq (d. 1225), neatly described it as 'a paradise surrounded by two misfortunes: famine and war' (Burns, *Islam under the Crusaders*, p. 3).

[5]In his *De Rebus Hispanie* (bk. VI, ch. 5) the historian and archbishop, Rodrigo of Toledo, also commented on the strength of the kingdom of Valencia's defences.

[6]12 June 1231 (ch. 120).

[7]Sanç and Garcia witnessed the treaty of submission of Menorca (17 June 1231), while Pedro López de Pomar was with the King at Barcelona on 1 September 1232 (*S*, p. 255). The occasion of Pedro's embassy remains uncertain, with dates of 1231, 1232, and 1236 all suggested. This passage suggests the event is before June 1231, perhaps relating to the time when a large Christian army had arrived at Xàtiva and demanded a tribute which the *qā'id* Abū al-Ḥusayn could not pay. He successfully sought assistance from Ibn Hūd (Burns-Chevedden, *Negotiating Cultures*, pp. 73, 76, n. 36).

and all that kingdom, all this would appear as nothing in comparison.[8] What you would find at Valencia is that five or six thousand crossbowmen with two-footed crossbows,[9] and many more besides, would come out and prevent any army from approaching the town, such is the strength of the crossbowmen and such the power that is there. And were you to take it, you would rightly be able to say that you are the best king in the world, for achieving so much."

[130] After that, we were unsettled by these words, because they questioned the merit of Majorca and praised Valencia. And we said: "Now then, do you want us to say how we think we can take it? We did not have a wife, and they spoke to us of marriage with the daughter of the king of Hungary and with the daughter of the duke of Austria, and the pope sought to arrange it.[10] Yet we have taken for a wife the daughter of one of the most honoured kings of the world; for, though they wished to give us the daughter of the duke of Austria, we would not take her for all her riches, because we preferred the daughter of the king of Hungary. If we were given the daughter[11] of the King of Castile Don Alfonso when we were not so powerful, surely it is only right that, being even more powerful now, we should take as a wife the daughter of a king. So, now we shall tell you how we shall take Valencia and all the other territory. We will go to Borriana, and we will carry all the provisions that we can bring from Teruel on mules; and we will have provisions brought to us, from another place, by sea, so that we have sufficient to supply the army. And we shall also

---

[8]The project of the conquest of Valencia predated that of Majorca, and many Aragonese nobles and the Lleidatans had argued for an attack on Valencia first, but the Catalan nobles had carried the day, since James ultimately decided that the cutting-off of Muslim maritime support through the Balearic campaign would aid the Valencian conquest (Burns, 'Rei Jaume', p. 48). When issuing the crusade bull in February 1232, Pope Gregory IX was uncertain of the direction of the crusade (Auvray, *Registres*, 1, p. 266; Burns, 'Many Crusades', p. 173). At a council at Lleida in March 1229, the papal legate, Cardinal John of Abbeville, gave his blessing to the Balearic venture and prohibited the sale of arms and other strategic materials to the Moors (Goñi, *Historia de la Bula*, p. 158; Linehan, *Spanish Church*, p. 24).

[9]The 'balesta de dos peus' would have been a standard centre shot crossbow, supported by a lever that made it look like it had two feet.

[10]In September 1235, James married Yolanda (at times called Violant in Catalonia) of Hungary 'whose endowments in northern France and Flanders seemed to an approving pope to pose no threat to Capetian interests in the Midi' (Bisson, *Medieval Crown*, p. 65). Also, Gregory IX's Austrian offer could have placed James in direct conflict with Emperor Frederick II, whose rebel son Henry had married with a daughter of the Austrian duke. Hungary was the traditional enemy of Austria (Engels, 'Rey Jaime I', p. 234). Yolanda (1215–51) was the granddaughter of the Latin emperor of Constantinople and daughter of King Andrew II of Hungary. She was mother of Peter III of Aragon, James II of Majorca, Ferdinand, Queen Violante of Castile, wife of Alfonso X, Constance, wife of Prince Manuel of Castile, and Isabel, wife of Philip III of France.

[11]Though James has made no previous mention of it, the annulment of the marriage to Eleanor was approved by a papal letter of February 1229 (Linehan, *Spanish Church*, p. 23). Their son, Prince Alfonso, was accepted as the legitimate heir.

take two *fenèvols* there. When we have taken Borriana, we will have the queen our wife go there, so that the people understand that we are determined to stay there. And those castles that are beyond, such as Peníscola, Cervera, Xivert, Polpís, les Coves de Vinromà, Alcalatén, Morella, Culla and Ares, which depend on the provisions of the fields of Borriana, and will stand between us and the land of the Christians, all of them will have to surrender.[12] For we will be before them and they will be unable to receive the provisions that normally reach them from Borriana."

[131] "When that has been done, and we have those castles, we will go to a place that the Christians call Puig de la Cebolla,[13] which is only two leagues away from Valencia. And we shall order raids to be made on Valencia from there, and shall devastate the land on our return, as a plan to bring them to great weakness and great need through hunger. Then we shall attack them before they can harvest the wheat again; and we will besiege them, so that, by the will of God, we shall overcome them."

Then Don Blasco and the master said to us: "If the Saracens of Valencia had dictated this to you, they could not have said it better; for it seems to us that Our Lord wishes to guide you, in giving you so good a plan."

And there it was agreed what had to be done and what not done.

Afterwards, when we were in Teruel,[14] Don Pedro Fernández de Azagra, Lord of Albarracín, invited us to hunt boar and dine with him in a village of Albarracín, called Ejea (which is where he said we would find him); and we granted this to him.

[132] When we had eaten, and it was nearly the hour of vespers, a messenger came to us saying that some foot soldiers of Teruel and of the frontier had taken Ares. And Don Pedro Fernández and Don Atorella were there with us. The man who came asked for gifts in return for the good news he had brought; and we said that we would give them to him. Don Pedro Fernández knew nothing of that frontier, but Don Atorella said: "Lord, a great good has befallen you and you have gained much today, because this is a way to begin the conquest of the kingdom of Valencia."[15]

---

[12]It is probable that James, in retrospect, gives to his speech here a clear plan of action that at that stage was as yet unformulated.

[13]Puig de Santa María. Cebolla is merely a Christian form of an Arabic word for a hill. Both James's father and grandfather had planned to conquer it, build a monastery and be buried there.

[14]On 30 January 1232, at Teruel, James imposed on Abū Zayd a new agreement in which most of the rights of the former ruler still possessed on Valencia were ceded (*S*, p. 131; Roque Chabás, 'Sección', p. 297). But if the hunt occurred immediately before the taking of Ares it is necessary to date it to the autumn of 1232.

[15]The events of the following chapters do not appear to be in chronological order. It seems Morella was already taken by Don Blasco at the end of 1231 or the beginning of 1232 (ch.

And we said: "May God wish it to be so."

Then he said: "Lord, do not delay, as Ares is a very good place and very strong, so you can hold it against all the Saracens in the world. Make haste in riding there. For I know the place, and you will see the same when you get there, and then you will say that I have spoken the truth to you."

[133] Then we sent to Teruel for Fernando Díaz,[16] Rodrigo Ortiz, and for the knights who were there, that they should come out to meet us at Alfambra.[17] Arriving at Alfambra before nightfall, we dined there and we had oats given to the horses, and after midnight we pressed on. At dawn we reached the end of the Campo de Monteagudo, then we passed through El Pobo, and went to Villarroya, which belongs to the Hospitallers.[18] When we found ourselves at the other end of the range, which was about half a league on, a mounted crossbowman came towards us, trotting and at the gallop, as fast as he could. And he said to us: "Lord, Don Blasco salutes you, and says to you that Morella is his."

When we heard these words we were very troubled. And Fernando Díaz said: "Lord, consider what you must do, as it is necessary to come to a decision."

We ordered the crossbowman to withdraw to one side, then we called on Don Pedro Fernández and Don Atorella. While they were coming, Fernando Díaz whispered in our ear and said to us: "Give up the journey to Ares, as Morella is an important thing, and it would be better for the Moors to have it than Don Blasco, as you can sooner take it from the Moors than from Don Blasco. Though Don Blasco is my lord, you are my natural lord, and I am not about to leave off giving you the best advice for a lord whom I can change when I feel like it. For you must understand that I hold myself to be your subject."

Then we asked the opinion of Don Pedro Fernández and Don Atorella, and other knights, as to what we should do. Don Pedro and Don Atorella, who had mounted that foray to Ares, said that we should go there and then afterwards we could go to Morella, and in that way we would have everything. But Fernando Díaz said: "Lord, I am here one of the least of your council, but

---

133), and that the assault on Ares (autumn 1232) was not only an attack on the Moors but, perhaps primarily, to give James a castle near Morella from where he could force Don Blasco to surrender that important castle (López, *Conquista y Repoblación,* pp. 45–7).

[16]From Albarracín, he was the right-hand man of Pedro Fernández de Azagra. He is described as 'majordomus camere' in 1224 and 1229 and 'majordomus curie' in 1233. He played a signal part in the Valencian campaigns and received many donations in the *Repartimiento* of Valencia (Martínez, 'Turolenses', pp. 114–15). Rodrigo Ortiz is perhaps a son or relation of Pedro Fernández.

[17]A town in the diocese of Teruel, to the left of the river of the same name.

[18]Villarroya de los Pinares (province of Teruel) had been donated to the Hospitallers in 1190 by Alfonso II (Miret, *Cases,* p. 206).

whatever they may say to you, go to Morella; and order the footsoldiers of Teruel and of the villages to arm themselves for battle, and to follow you as quickly as they can, leaving all their knapsacks."

Now, we understood that he gave us the best advice, because one should always attend to great affairs before lesser ones. And he said to us that we should make haste, as it was a long journey from that place to Morella.

[134] So we ordered some of the foot soldiers to remain, whereas the others should take up their weapons and come as quickly as they could; and they did so. Then, trotting and at the gallop, we crossed the river of Calderes[19] and pressed on to the river that runs to the foot of the slopes of Morella. When we had arrived there, two lightly-armed footmen came to us, and we asked them where the others were. And they said that they were on their way. Then we went up the slope, to a little hill that was there on the slopes of Morella, and was later called Puig del Rei. There we awaited the arrival of the rest of the company, positioning our watches, on horse and on foot, so that nobody could enter or leave Morella until the next day, when we had decided what to do. And we spent the whole night on that hill.

Now, it was the snowy season, as it was already past the Feast of St Michael.[20] And it snowed heavily, and the snow fell mixed with rain, so that nobody dared to uncover his face for fear that the snow might touch him. And the horses and the beasts sheltered in a hollow that was big enough for them, and here and there, wherever else they could. Because of this the pack-mules were unable to bring up the provisions to us that night. Nor could we go down to them, for fear that those of the castle would let Don Blasco know and he would position more forces there. Thus we were forced to fast,[21] for neither we nor the knights nor the beasts had eaten since the night we ate at Villarroya towards the hour of vespers.

[135] At sunrise Don Blasco arrived with five knights, mounted upon their horses and vested in their purpoints, and with squires carrying their weapons; and our watch saw him going down to the bottom of the hill. Don Fernando Pérez de Pina, who was head of the watch, sent a message to us saying that Don Blasco wanted to enter there, and that we should send instructions. And we sent word to them that, if he wished to enter there, they should not allow him to do so, but that he should come to our presence. Before our message arrived, Don Blasco hurried to enter there as quickly as he could, but Don Fernando Pérez de Pina went up to him and said: "What are you doing, Don Blasco?"

---

[19]A tributary of the Bergantes.

[20] 29 September.

[21]Thus, it was sometime between 29 September and the beginning of Advent 1232.

And he replied: "I wish to enter Morella where I will tell them what they must do, before going to see the king."

Meanwhile, the man whom we had sent went up to Fernando and whispered in his ear that we had ordered them not to allow Don Blasco to enter. So Fernando Pérez said: "Don Blasco, the king wants you to go to him."

And he said: "Tell the king that I will be with him shortly, but that I have to ask for a little time."

And Fernando Pérez responded: "You must know that nobody will allow you to enter there until you appear before the king, for that is the message he has sent to me."

Then he went up to Don Blasco, in such a way that if he wanted to escape he would not be able to do so. And Don Blasco, seeing that he had no other choice, pulled round his horse and came to us, and our watchmen with him.

[136] He dismounted before us and we rose to receive him; and afterwards he sat down in front of us, he and Don Pedro Fernández, Don Atorella, and Zeit Abuzeit,[22] saying that he wished to speak with us privately. So we ordered that everybody should go from there, except him and us, and he said to us: "Well, lord, what do you want with me?"

And we said: "We will tell you what, Don Blasco. You are here, and you are my major-domo,[23] and you are a man whom we have loved a great deal and have treated well, for you hold land in our name. And, according to the message you sent to me, God has given us this place. Now, this place is so strong and of such renown that, even though you deserve everything that you can have, it does not pertain to any other man in the world except a king. For which reason we entreat you, as our subject and for the good that we have done you, and because you are our major-domo, that you wish this castle to be ours. In this way we will do such good to you and yours, that everybody will say what a great reward we have given you for the service you have done us."

But he said: "Lord, do you not remember the charter[24] that you have made for us?"

---

[22] In 1229, Abū Zayd had entered a treaty of alliance with James by which the king was to keep in vassalage all he could conquer from Zayyān plus a fourth of Valencia's general revenues (*H*, 1, no. 119). From the agreement of January 1232 (Roque Chabás, 'Sección', p. 297) Abū Zayd was little more than a puppet in James's hands, here to consent to the hand-over of a castle where no actual power remained to him.

[23] Blasco was certainly acting as major-domo between June 1233 and April 1234 (*H*, 1, nos. 181, 200).

[24] In 1226, in return for his support during the minority, James had granted to Don Blasco all the castles and towns that he could obtain in the land of the Moors (*H*, 1, no. 85). Possibly, after the failure of the siege at Peníscola in 1225, James did not reckon on major successes for Blasco but in 1231–2, Blasco took the strategically important fortress of Morella, though not necessarily by force. James did not feel he could allow Morella to remain in Blasco's hands (Arroyo, 'Blasco', pp. 71–99). Indeed, Blasco's action may have precipitated the Valencian

And we said: "Yes, we remember it so well that we will tell you what it says: 'Whatever you gain from the Moors, it may be yours'."

Then he said: "Lord, that is right."

And we said: "Don Blasco, you know very well that this gain does not pertain to you, because this is a castle that is worth as much as a county with all its appurtenances. And this is what it falls to you to do. As God has given you so good a place and you are able to deliver it to me, you should deliver it to me, and I will do you such good that men will recognize what a great service you have done me. And I will do it willingly."

And he said: "Lord, I must consider the matter before I respond to you."

[137] Then he went out with four knights who had been standing to one side, and when he had taken a decision, he came to us and he said: "Lord, do you wish absolutely to have Morella?"

And we said to him: "Don Blasco, I think you are well able to understand that we wish to have it; and it is right for us to have it, and for you to have the other things that we have offered you."

Then he said: "As I see that it is your will to have it and you have offered me so much good, I will follow your will, and it pleases me that you have it. But I ask you one thing. Since you wish to have Morella, show me so much love that I may hold it in your name; for it stands to reason that, being the one who gave it to you, I would hold it for you better than any man in the kingdom."

We replied to him that this pleased us, and said: "Since it is so, let us go before Don Pedro Fernández, Don Atorella, Zeit Abuzeit, and the other knights, so they may know that you hold it in our name."

And he said that that was pleasing to him. Then we went before them; and he said that we should speak first, but we said: "Don Blasco, you speak, as it pertains to you to speak."

And he said: "Lord, you made me a charter saying that any place I took from the Moors would be mine. But, so great is the good that you have done me and which you say you will do, it stands to reason that if I can do you some service, I should do it for you. And it is my will that, as you wish this castle to be yours, it should be so, if I wish it so. And I ask that it should be your will for me to hold it in your name, as it makes more sense for me to have it than any other man of your kingdom."

We said to him that we thanked him for it, and that we would recompense him for the service he had done us. And after that, he went down on his knees

---

conquest, forcing James to act so that it was royal power and not that of the Aragonese higher nobles which was extended in the region (Font Rius, 'Conquesta', p. 255).

before us and did homage to us with his hands and mouth,[25] because through us he had the castle of Morella.

We stayed there that day, and when we left the next day, we went to Ares and took possession of it.[26] We gave so much to the foot soldiers there, for taking it from the Saracens, that they were well pleased with us.

[138] At that time lived King Don Sancho of Navarre,[27] son of King Don Sancho, who was the best king there ever was in Navarre. And the king of Castile[28] was attacking him through Don Lope Díaz,[29] Lord of Vizcaya, who had already taken two or three of his castles. So the king of Navarre sent a message to us saying that if we wished to treat with him, he would treat with us, and would show us as much love and grace as had ever been shown by one king to another. Now it seemed to us a good idea that we should go to see him in Tudela, for it was some twenty-five years since he had been able to leave Tudela,[30] nor had he ridden anywhere. And upon that matter we spoke with Don Blasco, Don Rodrigo Lizana, and Don Ató Foces, and we told them that they should come with us to that meeting; and they went there. When we arrived,[31] he could not come down to receive us in the town of Tudela, because he was so exceedingly and unbelievably fat that he was greatly ashamed of people seeing him, unless it were in a sheltered place; and so we had to go up into the castle.

The first day, at the hour of vespers, we went up there, and he received us as well and as gracefully as he could, for he came to receive us at a place he had not entered nor gone down as far for ten years. We embraced, and he was at least as tall as we were;[32] and he did this happily and laughing. Then, hand in hand, we went up into the castle by some steps, and we found seats placed in a

---

[25]James made a donation to Blasco of the castles and towns of Sástago and María on 24 February 1232 or 1233 (García Edo, 'Blasco', pp. 415–6). In January 1233, Blasco fixed the boundaries and arranged the repopulation of Morella (Puig, *Conquista*, p. 139). Problems between James and Blasco over Morella continued until 11 May 1235, when James granted the town of Morella and its appurtenances to Blasco but retaining the castle through Fernando Díaz. In compensation, Blasco received the castles and towns of Culla and les Coves de Vinromà (Ubieto, *Orígenes*, p. 56).

[26]Autumn 1232.

[27]Sancho VII 'the Strong' (1194–1234), son of Sancho VI 'the Wise' (1150–94).

[28]Ferdinand III (1217–52).

[29]Diego López de Haro, encouraged by Ferdinand, attacked the Navarrese. Lope Díaz was his son.

[30]The events James now relates are from the beginning of 1231. Since Sancho had fought alongside James's father, Peter II, at the battle of Las Navas in 1212, James could hardly have been unaware that he is exaggerating a little. Sancho's decision to reside in Tudela was a conscious and symbolic one, since Tudela stood near the borders of the kingdoms of Aragon and Castile (Leroy, 'Ribera Navarraise', p. 442).

[31]February 1231.

[32]James was measured as 182 centimetres high (just over six foot) in an examination of his remains undertaken on 22 July 1855 (Salvat, *Tarragona*, doc. 15, p. 154).

cloister that was of his chapel, and here he said that he was very glad for two reasons: Firstly, for the meeting, and secondly because we had such a great desire to see him. When he had gone on a while in this pleasant manner, we said to him that in fact it was he who had sent us a message, and that it was he who wished to see us, to our honour and to our profit. And this we had believed, since he had sent word to us to say so. "And as the words of the message were good and to our liking, it is only because you sent word that we should come to see you that we have come to see you this night. But now it is vespers, and in the morning we shall come here, and you will be able to speak with us then of the things of which it will please you to speak."

Then he replied to us that he would speak with us of the greatest good of which anybody had ever spoken to us. And we thanked him very much for it. And with that we took our leave that night from the meeting.

[139] When the morning came, we heard our Mass, and afterwards we went up to see him. And he began to speak in this manner: "King, I believe that you know, or at least ought to know, how much love and kinship there is between you and us. In kinship, there is nobody closer to us, except for the son of the countess of Champagne,[33] who is our nephew. But we consider you to be closer to us than he, because we love you more, since the love we showed him was very poorly received. For we showed him favours and love, but he behaved very badly towards us, so badly that he was speaking and treating with our men of Navarre to overthrow our power and be king. And for that reason we have sent for you, as we would rather the kingdom be yours than go to him or any other man in the world. And I prefer to say it to you from my own mouth rather than have others mediate between us. But, in this way, so that nobody shall say that there is anything underhand about it: we wish to adopt you, and you likewise to adopt us; for it is natural that we shall die before you, since we are seventy-eight and you are not yet twenty-five. We do this for the people, so they may not take us for a man of little wisdom in our deeds."

[140] On hearing these words, we were very pleased, as it truly seemed that they proceeded from great love. But we besought him that he should not feel aggrieved if we discussed the matter with the nobles who had come with us, and said that at vespers we would return to see him and give him our response.

---

[33]Thibaut IV of Champagne, who became King Teobaldo I of Navarre (1234–53). Famed as a troubadour, he was the son of Blanche of Champagne, sister of Sancho VII. Sancho had many sons but because they were all illegitimate he ruled out the possibility of any of them succeeding him. He also fell out with Thibaut, who was rejected as a possible successor by much of the higher nobility of Navarre. Based on the rather remote precedent of the treaty of Vadoluengo (1135) between García Ramírez of Navarre and Ramiro II of Aragon, Sancho suggested the treaty of mutual adoption of which James now talks.

It was necessary to discuss the matter for the following reason: we had a son[34] by queen Doña Eleanor, daughter of the King of Castile Don Alfonso, and we had made all the nobles, knights and cities of Aragon and the city of Lleida swear allegiance to him. Thus, we sent Don Blasco de Alagón,[35] Don Ató Foces, and Don Rodrigo Lizana to King Don Sancho, in order that, in secret, they might explain this matter to him, together with whomever else he wanted to participate in the talks. And they went there and they said to him: "The king sends us to you, and we wish to say to you, on his behalf, these words that he does not wish to say to you face to face, but instead sends us to say them to you. The king is well aware that you know that he has a son by his wife, from whom he has separated by order of the pope;[36] and he has ordered Aragon and Lleida to swear to that son. Now, the death of man is in the hand of God, and so young men may die as suddenly as old. And this is the greatest difficulty that the king has. He cannot take away his son's right while he may live. If it were not for that, you should know for certain that he would greatly wish it to take place and it would please him, for he knows only too well that you show him great love."

[141] Now he said that he would consider that matter. And he discussed it with Don Sancho Fernández de Monteagudo[37] and Guillermo Baldovín, who was then the best and most powerful man in Tudela, and with the justiciar of Tudela, and with others whose names we do not recall. And this was what they replied to us in the early morning of the second day: that it was a very serious matter that he, who was so old, should throw in his lot with two people such as we and our son were. But, for the great love that he had for us, as long as we helped him against the king of Castile, who did him harm and took his lands from him, he would do it. Moreover, he would include our son, with us, so that if he died before us, the land and all his kingdom would come to us, and if it happened to the contrary, that we and our son Don Alfonso died first, our kingdom and our land would go to him. An oath was to be sworn to that effect, and he would have his men swear allegiance to us first, and then we should have ours swear to him, that this treaty and these documents should be

---

[34]Alfonso, who died in 1261. In February 1228 James had secured the allegiance of the Aragonese to Alfonso in a general court at Daroca.

[35]The presence of Don Blasco here is a curiosity since he appears to have been in exile at that time and is not mentioned in any documents of the king in this period. Soldevila suggests that James is referring to Don Blasco Maza, who was certainly with the king at this time (*S*, p. 260).

[36]Gregory IX annulled the marriage of James to Eleanor in February 1229.

[37]Sancho Fernández de Monteagudo was seneschal of Navarre (*M*, p. 238) and on 4 April 1231 swore the oath of fealty to James and Sancho VII (*S*, p. 261; *H*, 1, no. 151). He governed Navarre for most of the period 1243–1253. Guillem Baldovín witnesses the treaty of mutual adoption of 2 February 1231 between James and Sancho (*H*, 1, no. 147; *Marichalar*, no. 187), and with the title of justiciar of Tudela (*S*, p. 261).

fulfilled. Then our men returned to us and told us of what they had spoken with him and how they had arranged the manner in which to proceed.

[142] When we heard the news, we and those who were with us were very glad.[38] For although we would have to enter into a war with the king of Castile, even so we found the pact to be a good one, for three reasons. First, because of the very great offence that the king of Castile had done him; second, because he was seventy-eight years old and yet still was prepared to join forces with us, even though there were two of us and as each of us might live for at least as long as he had, by right and by nature, it seemed a sensible course to join with him; and third, that, if the king of Castile did him harm unjustly, and he made us heir to all he had, as if we were his son, we could rightly enter into that war with good motive. For, as he had made the donation of Navarre to us, so we could justly defend the land of our father, since he had adopted us.

[143] Afterwards, we went up to see him with our nobles and we found him with two or three nobles who had just arrived. And we responded to him in this manner: that we thanked him very much for the honour and love of which he had sent word to us, and that we accepted and would do just as the nobles had agreed with him, helping him against the king of Castile and against all men who sought to offend him or do him evil.

After that we signalled a day to him, three weeks from then,[39] when he should order all the nobles and knights of Navarre to come, and from each city ten men with power delegated by all of the others, so that whatever they did would be sanctioned, praised and confirmed by them; and from all of the great towns, four men of each town, with the authority of all the others, who would accept what they did. And we would do the same, sending to Aragon, for the nobles, and all the others, just as he had done. When his men had taken the oath and homage of lordship and fealty to us, our men would do the same for him.

[144] On that day we met at Tarazona;[40] and, as he was unable to come out, we entered Tudela, with our nobles and the men of the cities, and we took the homage and oath of lordship and fealty from all those we have mentioned above, who accepted that, when his days had ended, we would be king of Navarre, either we or Prince Don Alfonso, if he lived longer than us, and so to

---

[38]The reincorporation of Navarre, lost on the death of Alfonso I of Aragon in 1134, had long been an ambition of the rulers of Aragon.

[39]The treaty of mutual adoption was agreed on 2 February 1231 at Tudela (*H*, 1, no. 147). On 26 February, James pawned various castles to Sancho in return for a substantial loan (*Marichalar*, no. 187). The oaths of the Navarrese and Aragonese were not received until 4 April 1231 (*H*, 1, no. 151).

[40]4 April 1231.

our descendants forever more.[41] In the same way, we ordered the nobles and the representatives of the cities to enter Tudela, ten men from each town, and all those of our lordship, so that they would make the oath and do him homage, just as he had ordered it to be done to us. Moreover, we assigned a man to go through Navarre taking the oaths and homage of all those who had not already made them; and he ordered the same to be done in our land.

[145] Having done these things, we held a meeting, we and he, about how to deal with the matter of the king of Castile. And in that meeting, four or five nobles participated on his part and the same number on our part; and also there were some citizens of Zaragoza present both on his part and ours.[42] These all swore, placing their hands upon the Holy Gospels, that they would keep it secret, and that each would give us his advice on what should best be done. Then we adjourned the meeting until the following morning, as it was almost night then and great matters are better treated in the morning, if it is possible to do so, than at any other hour of the day. Having heard the early morning Mass, all those who participated in the secret meeting came before the king of Navarre and us to say that they had considered those matters that night, for as Solomon says in his proverbs, the night gives good counsel.[43] And so that we could think better through all the night, we had convoked them in the morning.

[146] When the morning came, we said to the king of Navarre that he should speak first, as he was older and knew more about things than we did. And he began his speech in this manner, saying: "King, when it comes to the deeds of Spain I do indeed have great understanding, and for the following reason: because I have seen them, and I have experienced the things that have been done in my time. Now, there was already war between the king of Castile and my father,[44] and by the mercy of God, each time his men came into conflict with ours, the Navarrese showed themselves to be well prepared. But, such was Castilian superiority – as they were many and we were few – that it always went against us. With the grace of God, and with you alone to help us, I will be

---

[41]The agreements do not mention the safeguard of the right of Alfonso (*S*, p. 260) and it has been suggested that James invented this clause to justify his actions (Swift, *James*, p. 51). Moreover, the agreement may simply have applied to Aragon, so that the union of Aragon and Catalonia might well have been broken had Sancho outlived James (*G*, 1, p. 240).

[42]An indication of the strong Navarrese influence in Zaragoza.

[43]Not a direct biblical quotation but a very common proverb [Riera suggests the influence of Sirach, 40:5–6 ('Personalitat eclesiàstica', p. 586) but the sense is surely quite different there, because there the night brings confused sleep and troubling visions].

[44]There were many disputes between Alfonso VIII of Castile and Sancho VI of Navarre. Like Aragon, Castile sought to annex Navarre and there were various agreements between them to divide the kingdom. The main losses to Navarre had actually come early in Sancho VII's own reign, in incursions made by Alfonso VIII and James's father, Peter II (Ubieto, 'Navarra-Aragón'; González, 'Reclamaciones').

good enough to face them. And let us do it in this way. I have helped you very much, and with all my heart; so you should help me in accordance with my consideration of you as a son. For if we both help each other well, we shall overcome them, with the will of God, as we have right on our side and they do not."

With that he brought his words to a close, and said that we should speak. However, we said that his nobles knew the frontier better than either our nobles or us. And it fell to Don García Almoravit[45] to speak, and he said: "King of Aragon, I will tell you what has happened in this land, although all the men of Navarre who are here know at least as much of the evil that Don Lope Díaz de Vizcaya has done the king: for whatever evil he does to the kingdom, he does to the king. And he does it with the very great power that he himself has; moreover, the king of Castile has ordered his men to help him, if he needs them. But, since Our Lord God has granted us such good that He has brought together your love and that of the king of Navarre, we have hope in God that together you will put an end to all of it; and you will honour both the king and yourself in such a manner as will please the whole world, for the great offence they have done to him."

Then they said to Don Sancho Fernández de Monteagudo that he should speak, and he said: "Lord king, what more do you want? For what we hoped to have by God's mercy, we now have. And if you both wish to undertake this deed, the thing will come to a good end. And what more could anyone say? For if you prepare well for the task, the king and you will bring this deed to a good end."

After this, we said to the nobles and to those of the council, as there were many there, that they should speak; and they said with one voice: "All that has been already said, we all agree and confirm; for just as Don García and Don Sancho have said, if the two of you have the will to undertake it, the deed shall be completed to your honour; and we will serve you as much as we are able."

Then the king of Navarre said: "Since you have wished that my nobles should speak here, now let yours speak."

And Don Ató Foces said: "This is what we who are on the side of the king of Aragon will say. If you two kings will give us that with which we might serve you, I shall put into it as much as you give me, and what I place there of mine own shall relieve us from the pledge for five years, for if we must put our persons into it, surely it would be unfair if we had to put in our belongings too."

Then Don Blasco de Alagón said: "Lord, the nobles of Navarre speak well to you; for if you two strive to bring the matter to a good and righteous end, we

---

[45]Long influential in Navarrese affairs, he was witness to the treaty of friendship and alliance between James and the widow and son of Teobaldo on 1 August 1253, and in the treaty between James and Teobaldo II of 9 April 1254 (*S*, p. 262; *M*, pp. 231, 238).

shall all be worth more, both you and us. And as God has joined your love to that of the king, you will both be able to achieve great things, if you wish to."

After that Don Rodrigo Lizana said: "Take counsel, you and the king of Navarre, that you have enough assets for those who serve you in this deed, as it is with men of valour that you and he will win this enterprise of which we speak, and bring it to a fitting end."

And the king of Navarre said: "Speak, king of Aragon."

And we said that we would do so.

[147] "Well you know, king, that we who are kings take nothing from this world when the hour of our death comes but a single shroud, though it be of finer cloth than that of other people. Even so, this at least remains to us, that because of the great power that we have, we are able to serve God, and leave great fame for the good works that we have done, and, if in this life we do not do them, there will not come another time when we will be able to do them. Thus, if you wish it, I will show you how we can win this war in the following manner.

"It is true that I have three or four times more land than you, but you have more assets than me,[46] and wheat, and other things that will be advantageous in campaign. Now, I offer here to provide you with two thousands knights, and you will need to have another thousand; as from your land you must be able to assemble, among knights and men of lineage, enough who know very well how to manage horses and arms. And you should also send word to the count of Champagne, your cousin, that he should come to see you; and beseech him to help you with one thousand knights, as he must easily have them.

"If by chance the count of Champagne does not wish to help, because he has heard of these treaties that there are between us, you should assemble two thousand; for, by God's grace, you are easily able to pay them, and to have money profits nobody if it is not used. For what can you better spend it on than avenging the dishonour that the king of Castile and his men have done to your father and you? Through that, you shall be honoured, and when you die you shall die with honour, as shall we.

"And I will tell you how it will go, if we have four thousand knights of lineage and we enter Castile. The Castilians are very pompous and proud, and they will fight with us; and probably we shall not be able to avoid fighting a battle, which we will win, with the help of God, because we have right on our side and they do not. Then, having defeated them in the field, everybody will

---

[46]Sancho's wealth, gained through prudent administration, heavy taxation and war booty, had long made him one of the chief creditors of the Aragonese realm and had strengthened his bargaining power with it. During Peter II's later years and James's minority, he had built up a coherent line of advanced positions in the interior of Aragon that strategically reinforced his frontier from the Pyrenees until the Ebro (Martín Duque, 'Relaciones financieras').

be able to enter through the villages of Castile as they would through a field, because none of them have moats or walls. And we shall sack them, and our men will win so much that those who are not our men shall come to us for the profit that they can gain. For they will indeed gain much with us."

[148] Yet he responded to us very gruffly and rudely, and said that we should do our work in our manner and that he would do his in his manner. And when we heard these words we were much aggrieved, and we said to him that he ought to have taken well all that we had said, as we had not said anything which was not to his honour but so that he might recover what he had lost. And his men did not dare to say a single thing to contradict him. So much so that we said to Don Sancho Fernández: "Don Sancho Fernández, you do great wrong, in not telling the truth to your lord."

And he said: "You go ahead, just as you have set things out here to the king, and, if God wills it, all will be to your honour and profit."

Because of the pact that there was between us and King Sancho we did not wish to oppose him, and we left him until the morning, saying that we would have to speak of it the next day. And so we left him, on seeing him so upset.

[149] The next day we returned to see him, and we sent to ask him to lend us one hundred thousand sous; and he said that he would do it, if we could give him a guarantee. And this was the treaty between us: that we would deliver to him Ferrera, Ferrellón, Peña Redonda and Peña Faxino and he would then lend us the money.[47] And we said to him that we would be very glad to do so.

We then arranged that on Easter day[48] we would bring one thousand knights to him, and, afterwards, at Michaelmas, we would bring another one thousand; and that it would be done in such a manner that it would have to please him, and he would provide the other thousand. And we left there after discussing the matter.

So, Easter came, which was when we were supposed to see him. But, because we were occupied by other affairs, since we had to spend some time at Majorca,[49] we delayed seeing him for some two months, because we were

---

[47]*H*, 1, no. 149; *Marichalar*, nos. 176–8.

[48]23 March 1231.

[49]There are again some chronological problems here. Ubieto (*Orígenes*, p. 58) suggests a second visit to Majorca in March 1231 and then a third visit in June–July 1231 but this seems very uncertain. James was in the Balearics in May–July 1231 and again May–July 1232. It appears James was with Sancho in November 1231 (Baró, 'Relaciones', p. 167) and again in March 1232 (*Marichalar*, no. 181). James may well again have jumped a year (making these events of 1232). Either way, James seems to be minimizing the period of his delay. Essentially, James was reticent about the agreement with Sancho because he was already deeply involved in the conquest of Majorca and had his mind set on the campaign for Valencia. In these masterly passages, James places all the blame for the failure of the agreement at Sancho's door when, in fact, he himself had failed to fulfil his part of the bargain because he was occupied

unable to come to his presence. When at last we went there, he tried to reproach us for it. Before we saw him, a knight who had been with him for some twenty-one years came, and he was our friend and was called Don Pedro Ximénez de Valtierra,[50] and he said to us: "Now let us see what you can do, for the king of Navarre wishes you evil, and to accuse you of not having come on the day that you had fixed with him."

And we said to Don Pedro Ximénez: "I thank you very much for letting me know, but we shall see each other in the morning."

And we said to the king of Navarre: "We have come here to see you, and we beseech you not to be annoyed that we did not come on the appointed day, as we had to do various things for the good of this enterprise, so that we can better help you."

And he said: "What you say may be so, but you have not come on the appointed day."

To which we said: "But if things are so much better, for you and for us, than if we had come on that day, it ought not to trouble you."

[150] "Now show me," he said, "why things are so much better, and then I will understand it."

Then we said: "With this delay, we have gained two hundred knights, who you will have to help you. But tell me, have you prepared the thousand knights? For we did not find, through all Navarre, more than three hundred knights prepared, and I will have more than a thousand for you. And if you, whose concern this deed is, have not prepared or given anything, how can you censure me, when I have prepared one thousand knights, if you want them? For I will defy the king of Castile only if you have the other one thousand knights."

After that he said he would take counsel; and we went from there.

As we were descending from the castle of Tudela, we came across one of Don García d'Almoravit's knights, who was carrying a message to the king, on his behalf and on that of Juan Pérez de Baztán,[51] who was to be found at the frontier. And he said: "Lord, I have come here with a message for the king, and I have been here four days without being able to see him."

And we said to him: "What message do you bring?"

And he said: "If God helps me, lord, I will tell you, as you share so much with the king that I do not wish to hide it from you. The nobles send word to

with matters which he considered more important. The possibility of Aragonese succession in Navarre rose again in the 1250s and, most of all, in the 1270s. Perhaps these passages were related at a time close to the event, but they could also have been related in the 1270s at a time when James's son Prince Peter was pressing his own claims to the Navarrese throne.

[50] A witness to the treaty of mutual adoption who is found among the king's following during these years (*S*, p. 265; *M*, p. 120).

[51] He was one of the Navarrese knights who swore to the agreements between James and Sancho (*S*, p. 266).

the king that, if he sends them two hundred knights, they will defeat Don Lope Díaz de Vizcaya and will win the war, and you can be certain of it."

Then we said to him that we would let the king know it, although we would be unable to tell him at that moment, since we had already left the castle, but we would notify him of it at vespers.

[151] In the evening, we returned to the king and we said to him: "King, why do you act so? There is a knight here, at the gate, who comes on behalf of Don García d'Almoravit and of those who are on the frontier and are of your household, and he says that during four or five days he has not been allowed to come to your presence. But I will tell you his message, as there is good news."

And he said: "What news?"

And we said: "In good faith, I shall tell you; but do not reveal that I have disclosed it to you. He says that if you can assemble two hundred knights and send them to the frontier, with them they could defeat Don Lope Díaz; and, when he is defeated, your war will be over. So let him enter here before you."

Then he said: "Let me speak of this to you. Do you not realize what is happening? All the nobles wish to trick us,[52] and they wish to take our money."

Then we said to him: "They are not asking money of you, but rather they ask you for two hundred knights; and you should send them, or else you will lose the great honour you could have gained, and perhaps never again will you have so good an occasion as you have now. I would go willingly, with the sixty knights that I have here, but I have not yet defied the king of Castile. Even so, if we can find some excuse, order the towns to arms, and I will order my men that they should follow those who you appoint for their leaders, and I will give them provisions for eight days, and they will do what you order them to."

And he said: "That is not for you to worry about."

When we saw that he was not concerned with his own affairs, we had to keep quiet; and we thought to ourselves: "It will not be our fault, for we have done here all that we could."

[152] On seeing that he was not giving the matter a second thought, we went from the house, to speak with our nobles, and we said to them: "You see what has happened to us."

Then we told them all about it, just as it had happened. And Don Blasco said: "Lord, if the king is not bothered about his own business, why should you concern yourself more than he does? Depart from him tomorrow and say to

---

[52]The Navarrese nobles generally did not agree with the course Sancho had taken, but, even so, they were to find it impossible to negotiate with the reluctant James after Sancho's death in 1234 and preferred to place their country in the orbit of the king of France (Batlle, *Expansió*, p. 27).

him that if he needs you, he will find you prepared, as long as he fulfils the agreement he has made with you."

And we and all the others said: "Well said, Don Blasco. That is what we shall do."

When the morning came, we went up to the castle, and we said to him that if he fulfilled the accord that he had promised us, he would find us prepared, with two thousand knights. And that it was all in his hands, and did not depend on us. And we remained there one more day, and then returned home.

[153] When we found ourselves outside Tudela and had arrived at Tauste, we agreed that, as this enterprise was unprofitable both for our own affairs and his, we should go to the land of the Moors and take Borriana. So we fixed the day, at the beginning of May,[53] for the nobles and the masters of the Temple, Hospital, Uclés[54] and Calatrava, who were in our land, to be at Teruel with us. But nobody came on the day we had fixed for them to be in Teruel. Then the Bishop of Zaragoza, whose name was Bernardo de Monteagudo,[55] Don Pedro Fernández de Azagra, and men of our household came to us. And we were about one hundred and twenty knights and the militia of Teruel.

On the third day after having left Teruel, we went to camp at Xèrica;[56] and some seven hundred or eight hundred Moors came out to us, so that we did not dare camp on the plain of Xèrica, but rather we camped opposite the castle of Xèrica.

The Moors kept guard to prevent the Christians from daring to enter the plain, except in the fields near to us, and they defended it with crossbows and lances. Because of that, at night, we decided that we should devastate the land above the town, facing Viver; and that we should leave thirty armoured horses with those who remained at the tents, numbering some thousand men. With the others we would go to devastate the land above the town. And this is what we did.

When the Moors heard the armoured horses they did not dare to go out from there. The next day we devastated the land below the town, in the same manner as we had done to the upper part, leaving the armoured horses at the tents.

[154] When we returned from the devastation, Raimundo Samenla,[57] who was commander of Aliaga, came with another brother, who was of the Temple, also a commander, whose name we do not recall. They entered the camp, lightly

---

[53]May 1233 (Gual, 'Reconquista de la zona', p. 431).

[54]Uclés being the major house of the order of Santiago. Its commander at this time was Pedro Álvarez (1227–38) (Lomax, *La Orden de Santiago*, p. 287).

[55]The bishop of Zaragoza was Sancho Ahones until September 1235 (so he is the bishop here) and then Bernardo de Monteagudo from 1236 until 1239 (Ubieto, *Listas episcopales*).

[56]On the left bank of the Palància, in the province of Castelló.

[57]Aliaga was from 1163 a comanda of the Hospitallers.

armed upon their horses, with their lances in their hands, and they came to us. And we sent for the bishop, the nobles, and the good men of Teruel and for those of our own household. And this is what they said: "Lord, the master of the Temple salutes you, and he of the Hospital, and the commander of Montalbán;[58] and they say that they have been to the hill of the Pasqües, which is found before the Morvedre, three miles away. And they have been there for two days, just as you ordered, and they have travelled the length of the valley of the Segó. And now they are there they ask you to go there rapidly, as, if you do not, they will be unable to resist, because they are few and great is Valencia's power."

On that we said that we would take a decision; and they left the tent saying plainly that if we did not go, they would return there.

[155] Then we assembled our council, and all said: "It would be a good thing for you to go there to their aid."

And with that response that we gave them they left. But afterwards we said: "How can we leave these beautiful wheatfields before us without laying waste to them?[59] Are the Saracens going to prevent us by force from devastating them? Let us send the masters word to wait a day, and tomorrow we will be with them. And I will show you how we should go about devastating the fields."

"By God," they all said with one voice. "It is a good thing that you do not depart from here until all has been destroyed, but how shall we destroy them?"

"I will tell you," we said. "I have never been on this frontier, but it seems to me that these Saracens know their weapons and are very skilful. Yet all have a particular way of handling weapons: and for all the skill with which one attacks, if the adversary knows how to parry, he will overcome him. Now, these knights of ours only have lances, whilst the Saracens have lances and crossbows; yet we run better than they do. So I will tell you how we will devastate the fields, leaving them unable to defend them. Let us place twenty armed knights on the upper road and twenty more on the lower road; then we shall give shields to the squires, and the crossbowmen shall go behind the shielded men, and the men who are to destroy the crops shall go close behind the crossbowmen."

And we did it in the manner that we had decided. When it was morning we cut all the crops, in such a way that the Moors might understand that if they defended the wheat, it would profit us and harm them. And we cut the wheat from all the fields except two.

---

[58]The master of the Temple was Ramon Patot, of the Hospital, Hugh de Forcalquier, of the Santiagans, Pedro Álvarez (though here James appears to refer to the local commander).

[59]The destruction of the Valencian Muslims' crops was one of James's most often used and most effective tactics throughout his campaigns.

The next day, early in the morning, we went to camp at Torres Torres, and that evening we devastated all the fields there. And from there, through scouts, we let the masters know that we were coming.

[156] When the next morning had come, and we had heard our Mass, we went down through the valley of the Segó, and encountered the masters of the Temple, and the Hospital, and the commanders of Alcañiz[60] and of Montalbán. And all together we went to besiege Borriana.

The siege of Borriana began in the middle of May.[61] And there we made a *fenèvol* and a *manganel*. And the Saracens who were inside sometimes came out to skirmish. Whenever they saw that there were sheep and cattle near the town, they came out, at times a hundred on foot, and at times just seven men on horseback. And before going out, they placed crossbowmen to do damage at that gate, if the army surrounded it. At times they took a part of the cattle and then returned inside, but, on other occasions, the beasts would be recaptured by those of the host. Because of this, we forbade those of the army from bringing the cattle or the sheep to pasture between the army and the town.

One day, though we do not recall to which company of the army they belonged, there were seven beasts, pack-horses and mules, and those seven men on horseback came out by the gate that faces Valencia, and they cut off their path. And a knight of the army, named Guillermo Das, who was with Don Blasco de Alagón, went to guard the pasture with his men, and went with his horse, vested in his purpoint, and with a squire who carried his weapons near to him. And he took his weapons and his iron cap and went against the Saracens who were taking in the beasts. And if then he had wished to defend them, he would have been able to defend them well, as the army was already on its way; but he did not have enough courage to attack the Saracens well, so they were able to take four beasts inside, and two returned to the army.[62]

[157] Now we wish to name the nobles who were with the army. Firstly, there was our uncle Don Ferdinand, Berenguer d'Erill, Bishop of Lleida, and the bishop of Tortosa,[63] the masters of the Temple and of the Hospital; and also there was Don Blasco de Alagón, Guillem de Cervera, who was lord of Juneda, and Guillem de Cardona, who was brother of Ramon Folc; and there was Don Rodrigo Lizana and Don Pedro Fernández de Azagra, Lord of Albarracín, and Don Jimeno de Urrea, and Don Blasco Maza, and Don Pedro Cornel, and Bernat Guillem, who was father of the one who lives now and was our uncle,

---

[60]Rodrigo Pérez Pons.

[61]James was certainly at Borriana from 5 June until 25 July 1233, when the town was already taken (*H*, 1, nos. 181–5).

[62]Not only the destruction of crops but also the capture of animals played an important part in James's attacks. Here one beast seems to have got away from both sides.

[63]Ponç de Torroella (1212–54).

the prior of Santa Cristina, the commanders of Alcañiz and Montalbán, the militia of Daroca and of Teruel and afterwards those of Calatayud. And those of Lleida and Tortosa were there, too. And the militia of Zaragoza came, but Borriana had already been taken by the time they arrived.

And a master of Albenga, named Nicoloso,[64] who made our *trebuchet* at Majorca, came to us, and said to us: "My lord, it is not necessary for you to be here any longer if you wish to take this place, as you can have it, if you want, in fifteen days."

Then we asked him how it could be done. And he said: "Give me wood, as there is much here of the lote, and of some trees and others, and eight days from now I will have made you here a wooden castle,[65] and we shall make it go there, just as you know we moved the *trebuchets* at Majorca."

And we said that he spoke the truth, but that we wished to consult with the nobles.

[158] So we sent for Don Ferdinand, the bishops, and the nobles, that they should come to us; and we said to them: "A master who was with us at the conquest of Majorca, and who made our *trebuchet*, has come to us here, and says that he will make a wooden castle here in eight days, with which we will be able to take the town of Borriana."

What is more, we said to them that we had already seen it done, and we knew for certain, that if the castle were made, everything else would be achieved. But they asked in what manner could it be done. And we said: "I know very well how, but let us call the master to our presence and he will tell you about it."

And, while he was coming, we told them how it could be done, as we had seen it done in Majorca: "The wooden castle will have two supports on each side, so there will be four, besides two others across the ends of each side, front and back, to secure the supports. And there will be two platforms, the one midway up the castle and the other on the upper part; and on the top there will be crossbowmen, and in the middle men who will throw stones at the Saracens who go up on to the wall. Then the Christians will climb up that ruined tower and the Saracens will be unable to stop it, because of the crossbows and stones that are fired from the castle; and the castle will be on the other side of the moat. And in this manner the town can be taken."

---

[64]Of Albenga, port of the Liguria. His participation in the siege of Majorca has not been mentioned previously. A document of 1275 (*M*, p. 254) speaks of 'Ser Nicholos' in connection with siege-engines. The fact that James had recruited an Italian military engineer demonstrates the importance of siege-artillery in James's thinking.

[65]A siege tower.

[159] Afterwards the master came, and he explained it in the same manner as we had told it to them. And all said we should have the siege tower made as quickly as we possibly could. So we hired masters whom we found there, and we ordered wood to be cut and we ordered it brought to the camp; and we had the siege tower made. Throughout that time the *fenèvol* did not stop firing; and from inside there were two very fine *algarrade*s that fired.[66] However, we had greatly protected the *fenèvol* with hurdles, and it was low down, and once it began to fire, the *algarrade*s did not fire so often for fear of the *fenèvol*. When the wooden tower was made, we had our bows prepared, some hundred of them, well-anointed and greased, and the master secured two anchors on the land, with a mantle of hurdles that went in front, and had men with shields and armour fix the points of the anchor inside the ground near the side of the pasture land at the moat, by the blows of a mace; and through the rings of the anchor some large stakes were driven, and irons for each one, with wooden maces, and to these we attached the tracks along which the wooden tower would run. Then the master said to us that in the morning we should assemble men prepared to pull it, and he would demonstrate how to move it there.

[160] When the sun rose, we mounted and rode to the army at Daroca and Teruel to tell them they should each send two hundred men, and to do so immediately. And we said: "Master, have you prepared it?"

He said that he would have it ready immediately, and he would place the ropes through the ways.

"Master, if you follow my advice, you should delay moving the castle for two days."

And he said: "Why, my lord?"

"For this reason", we said, "For they have two *algarrades*, and if they use them against the wooden castle, the castle has no defence and they will hit it as if it were a board."

Then he said: "If it pleases you, we should let it go now; as even if there were ten *algarrades*, it would not care more for them than for an ant."

But we said to him: "If you wanted to, today we would be able to protect it, as I would send many carriers to the sea, and we would have them bring all the rope and cord mesh from the ships. And we should have around thirty of them; and we could place the wooden crossbeams that we have at the top of the wooden castle, so that they stick out an arm's length, and afterwards we shall tie them on, and they will hang down and fend off the blows of the *algarrades*."

But he said: "My lord, it is not necessary, as this is not a place that requires such artifices."

---

[66]'These machines were most probably positioned on the platforms of the towers or on the wall walk, so that they could achieve greater range' (Chevedden, 'Artillery', pp. 68–9).

And we said: "You know better than I do on these matters; and if you think everything is fine, I will not argue with you."

[161] Then we set our hands to it, and we ordered that the men should take the cords and we cried "Ayoç!",[67] just as is done in launching or hauling in a ship, and they moved the castle. And, when it had gone a little way, it stopped because the supports would not move, and arrows rained down, and they wounded four or five immediately, right at the start. And we were in our vested purpoint, our hauberk, with our iron cap on our head, and shielded ourselves with our sword, and there were some twenty men with shields who shielded those who pulled. And we had the men go so close together, that we did not allow those who were wounded to go from the ropes, but we made them sit and cover themselves, and afterwards we sent them back under cover. Even so a good eight or nine were wounded, as we were unable to shield them so well that the arrows did not pass between the shields that the men held. And when we had dragged the wooden castle about half the way we had to take it, the master said: "Order these men to go, as they are receiving great harm, and I will arrange it in such a manner that, when the Saracens look out, at dawn, they will find it there before them, if only you give me a select group of people and experienced men who shall do silently what I order them."

I said to him that he spoke well. And so we left there. Afterwards, there was nobody there who drank as much, in a single day, as we drank in those moments, for we drank two jugs of watered wine before we had eaten, because we were so thirsty; and then we went to eat.[68]

[162] In what we were doing, nobody helped us, nor did anybody offer to do so. And when the time came for us to eat, the *fenèvol* stopped firing. Then the Saracens set to work with the best of their *algarrades*, and they hit the castle some ten times before we had eaten. And it pained us as much as if somebody had struck us in the side with their fists. In fact, even that would not have hurt us as much as the blows that we heard given to the wooden castle, while we were eating. So we sent for the master, who came to us when we had finished eating. When he had arrived, we said to him: "Would it not have been better to have done what I said and to have followed my advice, although now it is too late for that?"

After that, we could not find men willing to go there during the day to draw it back to a place where it could not be attacked, in order to repair it. So we left it, that night, abandoned in that manner. All night long the *algarrades* did nothing but fire, striking the castle more than one hundred times.

---

[67] Here 'Heave'. Cf. ch. 59 (when disembarking in Majorca).
[68]Burns ('Spiritual life', pp. 31–2) has remarked upon James's preoccupation with food and drink (for instances, chs. 11, 28, 134, 183, 184, 228, 252, 253, 259, 497, 501).

[163] When morning came, we saw it would be destroyed completely if it stayed there. So we sent word to the master, before dawn, to tie the ropes in the rings, so that we could go there in the morning and draw it back. And when the morning came, before sunrise, we ordered the castle to be pulled right back to the camp, so that the *algarrades* could not reach it there. But we and the others saw that the castle could not be reused, because the blows of the *algarrades* had destroyed a great part of it. So we abandoned it, and from that moment on we had no desire to use the castle artifice.

Then we and the nobles and the bishops agreed to fire our *fenèvol* and dig tunnels, for we would take the town in that way without any difficulty. And the *fenèvol* and the *manganell* fired, and we dug the tunnels.

[164] Meanwhile two galleys arrived from Tarragona, one belonging to Bernat de Santaeugènia,[69] the other to Pere Martell. We did not have any galley, and feared that the king of Valencia might arm two or three galleys to attack the provisions that came from Tarragona and Tortosa. And the sailors and those who were wise in matters of the sea advised us that we should retain those galleys and on no account allow them to leave.

Then we went to the tent of the master of the Temple and we sent for them and we besought them, in every way possible, that since the galleys were there, they should stay there, and we would pay them what they had spent on equipping them, and give them much more besides. But they said that the galleys had cost them a lot of money, and asked us to allow them to depart. But we said to them: "Bernat, you are such a good and honourable man, and you, Pere Martell, are such a good townsmen, that you must always look to my honour. So how can you wish me to go from here without capturing this place? Let us leave aside the harm and dishonour I and all my army would receive; for to hold my kingdom, I have fought and subdued, in Aragon and Catalonia, all those who rose against me,[70] and I have conquered the county of Urgell and Majorca; and this is the first place I have besieged in the kingdom of Valencia. And for me to leave here? I would not do it. But it would have to be done if there were nothing to eat. For which reason I ask you, for God, and because you are my subjects, not to wish me such great harm nor so great a dishonour."

[165] Then they said that they would take a decision. And messengers went between them and us while they were deciding. And it came down to us having to pay them sixty thousand sous, and that it had to be paid then and there. And we said to them: "We will willingly give them sixty thousand sous; but concerning what they say, that it should be paid here, that I cannot do, as now I

---

[69]Bernat appears in a document dated 9 July 1233 at the siege of Borriana, so these events must be before that date (*S*, p. 270; *M*, p. 105).

[70]Referring to the struggles of the minority.

could not pay them one thousand sous, unless somebody loaned it to me or I were to pawn horses or other things; and now is not the time for pawning horses."

So, we offered them pledges. And they said that they would not accept it for anything in the world, if we did not include as surety[71] the masters of the Temple and the Hospital. So we asked them to enter the agreement. And the master of the Hospital said: "Give me your assurance, and I will enter the agreement."

But the master of the Temple, Ramon Patot by name, said that they were not in the habit of acting as surety for a king or anybody else. And we had to leave things as they were at that time. Then the master of the Hospital said: "I will speak with the master of the Temple and I will see what I can do."

And the master said: "I know what we can do. Let us act as this surety for the king, and then he can confirm in charters the privileges that we hold from his lineage, and it will be worth more to us than if he were to give us one hundred thousand sous."

The master of the Temple said that he would consult with his brothers; and the brothers advised him to do so, and afterwards he said that he would do it.

Then the master of the Hospital came to us and said: "If someone were to come up with the solution, would you thank him for it?"

"Aye," we said.

"It can be achieved in this manner: you draw up a charter confirming those privileges that we have from your line, and then we will have it done."

And we said: "You should know, master, that we will not do that, as you ask for too great a privilege."

"The devil take you!," said the master, "You are a strange man, since you say aye and then you do nothing!"

"Because of what you have said, I will do it; but it would be a good idea if there was another person here, as I am the king and you are the master of the Hospital."

And he said: "If any other person participates, all will be lost, and there is enough with you and me; for if the master of the Temple or his brothers knew about it, it would not be done."

"Then," we said, "Let it be done. But remember, if the occasion arises, what I have done for you."[72]

---

[71] Personal sureties were individuals who served to guarantee transactions by encouraging or forcing a debtor to perform, compensating the creditor in case of a debtor's failure to perform, or performing the debtor's obligation itself (Kosto, *Making Agreements*, pp. 124–33).

[72] At Borriana, James conceded to the Templars the castle of Xivert and a portion of the town of Borriana. Also he confirmed all the privileges of the Hospitallers granted by his predecessors (*H*, 1, nos. 183–4; *M*, pp. 104–5; *S*, p. 271).

[166] After that we assembled and we ordered Bernat de Santaeugènia and Pere Martell to come, and we gave the masters as sureties. In this way we kept the galleys. And provisions arrived to us by sea, once people knew we had the galleys. And there was enough to satisfy the whole army.

However, Don Ferdinand, our uncle, said that he and some of the nobles wished to speak with us in the morning. And we said that it would please us greatly. When it was morning they came to us in our tent. And he came with Don Blasco de Alagón, Don Jimeno de Urrea, Don Rodrigo Lizana and Don Blasco Maza; and they had not said anything to the bishops or the nobles of Catalonia regarding the words they wished to say. And they called for Don Jimeno Pérez de Tarazona[73] and the justiciar of Aragon, so that these alone of our household were with us.

Then they asked Don Blasco de Alagón to speak for them; and he began his speech in this manner: "Lord, Don Ferdinand and we have come here with you to serve you in the deed of this siege you have undertaken upon Borriana. And it is certainly the case that kings often begin to undertake and attempt to do things, such as you have done in besieging this place, but not all the things they begin can be completed as kings would wish. For if you kings were to achieve everything you wanted, all the lands would be yours. Now, in this deed of Borriana we see a great problem facing you, for you will not be able to keep the militias here, as they wish to go and reap the crops. Moreover, we, the nobles, have nothing to eat. Now, we do not wish to have to say this to you, but we do not have anything to eat, and we shall have to go from here gradually. And you will remain here in such a way that you will be forced to leave in dishonour and shame. But, if it were agreeable to you, we would be able to arrange it in such a way that you might obtain great assets. And then, at another time, when you have better arranged matters, you will be able to take Borriana, God willing. And we will help you, for Zaén[74] will give you so much of his

---

[73] Jimeno Pérez appears many times in the *Llibre*. He is greatly praised by the king for his abilities (ch. 168). He was to be lieutenant of the king in Valencia (ch. 328), steward of Aragon (ch. 286), commander of Alcañiz (*M*, p. 155), and lord of Arenós (*S*, p. 271). Curiously in chapter 273, when he seeks a joust against the Saracens, he appears to be referred to as a great sinner. The justiciar of Aragon, Pedro Pérez, certainly participated in the siege of Borriana (*S*, p. 271).

[74] Zayyān was of the locally celebrated Banū Mardanīsh lineage, which opposed the rule of the Almohads. He was the great nephew of the celebrated 'King Lobo' of Valencia. In 1229, he had captured Valencia where he remained as governor until 1238. He was governor of Murcia from April 1239 to early 1241, but was overthrown. He fled south to Alicante until this city fell into Christian hands in 1246. He abandoned Spain for Tunis, where, in 1250, he saved the sultan's life.

riches, that you will be able to cover the expenses that you have made in coming here, both for yourself and for the nobles."[75]

[167] And we asked Don Ferdinand: "Don Ferdinand, and you nobles who have come here, do you really think that I must do this?"

And Don Ferdinand said: "In good faith, Lord, it seems to us that due to the great misfortune that Don Blasco has said you and we are in, you would suffer the indignity of the men beginning to leave for lack of food."

We immediately replied to him that we did not think it necessary to consult on a matter like that. And we said: "We respond to you in this manner. Our Lord has done us much good and much mercy in our youth, and the things we have undertaken we have brought to a good end by the grace of God. And to think that in our youth we should have taken a kingdom that is upon the sea, and yet now that we have entered the kingdom of Valencia, for the first time,[76] undertaking a siege with you of so vile a place as this, which is no more than a farmyard, you should wish me to leave here for assets that I might gain! Believe you me that I will not do it. Rather I ask you and I order you, for the lordship I hold over you, that you will help me to take it, and that you give me no more advice such as this. For I could not return to Catalonia and to Aragon with greater shame than if I did not capture a place such as this."

[168] After the hour of vespers, we went for a stroll outside the camp; and we sent for Don Jimeno Pérez de Tarazona and the justiciar of Aragon. Now, they were brothers; and the justiciar of Aragon was the elder in days, but the other was wiser and more resolute and able in every way, except that the justiciar of Aragon knew the *fueros* of Aragon better because he very often judged according to them. And we said: "I have sent for you for this reason, because my father made you knights and I have dignified you further; and because of my misfortune, and the bad faith of my men, I am unable to confide in anyone in the army as I am going to confide in you two. Today, in the morning, Don Ferdinand and the nobles of Aragon asked to meet with me and they came before me; and you, Don Jimeno Pérez, heard what was said. They gave many reasons to discourage me from taking Borriana, and they offered me the recompense the King of Valencia, Zaén by name, would give if I would depart from Borriana. And I believe that by the way they were offering it to me, they must be going to get a good share. And, when I heard those words, they were very hard and cruel words for me to hear, and we ordered them that they should not say them to us, as it is something that we would not do for all the world, so

---

[75]James often portrays this difference between his own objectives and those of the Aragonese nobles, who are depicted as seeing the conquest in terms of economic gain and who would prefer riches to Christian conquest.

[76]James has erased the failed siege of Peníscola from his memory.

great would be the dishonour we would receive if we raised the siege. And we could not help crying, because of the great evil that we saw they would do us, because they preferred to have the goods of the king of Valencia, than to guard our honour and the faith that they owe us. And they, seeing us crying, took to crying with us."

[169] And the justiciar said: "Well, lord, what can you do with these men who, when you wished to avoid it, have left you alone here? For they are not the sort who will not be separated from you until death."

And Don Jimeno Pérez said: "Lord, you must take a decision, since you are in the midst of false and disloyal people; and I would rather be dead, confessed and absolved, than see the great evil that I see your men are doing to you. I have here about fifteen knights, but I believe that I can retain more than one hundred in the camp who will not abandon you. Meanwhile, have your councils, as Our Lord will help you and show you how you may take Borriana."

And the justiciar said to him: "Don Jimeno Pérez, you are my brother and you speak well, but the king will not be sufficiently accompanied with a hundred or even two hundred knights, finding himself as far inside the kingdom of Valencia as he does now."[77]

After that we said to them: "Do you wish me to speak the truth? Of this you may rest assured. I would rather be wounded by an arrow, in such a way that I did not die, but might have reason to stand before the people, so that they would say that I only left because of a blow that I had received. That notwithstanding, I will tell you how it will be. In the morning I will send for the bishops and the nobles (for there were some there from Catalonia[78]), and Don Bernat Guillem, who will do all that I order him to, and the notables of the cities who are here,[79] and I will consult them upon this matter as carefully as I possibly can, that they might remain with me here until God gives me Borriana. And I believe that they will have to grant me that. And when the others see the falseness of what they advised me, and that these men will remain with me, they will not dare to go from there; and because of the shame that they feel, they will remain here. And so we will take Borriana, in spite of the devil and the evil men who advised us badly."

[170] Then we did it in that manner. We sent for the nobles and we spoke to them, just as we had planned. And when they had heard our words, first the bishops and then the nobles said that it had not been fitting advice and that

---

[77]Seventy kilometres from the Catalan frontier (*S*, p. 272).

[78]Including the bishops of Lleida and Tortosa, Guillem de Cardona, Guillem Guardia, Guillem d'Aguiló, and Guillem de Montcada (*S*, p. 272; *M*, p. 105).

[79]From Daroca and Teruel (ch. 157).

those who had advised us so had done us evil; and that, since they had come there, it would not be through any fault of theirs that they did not help me to take it, and they would act in such a way as we should understand that it would not be abandoned because of them; and that regarding the expenses, they would have to bear them, and they would help us willingly. After that, Don Bernat Guillem came to us and he said: "Lord, already you have seen what advice they gave you, in saying that you should go from this place. But you would have no need to do it for any reason if you gave me this gift. Order up to three hundred hurdles to be made by the militias, and I, with my company, will go to place them around the moat. And order your company[80] that if the Moors go out to us, they must come to our aid, as we would be poorly helped by the others. And I will be there night and day, and I will not move from there until God gives you Borriana. I will even eat there. Every so often, order your company to come to help me by night in turns, and to come to my aid."

[171] And we replied that we thanked him very much for that and that we well understood that he desired to do us this service. Then we called Don Jimeno Pérez de Tarazona and we told him what Don Bernat Guillem d'Entença had shown us and asked of us, and he said that he had spoken to us as a good and loyal vassal, for it certainly seemed that he was of our lordship; and Don Jimeno Pérez asked us if he could help him, and called on our mercy that he might be there.

And Don Bernat Guillem undertook the deed. And those men of the army who had wished for us to go from that place learnt of it and it grieved them greatly, according to what we heard said by those who spoke with them. When Don Bernat Guillem had his hurdles ready, he ordered his armed knights and squires to carry them to the place where they wished to position them, which was near the moat. And when he had prepared the mantelets which he had had made for him by a master, he was at the hurdles and he did not move from there by day or night, but ate there and did not wish to go into the camp. Moreover, Don Jimeno Pérez, with his company, did not leave his side. And we divided the companies by shifts so that they would best be able to bear the difficulty of the task.

[172] One night between the first watch and midnight, the Saracens went out against the mantelets of Bernat Guillem d'Entença, where the hurdles were, and they came with fire. And there were some two hundred of them; and the others were positioned on the walls, with two-footed crossbows prepared to fire if anybody went to his aid. And the cry went up in the camp: "To arms! To arms! The Saracens have gone out against the hurdles of Bernat Guillem!"

---

[80]The knights of the king's household.

And we heard that noise; and those men who slept in our tent around us asked us if they should saddle their horses. And we said: "No, but each of you should go to help there as fast as your legs can carry you."

And, as quickly as possible, we put on our purpoint over our shirt, not waiting for anybody to put our large tunic on us. Along with some ten men who had been sleeping in our presence, with our swords on our arms and our iron caps on our heads, we went running right to the hurdles where Don Bernat Guillem was, and we said to him: "What is happening, Don Bernat Guillem? How goes it?"

And he said: "Right and well, Lord. And you see there those Moors who tried to set fire to the hurdles, well, thanks to God, we have defended them well."

[173] Then a squire said to us: "Lord, Don Bernat Guillem has been wounded in the leg by an arrow."

And we said: "Let us send for lint from the camp, and draw the arrow out."

And we did so. And we ourselves pulled out the arrow and we put lint with water on the wound, and we had the wound bound with a piece of the shirt of a squire.[81] And when the wound was bound, we asked him to go into the camp, and said that we would take charge there, and would excuse him from any service until he was better. And he said: "Lord, I will not do it, as I will get better here as quickly or quicker than if I were in the camp."

And not one noble came to his aid, but we alone. And we recognized that he was showing great courage, so we permitted it.

[174] Meanwhile we positioned the hurdles that we had made to protect the camp, and on the left-hand side, where Don Bernat Guillem d'Entença was, we ordered two mantelets to be constructed. And as for the guard, at night, each would take their turn every five nights to guard the *fenèvol* with knights and squires on foot. We placed those mantelets there, as close to Don Bernat Guillem as we could. And one Friday, after we had eaten, our company sent word to us that they had abandoned the mantelets and that we should send a company to guard them. Then we put on our purpoint and our iron cap, and with our sword in our hand, and with nine knights who were equipped in the same fashion, we went to the hurdles, ordering a mattress and a bolster to be carried there.

While we were there, resting and with our purpoint unlaced, the Saracens saw that the camp was sleeping. Being well aware that our shield was there and

---

[81]The case is interesting for the history of medicine. Crossbows were accurate, penetrating and deadly. There were no medics on hand. It seems James personally and swiftly pulled out the arrow from the wound and then immediately sought to stem the flow of blood. Not all Medieval medical opinion would have been on his side (Burns, 'Medieval crossbow').

that we were there, they made an attack with some one hundred and seventy knights, forty of them with shields. And they had their crossbows ready on the wall and on the barbican, and they brought fire with them. There were two squires on two hurdles, who kept watch over the town, and they said: "To arms! To arms! The Saracens are here!"

We all got up at once, and we tied our iron caps on our heads. And they had brought us a sword from Monzón, called Tisó,[82] which was very good and brought good luck to those who wielded it. We preferred to carry it rather than our lance, so we gave the lance to a squire who assisted us there. And the men of the army heard the noise.

All nine of us went out, just as we were. And the Saracens left two burning torches near the hurdles that were a little ahead of us. And we placed ourselves before them there, and they retreated right up to the barbican, and we drove them back into the barbican. When we saw that we could not catch them as they were quicker than we were (because they were not armed with hauberks or purpoints, but only carried shields and lances), they went in through the barbican. Meanwhile, the other Saracens defended them by throwing stones from the wall. And when we saw that we could not do them any harm and yet might well receive it, we returned to the camp, protecting ourselves with our shields. And believe you this, in truth, that twice we uncovered our entire body to allow those inside to wound us, so that, if we had to raise the siege, it could be said that we raised it because of the wound we had received.[83] But Our Lord Jesus Christ knows how things should be done and what must be. He makes those whom He loves well always do what is best; and this is how He acted with us. He did not wish for us to receive receive harm or a wound, and we took the town, just as is written below.

[175] Later on, the tunnels were dug that went into the moat. And we had an idea: to position up to one hundred armed men, at night, before dawn, between the hurdles and the tunnels. And that, when it was dawn, all should arm themselves in the tents, quietly, without making a sound, and, when we sounded the horns, the men should go out of the mines and invade the town, going up by that tower that the *fenèvol* had destroyed, because one could easily climb up there. We sent a messenger, by night, to the bishops and the nobles to tell them what had to be done in the morning; and we said that if they kept it a close secret, the town of Borriana would be taken in the morning. And they said: "May God will it to be so! But tell us how."

---

[82]More commonly, La Tizona. The name of one of the swords of the Cid.

[83]James was ruthlessly determined to gain Borriana as he considered it the crucial step on the path to Valencia, and knew that the appearance of defeat or renewed failure would give a great boost in morale to the Moors, who were equally determined to hold it.

So we told them how we had planned it, and it seemed a very good idea to them; and they said that they would prepare their companies, and that when dawn came they would be ready. And we said: "Go in peace, and take care to prepare yourselves properly. For we will make sure things are arranged so that it can be done."

[176] When morning came they sent a message to us to say that they were ready, and that we should order them how to proceed. And we said to them: "Be at the ready, as very soon the horns will sound. And when you hear them sound, hurry to go up, and God speed."

Now I come to what happens as it began to get light. We ordered the horns to be sounded, and the men went out of the tunnels and began to climb. And the Saracens heard the horns sound and saw the army surging, so they began to shout and to sound their trumpet, as soon as they could. Thus, before our men could arrive at the top, six or seven Saracens came, who had no other weapons, but only their tunics. And there was one who rolled up his sleeves and took a great stone and threw it at the first of the climbers, and he struck him a blow but was too close to do him any harm. Even so, when he wished to climb further, they gave him five sword wounds through the legs and he was unable to do so. Meanwhile, the others threw such large stones from above that they broke all the shields, so that, no matter what our men did, they could not climb up. And because of this incursion that we had attempted, and with the *fenèvol* firing and the tunnels so very close, the Saracens inside lost their nerve.

[177] After two days they asked to negotiate; and they said that if we gave them the space of a month and the king of Valencia had not helped them, they would surrender the town. And we told them that we would not wait three days for them: "We will not say a month." And, if they did not wish to surrender, they should prepare themselves for battle, for whether they liked it or not, we would have one. After this they asked us for fifteen days. But we said that we would not give them fifteen, eight or five days. Seeing that it was so, they said that they would make this pact: if we allowed the people to leave with all the goods that they could carry, they would surrender the town. And that they would do that in five days to give enough time to prepare things, then they would go; as long as somebody guided them to Nules, and we swore that nobody would interrupt that escort until they were safe and sound in Nules. And we said we would consider the matter.

[178] And this is what we decided: that taking account of day-to-day expenses, and that it would be easier to win the kingdom of Valencia through this place than any other; and considering, moreover, that on storming the town, there might be great disputes between the Catalans and the Aragonese and the many

other foreign people who were there;[84] and, on the other hand, that there was much bread in the town which would be of benefit to those who guarded the frontier; for that, and for many other reasons, we thought it right to accept those pacts. Hence it was agreed that they should all leave from there inside four days, with what they could carry on their backs and in their hands. And in this way we took Borriana.[85] And so that people may know how many men, women, and children there were in Borriana, there were seven thousand and thirty-two.[86] And the siege lasted two months before the town was taken.

[179] When Borriana was taken, Don Pedro Cornel said to us that if we gave him a reasonable amount, so that he could stay there and could provide what was needed for the knights who stayed with him, he would remain there with one hundred knights until the summer.[87] So, the two of us calculated how much the knights would need and how much food they would need, and we agreed that we should give him sixteen thousand *morabetins*, and that he would remain there until the summer. And we told him that if he could remain there now and send for his knights, we would have money given on his behalf to whomever he wanted. But he said he could not do that because in so important a matter he needed to assemble his vassals and speak with them. And we understood that he spoke wisely.

Then we thought that we could speak with Don Blasco de Alagón and with Don Jimeno de Urrea,[88] who had knights there whom they had brought to the camp, and ask them to have them remain there two months,[89] for Don Pedro Cornel would return at the end of that time. This we did, and we entreated them most earnestly that, for love of us, they would remain for two months. They made their excuses, saying that some of the men could not do so. But we spoke with them and entreated them for such a long time, showing them that it was something that could be done and must be done, and to which they must not say no, or else, lest through the dwindling of the number of vassals, we should lose the very great gift that God had given us. Seeing how greatly we desired it, they said that they would do it, as long as we gave them what they needed for themselves and for their company. And we thanked them very much for this.

---

[84]Both an indication of the friction between the Aragonese and Catalans and the presence of troops from outside the Crown in the crusade.

[85]Between 15–22 July 1233 (*M*, p. 105).

[86]Burns (*Islam under the Crusaders*, p. 77) revises the figure to about two thousand five hundred.

[87]Presumably meaning the next summer.

[88]After the taking of Borriana, James conceded to Jimeno the castle of Alcalatèn and its appurtenanaces for services rendered (*S*, p. 277).

[89]Until mid-September 1233.

[180] After that we left our camp, borrowing from merchants all we needed to provision our army during two months, and we went to Tortosa.[90] And with us there were Berenguer, Bishop of Lleida, and Guillem de Cervera,[91] who had been lord of Juneda and then became a monk of Poblet. When we had spent one day at the castle of Tortosa, where we lodged, both of them came to us, and said that they wanted to speak with us of a great secret which would be to our profit. And Pere Sanç and Rabassa,[92] who was our notary, were present. Then the bishop of Lleida said to Guillem de Cervera: "You speak first, just as we agreed."

But he said that he would not do so, as Berenguer was a bishop and of greater worth than him, so much so that he should speak before him. "For, so great is the deed, that both of us will have cause to advise the king."

Then the bishop began to speak: "Lord, you know well the great duty we (that is I and Guillem de Cervera) owe you because you are our lord, and that we must desire our profit and your honour. Moreover, we see you have committed yourself to such a great expenditure, so great that we know you cannot meet it."

And we asked them what they were referring to. And they said: "This enterprise that you have undertaken at Borriana. Because you know, and we know it as well as you, that you have neither treasure nor great revenue, and you do not have grain in any place in the world, but are obliged to live by travelling through your land. How then do you think to meet the great expense in that place, which is two days' journey into the land of the Moors? And how do you intend to keep so many knights here, who cannot live without fighting or dying, if you cannot help them?"

And Guillem de Cervera said: "Lord, the bishop has said to you what I wished to say, and we are agreed and of the same mind. But I will say something more: that the king of Castile and you together could not hold Borriana."

[181] When we heard their words (they troubled us greatly because they were spoken by the wisest men that we had in our kingdom), we responded thus: Although we had hoped they would encourage us, instead they discouraged us.

---

[90]James was certainly at Tortosa on 22 November 1233 (*H*, 1, no. 191) but this visit is possibly between 25 July at Borriana and a stay at Barcelona in early August (*H*, 1, no. 186), before returning to Borriana in mid-August (*H*, 1, no. 189). Perhaps all these events are of 1234.

[91]Conversely, Guillem was with the king on 22 November 1233 when James made a donation to Poblet (*H*, 1, no. 191) but there is no indication he was with James in late July–early August.

[92]Both of them royal notaries and trusted advisers of the king. Rabassa has already appeared advising the king in his early years (ch. 32), and Pere Sanç was to be the ambassador James sent to Zayyān to demand the fifths of Valencia and Murcia (ch. 275).

But Our Lord helped us, because of the good that we had to do in other things still to come. And so we took little notice of their words and we rejected them. We said to them that although we believed that they spoke with the best intentions and to protect us from trouble and expense, we wished to bear and we would bear that trouble and that expense; and that this time we would try everything we possibly could to hold Borriana, since God had given it to us; and that it should not upset them if on this occasion we did not follow their advice.

[182] With that, I left them and went to Aragon.[93] And one morning while we were at Teruel, between sunrise and dawn, a messenger arrived to us from Jimeno de Urrea, who was at Borriana. Whilst we were lying on our bed, they knocked at the door; and one of our officers said that there was a messenger from Jimeno de Urrea and that he brought good news. And we said that he was welcome to enter, since he brought good news. Once he had entered, the messenger asked us to give him a gift in return for the good news. To which we said that the gift that we gave him would depend upon the news that he brought. And he said that he was happy with that. Then he told us that the Saracens of Peníscola[94] had sent two Saracens to Don Jimeno de Urrea, saying that he should send for us, as they would surrender Peníscola immediately: "And he sent me here to you with the letter that the Saracens have sent him."

We had the letter read by a Saracen who was there at Teruel and who knew how to read Arabic, and we found that the words of the letter accorded with what the messenger had said.

[183] After that, we heard our Mass of the Holy Spirit and the office of Saint Mary, so that Our Lord and His mother would guide us in this deed, and in all the others we might undertake. While we were hearing Mass, we had food prepared, and then we ate, getting on our horse immediately afterwards. With us there were only seven knights, as well as the squires who served us, and some of our officials. And we did not ask any guide to direct us, since, through the boar-hunting which we used to do in those mountains from time to time, we were confident that we would find the route.[95]

A day after we left from Teruel, we passed through the Campo de Monteagudo, and on to Villarroya, which belongs to the Hospital. Then we rose before it was day and passed through a place that was called Atorella,

---

[93]Perhaps in the last week of July or the first week of August 1233 (*S*, p. 278).

[94]Once Borriana was taken, the northern zone of the kingdom of Valencia was very difficult to defend against the Christian advance and many surrenders quickly followed. The surrender of Peníscola has a particular satisfaction for James since he had failed to take it in 1225.

[95]An important indication of the part played by hunting in giving the ruler knowledge of the lie of the land.

where there is a town now; and afterwards we crossed the River of Truites,[96] and went through the gorge of Ares, and from the Ares gorge we went to the pass of Prunelles, and to Salvasòria,[97] and to Atemí. Afterwards we crossed the plain of Sant Mateu, which was wasteland then, and came out upon the River Sec, which runs above Cervera. And when it was the hour of vespers, we were before Peníscola, on the side where the vineyards are, above the wetlands.

[184] At once we sent our messenger to the Saracens, telling them that we were there, and they were very glad. Four of them came out to us, to say that they were very happy at our arrival. They said they wished to send us a present, and that it was late then, so they would do our will in the morning. Then they went back and brought one hundred loaves of bread and two pitchers of wine, raisins, figs, and ten chickens, as a present from the town sheikhs who were there. At night, because it was a calm night, we ordered sleeping quarters to be made out of rugs and blankets that we had brought, as we had forbidden anybody to cut down the trees, since it would have greatly upset the Saracens if we had cut them down on our first visit.[98] And apart from the bread, wine, and cheese that we brought with us, we had no other food except what they had brought us.

Early in the morning, at the rising of the sun, we went, with the small company that we had with us, to the sandy plain in front of the castle, dressed in our purpoints and with our swords girt and our iron caps on our heads. When they saw us coming, the Saracens all came out towards us. All the men, women and children who were in the castle came without carrying any weapons and they greeted us.

And we said to them that Don Jimeno de Urrea had sent us a message on their behalf, to Teruel, saying that we should come, and that they would give us the castle of Peníscola, and that they would give it to nobody but us: "Now let us see your letter, which Don Jimeno de Urrea sent to us."

Then they confirmed that they had sent that message and that they would make treaties with us and surrender the castle to us. And we conceded to them the use of their law and those liberties they had been accustomed to enjoy in the time of the Saracens.[99] And they said they were ready to surrender the town and the castle to us. We told them that our notaries were not there because we

---

[96]Literally, Trout River.

[97]Bruguera suggests this is a Mozarabic term for a place in the district of Morella (*Vocabulari*, p. 96).

[98]James prided himself on his understanding of the Valencian Muslims and his considerate treatment of them.

[99]In spite of James's expressed aim of expelling the Muslims from his lands, in reality, during his reign, in the vast majority of cases, they remained, and with arrangements which could not have been too dissimilar to their situation under Muslim rule (and on occasions were better).

had come in such a hurry, but that they should write down those things that they would ask of us, and we would agree it with them; and that when we had agreed it with them, we would promise to fulfil and respect what they wrote. Then they said to us: "Lord, do you wish it to be so? For we wish it and we will trust you and give to you the castle to hold on your trust."

And they chose two Saracens, the *alfaquim* and another, and we gave them all our men so that they could go up there. The other Saracens, a good two hundred of them, were in front of us and remained with us; and we made sure that none of them could seize the reins of our horse.[100] When we saw that our men cried "Aragon!",[101] we went up, together with the Saracens.

The next day in the morning we went straight to Tortosa, with some Saracens who they delivered over to us to carry the clothes, provisions and cattle that we were to give them, just as was written in the document between us and them. And the day that we entered Tortosa we did all that was required, so that the next day we were able to return to Peníscola; and our notaries came and drew up the documents for them.

[185] When the masters of the Temple and the Hospital heard that we held Peníscola, after a few days the master of the Temple went to Xivert, and the master of the Hospital to Cervera (for our father and our grandfather had given these places to those orders).[102] And immediately they told the Saracens who lived there, that, since we held Peníscola, they should surrender the castles, as they held charters from our father and our grandfather. For, since Peníscola was the most important place that there was in that land, and it had already surrendered, there would be no dishonour or shame if they surrendered. And they surrendered the castles at once; and immediately afterwards we took Polpís.[103]

[186] Now, we had informed Don Pedro Cornel that at the end of two months we would go to Borriana. And at the end of one month we went there.[104] Some twenty-five knights came with us, and we entered the town with our falcons for hunting crane, and with Don Pedro Fernández de Azagra, who had come with us with fifteen knights. When we arrived there, those we had left there were

---

[100]James took these precautions in case any of the Saracens might be carrying concealed weapons.

[101]When the royal pennon was raised on the tower.

[102]James's grandfather, Alfonso II, had granted Xivert to the Templars in November 1169. James's great-grandfather, Ramon Berenguer IV had given Cervera to the Hospitallers in 1157, and the donation was confirmed by Alfonso II in 1171 (*S*, p. 280). Xivert appears to have surrendered to the Christians in November 1233 (Gual, 'Reconquista de la zona', pp. 435–6).

[103]Santa Magdalena de Polpis.

[104]James had certainly returned to Borriana by 17 August 1233 (*H*, 1, no. 189). He was at Vilafranca on 14 August 1233 (*M*, p. 107). If James is entirely accurate, this would place the taking of Borriana between 15–17 July 1233.

overjoyed. And while we were there, our knights carried out raids. Meanwhile, we spent all our time hunting: so that, in our house, what with boars, cranes, and partridges, we, who were some twenty knights, plus the other officials who accompanied us, were able to live on meat from the hunts. And raids were made from there, so that we were able to gain Castelló de Borriana, Borriol, les Coves de Vinromà, and Alcalatén and Vilafamés.[105]

[187] Whilst we awaited Don Pedro Cornel between Michaelmas and Christmas, we agreed to make a raid on La Ribera del Xúquer, and we had some one hundred and thirty knights of lineage, one hundred and fifty almogavars and seven hundred footmen. We marched by night from Borriana and when we arrived very near Almenara,[106] going along parallel to the sea, they made five or six beacons further down the coast. And they spotted us, and they immediately made another at the mound of the hill-range which lies between Morvedre and Puçol;[107] and they made it so that everyone could know that a great cavalcade was coming towards La Ribera del Xúquer, for that was their signal.

When we had reached the Morvedre hill-range, they began to send signals from all the towers of Valencia. Then we went by the upper pass. And as we had already been spotted, we marched as quickly as we could, flogging the mules that had been left behind by those of the vanguard and our own as well.

We passed nearby Paterna and Manises[108] to a ford that a guide knew, through which all the others had passed. When we arrived there at the plain, day broke; and it was Friday.[109] And we went to sleep at the tower of Espioca. And as we were going through Alcàsser,[110] some two hundred men of the mule-train went to the town and brought away booty in spite of the Saracens. This annoyed us, because we wanted to do battle. But we went to Espioca, and we pitched camp there, because the mules could not go further.

[188] When we had already pitched camp, a Saracen said that if we waited for Zaén until sunrise, he would meet us in battle. So we sent word to him that we would wait until sunrise and he could send word to us there if he wanted to. We awaited him until the morning, but when we saw he was not coming, we

---

[105]These were all taken during the second half of 1233 (Gual, 'Reconquista', p. 435).

[106]In the province of Castelló.

[107]Puçol is immediately to the south of the Morvedre hill-range, and is the first town of the district of L'Horta de València.

[108]Paterna in L'Horta de València to the left side of the Guadalaviar. Manises, also in L'Horta, in the far west.

[109]Perhaps 7 or 14 October 1233 (S, p. 281). However, López (*La Conquista*, p. 55) dates the following events to the second half of 1234.

[110]In the district of La Ribera del Xúquer, to the south of the district of L'Horta de València.

loaded our mules, and went to encounter our advance party at La Ribera del Xúquer. Then we went to stay at Albalat,[111] and we remained there four days.

Now, the land was so subdued that we were not able to take more than sixty Saracens between us on the entire raid. But we found much barley and many chickens. And we loaded all the mules with as much barley as they could carry. Then on we went to the bridge of Quart,[112] and in three days we returned to Borriana.[113]

[189] And while we were at Borriana, Don Pedro Cornel arrived, near to Christmas.[114] And he had brought as much as he could by way of supplies, as well as money for the other things, because there was a market there for flour, oats and wine, all of which came by sea. So we left that land and Don Pedro Cornel remained there with one hundred knights. And they began to make war on Onda, Nules, Uixó, and Almenara,[115] for they did not dare to go further into the land of the Saracens. Even so, they made good raids.

Now, a squire of his called Miguel Pérez,[116] knew Arabic, and would go at times to Almassora[117] to ransom captives from the Saracens, because many were taken there. Two Saracens said to him that if he did not give them away and they received a reward from him, they would obtain great gain for his lord. And the knight said to them that he would not give them away and that he would arrange that his lord rewarded them if they would say what the gain was to be. They said it was Almassora. The squire said that they had spoken well, and that he would go to his lord and would speak with him. So he went to Don Pedro Cornel and he told him the news, and he was very happy and satisfied with it.

[190] After that, Don Pedro Cornel arranged with the squire that he should get those Saracens, or one of them, to come, and that he would negotiate with them and would reward them well. So the squire returned there; and one of the Saracens came back on behalf of himself and the other one. And Don Pedro Cornel said that he would arrange for us to give them inheritances, and he would give them each horses and garments. But they said that it was so great a deed that they could not do it without the participation of other Saracens who

---

[111]Albalat de la Ribera de Sefort, on the left side of the river Palància.

[112]Back in L'Horta.

[113]Perhaps 13–15 October 1233 or 20–22 October 1233 (*S*, p. 282) but it is possible that James has made one of his habitual leaps and the events are of 1234.

[114]If the events are of 1233, he had arrived by 16 November 1233 (*M*, pp. 107–9; *S*, p. 281).

[115]All towns of the district of La Plana de Castelló.

[116]Possibly the same who later leads raids against the Muslims in Valencia contrary to James's wishes (ch. 554).

[117]Another town of the district of La Plana de Castelló. Linguistic skills were required or at least preferred for those who undertook ransoming.

were their friends and relations. So Don Pedro Cornel said: "What are you asking me to do for them?"

The Saracen said that he would have to give them inheritances and allow them to remain in that land. And Don Pedro Cornel said that he would arrange for us to do that, and he had a charter drawn up for them there. And between them they decided the night on which they would surrender it.

Don Pedro Cornel was there in an ambush, with his armoured horses, a good half-mile away. And one of the Saracens came outside and said to them that they should send twenty good knights, and others, and that he would put them into two towers, and that the rest should come when they let out a cry or when they made a signal by fire.

[191] Thus, some twenty armed squires went there, with purpoints, hauberks, iron caps, and swords that they carried, but they did not carry lances, because they could not have wielded them in the towers they were in. They entered inside; but, as they were entering, they were pushed into a building. And inside the house there were some thirty Saracens who immediately seized them and bound them. Three of the squires realized that they had been betrayed, so they drew their swords and went up a staircase, which went out into a tower. And the Saracens went after them but they could not catch them. Our men went up to the tower and they defended it well; and they began to cry for help. And the men of the ambush heard them and went there; and the Saracens of the town of Almassora fought them closely.

Meanwhile, the full force of knights and the men of the ambush arrived there; and on arriving they found a beam[118] which the Saracens had cut down to use for an *algarrada*, but they had not finished preparing it. And they crossed the moat and placed the beam at the side of the tower, and they climbed up there with leather belts that those who were above had lowered to them, in such a way that the Saracens could not prevent it. When the Saracens saw that, they left the town, and many fled from there, with all their goods and provisions. And so Almassora was taken.

[192] Later we returned to Borriana. And after we had been there two months, we went back to Aragon and Catalonia. And later on, in the summer, we went to Borriana.[119] And our uncle Don Ferdinand was there with us, together with the bishop of Lleida, Don Blasco de Alagón, Don Pedro Cornel, Don Jimeno de Urrea, Hug de Montllor, master of the Temple, and Hugh de Forcalquier, master of the Hospital.

It was decided that we should make a raid on Alzira and Cullera. As we had already seen Cullera, we had decided that we should secretly bring two

---

[118]The rotating-beam of a *trebuchet* (Chevedden, 'Artillery', pp. 64–5).
[119]June 1235.

*fenèvol*s that we had at Borriana, so that nobody would know about it. So, if the army were to need a *fenèvol*, they would find them prepared and would not need to send for them; and we had them placed secretly on a ship.

When we arrived at Cullera, we pitched camp above it, just before the town, between the Xúquer and the castle of Cullera. And all the Saracens from the farms were down there, with all their cows, asses and goats. And that entire slope that went down from the castle to the tower below (where they took water) was full of Saracen men, women, children, and cattle.[120]

[193] When the men of the army saw that, the majority said: "Mother of God! If only we had a *fenèvol*! We could kill them all from the top of the hill, and capture them in three days."

When vespers came,[121] the bishop of Lleida, Don Ferdinand, and the nobles came to our tent to see us and relax with us. Then they drew me to one side, and made all the people go out, and they said to us: "Lord, what do you think about this place?"

We said: "If God helps me, I think it will be easy to take, if there was anyone here who would do it!"

Then they said: "There will certainly be those who will do this with you, as one, if means there were."

And we said: "What do you need?"

And they said: "We will need a *fenèvol*."

And we said: "And you believe that we could take it, if we had a *fenèvol*?"

And they said: "It could be done."

Then we said: "We will give you two."

And they said: "Where do you have them?"

And we said: "You can see them here, at the river's mouth, for they are on a ship."[122]

Then they said: "It seems you guessed what would be required."

And we said: "Better the man who guesses beforehand than he who has to find out afterwards."

And they said: "Now tell us how you think we should proceed."

And we said: "We must go to see where we can position the war machines. We shall go with thirty knights of our company and we will go up there. Give us one knight of your company and we will work out where we can position the machines."

Then they said: "You have spoken very well indeed."

---

[120]As was customary during sieges, the people from Cullera and the farm lands sought protection at the castle.

[121]23 June 1235.

[122]Their view had presumably been impeded by the mountain and the castle.

[194] When it was morning, at sunrise, we heard our Mass, and we immediately sent for Don Pedro Cornel and Don Rodrigo Lizana. Once we had assembled some thirty knights we went up the hill above the sea; and when we were at that place where there had once been two towers, just above the castle, we left the horses and we took our weapons, and we went down towards the castle, by the downward slope below us. And we were so near the castle that the crossbowmen could hit it easily. From there we examined the place, and we found it to be right for the two *fenèvols*.

When we had seen and examined the place, we went down and we sent for them. We went to the tent of the Bishop of Lleida, Berenguer, to see him and to hold our council there. And it was Saint John's day.[123] We said to them that the thing could be done, and that we could fire from there, and whenever a stone missed the castle and did not hit there, it would strike on the side where we were, which was entirely full of women, children, and cattle.

When they saw that the thing could be done, the majority of them then asked what they would do about stone for the machines, as at La Ribera del Xúquer there was none at all; and they spoke the truth. So we said to them: "We know of three solutions, so let us see if we can have stone from this place. One is to send for it from the River Sec; yet each time one hundred armed knights with armoured horses, and five hundred footmen, would have to travel there. Another would be to send for it down there to the river of Bairén, but, even so, a great company would be needed, so that if the Saracens wished to prevent the stones being loaded on to the vessel, they could not do it. Whilst another solution would be to have stonecutters cut the stones from the mountains, and to prepare them as is done with *brigoles* and *trebuchets*."

[195] Then they said to Don Ferdinand that he should speak. And he said: "Lord, we will have to consider this. Do not let that upset you, for we will return here before you immediately."

So they deliberated, and when they returned to our presence, Don Ferdinand explained, on behalf of all the others, what they had agreed. And he said: "Lord, in this matter of which you speak, we see a great difficulty, for reasons we will now explain. Because it would not be fitting for you to begin an enterprise and not complete it, and in the entire army there is not food for five days. Moreover, Valencia is not yours but rather is held by the Saracens.[124] So that if a bad sea were to come and your vessels could not bring the provisions here or did not bring them, you would have to leave here. And to take stone from so far away and so far into the land of the Saracens would not be easy to

---

[123]24 June 1235.

[124]On this occasion, James allows his uncle Ferdinand to say something useful. Since Cullera is 38 kilometres to the south of Valencia, given the lack of men and provisions, James could have been left in a perilous situation, harried by Zayyān as he beat his retreat.

do. As for the stonecutters, there is not a single one in the entire camp, nor would you find so many at Borriana that they could cut as much stone as the machines would need to throw, and you still do not hold any other place in this kingdom."

As we saw that they were all of the same mind, we had to abandon it; and we acknowledged that what they had said was true.

[196] When we had left there, the next day[125] we went to Silla,[126] and we pitched camp there because it was easy to find wood and good pasture there. After we had slept, at the sixth hour[127] we sent for the master of the Hospital, Don Pedro Cornel, and Don Jimeno de Urrea, and we spoke with them in secret, as there was nobody there but them and us; and we said to them: "We have sent for you because we think that we are leaving this land shamefully, for if with an army as large as this one we do not bring out more than twenty or thirty captives, the Saracens (and the Christians, too) will hold us in low esteem. Yet if you help me, I will show you how we can undertake a good deed; for, if I am alone when I make you a proposal, and you are all against me, I cannot accomplish it. So then, when I finish my proposal and Don Ferdinand has spoken, do not wait for the others to speak, but each of you say that you consider what I have said to be a good idea. For I shall show you how we can achieve great and honourable gain. The towers of Valencia over there are like the eye of a man, because those towers protect Valencia from receiving harm each of the many times when it could receive it. One of those is the tower of Montcada,[128] which is the best tower in the whole huerta of Valencia.[129] And when we advanced towards it, only the men-at-arms were left in there, because all the women and children went into Valencia. Already you have seen, then, how they left the farmlands when we approached; yet as we did not attack them on our arrival, they will not fear that we will attack them on departing; and the women and children will have returned there. Thus, we will be able to force its surrender within the space of eight days, and besides the people there, we would certainly obtain much there by way of booty and provisions. And I will advise you upon the way to capture it."

[197] "I will go to Borriana, and I will give rations to the entire army for eight days, if only the army will give me one hundred captives of my choice when it has taken the tower. For I believe I will capture a thousand or more there. And I will bring you a *fenèvol*. To do this, I will not require more than the day I

[125]25 June 1233.
[126]A town of the district of La Ribera.
[127]Midday.
[128]So-called because it was given by James to Pere de Montcada, VI seneschal (*S*, p. 286).
[129]Referring both to the area of L'Horta de València, and the fertility of the 'garden' of Valencia, which is one of the most fertile agricultural regions in the Peninsula.

depart and the next day, to get the rations; and on the third day I will return to you with the provisions and with the *fenèvol*. So that when we do go from here, you and we will depart with honour; and afterwards, when we return another time, they will not dare to await us at the towers of Valencia."

After that, the master of the Hospital, Hugh de Forcalquier, said: "God help me! Our lord the king has chosen a good path. Let us help him; for let me tell you that I will help him as much as I can."

When Don Pedro Cornel and Don Jimeno de Urrea heard that, they said that it seemed a good idea to them, and that it was good and noble counsel. But they asked how it could be done, since Don Ferdinand and some of the others would be against it. And we said: "With the power that we have and with the help that you will give us, our will shall be done."

Then we sent word to the others that they should come, since we wished to speak with them.

[198] Thus we sent for Don Ferdinand, Don Rodrigo Lizana, Hug de Montllor, Master of the Temple, the bishop of Lleida, the other nobles of Aragon and Catalonia, and some other good and honourable knights who were there and who understood deeds of arms. And we sent away those who had been with us, so that the others did not know that we had spoken with them; and they returned afterwards, when the others arrived. Then we assembled our council, arranging them all around the tent, and we said to them: "Barons, we have come here to do harm to the Saracens; and if we go from this land now, with so great an army, having done no more harm than taking sixty male and female Saracen captives, you and we will not depart with honour. Yet it seems to me that we can achieve a good capture and do a great deal of harm to Valencia. And, by God, we cannot fail in it."

Then they asked what it was. And we said the tower of Montcada: "And it is a very fine tower, and there are great riches there, and it is at the side of the city, and there is none better there, except the tower of Quart."[130]

And if we had to, we said that we could send for what was needed from Borriana, in such a way that those of Valencia could not prevent it, because we would be between Valencia and Borriana. "So let us go tomorrow to besiege it in the name of God. For we will capture it, and achieve great gain and honour in taking a tower such as that, a mere league from Valencia. Let me know what you think, as it seems a good enterprise."

[199] All said that Don Ferdinand should speak first. And Don Ferdinand said: "I think that it would definitely be a good thing to do, if it could be achieved;

---

[130]The tower of Quart, in the town of that name in the Pla de Quart.

but there are no provisions in the camp, and without provisions the people could not bear or endure it."

Then we said: "And if someone gives you the provisions, would you be happy to do it? Let us have the nobles and the masters who are here give their opinion; for, as far as I am concerned, I will agree to what the others agree."

And the master of the Hospital said to the master of the Temple that he should speak. So the master of the Temple said: "I say to you, for myself, that the plan is a good one, so long as the army has enough to eat. But, for myself, it seems to me that that place of the tower of Montcada is rather near to the Turks of Valencia."[131]

And we said: "Master, there are no Turks in this land!"

Then he said: "But I think it would be better for you to take Torres Torres,[132] which is a good place, and is on the road from Teruel to Valencia."

And we said to him: "Master, Torres Torres is a good place; but this place is worth seven times more than Torres Torres, and it will be of greater honour to us if we can take a place such as this, near to Valencia. And this place can be taken more easily, as Torres Torres is a stronger place than this, but this place is worth more in terms of *honors* and gain."

Then the master of the Hospital said: "I consider that the king has spoken well; and since he has the will to win this land, let him not be prevented from doing so because of us, and let us help him to gain it."

Don Jimeno de Urrea said: "Lord, I consider what you have said to be good, provided that you give us what we need to sustain ourselves until you have taken it. For, in my view, I think that you can do it."

And Don Pedro Cornel said: "I suscribe to the words that the master and Don Jimeno de Urrea have responded to you."

Then we told the bishop of Lleida that he should speak, and he said: "You understand affairs of arms, and I have come here to serve God and you; so, whatever you would do, I will do."

And we said to Don Rodrigo Lizana that he should speak, and he said: "Lord, this is what you want, and I see that all or the larger part wish it and advise it; so I will do what you wish, but you already know how the Moors defend their fortresses, and it would not be fitting for you to begin something and not to finish it."

[200] Then we replied to Don Rodrigo Lizana and to the others: "We will tell you how we will do it. We will go and pitch camp near the tower, and when the

---

[131]The master of the Templars is from the Midi and here in the Catalan text, as elsewhere, James indicates he is speaking in the language of his region. Being more accustomed to battles in the Holy Land he refers to the Valencian Muslims as Turks. There are various gentle plays on words here in the Catalan with torre, turchs, Torres Torres, terra, and Terol.

[132]A town to the right of the River Palància, 40 kilometres from Valencia.

next day comes, in the early morning, we will attack the town. And they will defend it. And in defending, as they struggle to hold the stockades, our men will break them. And once they enter they can cause great harm to the Moors, because the ones who defend there will probably be better than the others, and those who have remained at the tower and the *albacar* will be worthless. Then we will proceed according to how we see the battle going. Thus, if you and we believe that we can take it, we will go to Borriana, with only fifteen knights, as it is a good idea not to break up the company. And on the third day we will return here with the *almajanech* and with rations for eight days."

They all said that it seemed a good idea, since we had said it was so; but on this condition: that they would give us one hundred captives, as more than one thousand would be taken there; and that they would give us those whom we chose, to cover the expenses we would have made in taking the tower. They recognized that what we had said was fair, and they agreed to it.

[201] When the morning came, and we had heard the Masses, the squires and a large part of the knights started to arm themselves; and they began on the common outside the town, and began to enter the town on foot. The best of the Moors were all at the stockades; and, on our entry, seven or eight Moors died. And our men pursued them so that they could not take refuge in the *albacar* or the tower.

When we were near the *albacar*, we saw that the Saracens were defending poorly and were in disarray; so we called the masters and some of the nobles, and we said to them: "Do you think that I should go to Borriana, since these men can easily be taken?"

And they said that they thought it a good idea. And we said: "Now, order your men to send all the mules they have, and they will return with us, laden with all you need."

And we took only twelve knights with us.

When we arrived near Morvedre,[133] we awaited the mules and we unfurled our banner; and all together we went down to the sea, and we went to Borriana along the shore. And it was probably about the hour of vespers when we entered Borriana. Before eating, we obtained wheat, wine, barley, and mutton, according to the amount each of the nobles, the master and the bishop had indicated to us in writing that they would need as rations.

[202] Then, the next day at sunrise, we ordered the rations to be given to us, and everything was collected that day. And the next day[134] we left Borriana, in battle formation and with our armoured horses (of which there were twelve to fifteen). We passed in front of Morvedre, with our *fenèvol*, and by the hour of

---

[133]26 June 1235.
[134]28 June 1235.

vespers we had returned to the tower of Montcada; so that at night, before the stars were in the sky,[135] we had the *fenèvol* set up by the side of a house, and by night we attached the ropes, so that the next day at half-terce[136] we could begin to pull it.

And the throng of women, children, cows, and other cattle inside of the *albacar* of the tower was so great, that the stones which the *fenèvol* fired (and it fired day and night without ceasing) killed the cattle. And the stench produced by the dead cattle was so strong that on the fifth day they surrendered the tower,[137] and themselves as captives. Now, one thousand one hundred and forty-seven Saracens came out from there. And many fine goods, and pearls, necklaces, and gold and silver bracelets, and many silk cloths and many other clothes, were taken, so that with the Saracens and what they had there together, the booty easily amounted to one hundred thousand *bezants*.

With us we had Saracens who were from Valencia, and they chose one hundred of the others for us from there, as had been agreed. And one of the Saracens who had come was at our side and indicated to us which ones we should take.

[203] Then we decided to demolish the tower and to stay there for two days[138] to demolish it; and after that, when we left there, we would go to the tower of Museros[139] and we would take it with the *fenèvol* and with battle, if they expected it. So we demolished the tower of Montcada, and afterwards we went to Museros and we besieged the tower. When we began to set up our *fenèvol*, we knew for certain, from a Saracen of the tower, who had been captured by an *almogàver*, that Zaén had ordered them that no more than sixty should remain there to defend the tower, and that the women, children, and others had entered Valencia. The next day the *fenèvol* began to fire, and it damaged three or four of the merlons of the tower; and they, at night, placed baskets full of earth there, so that if the stones struck, they would do no damage to the roof of the tower. Then we ordered arrows to be made in the form of spindles, and inside we put tow lit with fire; and the crossbowmen fired them at the baskets full of earth and they began to burn. And when the third day came, and the Saracens inside saw that their strategy was not good enough, they began to negotiate, saying that they would surrender if their lives were preserved; and we agreed to that, because we thought they were worth more alive than dead.

---

[135]Cf. ch. 67.
[136]At nine o'clock in the morning, 29 June 1235.
[137]3 July 1235.
[138]4–5 July 1235.
[139]Museros is 11 kilometres from Valencia and near to the tower of Montcada.

[204] When we had taken them, Guillem Saguàrdia,[140] who was the uncle of Guillem d'Aguiló, a captive in Valencia, asked us very humbly that, as his nephew was a captive, we should hand over those sixty Saracens of Museros, as he believed that he would be able to exchange them for Guillem d'Aguiló.[141] We said to him that we would give them, if the nobles agreed, but with the promise that if he could not exchange him, the army would recover the captives. And he kissed our hand and was overjoyed. Then he sent word, through a Christian who could enter Valencia safely, to ask if they would give Guillem d'Aguiló in exchange for those sixty captives of Museros. And they conceded that to him and returned Guillem d'Aguiló in exchange for those sixty captives from Museros.

[205] Having done that, we went to pitch camp at Torres Torres. And before we had passed Albentosa,[142] they gave us seventeen thousand bezants for the hundred Moors that we brought. And we would have got thirty thousand bezants had we kept them a month longer; but we had to give them up for such a small amount because the merchants were pressing us for the money we had borrowed from them to provide for the needs of the army.[143] So we paid that debt and others, and then we went to Zaragoza, and then on to Huesca.[144]

---

[140]Guillem was with the king at Borriana in late 1234/early 1235, having previously participated in the siege there (*S*, p. 289).

[141]He had also taken part in the siege of Borriana, and was still free on 10 January 1235, when he was at Tarragona with his uncle. He must have fallen into the hands of the Saracens between then and July 1235 (*S*, p. 289). He was one of the principal defenders of the Puig (chs. 219–35) but he later fell out of favour with the king when he attacked the Muslims of Valencia in James's absence and against his wishes (chs. 295, 306).

[142]In Teruel.

[143]ch. 180.

[144]There is a leap here either to 1236 or even to early 1237.

4

Valencia – The Capture of the City

[206] While we were in Huesca, we went through our land towards Sarinyena, for we had decided to take the castle which the Saracens called Enesa and the Christians Puig de Cebolla, and which now has the name Puig de Santa Maria. We considered which noble of our land we could leave there when we had taken it. As we considered that men cannot gain in honour or worth without good works, we decided we had to entrust a place such as that, once it was taken, to somebody who loved us greatly and in whom we trusted.

Thus, because Don Bernat Guillem d'Entença was our uncle on our mother's side, and because the goods that he possessed, he possessed in our name, we thought it better to entrust it to him than to any other, whensoever God allowed us to take that place. So, as we were going along the road, we called him and drew aside with him from the road, and we said to him: "Don Bernat Guillem, you are a man whom we love and we trust, and you are very closely related to me, and I would like you to prosper and to give you the occasion to do us such a service that, because of the good that we do you, everybody will know that we have done a good thing in conceding it to you. Now, we have thought of something in which you can greatly serve us, and for which we would be obliged to do great good to you in return for the service that you would have done for us."

Then he thanked us very much for that, and he kissed our hand because of the mercy we had promised him, and asked us to tell him what the service would be. And we told him that it was our will to go and besiege Puig de Cebolla, which lies nearly two leagues distance from Valencia; and that, when we had taken it, we would place him there with one hundred knights on that frontier.

We explained to him that the castle was located on a hill, and it was good and strong and well constructed; and that we would give him provisions for a year, and that all through the winter[1] he would have to maintain the frontier there; and that when the summer came we would go there and we would devastate Valencia, and with the damage that they would receive from our raids and with the devastation we would do them, we should have ripened it just as one would with a fruit that one wishes to eat. And when we saw that it

---

[1]Winter 1237–8.

was the hour to besiege València and that the city was in a grievous situation through lack of provisions, we would summon all our nobles and townsmen: "Come to help us besiege València and, with the will of God, Who will help us, we shall take it. And when València is taken, that entire kingdom shall be conquered down to Xàtiva."

[207] When he had heard our idea, he did not speak or respond, and he hesitated for a long time. And when we saw that he had doubts about the words that we had spoken, we said to him: "Don Bernat Guillem, do not doubt, as this plan which we have revealed to you is a very good one. Keep it a secret, so that nobody knows about it until we have done what is necessary to arrange the deed; but accept what I tell you, as it should please you greatly, because one of two things will certainly happen: if God allows you to fulfil this service which we have ordered you to do, I will make you the most honoured man in my kingdom, and if you die in God's service and ours, you shall certainly obtain paradise. And for these two reasons you should not have any doubts in this matter."

Then he came to us and kissed our hand, and said that he would take the gift that we granted him since we had given him good counsel, for he could not come to any harm through either of the two things of which we had spoken.

[208] Meanwhile, together we agreed with him that we should summon our army for Easter; and we sent for it from the nobles, the cities, and the towns. And later on, at the beginning of Lent,[2] some men who came from València told me for certain that the castle of Puig had been dismantled. When we heard that, we were very upset; but in spite of the sadness that we felt, we said that it did not bother us, because we would build another castle there when we went there with the army. And for that purpose we ordered twenty moulds for walls to be made at Teruel, secretly, so that nobody knew about it.

Now, we were at Teruel on Easter Sunday.[3] Before our army arrived, we started on the road, and Don Jimeno de Urrea, our household, Don Pedro Fernández de Azagra and the militias of Daroca and Teruel came with us. And when we were leaving Teruel, on the road we were on, the men of the army saw the laden beasts which carried the walls (as none of the army knew our secret, or where we were going or not going).

When we were before Xèrica, and were laying waste to it, Don Pedro Fernández de Azagra and Don Jimeno de Urrea came before us, after we had eaten, and they said to us: "Lord, what is this that they tell us? You are carrying walls?"

---

[2]Early March 1237.
[3]19 April 1237.

But we said that we would not respond to them in front of everybody; but if the others left, we would speak with them and we would tell them what was and what was not going on.

[209] When the others had gone from there, we said to them: "We have done this thing very secretly, and I ask you and I order you that you will keep the secret until people may see why we are doing it and why not. For I have had them made because I wish to settle the hill that is now called Enesa and which will have the name Puig de Santa Maria. They have pulled down the castle that was there,[4] and I wish to rebuild it; and when we have rebuilt it, we will position our frontier there, good and strong; and from there we will wage so great a war upon them that Valencia will find itself so starved of provisions that we can besiege it and we can take it."

Then they said: "You should certainly have made that known to us, so that we might be better prepared with provisions and other things which we now do not have."

And we knew from their faces that they were not happy about it, and from their words that they were not fully behind it. So we said to them: "Barons, be glad of what we have done and what we shall do; as in this way Valencia shall be conquered better than in any other way in the world."

[210] With that, the next day we went to Torres Torres, and, on the third day, after we had laid waste to it, we left Torres Torres. Then we went through Morvedre, over a hill there is there, and near to the castle, no more than three or four crossbow shots away. We gave the vanguard to Don Jimeno de Urrea, and the foot soldiers were between us and him, and we had the rearguard. When we arrived down there on the plain, having gone past Morvedre, Don Jimeno de Urrea sent us a message letting us know that we would have to go into battle, since Zaén was at Puçol, with his entire force, and that we should be very glad about it. We said to him that it pleased us very much that that was so.

The men of the mule-trains, and those who went in the middle, all fled to the hill, except some brave men who stayed. These were the master of the Hospital, the commander of Alcañiz,[5] and the men of Alcañiz and of Castellote; so that we were a good two thousand footmen and a hundred horsemen, with the men of Borriana and some thirty armoured horses.

And we had already sent runners to Valencia, and they were to lie in ambush, so that if Zaén, King of Valencia, came out, they could fight him. But Zaén did not come out.

---

[4]Since Zayyān felt he could not feasibly defend El Puig, it was abandoned and destroyed in order that the Christians did not have a strong military base for their attack on Valencia.

[5]Of the order of Calatrava.

[211] When we heard that they were our men we were very glad. And we went to the hill and we pitched our tent on the plain below the town; and we camped, happy and satisfied, with those who had come from the watch and with our men. Then, after a few days, those of our nobles who had not yet come began to arrive, along with the militias of Zaragoza, Daroca, and Teruel. When they had arrived, we assigned to each one, according to the people that they had, a fair share of the work, so that they would do it; and if they could finish it in fifteen days or in three weeks, then they could go on their way, as long as they had done good work. And the building work lasted two months.[6]

[212] While we were here, raids were made; and so great was the grace of God when that place was settled, that nobody ever went on a raid against the Saracens to do them harm without returning to the camp with either a little or great gain. Indeed, so well were they guided by Our Lord, that not one raid that went from here was defeated by the Saracens. And for the vessels which arrived by sea, we ordered a roadway to be built near that hill, which was next to it, so that people could cross to the sea when the ships came, to get what was necessary for the army, and to bring the provisions from the sea.

[213] When we had been here three months waiting for Don Bernat Guillem d'Entença (for he was supposed to come to take over that place, and we did not wish to leave until he had arrived), two knights came with a message from him that he was at Borriana. Now, we had not been in good health, yet they asked us on his behalf to go to Borriana. But, when we heard the entreaties that they made us, we thought to ourselves that he had not prepared everything that he needed, and we said to them: "What does Don Bernat Guillem want with us in Borriana? We will be more useful here than in Borriana."

And they said: "All the same, we beseech you to go there."

And we responded to them: "We would go there willingly, but we have been ill, and now it is July,[7] and if we expose ourselves to the heat, we fear that the illness will worsen. Tell him to come in peace, since he will better be able to speak with us here than he can do there."

After that they left, and he arrived the next day. When we knew that he was coming, we went outside towards him to receive him and the hundred knights or so who came with him. On encountering us, he kissed our hand, and we greeted him. And after we had greeted him we asked him how things were coming along, and he said that they were coming along well. Then we said: "We can well see how things are going, as you go in good company, but what about the provisions?"

---

[6]Until late June 1237.

[7]Bernat had arrived by 9 July 1237 (*S*, p. 292), James having been there since the last third of April.

When we had said that, he said to us: "Let us enter inside, and I will speak with you."

Now, when he said that, and did not reply to us on the road immediately, we surmised that things were not going well. And he said to us that there were still forty knights yet to come. As soon as we realized that he had brought more knights than we had ordered him to do, we thought that he had spent on the knights what we had given him for the supplies.

[214] After these words, we went inside and he ate. And when he had eaten and we had slept, we sent a message to him telling him to come to see us. And he came and said that he wished to speak with us in private, and that nobody should be there. So we withdrew to one side, so that nobody was there, and he said to us: "I did not want to speak about this matter of the provisions, when you asked me, because I have spent the greater part of what you gave me for the supplies on the knights."

"How is that?" we said, "You have not brought supplies to Borriana by sea or by land? Because we have none here, rather on the contrary, the nobles who are here press me because of the time I have remained here. We have nothing to eat, and you have not brought anything! It's a mean trick you have played on us!"

Then he said: "I do have three hundred *cafizes* of Aragonese measure, at Tortosa, and fifty pigs, but I have pledged them for one thousand five hundred sous."

And we said to him: "For God's sake, Don Bernat Guillem, you have played a mean trick both on me and on yourself! For I trusted you and did not prepare myself for this, and now you cannot help me, nor I you. And the situation is so dire, that the knights who are here with me will not remain here if they have nothing to eat, and neither will your knights. And you should know, for certain, that if you were not so closely related to me and I did not love you so much, I do not know any man in the world on whom I would not avenge myself more for what you have done to me. For if this place cannot be held, Valencia is lost, now and perhaps forever after, since we will never again have so good an opportunity."

Then we said to him: "Go away, and think hard on this tonight, and we will pray to Our Lord to give us good counsel, as you have given us downright useless counsel."

And he left us.

[215] When morning came we had already considered what we should do, and we said to him: "I see no other solution but this: I will go to Borriana, if you give me all the mules that you have here. And if I find food there, I will send you all that I find to last for fifteen days, saving what the men who are there

will need just to be able to eat. From there I will go to Tortosa, and I will send you provisions for two months."

Thus, we went to Borriana. And when the moment had arrived when we wished to raise camp, a swallow had made her nest on the pole of our tent; and we ordered our men not to take down the tent until she and her little ones had gone, since she had trusted us.[8] They sent us the mules, and we loaded them with bread, wine, and barley; and we bought sheep in the camp, and cows and goats, which had been taken in raids. And there and then we gave them meat rations for one month. Then we left Borriana for Tortosa, entering there two days later. There we ordered four vessels to be loaded with enough wheat, wine, barley, and salted meat for two months, and we sent it to them. And when we had left there, we went to Tarragona.

[216] As we entered Tarragona by the road from Vila-seca, we saw, in the morning, the masts of many vessels at Salou. And we remained there all that day. When it was night, around the time dawn broke, Fernando Pérez de Pina was sleeping in our presence, and we said to him: "Don Fernando Pérez, are you asleep?"

And he said: "No, lord."

Then we said to him: "We have been thinking about something: as we believe we have found a solution to the Puig problem. Yesterday, when we passed Vila-seca, we saw the masts of vessels at Salou, and we believe they are taking supplies to Majorca. Get up at once, and I will give you two officers to go with you. Then take possession of everything, and tell the lords of the ships to come to my presence. And before you leave there, find out what is and is not there, and note it all down; and bring me the rudders and the sails."

It was done just as we instructed, and they brought the owners of the vessels to us and, in a document, all that the vessels contained. And we found that we could give Don Bernat Guillem d'Entença, who had remained at Puig, three months supply of flour, wine for six months, and that there was salted meat and barley for two months. Then we drew up a document for the merchants for what we would pay them. And we went to Lleida,[9] where we borrowed sixty thousand sous from the notables, and then we paid the merchants. What was left over we sent by river, to complement the rations of flour and wine. And from there we went to Huesca.

---

[8]'Far from demonstrating his sentimentality…this charming vignette showed that victory on the battlefield was ultimately to be subordinated to a set of chivalric and royal certitudes which put protection of the weak above defeat of the strong' (Kagay, 'The Line between Memoir', p. 173).

[9]August 1237.

[217] While we were at Huesca, a message arrived for us, with a knight called Guillem de Salas, who was a native of the region of Huesca, and who came on behalf of Don Bernat Guillem d'Entença and Don Berenguer d'Entença and all the company we had left at Puig. He greeted us on their behalf, and his face was wounded and he wore a bandage with lint. Then he asked for a reward for good news, and we said that we would give him a reward according to the news that he brought. And he said: "The news is such that it will please you and you will be happy."

And he said: "Here you have letters from the nobles and knights whom you left at Salou."

The letters said that Zaén, with all his forces from Xàtiva to Onda,[10] (which comprised some six hundred knights and some eleven thousand footmen[11]), had gone one day, early in the morning at sunrise, to attack the Puig. Yet ten horsemen who had gone to make a raid in Valencia, had returned to Puig and had informed Don Bernat Guillem d'Entença and Don Berenguer that Zaén was coming with his entire army. Then, when they had heard their Mass, and those who had not already received it had received the Body of Jesus Christ, they all went outside of Puig, armed, since they said that if they shut themselves in, it would be worse for them, for they would be more quickly captured there than if they were outside. Then they commended themselves to Our Lord and determined to wage a battle with them.[12]

[218] Meanwhile, the Saracens came and positioned the foot soldiers of the frontier of Xèrica, Sogorb, Llíria, and Onda as the vanguard, placing those who knew most about fighting at the front; and the knights, with the rest of the infantry, went behind. In such a way that, with the first attacks that they made, they had to defeat our men. But afterwards our men returned another time down the slope and recovered the part of the field they had lost. Then the Saracens began to shout out and recovered that place again, and the Christians retreated to the side of the castle. But as they retreated, a shout reached them from high up in the castle from those who were watching: "They're running away! They're running away, for they are defeated!"

And our knights heard it and shouted out: "For shame, knights, for shame!"

Then all cried out with one voice: "Santa Maria! Santa Maria!"

---

[10]In the province of Castelló.

[11]The number of Zayyān's forces seems much exaggerated. It is unlikely it would have been possible to rebuild and defend El Puig if Zayyān had such forces available, nor would the troops of Bernat have gone out to do battle against such superior numbers. Though the figures are here exaggerated, the importance of the action is not, since even in James's absence Zayyān was unable to oust the Christians from their operational base. After the battle of El Puig the writing must have seemed on the wall for Valencia City.

[12]Desclot (ch. 49) gives a slightly more detailed but not dissimilar description of this battle.

The Saracens who were in the rearguard and who had crowded in upon the others, then began to flee prior to those who were in front; and our men attacked the vanguard of the Saracens, and broke them. At that moment the battle began to be won. And the pursuit lasted as far as the River Sec, which is between Foios and Valencia.

There were many who died there from sword wounds, and others without receiving a blow.[13] And of our men there died there Ruy Ximénez de Luesia, who went in so deep in the first attacks that nobody saw him again until they found him dead; and his eldest son, Don Jimeno Pérez de Terga, as well as another who carried the standard of Don Bernat Guillem.[14] And there were other knights who were wounded, but they did not die.

[219] When the men of Teruel heard that the Christians had won the battle, but that many knights[15] had been lost there, some seventy or eighty of them went to Puig, and on the second day, at terce, they were with them.

When we heard the news, at Huesca, we made it known to the Orders, and we went to the cathedral. There before Jesus of Nazareth, with the bishop[16] and the canons, we had everyone sing the *Te Deum Laudamus*. Then at once we went to Daroca and we sent a message to the nobles that they should come to our presence. And while we were at Daroca we sent for the headmen of the villages and we assembled the good men of the towns, and we asked them and we ordered them that, without fail, they should have one thousand mules prepared in the space of five days, at Teruel. They said that since God had guided us so well and we wished it, they would do this.

Then we left for Teruel, and from there we sent messages to the villages, and they came as well; and we ordered them that within the space of three days they should have one thousand mules prepared, because we wished to carry provisions to Puig. They said that they would do this, and that they would do everything that we ordered, but that there were already a good eighty horsemen from Teruel there, and that we would find them there. Then we asked Fernando Díaz to lend us wheat to load onto those two thousand mules, and he said that

---

[13]Desclot (ch. 49) also reports this, putting the number at ten thousand who died from fear and panic during the flight. *The Chronicle of San Juan de la Peña* (ch. 35) speaks of the intervention of Saint George who turned up with many celestial knights so that not a single Christian was lost in the battle.

[14]Desclot (ch. 49) also puts the figure at three knights, but adds seven footmen. He reports that there was great rejoicing since for every Christian killed, one thousand Saracens had been killed.

[15]The Catalan text should perhaps read horses (cavalls) rather than knights (cavallers) here since James has just said only three knights were lost, while here in ch. 219 it says that eighty-six horses had been lost in the battle.

[16]Vidal de Canyelles, lawyer and bishop of Huesca (1238–52). Educated at the cathedral in Barcelona and at Bologna, he compiled the revised *fuero* of Jaca (the Huesca code) which was promulgated in a general court at Huesca in 1247.

he would do it; and that they would send round to the villages to bring the wheat to Sarrió,[17] and that they would find us on the road, in order not to keep us waiting.

Thus, we started on the road with our train, and with some hundred horsemen that we had, and we went to pitch camp at Alcubles.[18] And at Alcubles they told us that King Zaén of Valencia was at Llíria with all his forces, and that he would fight us. And we said: "Whoever may come, we shall enter there!"

We left Alcubles with our mules laden and with our horses armed, and with our banners spread, we entered Puig.[19] And Don Bernat Guillem, Don Berenguer Entença and the orders who were there, came out to receive us, together with Guillem d'Aguiló and others who were in there with them. And we were happy with them, and they with us, because of the good fortune which had befallen us. But not everybody could come out to receive us, since they had lost eighty-six horses in the battle.

[220] After that we sent a message to Jimeno Pérez de Tarazona, who was in Aragon, telling him to send us forty horses, and the one that was worth most should be worth one hundred *morabetins* or more.

While we were at Puig, Don Ferdinand, Don Artal de Alagón,[20] and Don Pedro Cornel came to us because they had received our message summoning them to Puig. And we received a message saying that the horses for which we had sent were at Teruel. So we said to Don Bernat Guillem d'Entença, Don Berenguer, Guillem d'Aguiló and those knights who were at Puig, that before we departed we would replace all those horses that had been lost, and they thanked us very much for that. And we said to them, moreover, that we would cede them our fifth,[21] as they had acquitted themselves so well in the battle, and they said that they thanked us for all that and that they recognized we had done them a great favour. Meanwhile we sent a message to those who brought the forty horses that were at Teruel, that they should bring them to Sogorb, as those who brought the horses did not dare to come without the protection of knights. Then we left there and we went to Sogorb with those nobles.

When we arrived at Sogorb and we had been there one day, the horses arrived. And we besought and ordered the nobles that they should tell their knights that the horses had arrived, and that they should not sell them too dear because we needed them urgently, and that they should make things easy for

---

[17]In the province of Teruel.

[18]On a plain surrounded by hills, about fifty kilometres from Valencia.

[19]Autumn 1237.

[20]Soldevila suggests that Artal de Alagón had already passed to the side of the Saracens at this point (ch. 227) and here it should say Artal de Luna, who was certainly with the king at El Puig in July–August 1237 (*S*, p. 296).

[21]The fifth part of the takings won in the battle, to which the king was entitled.

us, as we would give them what they were worth and more. They said they would do that willingly. Then we spoke with the knights, and chose the horses that pleased us, buying forty-six, which cost us sixty thousand sous;[22] and together with those forty that we had arranged to come, there were eighty-six. The nobles then went back to Aragon, whilst we remained there with thirteen knights.

[221] Having done that, we returned to Puig by the Morvedre road. And when we arrived near Morvedre, we asked if we should cross by the hill which is above the castle of Morvedre, at no more than two crossbow shots' distance. The others said that it would be better to cross through the valley of Segó. But one knight, whose name we do not recall, said that we could cross by the hill, as we would be across before anyone noticed. And I thought that what he said was for the best. Then we said to them: "You will do just as I tell you. I do not have here a pennon or banner; but let us take one of the covers the horses are carrying and make a banner, and then the horses and we will form into a tight group. Taking our lances, our shields, and our iron caps, we will all go on the side between the horses and the castle, so close to the horses that they will think that there are more knights than there are."

This is what we did, as it seemed a good idea to all those who were with us. And as we went past, a good thousand Saracens came out on to the hillside of Morvedre, with five horsemen, and they shouted out and insulted us, but they did not dare to come near us. Thus, by the will of God, we passed and we went to Puig. And the day we arrived at Puig we divided the eighty-six horses among those who had lost theirs.

[222] When we had done that we took leave of Don Bernat Guillem d'Entença, Don Berenguer d'Entença, Guillem d'Aguiló, and the knights who went with us far as Puçol, whom we ordered to go back, as we did not wish Puig to be left without knights. We even left there the horses of four or five knights who came with us.[23] Then we went to Borriana, and it was a fast day. When we had eaten, Guillem d'Aguiló arrived unarmed, so we asked him why he came without armour. And he said that he had come by sea, on a boat. We then asked if everything was going well for the men at Puig; and he said aye, very well, but that there were new developments. And Don Pedro Cornel was there with us. And the men of my company said: "What are these developments?"

And he said: "The men of Puig say that Zaén will be there tomorrow morning with his entire force."

And we and all those who were there said: "But we left there today in the morning, and nobody mentioned it. How can it be so?"

---

[22]Approximately 1304 sous per horse.
[23]A Friday in September 1237 (*S*, p. 297).

And he said: "Know that, in truth, they say he knew of your departure, when you left Puig; and all the Saracens who are there, from Castalla and Cocentaina,[24] united to go there, as soon as they found out you had gone. Such is the talk in the garrison."

Now we and all the others held it to be nothing, as it could not be, so we did not heed that news.

[223] But when midnight came, someone knocked very loudly at the town-gate. And the gatekeeper came to us and said: "There is a loud knocking at the town-gate, and there is a horseman there, and he wishes to speak with you."

So we told him to open the gate to him. And Don Pedro Cornel was sleeping in our presence, and we said to him: "Hey! Do you hear? What if the news Guillem d'Aguiló said was true?"

And Don Pedro Cornel said: "By my faith, it may be!"

Then Sanç de Mora entered, wearing his purpoint and with his sword girt, and carrying his iron cap, which he had taken from his head; and he said to us: "God save you, lord. I have come here by order of Don Bernat Guillem d'Entença to speak to Don Pedro Cornel, since he did not wish to send word of it to you."

And Don Pedro Cornel said: "What is the message?"

And he said: "Don Bernat Guillem sends word to you that Zaén, with all his forces, will be at Puig tomorrow morning, and that he must do battle with him. Now, if he saw you in such a plight, he would not fail you, so he asks that you will go to help him."

And we said: "A battle?"

And he said: "Yes, Lord. So we must certainly go there this morning."

Afterwards, Don Pedro Cornel said: "Lord, I will tell you what you have to do. We will go with you as far as the estuary of Orpesa, and from there on you need fear nothing. And if you can arrange to go at once, I will still be there in time for the battle. For since Don Bernat Guillem has sent word to me, I will not let him down."

But we said: "By the faith that I owe to God and you, Don Pedro Cornel, it shall be otherwise. As I have left them in that place and they have remained faithful to God and me, and given that we are so near to them, they will not fight this time without us."

Then he said: "Lord, do not do it, as it is not for you to do. In matters such as this you should send us, not go yourself."

Yet we insisted: "Be aware, Don Pedro Cornel, that nothing in the world will stop me from going there. So do not speak such words to me, as I will not be persuaded by them for anything in the world."

---

[24]Two towns to the south of Xàtiva which are near to the border with Murcia.

Afterwards there were some there who said: "Indeed he would seem to be king, who does not slyly abandon his servants."

And we clearly heard what they were saying. And Don Alaman de Sádaba[25] was ill at Borriana, but had one good horse, so we sent our servant to him asking him to lend it to us, in order to return to Puig for the battle. He lent it to us willingly and gladly.

[224] Immediately, at midnight, we mounted our horse, and rode along the seashore. When we had passed Almenara our chaplain was with us, and we said that we ought to hear Mass and go to confession, in case there was any sin that we had forgotten, and that we should each receive the Body of Jesus Christ. So we heard Mass and whoever wished to do so was able to receive Him. And as we rode along, Don Fortuny López de Sádaba, who was a good knight and who used to call everybody he liked 'sobrino'[26] came up to us and said: "What do you think will happen today?"

And we said: "By my faith, today the wheat will be sorted from the bran."

Then he made as if to to embrace us and said that he wished that God might give us good fortune.

When we were near the river of Morvedre, Don Martín Pérez,[27] who was later justiciar in Aragon, came to us and said: "Lord, you should send two knights to Puig in order to know what is and is not happening and how things stand."

So we said: "Go there, then."

And he said: "Give me a companion to accompany me."

And we gave someone, and he went there. Before we were at Puig, when we were half a league away, he came running straight towards us. When we saw him coming in that manner, we feared that it was true. And we said to him: "What news do you bring?"

And he said: "Good news. That the men at Puig are very well and there is nothing in what they told you."

[225] When we got there, we decided, with Don Bernat Guillem d'Entença and the others, that we should make a raid on Valencia, so we sent scouts there. Fifty horsemen went, bringing back some twelve Saracen men and fifty Saracen women, who had gone out, some to look for wood, others to find something to eat. When they arrived, we asked each of them if the Saracens had again levied the people to come to Puig; and we asked them one by one, so they could not falsify their responses. And they said that there was no levy, except of those men who were in the town. On hearing this news, we told the

---

[25]He had participated in the siege of Borriana in 1233 (*M*, p. 104).

[26]Meaning 'nephew', this is a mark of familiarity and affection.

[27]Justiciar in Aragon between 1247 and 1263 (*P*, p. 125, n. 3).

knights that we would leave, because it was more fitting for us to go than to remain there; for we could send them better counsel and meet their needs better from Catalonia and Aragon than if we remained there with them. And that day each knight left to his friend his iron cap and a good lance, if he had one.

Then we left for Borriana. And we said to Don Bernat Guillem that he should turn back from that village called Puçol and, by our order, he returned. And Don Berenguer d'Entença said that he had to speak to us, so he followed us to near the river of Morvedre, with up to twelve knights who had horses, weapons, and purpoints. And afterwards he went back.

[226] When he had gone back and we had crossed the river near the beginning of the marsh that comes from the sea, Miguel Garcés, who was from Navarre and now lives in Sariñena, and the scouts who went ahead shouted out: "To arms!"

Don Pedro Cornel, who heard the call to arms, took up his weapons and spurred forward. But we raced after him and took him by the reins and said to him: "What is it, Don Pedro Cornel? Is that the war-cry of Ejea? Halt and let us first see what it is, before attacking."

With us were Don Jimeno de Foces, Don Fernando Pérez de Pina, and Don Fortuny López de Sádaba; so that all together, with our company and those of Don Pedro Cornel and Don Jimeno de Foces, there were up to seventeen of us. And Don Fortuny López had nothing but a chinpiece to put on his head, and a tunic to wear, and a mule to ride, and the lance that he held.[28] And we had not a single armoured horse, but only our purpoints, iron caps, and lances. In the meantime, our scouts went into the sea, as they wished to take refuge in a boat in which Don Guillem d'Aguiló sailed.

[227] Then two muleteers arrived and we asked them what they brought; and they said that they carried seven suits of armour for man and horse. So we ordered them to unload them immediately and arm the horses. And a knight (though we do not remember his name) said: "Why do you not send word to Don Berenguer, as he could still get here in time?"

So we ordered Domingo de Fraga, our officer, to go there and order him to come as quickly as he could, since he could already see the state we were in. While we were having the horses armed, we put on our hauberk and we put cuisses[29] on our feet. Just as we had put the right one on, our men said: "Here you have them! Already they are coming!"

---

[28]He seems to have been an object of amusement to James (cf. ch. 224). He had presumably left most of his armour and his horse to someone at El Puig (ch. 225). He must have been quite a sight, riding a mule rather than a horse, wearing a chinpiece (barbuda) but no iron cap, a tunic (garnatxa) but no hauberk, and wielding a lance.

[29]They are to protect the legs and the thighs (*P*, p. 128, n. 7).

So we kicked off the cuisse from our leg and said: "We need not bother with that, as our body and horse are already armoured."

Then we got on our horse, and the others were ready to come against us. And we reckon there were some one hundred and thirty knights on horses, including Don Artal de Alagón[30] and his company and the Saracens. But we did not know that Don Artal de Alagón was there.

Before we had armed ourselves, the Saracens had captured Miguel Garcés, and an ass that carried the bed of Don Jimeno de Foces; and that had been when we had ordered Don Pedro Cornel to stop. When we had mounted, a knight who carried the pennon of Don Pedro Cornel held it behind us; and Don Fortuny López de Sádaba said to him: "You utter fool of a man; carry the pennon in front of the king. Do not hold it behind him!"

And the knight put the pennon in front of us. Then Don Fernando Pérez de Pina said: "There are many of them and you have few men here with you; there is nothing we can do except face them head on, and those who cannot avoid it will die, until we can withdraw to Puig."

But we said: "Don Fernando Pérez, I will not do that as I have never fled nor do I know how to flee, but I tell you that whatever God wishes to give me, I will receive it here with my men."

And we were on a hill, and they twice turned straight towards us to come and charge us, but Our Lord did not will that they should reach to us, so we went from there. Now some people said, not even a whole month after the event, that Don Artal knew that we were there and had forbidden them to attack us. But that was not the case, since Miguel Garcés, who had been captured, had not yet come to him, and we did not have a standard or banner there by which they could identify us, but only that of Don Pedro Cornel. For I believe that it was only afterwards, when the event was already over, that Miguel Garcés told them that we were there.

In the meanwhile, they saw Don Berenguer d'Entença approaching, and took off for the olive and fig groves of the valley of Segó, going little by little to Almenara. And we were very relieved when we saw them going away.

[228] Afterwards, as they were leaving, Don Berenguer arrived. We told him that he should come with us to Borriana; and he said that he would do so willingly, and that he would not part from us until Borriana at such and such an hour. For we thought that they would come to attack us from La Ràpita, but they did not come out. When we arrived at Borriana, Don Pedro Cornel said that we should eat and rest there for the entire day; and we said to Don Pedro Cornel: "Don Pedro Cornel, that is not the way of arms, because one may lose much by resting; and, by the faith that I owe you, we shall neither eat nor stop this night until we are at Orpesa."

---

[30]The son of Don Blasco.

And he said: "Why ever not?"

"For this reason," we said. "If the Saracens arrive this night, riding by night, at the estuary of Orpesa, they would certainly ruin everything, and they would destroy us; but now they cannot have advanced so much that they are in front of us. Let us, then, pass the night at Orpesa and rest there, and from there, we can go forward securely. And Don Berenguer shall return there this night, riding through the night, and he will have nothing to fear, for they will know less of his plans than they know of us."

And he took his leave of us and went there.

[229] We ordered that none of our men should remain at the town but that they should follow us; but only we, Don Pedro Cornel, and Pedro Palazín left the town. And when we had crossed the river Millars, a crossbowman came rushing towards us; and he came on horseback and wearing his purpoint, with his iron cap on his head and his crossbow bent. And Pedro Palazín said: "Here is a horseman who comes at the gallop towards us."

And Don Pedro Cornel and we wished to go towards him. But Pedro Palazín said: "I will go, as it is not for you to do."

So then we halted, whilst he went towards him and asked him: "Why do you come here so, galloping and with your crossbow prepared as if you wish to fire at us?"

And he said: "Lord, I am dead!"

Then he asked him what had happened, and he said that Aven Lop[31] had attacked the commander of Orpesa at the pine trees at the river mouth, and that he had taken the commander prisoner. Now we said to him: "And were you with the commander?"

And he said: "Aye, lord."

"And how is it that you have dared to come here, if your lord has been taken. And with your crossbow armed against us? It would have been better if you had fired at the Saracens than against us."

And we said to him: "You foul-smelling villain, how could you abandon your lord? If you had been taken, you could have got out of prison for one hundred and fifty or two hundred sous. Yet you have abandoned him and the field? By Christ, you can never have done a worse thing! Dismount from your horse."

And he said: "Lord, why must I dismount?"

And we said to him: "Because of what you have done."

---

[31] Ibn Lūb was most probably a relation of Zayyān and, like him, a descendant of King Lūb (Lobo) (1147–72), the *wālī* of Valencia who made himself ruler of Valencia and Murcia in the face of the Almohads.

Then we took from him his horse, his purpoint, his iron cap, and his crossbow, and we left him with nothing but a tunic;[32] and he followed behind us on foot.

[230] When we had travelled a mile along the riverside, we awaited the company. And when they arrived, we all crossed the estuary together, and we lodged at Orpesa, because it was already dark. We had brought meat, bread, and wine from Borriana; and we ate. And then we went straight to sleep; and we slept until morning. In the morning, we heard Mass, because the Hospitallers then held that place.[33] And that same day we went to Ulldecona, and the next day we entered Tortosa.[34]

We ordered tribute to be collected from the towns of Aragon and Catalonia, and we then ordered all the men who held some fief in our name, and the cities, that on Easter Day they should be at Valencia with the forces they commanded. Then, at once, we entered Aragon. And when we arrived at Zaragoza,[35] Don Ferdinand, Don Blasco de Alagón, Don Jimeno de Urrea, Don Rodrigo Lizana, Don Pedro Cornel, Don García Romeu,[36] and Don Pedro Fernández de Azagra presented themselves, and received us in the manner of a *Cort*, although we had not convoked the *Cort*.

[231] When we had been at Zaragoza for eight days or more, a message reached us saying that Don Bernat Guillem d'Entença was dead.[37] And the nobles found out about it before we did, and they decided to come before us to inform us of the death of Don Bernat Guillem, so that we could all discuss the best thing to do about Puig de Santa Maria, now he was dead.

They all came before me grief-stricken; and all the nobles said to Don Ferdinand that he should show us the message and inform us of the death of Don Bernat Guillem. And we knew from their faces that they had received terrible news. They said to us that we should order everybody to leave the

---

[32]James left him with nothing but his 'gonella' (the tunic worn under the hauberk) since he had abandoned his lord in battle when he could have helped him.

[33]The Hospitallers held it until 1249 when they exchanged, with Fernando Pérez de Pina, Orpesa for Borriana (*P*, p. 132, n. 14). Thus this section of the text was written after 1249.

[34]James was at Tortosa on 2 October 1237 (*M*, p. 129).

[35]James was at Zaragoza on 27 December 1237 (*S*, p. 303).

[36]His family rose out of Lleida but he was a high magnate of Aragon proper, appearing in the following of the king regularly between 1228 and 1271. He married Teresa, a daughter of James's son, Peter III of Aragon (1276–85). He betrayed James during the second siege of Xàtiva taking one hundred knights over to the Muslim side but later James was careful to keep him on his side and he did the king great service.

[37]Late December 1237 or early January 1238. James was certainly at Zaragoza on 27 December 1237 (Ubieto, 'Reconquista de Valencia', p. 159).

room, except them and Fernando Pérez de Pina and Bernat Vidal,[38] a wise man who went with us. So we had them leave.

And afterwards Don Ferdinand began to speak, for himself and for the others, and he spoke in this manner: "My lord, Our Lord has made all the things in the world, and He undoes them when it pleases Him. Now we are obliged to do anything that may be to your profit, and that would please us greatly; whilst we would lament any misfortune that were to befall you. For we have received some news through which you could suffer harm, unless you take counsel on it rapidly. And we are greatly saddened by the news, both for him, who was so worthy, and for you: for we have to inform you that Don Bernat Guillem d'Entença is dead, and we know this for certain. Moreover, as he held so great and honourable a position through you, on the frontier, it is important that you take counsel."

[232] Now, we were deeply upset when we heard these words, and for a good while we could not respond to them, because of the great sadness that we felt at his death. Then, after a while, we made an effort to respond to them, and we said to them:

"We are deeply saddened by the death of Don Bernat Guillem for many reasons. First, he was our relation, since he was our uncle on our mother's side,[39] and we had entrusted to him a place as prized to us as Puig, through which one can take Valencia and the entire kingdom. Furthermore, we grieve for a reason that is greater than all that we have said: because he was a very good and loyal person, who had a great desire to serve us, and he has died serving God and us. But let us console ourselves about him, because his soul, as all good Christians must believe, will go to a good place. Even so, these words and the news of his death have upset me; and tonight, because of the sadness that I feel, we cannot see anyone nor come to any decisions. But tomorrow, at the morning Mass, come before us, and together we will decide what to do with that place."

Everyone said that we had spoken well and that they would come to our presence.

In the morning we heard Mass at our house, because we did not wish to go outside, so the people would not see the grief that we felt. And when everyone was there, we put them in a room, and we asked them and we ordered them that they should advise us and help us to decide what should be done in a matter as serious as this one. They said to us that they would withdraw to one side, and that they would reach an agreement, and that afterwards they would

---

[38] A lawyer (*S*, p. 303) from Besalú (*Desclot*, ch. 50), he was with the king in May 1238, during the siege of Valencia (*M*, p. 132). He helped reconcile Alfonso X of Castile and James after their disputes concerning control of the kingdom of Navarre in 1254 (*Desclot*, ch. 50).

[39] As he was a son of William VIII of Montpellier, father of Marie of Montpellier.

come before us and give us their advice. We said to them that they did not have
to withdraw, but since that was what they wanted, we would accept it. Then
they went to discuss things, and after an hour, they returned, and they said to
Don Blasco de Alagón that he should explain what they had agreed, because he
knew more about the deed of Valencia than they did, since he had been there
for a good two or three years. Yet Don Blasco refused for a while and did not
want to speak, but everyone said with one voice that they wanted him to speak
on it, because he was better informed than them. So then, Don Blasco said that
he would explain what they had agreed, and he said:

[233] "Lord, this is the agreement we have all considered and thought about.
We have to take into account your circumstances, and not only your
circumstances but also the expense that you would have to undertake to
preserve that hill. And we see that you do not have such riches that you can
sustain so great an enterprise as you have begun. So we think it would be better
that you order your company to return, and on another occasion you may be
better prepared than now to besiege and take Valencia. For, the more that place
costs if the matter is not successful, the worse it will get for you and for us.[40]
And in spite of everything, you can return later and take Valencia, and with the
will of God, you will take it."

When he had finished his speech, Don Ferdinand said: "Lord, do you not
recall that when you began this enterprise at Puig, I said to you that you could
not finish it, and that you would spend a great amount for nothing?"

"We all agree to this," Don Blasco said.

And we wanted to know from the others if they all agreed to this, and they
all admitted that they did.

[234] Then we responded that we had not thought we would receive such
advice from them, for what we did, we did in the service of God, and this was
something that nobody of my line had ever done. And if people said that I had
abandoned the Puig because of the death of Don Bernat Guillem (a nobleman
of ours who had defeated the king of Valencia's forces on the battlefield), and
had done so after we had achieved the larger part of the deed through which the
kingdom of Valencia could be won, everyone would think that the merit of
holding that place was his alone. And I would rather demonstrate, at all times,
that my valour was such that the death of Don Bernat Guillem would not affect
me, nor would it even if four or five men such as he were to die. "So let me tell
you that the place shall not be abandoned, but that, through that place, we will
win Valencia and all the other land."

---

[40]Again James emphasizes how the nobles see his expeditions purely in terms of economic
gain.

None of the nobles agreed with the counsel we gave except Fernando Pérez de Pina and Bernat Vidal; but these did not dare say so in front of the others, but only in private. Even so, we ordered everyone who was there to be with us at Easter: "Because we shall go immediately to Puig."

[235] We went to Puig[41] with some fifty knights of our household. And Don Jimeno de Urrea came with us. And we ordered the son of Don Bernat Guillem d'Entença, whose name was Guillem d'Entença, and who was perhaps ten or eleven years old, to come with us. When we arrived there, we found Don Berenguer, Don Guillem d'Aguiló, and the companies of the Hospital, Temple, Calatrava, and Uclés, all distraught. And we found that they had him in his coffin, waiting for us to order them what to do. So we comforted them with our words and we told them not to be afraid because their lord was dead, since we would be their lord and we would do all that he had done for their good and their profit, and more besides. Then we ordered Don Bernat Guillem to be buried, until they could carry him to Escarp,[42] where he had promised his tomb would be.

[236] On the morning of the following day, after hearing Mass, we sent for his son, Guillem d'Entença, who was there with us, and we made him a knight, and we gave him all the land that his father had held from us. And the knights and the others who saw how well we behaved towards his son and towards the knights who had remained there with his father, thanked us very much, and asked Our Lord that he should give us a long life for the very good example we had given regarding the son, and in holding that place. When we had arranged all that, and had provided for their needs until Easter (when we would come with our army), we chose to make Don Berenguer d'Entença the leader of that company, now that Don Bernat Guillem was dead.

But when they realized that we desired to leave there, they all deliberated amongst themselves and decided, in secret, that the majority of them would leave the Puig, some because of business that they had to attend to in their lands, and others with some other lame excuses that they found because they did not want to stay. Yet we knew nothing of all that. And there were two friars preacher there to give penance and to preach, one named Brother Pere de Lleida and another one, and they came before us. Brother Pere said that he wished to speak with us in private; and he told us that he wished to come with us and that he would not remain there. So then we said to him: "Why do you want to go? For you are greatly needed here. On the one hand, to preach to them, and on the other, because if anyone arrives at the hour of his death, you

---

[41]Both the king and Don Jimeno were at El Puig by 24 January 1238 (*S*, p. 304; Ubieto, 'Reconquista de Valencia', p. 160).

[42]A Cistercian monastery to the right of the Segre.

would know better how to give him absolution than would a chaplain who understands nothing."

Then he said: "I will tell you why I want to go: more than sixty knights and honoured men, some of the best of the place, have spoken with me, and they say that they will leave, by day or night, when you leave."

And we said: "That is news to me! When they have won in battle, and we replaced the horses that they lost and secured them all their needs. Why is it that they cannot hold out until Easter, which is barely two months away, when we will come here with our army and go to besiege Valencia?"

"You must know," he said, "that the via fora[43] is already given; and if you go, they will go. Therefore, I am telling you that I will not stay, as, if I can avoid it, I do not want to die until God wills it."

Then we said to him: "Go now, and we will think about it throughout the night, and in the morning we will give you a response."

And he went. Yet he left us greatly troubled, feeling that our labours were like those of a spider, as having done so much there, we could now lose it all in an instant. For as we had held it at so great a price and with such great honour, if we abandoned it now, great harm and great evil would befall us, together with shame.

[237] After that we went to sleep, and we did not want to disclose this conversation to anybody who was with us. Even though it was then January and it was very cold, during the night we tossed and turned on the bed more than a hundred times, from one side to another, and we sweated as if we were in a bath. When we had deliberated for a long time, we went to sleep, from fatigue at the vigil we had kept. But when it was between midnight and dawn, we woke up and returned to our thoughts; and we considered that we must be dealing with evil people, because usually in the entire world there are no people so proud as are knights.[44] Yet these, when we had gone, would not feel any shame in fleeing by day or night and going to Borriana, which was only seven leagues away. And they, the few or many who wished to go, would travel across the land that we had already conquered, since they need have no fear to do so.

And we considered how with the help of God and His mother we had conquered from Tortosa to Borriana, but that, if that place was abandoned and lost, so those others places which we had won would be lost. For which reason,

---

[43]Essentially, here, 'Everybody out!'. According to Soldevila, it was the cry that went up in a town to summon a posse to set out on the road in pursuit of malefactors (*S*, pp. 304–5).

[44]James had already written to the pope concerning the bad faith of his vassals whom he said were conspiring against him while he attempted to prosecute the crusade. On 9 February 1238, Pope Gregory IX instructed the bishop-elect of Huesca to take measures against those who impeded the king's enterprise and on 5 March he took the king and the kingdom under his special protection until the termination of the crusade (Auvray, *Registres*, 2, nos. 4070, 4116).

we decided to go to the church of Santa Maria the next morning, and to convoke the knights and all the others. And we asked brother Pere if he wished us to keep secret what he had told us, before we spoke to the others. And he said no, but rather he would be pleased if we revealed it.

Thus, when they were all assembled before us, we said to them: "Men, we know only too well, and believe that you and all those who are in Spain know, too, the great grace that Our Lord has done us, in our youth, in the deed of Majorca and the other islands, and in conquering from Tortosa to here; and you are assembled here to serve God and us. Now, Brother Pere of Lleida spoke with us last night and told us that the majority of you wish to leave here if we leave; and we were amazed by that, because we thought to make our departure for your profit and to achieve that conquest. But since we see that our departure troubles you (we stood up now to speak these words), we promise here before God and this altar of His holy mother, that we shall not go beyond Teruel nor the river of Ulldecona[45] until we have taken Valencia. And we shall send for our wife the queen, and our daughter (who is now queen of Castile[46]), for them to come, so that you may appreciate the great determination we have to remain here and to conquer this kingdom, in the service of God."

[238] When they heard my words, there was nobody in the church who did not begin to weep, and we wept with them. And we said to them: "Now then, take heart, for we shall not go from here until we have taken the city of Valencia."

And they all went away, happy and content with the good nourishment of the words we had spoken. And after we had said these words and they had left our presence, we immediately sent our messengers to the queen telling her to come to Tortosa, and to Don Ferdinand, our uncle, that he should come with her.

We remained at Puig, after we had said that, for a full fifteen days, and then we left for the region of Peníscola,[47] since we did not want to cross the Ebro because of the words that we had spoken to them.

[239] The day on which we had fixed for the queen to come to Tortosa, and Don Ferdinand with her, they sent a message to Peníscola telling us that they were at Tortosa. So we sent them a message telling them to hurry to Peníscola, since we could not cross the Ebro because of the pact we had made with the knights who were at Puig; and when they were with us we would tell them why we had made that pact. But when they left Tortosa to come towards us, it began

---

[45] The Riera d'Ulldecona to the south of the Ebro.

[46] Violante, daughter of Yolanda of Hungary and wife of Alfonso X of Castile. Violante married Alfonso on 1 December 1249 but she did not become queen until the death of Ferdinand III (30 May 1252). This section of the text must therefore have been dictated after that time.

[47] Early February 1238. By 16 February 1238 James had returned to El Puig (*M*, p. 130).

to rain very heavily. And it rained so much on that occasion that when they wanted to cross the river Ulldecona, only one knight could cross on his horse, and had to swim across. They told him, before he crossed, that he should come to us at Peníscola, and that he should inform us that the queen and Don Ferdinand had arrived at Ulldecona and that they could not cross the river with the ladies there, and that we should tell them what to do. So we told the messenger that we would go there.

As we had already eaten, we got on our horse. And the rain had stopped, but there was such a sea, raised by the south-easterly wind, that when the waves came towards the castle of Peníscola in the direction of the delta of Tortosa, they reached well beyond the castle, and when they came from the direction of Orpesa they also crossed, over the sand, to the other side of the castle. And we left there. And the water level of the river Ulldecona had fallen, but not very much; and we crossed without having to swim, but the water was still high, and went up as far as the horses' saddle flaps.

We met with the queen and Don Ferdinand there, in private. And we told them how we had acted at Puig, saying it was because the knights all intended to return home if we had left at that time and in that way and also because we understood the knights' intentions (even though there was nothing for them to fear, as the battle had been won, and we had replaced the horses that had been lost and had left them enough to eat). But in spite of all that they did not wish to remain in that place, and they were unashamed of the harm they would do. And we said that that place was so significant to us for the good work we had done there, and all would be undone by their evil actions and cowardice, if we did not make the pact. And we feared two things: one, that it would grieve God that we should throw away what we had done well; the other, the shame of this world, since people might then blame us and be speaking the truth.

[240] After that, our uncle Don Ferdinand responded, saying that he was amazed that we should wish to act upon this plan that we had made; because to take Valencia was a great thing, and we were trying to do something that none of our line had ever been able to achieve; and not to go back into our kingdoms, when we wished to do such great things, and not to speak to our men, nor they to us, as we would not be able to, was no way to fulfil such a great enterprise. And the queen agreed with what he had said, because on the road both had decided to say that.

[241] Now we saw their intentions, for they desired us to go to Catalonia and Aragon. But in spite of everything that they said, we did not abandon the good proposal that we had, and we told them that we had come from the deed, and we knew how things stood, having seen them and heard them, whereas they could not know about them.

Then we said to them: "Don Ferdinand, how could we take Valencia if the Puig was abandoned before we besieged Valencia, and before they could harvest what they have sown? Because, if we entered into Catalonia and Aragon before we had deliberated with our men about what was necessary, and they with us, the Saracens would harvest the wheat they have sown. For Valencia and its kingdom are of very temperate climate; thus we must conquer a town such as Valencia through famine, without giving them time to receive wheat or provisions or help from any place. And if we are to take Valencia, that is the best course we can take. Besides that, we have promised them that we will not go beyond the Ebro or Teruel until Valencia is taken, and we cannot break our agreement. And so with the help of God, and with those who hold fiefs from us in Catalonia and *honors* from us in Aragon, and with the archbishop and the bishops (who promised to help us when we held the *Cort* at Monzón and took the cross before us[48]) for whom we have sent so that they should come to help us, as they have promised, by the will of God, we will have done so much when you arrive that all will be prepared for the taking of Valencia. And we will hold it well so that they will not be able to harvest the wheat or barley before you arrive. Thus, we commend you to God; and ask you to come quickly, as you will find the table prepared. And we do not intend to do otherwise."

Seeing that it would not be otherwise, he and the queen asked for some letters that would profit them, and we granted this. And Don Ferdinand returned home, and in the morning, the queen and we crossed the river, which had now subsided; and two days later we entered Borriana. We left the queen there and the next day we returned to Puig,[49] and the men of Puig were greatly pleased at our return, as we had remembered them so well.

[242] Zaén knew that we had this matter in our heart, and he also knew that we had ordered our wife to come, and he was greatly afraid. So he sent Alí Albaca to Fernando Díaz, and he made him swear upon the Gospels that he would not expose him; and when he had done that, Fernando Díaz came to us, and said that he wanted to speak with us in secret, for our great profit. When we heard that, we chose a part of the house where we slept, and he said that we had to keep the secret. And we said to him: "Since you say that it is to our profit and to our honour, it is reasonable that we keep it secret."

---

[48]Having renewed his alliance with Abū Zayd in May 1236, James had convoked the general court at Monzón in October 1236 calling for a renewed attack on the Moors and the siege and capture of Valencia City. The peace and truce was proclaimed and Pope Gregory IX, in early 1237, issued a series of bulls in support of the enterprise and called for the preaching of the crusade in Aragon, Catalonia, and the south of France (Auvray, *Registres*, 2, nos. 3480, 3483–6, 3488, 3493; Goñi, pp. 165–6).

[49]Before 16 February 1238.

And he said: "The greatest gain and greatest honour will come to you that has come to any of your line, because Zaén has sent a message to me through Alí Albaca, and has made me swear upon the Holy Gospels that I will disclose it to nobody except you. And he has said to me that, for his part, he would fulfil it, and that he would give us all the castles there are from Guadalaviar to Tortosa, and from Tortosa to Teruel, and that he will build you an alcazar at the Saidia;[50] and, moreover, he will give you each year, as long as the world lasts, two thousand bezants rent at the city of Valencia."

When we heard that proposal, we held it, in our heart, to be a good and a fine one, and that he was giving us a great thing, but we said that we would think about it.

And we remained thinking for a long while, so long that one could have walked a mile of land in that time, and afterwards we said to him: "Fernando Díaz, we well know and recognize that you seek our profit and our honour; but this is a thing which we will never do, for this reason: because we have arrived at the hour and at the point when we can obtain Valencia, and so we may have the hen and afterwards the chickens."

He marvelled at this and crossed himself, saying he was very much surprised that we should refuse this offer; because if this offer and this deal had been made in the time of our father or our grandfather, they would have jumped and danced at having received such great fortune.[51] And so Alí Albaca returned without being able to accomplish that for which he had come.

[243] While we were at Puig, a message arrived to us from Almenara,[52] from the *alfaquim* and another Saracen who was very powerful there, saying that, if they could speak with us, they would surrender Almenara to us. And we were very glad at that message. So we got on our horse and rode the next day in the morning as one who goes to Borriana, and we spoke with them both; and they said that they would speak with the *aljama* and that they would arrange the manner through which we could hold that place. Then we went to Borriana to see the queen and to comfort her so that she would be very happy that she had come to the frontier.

The next day we left Borriana,[53] passing through Almenara, and sending a message to those two that they should come out to us. On seeing our pennon, they came to our presence. Then we asked them to signal the day on which they could surrender Almenara. And they said to us that the castle of Almenara

---

[50]The citadel of Valencia, now known as La Saeria.

[51]It is probably the case that both Alfonso II and Peter II, both of whom enjoyed moderate success in their Valencian campaigns, would have been delighted at such an offer. It should be said that until the defeat of the Almohads at Las Navas de Tolosa in July 1212, the Christian rulers faced opponents who were less dejected and divided.

[52]About halfway on the road from Borriana to Puig.

[53]Early March 1238.

was such that, for the service that that they would do us, we should do great things for them, since, as soon as the other Moors of the territory heard that we held Almenara, all the country, from Teruel to Tortosa, would surrender to us.

But we said to them that it was better that they should hurry to do so before the others, as other castles were negotiating their own surrender; and that if they had the advantage over the others, they would receive better treatment from us for the good beginning that they had made.

Each of them asked us for an inheritance of three *jovates*[54] of land each, apart from what they possessed at Almenara, and that we should give to their relatives who would help in this deed, thirty *jovates*, and that all those *jovates* were to be taken from the alguebers,[55] that is to say, from those who had abandoned the place and fled; and that we should give them two hundred cows and a thousand sheep and goats, and that we should give scarlet cloth to forty of their relatives to wear, who would participate with them in the deed, and that we should give to the two of them a rouncy each, in lieu of knights' horses.

[244] When we heard what they said to us we were very pleased and we agreed to it, because, as the old proverb says: "He who does not give what grieves him, does not get what he wants". After that, we asked them to say on what day this thing could be accomplished. They said that first they would have to speak privately with their friends, and that they would prepare the deed in such a way that within eight days they would inform us of the day that we should go there.

After that we departed from them. And in front of the castle of Almenara, in view of those who had spoken with us, who were on the hill-side, we captured a crane, just as we would wish it to be captured, up high and cleanly. And we were among the first runners to get there.

We did not allow the crane to be killed there, but we took it from the falcons and we had them fed with chicken meat, and then we sent the live crane to those two men with whom we had made our agreement, saying that for the gift of Almenara they should eat the crane, and that we sent it alive because we knew their custom,[56] and they would not want it dead. And they were very happy about that, and they whispered to our messenger: "Tell the king to be of good heart, since what he desires of Almenara, he will soon see."

Then we were very satisfied with the message that they sent us, and we returned at night to Puig.

---

[54]Though there was a good deal of variation, the unit of land measurement in Valencia was usually a fanecate (eight hundred and thirty-one square metres). Six fanecates made a *cafiz* and six *cafizes* made a *jovate* or yoke (Burns, *Crusader Kingdom*, 1, p. xii).

[55]Absentees or emigrants.

[56]Of cutting the jugular vein.

[245] After eight days they secretly sent a Saracen, who entered the camp at night, with a letter from those Moors with whom we had spoken. The letter said that we could go to Almenara when we wanted, as what they had spoken of to us had been fulfilled, if we brought to them one part or more of the cattle which we had promised them. So we took from the camp cows and goats, which we had taken in raids, and we brought some seven hundred sheep and goats, and two hundred cows.[57] Then we ordered Pere Ramon de Tortosa (who was to be found amidst the army and had a workshop at Borriana) to come with us, and, along with three or four others who were also there, and from whose workshops we could take the clothes from their shops as well as from his, and were also there.

After that we went to Almenara, and we found all the Saracens there, except the *Alcaid* of the castle, who held it for Zaén, and who perhaps had with him up to twenty men who were not natives of the town. All of the Saracens of the town and region who were there said to us that they would surrender the two towers to us, and the *albacar* of the castle, and that they would fight at our side, for we could be sure that we would take these places.

[246] In the meanwhile, we delivered the cattle to them, and we said to them that in the morning, after they had surrendered the castle, they should come with us to Borriana for the clothes, and that we would fulfil everything else. Now, it was already vespers, and we, with twenty knights who came with us and our squires, went up inside the *albacar,* and they delivered to us a building that was a mosque, which was so near the castle that afterwards they would throw great stones down at us, so that nobody dared go outside to do his work, for fear of the stones that they were throwing.

When the morning came and it was already daylight, we sent two armed knights outside. Then they went outside of the house and they asked who was the lord in that castle. And those inside said that they would make him come out, so that he might speak with them. Then the two knights said in our name: "The king tells you that he is here, and he orders that you choose which of these two things you prefer: if you want, he will give you so much of what is his that you could not fail to accept it; but if you do not wish that, and you rather prefer death to life, it is prepared for you, because he will take you at once, before it is the hour of terce."

[247] After that the lord of the castle said that he wished to speak with us. So we went outside with our shields and with our iron caps, so that they could not do us any treason. Then we asked him what he wanted, for we were there.

He said that he had recognized us, but that he wanted to know for certain if we were there, because he wished to tell us that he was in that castle for Zaén,

---

[57]They had asked for a thousand sheep and goats and two hundred cows in total (ch. 243).

King of Valencia, and he was a knight, and he understood very well that he was unable to defend himself against us, since the Saracens were with us and with our force, we could easily storm the castle. But he asked us that as he was surrendering the castle to us, we should treat him well, as well as the others who were there in that place.

We said that we would do so willingly, and that he should prepare to come out; and that he should come to us and we would give him an appropriate reward.

He responded that he would do so, and he came to us and asked that we should give two horses to him and to a relative of his who was there, since they had eaten the horses that they had while defending the castle in the name of their lord; and he asked that we should give clothes to the company that was there. There and then we gave him two horses. Then we sent to Borriana, to Pere Ramon, for the clothes for the men of the castle and those of the town, so that he would supply us with the clothes that we had to give to them. And so, with that, we had the castle.

[248] Meanwhile, we sent two knights to the queen, telling her that she should come quickly, as Our Lord had shown us such grace and mercy that He had given us the castle of Almenara, and she would be better off and more comfortable there than at Borriana. When the message reached her she had already prepared to eat, so she said that she would come after she had eaten. And it was in Lent.[58] But the knights said: "The king orders you to come, as he has dinner prepared, and you will dine better and more merrily there with him than you would do here."

When she heard that, she left her meal. And we waited there until she arrived, then we went out to the slopes at the foot of the castle, and we and she entered the castle happily and ate with great joy.

[249] When the next day came, messages arrived from Uixó, Nules, and Castro, saying that, if we wished them well, they would surrender the castles to us, since we held Almenara.[59] For they recognized only too well that Our Lord wished for us to have that land.

We said to them that they should come in peace, and that we would come out to them at a forked tower dividing the districts of Almenara and Uixó, and which stands facing Almenara, near La Ràpita, which was called Mencofa in the time of the Saracens. But we did not wish to fix the same day for all the

---

[58]Ash Wednesday fell on 17 February and Easter Sunday on 4 April. In ch. 254, James says Yolanda spent the second half of Lent at Almenara. So the date here should be about 11 March 1238.

[59]This was the normal course followed by James throughout the Valencia campaigns with the surrender of centres of strategic importance followed by the surrender of the surrounding castles (López, *Conquista y Repoblación*, p. 61).

castles, because we did not wish one to know the treaties we made with the other.

So we told the men of Uixó that we would come out to see them next day at the hour of terce. And we set a day to meet the men of Nules three days later, telling them to go out to the fig-gardens that are above Mencofa, which is in their region. For we would draw up our treaties with each of them there. And from each of the *aljamas*, there would be ten of the best and most powerful sheikhs.

And when we spoke with one group, the others were not there. Meanwhile, we ordered the men of Castro that they should remain here with us, and that we would make treaties here; and we made the treaties giving them a quantity of sheep and goats, and we robed the five sheikhs, and gave them two mounts. And we recognized their law and their liberties, exactly as they had held them in the time of the Saracens; and we gave them five of our mounted squires to protect them, and ten footmen.

[250] When the next day came, we had five sheep and twenty hens carried and went with our bread and our wine to the forked tower, exactly as we had promised the men of Uixó. And when we had been there a while they arrived.

We had kept back two live sheep and five chickens for them so that they could dine with us. And when they arrived, we did not wish to speak with them until we all had dined, so that we would be happier from having eaten and from the wine we would drink. We gave them up to one thousand five hundred sheep and goats and sixty cows, and robes for thirty people, and three rouncies. And we had charters made for them respecting their law and their customs,[60] such as they were accustomed to have in the time of the Saracens, recording that they should render fealty to us, as they had done to their king.

Then they asked who would give them that; and we said that we would give it to them in the space of three days, and that they should not delay in surrendering the castles to us, because then we would fulfil all that for them. And they believed it of us. There were only Don Ladrón[61] and nine knights with us. And the Saracens said to us that we should approach the castle, and they would surrender it to us.

[251] And so, we set out on the road with them; and some two hundred Saracen men and women came out to receive us, with great rejoicing, at the foot of the hill. And as soon as they were before us, they put down their lances. Of the

---

[60]The generous terms were reproduced in a surrender document of 1250. Uixó's Muslims were assured of their marriage customs, and were allowed to instruct their children in the Koran, travel freely, appoint their own judges, and prevent Christians from taking up residence amongst them. They were required to pay a tax of one-eighth (Guichard, *Musulmans de Valence*, 2, pp. 264–5; Burns, *Islam under the Crusaders*, p. 122).

[61]Don Ladrón was certainly at El Puig with James on 23 April 1238 (*S*, p. 310).

nine knights there, we sent eight to the castle, whilst we remained below with Don Ladrón and with all the remaining Saracens. Then, when our pennon was on the alcazar, we went up there, and the Saracens went up the hill with us. And we said to them: "Wait for us here, for we will be back with you soon."

Then we took our castle and we left our men there. And afterwards we came down again, and went to Borriana. There we took the cattle that we had promised, and the horses and the clothes, and we gave it to them. And we finished all that the next day, instead of waiting for the third day, sending it all to them as quickly as you now write it.[62]

[252] After that we went to see the men of Nules; and we took our dinner with us, and the Saracens ate with us, as we did not wish to speak with them until they were warmed up by food and wine. When we had eaten, we drew up our treaties and we gave them a thousand head of sheep and goats, and fifty cows, as well as robes for twenty people, and two horses.

Then we went with them to the castle, and they surrendered it to us there and then. And we left our castellans and our men there and we stationed guards at each of the castles, just as was necessary.

[253] And before we left Almenara, Alfàndec surrendered immediately the next day. Thus we had won those five castles.[63] Then we went to Puig, where our company was, and they greatly rejoiced with us, for the grace that God had given us.

[254] Whilst we were at Puig, we had Lent there. And the queen spent half of Lent at Almenara, until Easter, and we went to spend Easter with her; and after Easter, we went together with her to Puig.

And, immediately, on the third day of Easter,[64] a message reached us from a Saracen of Paterna telling us secretly, with letters from the entire *aljama,* that they would surrender the town and castle to us. And we said to them that we would go there and that, when we were there, they should be ready to deliver those castles, and that we would respect their law and all the customs which they had in the time of the Saracens, and that we would treat them very well.

When the fourth day came,[65] in accordance with what we had agreed with them, we went there with some one hundred knights, and the queen was with us. And all the Saracen men and women came out to receive us with great rejoicing, and we said that we would treat them well, and that we would give

---

[62] 'ab aytant aquí meteys'. Once again, we find reference to the mode of composition of the text, by oral narrative and dictation.

[63] Almenara, Castro, Uixó, Nules, and Alfàndec.

[64] 6 April 1238.

[65] 10 April 1238.

them franchises for two years because of the trouble they had taken. Then they gave thanks to God for the fine words we had spoken, and they opened their gates to us and we entered inside.

And we left the queen there with some ten knights as a garrison. And afterwards we took Bétera[66] and Bufilla, before returning from there to Puig.

[255] When the Saracens of Valencia found out that we held Paterna, the anger and sadness they had felt at first doubled, on seeing how close we were to them.

And while we were at Puig de Santa Maria, we took a decision not to wait any longer, but to go and besiege Valencia. With us were the master of the Hospital, called Hugh de Forcalquier, and a commander of the Temple, who had some twenty knights there, and the commander of Alcañiz,[67] and Don Rodrigo Lizana, who had some thirty knights, and the commander of Calatrava, and Guillem d'Aguiló, who had some fifteen knights there, and Don Jimeno Pérez de Tarazona,[68] along with our household who were with us. All in all we were perhaps some one hundred and thirty or one hundred and forty knights of lineage, and there were fifty *almogàvers*, and a good thousand foot soldiers.

[256] It was our decision that the next day, in the early morning, we would mobilize in the name of Our Lord and that we should go to besiege Valencia.[69] And we crossed the marshland through a pass that we had made, and we went along the seashore until the Grau,[70] and there we crossed at a ford. When we and our mule-trains had gone beyond the water to some houses that were between Valencia and the Grau, but perhaps nearer the Grau than Valencia, we had our standards and our tents set up, and we remained there. And there was perhaps a mile from this place to Valencia. We intended to wait here for more people of the company that were to come to us from Aragon and Catalonia, with whom we would go to besiege Valencia. And that day we saw Saracen knights, who went between us and the town, to see if they could take anything from the army. But we ordered our knights to be very vigilant and not to do any foraging until we knew the territory.

---

[66]In Valencia province, Bétera and Bufilla are a very little distance apart, above the Guadalaviar, and to the north-west of Valencia city.

[67]Rodrigo Pérez Pons.

[68]Jimeno was with the king in December 1237 (*M*, p. 127) and again in November 1238 (*M*, p. 137) after the surrender of Valencia. He was then steward of the king.

[69]22 April 1238.

[70]Where the river meets the sea, by the city of Valencia.

[257] When the next day came, before the dawn, without us knowing it, the *almogàvers* and the foot soldiers went to take Russafa,[71] which is two crossbow-shots from the town of Valencia. And at the time, we had a sickness in our eyes, and we could not open them unless they were washed with hot water. And they told us that the *almogàvers* and footmen had gone to take quarters at Russafa, which they had taken. And Hugh de Forcalquier, Master of the Hospital, came to us and said: "What do you order us to do? For everybody has gone to take quarters at Russafa."

And we said: "Let us arm our horses and, with our banners spread, let us go to help them; for if we do not, they are all dead."

And he said: "Your order shall be fulfilled."

And so we all armed and made haste straight to the little village called Russafa. And if we had not made such haste to go there, all those who were at the village would have been dead or captured. For when we went into the village, the Saracens were at the other end, and we held them in a square that was there.

[258] In the meanwhile, Ramon Canella, commander of Aliaga, and Lope Ximénez de Luesia, came to us and told us that we could easily capture fifty Saracens, if we spurred on against Valencia. And we said that we would like to see it. So we remained at that gate from where one can see Valencia. And we saw Zaén, with all his force from Valencia, at a tower that is half way between Valencia and Russafa, where there are some rocks and where the water collects when it rains or from the irrigation channels – and which Ramon Riquer now holds.[72] We observed that there were perhaps up to four hundred horsemen there, and of foot soldiers, the major force of the men of Valencia. And it seemed to us and to those who were with us that there were there, more or less, some ten thousand men.

Close to us, at little more than a stone's throw, there were some thirty or forty Saracens in a beanfield gathering beans. And they said that they could capture them if they spurred on. And we told them that they had spoken unwisely, because in a charge it is usually the case that if one does not take the place, those who make the charge have to turn round in flight. "And, what is more, we do not know if they have watered the fields, because if they have done that, on returning, the knights would have to return through the fields and they would have to enter through the irrigation channels, and some might fall there and do themselves great harm; and if by chance they were to drive us back in flight to the village, we would have to abandon the village, because they would have been able to take the other square."

---

[71] A suburb of Valencia.
[72] On 14 May 1238, during the siege of Valencia, James donated this tower to Ramon Riquer (*M*, p. 131).

For which reason we said we would not accept that advice, but that instead that night we would order valiant men to be found who would look to see if the fields were irrigated or not; and if they had not been irrigated, they should come to us, and we would hold it for good that a charge be made, and we said that, through the mercy of God, we had already done enough on the first day, having camped two crossbow-shots away from the town.

[259] We remained armed all day, so much so that nobody ate unless it was on horseback, and then only bread, wine, and cheese. When it was the hour of vespers, the Saracens turned tail and went back to the town. Then we dismounted and quickly took off our armour and ate. When we had eaten, we ordered fifty knights to arm who were to watch the camp at night. And when morning came, and we had heard our Mass, the Saracens did not come out to us but allowed us to rest. And we were there in that manner for five days.[73]

[260] Meanwhile, nobles kept arriving from Aragon and Catalonia. And among the first, the archbishop of Narbonne arrived,[74] with forty knights and six hundred footmen, and he was called Pierre Amell. So the army continued to grow, and the Saracens were hemmed in in such a manner that they did not dare to come out against us, except for some skirmishes they had with some of the army. For that reason, we did not need to arm the horses, as they did not come so close to us that we would be able to catch up with them. And the nobles and the cities, as they arrived, besieged Valencia on all sides, and they went closer to the town than us (who had been the first to arrive). And the city[75] that encamped nearest was Barcelona.

[261] And then we considered from which part to besiege Valencia. The majority said that it was more fitting to besiege it at Boatella,[76] and this was the opinion of the archbishop of Narbonne and the other nobles who were with us; but we disagreed with what they said and we showed them, with three reasons, that we could not besiege it at any place better than at that place where we were then.

The first reason was that if we set up the war-machines in front of the gate, it would be easier for the Saracens to come out to them and set fire to them, since they would be found near their gate, something which they could not do where we were. "And as this place is further from the gate, they will not dare come out." And so, now, exactly where we were, we would set up the

---

[73]Perhaps until 30 April 1238.

[74]Pierre Amell. His presence during the siege is confirmed by an exchange between James and the archbishop of Narbonne dated at Montpellier on 7 April 1259 (*M*, p. 286). In 1237, Pope Gregory IX had called on the archbishop and his suffragans to assist the campaign.

[75]That is, the militia of the city.

[76]The gate of the Boatella corresponding to the carrer de Sant Vincent (*S*, p. 314).

machines, so that if the Saracens came against them, the army might easily capture them before they returned to the town, because at that time there was no gate there between Boatella and Xerea.[77]

The other reason was that here the town jutted out, and when the barbican or wall had to be undermined, they would be unable to prevent that from the towers, because the wall came out here where the battle would be, and stuck out more than any other wall of the town.

The third was that if the army was moved to Boatella, the men of the town could come out[78] on horseback to intercept the reinforcements that would come to the army by sea, and one would need to have a full hundred armed knights to guard the camp, which would leave a shortage in the army, and would be troublesome for those who were the guard.

When they had heard our speech, all agreed to the advice that we had given, and they held our plan to be the best.

[262] After that the archbishop of Narbonne who was a courageous man, asked why we were there if we were doing nothing. And we told him that we would act when the army had come, and we would attack Boatella. Meanwhile a *trebuchet*, which we had had made at Tortosa, and two *fenevols* arrived. And we had them set up, and we fired from that place where the camp was.

Then we had mantelets made which we set beyond all the machines with armed men in garrison. And soon afterwards these brought the mantelets closer to some mud-walls near the moat, and from there they threw wood and vine branches inside the moat, which was full of water. Then, around three armed men crossed to the barbican.

When we were told that three armed men had crossed to the barbican, we could not believe their words, so we went to see if what they had said was true. And when we saw that the men could remain there and the Saracens could not put them to flight, we ordered two pickaxes to be sent there, and they hacked three hollows into the barbican and into each of two of the hollows two men could enter very easily.

[263] While we were there we sent two of our nobles, Don Pedro Fernández de Azagra and Don Jimeno de Urrea, to Silla, with our *fenevol*.[79] And they attacked for the space of about seven days. And at the end of eight days they surrendered, and in this way we took Silla.

---

[77]The gate of the Xerea corresponds to the carrer de Xèlpolella (*S*, p. 313).

[78]Desclot (ch. 49) says that after the battle of Puig, Zayyān had closed and fortified all the gates of the city except for one from which they could enter and leave.

[79]Both Pedro and Jimeno appear in documents of the king at this time, dated 28 May and 11 June respectively (M, p. 132).

[264] We ordered the barbican to be mined, whilst the Saracens defended it as best they could, but then twelve galleys and six atzaures[80] came from the king of Tunis,[81] between the first sleep and midnight, to the Grau of Valencia. And a message arrived to us, at night, from those who were at the Grau of Valencia, saying that many galleys had arrived there, and that they calculated there were between twelve and fifteen of them.

When we heard this, we took fifty knights with armoured horses, and some two hundred footsoldiers, and we had them placed in ambush on a bank a little distance from the sea, between some reeds and the bank, where they could be placed very easily. And we warned them not to go out until the Saracens were well on land, and to remain there, without leaving the ambush, until the hour of half-terce. And the Saracens, for fear of being ambushed, did not disembark.

When night came, they made a good hundred beacons of light in the galleys, so that the men of the town could see them, and these beat their drums to show the king of Tunis that he was their lord. And when they had made this din, we ordered the men of the army to make torches in every tent, so that, when it was dark, they could light them all, and let out a great cry. And it was done as we ordered, so that they would understand that we cared little for their displays. The men of the army threw a good five hundred torches inside the moat; so that those of the city might understand that we thought very little of what they had done, and that the galleys would not be able to help them.

[265] Then we went along the coast up to Tortosa and Tarragona to tell them to be on their guard and all to come together; and they did so. Now, we had three galleys, between Tarragona and Tortosa, and we ordered them to be armed immediately. Meanwhile, the Saracens' galleys, after having been there two days, went to Peníscola and they disembarked there in order to attack Peníscola. And Don Fernando Pérez de Pina went out of the castle that he held for us there, with his squires, and with ten horsemen, including him and Don Fernando de Ahones and the other men who had gone there. Together with the Saracens of the town, who helped them very well, they defeated the men of the galleys, and some seventeen of these died there.

And the caravan[82] from Tortosa, which was formed of twenty-one sails, armed seven vessels in such a way that each of these could capture a galley if it went alongside the vessel. And with the three galleys and seven vessels, they came, all together, in such a way that the galleys recognized the plan and fled, not daring to await them.

---

[80]Applied to any Muslim sailing ship (auzār – the sail of a ship), probably these were transports carrying men and provisions.

[81]Abū Zakarīyā' Yahyā. He was not one for lost causes and did much trade with Aragon. Probably the small fleet was under instruction only to intervene if the situation could be saved.

[82]'Caravana' or caravan is the word normally applied to the Tunisian fleet under sail, but is here applied to the Tortosan relief force.

Thus, a great supply of wheat, wine, barley, cheese, fruit and other small things arrived to us, for the army was so large that there were a good thousand knights and a good sixty thousand foot soldiers. But, even so, one could find all that one wanted to sell or to buy, just as one would in a city. There were even apothecaries from Montpellier and Lleida who sold herbs and spices there (as is done in a big town), both for the sick and the healthy.[83] And we ordered our machines to fire, and the men of the army had many skirmishes with the men from inside, and they made charges. In this way, at one time, the Saracens lost Xerea,[84] so that more than a hundred knights of the army were able to enter there. And the Saracens lost some fifteen men defending it.

[266] Another time the men of the company of the archbishop of Narbonne had a skirmish with those from inside, but did not know the customs of the Saracens, who fled in order to be able to draw them near to the town. Now, we saw that the foot soldiers were beginning to be drawn on by those who were fleeing, so we sent word to them that they should not pursue them, for if they did so the Saracens would do them great harm. Yet they did not wish to stay, despite our message; and because we were afraid for them, lest some thirty or more would die there when the Saracens attacked them, we went up to them on a horse we had mounted and we ordered them to withdraw.

As we returned from there with the men, we turned our head to the town to keep an eye on the Saracens, as there was a great company outside; and a crossbowmen fired at us, and running through the brim of the helmet and the hood of mail, the arrow hit us, near our forehead. By the will of God, the arrow did not go right through our head, but the point drove halfway into my forehead.[85] And we, because of the anger that we felt, gave such a blow to the arrow that we broke it; and the blood was running down our face. Yet we wiped the blood off, with the silk cloak that we were wearing, and we went along laughing so that the army would not be alarmed.

Then we went into our tent where we rested; and our entire face and our eyes swelled up so much that we could not see out of the eye on the wounded side of our face for four or five days. When the swelling on my face had gone down, we rode through the whole camp, so that the people were not completely disheartened.

---

[83]The armies of the Crown were unusually fortunate for the time, since they had the advantage of considerable Christian and Arab medical expertise. Moreover, Montpellier was especially noted for its faculty of medicine.

[84]The gate of this name.

[85]The king made light of the blow but the wound above the left eye was serious. After the monastery of Poblet was sacked in 1835 and the royal tombs despoiled, the remains of James were easily recognizable both because of his height and the wound to his skull.

[267] Meanwhile, Don Pedro Cornel[86] and Don Jimeno de Urrea decided to attack the tower that is at the gate of the Boatella, on the street of Sant Vicent; and they concealed this from us and from everybody else in the camp. Yet after they had attacked it for a while, because of the reinforcements that came out from inside the town, who defended very well, they were unable to take it and they had to return from there. And we told them off for undertaking so important an action without consulting with us or the nobles of the camp, and we said to them that it was only right that it had gone so badly for them.

[268] Then we sent for the bishops and the nobles of the army, and we decided that, since the action had already commenced, it was necessary to take the tower the next day; and that we should arm up to two hundred knights and all the crossbowmen of the army and at sunrise we should go there and fight them. And, come what may, we would take it, and nobody should leave there until it was all taken. Thus, at sunrise, we went there; and there were some ten Saracens prepared to defend the tower, and we fought them.

They defended very well and with so much skill that nobody could have defended themselves better than they did; but such was the power of our crossbowmen, and of the stones that we fired at them, that nobody could stick out his hand without it being wounded by an arrow. Despite all that, they did not want to surrender the tower to us, when we told them to do so; but one of our army set fire to the tower, and when they saw the fire they were afraid and said that they would surrender. Then we said that we would not show them mercy, since they had not surrendered before.[87] So we burnt them there and we took the tower, and then we returned to the camp.

[269] When this action was completed, those inside were greatly afraid, because we had taken a tower from them; and we ordered our war-machines to fire night and day. After a time, when perhaps a good month had passed,[88] a Saracen merchant came out towards us under our safe-conduct. And the company of Ramon Berenguer d'Àger[89] met him, and one of them brought him on the haunches of his horse. He came before us and gave us news of Zaén,

---

[86]Don Pedro's participation in the siege of Valencia is indicated in documents of 11 July and 11 September 1238. He was also one of the first to witness the surrender of the city on 28 September 1238 (*M*, pp. 133–4).

[87]At Muret, James's father refused to show mercy to Simon de Montfort though it was requested and had, in James's opinion, suffered the consequences for this sinful act (ch. 9), but here, since James had offered mercy and the Moors had refused it, the king considered his ruthless action to be justified. Most importantly, it sent a clear signal to those inside of the city of the treatment they could expect if they resisted too long.

[88]June–July 1238.

[89]He appears at the siege as witness to documents of 23 May 1238 and 28 August 1238, and was one of the witnesses of the surrender of the city (*M*, p. 134).

King of Valencia, of how he conducted his affairs and what his intentions were.

And he said that there were three things which had greatly disheartened him: the first was that the galleys of the king of Tunis had profited him so little;[90] the second was the tower that we had burnt; and the third was that he had seen so great an army around him that now almost the whole of Valencia was surrounded. He believed they could not hold out for a long time, because they did not have provisions for the amount of people who were in Valencia – men, women, and children – since we had surprised them and we had besieged the town before they had collected the harvest; and that certainly he believed it would not be very long before we conquered it.

[270] When we heard the words the Saracen spoke to us, we were very pleased; as were the men of the army when they knew of it. Now, because this book is of such a nature that one should not put trifling matters into it, we leave off telling of many things that happened, and wish only to speak of the most important matters so that the book will not be too greatly lengthened; nevertheless, we do wish to treat and speak of those matters which were great and good. And this much we can tell of that camp: that we, who have made some thirty camps, have never seen, on any occasion, an army so well provided as that one with the things which are necessary to support a man; so that the sick were able to find help from apothecaries just as if they were in Barcelona or Lleida.

[271] Later on, fifteen days before the eve of Saint Michael,[91] Zaén sent us a message saying that if we wished to give safe-conduct to a Saracen who was called Alí Albaca[92] and who was a native of Peníscola, he would send him to us, and he would speak with us. And we told him that we were very pleased that he should come, and that we would grant him safe-conduct. When he arrived he told us why the king of Valencia had sent him; and we said we would consider the matter and that shortly we would respond. Now, we thought that it was not a good idea that any man of the army, neither the nobles nor the others, should know anything of these words, because there were many who did not want Valencia to be taken,[93] and would rather it belonged to the

---

[90]Zayyān was heavily dependent on maritime support from the Hafsid dynasty and once the fleet had failed to relieve Valencia, the city was essentially lost.

[91]So, 13 September 1238.

[92]Alī al-Baqā clearly enjoyed the confidence of Zayyān who had sent him two years previously as negotiator (ch. 242).

[93]Another indication of the ill-will of the nobles who would have preferred the economic benefits of the tributes to the capture of the city and did not want to see the increase of the power of the king.

Saracens than it should fall into our power. Afterwards we will see proof of this.

So we went to see the queen and we told her the words that Alí Albaca had said to us, and we communicated our thoughts to her, to see if it seemed good to her.[94] And we asked her and we ordered her that none of the army should know about it, but only we and she, and the messenger, who was the interpreter. She said that the words that we had said to her pleased her greatly, for nobody had so great a share in our honour and our good as she did, and if God had honoured us and loved us, she thanked Him for it, since any hope of her own good was entirely in us. Furthermore, she considered it a good idea that nobody else should participate in that agreement, so that nobody might oppose it in any way; because she had already seen in other places, which were castles, that our nobles wanted them more for themselves than for us, and that they did many things to us there that they should not do. For which reason she believed that, if in little things they acted so, in the case of Valencia they would again use their power to stop it from being ours. Therefore, she considered it a good thing, above all else, to keep the secret, until we were certain of possessing Valencia.

[272] We sent word to Alí Albaca that he should return to our presence, and we said to him that he should explain why he had come. And he told us that they were significant words and of great importance: "And it is not fitting that we speak; but Zaén, King of Valencia, has sent word to you through me that he will send you the *Rais* Abulfamalet,[95] who is his nephew, the son of his sister, and who after him is the most powerful man in Valencia and the kingdom, and the man in whom he most trusts. If God wills it, before you and he part, we trust in God that the deed will come to a good conclusion."

After that he told us that he would enter inside the town and that he would come to us with some plan or other; so we gave him a knight to guide him as he returned to the town. Then he gave us an hour the next morning, at the hour of sunrise, when he would come to us, that then we might send a knight to protect him. And we promised him that we would do so.

When morning came we sent a knight to him, and he came. And when he was in our presence he said that Zaén, King of Valencia, warmly greeted us, and he told us on his behalf that when the morning of the next day came, between the hour of terce and sunrise,[96] we should send two nobles to protect

---

[94] The participation of Yolanda, without whom little is done, indicates both the very important role that was often played by the wives of rulers in negotiations and the high regard in which James personally held his wife.

[95] Abū l'Hamlāt.

[96] At about eight o'clock in the morning.

the *Rais* Abulfamalet, who would come to us. So we ordered Don Nunó [97] and Don Ramon Berenguer d'Àger to prepare to go out to receive the nephew of Zaén, the *Rais* Abulfamalet, early in the morning, and that they should protect him until he had come to us; and they said that they would do it.

[273] Meanwhile, two Saracen knights challenged any two of our knights in the army to a joust, and they made it known to us. And Don Jimeno Pérez de Tarazona, who was afterwards lord of Arenós, came to us and asked us to give him permission to undertake that joust, along with Miguel Pérez de Híjar. [98] Now, we said to him that we were very surprised that a man such as he, who was so great a sinner and of such an evil life, should ask for a joust, and we feared that we would be shamed. But he pressed us so insistently that we gave him permission. And he jousted with the Saracen, and the Saracen overthrew him. Another Saracen came out and went against Pere de Clariana, and during the joust the Saracen turned his back on him and fled; but he pursued him until he crossed the river Guadalaviar where the Saracen took refuge among his own people.

[274] When the next morning arrived, very early in the morning, the *Rais* Abulhamelet came out, with that Saracen who had jousted, and with ten other knights, fully equipped and dressed, and with good horses and fine new saddles, and they would have been able to enter any court as very distinguished men. And when he entered our quarters (which were very tidy and adorned) and was near us, we got up for him. Yet he did not wish to kiss our hand, but prostrated himself before us and came to embrace us. And he was seated before us, and greeted us on behalf of Zaén, King of Valencia, and he told us that he had never seen us before and so was very pleased to meet us. We said to him that we wished God might give him good fortune and that we were overjoyed that he had come to us and had come to see us, because we would honour him and treat him so well that he would have to thank us. He told us that that is what he hoped of us, for we were of such a nature that those whom we loved always received good and honour from us.

Now, we invited him to eat, but he told us that though he thanked us very much for the invitation, he would not eat outside the town, because he had been forbidden to do so by his lord. [99] Nonetheless, he already felt himself to be

---

[97]During the siege, Nunó witnessed documents of 28 August 1238 and 17 September 1238, and he also witnessed the surrender of the city on 28 September 1238 (*M*, pp. 133–4).

[98]Perhaps the king really wished to describe Miguel as a great sinner rather than Jimeno, whom he has already praised and who was one of his closest advisers. But it is also quite possible that the event was an in-joke with the knights present while James was narrating the tale (perhaps Jimeno himself was there).

[99]Offering food was more than simply a matter of politeness. Rather it shows the king's understanding of the importance dining ritual held in the mind of the Medieval Muslim. James

very fortunate to be invited and honoured by us. Then we said that if he did not want to eat there, we would send food to the town for him; and he said that he thanked us very much, but another occasion would come when he could receive it better than he could do now, since he could not do so. After that, we said to him that, if he wanted, we would order everybody in the room to go outside so that he could speak with us in private. And he said that he did want that, and that he would not speak in our presence unless we were alone or with one or two people who were our confidants. So, we ordered everybody to leave the room, except us, him, and the interpreter.

[275] Then we asked him what he wanted to say. And he said that Zaén was surprised that we had so offended him in ordering our armies and our power against his land and the power that he had; for he considered that he had not done anything against us that he should receive so much harm from us.

Upon that we responded to him, saying yes he had done so, because when we went to Majorca to conquer it, he came to attack our land, and went as far as Tortosa and Amposta, and all the harm that he and his men were able to do to our men and cattle, they did to us.[100] Similarly he attacked us at Ulldecona, which was inside our kingdom. Furthermore, he had done us wrong in another thing, too. We had sent our messenger to him to tell him that we wished to have a peace and truce with him, and that since in our childhood we were accustomed to have and to take the fifths of Valencia and Murcia, we sought for him to satisfy that which he had failed to give us from Valencia.[101]

Thus, we made a claim for one hundred thousand bezants; and we sent to him Don Pere Sanç,[102] our messenger, who was our notary, and he, scorning our love, offered us no more than fifty thousand bezants. After that, we did not wish for anything of him nor his love, so we had to come against him; for he preferred to have fifty thousand bezants than to have our love.

[276] And he responded to our words, and said that he did not think we should be angered by that, since, when we had taken the fifths of Valencia, he was not lord of the kingdom of Valencia, because Zeit Abuzeit was the king. Yet he then went on to say that things had to follow the course that God willed: "And upon that matter which is now between you and us, we have to seek a means of resolving it well and to your honour, since that is what Zaén desires."

We responded that he spoke well, and that we should arrive at an agreement on present matters and not upon past affairs. Then he said that he wanted to

---

was fully aware that if Abū l'Ḥamlāt were to accept the offer then a friendship was established between them and implicitly the first step to a negotiated surrender had been taken.

[100]While James undertook the conquest of Majorca, Abū Zayd, helped by the Aragonese nobles, such as Pedro Fernández and Blasco de Alagón, sustained the battle against Zayyān.

[101]The tribute that Abū Zayd had agreed to pay in 1225.

[102]From Lleida, he was certainly king's notary from 1221 until 1246 (*M*, pp. 38, 184).

know from us what we wanted done, in those matters that God had ordained should befall them. For which reason he asked us insistently that we should not conceal our will from him, and that if we wished his lord to give us assets, he would give them to us, according to his means. For, as we were aware, the city of Valencia had received great damage because of the men who had been lost to our forces after the battle of Puig was waged, and because we had laid waste to the crops and the *horta* of Valencia, as well as to other places of the kingdom, in the greater part of them and in the best.

We then said to him that we believed it was necessary that the queen should come, and that we did not want any other person of the world to know anything of that except we and she and he who spoke those words. And he said that these were two things for which he greatly thanked us: one, that with the queen we would seek to make it worth more, and would hold the agreement in higher regard; the other, that he was pleased we would keep it a secret, since that was better for him and for us, because he knew well that we had to guard ourselves against many men who did not wish our profit in that matter nor in anything else.

[277] So we sent for the queen. And when she had come, we ordered all the women who had come with her and all the others to leave, and of them all, she alone remained with us. Then we repeated to her all the words that we had had with the *Rais* Abulhamelet, and he with us, as is written above. And we said to him that we preferred to respond to him before the queen rather than apart, and that this was our response: that we had come to that place, and that God had guided us in all the things that we had commenced until that day, and we had achieved them; and that as we were there, this was our plan and our intention: that we would never leave that place until we possessed Valencia. Hence, if the king of Valencia wished to avoid the very great harm that could be produced in the capture of the town, when so many Saracen men, women, and children, could die and lose all that they had, that seemed good to us. And we said that for their good and their profit, because we would take them under our protection and we would escort them with all that they could carry. "Because their death would grieve us. And if it were their will to surrender the town, voluntarily, we would prefer to have it that way than by force, since the greater part of the army wish to sack the town, but we do not wish it because of the pity that we feel for you. And this is our will, and we will not do otherwise, as long as you do not oblige us to do you harm through force."

He said that the words were very weighty, and that he could not discuss them with us without the agreement of his lord and uncle. And we recognized that he was right, and we said to him that he should go to do so in peace. Then we again invited him to eat, but he did not want to accept, and after that, he went back inside the town.

[278] When the third day arrived, he sent us a message to say that if we would grant him safe-conduct, he would come to us. And we sent him one of our nobles, and he came to our presence as soon as the noble had gone there. He said to us that the King of Valencia, Zaén, understanding that the town could not be defended in the long term, and so that nobody suffered more harm than they had already received from us, had agreed that he would surrender it to us, on the condition that the Saracen men and women could take all their belongings, and that nobody should search or maltreat them, and that both they and he would be accompanied under our protection to Cullera. For, as God willed that we should have Valencia, he, too, had to accept it.

We said to him that we would consult with the queen alone, who was in that council. And he said that he considered that a good idea and he left our chamber. We remained there with the queen and we asked her what she thought. And she said that if it seemed good to us, we should accept the agreement, because it seemed a good idea to her, as he who could have Valencia from one day to the next should by no means leave it to chance.

We recognized that she had advised us well, and we told her that we agreed with the advice she had given us, but that we wished to add one thing, and that, having added it, we would consider the advice good: If the town was taken by force, it would be difficult to avoid great disputes between the men of the army and us over vile assets or belongings, and we ought not delay that which our lineage had always desired to have and to take. Moreover, if we were wounded or became ill during the period of delay until the town was taken by force, all could be lost. For a deed such as that should not be left to chance, and it was necessary to make good haste to have it.

[279] With these words, we sent for the *Rais* Abulfamalet and replied to him as follows: "*Rais*, you are well aware that we have spent a great deal on this deed, but despite the money our men and we have spent, and the harm we have suffered here, we shall not give up fulfilling this deal, and we will protect you as far as Cullera, with all the belongings that the Saracen men and women carry there and can carry there. And out of love for the king and you, who have come here, we wish to do this grace: that the people may leave safely and securely, with their belongings and with what they can and want to carry."[103]

[280] Now it pleased him, when he heard it, and he said that he thanked us very much, although they would lose much by it. Even so, he thanked us very

---

[103]The Muslims were allowed to remain in Valencia under James's protection. Those who wished to leave were to do so within eight days with what they could carry. Those who remained would have to guarantee to live alongside the new arrivals. There was a seven-year truce with Zayyān. The city would be ruled by King James and his men, who swore to observe the pact. Zayyān was to deliver to James all the towns found to the north of the Xúquer, excepting the castles of Dénia and Cullera, within twenty days (*H*, 2, no. 265; *Alicante*, no. 5).

much for the mercy we had shown him. And after a while we asked him on what day it should be. And he said that they would need ten days grace. But we said to him that he asked for too much, and that the army had been calm for a long time and it greatly troubled them to do nothing, and that it was not in our interests or theirs. So, after much discussion, we agreed that they would surrender the town on the fifth day, and begin to leave.[104]

When this pact was agreed between him and us, we said to him that he should keep it a secret until we had spoken with the archbishop of Narbonne, the bishops and with our noble men. And he said that he would do so. And we said to him that we would speak of it that evening, ordering that from that hour forward nobody should do them harm.

[281] When that was done, and we had eaten and drunk and slept in a tent that was near our quarters, we sent for the archbishop of Narbonne, and he came. And when everybody was in our presence, we told them how Our Lord had conceded to us many favours and, among them, now he had conceded one to us for which they and we should thank Him greatly. And as they had a great share in this good fortune of ours, we wished to let them know it, so that they should rejoice in it: Valencia was ours.

When we had said these words, Don Nunó, Don Jimeno de Urrea, Don Pedro Fernández de Azagra, and Don Pedro Cornel went pale, as if somebody had wounded them straight to the heart.[105] And except for the archbishop and some bishops,[106] who said that they thanked the Lord for this good and this mercy that He had done us, none of them began to praise it or thank God for it, nor held it for something good.

But Don Nunó and Don Pedro Fernández de Azagra asked us how that could be and in what manner. So we said that we had assured the king of Valencia and all the Saracens who lived at the town, men and women, that they could go under our protection to Cullera and Dénia, and that in this way they would surrender the town on the fifth day.

And they said that it seemed reasonable to them, since we had done it. And the archbishop of Tarragona said: "This is the work of God, and I do not believe that of these three things, one of them is not to be found in you at all times: either you have served God, or now you serve him, or you shall serve him."

---

[104]28 September 1238.

[105]The nobles were again furious because James has taken the city without their help, without an opportunity for battle or plunder, and increasing his own power at their expense.

[106]The archbishops of Narbonne and Tarragona were both present, as were the bishops of Barcelona, Zaragoza, Huesca, Tarazona, Segorbe, Tortosa and Vic. All witnessed the surrender.

Then Ramon Berenguer d'Àger said: "We must greatly thank Our Lord for the love that He has shown you. As that which your line and you have desired has now been fulfilled through you, we have to thank Our Lord."

[282] When the next day came, at the hour of vespers, we sent word to the king and to *Rais* Abulhamelet that, in order that the Christians might know that Valencia was ours, and thus not harm them in any way, we would place our standard on the tower that now belongs to the Templars. They said that that was agreeable to them.[107] And we were then between the gully and the camp and the tower. When we saw our standard upon the tower, we dismounted and we turned towards the East, tears falling from our eyes, and kissed the ground for the great mercy God had done us.[108]

[283] Meanwhile, the Saracens hurried to leave, inside the five days they had agreed with us, and by the third day all were prepared to depart. With knights and armed men near us, we brought them all outside, to the fields between Russafa and the town. As we did so, we were forced to wound fatally men who wished to rob the belongings of the Saracens and seize some Saracen women and children. Thus, even though such a great multitude of people departed from Valencia, in which there were some fifty thousand men and women,[109] by the mercy of God they did not lose a thousand sous in value, so well did we protect them and did we have them protected until Cullera.

[284] When we had done that, we entered the town.[110] And when the third day came we began to divide the houses with the archbishop of Narbonne, the bishops and the nobles who had been with us, and with the knights who had been given inheritances in that district. We also gave portions to the corporations of the cities, each according to the company and the men-at-arms they had sent there.

---

[107]James does not mention the ceremonial signing of the surrender treaty but Ibn al-Abbār, Zayyān's secretary, recalled the Christian king coming from his camp at al-Rusāfa in his finest clothes and surrounded by the nobles in order to draw up the treaty in full sight of both armies (Ibn al-Abbār, 'Traité inédit', p. 33).

[108]The news of James's conquest of Valencia was greeted ecstatically by Pope Gregory IX, Louis IX of France (who sent a thorn from the crown of thorns to Valencia), the north Italian cities (who wished James to lead a crusade against Frederick II) and in much of Christendom (though not necessarily in Languedoc, since the troubadours lamented James had not paid sufficient attention to protecting their region). In England, Matthew Paris recorded, gleefully and inaccurately, that the king of Aragon had ravaged the great city of Valencia through bloody war (Burns, *Crusader Kingdom*, 1, p. 1). The chronicle of Saint Denis *(RHGF, 21, p. 108)* more accurately said that, in order that James did not have to wait a long time, he settled for terms.

[109]Burns puts the number at fifteen thousand *(Islam under the Crusaders*, p. 76).

[110]9 October 1238.

[285] Later on, some three weeks having passed,[111] we appointed partitioners to divide up the land of the district of Valencia; and we examined the charters detailing the donations we had made, and we found that there were more documents than there was land in the district, because of the donations that we had made to some men. There were other men, too, who had said they wanted very little, but afterwards it would be found that it was two or three times as much. Because of the trickery they had done to us, and because there was not enough to meet the donations in the documents, we took land from those who held too much, and redistributed it fairly, so that all had adequate land there. And in this way the land was divided.[112]

[286] Though we wished to divide the land ourselves, we had appointed as partitioners (as it would have been too much work for us), Don Assalit de Gúdar and Don Jimeno Pérez de Tarazona, who was then our steward in the kingdom of Aragon.[113] However, the bishops and nobles came to us and said: "We wonder that you should give as important a city as this, which is the foremost in all the kingdom of Valencia, to be divided by Don Assalit and Don Jimeno Pérez, for, although they may be good and well versed in law, it does not pertain to them to divide it. Rather you should appoint the most honourable men that you have here. Hence, we ask you and we advise you to do this, because all the people speak of it, and they say you have not proceeded well in the matter."

We said to them: "So then, who do you think we should have appointed?"

And they said: "We think it right and advise that you appoint two bishops and two nobles; for just as it is an honoured place, so you ought to appoint honoured men."

Then we said: "So that we may better respond, tell us who you wish us to appoint and upon that matter we shall deliberate."

They said that they thought it right that it should be Berenguer, Bishop of Barcelona, Vidal de Canelles, Bishop of Huesca, Pedro de Azagra and Jimeno de Urrea. And we said: "We will take a decision upon that and will respond to you."

[287] Meanwhile we sent for Don Assalit de Gúdar and Don Jimeno Pérez de Tarazona, and we said to them: "Look what the bishops and the nobles have

---

[111]Late October–early November 1238

[112]The *Repartiment* has now been edited in a number of editions: *Repartiment de València: edición fotocópia*, ed. J. Ribera y Tarragó, Valencia: Centro de Cultura Valenciana, 1939; *Libre del repartiment del regne de Valencia*, ed. M. Cabanes Pecourt and R. Ferrer Navarro, 3 vols, Zaragoza: Anubar, 1979; *Llibre del repartiment de València*, ed. A. Ferrando, 4 vols, Valencia: Vicent Garcia Editores, 1978.

[113]Both Assalit and Jimeno were with James during and after the conquest (*M*, pp. 131, 136).

said to me; that I should remove you from the office of dividing the inheritances and replace you with the bishops of Barcelona and Huesca, and Pedro Fernández de Azagra and Jimeno de Urrea."

And they responded: "We already knew that you wanted to say this, but we ask you not to remove us, as we would receive dishonour."

Then we said: "To my mind you are not thinking straight, for by this we can undermine their plans."

And they said: "In what manner?"

And we said: "Like this: we shall follow their will because we know the land will be insufficient for the donations. Then they will have to return it to us because they will not know how to resolve the matter."

Still they said: "We ask you not to take it from us, because we would receive dishonour."

But we said to them: "Leave it to us, for in the long run we will protect you from dishonour and shame."

And they said that it should be as we wished.

Then we sent for the bishops and the nobles, so that we could respond to them on that which they had said to us.

[288] When they were before us, we said that we would grant them what they had asked of us, and that we were pleased that they would take charge of it. And they thanked us very much and kissed us on the hand. After that, we waited fifteen days for them to divide it, but they did not do so. Then Don Assalit de Gúdar and Don Jimeno Pérez de Tarazona came to our presence and they said: "Now we understand that what you told us is true. For we know from men of their counsel that they can neither agree nor resolve the matter."

We said that in the morning we will send for them, and that we will want to find out if they were dividing the land or what they were doing. And they came and they said to us: "Lord, you have to know that, truly, we find ourselves in great difficulty concerning this business, and we believe that we will have to return it to you."

Yet we said: "What, return it? Since you have started to do it, it is absolutely necessary that you finish it."

Then they left our presence, but on the third day they returned, because the people were crying out, and saying that those partitioners were good for nothing, since they did not divide the land, but made them spend their money in exchange for nought. Again they said they would return the business to us, because they did not believe they could resolve it. And we said: "Since you wish to return it to us, we shall send for the nobles, the knights, and the men of the city", and that in front of all of them they should return it.

And we ordered a great council to be assembled in the houses of King Llop,[114] and in front of everybody, they returned the charge.

[289] When we had recovered it, we sent for Don Jimeno Pérez de Tarazona and Don Assalit de Gúdar, and we said to them: "Is not the shame they have received, in not knowing how to divide the land, better than if we had done it in spite of them and had entrusted it to you?"

And they said that they thanked us very much for it, and that we had taken the better course. Then we said: "Now we will show you how to divide the land, and you will do it just as it was done at Majorca, for it cannot be done in any other way: You shall reduce the jovate to six cafizes,[115] so it will both have the name jovate and will not be one. Moreover, to those whom we have given too much, let their lands be redistributed fairly, according to their value."

Now, they said that we had spoken well, and that we had no other choice, so they would do it so. Furthermore, we said to them that they should ask for the charters of the donations, and we, depending on what we saw fit, would give of it to them in proportion to the value shown. And they did it, and in this way the land was divided.

And so that all may know when Valencia was taken, it was on the eve of Saint Michael's day, in the year MCCXXXIX.[116]

---

[114]King Lobo (1147–71).

[115]That is, from twelve to six *cafizes*.

[116]Valencia surrendered on 28 September 1238, not 1239.

5

Valencia – The Southern Campaign

[290] When Valencia had been taken, Ramon Folc de Cardona[1] arrived. And, what with his relatives and his men, some fifty knights came with him. They said that, as they had not been at the siege, they besought us to permit them to make a raid through the lands of Murcia. And it pleased us that they should do so. With them they took Artal de Alagón,[2] son of Don Blasco, who knew the land, because he had already been there. The first place they came upon to which they wished to do harm was Villena.[3]

When they arrived near Villena, they caparisoned the horses, and having armed the whole company with the weapons that were there, they charged against the Saracens of Villena, and took from them two parts of the town of Villena. Yet, as they could not hold out if they stayed longer, because of the strength of the Saracens who were inside, they were forced to leave the town. Nevertheless, they brought away a great deal of booty that they found in the houses.

[291] Then they went to Sax,[4] and made a raid there, taking a great part of the town. However, a Saracen threw a great stone from a rooftop, hitting Artal de Alagón upon his iron cap, with such force that he fell from his horse. And from that blow he was to die. When they saw that Artal de Alagón was dead, they brought him outside, and they were forced to depart because of the evil they had received there. Thus, even though they had intended to go further, they came to the decision to return, because of the death of Artal de Alagón. Within eight days we had them back. And the raid did not profit anybody, except that they obtained cattle for the army to eat. And when that had happened, Ramon Folc went home.

[292] Now, we were advised by the nobles and the knights who had been with us at the siege, that we should find out to how many men we had given inheritances. And we found that we had given inheritances to three hundred

---

[1]The son of Guillem de Cardona.

[2]Artal had certainly participated in the siege of Valencia (*M*, p. 131).

[3]To the north-west of Alicante and by the river Vinalopó. The raid, therefore, travelled far from Valencia.

[4]A little to the south-east of Villena.

and eighty knights, besides the nobles. And we ordered them to come to our presence and we began to speak to them in this manner: Our Lord had favoured us so greatly, that though there had been other kings in our position who were as good or better than us, He had never wished to concede that grace nor give to any of the others the victory that we had gained. And so, we and they had ought give thanks to Our Lord, for having seen the day on which we had won Valencia. Having won Valencia, we had won all the rest of the kingdom. For which reason, it was necessary, since God had given to us and them so much good and honour, that we should hold this land that we had conquered. And since we had given inheritances to three hundred and eighty knights in the kingdom, besides the nobles, we asked that those who had been given inheritances should remain a year with us, and that at the end of a year they could return to their lands and attend to their affairs, and sell what they had there in order to come here; and that, while they were away, we would guard their land, for a reasonable length of time.

Speaking for himself and all the others, Don Ferdinand[5] said that they would deliberate, and that they would give such a response that we would be satisfied with them. Thus, they went to deliberate, and they did not delay long in replying, saying to Don Ferdinand that he should respond on behalf of all of them.

[293] And he got to his feet and said that they thanked God very much, he and the nobles and the knights, for the mercy God had done us, for they well understood that we had given inheritances to them there, and that they ought to serve us and help us, but they besought us and called on our mercy that we would wish to attend to their requests. And these were the requests that he and they made of us: that, since we had asked for three hundred and eighty knights to remain in our service, it should please us – for this was a reasonable thing they were saying to us, and they would take this favour that we had granted to them just as if they had been given inheritances by us – to accept that one hundred knights serve us during four months, and during another four months, another hundred; and that in the other four months that would complete the year, another hundred would serve us. In doing them this grace they would consider themselves to have been given inheritances by us, and we would have given them the greatest show of love that a lord had ever given his vassals.

Thus he ended his speech.

[294] And we replied to him in this manner: "Ferdinand, will you, the nobles, and the knights be satisfied with me if I grant this favour that you ask?"

---

[5]Ferdinand certainly took part in the siege of Valencia, signed the document of surrender, and was still in the city in January 1239 (*M*, pp. 133–4, 138).

And they said to us that indeed they would be satisfied, and that they would consider it a great gift and a great favour. So we said: "Since you consider it a gift and a favour, we concede it to you in the way you have dictated. And we give to you these favours and others so that you may recognize what kind of lord you have in us."

Then they got up and approached us, and kissed our hand for the favour we had done to them.

[295] We ordered a galley to be armed to go to Montpellier, to ask them to help us with the expenses we had incurred in conquering Valencia. And we went there,[6] leaving behind us in the land Astruc de Belmont, who was master of the Temple, Hugh de Forcalquier, Master of the Hospital, Don Berenguer d'Entença, Guillem d'Aguiló, and Don Jimeno Pérez de Tarazona.[7] Now, Guillem d'Aguiló rose up, with knights, footmen, and *almogàvers*, and did harm to the Saracens, as much to ours as to theirs; and, moreover, they besieged Rebollet[8] and took it. But when that happened, we had already left for Montpellier.

When we arrived at Lattes,[9] the consuls and some hundred notables of Montpellier came out on horseback to receive us, and Pierre Boniface[10] with them; and he was then the most powerful man in the whole town. Don Pedro Fernández de Azagra[11] and Don Assalit de Gúdar came near to us, but Pierre Boniface said: "Leave the king to us, as we have not seen him for a long time, and we ought to be near him."

Don Assalit told him that it was more fitting for them to be in that place than for Pierre Boniface or the others. But Pierre Boniface replied that in their land it was fitting for them to travel at our side. And we indicated to Don

---

[6]From June to October 1239. The reasons for James's visit to his hometown went beyond what he mentions here. James felt the increasing power of the northern Franks in Occitania had to be opposed as it threatened his interests in the area, including Montpellier. James tentatively gave his support to Raymond VII of Toulouse and Raymond Berenguer V of Provence in their proposed league against the Franks. Here, as in 1245, James left off the Valencia campaign considering events in southern France of more pressing importance.

[7]The presence of Berenguer, Guillem, and Jimeno at the siege and conquest of Valencia is well-documented (*M*, pp. 130–4).

[8]The castle of Rebollet just to the south of Gandia. James appears to have condemned the attacks on the Saracens but not the taking of Rebollet which he entrusted to Carròs on 18 July 1240 (*Llibre del Repartiment*, no. 2258).

[9]Probably on Thursday 2 June 1239 (*M*, p. 140; *S*, p. 319). Lattes is seven kilometres from Montpellier. In 1238, while James was occupied with the Valencia campaign, it appears the bishop of Maguelonne, Jean de Montlaur, had suppressed his rights on Montpellier and Lattes and transferred them to the count of Toulouse. The chief supporters of the bishop and Toulouse were Pierre Boniface, Guerau de la Barca, Raymond Bessède, Guillem d'Anglada and Bernard and Guillem Regordan. They were opposed by the king's lieutenant, Atbrand (Baumel, *Histoire d'une seigneurie*, 2, p. 86).

[10]Bailiff in Montpellier in 1236, and consul in 1238 and again in 1246 (*S*, p. 319).

[11]Both Pedro and Assalit were present with the king on this trip (*M*, p. 140).

Assalit that he should not take issue with him about it. And on seeing that we took issue with him, Don Assalit fell silent. Now, we pretended that those words had not affected us, but they troubled us greatly as they showed how very arrogant Pierre Boniface was.

[296] In those times, it was Pierre Boniface, Guerau de la Barca,[12] Bernard de Regordan,[13] who was well-versed in law, and Raymond Bessède who held the greatest power in the consulate. But we dismounted at the house of Atbrand,[14] who was our bailiff. These others wished to do him great harm, and had decided in the consulate that if we did not come immediately, they would pull down his houses. And they had made a battering ram, to the end of which they had bound with iron a beam, on which, here and there, there were rings through which ropes could be attached, and with which they could demolish the houses of Atbrand and any other who wished to support him.

When we had taken up quarters in the house of Atbrand and the bells tolled for vespers through the town, the consuls came to us, with other men, at the house of Atbrand, where we were staying. And there were perhaps some twenty of them and they said that they wished to speak to us in private. So we went up onto a little terrace belonging to Atbrand, which was in the open air; and Pierre Boniface got to his feet and said: "Lord, the consuls and one part of the council of Montpellier have come here, and we are very pleased at your arrival. Now we wish to tell you as much, and I say it to you for them and us: that we desire to honour you and give you much love, just as we ought to do for our lord. Now, we know that Atbrand has you believe that he can give you Montpellier and you must know that that is certainly not true, because he has no more power of action or law in Montpellier than any other resident of the town,[15] for it is we who have the power and the money. If it were not for you, there is no sewer so vile in this town from which we would not drive him, both him and those who wish to help him. All that we bear from him, we bear for your sake, for we have in our power men, weapons, and money, against which his power would be as nothing. This we beg you to believe of us."

After that, Guerau de la Barca got up and spoke on this subject.

[297] When they had spoken, we replied to them in this manner: "Worthy men, these words that you have just spoken to us are words that you should not have

---

[12]Bailiff in Montpellier in 1253 (Tourtoulon, *Don Jaime I*, 2, p. 22). Baumel refers to him as Guillem de la Barca (*Histoire*, p. 94).

[13]He figures as a witness with the title of 'Jurisperitus' in the homage of James to the bishop of Maguelonne in December 1236 (*S*, p. 320; Benoit, *Recueil*, no. 264).

[14]Bailiff in Montpellier in 1222 and 1227, king's lieutenant in 1237, and he figures as both bailiff and king's lieutenant in October 1239. He had participated in the conquest of Majorca (*S*, p. 320).

[15]Pierre Boniface is here made to speak a mix of Catalan and Occitan.

to say to us, because we well believe that you have the heart to serve us; and Atbrand has served us and serves me as well as he is able, and he is your neighbour and one of the honoured men of lineage in this town. Thus, if you wish to act well, this is the path you must take: You and he, and whoever else you can count on, should preserve our rights and our lordship. For you are very much obliged by the great ties we have with you and you with us, and by reason of our seigneurie. Furthermore, the town is much improved since Our Lord wished that it should come into our power. And there must be no quarrel between you but one: to strive to be the best in our service. And we shall love you as it is necessary for one to love his men and his subjects."

And with that, they left us.

[298] We sent for Atbrand and we told him of these words which they had spoken, so that he would not be upset or angered; and he thanked us very much, paying little heed to their words and their worthless threats, and saying that we should recognize the service that he would do us on the occasion of this visit to Montpellier. And he spoke thus:[16] "I will make the different scales of Montpellier, or the majority of them, come to you."

We asked him how, and he said: "I have spoken with the farm labourers, the tanners, and the potters,[17] so that they come to you with torches, and that they should come to honour you; and, so, little by little, we will draw them to your side. And by the time those false people are aware of it, they will already be unable to do anything, and then I will place all in your hands and you will be able to act as king and lord, and revenge yourself on those upon whom you wish to take revenge, and who wish to take this town from you."

We said to him that he had spoken exceedingly well, but that he should act in a wise and prudent way, until we saw that our power was complete.

[299] In the evening, after we had dined and it was already night-time, some five hundred farm labourers, the leaders and the best of them, came to us; and they came with torches with candles; and they said: "Lord, we have come here before you, and welcome you one hundred thousand times, and we have come to fulfil and accept your commands."

---

[16]Here again, James uses a device to indicate the speaker is talking in his own language: '*Yeu faray* venir *las escalas de Montpeylier*'. Atbrand and his supporters continue to do so in chapters 299–303. For the convenience of municipal government, the inhabitants of Montpellier were divided according to their profession into seven categories (Tourtoulon, 2, p. 21).

[17]The Catalan 'Urgeria' seems to refer to the ward of the potters rather than to barley or barley merchants (which one might expect) (Tourtoulon, 2, p. 21). It is perhaps derived from Latin 'urceolus', usually meaning a holy water cruet but sometimes a pot (hence modern Catalan 'urcèola').

Then Atbrand spoke and said: "Lord, here you have a group of the farm labourers; and when they are here, all the others are here, and they are some six or seven thousand. And they speak to you thus, and I say it for them, because they have said to me that I should speak on the matter: They are disposed and prepared to do for you what they would do for their natural lord, in all things always; and for that reason we have come to say it, so that you may better believe it."

We replied that we thanked them very much for coming and for the good disposition they showed us, saying that we believed all that they had said, and that we had it in our heart to love them and do them good, and that from then on they would be more highly regarded by us because of the goodwill that they had shown towards us. After that, they went away from us very joyfully.

[300] When they had gone, the tanners came and there were some two hundred of them, with torches with candles. And they said that we were as welcome as the beautiful day of Easter, and that they had come before us to accept and do our will; because the tanners had never deserted the lord of Montpellier, and that now they had one who was more honourable than any they had ever had, it was with good reason that they should serve us. And then Atbrand said: "My lord, through your favour, I hold your place in this town when you are not here, both inside and outside, and I can greatly recommend to you the tanners, as you can count on them for help and advice whenever I ask them. And you should know that they are very much yours, for you to order and command, and they have come to declare this to you, so that you may better believe it of them."

And we responded to them that we thanked them very much for it, and we recognized the goodwill that they showed us, and that just as they had the good heart to serve us, so we had it in our heart to do them great good: "And, moreover, we thank them when they have helped us and been of use to us in our affairs; because when they help you, they help us."

And so those men went away, and Atbrand sent word to the others who wished to come, that it was already late, and that they should come to us the next day; and upon that they left off from coming.

[301] The next day,[18] at vespers, the potters came, with torches with candles; and there were some two hundred of them. They came to offer us their service and to tell us that they were disposed to do whatever we commanded, just as good vassals should do for their lord. And then Atbrand said: "Lord, well you can recognize the great joy that the town of Montpellier has through you, and, most of all, those who love you; so much so that you can say and command

---

[18]3 June 1239.

what you want them to do, as they are disposed to fulfil your commands. We do not want so many lords, for they have enough with you alone; and they have shown you that they wish to increase and advance your lordship."

We said to them that we were very grateful for the words that Atbrand had affirmed on their behalf, and that at all times we held this hope of them: that nobody in Montpellier could do us harm with their consent. And since they wished it, "with the power that we have here, we can do here all that we wish to do rightfully, for we must do nothing except what we ought to do by right." And we thanked them very much for the goodwill that we recognized in them.

[302] When those men had left there, those of the Saunarie[19] came, and they offered us their persons and their goods and all that they had; and they said that we were very welcome, since now we would put Montpellier in order, if anyone had wronged us there. And when these speeches had finished, Atbrand said: "Lord, now you can avenge yourself if anyone in Montpellier has wronged you, at whatever price, for you can do it."

And we replied to them: "Atbrand speaks well and wisely; but it is our heart and our will that, since you have so good a will to protect our right, and it would grieve you if anyone did us harm, that whatever we do, we have in our heart to do lawfully and rightfully, and with your advice."

After that, they left from there.

And we remained very happy and satisfied with the good words and good will that we had seen and heard.

And if we were not sufficiently encouraged to keep our right in Montpellier, it was not through lack of encouragement from Atbrand.

[303] When morning came,[20] we went to Mass at the house of the Friars Preacher. And when we came out from the Mass, we found a good five thousand men of each one of these groups and others who were there, and all with one voice said that we should now have those who had wronged us in Montpellier make amends, and that we should ask in truth who was wronging us, and that we could now exact reparation from anyone who had done so. And we ordered them all to be quiet, and we said to them that we had always thought that they loved us greatly, but that now we believed it completely, because we recognized the good will they had towards us. Because of what we could see in them, we would be ever bound to love them, to protect them, and defend them in all they possessed and would win; and that they should go, for from that time on we would maintain our right and theirs in Montpellier.

---

[19]The area where the salt was stored (Tourtoulon, 2, p. 21, n. 2).
[20]4 June 1239.

[304] Immediately afterwards, we sent a message to Pierre Boniface, Guerau de la Barca, Bernard Regordan, Raymond Bessède and to others who were of their party, telling them to come before us the next morning. And they were aware of the great stirring among the people, and had realized that the people had come to us in the night; and they took their goods from their houses at night, and placed them in religious houses and in other places of the town.

And on the third morning after our arrival in Montpellier, which was when they were supposed to have come before us, and our officers had gone to their houses to tell them that they should come, a message arrived to us saying that they had left. And we ordered it to be declared to them that they should return within one month to answer to us by law. And they did not return to us inside that month, so we ordered all the goods of theirs that we found to be confiscated, as well as their inheritances. Afterwards we took the battering ram that they had made to pull down the houses of Atbrand and some of the friends of Atbrand. And with that same battering ram, we ordered the houses of those who had fled to be pulled down, that is to say, three or four houses of those who had stood out as leaders of those who had escaped us. And we left the others so the town would not look ugly afterwards. In this we did evil to those who had given us motive to do so, and good to Atbrand and those who had supported him. From among them, we appointed the consuls, the councillors, and the bailiff. And from the time we appointed them, they and those whom they have appointed have kept their offices until this day.[21]

[305] During the time that we were in Montpellier, the counts of Toulouse and Provence came to see us;[22] and we held great courts of the honoured men of those lands who came to see us. And that happened a year after the capture of

---

[21]On 17 October 1239, at Lattes, James granted an amnesty and pardoned those of the inhabitants who had sworn false oaths against him (but excluding Pierre Boniface, Guillem de la Barca and five others). Moreover, the bishop of Maguelonne was no longer to have any say in the election of the twelve consuls or receive the oaths of the consuls. Considerable problems continued between the bishop and the king's officials (Baumel, *Histoire d'une seigneurie*, 2, p. 88). Pierre Boniface returned to Montpellier and acted as bailiff again in 1246 and 1250, as did Guillem de la Barca in 1253 (Baumel, p. 94; Tourtoulon, 2, p. 22). This may suggest that these passages of the chronicle were related before then.

[22]Raymond Berenguer V of Provence was with James on 15 July (*M*, p. 140). James is very discreet about his Occitan business, which perhaps suggests that when he was telling this section of his story the events were recent and it would have been inadvisable to say more. In 1240, he supported the ill-fated uprising of Viscount Raymond Trencavel of Béziers (one of the nobles who came to see James during this visit to Montpellier) and in 1241 allied himself with the count of Toulouse, but he did not participate in the grand alliance led by England that saw Henry III defeated by France at the battle of Taillebourg in 1242. The presence of Raymond VII of Toulouse at Montpellier at this time might suggest he had made no attempt to wrest the town from James, whatever the intentions of the bishop of Maguelonne.

Valencia.[23] We entered Montpellier on Thursday; and on the Friday, between midday and nones, there was the greatest eclipse that has ever been seen in the memory of those men who are alive now, for the sun was entirely covered by the moon, and one could see full seven stars in the sky.[24] After that, when we had seen to our affairs in Montpellier to our honour and profit, we ordered the ship of Montpellier, which had eighty oars, to be armed, and we went in it to Colliure, and afterwards, by land, we went to Valencia.[25]

[306] When we arrived in Valencia, we received great complaints from the Saracens who had surrendered to us, saying that Guillem d'Aguiló[26] and his company of *almogàvers* and footsoldiers had done them that harm and that robbery. And we sent for them, but they did not wish to come to us and fled; and some went to the king of Castile,[27] and others to Aragon, and here and there. Then we sent for Guillem d'Aguiló, and he said that, if we gave him safe-conduct, he would come to us; and we, in order to hear from him why he had done us that wrong, gave him safe-conduct. And he came to our presence, and we asked him why he had done us wrong, and we said to him that he had not served us well nor in accord with the good that we had done to him. He said that he had done harm to the Saracens, and that he had not thought in doing so he had done us a disservice. And we said to him: "Yes you have done me disservice, for two reasons: one, because you have done harm to the Saracens; the other, because you have violated our order, since the Saracens were living in our trust, and you have broken the promise we had made to them."[28]

Then he went away; and we wished to seize what we had given him in Valencia, Algirós and Rascanya. But we found that he had pledged them to others, before doing this evil, and therefore we could not seize them. He sent word to us that he would return all that he could return; and we recovered a portion of the goods and the Saracens. And we spoke with the Saracens, and

---

[23]September–October 1239. Trencavel was with James on 6 October 1239 (Burns-Chevedden, *Negotiating Cultures,* p. 81, n. 5).

[24]The eclipse was recorded by many chroniclers. The *Thalamus Parvus* of Montpellier placed it between midday and nones on the first Friday of June 1239 (Soldevila, *Pere el Gran,* 1, p. 6).

[25]James is found again at Valencia on 22 November 1239 (*H*, 2, no. 302).

[26]James has already alluded to this incident in chapter 295. On 29 December 1239, Guillem witnessed two documents of the king (*M*, p. 141). Perhaps the incident had been dealt with by then (though López Elum (*Conquista y repoblación*, pp. 73–4) situates these events between January and July 1240).

[27]The mention of Ferdinand III may suggest that Castile in part backed these incursions into the Aragonese conquest zone during James's absence.

[28]Referring to the terms for the surrender of Valencia and the region. James here emphasizes his insistence on abiding by agreements he had made, whether with Christians or Muslims, providing they were not broken by the other side.

they asked that we should be greatly grieved by the harm they had received. And they recognized that it grieved us, and each returned to their villages and felt secure since we were in the land.

[307] After that had happened, we went into the valley of Bairén, and we spoke with the *alcaid* who held the castle of Bairén and with those of Vilallonga,[29] Borró, Vilela, and la Palma, which were castles of rock, large and strong. And they told us that when the *alcaid* of Bairén had treated with us, all those of the valley would surrender. And Zaén was still in Dénia, and he sent word that he would meet with us; and we sent word to him that he should come to us at the fortress of Bairén. And he came in an armed galley, and ordered two tents pitched; and there he disembarked, and met with us in our tent. He said to us that if we wished to give him Menorca, so that he held it in our name, he would deliver to us the castle of Alicante, since it was in his power and he could surrender it to us; and that it was necessary that we should give him five thousand *bezants* as a gift. And we told him that we would deliberate and that we would reply to him. When it was vespers, this was the response that we gave him: that we thanked him very much for the love that he had shown us, and that the love and good will he showed us was very clear, as he preferred that the castle of Alicante should go to us than to any other man; but he should not take it badly if we were unable to make that deal with him, since we had made pacts with the king of Castile, and we had already divided the lands in the time of our father and his grandfather, in a manner that the castle corresponded to his portion; for which reason we did not wish to break the agreement that we had made with him.[30] And Zaén said to us that we should recognize that the matter had not foundered because of him, and since it had not foundered because of him, that he had not wronged us in it. After that, he went away from us.

[308] The next day after that we spoke with the *alcaid* of Bairén and we told him that he should now recognize that Our Lord wished for us to have that land. Moreover, as He wished it, he should not delay us any longer there nor bring evil on us or himself; because it was not fitting to cut down the wheat and the trees, since the Moors would be our responsibility, and we had it in our heart to do them good. Thus, so that they would remain there always, he should do nothing to prevent it; and we said that we would do so much good to him and his family that they would forever more be honoured and rich.

---

[29]Four castles just to the south of both Xàtiva and Bairén (la Palma the most northerly, then Vilella, Borró, Vilallonga).

[30]James is almost certainly referring to the treaty of Cazola of 1179 between Alfonso II of Aragon (his grandfather) and Alfonso VIII of Castile (grandfather of Ferdinand III).

He said to us that he thanked us very much, but that he had so fine a castle, that we might well understand that he would do wrong to surrender to us so quickly. Then we said: "Well, since you do not wish to surrender immediately, we beseech you that you guarantee it to us in such a manner that the day we fix with you, you will not fail in the agreement."

And he asked what surety we would like. To which we said that we would like his eldest son; and we had learnt the names of his two nephews, and we said that he should give those two as sureties along with his son. And he said that he would consider it and reply to us the next morning; and we allowed him to consider it.

[309] The next day, in the morning, he returned to us and gave this response: that it must not grieve us if he did not include his son and his nephews, but he would make an oath, along with the twenty best sheikhs of the Saracens who were in the castle, that he would fulfil the agreement with us. Then we told him that we would immediately take a decision. And we replied to him that we accepted the oath that he and the twenty sheikhs of the best who were found in the castle would make, as long as they placed the outer tower in pledge that he would surrender the castle to us, and we said that he should have an outer wall built for us around that tower by the Saracens. He besought us that we should allow him to go and deliberate in the castle, that in the evening he might give us his response.

[310] At vespers he returned to us and told us that he approved the terms, and he would give the tower as security, and he would order the outer wall constructed. And we drew up our treaties and we signalled a day within seven months on which he should surrender the castle to us;[31] and that we would give him three horses and would robe fifty of his men in scarlet cloth, of strong weave, and that we would dress him in scarlet standard and his nephews in green; and that we would give him twenty *jovates* of land to share between him and his nephews, to add to those that they already had, and would refrain from taking from them what was left over. And he surrendered that tower to us, and we delivered it to Don Pelegrín de Atrosillo until God should give us the castle; and we told him that he would hold the castle for us when we had obtained it. The *alcaid* of Bairén behaved well and favourably, letting him go about his work, just as he had promised us.

---

[31]If these events took place after the king's journey to Montpellier then they were probably of 1240 [though López Elum (*Conquista y repoblación*, p. 74) argues that the treaties were drawn up in January 1239].

[311] When the day came that seven months had passed,[32] Don Ferdinand, with those of Calatrava, and with Don Pedro Cornel, Don Artal de Alagón, and Don Rodrigo Lizana went to besiege Villena; and they took an *almajanech*. And they went there by an agreement among themselves, which they had already taken before telling us of it. And we told them that we wished them good fortune, and that if they could take the town, they should take it. They went there and they besieged it, and they set up a *fenèvol* there. And Don Pelegrín de Atrosillo came to us, and told us that eight days from then would be the day when the *alcaid* of Bairén would have to surrender the castle to us, and that we should approach Cullera, and that, if he could, he would make him come to us. For, once he was with us, Don Pelegrín trusted in God that the castle would be surrendered to us. And having said that, he went away immediately.

We went away to Cullera;[33] yet we could not take many knights with us, because all had gone to Villena, so that we could not assemble more than some thirty knights. When we arrived at Cullera, Don Pelegrín de Atrosillo sent a squire to us, and he said to us that he had asked the *alcaid* to come to our presence and that he had agreed with him to do so. Then Don Pelegrín came down from the tower, and the *alcaid* from the castle, and some thirty men-at-arms went with him.

[312] When they arrived at a fountain that is under the rock of the castle, the *alcaid* said to Don Pelegrín that he should wait a little for him, as he would be there presently. While he waited for him, he saw that he was taking off the tunic he was wearing, and that he sat down in the fountain, and that he bathed himself and threw the water over himself. When he had bathed, he sent word to Don Pelegrín, through a Saracen who knew our Latin,[34] that he had been seized with fever and that he could not continue onwards.

And when Don Pelegrín saw that, he considered it a bad sign; and he sent us a letter through a boy of his, in which he informed us of what the *alcaid* had done, and he said that the *alcaid* did not dare to come to us, and was preparing to defend himself lest we should attack him. In the letter that he sent us he told us that if we attacked, he would make two fire-beacons, and by that we would know that they were attacking him; and if we did not attack, we should make one. And that happened on the day that the *alcaid* was to have delivered the castle.

---

[32]Then probably August 1240. Don Artal goes to the siege having already died in chapter 291 in the raid on Sax. Either James means to refer to Artal de Luna (*S*, p. 323) or the siege of Villena precedes the raid on Sax. Again here the chronological problems have yet to be resolved.

[33]Cullera seems to have been taken, perhaps without a fight, in 1239. (After April 1239, when Zayyān was named king of Murcia, the terms of the surrender of Valencia were not adhered to by James.)

[34]That is, Catalan.

When we had dined, we went up to the roof of the castle of Cullera; and when the sun had set (and that was in August), they made a fire-beacon, and immediately they made another; and we understood, according to the letter that he had sent us, that they had attacked him. So we immediately ordered barley to be given [to the horses] and after midnight we began to cross by boat. On seeing the signals that they had made, we had a boat sent to the mouth of the lake in the marshlands that come from Corbera.

Because it had rained a great deal, and because of the large amount of rainfall, a great amount of water had burst out from the mouth of the lake. For which reason, we saw that we could not cross without soaking the saddles of the horses, which would have to swim; so we placed the saddles of the horses and ourselves in the boat, and we went across in turns. And the horses crossed in groups of three or four, being held by the reins as they swam. In undertaking that crossing we had to stop for the time it takes to cross half a league. And when we had crossed, we left the boat so that the others of the company could cross and come after us.

[313] When we had gone further on, we came to that estuary that comes out from the valley of Alfàndec,[35] and we told a squire to go on horseback, with a lance, to see if there was a ford; but he could not find a ford where one could cross without having to swim the length of a knight's spear or more, as we did not have the boat with us. And we said: "Let us cross in peace, as it is necessary to do so."

Thus, we crossed in the same way as we had crossed the other time; and, when we arrived before the castle, at the fortress, it must have been about the hour of nones. And we ordered bread, wine, and salt meat to be brought by sea, since we could not have fresh meat there at that time.

When we arrived there, Don Pelegrín de Atrosillo came towards us, with a single squire who came with him; and we asked him what had happened and why they made those signals. And he said they had done so because the trumpet had been sounded by those in the castle, and they had made smoke signals to advise those in the farmhouses to assemble: "And we saw that they were assembling; and because of that we made the two beacons, because they gave every indication that they were coming to fight us; and we believe that they have not fought us because of the fire-beacons that we have directed to you."

Then we said to Don Pelegrín: "Approach the castle and tell the *alcaid* that we are here with our banner; and that he should come for we will speak with him."

---

[35]Alfàndec de Marinyèn refers to a valley in the mountains of Valldigna to the south of the River Xúquer.

So Don Pelegrín approached the castle and told the *alcaid* what we had said; and he replied to him that it was evening, and that he besought that we would give him time until the morning, and that afterwards he would come to us. And we saw that it could not be otherwise, so we granted that to him.

[314] In the morning he came to us, and we said to him: "Abencedrel,[36] you well know the agreement that you have made with us, and the treaties made between you and us, and how we will receive you as a vassal. For which reason we beseech you and we command you, by the agreements you have made with us, that you shall deliver the castle to us, and we will fulfil what we have promised to you, both to you and to your relatives."

And he said: "I will send for the sheikhs of the town and the villages, and we will come before you; and if you draw up the documents that we asked of you, with that, we will deliver the castle to you. And when you have this one, you shall have this entire valley, as no castle will dare to oppose you or rebel against you."

At the hour of vespers, he came with some twenty Saracens, the most honoured who were in the castle and the valley, and they drew up their documents with us, in accordance with the conditions that they asked of us; and we conceded those to them, because they were reasonable, as well as some others, so that we could enter so good a place as that was. And when we had drawn up the treaties, we had them given to them and we agreed with them that in the morning they would deliver the castle to us. We got up early in the morning and heard Mass and then we drew near to the town and the castle. Here he came into our presence, with his son and his relatives; and we had our banner sent up to the castle, with some armed men. So they delivered it to us, well and peacefully. And when we had supplied the castle with provisions and arms, we entrusted it to Don Pelegrín de Atrosillo, so that he should hold it in our name, and we returned to Cullera.

[315] When we had arrived at Cullera,[37] we heard news that Don Ferdinand, the nobles and those of Calatrava had withdrawn from Villena, because the men inside had made a sortie by day against the *fenèvol*, when Don Pedro Cornel was guarding it, and they had killed two of their knights and some others. Thus, because of that raid they had raised the siege. Then they all came back to us and returned to Aragon. Afterwards the commander of Alcañiz,[38] with the brothers and the *almogàvers*, constructed siegeworks at Villena. And later, while they were there, the men of the town came to us and said that if we

[36]Ibn Sīdrāy.
[37]Perhaps November 1239 (López, *Conquista y Repoblación*, p. 70).
[38]Rodrigo Pérez.

ordered them to do it, they would surrender Villena to the commander. So we ordered them to surrender it, and they surrendered it to the brothers.

[316] Later on, we had to leave the kingdom of Valencia,[39] and we went to Catalonia and, afterwards, to Aragon; and we left the land to Don Rodrigo Lizana, to take charge of it. While we were in Aragon, we heard it said that in a raid undertaken by the cousin of Don Rodrigo Lizana (who was called Pedro de Alcalá), he had attacked the Moors of Xàtiva on the way down the slope, and the Moors had attacked him on the way up the slope. And the Moors had been victorious and had taken Don Pedro de Alcalá with five knights.[40] Afterwards Berenguer d'Entença left Xàtiva to make a raid at the Cabanes de Terol;[41] and he passed between Riba-roja and Manises, and at no time did Don Rodrigo Lizana or the master of the Hospital or those of Valencia dare go out to him, but he continued on his way, and they did not dare to confront him. So they did not dare follow him beyond the river Sec, which runs through Torrent and Catarroja.

[317] And we heard this news in Aragon: that things were going so badly with the Moors who were in the kingdom of Valencia, that they did not dare to go out on raids, and that we should go to the kingdom as there was very great need. So we went there, and we lodged at Altura, which had surrendered to us. And the archbishop of Tarragona, called Master Pere d'Albalat,[42] came out to meet us, and with him, Don Rodrigo Lizana; and they received us well, saying that there had been great need for us to come, and that we had come at a good time. And we said that that pleased us very much. Yet only some twenty-five knights came with us.

When we arrived at Morvedre, Don Rodrigo Lizana spoke with us, and he told us, in front of the archbishop, that his cousin, with his company, had gone to Xàtiva, and had been captured along with five knights, and that he asked us as a favour that we would rescue them from there, as we alone could do so. And we said to him: "How?"

---

[39]Perhaps January 1240 (López, *Conquista y Repoblación*, p. 70).

[40]James had undertaken a short siege of Xàtiva in May 1239 which he had to abandon because of problems in the Languedoc (Engels, 'Rey Jaime I', p. 224). This second siege of Xàtiva begins in May 1240.

[41]It seems from this passage that Berenguer had passed to the service of the Muslims. Possibly he had supported the raids of Guillem d'Aguiló against the Moors but had then fled to Xàtiva to escape the king's justice.

[42]Bishop of Lleida (1236–8) and archbishop of Tarragona (1238–51), he was one of the great reforming prelates of the age and played an influential role in the battle against heresy (Linehan, *Spanish Church*, pp. 54–82).

And he said: "If you only go out from Valencia, and order your army to assemble to advance on Xàtiva, giving the impression that you will lay waste to the land, they will immediately surrender my cousin and the knights."

And we told him that we would do it, and that we had come for that reason, and that whatever we could do to help, we would do there.

[318] Then we ordered our army to be assembled; and we went to the ford of Barragà, and there we awaited our army for a day. And the *alcaid* of Xàtiva knew that we were coming against him, and he sent to us Abenferri,[43] who was once of Llíria and now was with him. And he said that he wondered that we should do this, because he was of the heart and the will to do all that he could do for us, within reason, but they had broken the truce that we had given him, and, therefore, he had had to defend himself; and if he had done harm, he had done it for that reason.

And we replied to him that if anybody had done him harm, they would pay for it, but we wished that he immediately deliver to us Don Pedro de Alcalá with the knights; for we would not tolerate that for anything, and we would challenge him for it and ravage the lands. Then Abenferri left us.

At vespers we said to Don Rodrigo: "Let us take some thirty knights, as we have never seen Xàtiva[44] and we wish to see it."

And we went to that peaked hill that is at the side of the castle, and we saw the most beautiful huerta that we had ever seen of a town or a castle, and there were more than two hundred terraces in the huerta, the most beautiful that one could find, and many farmhouses around the huerta; and, moreover, we saw the castle, so noble and so beautiful; and such a beautiful huerta.[45] And we felt great joy and great happiness in our heart; for it seemed to us that not only for Don Pedro de Alcalá did we have to go upon Xàtiva with our army, but also to win the castle for Christianity, so that God might be served by it. But we did not wish to say anything to Don Rodrigo of our intention.

[319] The next day in the morning Abenferri came to us, and said to us: "Lord, the *alcaid* wished to deliver the prisoners to you willingly, but he could not do it, because those who have bought them have them and do not want to surrender them, and they ask for so much, that he does not have enough to ransom them." When he gave this response, we were very pleased, although we kept quiet, because our desire to take Xàtiva was greater than our desire to

---

[43] Ibn Fīrruh. He was perhaps of the family of Ibn Fīrruh al-Shāṭibī, a noted Xàtivan scholar who died in 1194 (Burns-Chevedden, *Negotiating Cultures*, p. 83, n. 9).

[44] The king's memory appears to be playing tricks on him. He had besieged the city briefly in May of the previous year and presumably had said these words to Rodrigo on that occasion.

[45] This sentiment concerning the castle was echoed by *Desclot* (ch. 49) and *Muntaner* (ch. 9), while the Moors considered the huerta (the countryside around Xàtiva) to be 'the Paradise of the Occident' (Tourtoulon, 2, p. 30).

recover the knights. And we sent the Moor away, and we told Don Rodrigo Lizana that the *alcaid* had sent word to us to say the following: that he could not deliver Don Pedro de Alcalá because he did not have enough to ransom them, and we said that we were thinking more about the castle than the knights.

[320] Meanwhile, immediately afterwards, we went to besiege the castle on the plain; and, when we were in place there, Don Rodrigo Lizana was with us with ten knights. On arriving, we had inspected to see if that hill was any good, and we found a small spring there. And Don Rodrigo Lizana said that that was not enough water for the army, and we said to him that he spoke the truth. Then we sent a message to Beltrán de Ahones,[46] saying that he should go up to the Escardenyo hill with three knights and with four squires; and he went up there, and he told us that we would not be able to pitch tents there: "Because, apart from goats, nothing else can stay there."

And we went up another hill that was there; but we could not decide on any of the three; and also we had seen an adjoining hill that was very steep. We sought a hill that was lower and that was near to water, but we could not decide on any of all those hills. So we returned to the camp and we dined.

[321] When we had dined, we sent for Don Rodrigo Lizana, and we said to him: "Don Rodrigo, let us hear Mass in the early morning, as we have seen a hill which we believe will be a good place for siegeworks."

And when the next day came, and we had heard Mass, we ordered the horses to be saddled. But, while they were saddling the horses and taking up their weapons, Abenferri came and said to us in private, before our interpreter, that if we did not lay waste to the land, he would give us the captives. But we said to him that he should go away, for he had delayed so long that from today on we would no longer agree to that. Yet we told Don Rodrigo Lizana that they did not wish to deliver them, so hiding our intention from him. For we considered that it was of more worth for them to continue in prison for a while so that we might obtain Xàtiva, since God had arranged it so for us.

After that, we went up the hill; but the hill had deceived us, because although it was steep on the side we had seen, on the other side it was flat, so that one could easily walk up it. And God gave us a village at the foot of the hill, in which there was a very good fortification, and water from a river that passed at the foot of it, just as we required; and there we built our siegeworks. And we ravaged their lands and broke up their dams and their mills. And when we had broken them, they repaired them. The little villlage was called

---

[46]An Aragonese noble of the family of Pedro Ahones, he was also to be found in the following of the king from 1245–57 (*M*, pp. 174, 258; *S*, p. 325).

Sallent;[47] and a river passes there that passes through Ana, and whose water comes from the spring of Ana. From there we knew, from the people that we had captured, that we had done great damage in breaking the irrigation channels and destroying the mills. And we knew what great harm it would do to the town, where there were so many people, if we took away the water they needed to irrigate, and for the mills. But we were unable to destroy them all, since we had only a small company, and there was a large company in power there, and the place was narrow.

[322] Now, the *alcaid* sent a Moor named Setxi[48] to us, who was very powerful in the town and was of the *alcaid*'s council; and he sent him to say, in his name, that he was disposed to deliver to us Don Pedro de Alcalá and the other knights. And we gave him this response: that, because at the start, when we asked for them, he did not give them to us, now we wanted Xàtiva more than the knights. And he, when he heard these words, went back greatly afraid. And those of the army made raids on the castles that were around us at Xàtiva.

[323] One morning as we went down to our quarters, which were at the foot of the village, there was a tent from Outremer[49] that we had lent to Don García Romeu[50] (who was the son of Don García Romeu Lobo, who lived in the time of our father), who had come with us with one hundred knights when we had paid him with land and money; and while we were going down, Bartomeu Esquerdo, who was a scout, in the course of a dispute which he had with a man, wounded him with a knife right in front of us, and entered the tent that we had lent to Don García Romeu. We galloped after him and, as he entered the tent, we took him by the hair and dragged him from there. And neither Don García nor any of his men were in the tent. Then we ordered him to be delivered to the guards for them to guard him, so that, if that man whom he had wounded died, he would receive what he deserved, and, if not, we would have him released.

[324] After that, two knights of Don García Romeu came to us, the one named García de Vera,[51] and another. And they said to us on Don García's behalf that

---

[47]A charter of 7 May 1240 granting houses in Dénia (*Llibre del Repartiment*, no. 2166) was dated 'in Sallent, at the siegeworks of Xàtiva'.

[48]al-Shajasī.

[49]The tent had possibly been a gift to James from the sultan of Egypt (*S*, p. 326; Dufourq, 'Vers la Méditerranée', p. 11).

[50]He was one of the most important Aragonese nobles of the period and was often in the king's following. He had served at Puig de Santa Maria, in the siege of Valencia, and in the first siege of Xàtiva. His son was to marry Teresa Pérez, a natural daughter of Peter III. García's father had been a constant companion of Peter II and had fought at Las Navas in 1212.

[51]Presumably the same who appears in a document dated at Valencia on 16 May 1240 (*M*, pp. 141, 144).

he sent them to us, as he was very surprised that we, who ought to honour him, had given him so great an affront. For he had come to serve us, and he did not think to receive so great an affront for the service he had given us. And we asked him what affront we had done to Don García that he should send them to say such strong words to us. And they said: "Lord, we will tell you of them. You know well that if anybody places himself in the house of a knight, even though he may have done an evil deed, he ought to be secure there, and especially in the house of Don García Romeu, who is one of your nobles and is greatly honoured."

And we said: "Has Don García any complaint against me other than this?"

And they said: "No, but he considers this to be a very serious complaint, and so do we."

And we said: "God be praised that he has no other complaint against us but this! And in this complaint, have it from us that he does us wrong, because your houses are not churches from which those who have wounded or killed a man cannot be taken.[52] Moreover, that was not the house of Don García Romeu, but rather a tent that we had lent him, and we were not doing anything so unseemly that he should resent us for it. Because if we saw a man wound with a knife in our presence and we seized him or ordered him seized, we would have done justice in his opinion and in that of those who were with us. Moreover, when we took that man from our tent, we did not think to have done Don García any wrong.

"And tell him another thing on our behalf: that as we have done him good and we have called him, as is fitting, to our service, we beseech him that he should not seek occasion to provoke us, above all at this time, when we are upon so good and honoured a place as Xàtiva is. And on that matter we send word to him, to beseech him to do what he must; for if he were to do otherwise he would err greatly against us and against himself, because no man should seek any occasion on which he can start a quarrel with his lord or his friend, and especially when he is in the wrong. And if he does not accept that from you, tell him that we will speak with him face to face."

---

[52]The dispute is, therefore, again related to the conflicts between the nobility and the Crown over the customs of Aragon. The opportunities that the Aragonese had expected in the Valencia campaigns had been limited by Catalonian enterprise and further when James, in 1239, had law-codes drawn up for the new kingdom which were not based on Aragonese laws. The nobles considered the king's power had been increased while they were marginalized. García Romeu considered that when Bartomeu had entered into his house (even when the house was a tent which he had been lent) he was just as safe under his protection as he would be claiming the right to asylum in a Church. The new law-code of Valencia specified that the one major church of each place of the realm of Valencia shared with the cathedral the right to asylum (Burns, *Crusader Kingdom*, 1, p. 74). James did not consider that the law extended to include knights' residences as places for asylum.

And on that they went from our presence. And neither for the message that we sent him, nor for what we said to him ourselves, did he wish to leave off the charge that we had offended him.

[325] After that, Setxi Abenferri[53] said very secretly to the *alfaquim*, who was called Don Bahiel: "Why is the king so preoccupied with the deed of Xàtiva against the *alcaid*? We could have the best men of his company if we wished to have them."

And the *alfaquim* answered them: "By the faith that you owe, you should say who they are."

"By the law that we have," they said, "We could have García Romeu with his company who would change to our side against him."

And the *alfaquim* said: "Can you prove that it is so?"

And they said: "Indeed. We can prove it, and tell you how. Let the king give us a man in disguise, and then, when García comes to speak with the *alcaid* and with us, and he goes out, the man will be able to see it, because no one should come without the will of his lord. Or, if you want, we will put him behind a curtain or in a hiding-place, in order for him to hear how García Romeu speaks with us; and then the king will know that we are telling him the truth."

And the *alfaquim* brought them before us and said: "Tell them to tell you the truth, by the faith that they owe to God and to you, as they must, being your subjects; and let them tell you what they have told us."

And we asked it of them; and they told us the same words they had told the *alfaquim*. And so we learned of the great treason that García Romeu wished to do to us; and we told them that we cared very little about it, and that it mattered little to us whether he was inside or outside. And we departed from them, giving them to understand that we were little concerned with the matter.

[326] Moreover, to one side, we told the *alfaquim* that he should speak with them privately, and that they should say what it was that the *alcaid*[54] wanted us to do: "And if they ask what it is that we will do, tell them that we shall never leave here unless he gives us one of the castles of Xàtiva, or Castelló."

And they said that they would enter to speak with the *alcaid* and that they would press for him to begin negotiations. And they went in to speak with him.

---

[53] Here Ibn Fīrruh and al-Shajasī are treated in the text as if they are the same person but it is clear from the subsequent conversation that both are talking with the *ḥakīm*.
[54] Abū Bakr.

[327] The next day they returned to us and they told us that he would give us Castelló,[55] and that from that moment he would recognize us as lord; and that, if he had to give Xàtiva, he would give it to nobody but us. And so we made this treaty with him. And on the third day he gave us Castelló; and we recovered Don Pedro de Alcalá and the four knights of Don Rodrigo Lizana who had been captured with him. And we told them that the *alcaid* should come outside to us, with the best hundred men of the town, and that he should receive us as lord; and that he should never deliver the place to anybody except us, if he abandoned it. And all participated in that oath. And we had seats prepared in the *reyal*[56] we had given to the bishop of Valencia, Andreu by name,[57] who was a Preacher and then bishop. And this was the beginning of the pact that there later was between us and the people of Xàtiva.

[328] After that had happened, we went to Aragon; and we stayed between Aragon and Catalonia a whole year or longer, and Jimeno Pérez de Tarazona remained in Valencia in our place. And after we had been a year or longer in Aragon and Catalonia, we returned to the kingdom of Valencia,[58] because it was the time and opportunity to finish what we had started, so that we might also have all the rest of the kingdom, just as we had up to the Xúquer.

[329] On our return, the *Rais* of Alzira left there because he was afraid of us; and he had left with some thirty knights and went to Murcia. The government of the town remained with the Saracens and with the council of elders. And they sent their messengers to us saying that Alzira was a good and honoured place, among the best there were in the kingdom of Valencia; and that, if we liked, they would come to an agreement with us, provided that we allowed them to remain in that place. And the proposal that they made to us pleased us very much, and we told them that we would receive them into our grace and we would give the place over to them, if only they gave us possession of those towers that are at the Valencia gate. And they told us that they would deliberate and then respond to us. And we asked them when they would give us their response and they said on the third day, and that pleased us greatly.

---

[55]As the castle was some distance from Xàtiva, it might seem poor reward for James's labours, but since it gave the Christians access to the city through the valleys of the Sallent and Albaida, the deal was sufficiently acceptable for James not to suppress an otherwise embarrassing incident.

[56]In 1249, the king locates a grant "next to the *reyal* in which we made the first treaty with the *qā'id* and Saracens of Xàtiva" (Burns-Chevedden, *Negotiating Cultures*, p. 86).

[57]Andreu d'Albalat, the brother of Archbishop Pere d'Albalat of Tarragona, was elected in December 1248, acted as chancellor to James, and proved the most effective of Valencia's post-conquest bishops. He died in 1276 (Burns, *Crusader Kingdom*, 1, pp. 25–6). The grant of the *reyal* was actually made to Andreu on 30 March 1249 (*H*, 2, no. 48).

[58]April 1242.

[330] On the third day, some of the best sheikhs of the town came to us at Valencia. And there were four of them there on behalf of the rest. And they said that they would give us the biggest tower, which is near the bridge of the Calçada, that was at the gate we were asking for.[59] And we said that we were very pleased since they so readily agreed to do our will, and that we would love them and do good to them. And they drew up their treaties with us, as to how they would remain at Alzira with the law-codes and customs they had in the time of the Almohads,[60] and they could practice their services in the mosques as they were accustomed to do; and that all Saracen captives who arrived at Alzira would be free, and that we could not recover them, nor could anybody do so in our name. And they signalled a day that was five days hence for us to come to occupy the tower. And we told them that we would be there on that day, and that they should have all the sheikhs of the town and other people come out on that day to swear fealty to us and also that they would be loyal to us, and to our kin, and to our men.

[331] Thus, we went there on that day, and all the sheikhs came out to us, and they swore upon the book of the Koran that they would be good and loyal to us and that they would defend our body and members, as well as our men who we put there to act on our behalf. After we had occupied the tower, we asked them that they should wish to give us as far as the third tower, and that we would make a wall there so that the Christians could not enter into Saracen places, nor the Saracens into Christian places. And they asked that we might make a little gate which went out to the road, through which they could enter the town, so that they could not say that they had received harm from the Christians. And they told us that they could not respond without consulting the other Moors, and that in five days, having consulted, they would respond to us. And we asked some of the leading Saracens that they should advise it to be done, and they said that they would do it in such a way that we should be satisfied.

[332] When that day arrived,[61] they responded to us that they were agreed on it and that they granted it to us. And we ordered a dividing wall built between us and them; and so the castle was enclosed and fortified. And in this way we obtained Alzira and we took the rents that the *Rais* of Alzira (that is, their lord) was accustomed to receive.

---

[59] By which, James controlled entry to the town (*Desclot*, ch. 49).

[60] 'In the time of the Almohads' in Alzira would have been until the revolt of Ibn Hūd in 1228, but James is perhaps using the expression loosely.

[61] 30 December 1242.

[333] Later on, around a year and four months later,[62] during a raid made by the company of Don Rodrigo Lizana and the *almogàvers*, the Moors whom the *alcaid* of Xàtiva had under his lordship, together with the Moors from Tous, Tàrbena, and Càrcer,[63] came upon them as they returned with the booty. And that raid was not upon Moors whom the *alcaid* had in his lordship, but against other Moors who were still at war with us. The Moors of the *alcaid* and the knights of Xàtiva attacked them and took the booty from them as well as five or six mules and packhorses, and they killed two warhorses there. And Don Rodrigo Lizana immediately informed us of the harm that the *alcaid* of Xàtiva and his forces had done him. When we learnt of that, we were pleased for this reason: because he had broken the agreement he had made with us, and therefore we had a reason to go against Xàtiva. Thus, when we heard that, we went from Aragon,[64] where we were, to Valencia, and from Valencia to Alzira.

[334] And we sent a message to the *alcaid* of Xàtiva, telling him that he should come, because we wished to see him, and that he should come to our presence. We took up quarters in the town, in the houses of ours belonging to the camp, and he came to that place. But we did not wish to speak to him on the day that he came, for he came with a sizeable company and we wanted him to think all was well. The next morning he came to our presence, and told us that he had come at our command and because of the letter we had sent him, and we told him what we wished to say to him: "*Alcaid*, we have sent for you for this reason: your Moors and the force of knights you have in your pay have done us harm and have destroyed a company belonging to the man we left to govern Valencia. And you well know the agreement that you made with us, and that the charters are divided clearly according to a. b. c., and we have the one part and you have the other.[65]

"According to what is contained in those documents, you have broken the pacts that you had with us. And not only in that matter have your men and those you have in your pay done us harm, but they have done us harm in two or three other matters; and they have killed men who would not have died had it not been for you. Therefore, regarding the pacts that we had with you, since you have broken them, it does not seem to us that we need be bound to you by them. Thus, since we have the greater part of the kingdom of Valencia, and Xàtiva is of that kingdom, we wish to take it, and since you hold it, we order you that you should surrender it to us."

---

[62]The third siege of Xàtiva was underway by 7 January 1244, which suggests there was less than a year between these events.

[63]Tous and Càrcer are just to the north-west of Xàtiva, while Tàrbena is far to the south.

[64]James had been in the kingdom of Valencia from September until November 1243, and then spent much of December involved with the *Cortes* at Daroca in Aragon. These events appear to be of late December 1243.

[65]Referring to the treaty of 1240.

[335] When he heard these words, he went white, considering himself to be a prisoner, and while he was in this state and could not reply because he was so afraid, we said to him: "*Alcaid*, be not afraid, as you are as safe here as if you were at the castle of Xàtiva. And we do not want you to respond to us here, but for you to return there and deliberate with your sheikhs and with whomsoever else you want to. When you have reached an agreement you should either come to our presence or send us your response, as our court is such that we never take away the liberty of any man who comes to us, however much wrong he has done us. But if you do not wish to make amends to us, you may well believe that we will demand it in such a way that you will have to do what we tell you to. And it is better that you do it with love and willingly than if it had to come about in any other way."

After that, he and the other Moors kissed our hand (and he was first) and said that they could well recognize the great faith and great loyalty that was in us. And so they went to dine and they were there all that day. And we said to them before they left there, that they should fix a day with us for their response. And they said that as we asked for so great a thing from them, they would need a full eight days to make a decision, and they besought that we should give that to them, and they added that on the eighth day either he or his messenger would come to us. And we granted that to him, and the next day they went to Xàtiva, and we went to Castelló, and we took the queen there, along with our uncle Don Ferdinand and other nobles.

[336] On the eighth day he sent a learned Moor to us named Almofois,[66] who was the most learned man in Xàtiva and one of the most important men; and another Moor came with him. And we had Don Ferdinand with us and the other nobles who were there with us; and we told the Saracen that he should respond. He got to his feet and said: "Lord, lord, the *alcaid* and the other sheikhs of Xàtiva greet you warmly, and speak to you on the day you ordered them to come to your presence, and they respond to you the following: that they had good reason to do this misdeed of which you accuse them, for the Christians were taking as many possessions of the *alcaid* of Xàtiva as they would have done in war; and upon a call-to-arms they received, our men had to go out from there and recover what had been taken, and they did them no other harm. And the *alcaid* replies to you concerning the demand that you have made of the castle of Xàtiva, that you already know the great value of the castle of Xàtiva, because there is none better in all Andalusia,[67] so that if he surrendered the castle for so small a matter, both Moors and Christians would hold him in contempt. And although the *alcaid* and the Moors do not follow your law, they

---

[66]al-Mufawwiz.
[67]Here referring to the lands of the Iberian Peninsula in Muslim hands.

would be shamed before you if they did something so base; therefore, they beseech that you would not wish them to do that."

And after that, he sat down.

[337] And we responded to him without consultation and we said to him: "Almofois, you are a learned man, and it seems so for two reasons: first, because of the reputation that you have; and the other, because you have explained your case well. But if in the affairs of this world that are disputed by many people, or between one person and another, there was no judge who knew which side was right, nothing would ever be accomplished. And the *alcaid* is our vassal, since in making that treaty with us, at the camp that is near the town, he made himself our vassal[68] and said that he would obey us and defend us and ours. And, as our vassal, he must submit himself to our authority, and since we must give him a judge, we will give him as a judge Don Ferdinand, who is one of the greatest men in Spain both in lineage and in nobility. And if he recognizes that our plaint is right, let him make amends to us, and if he decides that it is not, we shall withdraw this plaint that we make of him. For the words that we would have with you on behalf of the *alcaid* would have no substance if there were no judge here to decide, so we give you a judge."

[338] Then he said to us that it was not the will of the *alcaid* nor of the elders that he should accept any judge, but he would go back there and after consulting, he would respond to us. And we asked him when we would have a reply and he said on the third day. And we agreed to that, since we did not want to argue with him over the number of days, since he asked for a reasonable length of time. And he went away and on the third day he returned, and responded, before Don Ferdinand and before our court, that in this business no judge was necessary, but rather we should tell him what it was that we demanded, and he would respond to us.

And we took a decision and we said to Don Ferdinand: "What Almofois says is wrong, because in any matter when the lord makes a complaint of his vassal, or one man against another, there has to be a judge, in case one does not admit the plaint the other has of him. Moreover, the judge has to have an assurance from both parties that his judgement will be fulfilled. Therefore we reply to you, as you are the messenger of the *alcaid*, that if the *alcaid* wishes to accept Don Ferdinand as judge and to ensure that if we win he shall fulfil the sentence, we will be satisfied."

---

[68]The whole episode, referring back to the treaties of 1240, written for both sides in both Latin and Arabic, demonstrates the lack of understanding between Christians and Muslims. Abū Bakr did not define himself as James's vassal who had to accept the binding decisions of a feudal judge appointed by the king.

And he said that he could not do any more than he had been ordered. And then we ordered the nobles and the citizens of Valencia who were there to witness that the *alcaid* would not accept our judge, who we gave him. And when we had taken their testimonies, he mounted and went on his way. And from that moment, there was war.

[339] We then sent for the knights of the kingdom of Valencia and other men and the *almogàvers*, and with the other nobles we went to besiege Xàtiva.[69] And we pitched camp in the huerta beside the river;[70] and on the other side there was a ravine and above the camp we built a moat; and so the army was enclosed. And while we were in that camp, there were many skirmishes between us and them.

And there was a man there who was a relative of the bishop of Cuenca and was a native of Cuenca, and he told us, before we went to besiege Xàtiva, that Prince Don Alfonso wished to have a tent made at Xàtiva.[71] However, with the pretext of having the tent made, while they were making it, he conducted negotiations between the *alcaid* and he who is now King Don Alfonso and was then the prince.[72] And we understood that that tent was only being made as a ruse so that the *alcaid* of Xàtiva and Prince Don Alfonso could negotiate. And so the tent was being made to conceal the fact that they were negotiating. And that man of Cuenca, when he learnt that we were besieging the town, came from Cuenca, on the advice of the bishop,[73] so that he could find occasion to speak with the men of the town and tell them that Prince Don Alfonso was coming, and that they could reach an agreement with him. And we suspected what was being done, and we knew very well that that tent was being made as a stratagem, through which we might lose Xàtiva.

[340] Hence, we ordered it proclaimed throughout the army that anybody who conversed with the Moors without having asked permission from us, would be arrested and brought before us. And one day the Moors came out against those of the army who intended to forage and ravage the land, and the call-to-arms

---

[69]The first document dated at the siege of Xàtiva is of 7 January 1244 (*M*, p. 165).

[70]The River Montesa, a branch of the Xúquer.

[71]Xàtiva specialized in tent manufacture.

[72]Following the death of Ibn Hūd in 1238, Castile had conducted a continuous campaign against the kingdom of Murcia. Crippled by internal divisions, Murcia surrendered in March 1243 and became a tributary of Castile. Prince Alfonso occupied Murcia city on 1 May 1243. Alfonso, seeking to subdue the nothern castles of the kingdom, pushed towards Xàtiva, which during the Huddite period (1228–38) had usually declared itself under Ibn Hūd at Murcia rather than Zayyān at Valencia. Xàtiva now sought to negotiate favourable terms for a surrender to Alfonso. James and Prince Alfonso were inevitably drawn into conflict as each pressed upon the other's conquest zone.

[73]Bishop Gonzalo Ibarra Ibáñez . He was known as 'the hammer of the Saracens' (Burns-Chevedden, *Negotiating Cultures*, p. 88).

went up in the camp, and they went out against the Moors. And Don Pere Llobera[74] came upon that man of Cuenca who was negotiating with the Moors and, according to our proclamation, which he had heard, that any man who spoke with the Moors should be arrested, he went up to him and told him that he should come to our presence. And the other said to him: "Why do you want to take me to the king?"

And he said: "Because the king has forbidden anyone to speak with the Moors, yet you have spoken with them, and I want to know if the king ordered you to or not."

As he was unable to defend himself, he was brought to my presence by force.

When he came before us, Don Pere Llobera said to us: "Lord, this knight was speaking with those inside."

And he did not deny that he had spoken with them, but said that he had said nothing bad of us or of the army. And we asked him how much time he had been in the camp. And he said that he had been there for fifteen days.

"Then," we said, "If you have been fifteen days in the camp, it has already been eight days since we made a proclamation forbidding anybody to speak with the Moors if he had not asked for our permission. And you have not asked for any such thing. So then, why have you been speaking with them?"

And he said that he had not said anything that would harm us. And we said to him: "Yes, you have spoken there, because you are he who carried the letter from the bishop of Cuenca saying that you wished a tent made for Prince Don Alfonso, and with the excuse of making the tent, you have negotiated to our harm, so that they should surrender to him. And we know that for certain from the Moors of the town. And you heard very clearly the proclamation that we had had issued, for all those who were in the camp must have heard it. And for what you have done against us, while we trusted in you, we will punish you in such away that all those who wish to take Xàtiva from us will beware because of what we are going to do to you."

And we immediately ordered the guards that they should take him and that they should let him do penance and confess, and that they should hang him from a tree.[75]

[341] When a month had passed, they told us that Enguera and Moixent had already surrendered to Prince Don Alfonso, and we were very surprised that he should take anything which was in the jurisdiction of Xàtiva, since it was of

---

[74]He was among the witnesses of the first document surviving from the siege on 7 January 1244 (*S*, p. 329).

[75]The time that James spends on the incident suggests both that the hanging of the Castilian knight was notorious and that the king would stop at nothing to obtain Xàtiva.

our conquest[76] and he had our daughter as his wife.[77] And, to know if that was the case, we went to Enguera and we told the Saracens that they should surrender it to us. And they said that they had already surrendered it to Prince Don Alfonso and that his castellan was already there. And we realized then that the rumours about the tent had been proven to be true, because, if he had taken any of the castles of Xàtiva, he would readily take Xàtiva itself if it was surrendered to him. And we sent for the knight who was there to come to us. And he came and we asked him: "You, why are you here?"

And he told us that he was there for Don Pedro Nuñez de Guzmán,[78] and that the prince had encharged Don Pedro Nuñez to hold the place for him. And we said that we did not believe that the prince would occupy any thing of the world that was of our conquest.

[342] With that we left there, and we ordered for those in the camp who were commissioned to raid[79] that they should go to do them harm. And the next day we laid an ambush for those of Enguera, and those of our army took seventeen men and brought them to us, and we bought them from them. And the next day we went to Énguera and we told them that they should surrender and that, if they did not do so, we would put those seventeen on trial, and that we would do the same to all those whom we would take, until the place was empty. Yet, in spite of all that we sent to say to them, they did not wish to surrender the castle to us. So that, in full view of them all, we had half of them beheaded and the other half hanged.[80] And we returned to our camp, which was before Xàtiva.

[343] After fifteen days Prince Don Alfonso sent us a message,[81] saying that he wished to see us, and asked us that we should go to meet him at Almirra. And we sent word to him that he had wronged us and if he repaired the wrong he had done to us, we would meet with him willingly. And before we had his response, we arranged with a brother of Calatrava, who was holding Villena, that he should surrender Villena and Sax to us; and we obtained from the Moors Cabdet and Bugarra. And when the prince wished to occupy Villena, Sax, Cabdet and Bugarra, and they did not wish to receive him because we

---

[76]James considered both to be within his conquest zone according to the treaty of Cazola. Enguera lies fifteen kilometres west and Moixent twenty-five kilometres south-west of Xàtiva.

[77]Violante was married to Alfonso in December 1249 when she was twelve years old but the marriage had already been agreed in 1241 when she was three. Though such agreements were often broken, James would have already considered Violante as Alfonso's wife here in 1244.

[78]Pedro Muñoz de Guzmán was one of Alfonso's witnesses at the treaty of Almirra (26 March 1244).

[79]'Cavalcadors'.

[80]They were executed as traitors since James considered them within his jurisdiction.

[81]Early March 1244.

held them all, he sent word to ask us that we should come out to meet him. And we left in the camp two hundred knights and footmen who were there and we went to meet him. And there was noone with us but Guillem de Montcada, the master of the Hospital, Jimeno Pérez de Arenós and Carròs, and a part of our company.[82] And with Prince Don Alfonso there were the master of the Temple, the master of Uclés, Don Diego de Vizcaya and other nobles of Castile and Galicia, whose names we do not recall.[83]

And we attended this interview between Almirra and Cabdet, where he had pitched his tents (whilst we were at Almirra). And we had with us a third more knights than he had with him. And we met; and, after we had met, he came to our camp to see our wife, the queen. And we wished to deliver to him the castle of Almirra and the town, in which he could take up quarters, but he did not wish to accept it, and encamped outside, at the foot of the hill of Almirra, where he had ordered his tents pitched. And here we passed the time merrily and in good company.

[344] Then our wife the queen came, because she had asked us that we should allow her to attend the meeting, so that she might help to solve the dispute that there was between us and our son-in-law; and he came to see her as soon as she arrived there.[84] And that day passed in joy and happiness, since it was not good that one should speak of any business on the first day.

[345] The next day, after we had heard Mass, he came to see the queen again. And we asked him why he had sent word to us that we should come to meet with him. And, in his name, the master of Uclés and Don Diego de Vizcaya said to us that the prince had come for this reason: that he was married to our daughter, and he believed that we could not have married her with any man of the world better than him; for which reason he believed he ought to receive, with her, a portion of land for the marriage, and that we ought to give him Xàtiva, which we had assigned to him through Ovieto García, who had negotiated the marriage.[85] And we told them that we would deliberate and that we would respond to them.

---

[82]Guillem, Hugh de Forcalquier, and Jimeno all witnessed the treaty of Almirra, while Carròs witnessed another document at Almirra on 25 March 1244 (*M*, pp. 167–8). Others present according to the surviving documents were Bishop Andreu and the Archdeacon Martí of Valencia, the provincial master of the Templars Guillem de Cardona, Jimeno de Foces, Don Ladrón, Ramon de Belloch, Mateu Ferriç, and Pedro and Gil de Atrosillo (*S*, p. 330).

[83]The master of the Templars in Spain, Martín Martínez, the master of Santiago, Pelayo Pérez Correa, and Don Diego all witnessed the treaty at Almirra for Alfonso as did Bishop Gonzalo of Cuenca, Alfonso Téllez, Pedro Muñoz de Guzmán, Gonzalo Ramírez, and Pedro Guzmán (*S*, p. 331).

[84]Once again we see the influential part played by Yolanda in James's negotiations.

[85]We have no evidence that James had offered Xàtiva in dowry to Alfonso during the marriage negotiations and it seems unlikely.

And we deliberated with the queen and with the nobles who were with us, and we sent word to the prince that he should send the master and Don Diego to us, and that we would reply to them. And they came, and this was our reply: that we and the queen well knew that we had married our daughter well, but that we had never made any such offer to Ovieto García or to any other man of the world as to say that we would give Xàtiva or any other place; and that when we had married with Queen Doña Eleanor, his aunt,[86] they had not given us any land nor goods with her. "And we do not believe that we have to give more to any king for our daughter than he gave to us with his."[87]

And that he should not grieve, for we would not give Xàtiva to any man in the world, because it pertained to our conquest, and that he already had enough land and ought not to envy what was ours; and that we besought him that it should not grieve him, as we would not do anything other than we had already decided.

[346] And they took their leave, visibly dissatisfied with us, and returned to their camp. And at vespers they returned to us again, and said that they would prove that what they had said was so, through Ovieto García. And we said that we considered Ovieto García to be so fine a knight that he would not fail to tell the truth because of Don Alfonso, his lord, but the law forbad that the testimony of a vassal should be received against another. And it was a very important matter, and we did not wish to stake Xàtiva on the word of a man who was his vassal, since both God and we knew the truth; and that the prince ought not to ask for land with our daughter, since he could obtain from us other great and good benefits, to his honour and profit, so that if he needed one or two thousand knights, he could have them to help him, and us as well, and not only once, but two, three, or ten times if it were necessary.[88] And that was worth more with our love than the other thing would be without our love. And so that night passed with those discussions between us and them. And we told them that we would not reach an agreement in that way that they had asked. And so they parted from us that night.

[347] On the next day they returned and they said to us: "Lord, it would be a good thing for you to give Xàtiva to the prince, since, if you do not do so, he will have it anyway, because the *alcaid* will give it to him."

And we said: "And how will the prince have it? And the *alcaid*, how will he give it to him?"

---

[86] Alfonso's great-aunt. Eleanor was the youngest sister of Berenguela, mother of Ferdinand III, father of Alfonso.

[87] Perhaps referring to Ferdinand since Alfonso did not become king until 1252. Alfonso VIII of Castile had already been dead almost seven years when his daughter Eleanor was married to James in 1221.

[88] James fulfilled the promise in his Murcian campaign (1265–6) some twenty years later.

And they replied: "Because he very much wishes to give it to him."

And we said to them: "We do not fear anybody taking it from us. And the *alcaid* cannot give it, nor would he dare to take it, safely, for whoever wishes to enter Xàtiva, will have to get past us. And you, Castilians, just you try to get through with your threats, for I shall be ready for them. So, speak, if you have anything else to say; but, as we will hear nothing else except that, know that I will go on my way, and you may try what you may."

[348] After that we ordered to saddle and to prepare the mule-trains. And the queen began to cry and said that she was born in evil hour, as she had come to reconcile our son-in-law and us, and now she saw that the matter had gone badly. And they left and said to the prince that we wished to go and we had ordered to saddle.

And when we had already saddled up, the master of Uclés and Don Diego de Vizcaya came to us, and said to us: "King, is it fitting for you to be so greatly and so quickly enraged?"

And we said: "There is no man in the world whom you would not make lose his temper, because you do everything with such pride and you think that everything that you want ought to be done."

And they said to the queen: "Lady, speak with your husband and tell him not to be angered or leave in such a rage, as we will go to Don Alfonso and the matter will not be left as it is now left."

And the queen besought us, weeping, that we should not be in so great a hurry nor ride off, as they would go there, to Don Alfonso, and they would arrange things to the satisfaction of both. And we said that, as she and they asked it of us, we would do it, and that they should return soon with their plan. And they went to speak with Don Alfonso and they negotiated the matter in this way: that he would leave and give up his demand for Xàtiva and that we should divide the lands between us and him according to the division that there had been between the kingdom of Murcia and the kingdom of Valencia, and that we would deliver to him Villena, Sax, Cabdet, and Bugarra, and that he would deliver to us Enguera and Moixent.[89]

[349] This was the division of the lands: that the prince would have Almansa, Xarafull and the river of Cabriol, and that we would have Castalla, Biar, Relleu, Xixona, Alarc, Finestrat, Torres, Polop, la Mola that is near Aigües, Altea and all that there is inside those boundaries.[90] And we drew up charters, with bulls, between us and Prince Don Alfonso, and we departed as good

---

[89] Saturday 26 March 1244 (*H*, 2, no. 388).

[90] James's new boundary ran just below Biar, Castalla, Xixona, la Mola and Torres, while Alfonso's boudary ran from just above Xarafull, Almansa, Cabdet, Villena, Sax, Agost and Busot. The treaty removed the possibility of Castile giving aid to Xàtiva against James.

friends, and each turned over to the other what he held that was not his own. And we returned to Xàtiva,[91] to the camp, that was in very good condition just as when we had left it. And we were there two months without them speaking of any treaty that we could make.

[350] Two months later, the *alcaid* sent us a Saracen named Abulcàssim,[92] and we ordered everyone to leave our tent so that we could speak with him. And he, seeing that there was nobody there but us, told us that the *alcaid* greeted us and commended himself to our grace, as to the man in the world he had greatest desire to serve, love and honour, and that he sent to ask us why we besieged him, when we certainly knew that his father[93] had ordered him that he should not surrender the castle to any Christian of the world nor any Saracen, if it was not to us, if he had to lose it; and that we did not have to besiege it or to do him harm, because he held it for us and would not follow any other road but ours.

And we replied to him that we knew well from report the orders which his father had given him, but that, since God willed that we should be king of the kingdom of Valencia, and Xàtiva was the most notable place that was there, after Valencia, he had to accept that. Because, on the one hand, we would be able to do him good so that he and his lineage could live honourably, and on the other, the castle of Xàtiva pertained to us, for the castle of Xàtiva was the key to the kingdom, and we could not be king of the kingdom of Valencia if Xàtiva were not ours. And therefore we asked him to accept it, as we could in no way go from that place until we had obtained it. "And however much he has made it cost us, he himself will not escape the expense he must put into maintaining the place; so if he persists in this way we will both suffer. Yet, he can avoid this through our love and with the benefits that we will give him; and so, what we give him will seem better to him, and Xàtiva will seem better when ours."

[351] "Lord," he said. "What would you wish for the *alcaid* to do with Xàtiva?"

And we said to him: "Give us the castle, and we shall give an inheritance to him, both to him and his lineage."

And Abulcàssim replied: "How could he part so rapidly with Xàtiva, which is so fine a place, without thinking first what he might request of us and what not?"

---

[91] James had already returned by 29 March 1244 (*M*, p. 168).
[92] Abū al-Qāsim Ibn ‘Īsá, the brother and chancellor of Abū Bakr.
[93] Abū al-Ḥusayn.

And we said to him: "It is necessary that he parts with it to one who will be his lord and will protect him from harm and will give him ten times more than his lineage has ever had."

Then he said: "Lord, the words that you say are of very great import and, if it pleases you, I will return to the *alcaid* and tell them to him."

And we said: "It pleases us well that you should go there and tell them, and that you represent us well there, as you are the chief scribe of Xàtiva, and we shall reward you well, with more than you have ever had, for you know very well that you cannot save yourselves from us."

[352] After that he went back inside. On the third day he returned to us, and told us that that the *alcaid* did not contemplate surrendering Xàtiva on any account. To that we said to him that, since he did not wish to give it to us, they should prepare to defend it, as we would attack it, and we would not leave for as long as it took to take it. Then they asked us that we might send to him Jimeno de Tovía,[94] who was his confidant, and in whom he greatly trusted. So we sent for him, telling him that the *alcaid* demanded it, and that he should enter into Xàtiva with Abulcàssim, and that now we would know the love and the duty he had for us. And that was on Wednesday.[95] The messenger asked us that we should not do any harm to the town, nor would they to us, until Sunday, since on Friday the sheikhs would go to the mosque, and there they would deliberate until Saturday, and therefore the truce should last until Sunday. And we granted that to him. But we do not wish to give a long account of this, for the negotiations lasted a long time, and so would greatly lengthen this book.

[353] The next day Abulcàssim, Setxi, Almofois,[96] and Jimeno de Tovía, came to us: "Lord, here the *alcaid* sends all his council and all his heart; for whatever these men do you may consider it to be just as surely done as if he did it."

And this was their proposal: that he would deliver the lesser castle of Xàtiva to us, and retain the greater for two years from that Pentecost,[97] if we might make it known to him what honoured place we would give to him. And we asked what inheritance might be suitable to give to him; and he asked for Montesa and Vallada,[98] which are good castles and are near to Xàtiva, and we said that we would deliberate.

---

[94] An Aragonese knight of the Tovía lineage.

[95] Jimeno was certainly present at the siege on 10 May 1244 (*S*, p. 333). Burns (*Negotiating Cultures*, pp. 100–2) argues that the Jimeno meeting was on Wednesday 25 May 1244.

[96] Abū al-Qāsim, al-Mufawwiz, and al-Shajasī.

[97] 22 May 1244. James does not indicate here whether or not Pentecost had passed.

[98] These were important castles. Montesa was later home to the important military order of that name. In 1370, the official Crown history (*Chronicle of San Juan de la Peña*, p. 70) described Montesa as 'an awesome stronghold'.

Then we left our tent and went to the houses that we had had made,[99] where the queen was. And the master of the Hospital, Hugh de Forcalquier, Guillem de Montcada, Jimeno Pérez de Arenós, and Carròs attended our council. We told them of the treaty that the *alcaid* had proposed, and that they should advise us on it. And they said to the queen that she should speak first. And the queen said: "Lord, what advice could I or anyone give you in this matter? I advise you that since you can obtain Xàtiva, you should not delay matters for a castle or two, because it is the most beautiful and richest castle that I or anybody has ever seen."

And the master of the Hospital said: "I will not say anything more, because the queen has given you good advice."[100]

And all the others assented to that. And we said that they had advised us well on the matter, and we considered it done. For we thought that as he was giving us the lesser castle, the greater was already no longer in his hands.[101]

[354] After that we sent for Jimeno de Tovia and the Saracens, and we responded to them in this way: that we had so greatly loved the father of the *alcaid*, and we so greatly loved his son, whom he had left in our care,[102] that, even though we had not resolved the matter entirely to our satisfaction, for love of him, we wished to do so. And they besought us on behalf of the *alcaid* and the sheikhs, that we might wish for Don Jimeno de Tovia to hold the castle, since the *alcaid* trusted him greatly and we also trusted in him. This we granted to them, and we took the lesser castle.[103] Then we withdrew our army and, having provisioned the castle very well with food and men, we returned to Valencia.[104]

[355] While we were in Valencia, two Saracens came to us from Biar, and they were old men (for each was more than fifty years old) and they said to our officers that they wished to speak with us, and that they came for our great advantage. And we had them enter to our presence and we asked them what they wanted. And they said that if we wanted to go to Biar, they would give us the castle; and that it was the best castle of that frontier, and that if we held it,

---

[99]Marsili (*Crónica latina*, Bk. 3, ch. 60, p. 318) suggests the houses were built for the occasion.

[100]Again Yolanda played a vital part in advising the king and influencing the advice given by his council. Burns (*Negotiating Cultures*, p. 102) dates this meeting to Monday 30 May 1244.

[101]Because James would have it eventually.

[102]James considered Abū Bakr as his vassal, though it is unlikely the *qā'id* would have viewed matters so.

[103]The treaty was sealed on Sunday 5 July 1244.

[104]James was at Valencia through most of August 1244 (*M*, pp. 168–9; *H*, 2, nos. 392–5).

we would hold all that frontier. And we said to them: "Now tell us how you can give it to us and how it might be done."

And they replied that they were among the most notable men of that town, and that they had spoken there with some people of the town, with such who could deliver it to us easily, and that they certainly knew that if they saw us, it would be done. And we said: "Go there and we will assemble some hundred knights here and we will be at Xàtiva. And bring to us there certain news of whether the thing can be done or not."

[356] And, when that day came, we were in Xàtiva,[105] and one of those two Saracens went there, and we asked him what had become of his companion. And he said that all the Moors of Biar had agreed to the deed, and that his companion had remained there to lead them all before us, so that they should come to our mercy when we approached the castle. And we went there with this guarantee, since no Saracen had ever before broken a promise to us having promised to surrender a castle, except al-Azraq in the matter of Rugat.[106] And this Saracen presented it to us so well and so persuasively, that we had to go there. And when we arrived there we found all the Saracens of Biar armed with their weapons, and they had come outside the town. And we said to the Saracen: "Approach them and tell them we are here."

And he approached them and they said to him they did not wish to speak to him and that, if he went near them, they would throw stones at him. And we were there for a good three or four days,[107] on the side where one goes from Ontinyent to Biar, towards the water.

[357] Afterwards we moved on to a hill that overlooks Biar, towards the side from where one goes to Castalla; and it was around the Feast of Saint Michael.[108] And we ordered our houses constructed there, and whoever could not have a house made a good hut, and some of us in houses and others in huts, we stayed for some two months. During those two months[109] we made a *fenèvol*, and few days passed that our men did not have hard-fought skirmishes with those of the town, because there were some seven hundred footmen inside, well-armed and skilled.

---

[105] August–September 1244.

[106] The incident is related below in chapter 375.

[107] The king was 'in exercitu de Biar' on 5 September 1244 (*M*, p. 170). The attack on Biar in all lasted from September 1244 until February 1245 (Font Rius, 'Conquesta', p. 263).

[108] 29 September 1244. James returned to Valencia where he was found on 12 September but he had returned to Biar by 22 September (*M*, p. 170).

[109] September–November 1244.

[358] Then one day we ordered our nobles to assemble,[110] those of the orders who were there, and Guillem de Montcada who had come there with sixty very good crossbowmen from Tortosa.[111] And we attacked the town in order to take up quarters there. And they defended it very resolutely so as not to lose anything except by force, and knights of our side were wounded there, and other men of their side. And we were there from mid-September until the beginning of February.[112] And we do not wish to recount all those deeds of arms that were done there, nor all the treaties that they spoke to us of there, and we to them, since they would be lengthy accounts.

[359] But towards the end, when all that had passed, the *alcaid* who was there, and was called Muça Almoravid, surrendered the castle to us and we retained the Saracens in that town, and we drew up the charters of their sunnah,[113] so that they should remain for all time with us and with ours.

[360] When we had completed that, we returned to Valencia from there and we wished to ask of Zeit the right that he owed us of Castalla, according to our charters.[114] And Don Jimeno Pérez de Arenós told us that it was not necessary, as he held it and that they could easily reach an agreement with him. And we asked him how he held it. And he said that Don García Pérez de Castalla held it for him,[115] and that he could deliver it to us when we agreed to terms with him. And we asked him in what manner would he agree, and he said that he would take places in the kingdom of Valencia five times less than that place was worth. And after we had spoken a great deal, we made this agreement: that we would give him Xest and Vilamarxant.[116] And we gave them to him, and in this manner we obtained Castalla.

When they saw that we held Xàtiva and Biar, the rest of the kingdom from Xúquer to the lands of Murcia surrendered to us, according to the agreement that we had made allowing them to remain in the kingdom. And so we had it all.

---

[110]The nobles included Prince Ferdinand, Guillem d'Entença, Artal de Luna, Pedro Fernández, Rodrigo Lizana, Pedro Cornel, and Pedro Maza (*M*, p. 170).

[111]The crossbowmen of Tortosa (here with their lord, Guillem II) enjoyed a great reputation. Possibly, they were Moors (*S*, p. 335).

[112]The king was at Valencia by 14 February 1245 (*M*, p. 171; *S*, p. 335).

[113]Here used to indicate all the laws by which the Muslims of Biar had been governed.

[114]At Valencia, on 14 February 1245, James confirmed Abū Zayd in possession of his goods (*H*, 2, no. 401).

[115]At Lleida, on 13 October 1262, García Pérez, at the king's 'wish and command' gave 'sworn homage' to Abū Zayd for the castle of Castalla (*Diplomatarium*, 2, no. 405a).

[116]Xest, between the Camp de Llíria and the Pla de Quart, and Vilamarxant, a town of the Camp de Llíria (*S*, p. 336).

[361] Then we went to Aragon, and we passed through Teruel and Daroca, and we went to Calatayud.[117] And one day we went to the Mass at the major church of Santa Maria de Calatayud; and, when we had heard Mass, Don Jimeno Pérez de Arenós came up to us and said: "Lord, you will need to take a decision concerning your affairs, as conflicts are arising of which you are unaware."

And we asked him what conflicts they could be. And he said: "You will soon know it well enough."

And we said: "You do me wrong, Don Jimeno Pérez, for if you know something to our profit, it would make us glad and would please us greatly; and if it was something to our harm, we would take counsel; for if one can take counsel beforehand, it is worth more."

And he said: "Do you want me to tell you about it, then?"

And we said: "Yes, we certainly do."

And he said: "al-Azraq has captured some of your castles in the lands of Valencia, and we did not dare to tell you."[118]

And we said: "They did us evil by not telling us, since they understood that we were losing something of ours. Yet it pleases us much, because we could not expel the Saracens from the land because of the agreements that they had made with us. And now they have done something by which we can expel them. And as it pleases God, it greatly pleases us that there where the name of Mohammed has long been proclaimed and invoked, the name of Our Lord Jesus Christ will be invoked."

And we said: "Do you know what castles he has taken from us?"

And he said: "Gallinera,[119] Serra, and Pego."

And we said: "Since the news is such, we will see who has done us this evil; and we will go there and we will take counsel."

And then we told the queen what Don Jimeno Pérez de Arenós had said. And she said that she already knew that, but she had not dared to tell us.

---

[117]The king has moved forward a little, to October–November 1247, when al-Azraq had renewed attacks in Valencia.

[118]al-Azraq proved James's most formidable Muslim opponent. Without the possibility of outside help from Granada or North Africa, in 1245 he had signed a three-year truce with James, who himself was keen to turn his attention to protecting his interests in southern France (Burns-Chevedden, *Negotiating Cultures*, p. 10). It is curious that an eleven-year war from 1247–58 (really a continuation of the Valencian campaigns), which involved many rebels, and which had in its early phase been the subject of many crusading bulls issued by Pope Innocent IV (Burns, 'A Lost Crusade') is treated in just fourteen chapters here. This may be out of a deep-seated contempt, on James's part, for his opponent. James refers to him in his documents as 'al-Azraq our traitor' and 'al-Azraq our betrayer' (*Diplomatarium*, 2, nos. 79, 85, 91). But it could also be that the king had returned to the construction of his autobiography at a much later date and felt that the events of the revolt *had* to be included even though he preferred to move on in his narrative to the Murcian campaign.

[119]The Vall de Gallinera, which included eight towns and two castles.

And we said: "You were seriously wrong in not telling us, for the sooner one takes counsel on the harm one has received, the better it is; and it is our will that we go to Valencia and recover our land, since the more land al-Azraq takes control of, the harder it will be to recover it."

And she said: "You speak well, and may it go well for you, and I beg you to take me there with you, that I may accompany you."

[362] Then, we and the queen departed and we went to Valencia.[120] And while we were at Valencia, the *alcaid* of Xàtiva came to us, with a great company of Saracens, and with a good ten of the sheikhs of the town; and he entered very happily before us, and kissed our hand and asked us how it went with us. And we said that well, thanks be to God, but the evil al-Azraq had done to our castles greatly grieved us, and that we wondered how they had allowed it. And they said: "Lord, if anybody has done you evil, you must know that it greatly saddens and grieves us."

And we could see that they were very content and satisfied, and we had never seen them so content and satisfied. And we expected the evil that al-Azraq had done to grieve them so that they would offer us help, but not one of them offered it to us beforehand, but rather said that they had come to see us, and that they were overjoyed at seeing us; and moreover they said that, through the grace of Our Lord and us, Xàtiva was so full of people that the men rubbed shoulder to shoulder. And after that they remained with us for two days, and on the third day they left. And we said to the queen: "Have you noticed what these Saracens have done, for they have entered joyfully before us and have not lamented at our misfortune, but held it of little account?"

And she said: "I had not noticed it, but now I can certainly see that what you say is true as they cared little about it, and said little about avenging you, nor did they suggest that you avenge yourself there."

[363] When they had left Valencia we went to hunt in Borriana. And having been there two days and one night, when we were in bed, they knocked on the door, and the guards told us that there was a messenger from the queen. And we thought that this message was something to do with a new deed that had occurred. And the messenger entered, and gave us her letter in which it said that al-Azraq had taken the castle of Penàguila.[121] And we were greatly perturbed at that, for on our arrival they ought to have repented of the evil they had done, but instead they did more evil to us, and in a place as fine and honoured as Penàguila was. And we were greatly perplexed by this. On the one hand we were upset by the affront they had done us, and on the other hand it pleased us, since they gave us the motive and the opportunity to avenge

[120]November 1247.
[121]In the province of Alicante.

ourselves. And that night we could not sleep at all, but we sweated as much as if we were in a bath.

[364] The next day in the morning, we mounted and went to Valencia, and there we found the bishop of Valencia, named Arnau,[122] who was of the lineage of Peralta, and who was afterwards bishop of Zaragoza, and we found there with him Don Pedro Fernández de Azagra, Don Pedro Cornel, Don Jimeno de Urrea, Guillem de Montcada, the castellan of Tortosa, Don Artal de Alagón, and Don Rodrigo Lizana. They came out to receive us and we told them that in the morning they should come before us, as we wished to speak together with all of them of an important and pressing matter. And they said they would do our bidding.

When it was morning,[123] having heard the Mass that we had had celebrated, we had with us two or three priests of the church of Valencia who were men of worth, and up to five citizens, and the nobles who were already there. And we began to speak, and told them how we had come from Borriana because of a letter that the queen had sent us, in which it said that al-Azraq had captured from us the castle of Penàguila. This had saddened and angered us greatly, as their audacity was so great that they had harmed us by taking two or three of our castles. Moreover, they did not wish to leave off harming us, even though we allowed them to stay in our land and live alongside us and our lineage.

"And now, to our shame, even with us here in our land, they have taken so little heed of our love and our lordship that it grieves us greatly. And you ought to take a share in our grief; for just as you would have a share in our good, so you ought to have a share in our misfortune and shame. So I beseech you and I order you, for the lordship I have over you, that it should grieve you, and that you help me to avenge this, since we are of the heart to make them pay dearly. For it seems to me a work of Our Lord, Who wishes that His sacrifice be for all the kingdom of Valencia, yet protects me so that I do not break the agreements I have with them. Rather they give me reason to go against them, having retained them in my land, and not thrown them from their dwellings nor done evil to them, so that they might not be prevented living richly with us and our lineage. Know, then, that, by the will of God, we shall make them pay dearly and heavily. What is more, that they should take my land and that in which I had settled them gives me good reason to settle the land with Christians. Now we must tell you what we think should be done, whilst always keeping in mind your counsel, if it is better than ours."

---

[122]He was bishop of Valencia 1243–8 and then bishop of Zaragoza 1248–71. The king speaks of Arnau as if he is dead and this may possibly indicate that this section of the text was constructed after 1271.
[123]1 December 1247.

[365] "This is what we have thought: that we should take around four hundred knights with whom to secure the castles that we have at Xàtiva, and the others. When we have secured them, let us speak in front of everybody, in the church of Santa Maria, at the next feast of the Epiphany,[124] which will be a month from now, and, having first demonstrated the harm and insults they have done us, let us say that I wish to take back the land and settle it with Christians. For when the men of our kingdom and of other lands know and hear that we have this good proposal to serve God, so many people will come that it will not be necessary to call for the army or a raid, as we will have more with these people and from the others than if we called for the army or a raid. But let us keep this in mind: that those who have not come against me, and have not seized my castles, shall receive no evil from me or from mine, but rather they should be given a fixed day by which to prepare themselves to leave the kingdom of Valencia with their wives and their children, and with as many of their possessions as they can carry, and that they shall be protected by me until they are in the kingdom of Murcia. And when they are in the kingdom of Murcia, they will have to make their own way to Granada or further."

[366] After that, having heard my words, the bishop of Valencia responded, and he said that he gave great thanks to Our Lord and His mother for the good proposal that He had given us; and that nobody had ever served Our Lord as well as we, since we had the will to do this; and that our name would be renowned in all the world, and that we could not give greater joy to the Pope nor to the church of Rome than by doing this.

And we said to the nobles that they should speak; and those that had Saracens spoke reluctantly,[125] since we did something that did not please them. And we said to them: "Why does this not please you and why do you not advise us to do it? Since, for your own benefit, you should not leave off from advising me according to God, and to my profit and to your own, as it surely shall be in the long term. For, even though your revenue will be reduced, because it will not be worth so much to you through Christians as through Saracens, mark well how great is the mercy that you and I will do there, since they have given me reason to expel them without breaking my word.

"The second reason, which is very powerful, is that if, by chance, and through the sin of Christians, some day the Saracens who are on this side of the sea and those who are beyond the sea should reach an accord, and the Saracen people from each of the towns should rise up, they would take so many castles

---

[124]6 January 1248.

[125]The nobles could not afford the disappearance of the Muslim populace. Nor, in reality, could the king or the Church. But James was able to uphold his reputation as a Christian champion by emphasizing that it was the reluctance of the barons that was the stumbling block to expulsion (Burns, 'Immigrants from Islam', pp. 40–1).

from us and from the king of Castile, that everybody who heard of it would marvel at the great harm that would befall Christianity. And it is better that the damage falls upon another rather than upon ourselves, since times change, and one should be prepared in advance so that nothing can come to harm one later."

[367] Then those of the city of Valencia, and the bishops, and the clergy, helped us to maintain the proposal that we had set out. And we were able to defeat the nobles by our natural wisdom, since our argument was better than theirs, in a manner that, when it came down to it, they had to approve it. And the council ended with them having recognized our proposal as the best.

Then we ordered that they should secure Xàtiva and all the other castles that we held. And we assigned Guillem de Montcada with sixty knights and armed squires to the castle of Xàtiva. In addition, we ordered that the other castles should be secured, and to those that we could not fortify sufficiently and to others we transmitted as large a company as was needed for each place. And we sent messengers to the Saracens with letters in Arabic with which we ordered them and fixed them a day within a month by which they should be prepared to leave our land with all their possessions and provisions,[126] and all that they could carry, since we did not wish for them to remain, since they had behaved towards us in such a way.[127]

[368] After that, the Saracens sent messengers to us, of those that they had and could find among them at some of the honoured places, saying that they greatly marvelled that we should expel them from our land, and that if we wanted them to increase the rent to us, they would give all that we considered to be right and fitting. And those of Xàtiva, who had wronged us, said that they would give one hundred thousand *bezants* each year in rent to us.

And we took counsel there, and we said to them that we well understood that they would increase the rent to us and that the land was worth more than it ever had been, but that, if now, without having help by sea, they had begun to act in that manner, we knew very well that when their power increased, they would revolt against us. Therefore we wished them to leave our land once and

---

[126]After the council at Valencia on 1 December 1247, revenue was collected for the war against al-Azraq in early 1248, and, very much in need of financial and military support, James requested the crusade which was formally proclaimed by Pope Innocent IV in November 1248 (*DPI*, 2, nos. 557–9). In March 1249, a provincial council at Tarragona, confirming a decision taken at a council at Tortosa a little before, voted the crusade twentieth for the expulsion of the Saracens from the kingdom of Valencia (Burns, 'Crusade against al-Azraq', p. 96).

[127]In these passages, the king exaggerates the extent of the exodus. The economic consequences of a large-scale expulsion of the workforce would have been catastrophic and it is evident that most of the Muslim population remained in place (Burns-Chevedden, *Negotiating Cultures*, pp. 108–9; Guinot, *Fundadors del Regne*, 1, p. 295).

for all, safe and secure with all their goods and belongings. And they, weeping and with great sadness left from before us, and they had to follow our order.

And each set to attacking the castles wherever they were able and where they saw that there was only a small garrison, and they were helped by their neighbours, and those who were nearby, attacking the castles with such force that in different parts of the kingdom of Valencia they took some ten or twelve of them. And there was a great war. And those that did not fight or could not take castles left the land, and all went to Montesa, so that a good sixty thousand men of arms, not counting women and children, collected there.

[369] Meanwhile, the Saracens became afraid that we would have the riches which they carried taken from them and whatever belongings that were valuable, and they deputed Don Jimeno Pérez de Arenós to speak to us, saying that they would give to us half of the money and half of their valuable belongings. And they negotiated that so that we would safeguard them with the other half.

But we said that we would not do such a thing for anything, since we had promised that we would protect them, and that to have them robbed on the road now was something we would not do for anything. For we had already spoken to them on that matter, saying that they would be under our protection. And to take advantage of them, when they were losing their houses, their inheritances and their homeland, and after we had given our word to them that they might leave safely and securely from our land? On no account did we wish to do so. For we were pained at the harm we were doing them; and our heart could not bear the idea that we should give them further pain on top of that, by taking anything from them that they were carrying.

Thus, we had them guided as far as Villena, and the knights and the nobles who protected them in our name reported to us that they occupied some five leagues from the vanguard to the rearguard. And they said that at the battle of Úbeda,[128] what with men, women, and children, there had not been seen more people than were gathered together there.[129] And Don Frederick,[130] brother of the king of Castile, was at Villena, as he held it for the king, and he levied a bezant on each Saracen head, whether male or female; and that came to one hundred thousand *bezants*, so they told us. And they entered into Murcia, and

---

[128]Las Navas de Tolosa (16 July 1212).

[129]The *Repartiment* of Valencia indicates a great deal of activity in Xàtivan territory in 1248 which ties in with the expulsion of some Muslims (though less than James suggests) and the repopulation of the lands with Christians (Burns, 'Crusade against al-Azraq', pp. 87–8). James had besieged Llutxent through much of March and then arranged the settlements around Xàtiva from March to July.

[130]Son of Ferdinand III and brother of Alfonso X of Castile. This section of the text must be dated to after 30 May 1252 when Alfonso became king.

some left for Granada and others into the land of the king of Castile. And so they were all scattered.

[370] Meanwhile, those that remained in our land made al-Azraq their leader. And one day a message reached us saying that they were attacking Benicadell,[131] and that they were preparing *algarrades* there and attacked them closely with shields and lances. And we were at Valencia. And we sent for the bishop, our nobles and some knights who were there, who knew of deeds of arms, and the notables of the city, so that they should prepare to go with us, because a message had arrived saying that they were attacking Benicadell, and we wished to go there to put them to flight. For if Benicadell was lost, the port of Cocentaina would be lost, since nobody would dare to go to Cocentaina, nor Alcoi, nor to the lands of Xixona, nor to any place in Alicante, and that would be a great setback for the Christians.[132] Moreover, from the side of Eslida and of Veo,[133] the Saracens had defeated some three thousand Christians who had entered against them to do them harm; and our men were from the districts of Tortosa, Alcañiz, Castellote, Horta, Vilallonga, Alcanar, Valderrobres[134] and other places that were isolated villages; and that between four and five hundred had died in that disaster. And that if they took Benicadell, it would be a great setback for the Christians of the kingdom of Valencia. And the bishops and the knights were there considered it right to help them.

Yet Don Jimeno Pérez de Arenós said: "Saving the honour of you all, I do not think this is good advice, because the Moors are many and they have been very heartened by this defeat that they have inflicted on the Christians and because of the castles they have taken. For it is a mountainous land, and there is a very large company there, and it is not a land where armoured horses can go easily at the gallop. And if we risk the king going to a place where he cannot complete things, or where they will make him retreat from what he would wish to begin and end, afterwards there would be no way of repairing it. Whereas, while the king is in Valencia, if we receive harm, such is his power that he can repair everything."

And all those who were there agreed he had spoken truthfully and wisely; and they besought us dearly and insistently that we should not wish to go there

---

[131]To the south of the Vall d'Albaida, it gives its name to the Serra de Benicadell but here refers to the castle of that name.

[132]These events seem to relate to the period August 1249. al-Azraq's victories were a serious setback to James and threatened Christian communication through much of southern Valencia (Burns, 'Crusade against al-Azraq', p. 95).

[133]Probably Alcúdia de Veo. Both places are in La Plana Baixa.

[134]Valderrobres and Horta de Sant Joan are both about halfway between Tortosa and Alcañiz, while Castellote is south-west of Alcañiz and north-west of Morella. Vilallonga perhaps treats of Vilallonga del Camp which is just north of Tarragona. Alcanar is south of Tortosa and north of Peníscola.

and that we should send them. And we recognized that they were right and that they gave the most sound advice, and we agreed to it because of the entreaties that they made of us.

[371] And then they went there.[135] And the Saracens held two hills, one on this side of the rock, the other beyond it, so that our men with armoured horses and with footmen had to attack them and take from them the hill that was on our side. And here Abenbassol[136] died, and he was the best man that al-Azraq had, and the most powerful, and in valour he was worth more than al-Azraq himself. And with the help of God, the Christians saw that those of the other side were also losing the hill and the Saracens who were there saw that Abenbassol had died and they abandoned that hill on the other side. And the Christians had not thought that they would abandon it, and had not placed guards at the foot of the hill. So the Saracens all left there, and went to take refuge at Alcalà,[137] in the land of al-Azraq. And from then on, the Christians took heart, and so the power of the Saracens decreased. And the war lasted some three or four years,[138] and hence al-Azraq negotiated first with Don Manuel,[139] brother of the king of Castile, and then with the king of Castile.[140]

[372] And the king of Castile asked us to give him a truce out of our love for him: for he had sent him his banner, along with another that he already had there from Don Manuel. And the king of Castile had sent another to them, so that he already held them under his command. And as far as he could he would defend them, as long as al-Azraq forbade his own people and others from telling us (so much so that he threatened Don Jimeno de Foces, because of the

---

[135] James now makes one of his customary leaps. Pope Innocent IV continued to provide vigorous support for James against the rebels and those (including Christians) who were helping them (Burns, 'Crusade against al-Azraq', pp. 99–103; Burns, 'Lost Crusade', nos. 7–13, pp. 445–9; *DPI*, 2, nos. 616–20) but the war now appears to have waned and entered a diplomatic phase with al-Azraq negotiating terms with Queen Yolanda in 1250. Diplomacy may well have been the result of financial exhaustion on both sides.

[136] Ibn Baṣṣāl.

[137] Alcalà de la Jovada (or de Gallinera). James is here referring either to the hamlets of the Vall d'Alcalà or the castle of Benissilí, the main stronghold of al-Azraq.

[138] James is perhaps suggesting that this phase of the war lasted three or four years (1254–1258).

[139] Don Manuel governed Murcia to al-Azraq's south. Manuel (d. 1283) was the youngest child of Ferdinand III and Beatrice of Hohenstaufen. Loyal to Alfonso until their final years (when he supported the succession of Prince Sancho), he received generous issues of land, particularly in Murcia. He is best known for being the father of Don Juan Manuel (Lomax, 'Padre de Don Juan Manuel').

[140] Relations between Aragon and Castile were very poor after the accession of Alfonso X and until 1256, when James and Alfonso patched up their differences over Navarre, borders, and Alfonso's treatment of Queen Violante, war was anticipated (*H*, 3, nos. 659, 666, 682, 687, 702, 710; *CDCZ*, 1, no. 77; *Alicante*, nos. 140, 147). al-Azraq appears to have taken advantage of the mutual distrust of the two monarchs to ally himself with Castile.

king of Castile). And in a meeting between him and us, we gave al-Azraq a truce from one Easter until the next,[141] because the king of Castile had begged us to do so.

[373] Now, when it was the beginning of Lent,[142] a Saracen, who was a close confidant of al-Azraq and who accompanied him and by whose advice he did a great deal, sent us a messenger. And the messenger was a Christian who he sent us, and with whom he had spoken very secretly, and he said: "Lord, this Saracen (and he told us his name) greatly salutes you, and says to you that if you do him mercy, he will arrange for you that al-Azraq shall sell all the wheat that he has, so that if you wish to attack him this Easter, you will find him without any provisions, as he will arrange for him to have sold them all."

And we asked him if that Saracen was of al-Azraq's counsel and he told us that he was, more than any other of his company; and that we could believe it, because he did not wish to have anything of ours until he had fulfilled this in such a way as would satisfy us. And we said to him: "Now say then, what is it that he asks?"

And he said: "He asks that you give him three hundred *bezants* and four *jovates* of land in Benimassor,[143] and that you draw up a charter saying that, if he fulfils that, you will give him the *bezants* and the land."

And we said that we would do it. And we had him draw up the charter in the manner that he had agreed with us. And furthermore he said that, when he had arranged for al-Azraq to sell all the wheat, he would come to us and would leave his company; and that we need do nothing more than go against al-Azraq at that time, because all his assets would be lost, and that we could do with him as we wished.

[374] Then we arranged for Ramon de Cardona,[144] Guillem d'Anglesola,[145] and other nobles of Catalonia and Aragon to be with us without fail on Easter

---

[141]Until 24 March 1258. That al-Azraq was in a sufficently strong position to threaten James's lieutenant in Valencia may have persuaded the king to grant him a truce. But an alliance with Alfonso which potentially threatened James's possessions in southern Valencia was inadvisable, as al-Azraq should have known and Alfonso surely did.

[142]6 February 1258. James was at Tortosa (*M*, pp. 270–3). On 28 February, at Tortosa, the king summoned Àlvar, Count of Urgell, to come to serve in the war against al-Azraq and then again on 18 March (*Diplomatarium*, no. 79a; no. 85a).

[143]Perhaps Benimassot in the Vall de Ceta, in the province of Alicante (*S*, p. 340).

[144]Ramon Folc IV, Viscount of Cardona (1233–76). From 1251 until his death he was in an almost perpetual state of rebellion and, ever opposed to the designs of James I, in open war against the king from 1251–53 (*H*, 3, nos. 619, 629) 1259–1262 (*H*, 4, nos. 1135, 1138) and 1268–9 (*H*, 5, nos. 1594, 1596, 1598–1600, 1611). Moreover, in 1274, the refusal of Ramon to deliver to the sovereign the power over the castle of Cardona was the catalyst for the great noble revolt (Sobrequés, *Barons*, 101–2).

[145]A relative of the bishop of Vic, Ramon d'Anglesola (1265–98), he was often in the king's following and was with the king at Valencia on 28 March 1258 (*M*, p. 273). He later took part

Sunday,[146] because we had great need of them, and their coming would be to our great profit and honour. And the Saracen spoke with al-Azraq and told him: "al-Azraq, you have provisions but you have no money, and yet you give wages to the footmen, and you owe them a great amount. Now the king of Castile is your friend, and just as he has craftily obtained a truce with the king of Aragon for you, send to ask him to obtain another for this year. And the king of Aragon loves him so much that he will not say no either to that or to something greater, if he asks it of him. And we have good harvests, and you will get money from the bread you sell that is now here; and you will have enough wheat from what we collect in these harvests. And thus you will have sufficient for your company of all you require."

[375] And al-Azraq responded to him, and said to him that he had advised him very well, and that he would follow his advice. And immediately he sent a message to the king of Castile asking him that he should obtain for him a truce from us for another year, (because that which he held, he held it for his service and under his orders). And the king of Castile, when he saw the letter of al-Azraq, sent another to us, asking the same thing of us.

That happened around Lazarus Sunday,[147] a little before or after. And the Moor came to us and told us that he had fulfilled what he had told us he would do, and that we would see that it was true. We asked our men of Cocentaina and of other places that were near al-Azraq, and we found it was true that he had sold all the wheat that he had. So we replied to the king of Castile that we found it very strange, for he asked us something that was to our prejudice, as he well knew that al-Azraq had done great evil and great damage to our land. Furthermore, he had come to us and had said to us that he wished to become a Christian and wished to take a relative of Carròs as his wife; and yet when we had been riding, by night, to a castle of the Moors that he held, called Rugat,[148] he tried to doublecross us, because there were only thirty-five knights with us, and he attempted to ambush us with seven Moorish ambushes, with a great clamour of horns and trumpets, and with crossbowmen (of whom there were many), and other men with shields. And if Our Lord had not helped us against him, he would have killed and confounded us. Moreover, he captured and held eighteen Christians we had sent to secure a tower near the castle. So then, we were sending word to the king of Castile that he ought not to show love for any man who had plotted our death, nor respect him, nor intercede for him; and that we would do nothing in response to his entreaties. And to the Moor who was

in the great noble revolt of 1274. Possibly it was 1274 when James narrated this part of his story.

[146]24 March 1258.

[147]Lazarus Sunday. The fourth Sunday of Lent (10 March 1258).

[148]In the Vall d'Albaida, province of Valencia. James has already referred to the matter in chapter 356.

with us and who had arranged all that, we sent the full sum of the *bezants* and we granted him a charter of inheritance, just as he had arranged with us.

[376] We spent Easter in Valencia,[149] and on the Tuesday, we went to Xàtiva; and no more than fifty knights went with us. And on the Friday after Easter, we left Xàtiva,[150] and we went to Cocentaina;[151] and we learnt that the nobles were coming, and that a number of them were already in Valencia. On the following Thursday we held a meeting with the *alcaids* of Planes,[152] and of Castell, and Pego. And the next day, having heard Mass, we went to Alcalà, yet al-Azraq did not dare await there, but moved on to Gallinera. And we went to Alcalà,[153] since al-Azraq's quarters were there more than in any other place. But we do not wish to speak of all that was done there, since it would lengthen this book. Nevertheless, on the eighth day[154] we recovered Alcalà, Gallinera, and sixteen castles that he had taken from us, and he agreed with us that he would leave our land for always, never to return again. And we gave Polop to a nephew of his,[155] to hold during his lifetime, and that was the agreement between him and us.

[377] Before this came about,[156] the king of Castile came to Alicante, and he sent a message to al-Azraq to come out to him; and he met him. And the king of Castile was hunting, and al-Azraq came with ten Moorish knights and with his personal guard who preceded him. And they told him that al-Azraq was coming and he stopped. And al-Azraq went to him and kissed his hand. And the king of Castile asked him if he knew how to hunt, and al-Azraq said to him that if he wanted, he would hunt castles of the king of Aragon. And a Galician who was with the king of Castile said it was a poor Moor who could hunt nothing but castles. And there was a knight of our land there, called Miguel Garcés, who heard these words, and he told it all to us.

---

[149]The king was still at Tortosa after Easter (*Diplomatarium*, 2, no. 89a (26 March 1258), (where he waived taxes on the town of Ontinyent, which had just been victim of a serious earthquake) but he was at Valencia soon afterwards (*M*, pp. 272–4).

[150]These events, however, appear to refer to May 1258 when the king was certainly in Xàtiva (*Diplomatarium*, 2, no. 124a).

[151]The king was at Cocentaina on 22 May 1258 (*M*, p. 275) and still on 26 May 1258 (*Diplomatarium*, 2, no, 131a).

[152]Three towns of the province of Alicante.

[153]Referring to Benissilí castle.

[154]James was laying siege to the castle from 29 May–3 June (*M*, p. 275; *Diplomatarium, 2*, nos. 133a, 139a (of 2 June, but not dated 'at the siege of'). Again James may have been forced to do some sort of a deal because French affairs (this time the Treaty of Corbeil with Louis IX) interfered.

[155]Abū Ja'far. James had granted the castle to al-Azraq, who, in turn had granted it to his brother Bāsim and his nephew Abū Ja'far. James confirmed the grant on 9 April 1261 (*Diplomatarium*, 2, no. 354).

[156]Ballesteros (*Alfonso X*, p. 97) places this earlier event in July 1254.

And when we had taken from al-Azraq all that he had and we had expelled him from our land, we remembered these words; and we had a letter written to the king of Castile, and we sent word to him that we had been told that al-Azraq had gone to him and had said those words mentioned above. And we let him know that we had taken sixteen castles from al-Azraq in eight days, and that we knew how to hunt in the way that we related to him, whereas al-Azraq had hunted just as he had heard from our letter.

6

The Reconquest of Murcia

[378] And, later on, when we had completed the deed of the kingdom of Valencia and recovered what we had lost, we went to Aragon.[1] And we had already heard that the king of Castile had fallen out with the king of Granada,[2] and that the king of Granada had, for a long time, had recourse to the Moors on the other side of the sea; and that horsemen had crossed to his land, so that later they might recover all the land of the king of Castile and all that they had lost, because of us or any other man in the world, throughout the whole of al-Andalus. And the king of Castile, who was at Seville, when he found that out, defied the king of Granada.[3] For a great company of horsemen had already crossed in secret.

---

[1]The events now related are of the Murcian revolt of 1264–6. After the assassination of Ibn Hūd in January 1238, Muslim Murcia descended into a political chaos which was happily nurtured by Ferdinand III of Castile. In April 1243, at Alcaraz, the kingdom was ceded in fief to Ferdinand, providing the rights of the Muslims were respected, and on 1 May 1243, Prince Alfonso entered Murcia city, but many towns refused to surrender, which led to a long campaign of subjugation. From 1257, Alfonso X determined on the Christian repopulation of the kingdom of Murcia to secure Castile's control of the territory. The Muslim population was discontented by many infringements of the agreement of Alcaraz. In 1263, the son of Ibn Hūd, al-Wāthiq, who had governed Murcia briefly in 1238, returned to the scene, as the spirit of rebellion spread, and even complained to the pope of the Castilians' bad faith. In Spring 1264, taking advantage of similar uprisings sponsored by the sultan of Granada, the Murcian Muslims rose in revolt and, in the absence of a strong Castilian military presence, took many of the major towns and castles of Murcia.

[2]Emerging from the ruins of the Almohad Empire, Ibn al-Aḥmar (Muḥammad I), a warrior of the Banū Naṣr family, was declared sultan in 1232 at Arjona, and, through rigorous government, and often in alliance with Castile, formed the kingdom of Granada, which city he entered in May 1237. He aided Castile in the conquest of Seville in 1248 but also often gave support to the Ḥafṣid dynasty of the eastern Maghrib. In 1262, Ibn al-Aḥmar, seeking the conquest of independent Ceuta in order to improve Granadan commercial activity, sought help from Alfonso X but the Castilian ruler's demands seemed excessive. While Alfonso pushed ever further south in Spain, the Granadans acted alone against Ceuta and their fleet was destroyed. While outwardly maintaining good relations with Castile, Ibn al-Aḥmar sought support against Alfonso from North Africa and the Muslim communities in southern Spain who paid tribute to Castile.

[3]Disaffected Marīnids had been crossing to Granada steadily since 1262 in search of Holy War. Ibn al-Aḥmar sent word to Alfonso that he broke his vassalage to Castile, as Alfonso recognized in a letter of 20 June 1264 to the bishop of Cuenca (Torres, *Reconquista de Murcia*, p. 65).

And the king of Granada had arranged with all the castles and the towns that the king of Castile held where there were Moors, that all would rise on a fixed day, to fight with all the Christians, capturing the king of Castile and his wife, and recovering the towns and castles all at one blow. And they did so. So that, if the king of Castile had not discovered that Seville plot, he and his wife and his children would have lost their lives. But even though he was spared the Seville plot (because the Saracens, who formed a great multitude inside, did not rise), inside three weeks the king of Castile lost three hundred cities, great towns and castles.[4]

[379] And we were at Sixena on Palm Sunday,[5] that we kept there in honour of the monastery that was built by Queen Doña Sancha,[6] who was our grandmother. And here they told us that the queen of Castile[7] was sending us a messenger who was at Huesca. And the messenger was Beltrán de Villanueva,[8] who was our subject and a man whom we knew well and loved. And we, on learning that, went to Grañén, one of our towns, which is four leagues from Huesca.[9] And we found Beltrán de Villanueva there, and he gave us the letters from the queen.

And they said this: that we well knew that she loved us dearly, as a daughter should love a good and loyal father, and that we had married her to the king of Castile, who was one of the most important and powerful men in the world,

---

[4]The Muslims rose up in June 1264 and, although Alfonso escaped, many Christians were killed and many important fortresses were captured including Jérez, Arcos de la Frontera, Rota and Medina Sidonia. Alfonso reacted vigorously, having the crusade preached on the basis of bulls of Innocent IV (1246) and Alexander IV (1259), while Clement IV issued four further crusading bulls in March 1265 (Goñi, *Historia de la bula*, p. 192). Alfonso defended Seville and, with the aid of the order of Calatrava, recaptured Jerez, Arcos and the zone to the south of Seville. Alfonso then allied himself with the Muslim governors of Málaga and Guadix and with reinforcements from Castile he forced Ibn al-Aḥmar to terms in Autumn 1265, though both sides were only seeking a truce while awaiting outside help (Torres Fontes, *Reconquista de Murcia*, p. 71). al-Wāthiq threw himself on Alfonso's mercy in the closing months of 1265 but this did not end Murcian resistance.

[5]Palm Sunday fell on 20 March 1264. James may have been at Sixena then, but he was certainly there on 24 June 1264 (*M*, pp. 352–3) and probably during that visit he received news from the queen of Castile.

[6]Sixena was a Hospitaller foundation which acted as something of a finishing school for young ladies. It had been founded by Sancha who retired there after Peter II reached his majority.

[7]Violante, daughter of James, wife of Alfonso X.

[8]He later intervened as partitioner in the *Repartiment* of Murcia, for which he was generously rewarded. In Huesca, on 1 July 1264, James would concede to Beltrán safe-conduct in order that he might take his wife to Castile (*Alicante*, no. 329; Torres, *Reconquista de Murcia*, p. 113, n. 79; Garrido, *Jaume I*, p. 70; *S*, p. 342).

[9]James was at Sixena on 24 June 1264 and at Huesca by 29 June (*M*, pp. 352–3).

and that, already she had eight or nine sons and daughters from him.[10] For which reason she besought us, for God, our reputation, and our valour, that we would not allow him to be dispossessed, and that we would give advice to help them, since she had no other adviser or refuge except us; and the Moors had taken all the land from them except for a little, and she besought us as her father and lord, in whom was her trust and her hope, that we would help her husband, so that she would not see the day when he or her sons were dispossessed.

When we had seen the letters, we responded to Beltrán that we could not reply to him there, but that we would go to Huesca and we would assemble our council, and we would give such a response as the queen might be satisfied with us. And he kissed our hand, and he thanked us on her behalf as much as he could.

[380] On the morning of the next day, having heard Mass at Huesca, we ordered the nobles who came with us and others who we found there, that on the following morning they should be there with us and the others who were there, because we wished to speak with them of an important and urgent matter. And the bishop of Huesca,[11] the abbot of Montearagón, Fernando Sánchez de Castro,[12] Don Bernat Guillem d'Entença,[13] Jimeno Pérez, Don Gonzalvo Pérez, who was the nephew of Jimeno Pérez de Arenós, and the archdeacon of Valencia were there.[14]

And we showed them the letter of the queen, and we asked them to advise us in what manner we should proceed in that matter on which queen had sent word to us. And everybody said to the bishop of Huesca that he should speak.

---

[10]The children of Alfonso and Violante were Sancho IV, Ferdinand, Peter, John, James, Berenguela, Beatrice, Violante, Isabel and Eleanor. Though it is reported speech, presumably it is the grandfather rather than the mother who cannot remember how many children she has.

[11]Domingo de Sola (1253–69). In the previous October he had been designated by the pope to collect from the Aragonese Church subsidies for the Holy Land (Linehan, *Spanish Church*, p. 206).

[12]Illegitimate son of the king through his relationship with Blanca de Antillón and one of the most important figures in the later part of James reign. In 1261, Fernando was envoy to Naples to agree the marriage of Prince Peter to Constance of Hohenstaufen. In 1265–6, he participated in the Aragonese revolt against James's support of Castile. In 1269, he arrived at the Holy Land in spite of the failure of James's expedition. In 1270 at Naples he placed himself in the service of Charles of Anjou, enemy of Prince Peter. On his return to Catalonia, there was open war between him and Peter. In 1274–5, he was one of the nobles who revolted, refusing to give help to Alfonso X of Castile against the Moors. Prince Peter was sent to put down the revolt, besieging Antillón and Pomar. While fleeing in disguise, Fernando was captured and Peter had him drowned in the Cinca.

[13]One of the sons of the Bernat Guillem d'Entença who died at Puig de Santa Maria.

[14]Gonzalvo Pérez (referred to as 'de Tarazona' in ch. 381), Jimeno and Bernat Guillem had certainly been with the king at Zaragoza on 20 June 1264 (*M*, p. 352). The archdeacon appears to be Gonzalvo himself (*Alicante*, no. 305) (or perhaps Martín López (*M*, p. 294)).

And he said: "Since you and the king wish it, I will speak on it. Lords, this is a very important matter. And is it for me to advise the king to proceed with us alone, when there are so many nobles in his land, as well as archbishops and bishops? So that he may take counsel upon so important a matter, which is greater than the battle of Úbeda or any other there ever was in Spain, I consider it right that the king assembles the *Cort*, and that he explains this matter to them, and with their advice he does what he wishes to do."

[381] And we said to Fernando Sánchez de Castro that he should speak. And he said: "Let Don Bernat Guillem speak, as he is older than me, and afterwards I will speak on it."

And Don Bernat Guillem argued with him, but even so he spoke first. And he said: "I say this: that it seems to me that the king cannot let the queen down, when she has sent as warm a letter as she has sent him; but it seems to me that the king can now receive reparations for the ways in which the king of Castile has insulted him, and he can do so with good reason, since his help will cost the king so much, and he will do it in the greatest hour of need at which any king has ever gone to another. In this way, the castles that the king has asked of him many times and has not obtained, he will now obtain by right. But that he should not help him? That I would not advise for anything, as he greatly needs help; and when in need, a man knows his friends."

When he had finished his speech, we said to Fernando Sánchez that he should speak. And he said: "In the first place, I agree with the words that the bishop of Huesca has spoken: that the king should convoke his *Cort*. And I also consider what Don Bernat Guillem has said is good advice: that the king should obtain the castles, as he may never have a better opportunity than now. And that we should serve him in that as well as we are able. And I believe that the others will do the same. Thus, let the *Cort* be convoked, since without the *Cort* we do not have a complete council. For, in so important a matter as this, it is necessary to celebrate the *Cort*."

And the abbot of Montearagón, Don Jimeno Pérez de Arenós, and Don García Pérez de Tarazona said the same. And since we do not wish to lengthen this account, they said that it seemed a good idea to hold the *Cort*, and that we should send word to the king that he should deliver to us Requena[15] and other places of ours that he held, and that we had the intention and desire to help him. However, they added that we could not respond to him properly until we

---

[15]There had been many contentions between Alfonso and James over the boundaries of their conquest zones in the mid-1250s, as well as the struggles to gain control in Navarre, and there had been a renewal of contentions in 1262–3 (*Diplomatarium*, no, 421a; *Alicante,* no. 305). The Aragonese nobles now felt it was the time to take advantage of Alfonso's misfortunes.

had held the *Cort*, but after that we would respond to him in such a manner that he ought to be satisfied.

[382] After that they asked us to speak and we said that we were pleased by this: "Firstly, I will say that I do not agree with anything you have said, and I will tell you how this matter really stands. You have to know that this is the way in which a man who tastes wine and wishes to water it proceeds, because those who taste wine and wish to water it, need to know if it is already watered or strong. The king of Castile has used my daughter in this way, for because of the wrongs he has done me, he does not dare ask for my help, and tries to obtain it through her. And if he finds, through our letters to her, that we wish to help him, other requests will follow for us to help him.

"And I respond to your advice on the *Corts* that I think it right that the *Corts* should be assembled, and I will hold one in Catalonia and another in Aragon: and the first will be in Barcelona, and the other will be in Zaragoza. However, I do not agree that I should ask advice in this matter in any of these *Corts*,[16] for, in all the lands of the world, there is not to be found all the wisdom and valour that there ought to be; and we, who have tried do so, have found that they are divided when we ask for advice on a great matter, because they cannot agree well.

"But, when we speak with them, we will say to them that they should help us and support us, because this is something that I cannot refuse to do for three reasons: one is that I cannot fail my daughter and my grandchildren, now that people wish to dispossess them; the other (which is more important than all the others, and which you have not touched on), is that that even were I not bound by my valour and my duty to help the king of Castile, I have to help him because he is one of the most powerful men in the world. And if I did not help him and he escaped from the difficulty he is now in, for all time he might hold me as his mortal enemy, since I did not help him in his greatest hour of need. And if he could seek to do me evil, he would seek to do so all the time, and he would have good motive; the third (that is the strongest of all, and is one of natural wisdom), is that if the king of Castile were to lose his land, we would be in a weak position in this our land; for it is better to defend on his land than on our own.

"And no other advice is necessary, but that I send word to the queen that I will help him with all my power and that I will enter Catalonia and as soon as I am able celebrate the *Corts*, and I will do the same in Aragon. And in those

---

[16]In response to the nobles' assertion that the *Cortes* should be convoked in a matter of such importance, the king emphasizes the limited power of the *Cortes*. James says he does not have to seek their advice nor will he but rather he will demand their support. The insistence of James on supporting Castile with men and money against the advice of his nobles would lead to a constitutional crisis (González Anton, *Uniones Aragonesas*, p. 23).

Corts which I will celebrate, I will not tell them to give me counsel, but I will tell them that they should help me. And in as brief a time as I can, I will go to his aid."[17]

[383] Then we left there, and we went to Catalonia.[18] And firstly we convoked our *Cort* at Barcelona.[19] And when the *Cort* of the nobles, citizens, and clergy had assembled, we asked them that just as they and their lineages had always helped us in our affairs, and especially in that of Majorca, so it was necessary that they should help us in this, because the need was great. And they said that they would deliberate. And their decision was this: that on behalf of Ramon de Cardona and his lineage, we should repair some wrongs which, according to what they said, we had done him, and that if we spoke privately with him at once, they would give us such a response that we would remain satisfied. And we said that anybody of our land who had a complaint of us should come to us and we would repair it. And that for that reason they should not now place any obstacle to obstruct us in this business, as it did not seem reasonable that we should ask them one thing and that they should respond to us concerning another; and for that reason we asked them and we ordered them that they should take a better decision, as a response such as that did not seem appropriate for men as good as they were. And they deliberated again, and they responded to us as badly or worse than they had on the first occasion.

[384] When we saw how badly they behaved, we said to them that they had not sufficiently understood what could happen afterwards, because if the king of Castile lost his land, we would have more difficulty, we and they, in holding our land than we had now. And we said to the clergy: "What will you gain if the churches where Our Lord and His mother are worshipped are lost through ill fortune, and Mahomet is worshipped there? And if what belongs to we kings is lost, you can well understand that what is yours will not be restored. And I never thought that it would happen that you would respond to me in so wicked and villainous a manner; that convoking the *Cort* of the Catalans I would not obtain a fitting response. For if I had insistently besought something unfitting

---

[17]James does not mention that the Crown had already been planning attacks on the Muslims before the revolt. On 27 October 1263, James conceded licence to Guillem Grony to make war on the king of Tunis (*H*, 2, no. 1370; Dufourq, 'Vers la mediteranée', pp. 57–8 (nos. 92–5)); On 6 February 1264, James conceded to his son Pedro Fernández the command of a fleet to be sent to attack the Moors (*H*, 2, no. 1381); in May 1264, Prince Peter was ready to arm galleys to go against the Moors (González, 'Recull de documents', 2, doc. 71).

[18]The king was at Huesca until 2 July 1264, he was then at Pertusa and Monzón on 3 July (*M*, p. 353), and at Lleida on 5 July (*H*, 2, no. 1409).

[19]James was at Barcelona from 16 to 27 July 1264 (*M*, p. 354) though here he is referring to a later visit from 2 to 13 November (*M*, pp. 361–2). The *Cort* met at Barcleona on 12 November 1264.

from you, I could obtain it. And as I see that it is so, I depart dissatisfied with you; as displeased as any lord can be with his men."

[385] And we got up and we did not wish to hear any reply from them and we went to our house. And they insistently besought us that we should not be angry, for they would deliberate again and they would respond to us. Yet, in spite of all that, we did not wish to stay. And one group of them followed us to our house, while the others remained there; and afterwards those who had followed us returned to them.

[386] And while we were in this mood, not even wanting to eat, they sent to us Berenguer Arnau,[20] Pere de Berga and two other nobles, whom we do not recall, and they asked to speak with us. And, in private, we listened to what they wanted to say. And they said to us that not for anything in the world would they allow that which had never happened before to happen now, that is, that having asked advice or help from the prelates or the nobles of Catalonia, we should not receive it from them. And as we wished to leave the town and had already said so to some people, they said to us and they besought us that we should remain there, and they would act in such a manner that we would be satisfied with them. And they besought us so much and so insistently that we had to grant that to them.

[387] And, on the same day, at the hour of vespers, they all came to our presence and they said that not for anything would they act in a way which would give us reason to depart from them dissatisfied, and that we should listen to their arguments because they had not said what they had said with bad intent; moreover, they asked that, before we granted this to them, we should do what Ramon de Cardona had asked of us. And they said that they had the intention of giving us the *bovatge*, although we did not have the right to it, because we had already taken it twice: once, when we began to reign,[21] the other time, when we went to Majorca. But that now they would give it to us because we wanted it and they would serve us in that deed in such a manner that we would thank them for it. And we were satisfied with their response and we convoked the *Corts* in Aragon so that all were to be in Zaragoza in three weeks' time.

---

[20]Berenguer Arnau d'Anglesola and Pere de Berga both participated in the subsequent campaign against the Moors (*M*, pp. 384–5).

[21]Firstly at the *Cort* at Monzón in 1217, and afterwards in the first Majorcan expedition, as mentioned in chapter 50. The Catalans only conceded the *bovatge* to James on 23 November 1264 when he was already at Lleida (Torres, *Reconquista*, pp. 115–16).

[388] Then we left there, and we went into the districts of Aragon,[22] and we ordered the bishops and the nobles to our *Cort*, and we had them assembled in the church of the Preachers. And we explained the matter to them, and we got to our feet and we began with an authority from scripture that says: *Non minor est virtus, quam querere, parta tueri.*[23] And we said that although up to that time Our Lord had shown us great love and great honour in the conquests of Majorca and Valencia, and in other affairs of our land and in other places, now we found ourselves in the position of having to defend what we had conquered and what our lineage had left to us. For this reason: "For when He gives such grace to us and you that He will help us to remedy the evils that others have received, we have to greatly thank Our Lord, we and you, as through us and through you I can help the king of Castile (who is so closely tied to us) against this treason and this evil that the Saracens have done him. We ought to give Our Lord great thanks for this. And it is better we act upon the land of another than on our own.

"Therefore, we ask you, for the love that you owe us, for the good we have done you and for the obligation that we owe to one another, that you help us in this business. And the help will be such that what we receive from you will amount to little when compared with what we shall give you of ours, since for every *morabetin* of yours that you expend we will give you ten. And we do not ask this of you because of the duty that you owe us, but rather that we may better able to carry out this business. Because, if you were to consider how great is the honour that we and you shall take from this deed if we can remedy this matter, nothing ought to be more dear to you. Moreover, if we were to go to Outremer, we would not do a third part of the great mercy we do in defending what God has given to the king of Castile and to us. Because this is something from which we could receive shame and harm, since if he loses his land, we could lose ours. And, if you want us to say what we will do and how, let two nobles come to us, and we will tell it to you in private. And after that you can deliberate in order to give us a good response; one that may be to the honour of God, and of us and of you."

[389] And a Minorite arose and said: "So that the king and you may have greater resolution and comfort, I will tell you a vision that one of our brothers saw. And that brother, who was from Navarre, said that, while he was sleeping, he saw a man in white robes and this man called him by name and asked him if he was sleeping. And he made the sign of the cross and was afraid. And he asked him, "Who are you who has woken me up?" And he said, "I am an angel

---

[22]The *Corte* at Zaragoza met in December 1264.

[23]The quotation is from Ovid's *Ars amandi* (bk 2:13) with 'nec' changed to 'non'. It is repeated by the Dominican Pere Marsili, who recognized it was not scripture but misquoted the line.

angel of the Lord and I tell you that in this conflict that has arisen between the Saracens and the Christians in Spain, you can believe for certain that one king has to save everyone and to defend them so that evil does not befall Spain." And this brother who was from Navarre asked him which king that would be. And he replied that it was the king of Aragon who had the name James."

And he said that this brother who had this vision had told it to him during confession,[24] and had assured him that he had seen it and that it grieved the brother greatly that the angel did not say it was the king of Navarre. "And for this reason both you and the king should be of good heart, since Our Lord will redress so great an evil and will prevent it from happening, and I tell you that to comfort you."

[390] After that Don Jimeno de Urrea got up and said that visions were all very well,[25] but that they would come to our presence and deliberate upon whatever we said. And we said that they spoke well. And upon that, the assembly broke up, and it was in the church of the Preachers. And we went to our room and some seven or eight nobles came to us and we said to them: "Barons, we did not wish to say the things that we want to say to you in front of the people, for these things are best spoken of privately, so that you may help us in a way that will be to the profit and honour of both you and us.

"It is the case that we have convoked the *Corts* at Barcelona, and we can praise the clergy of Catalonia and the nobles because, when we explained the good proposal that we had to serve God and help the king of Castile, they showed their desire and their will to help us: firstly, saying that they would help us with money that they would give us for their men, and that would be *bovatge*; and then they asked us to help both our men and theirs, and that they would serve in all that they held in fief in our name, in what we would give them and, moreover, in the fiefs they held through us.

"Therefore we ask you that you consent that your men should help us in the same way in which they help us; and if this way does not please you, let you and us seek another way, but of equal worth to that way. Because if you consider it carefully, the most that we will have from your men will not rise to more than five thousand sous, and you can obtain thirty thousand from us. So it seems a good idea to put down five thousand sous for thirty thousand sous you will gain. And for a knight, however much I give him, it will not rise above fifty sous, but we will give it to you in a manner that you can give two or three thousand sous. And, moreover, we will draw up a charter so that that which we

---

[24]Perhaps while going to confession but not during his confession.

[25]It is likely that James shared the view of Jimeno which he repeats here. There is only a little talk of miracles throughout the text and James does not personally witness anything miraculous.

now ask of you, if you give it to us, shall not become a precedent against you or yours."

After that they were all silent and did not say anything. And we said that we found it strange that they were quiet, because we had not said to them anything base that might upset them. And when we saw that they did not wish to speak, we said: "We want to know from you, Fernando Sánchez de Castro, what your reply is to us on this matter."

And he said that as we wished him to say it, he would speak. And he spoke thus: "I do not believe they and I will come to an agreement on this matter now; but, for myself I say to you that if you want to set fire to what I have, that you begin at one end and ride out through the other."

And we said: "And can you not respond better, Fernando Sánchez. Because I am not here to burn lands but to defend them and to give lands to you, as I have already given lands to you. That is how we would burn you and not in the other way."

[391] Then we asked Bernat Guillem d'Entença to speak. And he said: "Lord, if you wish something from me or some places that I hold, I will give them to you willingly; but what you ask from me now, I cannot do it."

And Jimeno de Urrea said: "Lord, we in Aragon do not know what *bovatge* is; but we will deliberate and we will respond to you."

And we said: "Barons, it is necessary that the accord should be better than what you now say, because we do not wish anything but your good and ours."

And they went to deliberate. And they did not wish to come before us neither that day nor the next until evening, when Don Bernat Guillem d'Entença came to us. And we said: "Don Bernat Guillem, you delay in giving us the response that you ought to give us."

And he said: "We do not wish to give it to you for this reason, because we believe that it would not please you."

And he added: "Know for certain that they do not intend to respond to you well."

And we told him to go away. And we ordered our guards that they should go to each of the nobles and tell them that in the morning they should come to our presence.

[392] In the morning they came, and they stood before us without saying anything. And we said to them: "What have you agreed about what I have said to you?"

And the one said to the other: "You say it."

And they told Jimeno de Urrea that he should speak first. And he said: "In this land, lord, we do not know what *bovatge* is; and I say to you that, when they heard this thing said, all cried with one voice that they would have none of it."

And we said: "We greatly wonder at you: you people are too stubborn to listen to reason. You ought to think well on what the business is and you ought to consider whether we do it for good or bad reasons. Because we certainly believe that nobody would be able to consider what we do to be evil, since we do it in the first place for God, in the second place to save Spain, and in the third place so that we and you might win great fame and renown for together having saved Spain, through you and us.

"And by the faith that we owe to God, since those of Catalonia, which is the best kingdom of Spain,[26] the most honoured and the most noble (because there are four counts there, that is to say, the count of Urgell, the count of Empúries, the count of Foix,[27] and the count of Pallars, and there are nobles, and for every one there may be here there are four in Catalonia, and for every knight here, five in Catalonia, and for every cleric here there are ten in Catalonia, and for every honoured citizen here there are five in Catalonia),[28] and since those of the most noble land of Spain have not wished to keep from us what is theirs, you, who hold our fiefs, some of thirty thousand sous, others of twenty thousand, others of forty thousand, rightly ought to help us, and especially so since you will retain everything that is yours, together with what we add to you of ours."

And they said that they would not do it in that way for anything in the world. And we said: "Yes, you will do it, in some manner."

And they were silent. And we said: "Will you not do it in such a way that it will cost you nothing except the word that you give?"

"How?" they said.

"We will tell you how. Offer it to us in front of everybody, but you will not give us anything of yours. In this way we will not lose the contribution of the clergy, the orders, or the knights, even though you will keep all that is yours."

And they said that they would deliberate and they would respond to us.

[393] The next day in the morning they assembled in the house of the Preachers. And they sent two knights to us while we were assisting at a law-

---

[26]This famous eulogy to Catalonia is one of the indications in the text of an incipient nationalism. The Aragonese nobles were never comfortable with the Union and James was never comfortable with the Aragonese nobles.

[27]The county of Foix is outside Catalonia but the count had close familial ties and many possessions within Catalonia. As viscount of Castellbò, the count (at this stage Roger I of Castellbò (1230–65)), intervened in Catalan affairs a great deal and he was subject to the count-king for the viscounty.

[28]The repetition is there in the text. At times, especially when agitated, James rambles a little and his scribe has faithfully reproduced the king's words.

suit alongside the bishop of Zaragoza,[29] who was judge in a case from Azuer that Doña Teresa had with García de Vera and Miguel Pérez de Alagón. And when we came out from there, they sent Sancho Gómez de Balamazan and Sancho Aznares de Luna to us, and they said to us: "Lord, the nobles and the knights have sent us to say that they consider what you have asked the greatest thing that a king has ever asked of them; and that they will not do anything in favour of it, but would rather lose all that they had."

And we looked at the bishop of Zaragoza, who had come with us, and we began to laugh, and we said: "The barons do not respond fittingly, but on another occasion, if God wills it, they will give us a better response on this."

And when these messengers had returned to the knights, the knights all cried out and said: "Let us go from here and let us go to Alagón, and there we will take counsel."

And they all left the town, and only two knights remained with us.

[394] And when we had dined, Pedro Jordan de Ejea[30] came to us and said: "Lord, what I see greatly grieves and saddens me, as it has been done rashly and wrongly. Yet I cannot avoid going there. Do you wish for me to say something to them on your behalf?"

And we said: "No, we do not want you to say anything to them."

And he said: "Think about it, because if you order me to say something to them, I will say it."

"And are you telling us the truth, Pedro Jordan? You would say it to them?"

And he said: "Aye, Lord."

"Then, tell them this on our behalf: that tomorrow they will be sorrier than they are today, and in fifteen days, more than that, and in a month, more, and after a year, they will wish they had not done it. And God confound you, if you do not tell them that!"

And having secretly sworn oaths at Zaragoza, and afterwards in Alagón, they went to Mallén; and we to Calatayud.

[395] While we were in Calatayud,[31] we sent a message through the bishop of Zaragoza, saying that we would give them satisfaction if they had any complaint of us, and that we found it strange that they acted so, going against our lordship so cruelly and harshly. And then they sent a message to us saying

---

[29]Arnaldo de Peralta, an Aragonese who had first been an able bishop of Valencia (1243–8) is here hearing a case involving Teresa Gil de Vidaure, James's common law wife. García de Vera is perhaps the same who appears in the incident at Garcia Romeu's tent (ch. 324) in 1240. Miguel Pérez is probably a vassal of Queen Violante of Castile, James's daugher, and was conceded some houses at Huesca in January 1265 (*M*, p. 365).

[30]An Aragonese knight who had witnessed the treaty of alliance between James and Teobaldo II of Navarre in April 1254 (*M*, p. 238).

[31]December 1264–January 1265 (*S*, p. 347).

that they would send Don Bernat Guillem d'Entença, Don Artal de Alagón, and Don Ferriz de Lizana to us if we would grant them safe-conduct. And we granted that, and we sent them another message saying that we were prepared to do them justice. And they came to Calatayud.

Now, we were in the church of Our Lady Saint Mary. And there were more than a thousand men there to listen to the discussions. And we said to them that we wanted to know why they had taken that oath without asking us if we had done them wrong or not, and without first seeing if we wished to repair it, as it was very strange that someone should take an oath against his lord without him knowing why. And they said that they did so because we had broken the *fueros* of Aragon. And we said that they should show us in what way and we would make amends, and that we had the law-code with us and we would have it read in front of everybody, chapter by chapter, and they should say how we had broken it against them, and we would put it right, chapter by chapter. And they said that it was not necessary that we had it read, but rather they would tell us in words.

And we said that we would certainly listen to their words, if they put them in writing. And they gave us a document containing the complaints that they made, saying that we had gone against the laws of Aragon, because we were always accompanied by pleaders in law and decretalists, and we judged according to them; and that we were doing wrong to Don Bernat Guillem d'Entença in the business of Montpellier.[32] And they made other complaints that had neither rhyme nor reason and with which they only wished to cover their misconduct.[33]

[396] We responded to them that on their complaint referring to us having in our house lawyers and decretalists, we could not be held, because in all courts of kings it is necessary that there are decretalists, lawyers, and fuero lawyers, because there always appeared cases of all these types; and if we did not have

---

[32]This appears to relate to certain rights that Bernat Guillem claimed in Montpellier as grandson of the last of the Guillaumes of Montpellier and which he considered had been denied to him by the king's lawyers (Tourtoulon, 2, p. 270).

[33]Among many complaints, the Aragonese objected to the king distributing the honors to those who were not among the Aragonese nobility; they objected to the use of Roman Law and decretals rather than ancient custom; they considered the kingdom of Valencia should be ruled according to the *fueros* of Aragon; they complained that the king's officials overreached their authority in their treatment of the nobles; they insisted that the king was responsible for the education, marrying off and arming of his nobles as knights; they claimed that the attempt to introduce the taxes of *herbatge* and *bovatge* and the salt-tax into the kingdom were very offensive; the Aragonese reclaimed their ancient fueros; they insisted that nobles were not obliged to serve in wars which were outside of the kingdom and which were not in the interest of the nation; they said that the county of Ribagorça had been unlawfully separated from the kingdom of Aragon in order to unite it to Catalonia (Tourtoulon, 2, pp. 269–70; González, *Uniones Aragonesas*, p. 23).

in our court those who could resolve them it would be to the embarrassment of our court, because neither we nor laymen could know all the writings that there are of law in the world. Thus so that they could help us when it was necessary, we had to take them with us; and, because our dominions do not have one law-code or custom. And for this reason we took them with us.

But we asked them that they should say whether, in Aragon, we had judged the cases by a law other than the law of Aragon, when this was sufficient, and, if it had been so, we would make amends to them for it. Because the law of Aragon says that, where the law falls short one should be guided by natural wisdom and equity. And they did not want the laws of Aragon to be read, word for word, on those things in which they said we had done them wrong. And then, having answered the complaints that they had made unreasonably, and that they ought not to have made, we said:

[397] "Worthy men, it seems to me that you wish to act as the Jews acted towards Our Lord, when on the night of Thursday, at the Supper, they seized Him and they brought Him before Pilate to judge Him, and they cried out 'Crucify, crucify!'[34] So, you say that I have broken the *fueros*, but you do not say in what and in what not, and as you do not wish to receive justice from me, it is the most novel complaint and argument that anyone has ever made against his lord. But one thing I will say to you, worthy men: two things allow you to persist in this mischief and allow you to remain in our land: one is the help that we have to give to the king of Castile, whom we will not let down, since we have promised him; that our wisdom is such that it prevents us from going against you on this occasion. Because, if it were not for these two things, there is not a plain, nor wall, nor rock in the world from which we would not drag you, since for each knight that you have we would place three who would not be your friends nor refrain from doing evil to your person or your possessions. Moreover, we have all the towns of Aragon and Catalonia, which will be against you, and they know as much of war as you do.[35] And since we have the power, the knowledge, and the money, it does not seem that you ought to wait for us, having done us wrong."

And upon that they departed from us and left there.

[398] When they had left, we learnt that they intended to assemble at Almuniente[36] on a fixed day, and we knew the day that they would be there.

---

[34]Based on Mark 15:13; Luke 23: 21; John 19:6: Matthew 27:22.

[35]It is a testimony to a dramatic change in the political structure of Aragon-Catalonia since the beginning of James's reign that the king could now suggest the support of the towns was more important than the support of the nobles.

[36]In the province of Huesca.

And we decided to go to Huesca,[37] and we asked and we told the bishop of Zaragoza that he should come with us, because we would need him and we wished to send him to them. And he told us that he would do it. And when we arrived at Huesca we sent the bishop to Almuniente, where they had assembled; and we sent word to them that we asked them and we ordered them, for the lordship we had over them, that they should not commit so great a sin against us as they now did. And the bishop went there and he told them that. And, when he returned, he told us that Fernando Sánchez de Castro and Don Bernat Guillem d'Entença would come to us if we gave them safe-conduct; and we gave them safe-conduct. And we had already sent word to them that we would place the matter in the power of the bishops of Zaragoza and Huesca. Then they came to us; and, to shorten the story, since it would take a long time to tell, they would agree nothing with us nor we with them. And they left, although we continued to offer to do them right, but they did not wish to accept it.

[399] When we saw that this was the way things were going, we sent for Pere de Montcada,[38] Ramon de Montcada and other nobles of Catalonia, and the men of Lleida, Tamarite, Almenar and other places, telling them to come to our presence with the army, prepared with their men and their weapons, and that on a fixed day they should be at Monzón.

[400] And while the letters were on their way, we were in Barbastro.[39] And the knights sent word to us that if we gave them safe-conduct, they would come before us; and we gave them safe-conduct. And Fernando Sánchez de Castro, Don Bernat Guillem d'Entença, and Don Ferriz de Lizana (who were in that oath) came there. And we were in the major church of Santa Maria de Barbastro. And Fernando Sánchez spoke for them, and said that that oath which they had sworn was not against us, but was because we had broken their laws and asked unfitting things of them, and because in Ejea we had sent them away,[40] when Don Jimeno de Urrea, Don Artal de Alagón and other nobles and

---

[37]James stays in Calatayud through January and then we find him at Huesca on 8 February 1265 (*M*, pp. 364–6).

[38]Pere de Montcada was the seneschal and lord of Tortosa, while Ramon, his brother, was lord of Fraga. Ramon was with the king at Ejea on 7 February 1265 when James recognized a debt to Ramon of one thousand sueldos which he had lent for the war against the Moors (*Alicante*, no. 344).

[39]These events are probably of June 1265 (*S*, p. 349).

[40]The king is now referring to the *Corte* at Ejea of 26 April 1265. James was forced to make important concessions to the Aragonese, giving in to many of their earlier demands. The honors were to be reserved to the Aragonese; the nobles, knights, and the petite noblesse were exempt from payment of *bovatge* or *herbatge*; the witness of two knights would establish nobility; the justiciar of Aragon would be judge of civil and criminal plaints between the king and the nobles; the king could not concede land nor honors to sons born of the queen; the

knights, except Fernando Sánchez, Don Bernat Guillem, and Don Ferriz, had argued with us. And we said to these three that we had not wronged them by breaking any law, nor had we taken inheritances from them, but rather we had inherited them, for Don Ferriz had a good *honor* when he intervened in that, and we had inherited the father of Don Bernat Guillem with all that he possessed. Wherefore we marvelled that they had done so harsh a thing against us.

And to tell you more briefly, they could not agree with us, and we told them that since it was so, we would have to defend ourselves.

[401] We went to Monzón; and men of Tamarite came to us first of all. And we had them attack a fortress that was near Monzón, which Pedro Maza,[41] son of Arnaldo de Lascellas, had built. And we took it and we had it pulled down. Afterwards we went to Rafals,[42] and, with the men of Almenar and Tamarite, we took it, because they surrendered to us. Then we went to Lleida[43] and we asked and we ordered the notables that they should prepare to form an army with us, for they had broken from our lordship when we were preparing to go to the help of the king of Castile. We left there and went to Monzón, because the waters of the Cinca were high; and we crossed at the bridge, and lodged there for one night. From here we went to Pomar,[44] and we had a *fenèvol* prepared, and a castle of wood made. Yet, with a *brigola* they had inside, they prevented us from setting up the *fenèvol* or bringing the wooden castle close enough to do them harm. And when we saw that it could not be done, we sent to Tortosa for a *brigola* that we had had made there, with which to destroy their *brigola*.

[402] After that Pedro Martínez, a cleric and son of Martín Pérez,[45] who was the justiciar in Aragon, came and said to us that if we wished to lift the siege, they would be reconciled with us in the following manner. They would place the dispute between us and them in the hands of the bishops of Zaragoza and Huesca, if we gave them the *honor* that, as they believed and said, we had taken from them. In turn, they would assure us that they would do right by us

---

nobles could continue to exploit the salt mines in the manner to which they were accustomed; a noble who granted the cavalleria to an unworthy person would be deprived of his honor; the justiciar of Aragon would always be named from among the knights (Garrido, *Jaume I*, pp. 73–4; Tourtoulon, 2, 274–5).

[41]Perhaps the P. Maza who appears with the title of escuder (squire) in a royal document of April 1253 (*M*, p. 229). Arnau participated in the assembly at Lleida in 1214 (*M*, p. 19; *S*, p. 350).

[42]13 June 1265 (*S*, p. 350; *M*, p. 372).

[43]Between 20 May and 4 June 1265 (*S*, p. 350).

[44]James was at the siege of Pomar on 20 June 1265 (*M*, p. 372).

[45]Martín Pérez de Pina was still justiciar in Aragon on 21 December 1264 (*M*, p. 364). The king recognized his debts to Pedro Martínez de Luna on 29 May 1265 (*Alicante,* no. 350).

before we surrendered the land to them. This would be guaranteed into the hands of the bishops, in a manner that we might be satisfied. And if we gave a place where they could lodge they would approach us; and that was how the matter between us and them should be treated.

[403] Now, we were pleased with what Pedro Martínez had said to us. So we raised our camp and we entered Monzón,[46] and we ordered the men of Gil[47] to welcome them into the town, and they did so. And they came to Gil and lodged there. And they were perhaps some one hundred and fifty knights; among whom were Don Bernat Guillem d'Entença,[48] Don Ferriz de Lizana, Don Fernando Sánchez de Castro, and others; as well as the sons of Don Fortuny de Berga[49] and others who were close to us and were their friends. There we placed the matter in the hands of the bishop of Zaragoza and the bishop of Huesca. The nobles assured that they would give satisfaction for the wrong they had done us in going against us and against our lordship; and that if the bishops decreed that we should return them the *honor*, that we would deliver it to them. This was written in charters, and they gave us a truce until we had returned from helping the king of Castile, plus fifteen days. And this was set down in the charters.[50] Then we fixed a day when we would be at Zaragoza, and that they would be there. This we did for two reasons. Firstly, because we knew that they would be unable to give us satisfaction, since all that they had had fallen into our power and not only what they had but their very persons. The other reason was because it was harvest time, mid-June, and we could not retain the people there, so impatient were they to go. And we would not be able to make them remain, neither by beating them nor watching them nor by imprisoning them, even if we personally had them watched and beaten.

[404] On the day that we had agreed with them, we were at Zaragoza,[51] and they went there. However, the bishop of Huesca only went as far as Almudévar, where he fell ill, and he said that even if they killed him he could not go any further he was so ill. So he had to go back. We said to them that the bishop of Huesca could not come, and they said that they already knew it to be true. Then we said to the bishop of Zaragoza that we were ready to proceed

---

[46]The king was at Monzón on 30 June 1265 (*M*, pp. 372–3).

[47]San Gil in the province of Huesca, near the Selgua.

[48]Certainly all of these three were with the king at Monzón on 30 June (*M*, pp. 372–3).

[49]Whose wife was Sibília d'Entença, daughter of Bernat Guillem (Zurita, *Anales*, 3, ch. 66). They were thus close relatives of the king himself.

[50]On 30 June, James granted protection to Bernat Guillem, Ferriz de Lizana, and Fernando Sánchez and to all their goods and vassals, while he was away on the frontier of Murcia and Granada (*M*, p. 373; *S*, p. 351).

[51]The king had been at Zaragoza on 18 June 1265 (*Alicante*, no. 351) but perhaps these events are of late September 1265, when James was also at Zaragoza (*M*, p. 378; *S*, p. 351; *CDCZ*, 1, no. 116).

with his judgement, which would be worth as much as if both of them were there. The bishop said that he would speak with them, and would find out if they would agree to that. And he spoke with them and they said to him: "For what does the king wish us to give satisfaction to him and in what to recognize his right?"

"For that," said the bishop, "Which you have done to him; and then he will fulfil what has been stipulated between you and him."

And from what we know of the discussions, (for they were between the bishop and them), it seemed to us that the bishop understood that they were unable to give satisfaction for having sworn an oath against us, because all that they had would not be enough. And he explained to them that, legally, all that they had would not be sufficient and that they would have to place their persons in our power to do our will. Afterwards he spoke with us, and he said: "Lord, it seems to me that the knights have agreed with you to something that they cannot fulfil, and now they recognize that. Therefore, it seems to me that I cannot in any way say that they should give you satisfaction, because, with all that they have, they cannot."

[405] And we said to him: "Bishop, you ought not to disclose anything from one side to the other; rather whatever you say, you should say as a sentence, and we will return to them their *honor* so that they can fulfil whatever you decree."

The bishop said that he did not think that he could give a judgement that disinherited them of all they had. And we said to him: "What is it to you, if they have put themselves in that noose?"

But the bishop did not wish to say anything more on the matter, so the *honor* remained in our power, and they broke the agreement they had made at Monzón, because they did not wish to await what would befall them as a punishment. We, however, respected the truce that they had sworn, as it was contained in the charters that were agreed between us and them.

[406] After that we left, together with whatever forces we could muster, to help the king of Castile, during the truce that they had given us. Passing Zaragoza,[52] we went to Teruel; and there we sent a message to our sons,[53] to Ramon de Cardona and Ramon de Montcada, and to the others, that they should come to

---

[52]The king has said he is at Zaragoza, where he was until 29 September 1265 (*S*, p. 352). He was certainly at Teruel on 12 October 1265 (*M*, pp. 378–9).

[53]To Princes Peter and James. Prince Peter had already undertaken two raids into Murcian territory in March and June 1265. According to *Muntaner* (ch. 13), the first of these raids did particularly severe damage to the Murcian rebels and arrived at the capital itself, while the second was to cause such damage that it smoothed the path for James's arrival (*Muntaner*, ch. 14). *Desclot* also reports Peter's attack on the city itself, saying that there was a true battle but the Christian forces, in clear numerical inferiority, had to withdraw (ch. 65).

us at Valencia, with all they could assemble. Now, we ourselves had enlisted two thousand knights. And there was nobody there from Aragon, except Blasco de Alagón.[54] And of the two thousand knights we had enlisted and paid, we did not have more than six hundred.

At Teruel we spoke with the notables of the town, and we asked them to help us in the enterprise we had begun. We told them what had been done to us, and how we could not, for anything in the world, avoid helping the king of Castile, since we had promised this to him. And we besought them most insistently that they should loan us grain and cattle so that we would have sufficient for the army. And they said that they would deliberate, but that they did not wish to delay the agreement until the next day, so they would try to respond as soon as possible.

[407] After a short time they returned to us; and Gil Sánchez Muñoz[55] replied for all those of the town, and said: "Lord, you well know that never in what you have demanded or asked have you ever found us wanting. It has never happened, nor will it happen now. We say to you that we will loan you three thousand loads of grain (a thousand of wheat, and two thousand of barley), twenty thousand sheep, and three thousand cows. And if you want more you may take it from us."

We responded to them that we thanked them very much for it, and that we saw that in them we had good vassals, and that they loved us and greatly trusted us. And they said that we should give them an officer to go with them through the villages and, wherever they found what we needed they would take it, and would secure it very well, in such a manner that when we left Valencia, we would have it all. So we gave them the officer to go with them, and we departed from them very satisfied with the love that they had shown us, and that they should put it into effect so well.

[408] When we arrived in Valencia,[56] we spoke with the notables of the city and we asked them to remember how they had been settled there by us (since God willed that we should conquer the city). Moreover, we said we had more hope in them aiding us in helping the king of Castile to conquer the land that had risen against him, than in anyone else. For we had defied everyone else in our land, and for that reason we were in Valencia. Thus, we asked them, as insistently as we were able, and so that we might see that they knew we had established them there, that they should help us in such a way that we would

---

[54]On 18 June 1265 at Zaragoza, James had recognized his debts to Blasco for his financial support for the Murcian campaign (*Alicante*, no. 351) and he was with the king again on 6 October (*M*, pp. 378–9).

[55]It is reasonable to suggest that he is of the family of the Pascual Muñoz of Teruel, who some forty years previously had helped James out of similar difficulties (ch. 25).

[56]James was at Valencia by 26 October 1265 (*S*, p. 352).

gain honour from that deed. For they had a great share in my honour, and this would be one of the greatest honours we had ever achieved. And they said that they would deliberate and that they would return before us the next morning.

[409] When the next morning came they asked us what we wanted them to do that they could do, because they were prepared to do our will. And we told them that we needed provisions; that is to say, wheat, wine, and barley. "For which reason we ask you to proceed in this manner. Go through the town, and let whoever has wheat loan it to us, except what he needs for a year for his home. And if there are merchants, let them loan it to us, and we will give them as much security as they want. Be good to us in this, and find it for us wherever you know it may be."

They said that they would do so willingly, because they saw that we had need of it, and they saw the urgency and the need that there was, and, moreover, the dishonour and harm we might receive. And they did it. Then Prince James, Ramon de Montcada, and other persons[57] whom we do not recall came. And we went to Xàtiva, and from Xàtiva to Biar.[58]

[410] While we were in Biar, we sent a message to the Saracens of Villena saying that we asked them and we ordered them that they should come to meet us early in the morning. In the morning, we went there and they were awaiting us. And, when we arrived there, we took to one side thirty of the best men of the town. And we asked them how they could have done such a thing as to rise against their lord, Don Manuel.

Then we said that although they had committed a great error, we would have mercy on them and would obtain from him his pardon, since there was such great friendship between us that he would do what we said.[59] But if they did not wish to do so, we would have no option but to do them evil, because, as they could very well see, they would be unable to defend themselves against our power.

Therefore, it was better for them that I should reconcile them with Don Manuel so that they could stay in their houses with their inheritances, than for them to have to leave there and go to a foreign land, where they would not find

---

[57]It is a matter of curiosity that James does not mention the presence of Prince Peter in Valencia (Soldevila, *Pere El Gran,* 1, pp. 130–1) and generally underplays his important role in the campaign. It is possible that James narrates this section of the text at a time when he had fallen out with Peter. On 30 September 1265, Clement IV wrote to both Princes Peter and James to congratulate them on the zeal with which they had rebutted the Saracen attacks (*Documentos de Clemente IV,* no. 47; Goñi, *Historia de la bula,* p. 198). James had to cover expenses undertaken by Peter in the campaign (*Alicante,* nos. 359–62).

[58]James was still at Valencia on 1 November 1265, but was at Xàtiva on 5 November, still there on 8 November (*M,* p. 380) and was then at Alicante from 12 November until 18 December planning the campaign against the Moors (*Alicante,* p. 150).

[59]Don Manuel's first wife was James's second daughter, Constance.

help nor anyone who would do good to them. They said that they thanked us for the words that we had spoken, but that they had risen against Don Manuel because of his conduct. And they said that we might return to Biar and that they would respond to us at night.

[411] That night they sent two Saracens with their response; and one of them had Latin.[60] And they gave this response to us, saying that if we returned in the morning, they would swear, according to their law, that if Don Manuel came and agreed with the treaties that we made with them, and would pardon what they had done, they would deliver Villena. But if Don Manuel would not pardon them, they would not be held to the agreement. Furthermore, if we swore to them that we would not return Villena to the king of Castile or to Don Manuel, then we could go there and they would deliver it to us. We thanked them for what they had said, and we told them that we would go there in the morning and that we would deal with them to their satisfaction, and we would draw up our charters with them. And we gave one hundred *bezants* to the one who spoke Latin, so that he would represent us well in the matter; and he said that, with the help of God, he would have them do what we wished. (And we gave them to him secretly, so that the other one did not know about it.)

[412] In the morning, we went to Villena, and we drew up three charters to the effect that they would deliver Villena to Manuel when he went there; that we would arrange for him to pardon them; and that he would observe the initial agreements he and they had made. Having drawn up the documents, all those at Villena who were twenty years old or more swore to us that they would observe what they had agreed with us in those documents.

[413] Then we left there and we went to Elda;[61] but we did not lodge inside the town, as the Saracens had still not entirely surrendered themselves to Don Manuel, to whom they belonged. And they sent to ask us that nobody should lay waste to their lands or do them harm, and that they would act according to our will. Thus they came to us, so that we would give them officers and men who would protect their huerta so that nobody did them harm; and we did so.

[414] Then at once we sent a message to Petrel,[62] which Jofre had lost. And straight away two of the sheikhs came to us, along with a Jew who had been there in the time of Jofre and to whom the Saracens had not done any harm.

---

[60]'la u d'aquells era llatinat'. Either meaning he spoke Catalan or, as is perhaps more likely here, he knew how to read and write Latin, and therefore could help in drawing up the treaties.

[61]A town of the province of Alicante, to the left side of of the River Vinalopó.

[62]In the province of Alicante.

And we negotiated with them that they should deliver the castle to us, and that we would deliver it to Jofre.

We said to them that we would make them fulfil the agreements that they had with the king of Castile and Jofre. And they said they had risen against him because of his conduct towards them, but that if we swore that we would retain them, they would deliver the castle to us immediately, but that they were afraid of Jofre. We responded that one thing we would most certainly guarantee before we delivered them to Jofre was that we would make them observe their initial agreements. However, we said it would not be right for us to come to the help of the king of Castile and yet to retain the castles that we ought to return either to him or to those that held them for him.

After that they said they would go and make a decision and that they would respond to us in the evening. And they returned to us near to sunset and they said that, since we so greatly wished it, they would act according to our will. Thus, the following morning we went before them with our knights, and we had the men of Jofre hoist our flag on the castle, and we delivered the castle to them.

[415] The next day we went to Nompot,[63] which is a village in Alicante. And the day after that we entered Alicante, and we set our company in order there. While we were in Alicante we assembled our sons, Prince Peter and Prince James, the bishop of Barcelona, and the nobles, in the church of Alicante (the new one outside, not the major church).[64] And the knights were there, too.

We said to them that we were entering into the conquest of the king of Castile,[65] and we wished to lay down rules as to how they should conduct themselves in arms and in other matters.

Firstly, in arms, that when they were on the move, nobody should take up arms without our order, and, if they had to take them up, that they should not leave us without our permission. And that if we shouted, "'Via fora', for they have attacked such a place", all should take up arms and come around us, and do exactly as we ordered. In the same way, if they were in the camp at night and somebody shouted "To arms", so that the army had to rise, everyone should take up their weapons and equip whatever horses were there, and come to our tent (or to our house, if we were sleeping in a house). And that not for anything in the world should they break ranks without our command. Above all, they should take care not to quarrel among themselves nor with others, for quarrels are the worst thing that there is or can be in the army of a king or a

---

[63]Today Montfort, a village of Alicante.

[64]21 November 1265 at the church of San Nicolás de Alicante (*Alicante*, no. 366; *M*, p. 380).

[65]By virtue of the treaties of Cazola (1179) and Almirra (1243) the region of Alicante pertained to the conquest zone of the king of Castile.

lord. For by them a man places the whole army at risk of death or being lost, and afterwards the enemy can come and overcome all those in the army who remain alive. Moreover, if any dispute should arise over raids or anything else, it should be brought before two knights who we would appoint there as judges. And we would order them that if any man has done wrong to the other, they should have it set right, and that if they were unable to do so, then we would do so.

"For quarrels in this world are about 'yes' and 'no'; for no man should take the law into his own hands against another, when there is a lord. And if anybody wishes to take up arms and desires it, we will find him a way of losing his desire for it. For such damage can they do with their quarrels that all our army could be lost or thrown into confusion, and we would have to give up the campaign. Wherefore we beseech you and we order you, under pain of treason and on our love, that you do not violate this order that we have given you."

[416] When we had finished speaking with them, we sent a message to Elche through our exea,[66] and a dragoman, with the letter, saying that they should send two or three Saracens, of the good ones of the town, to speak with them; because, if they wished it, we would do them no harm, nor did we have the intention to do so, but rather we would help to save them. And they sent Mohamed Abingalip,[67] with another.

When they came to our presence, they saluted us in the name of the sheikhs and the *aljama* of Elche. And we said we hoped God would give them good. Then we said, "Let me make known to you the reason we have sent to you. We believe you know from those Saracens who have entered into battle against us how our Lord has helped us against them, and that He has carried us to victory in all we have begun. Also, we believe you know how generous we prove with those who wish to have peace with us, if they place themselves at our mercy; and how we always fulfil what we have promised them, if they do not lose it through their own conduct. And we have now come into this land for these two purposes. As for those who rise up against us and do not wish to place themselves at our mercy, we will conquer them and they will die by the sword. And for all those who wish to place themselves at our mercy, we will have that granted to them and they will be able to remain in their homes and keep their possessions and their religion. Moreover, we will make sure that the king of Castile and Don Manuel respect them and the treaties they have with them, and

---

[66]This refers surely to the 'exea' (an Arabic word meaning guide or companion). The exea had started out as a municipally licensed official involved in the ransoming of captives but in the thirteenth century became ever more a royal official though still primarily in a ransoming role (Brodman, *Ransoming Captives*, pp. 7–9). The exea set out perhaps towards 20 December 1265 (*Alicante*, no. 373).

[67]Muḥammad ibn Gālib.

also their customs, according to the charters they had, and if in any way they have broken them they will have to set that right."

[417] And that Saracen replied that he thanked God and us for the good words that we had spoken to them. And that this was what they hoped of us. For they had certainly heard it said that those who trusted in us were safe, and that we did not break faith with them, but rather we fulfilled what we promised them. And he said that we should send men to them to protect them and they would go there; and that afterwards they would report to the *aljama* the fine words we had spoken to them and then they would return to us. And so they went and told the *aljama* what we had said to them, and when they had done that, they came back to us and told us of what they had spoken inside. And we said to that Saracen, who was called Mohamed, that we wished to speak with him. Taking him to one side, we asked him to take care of our business. And we said that, as well as the share of the inheritance he held at Elche, we would give him so much for this that he and his lineage would be worth more for all time, if he would hold in our name (and afterwards in the name of Manuel) the town and all the revenues. And we had hidden away three hundred *bezants*, and we put them into the sleeve of his gown. And he was content with us and promised on his law that in this matter he would do all that he could do for our profit, and that he had confidence in God that he would accomplish it. Then he went away.

[418] The next day he came again with a guide that we had given him. And he came with a letter from the sheikhs of the town which contained the things we should do and not do for them. And these were the things that they asked. First, that they would be able to remain there with all their inheritances. Second, that they would be able to practise their religion, as to shouting from their mosque. And the third, that they could be judged according to the custom of the Saracens, and were not to be compelled by any Christian, but that Saracens should judge them, as was done in the time of Miramolino.[68] We granted that to them, and we assured them that if they had done anything to grieve Don Manuel, we would make sure that Don Manuel and the king of Castile would pardon them, and that we would make the latter observe all the agreements that they had with us. And they said to us that the day we went to Elche they would give us the tower called Calahorra, and they would draw up their treaties and conclude their agreements, and that when we passed through there they would fulfil all these things for us.

[419] Now, at that time we did not wish to reveal the matter to our nobles. And we had Prince Peter, Prince James, the bishop of Barcelona and the other

---

[68] Perhaps referring to the time before Castilian rule (1243) rather than the end of Almohad rule (1228).

nobles summoned. Meanwhile, two galleys that we had armed arrived, and they brought to us two small ships loaded with grain, that were worth some fifty thousand sous. And we asked advice from the above-mentioned nobles about what we should do and where we should go.

And this was the advice they all gave: that we should go to Elche for the following reason. Those of Elche were on their way, and if they went from Alicante towards Murcia and Orihuela,[69] they would be able to ransack them. Then we said that they should go via Elche, and we would speak with them, and perhaps Our Lord would give us such luck that they would deliver it to us.

And we did not wish to reveal to them what we had done, so that nobody would be able to obstruct it. In fact, we said to them that it was likely that Elche would resist more than Murcia, because it produced more wheat than Murcia.

[420] When we had agreed on what day we would move, we said to them that we would go in advance with one hundred knights, and we would find out if they would surrender the town to us and if they would deliver it to us voluntarily. If they would not, we would decide if we should continue on or if we ought to besiege it. And we went there before the others, and as soon as we had arrived there, the sheikhs and some of the best men of the town, some fifty of them, came to us, and granted the charters and the pact just as had been agreed between the messenger and us. And they swore, they and all those of the town, that they would abide by it in the manner that had been agreed.

When the army arrived, they found the Saracens with us, when we were drawing up our treaties, and that the Saracens had taken their oath to us according to the agreement that we had made with them at Alicante. And the army marvelled that we had been able to obtain it so quickly. Then, as it was evening, the Moors asked us that we should wait until the morning of the next day, when all the Saracens of the town would come to us. Then we would be able to make them grant the charters and the agreements, and they would deliver the tower of Calahorra to us, which is the strongest place of Elche. And we waited, since they had asked us to do so.

[421] In the morning, we drew up the documents, so that by the hour of terce they had already confirmed the agreements and all the other things, and they had delivered to us the tower of Calahorra. Having taken the tower, we left the bishop of Barcelona[70] there so that he could make sure that nobody might ravage their lands.

---

[69]A sizeable town at the side of the River Segura in the province of Alicante. It was one of the towns annexed to the Crown of Aragon by James II.

[70]Arnau de Gurb. At the end of November 1265, James indeed entrusted the tower of Calahorra at Elche to Arnau as guardian (*Alicante*, no. 369).

[422] All that happened on the same day. Then we went to Orihuela[71] and we left Astruc Bonsenyor[72] at Elche so that he could bring us the charters made between us and the Saracens of Elche. When we arrived at Orihuela, the son of Benhud, the *Rais* of Crevillente,[73] came to us and told us that his father had been captured and that the king of Castile had taken him prisoner. For that reason he came to us. Moreover, he said he would do all that we commanded and that our men could enter Crevillente safely and surely. And he said that he came to us in order to deliver to us the two castles that he had, and so that we could help ourselves to what was his as if it were our own.

Thus, we had freed and recovered all that we had lost, from Villena to Orihuela and from Alicante to Orihuela, so that everyone could go along the roads safely and surely.

[423][74] One night, while we were at Orihuela, where we remained some eight days,[75] two *almogàvers* from Lorca[76] came to us and knocked on the door. And it must have been near midnight. And they said that the people of Lorca reported to us that eight hundred light horsemen, with two thousand loaded mules and two thousand men-at-arms guarding them, were entering supplies into Murcia, and that at sunset they had passed before Lorca. And they informed us that if we went out there, we could take the whole train, because they would perhaps flee, since they had those fleet mares and horses. On hearing that, we ordered the guards to rise immediately and to go to Prince Don Peter, Prince Don James, Don Manuel, the master of Uclés,[77] as well as the representative of the master of the Temple,[78] the master of the Hospital, and

[71]The king was at Orihuela on 24 December 1265 (*M*, p. 381), though it is possible he was there in late November/early December as well.

[72]A Jew from Barcelona, a royal notary and specialist in Arabic documents (*M*, pp. 338, 393–4, 404). This probably treats of events of late November 1265 (Torres Fontes, *Reconquista de Murcia*, p. 132). The town and district had been softened up in the previous months both by conciliatory letters from Don Manuel and attacks by Prince Peter.

[73]Garrido (*Jaume*, p. 91) suggests that this passage treats of two people: one, Ibn Hūd, the grandson of Ibn Hūd Bahā'ad-Dawla who had governed Murcia after the fall of Zayyān; the other, the *Ra'īs* Ahmad ibn Hūd. Crevillente is in the province of Alicante.

[74]Here begin three narrative sequences which are told in the wrong order. The first, about the incident with the light horse of Lorca, takes place after the incidents in Alfama, but James either decides to tell it first because it is more dramatic than the others, or he remembers it first and then adds the other sequences because they are similar. All three sequences (423–8, 429–30 and 431) illustrate the king's prudence.

[75]24–31 December 1265. There is some confusion here since the king was at Orihuela for eight days over Christmas but in ch. 432 he relates a meeting with Alfonso X of Castile which took place at the beginning of December as if it were after all these events.

[76]A town of the province of Murcia, just below the River Sangonera.

[77]Pedro Nuñez, who was to be at Murcia on 23 June 1266 dealing with the matter of the submission of the capital to Alfonso (*S*, p. 356).

[78]The master of the Temple was Lope Sánchez and of the Hospital Hug de Malavespa (*S*, p. 356).

Don Alfonso García and all the other nobles.[79] They were to tell them to mount quickly and go to the gate of the bridge, where they would find us, because that message had arrived to us from Lorca, and to carry provisions for one day.

We left at once, and when we had crossed the bridge of the river called Segura, we waited for them outside. And when they had arrived, we set off. When dawn broke we arrived at a small village between Murcia and the mountain on the route to Cartagena, where the kings of Murcia are buried, on a little hill that rises above the village, and upon which Abenhud is buried.[80]

[424] When it was daylight, we held a council. And Prince Peter, Prince James, Don Manuel, the master of Uclés, Don Pedro Guzmán,[81] and Don Alfonso García were in this council.

Now, they considered it a good idea to leave from there, and to send scouts in advance to see if the horsemen were coming or not. But we told them that we did not think that was a good idea, because the usual course that light horsemen took with those whom they encountered was to tire out those who had armoured horses by circling around them. But we would have one hundred armoured horses of our household, and the others we would not arm. And our sons should be in the vanguard, and Don Manuel, the master of Uclés, and Don Pedro Guzmán on the flank. And we with those hundred armoured knights would form the rearguard. And if they were to fight us with the light horse, none should advance towards them until we had ordered the trumpets sounded. And when they heard the trumpets, those on unarmed horses should advance against them, and should not leave off until they had all been killed or they had captured them. And we would go after them with the armoured horses, and all that fell on the field we would gather up. And everybody considered this a good plan.

[425] When the council broke up, we sent Guillem de Roquefeuil,[82] with five or so other knights, to go and see if they were coming or not. And he sent a message to say they were coming. And the master of Uclés, Don Pedro Guzmán and Don Alfonso García came to us and they said: "Lord, look to saddle up and move, for you see the Moors are coming."

---

[79]Alfonso García de Villamayor was Alfonso X's governor and miltary commander in Murcia. Others present around this time included Guillem de Roquefeuil, Ramon de Montcada, Guillem de Canet, Jaspert de Castellnou, Guillem Hug de Serrallonga and Ramon d'Urtx (*M*, p. 385).

[80]Buznegra. Now Voz Negra.

[81]Pedro Núñez de Guzmán, Master of Uclés, mentioned in the previous chapter.

[82]King's lieutenant in Montpellier (*Alicante*, no. 334). He was certainly with the king on 12 January 1266 when James enfeoffed to him a castle in the region of Montpellier (*M*, p. 382). He played a major part in the reconquest of the kingdom of Murcia for which he was amply rewarded by James (Torres Fontes, *Reconquista de Murcia*, pp. 171–2, 213).

But we said: "Master, let us not be hasty. Let them ride down onto the plain, so that we can place ourselves between them and the town, and so, when they flee, we will have the mule-trains and those on foot that escort them. For many ambushes that are set fail through going out too hastily."

And the master said: "Do not do it, by God, since you do not know what kind of people these are. For you will think that they are near the huerta,[83] and, before you know it, they will have entered inside the town and you will have nothing at all."

And we said: "Master, we shall have the mule-trains and the foot soldiers."

And he said: "Lord, do not believe it, because they will be in the town, and it will be a wonder if you can overtake them."

And they insisted so much that at last they made us move. And when we were outside, we displayed our standards, and we arranged our battle-lines, with the vanguard and the flank as above, and we kept the rearguard, as above, with one hundred armoured horses.

[426] And when we were outside, in formation, an *almogàver* came to us and said: "Lord, a gift for good news."

And we said: "About what?"

"See the Moors!" he said. "Here they come."

And we said: "Friends, allow us to win the battle and then we will give you a reward."

The bishop of Barcelona went with us, and we called for Brother Arnau de Segarra,[84] who was a preacher, and we told him that we wished to make our confession to him. And he said that we should speak. Then we told him we did not consider ourselves to have done any wrong to Our Lord through which we ought to be lost, except in the matter of Doña Berenguera,[85] and we had it in our heart to live with her without sin just as a man ought to live with his wife. And that He already knew that we planned to conquer Murcia and all that kingdom, and that the good work that we would do in conquering that kingdom and returning it to the Christians should count for us, so that that sin should not bring us harm on the day of the battle.

---

[83] The cultivated plains outside the town.

[84] A Dominican who studied with Albert the Great, he was provincial master and then prior of the community of Girona, which he had founded in 1243. He also helped found missionary centres to preach to the Muslims and Jews. A close confidant of the king, he was used by him in many important law cases.

[85] Berenguera Alfonso, natural daughter of Alfonso de Molina, brother of Ferdinand III. James was greatly taken by her and, in order to marry her (though the relationship was incestuous), sought to put away his common law wife Teresa Gil de Vidaure who, according to James, had contracted leprosy (Chamberlin, 'Sainted Queen', pp. 308–9). On 17 February 1264, Pope Clement IV responded firmly in the negative to James's desire declaring it 'antagonistic to God, abominable to the angels, and monstrous to men' (*Documentos de Clemente IV*, no. 56). Berenguera died in Narbonne on 17 July 1272 (*Alicante*, no. 570).

Then we asked him that he should give us penance for that sin. Now he said that mortal sin was a great matter, but if we intended to free ourselves from it, he would pardon us. And we told him that we would enter into battle with that faith, and that we would free ourselves from mortal sin in one way or the other, and that we would serve God so well that day and in that conquest that He would pardon us. For we had not any ill will towards anybody in anything else, and that was sufficient for Him. And we told him that he should give us his blessing,[86] as we commended ourselves to God; and he did so.

[427] Then he left there, and we said that we wished to go to the vanguard to our sons. And we went there with a knight, and we ordered them to halt, them and all the others. In front of everybody we said to them: "Sons, you know well from where you come and who your father is. Act in such a way today in this deed of arms that all the world will recognize who you are and from where you come. And if you do not do so, we promise to God that we will disinherit you of all that we have given you."

And then Prince Don Peter and Prince James, both together, said that they would mark well from where they came, and that it would not be necessary to disinherit them because of that.

[428] Then we returned to our rearguard. And when we arrived at our line, Bernat de Vilanova[87] said: "Knights of Catalonia! Catalans! By the faith you owe to God, remember who is your lord, because today we must do such a thing that all the world will speak of the good that we have done."

And all those who heard this applauded it. And we advanced, and we saw the dust they raised. And a message reached us saying that they were fleeing and were turning back. And there were some who advised that we should pursue them, but we told them that we did not wish to do so, because Alhama[88] was no more than four leagues away, and there were some eight hundred light horse and they had some two thousand footmen, and at Alhama there were between six hundred and seven hundred. So that, by the time the knights arrived there they would be tired and they would not easily be able to pursue the footmen, and it would be necessary to enter into a fray. And they would charge out of the fortress and the castle, driving us and our men out of the town. So we forbade the pursuit.

---

[86]Though James does not say so straightforwardly, since he refused to abandon his mortally sinful relationship, Brother Arnau refused him absolution. Clement IV was to take the same line and while congratulating him on his victory in Murcia urged the king to regulate his personal affairs (*Documentos de Clemente IV,* no. 74).

[87]It is not clear whether this in fact treats of the Beltrán de Villanueva who appeared in ch. 379 and certainly participated in the Murcian campaign or indeeed a Bernat de Vilanova who appears one time in Miret's Itinerary in 1270 (*M,* p. 436).

[88]In the province of Murcia between the capital and Lorca.

[429] Then we went to a place which was called Alcantarilla. And with us were our sons, the master of Uclés,[89] and Pere de Queralt,[90] along with the master of the Temple, and of the Hospital, Hug de Malavespa, and another. And we sent for the nobles we have mentioned above, and we asked them advice on what we ought to do. And our sons and the nobles of our land said that the master of Uclés Don Pedro Guzmán, and Don Alfonso García should speak because they knew the territory better than they themselves did. And the master said that we could take the castle of Alhama if we wished to besiege it. And that if we prepared a machine of war, we could obtain it in a few days. Afterwards they said to Don Alfonso García that he should speak and he said that Don Pedro Guzmán should speak. And Don Pedro Guzmán said that he did not know anything about Alhama, but that Don Alfonso García, who had held the land, knew more than he did. And Don Alfonso García said: "I shall tell you, because I held Alhama for a time."[91]

"Then you know more about it than anybody."

And he said: "I will say to you the following: that if the king positions himself with an *almajanech* on the hill that is above there, inside eight days he will have Alhama."

And everybody said that it would be a good idea if that were done.

[430] Then we said to them: "Barons, we see four things that are against this plan. First, on a fixed day we have to meet with the king of Castile at Alcaraz," and until that day on which the meeting should take place, there were only seven days. And from what we could see, the castle was on the mountain so that it did not fear any *almajanech*, except on the side where the hill was. The second, that the Moors could defend a castle as well as any men in the world, for which reason it did not seem to us that we could be with the king of Castile on the day we had fixed; and that we believed that, though we attacked it for a month, we could not take it, for they had two thousand loads of grain there and it was too well fortified to be taken by force. The third, that Murcia was between us and Orihuela, and there was a great force of horsemen and footmen, and the mule-trains would be difficult for us to protect until Alhama. The fourth, that we did not have food for more than a day, since we had come to fight the Moors, wherefore we had not carried provisions, as battles are won quickly and they are given to those to whom God wishes to give them. And for this reason it was better and sounder advice that we should go to see the king of Castile and then together we would take a decision about Murcia. And our

---

[89]Gonzalo Pérez (1261–6).

[90]He was to be lieutenant of the master of the Templars (ch. 446) and later played an important role in the reign of Peter III as admiral and ambassador to Pope Martin IV.

[91]Here Alfonso García is made to speak a mix of Castilian and Catalan.

sons and those who were with us understood that we were right. After that, we returned the next day to Orihuela.[92]

[431] When we arrived at Orihuela, at the hour of sunset, we could see from the castle the dust of the companies that were going from Alhama towards Murcia. And word went through the town that the light horse were entering Murcia with the provisions. And our sons, and the masters of Uclés and of the Hospital, and the other nobles with them, came to us and said that they had seen dust between Alhama and Murcia, and that it was the light horse. So it seemed a good idea to them to arm the horses they had there and to go against them, for at least they would obtain the provisions that they wished to take into Murcia.

And we said that we did not think that it was a good idea for this reason: It was late, and by the time that they got there it would be dark night. Moreover, the men and the horses, if they went at the gallop, would be tired, so that when they approached Murcia and arrived at the huerta (where there were many watercourses that were difficult to cross), the Moors of Murcia could sally forth, on foot and on horseback, along with those others who had arrived there, and they could be defeated or could receive great harm, and then the ambition that we had of taking Murcia could be lost and confounded.

"But let us do one thing: we think that the dust is nothing, just that when it is windy, that produces dust. For we passed through there, and we did so this very day.[93] Even so, let us think the worst and imagine that they have got the provisions inside. There is not a day in these times when for every two thousand loads of grain there are in Murcia they do not eat two hundred. So, the fact that for ten days there should be food to eat in Murcia, because we have gone to visit the king of Castile, will not give them any advantage."

And these were our words to our sons, and they said that we were unsettling the men of the army. Yet we said that they did not speak the truth, and that the kingdom would be won by what we knew how to say and do, whilst by what they would say and do it would be lost, and we could not even believe they should begin such a thing as they said. Later we proved it to be true that what they said was dust in the wind, and that the light horse had not taken in any of the things which my sons had spoken of there.

[432] After that we left there and we went to Alcaraz, and our sons came with us, with three hundred knights. And we arrived at Alcaraz on the day that we had fixed with the king of Castile.[94] Before we entered Alcaraz, the king of

---

[92]Perhaps the beginning of December 1265, though the chronology here is very confused.

[93]That is, dust would have formed when James and his company passed through and then the wind would have made the dust rise.

[94]Beginning of December 1265.

Castile came out a league to receive us. And there were perhaps some sixty knights with him, and more than three hundred with us. We had also left another three hundred knights at Orihuela when we left there, as well as the *almogàvers*, of whom there were perhaps some two hundred. And when the king saw us, he was very happy and satisfied at our arrival. And we found the queen and her children at Alcaraz, and Doña Berenguera Alfonso, who afterwards came with us. And there we spoke of the deed of the Saracens, and we were there for eight days, with great joy and cheer.

[433] Then we went back towards Orihuela,[95] and on the road, there was a small skirmish with the light horse. And Don Manuel was with us. He was coming to Villena because of the agreement that the Saracens of Villena had promised us; that is to say, that they would deliver the town to him in virtue of the agreement they had with us, and even if he did not come, they would deliver it to us. We had the Saracens of Villena informed that we were coming and Don Manuel with us. Yet they did not wish to come out and broke the agreement with us and the oath they had sworn according to their law.

From Villena we went to Nompot and from Nompot to Elche. And when we had arrived at Elche,[96] we delivered the tower of Calahorra and the entire town to Don Manuel.

The next day we entered Orihuela and we found our company happy and satisfied, because they had made some raids into Murcia, and they had achieved gain on some of them. We arrived there before Christmas, and we remained at Orihuela until New Year's Eve.[97] Indeed, we entered there four days before Christmas, and we remained there until New Year's Eve.

[434] The day after New Year's Eve, at the beginning of January, we went to besiege Murcia.[98] And in the advance on Murcia with our army, we were among the first to arrive there in order to set up our camp, just as was necessary. Because in battle the king ought to be in the rearguard, but, in setting up the camp, he ought to go first, in order to lay the siege in the best possible manner, so that it is not afterwards necessary to move them, so well are they established. When we were at a place to which a guide had taken us, he brought us a tent and said to us that there we could set up the camp. And when he had brought us there, we asked where Murcia was, and they said it was nearby. And we said: "Where is it?"

---

[95]Late December 1265.
[96]22–25 December 1265 (*Alicante*, no. 375).
[97]31 December 1265.
[98]The first notice we have of the king besieging Murcia is on 5 January 1266 (*Alicante*, no. 382).

And the guide said: "I will point it out to you." And he pointed it out to us, and it was hardly a crossbow-shot away.

And we said to the guide: "You have given us a very dangerous place to camp, but though it be risky, know for certain that without fail we will have it, or it will cost us dear".[99]

[435] While we were setting up the camp, the Saracens came out, and those of our camp said: "Lord they are firing at us heavily with arrows and stones, and men and beasts have been wounded."

And we said: "Well we know the custom of the Saracens, and if one bears them for another day from now they will not return. So then, allow the army to arrive, when we will have crossbowmen to give you, and then we shall respond according to what the Sarcens do."

So we gave them some thirty crossbowmen and we took armoured horses, and we positioned them at the portels to defend our men from the shots that they fired. And when the sun was about to set, the Saracens went inside, and the next day they did not return there, and afterwards they did not come out against the army for a month.

[436] Then we sent an exea with a Saracen, to tell the governor[100] to come out to us as we wished to speak to him for his good and that of the townspeople. And he sent word to us that we should send him a knight, and we sent him a knight by the name of Domingo López, who was a settler in Morvedre, and knew Arabic, and Astruc,[101] a Jew who was our scribe for Arabic. The governor came with one of the most powerful knights of the town. Both of them had been made knights by King Don Alfonso of Castile. And when we learnt that they were coming, we had our house draped with good cloths and fine couches prepared. And we ordered that they should have live fowl, sheep and goats prepared, so that when they arrived these might be slaughtered, and that the guests should remain with us.

[437] We were sitting on our seat, and they came and they greeted us, and they knelt before us and kissed our hand. And we ordered everybody to leave our chamber, except them and Astruc, the Jew we have mentioned above, who was our interpreter.

And we told them that we had sent for them for this reason: Because they well knew that there were many Saracens in our land (those whom our lineage

---

[99]Perhaps the king accepted the dangerous position he had been given so that the defenders of Murcia would not take heart if he appeared to retreat (Torres Fontes, *Reconquista de Murcia*, p. 146).

[100]Abū Bakr (Garrido, *Jaume*, p. 106).

[101]Astruc Bonsenyor (ch. 422).

had had in Aragon and Catalonia in times past, and that we had in the kingdoms of Majorca and Valencia), and all practised their religion just as if they were in the land of Saracens. And these were the ones who had come to our mercy and had surrendered themselves to us; whereas those men who had not wished to surrender themselves, we had taken by force, and we populated their lands with Christians. And because we did not wish their harm or death, "We wished to speak with you first of all so that you might help us to protect the Saracens of Murcia and the kingdom." For we would obtain for them three things from the king of Castile: firstly, that he maintained the charters that he had with them; the other, that we would make them uphold and observe the agreements that they made with us; thirdly, that we would have them pardoned for all the things they had done him. And concerning these things that we said to them, we would have them draw up a charter for the king of Castile so that he would fulfil all that they agreed with us. Furthermore, we said that if they did not do that, nor wished to do it, we came with the intention of not leaving there until we had taken the city and all its land by force. However, we reassured them that we did not wish their death or destruction, rather we wished that they might live for always under the king of Castile, and that they could preserve their mosques and their religion, just as they had agreed with him in the initial charters.

[438] They thanked us for the words that we had spoken to them, but they said that they could not respond without deliberating with those of the town, and that they would bring us their response by the third day. Now, that was Wednesday,[102] and they said that they would assemble on Thursday, and that on Saturday they would come to us and respond upon what we had said to them. As we did not wish to hurry them into a response, we agreed to that.

Meanwhile, goats and chickens had been slaughtered. And they said that they did not wish to eat there, with us, and we said that we would have new cooking pots given to them in which they could cook the meat and that they could eat there.[103] And they begged us that we should not wish for them to stay, because those of the town would think the worst had happened to them, but on another day, as they had agreed with us, they would dine here. After that we sent them away.

[439] When Saturday morning arrived,[104] they sent us a message saying that if we gave them safe-conduct, they would come. And we did that and they came.

---

[102] 20 January 1266.

[103] It was necessary that the pots were not those that had been used for cooking meat destined for the Christians.

[104] 23 January 1266.

And we had prepared a meal for them, with the things mentioned above, and immediately they set about preparing the meal for their company.

And the governor and the knight, whose name we do not recall, returned to us. And those two had great power in the town, especially the governor, so that all that they agreed with us would have worth. And we had all those who were there with us go out, excepting only Astruc and those Saracens. And they responded that they had deliberated with the sheikhs of the city but that they had not wished that he who held the fortress for the king of Granada should participate in the deliberations.[105] And we considered that a good sign, because they had excluded from the deliberations the man whom the king of Granada had left as his representative and who was their leader.

And they said that they had related what we had said to them to the sheikhs and to the wise men of the town and that they thanked us very much for the fine words that we had sent to have explained and spoken to them, through which they well understood that they would find loyalty and truth in us, and that we would fulfil what we had promised them. In addition, they said that they wished we would tell them how they might preserve their law if they agreed to deliver the town to us, and that they had brought there a document of the conditions that they asked for. And that is the manner in which they said we should draw up the document for them.

[440] Then they showed us a document that they had been given containing a report of the meeting and the agreement that had been undertaken inside the town. And there were many demands, but this one was the most important (for so as not to lengthen this book we will refrain from including all the demands that they made). Indeed, this was the principal demand that they made of us: that they might observe their practices of shouting out their prayers and judging Saracens, just as was their law and they were accustomed to do, and as the king of Castile had promised them. And for what they had done in retaking the fortress and rising up against the Christians, they wished that the king might pardon them, and they would deliver the town to us in virtue of the charters that we and they had drawn up. Moreover, they said that we should send a letter to the king of Castile, and that a messenger of ours should escort the knight that they would send, in order to confirm the charters and the agreements that we would make with them.

[441] And we said that they should not delay in delivering the fortress and the town to us there and then, because we did not wish to send any message to the

---

[105]It is noticeable that although Ibn al-Aḥmar had negotiated a peace some months before with Castile, his officer is excluded from negotiations which it was assumed he would disrupt. The Murcian Muslims appear to have felt no more at ease with a Granadan commander than with a Christian one.

king of Castile until they had placed the town in our power. For we said they would not gain anything by that, seeing as they wanted to surrender to us, because we had there a great company of knights and footmen, who would lay waste to their lands, and who each day were doing them harm. And we said that since they intended to surrender it to us, we would not propose to lay them waste, and we did not wish them to be injured or oppressed in the tents or the huerta.

Then they said that they would deliberate on that, because they understood that what we said was in their interest. And we insisted to them that they should go inside and deliberate since it was both in our interest and in theirs. And they said that they would go to reach a decision, and that afterwards, the next day, they would come to us and respond. And so they left.

[442] The next day[106] they returned with their response and said that they would do what we had said, but they wished to know how we would divide the town. And we told them that we would give them the entire town above the fortress on the side where the camp was positioned. And that pleased them very much. And we fixed a day for them to evacuate the other part, and they said that on the third day they would abandon the fortress and would make the Saracen who the king of Granada had left as *alcaid* in Murcia leave there; and that on that day they would leave, and on the fourth day they would deliver the fortress to us. And they did so, and three days later they sent out the man who was there in the name of the king of Granada, and they abandoned the fortress to us.

[443] And on the fourth day,[107] we prepared fifty knights, with their squires, their armoured horses, and one hundred and twenty crossbowmen from Tortosa.[108] And we awaited them on the bank of the River Segura, near the fortress, waiting for them to reach the top so that they could place our banner on top and occupy our towers. And our men delayed a long time in going up there and we prayed to Santa Maria for what we desired, that there she might be adored and believed in, and that we might bring the enterprise to a happy conclusion and that she would pray for that to her beloved Son. And we were greatly afraid that they might have been captured, since they delayed so long. However, after a long while we saw our banner up on the fortress and the towers well manned with our men and crossbowmen. And we got down on to the ground from our horse and we thanked Our Lord God for the grace he had done us, and we knelt, crying and kissing the ground. Then we returned from there to our quarters.

---

[106]26 January 1266.

[107]30 January 1266.

[108]Renewed mention of the Tortosan crossbowmen who clearly had considerable expertise.

[444] In the evening, the governor came before us, and he said that they had fulfilled our will, but that the Christians were already entering into the town and taking what they should not take. And we said that we would send three men inside so that nobody should enter beyond the fortress and that in the morning we would enter the town and, in the presence of the sheikhs, we would divide it.

[445] And in the morning,[109] after we had heard Mass, we went up to the fortress, and the governor with us, with five of the best Saracens of the city of Murcia. And they said that we should divide the town just as had been agreed between them and us. And we said that from the mosque that was near the fortress down to the gate where the camp was should be of the Christians, and that that mosque should be included in our part. They said that that had not been agreed and their documents said that they would keep their mosques and that they would have them as they had them in the time of the Saracens. And we said to them that it had been agreed in that manner, but that they had not understood it. Because we wished that they should conserve the mosques but, "What would the Christians do without a church that they could go into? And that church shall be at the gate of the fortress. And that from there 'Alàlosabba'[110] should be cried near to my head when I am sleeping... that, as you can well understand, is not fitting. Now, you have some ten mosques in the town. Make your prayers in those and leave this one to us."

And they said they would deliberate.

[446] When we returned to the camp, our sons, Prince Peter and Prince James, came to us, with the master of Uclés and the bishop of Barcelona, as well as Pere de Queralt, who was there on behalf of the master of the Temple, the master of the Hospital, named Gui de la Vespa,[111] and other nobles of the army, such as the count of Empúries, named Huguet, who was there in place of his father,[112] Ramon de Montcada,[113] Blasco de Alagón,[114] Jofre de Rocabertí,[115]

---

[109]31 January 1266.

[110]Perhaps meaning "[ḥayya] 'alā 'ṣ-ṣalāt" or "[come] to prayer", but an alternative reading of the Catalan text here is "lo sabaçala", which would then refer to the muezzin himself.

[111]Hug de Malavespa.

[112]The count was Ponç Hug III (1230–69) and his son Hug V (1269–77). The fact that James calls 'little' Hug (Huguet) the count means this passage was dictated after the death of Ponç Hug.

[113]He witnessed a diploma at Murcia on 5 February 1266, two days after the taking of the city (*S*, p. 363). On 27 April, James recognized a debt of ten thousand sueldos to Ramon for the soldiers he had taken on the Murcian expedition (*Alicante*, no. 430).

[114]On 18 June 1267, at Zaragoza, James recognized a debt of six thousand one hundred and thirty sueldos to Blasco for the men and provisions he had brought to the Murcian expedition (*Alicante*, no. 432).

[115]Viscount Jofre III de Rocabertí (1229–82).

Pedro Fernández de Híjar our son,[116] Guillem de Roquefeuil, Carròs, and other nobles of the army.[117] And they said that the treaty we had made with the Saracens was not a good one, since what we had taken of the town was so miserable an amount that the Saracens could drive them from there, when we and the army were not there; and that, according to the charters we had drawn up with them, we thought to have won Murcia when, in fact, we had not gained anything. And we said to them that they were wrong in thinking that, because we had been in more places than they had been and we knew the custom of the Saracens better than they did. Furthermore, when a man is able to gain from his enemy – (and not just the Saracens) – two arms' breadth of land, he might well hope to have ten or a hundred. Thus, we said that we would bring them joy from this. And as they had not intervened in the negotiations between the Saracens and us, and did not know the secret deal that had been made, they were displeased about what we had not done.

[447] And here we entered into dispute, as to whether according to the treaty we had drawn up with the Saracens, we could still expel them from the town, since the treaty said that we had to keep them in Murcia.[118] Yet we said that the decree said that the suburbs of the town were the town, so that we could also put them in la Rexaca[119] or in the huerta (as these were inside the suburbs) as well as in the town itself, since they were attached to the town and were a part of the town. So we said that we would be able to make them leave the town to la Rexaca, which was a district of the city. And they said we could not do it. And we had the Brothers Preacher come and the clergy, and we proved to them by law that it was just as we had said. And they said that it was not their understanding that it was so. And we said: "If you do not wish to understand it, we cannot do anything about it. But we will give the town to God, in spite of all of you."

[448] After that had happened the governor and more than twenty of the sheikhs came to us from the town. And they asked that we should not occupy

---

[116]His mother was the Aragonese Berenguera Fernández. James gave him the barony of Híjar. He was named admiral against the Moors in 1263, lieutenant in Valencia in 1267, and took part in the Holy Land expedition of 1269–70. He was commissioned to defend Murcia in 1273, helped put down the Muslim revolt of 1276, and, after James's death, generally supported the crown, taking part in the conquest of Sicily in support of his half-brother, Peter. Pedro married first Teresa d'Entença, and then Marquesa, an illegitimate daughter of Teoboldo of Navarre.

[117]Including Guillem de Canet, Jaspert de Castellnou, Guillem Hug de Serrallonga, Ramon d'Urtx, Guillem de Cardona and Beltrán de Villanueva (*S*, p. 363).

[118]James does not mention that many Muslims left Murcia for Granada under guarantee of his protection but that they were attacked by *almogàvers* and many of them cut down (Torres Fontes, *Reconquista de Murcia*, pp. 164–6).

[119]A suburb of Murcia.

the mosque nor should we wish to take it from them, because it was the best place they had in which to make their prayers. And we said to them that just as they wanted the best place to make their prayers, we also wished to have it, and that it would not be in any other way nor could be, since it was a very reasonable thing that we should have a great place in which to make our prayers, since they had so many. And they said that they would not have it in any other way.

So we said that we were greatly saddened by the harm they would receive because of what was happening between us, since they did not wish to avoid it. For, whatever else happened, we would have the church. And we said that they should enter the town and consider well what they were going to do.

[449] Then we ordered the fifty knights who were in the fortress to arm themselves, and for the one hundred and twenty crossbowmen who were from Tortosa to be at the ready, so that if the Saracens did not wish to agree, the town was to be sacked. And when they saw that would certainly be done, the Saracens said that they would do our will. And so we had the church.

[450] On gaining the church, we ordered an altar to be set up to Our Lady Saint Mary, because in all the great towns that God has given unto us to win from the Saracens we have built a church of Our Lady Saint Mary. And as this was the greatest town of Andalusia, except for Seville, we wished to honour the name of the mother of God, so that she would be honoured there for all time.

[451] On the second day, when the altar was prepared, we had it decorated in the early morning with the cloths of our chapel, very honourably and nobly. And Bishop Arnau de Gurb of Barcelona, and the bishop of Cartagena[120] were with us. We had all the clergy who were there dressed in cloaks of samite and others in cloth decorated with gold. And with our crosses and with the image of Our Lady Saint Mary we went out from our quarters in the camp. On foot, we entered through the town into the church of Our Lady Saint Mary that we had built. And when we saw the altar and we approached there, we were seized with very great devotion through the grace and mercy that God had given us because of the prayers of His mother. For we had never gone past Murcia without praying that we might be able to place the name of the glorious virgin Saint Mary there, and she, praying to her beloved Son, caused our wish to be fulfilled. Embracing the altar, we wept so strongly and so heartfeltly that for the time it takes to go a mile, we could not stop crying nor leave the altar. And we had *Veni Creator Spiritus* sung, and afterwards the Mass *Salve, sancta*

---

[120]Pedro Gallego.

parens.[121] Having done that, we entered into the fortress, and with great joy we took up our quarters.

[452] On the third day we had our sons come before us, together with the bishop of Barcelona, and the nobles of Catalonia and Aragon who were with us, and we told them that they should deliberate upon what we ought to do. And everybody said to Prince Peter that he should speak. And he said that since God had done us so great a mercy that we had taken that place and many others, we should inform the king of Castile, that he might occupy the city and the land as we had sufficiently fulfilled our duty. And afterwards they said to Prince James that he should speak; and he said he agreed with what Prince Peter had said to us. And afterwards we said to the bishop of Barcelona that he should say what he thought.

And he said: "Since you wish me to speak, I will tell you what I think. I would not wait to deliver the town to the king of Castile, but instead would deliver the town to Alfonso García, who held it for the king." And he added that we would have sufficiently done our duty, if we delivered it to one who would hold it for him. Because we were spending a great deal here, and we might be spared further expense. Moreover, if we aimed to do more we might lose it. And the other nobles were agreed with the words of the bishop

[453] After that they said to us that we should say what we thought. And we spoke to them in this manner: that we thought what the bishop of Barcelona had said to be good, to surrender the city of Murcia to Don Alfonso García, and that was our intention. But we did not think it a good idea to go from there, leaving the land to the people of Castile, such as Don Pedro Guzmán and Alfonso, since, when they found themselves in possession of those places, they would lose them.[122]

And we said that we should not leave the city then, having built the altar to Our Lady Saint Mary here and that to leave her alone here was something we would not do under any circumstances. For if through our misfortune the Saracens recovered Murcia, we would feel great sadness. Wherefore we could not leave it in this way, neither we nor the others. "For all the good that I and you have received, and that God does unto us, we have through her, who prays to her beloved Son for us.

"And you must know that not for anything in the world would we abandon her at this moment and at this time. And I think that what Prince Peter says is good, that we should send a message to the king of Castile saying that we have

---

[121]The hymn *Veni creator spiritus* ('Come, Holy Ghost, Creator come'); *Salve sancta parens* is the Common of the Blessed Virgin Mary and yet another indication of the king's devotion to Our Lady.
[122]Judgement of the king on the Castilians and indication of national sentiment.

restored the town to Alfonso García, and that he should send to him such help as he might need to retain it, and then we will be able to leave."

And when they saw that that was what we wanted, and that we would bear the expense, they said that we should act according to our will.

[454] Now, we took two guides and we sent them to the king of Castile with our letters, so that he might occupy the city of Murcia and the other castles. And between Murcia, Lorca, and the other places, there were some twenty-eight castles, which we delivered to them. And we immediately delivered the city of Murcia[123] to Don Alfonso García and he took possession of the fortress and placed his guards in there. And we remained close beside him until a message arrived from the king of Castile announcing that he would send help very soon, and that he thanked us very much for what we had done and what we had reported to him. Then we left some ten thousand men-at-arms, from our own land and others, so that they should remain there with Don Alfonso García and help him.[124]

[455] Having left the town reinforced in the manner we have related above, we went to Orihuela and the next day to Alicante.[125] And there we ordered our sons and the nobles to come before us, and we said to them that if they thought it a good idea, we would make a good raid into Almeria before we left there. And that we would give them provisions for ten days. "Because it will take four days to get there and another four days to return." And that of the remaining two days, if it was necessary for us to be there we could consume the provisions there, if not we would have them on our return.

And they asked how they would transport their food, because the mule-trains were already fully loaded with the provisions that they carried. And we said to them that lands were not conquered so, adding, when we had conquered the kingdom of Valencia, we carried food for three weeks in this manner: the knights rode their horses, and they loaded the beasts with bread, wine, and barley, and they carried their lances in their hands, and the shields went upon the mule-train, and as they went forward lightening the load, we recovered their beasts one by one. And they said they could not do that. And we said: "Will you not do what we and those who went with us did?"

---

[123]Early February 1266.

[124]James's support for Castile was generous but we must keep in mind that he continued to take a great interest in the region, encouraged a large-scale Catalonian repopulation movement to the kingdom and, according to *Muntaner* (ch. 17), left Alfonso and Don Manuel in little doubt that the lands could be his by right of conquest (Rubio García, *Corona de Aragón*, pp. 16–17).

[125]We find James at Murcia on 1 March 1266 (*Alicante*, no. 387), still on 4 March (*S*, p. 365) and then at Alicante on 9 March 1266 (*Alicante*, no. 388), where he remained until 2 April (Torres Fontes, *Reconquista de Murcia*, p. 183).

And they said that however much we might do, they could only carry provisions for six days. But we said to them that we needed four days to arrive there, and that we would do wrong if on the sixth day we had nothing to eat, and that they were well able to do what we had suggested to them. But they would not do it, and therefore that raid was abandoned and not undertaken.

[456] After that we decided whom we had to leave on the frontier of Alicante and Villena,[126] so that, if it was necessary, they could aid Murcia by making fire-signals from Orihuela. And we left Don Artal de Luna[127] and Don Jimeno de Urrea at Alicante, with one hundred knights, and we put Berenguer Arnau and Galceran de Pinós[128] at Ontinyent and Biar with seventy knights, so that they could keep that road safe and secure for those who went by it, and so that, if it was necessary, they could aid Murcia. And we borrowed from merchants whom we found at Alicante, and we left our men enough to eat for a good fifteen months.[129] And we had given them so good and sufficient a ration in Murcia that the Aragonese knights sold full thirty thousand sous worth of that ration that we had left them; and that which they had sold was ours.

[457] After that we returned to the kingdom of Valencia,[130] and then we went towards Montpellier.[131] And at Girona[132] we found a great dispute going on between the count of Empúries and Ponç Guillem de Torroella upon a claim that the count made of him on Torroella, and the power over the castles (and of Rocamaura,[133] and another castle) and taxes that he ought to receive in Torroella. And having heard this plaint and their response, we went to Montpellier,[134] delaying the case until we returned. And we left a scribe there

---

[126]The towns which formed the two extremes of the frontier inside Murcia and the lands of the king of Castile.

[127]Probably the son of the Artal de Luna who appears earlier in the text (chs. 21, 25, 28). This Artal was certainly with James on 30 March 1266 (*M*, p. 385; *S*, p. 365; *Alicante*, no. 401).

[128]Galceran IV de Pinós (d. 1295) who later accompanied the king in the expedition to the Holy Land (ch. 489). On 2 July 1267, James recognized a debt to him for services undertaken during the Murcian conquest (*Alicante*, no. 433).

[129]Perhaps the text here should say five months rather than fifteen which seems an excessive length of time for the Castilians to re-establish themselves and for James to provision the garrison (*S*, p. 365). On 17 January 1267, James recognized a debt to Simonet de Modul and Conrad de Junta for thirteen thousand *bezants* he had borrowed to provision the army (Garrido, *Jaume*, p. 115).

[130]The king was still in Alicante on 2 April and at Valencia by 7 April 1266 (*M*, p. 386).

[131]The king went to Tortosa, Lleida and then to Barcelona where he was from 8 June to 20 August (*M*, p. 387).

[132]September 1266.

[133]A castle on a hill near Torroella de Montgrí.

[134]He was there by 26 October 1266 and remained there three and a half months (Baumel, *Histoire d'une seigneurie*, 2, p. 125; *S*, p. 366).

to take evidence and record what had been done, so that when we returned we could pass sentence.

[458] When we returned from Montpellier, and we arrived at Perpignan,[135] Don Ferriz de Lizana sent us a letter in which he said that he was defying us. And on the same day a message arrived from the king of the Tartars.[136] And we said that we considered ourselves even more shamed that on that same day that a letter had arrived to us, with great love, from the most exalted king in the world, Don Ferriz de Lizana was defying our lordship. And we said that we were not accustomed to hunt small game, but were accustomed to hunt crane and bustards. "But since he wishes it so much, I will go to hunt, and I will capture doves and magpies."

[459] On that we went to Lleida[137] and we spoke with the peacemen and with the notables of the town and we told them that they should help us against Don Ferriz. And they said that they would do so willingly: "But what will it serve?" they said, "For you will immediately pardon him. And so you embolden them to do evil against you."

And we said to them: "You shall see in what manner we shall act, so that all goes well."

Then we left the town and we went to Monzón.[138] And the men of Tamarite came to us, and they said to us that if we wished it, they would attack Castejón,[139] which they called Picamoixó. And we said to them that that greatly pleased us. And they attacked it and they took it, and we ordered it to be demolished.

[460] Afterwards we went to Lizana,[140] and we took two *fenèvols* with us. And we found that inside there was a *brigola* prepared. And Fernando Sánchez de Castro held the castle, by reason of the oaths sworn by the nobles of Aragon allowing that each could deliver his castle to another.[141] And he asked us that we might permit him to withdraw the men of his who were there, because Don

---

[135]February 1267.

[136]Abaqa Īlkhān (1265–81), son of Hülegü Īlkhān (1256–65) (hence nephew of Qubilai Khān (1260–94), and great-grandson of Chingiz Khān (1206–27)). Abaqa was son-in-law of Michael VIII Palaeologus, Emperor of Constantinople.

[137]April 1267 (*M*, pp. 397–8).

[138]26 April 1267 (*M*, p. 398).

[139]Castejón del Puente (ch. 20), near Barbastro. Picamoixó may have been the name of the castle there.

[140]James was 'at the siege of Lizana' on 21 May 1267 (*S*, p. 367).

[141]The Aragonese nobles had agreed to maintain a truce with James while he was involved in the Murcian campaign. Their grievances against James's support of Castile and their long-term dissatisfaction at what they perceived to be their subordinate role had not gone away and would remain for the rest of his reign.

Ferriz de Lizana wished to fortify it with his own men. And we granted that to him, since we preferred that the men of Don Ferriz, who persevered in doing me evil should be there, since Fernando Sánchez had come over to our side.

And those men who wished to enter Lizana were at Alcolea.[142] And Don Ferriz placed a nephew of his there as leader, and some knights and other men of lineage entered there with him. He put there those who with him had done us most harm, and who had ravaged our land most. They passed by outside our tent, and there were some whom we recognized, because they had been with men of our company. And we asked them: "Why do you enter there and for whom?"

And they said for Don Ferriz de Lizana, who was their lord, for since he had ordered them to enter there, they wished to fulfil his will. And we said to them: "We will make you a prediction, after you have entered there, you will never do harm again, either to me or to others."

And they said that it would be as God willed. And we said: "God wills what we tell you, because your sin shall thwart you, so that you will never do harm again to me or to others."

[461] Then they entered inside, and we sent for the two *fenèvols*, and we ordered them to begin to be set up. And they wanted to have truces with us; and that pleased us for as long as we were setting up the war-machines. And when we had prepared one, they began to set up the *brigola*, and they did not wish to fulfil the truce we had agreed with them. And they fired.

Yet, though they hoped to reach the camp, they could not reach it. And the cord of their *brigola* got entangled around the beam.[143] And we and the men of the army had made many slings. And we had the *fenèvol* prepared, with the base greased, so that it could advance when we wanted it to advance. And as soon as the *brigola* had fired and the cord was entangled, we had everyone called to arms so that they should all go to fight. And with the crossbows and the slings they acquitted themselves so well that the others could neither go up there nor disentangle the cord nor lower the beam of the *brigola*, however much they tried.

[462] Then we positioned the *fenèvol* so far forward that it could reach the *brigola*. And the master of the *fenèvol* fired the first stone and missed the *brigola*. And we went to take charge of the *fenèvol* and we fired and we gave such a blow to the *brigola* that we opened its box.[144] And after that blow, they could not be helped by it any more. And that evening, before it was night, he who fired the *fenèvol* broke the single-pole frame of the *brigola*.

[142]Alcolea de Cinca in the diocese of Lleida and the province of Huesca.
[143]The event is discussed in detail by Chevedden ('Artillery', pp. 75–6, 78–9).
[144]A box full of stones or other heavy materials which acted as a counterweight.

[463] Immediately, the next day, we set up the other *fenèvol* beside it. And we fired there for some five or six days, until the castle, which had not been fortified well enough to prevent it, was destroyed, and because it had damaged roofs, the stones that reached inside did even greater damage than those that struck the wall. So that, one night, when we had already gone to bed, and those of the company of Prince Peter had the watch, Bernat de Vilert came to us and asked us if we were sleeping. And we said to him that we were not.

"Lord, those from inside have spoken with us and they say that, if you wish to show them mercy they will surrender the castle."

And we told them that they should take no heed of those words, since for two reasons we did not wish to show them mercy: one, because they had done us such great harm and to such a great extent; the other, because those inside were among the worst malefactors Don Ferriz had in his service. But, if they wished to come to us in such a way that they would be subject to our will whether we showed them mercy or not, then we would receive them, and in no other manner.

[464] The next day we were on a little hillock that was near the moat, we, the prince and numerous knights. And a knight and a squire came out from the castle without our safe-conduct and they came to us across the moat. And the people who were at the camp surrounded them. And they said: "Lord, the castellan and those inside salute you, and they say that they will place themselves at your mercy and under your power, and that they will deliver the castle to you."

And when we heard these words, we did not wish to listen to any advice, since the majority would not have advised what we had the intention of doing with them. And we replied immediately that we would do no such thing, but that if they wished to come to us so that we might do with them what we wanted, even if we wished to judge them, then we would receive them. And if not, they should defend themselves, for we would have them anyway. And they said that they would return there, and they went.

[465] After a little while, they came and they said that they would place themselves in our power, that we might do with them as we wished. And they said to us that if we sent some men to occupy the castle they would deliver it. And we chose knights and other people who were there to witness the fact that we took them to do with as was our will and in no other manner. And then they delivered the castle to us. And we hanged from the wall of the castle those whom it was right to hang, and we did justice to the others of note, as one ought to do to men who have done such a thing against their lord.

7

The Twilight Years

[466] Having done that, we went to Tarazona,[1] where, in four or five places, they forged gold coins, of ours and of the king of Castile. And when we were in Tarazona the matter of the money forged there was notorious.[2] And we conducted an inquisition in two parts of the town, having them brought to our house under the power of a judge, who was called Master Humbert,[3] and travelled with us, as well as one other, and these conducted the inquisition on them. And we said that when they had taken it down that they should show it to us. And they struggled a good four days without being able to find out anything about those coins. And we would come in from hunting and Master Humbert would say to us: "Sire, what do you want us to do? For we cannot find out anything of the truth about the money, either of who forged it or where it was forged."

And we said: "How can it be that we cannot find the truth when the matter of the forging of the money is so notorious? This is a great marvel, as the bushes, if they knew how to speak, would be able to tell it. For they must forge it among the bushes and the streams when they cannot find a house in which to do it."

[467] And when we entered the town and we were in our house we thought about how we could find out about it. And then a man came to us and he said that he wished to speak with us in secret. And we ordered all those who were there to leave the room, and he remained alone with us, and he said to us that a

---

[1] A slight jump here. James went to Huesca, Zaragoza, Lizana and Zaragoza anew, Almudévar, Zaragoza again, Barcelona, Lleida, Huesca and arrived at Tarazona in late September 1267 (*M*, pp. 399–402).

[2] On 26 October 1267, James explained the circumstances of the case and dictated sentence. He said there that the matter had come to his attention because it was notorious (*S*, p. 368). Kagay points out how James's relation of events enhances our understanding of a significant matter for which the documentary record is sparse (Kagay, 'The line between memoir', pp. 175–6).

[3] The Provençal jurist Master Albert de Lavànya. He studied at Bologna and was the author of a number of treatises on law. One of the principal leaders of the Marseilles revolt against Charles of Anjou, he fled to James's court, acted as judge in many cases, received a castle and town for his services in 1268 and was specially recommended by James on his deathbed to Prince Peter (Burns, *Crusader Kingdom*, 1, p. 75). He was among the witnesses of the sentence of 26 October (*S*, p. 368).

man, whom we knew well, saluted us, and that, if we would grant him protection, he would put us on the right track on the question of the coinage that we might find out the truth; as long as we did no harm to his person or his goods. And we said to him that he should reveal to us who that was and that if we discovered that what he said concerning that matter was true we would protect him. And that other man wished to have an agreement with us that we would not do him harm, and he would come before us. And we agreed to that, placing our hand in his, and afterwards we said to him: "Now, since we have agreed it, tell us who the man is."

And he said to us that it was Marqués. But we did not know him well, so we asked who Marqués was. And he said: "A cleric who is the brother of that Domingo López who had Pedro Pérez[4] killed when he was leaving Tudela."

[468] Then we sent for Master Humbert, and he came immediately. And we said: "Master Humbert, we believe that we have found out what you and we have been looking for."

And he said to us: "About what?"

And we said: "About the matter of the coins."

And he said: "I am very happy and satisfied, because I was rather vexed that I could not find out."

And we said to him that it was better to pardon one and to know the truth, than to leave the matter unsolved. And we called for the man who had said those words to us and we said: "Friend, where is Marqués? Can we see him now?"

And he said that he was not in the town. "But I will make him come to you," he said, "Before you go to bed."

And we said: "Then do so, and we shall thank you greatly, and you shall gain more in our eyes when you have put me on the right track in this matter."

And we said: "Go, and get a move on."

And he went.

[469] And when we were about to go back to bed, he came back. And we went into the chamber with him and Marqués, who had come with him. And Marqués said: "We humble ourselves before you, lord."[5]

And we greeted him. And we had had prepared a text of the Gospel for him to swear upon and we had Bonanat,[6] our scribe, write down the words that he spoke. And we made him swear that he would tell the truth and that he would not avoid telling it out of love or fear, or for money that someone may give him

---

[4]Pedro Pérez appears to have been a ringleader of the dealers in false coin, according to the sentence of 26 October 1267 (*S*, p. 369, Zurita, *Anales,* 3, ch. 72).

[5]Here and in the following chapters, it is indicated that Marqués is speaking Aragonese.

[6]Perhaps Bonanat de Puig (*M*, p. 436; *S*, p. 370).

or promise him, or for fear of any man. And if he knew more than we had asked him, or might ask him, then he should say it. And he said: "Pardon me, lord, and I will tell you the truth about what has and what has not happened in this business."

And we said to him that we pardoned him, as long as he told us the truth, and that would raise his worth for us. And he kissed our hand for the mercy we had shown him, and he told us that, as we had pardoned him, he would tell us the truth, since he was one of the guilty parties and had consented to all that had happened. And we said to him: "You may well continue, as you have begun well."

And first he began to speak about the coinage of the king of Castile,[7] and afterwards about our own. And he told us they had forged money with false maravedis, and in what place, and who had been a party to it, and who the conspirators were. And he told us, moreover, that we should send for those of whom he had spoken, and, if they denied the fact, that we should bring him from behind a curtain, where he would be, and he would make them tell the truth: "And they will not dare to deny it, if I am there in front of them."

And we did it exactly in the manner that he had suggested, as there was no better way.

[470] In the morning, we immediately sent for one of them. And he came well primed because the others had instructed him very well. And he denied the business. And we said to him: "How can you deny it? Were you not in such a place, and were such and such not with you? For we can prove it."

And he said: "If you can prove it to me, I will not be able to deny it."

And with that we had Marqués come out, and when he was there before him, Marqués said to him: "Friend, were you not with me in such and such a place, and did we not speak of this matter and what we would do and not do? And do you not know that Don So-and-So and Don So-and-So were in our council?"

And when he heard these words, he went white. And when we saw it we said to him: "You have done wrong, to God and to me, your natural lord, when you have denied the truth, and this thing will be proved to you, and if you deny the truth, and I can prove it, you will fall under the penalty of justice. And if you tell me the truth, you will be able to find mercy in me, since by the truth one finds mercy from God and from earthly lords."

[471] After that he began to speak, and he agreed with Marqués concerning that affair. And he disclosed whom the others were who had also participated in this business. And each informed on the other, so that finally we had so many

---

[7]The sentence of 26 October specifically refers to false coin of Burgos being minted in the castle of Trasmoz.

testimonies that we knew how the matter had happened and how not, and where they had forged the money, and who had done it, and who they were. Moreover, it was proved that the sacristan,[8] brother of Pedro Pérez, had forged false maravedis of copper, and they had covered them with gold leaf. And we found that they passed through the hands of Pedro Ramírez,[9] at Santolalla,[10] and that they were also forged at Tortolés, at the town of Tarazona, and in many other places. Therefore, in that matter we visited justice on Don Pedro Ramírez and his son, and his wife Elfa de Tortolés, and we had them drowned.[11] And we did justice to others as was fitting,[12] and we took their goods, as the goods of men who had dared to try and forge coins in our land and that of the king of Castile. And as the sacristan was a cleric, we delivered him to the bishop, and he put him in prison, and he died in that prison. And when we had done that, that is to say, punished the very great evil and great harm that the peoples of the land had received, we left there and we went to Zaragoza.[13]

[472] After we had been to Zaragoza, we went to the kingdom of Valencia,[14] because we had not been there for a long time. And we spent Christmas at Alcañiz, and the New Year in Tortosa.[15] And when we arrived at Valencia, a message arrived saying that Princess Doña Maria,[16] our daughter, had died. And it was our wish to go there, and that she be buried in Vallbona alongside her mother.[17] And the people of Zaragoza, in spite of the nobles and the knights, buried her at San Salvador de Zaragoza. And when we learnt that they had already buried her, we remained in the kingdom of Valencia.

---

[8]Blasco Pérez. Both were sons of Juan Pérez, formerly the justiciar in Aragon (*M*, p. 299). Blasco had earlier been granted a license from the Crown for treasure-hunting in the Tarazona district (*M*, p. 366).

[9]Perhaps the Aragonese knight, Pedro Ramírez de Oria.

[10]The Castle of Santolalla near the River Aragón (*S*, p. 371).

[11]A form of execution reserved for great crimes. The son is perhaps Miguel Ramírez (*S*, p. 371).

[12]The sentence survives. Zurita, *Anales,* 3, ch. 72 says that the principal malefactors were people to whom Pedro Jordan had entrusted the administration of the town of Sanguesia at the time of his death, and that all was done with the consent of his widow Elfa. Through her confession and others it was proved that the sons of Pedro Jordan and others had minted false coin at Tortolés and at the castle of Santolalla. The sons were disinherited, all their goods confiscated to the crown, and they were perpetually exiled. This sentence was pronounced at Tarazona on 26 October 1267.

[13]By 17 November 1267 (*M*, p. 404).

[14]James was in Valencia by 17 January 1268, having not been there since April 1266 (*M*, pp. 562–3).

[15]James was certainly in Tortosa from 31 December to 7 January 1268 (*M*, pp. 406–8).

[16]The youngest of James's daughters by Yolanda of Hungary.

[17]Vallbona de les Monges, a famed Cistercian convent in the diocese of Tarragona.

[473] Then the bishop of Zaragoza,[18] Don Sancho Martínez de Oblitas and Poncio Baldovín,[19] who were her executors, came to us and said that they wished to show us her will. And we listened to it, and we found that she had left one thousand marcs for debts and wrongs, and also to pay her maidservants, and her household, to whom she wished to do well. And they said that they had nothing else but the jewels, of which they wished to inform us, because they would rather we had them than another, because they had been ours. And we told them that we would pay for everything, and we assigned them Daroca, Barbastro and Roda, so that with the revenues from these places they could pay those thousand marks. And so we recovered the jewels.

[474] After that had happened, Ramon de Cardona and some nobles of Catalonia challenged us to go to war over the business of the count of Urgell, who had died, since they wished to have the county of Urgell by force.[20] And the executors of the count had requested and demanded many times that we made them a loan, on security of the revenues of the county, to pay the debts

---

[18] Arnaldo de Peralta.

[19] We know Sancho was with the king at Perpignan on 9 October 1269 at the time of the failed expedition to the Holy Land (*M*, p. 431). On 11 June 1269, Poncio was paid three thousand sous by James for the expenses he had undertaken in paying off Maria's debts (*M*, p. 426).

[20] The highly complicated matter of the war of succession in the county of Urgell. Àlvar de Cabrera, Count of Urgell, born in Burgos in 1239, son of Ponç de Cabrera, arrived to take possession of the county in 1253. In his absence, his nobles, in agreement with James, had married him off to Constança de Montcada, the king's niece. But, led by Jaume de Cervera, his youthful advisers, enemies of the Montcada, sought to marry Àlvar to Sibil·la d'Anglesola. But on the wedding day, and at the church, Àlvar tearfully declared that he loved Cécile, sister of the count of Foix. In 1256, Àlvar married Cécile. Civil war ensued in the county of Urgell. In 1259, James, supported by the Montcadas, invaded the county, while many of the nobles of the region sided with the unfortunate count. An agreement was reached in 1260 and Àlvar accepted a previous ecclesiastical judgement that returned him to Constança. But Àlvar then proved reluctant to stay with Constança and the count of Foix persuaded the papacy to take a new decision which, in 1264, found in favour of the Cécile marriage. A tribunal at Barcelona in July of that year rejected the decision. In 1266, the papacy, advised by Saint Ramon de Penyafort, upheld the Constança marriage. But Àlvar refused to accept the decision, James invaded the county again, and the count fled with Cécile to Foix, where he died soon after at the age of twenty-eight. He had left children from the two marriages. From his marriage to Constança de Montcada there was Elionor. From the marriage to Cécile de Foix, there were Ermengol (who became the count) and Àlvar, Viscount of Àger. The Montcadas fought for the succession of Elionor, Ramon Folc IV de Cardona for Ermengol, and there was a third candidate, Guerau de Cabrera, brother of the late Àlvar. But only James could pay off the debts with which the county found itself crippled. So the king took the county, while leaving Constança, Cécile, and Guerau in possession of some castles. In 1274, Ermengol, supported by Ramon Folc IV, defied James and the war was renewed. Peter III returned the county to Ermengol and, though the troubles in the county continued, as Ermengol X, he proved a very loyal servant to the Crown. On his death in 1314, the county returned, through marriage, into the hands of the house of Barcelona (Sobrequés, *Barons*, pp. 68–73).

and wrongs of the count. And we, at their request, made a loan, on security of the county, to pay what he had owed. And upon that and because of that Ramon de Cardona went to war with us.

And while we were at Cervera,[21] where we had passed the Feast of All Saints, Prince Don Sancho,[22] our son, whom the pope had appointed as archbishop of Toledo, sent us messengers with his letters. In them, he asked us most insistently to be at Toledo for Christmas Day, as he had to celebrate the Mass. And he said in his letters that he would already have come to us as his father and his lord, but that we should forgive him, as he could not come to us as he was preparing to receive us. Instead, he would come to receive us at Calatayud and he would enter with us to Castile. And he asked us that we should go with him to Brihuega,[23] or to Alcalá,[24] and to other places he possessed on that road. And, understanding the claim he had on us, since he was our son, and as he behaved accordingly, we agreed to that. And as Christmas day was so near, we left our son Prince Peter in Cervera, so that he could hold the frontier there.[25]

[475] And, when the Feast of All Saints had passed, we left there for Aragon, and fifteen days before Christmas we arrived at Calatayud.[26] And the king of Castile learnt that we were going to Toledo, and he came out to receive us at the monastery of Huerta,[27] and he did not part from us until we arrived at Toledo. And the archbishop came out to receive us at Alcalá. And we travelled together in this way until we were at Toledo. And we remained in Toledo for eight days.

[476] On the eighth day that we were there, a message arrived to us saying that Jaume Alaric,[28] who was our subject, and whom we had sent to the king of the Tartars, had returned and was bringing us good news. And two Tartars came with him, two honoured men, though one was more honoured and more

---

[21]James was certainly at Cervera from 13 October to 6 November 1268 (*M*, pp. 413–16).

[22]The youngest of the sons of James and Yolanda, he was appointed archbishop of Toledo in 1266. He died in October 1275 confronting the invading Moorish army at Martos.

[23]In the province of Guadalajara, at the side of the River Tajuña.

[24]Alcalá de Henares, between Guadalajara and Madrid, at the side of the River Henares.

[25]Prince Peter arrived at Cervera on 27 November 1268 and remained there until 21 December (Soldevila, *Pere El Gran*, 1, pp. 292–3).

[26]The king was at Lleida from 8 to 10 November and on 17 November at Huesca, then at least until 29 November at Zaragoza. On 5 December he was at Ricla and then by 8 December 1268 at Calatayud (*M*, pp. 416–17).

[27]Santa Maria de Huerta, in the diocese of Sigüenza and the province of Soria.

[28]Perhaps a burgher from Perpignan (Tourtoulon, 2, p. 312), perhaps the castellan of Santa Linya in 1282 (*S*, p. 373), and perhaps a relative of Guillem d'Alarich who was sacristan of Valencia in 1271 (Carreras, 'La croada', 1, p. 110, n. 1).

powerful. Now, we told this to the king of Castile,[29] and he held it to be a great matter, and risky, and very marvellous. He told us that they were a very deceitful people, because of which he feared that when we had gone there, they would not fulfil what they told us, because it was a very great matter. Even so, he well understood that, if Our Lord wished to guide us there, for no king had ever before done so good and honourable a deed, the entire holy land of Outremer and the Sepulchre could be won. Yet he was unable to advise us on it in any way.

[477] We replied to him that we thanked him very much for what he had said to us, and it truly appeared from his words that he loved us. And we responded to him that it was a true and certain thing that the deed was great, for no king on this side of the sea had held any alliance or friendship with those Tartars. On the one hand, their power had begun only a little time before, and on the other, they had never sent a message of friendship to any Christian king except to us. Moreover, if they had chosen to send a message only to us among all the others, it seemed a work of God, and that God wished to commend it to us, and that we should do it. Thus, since He wished it, we would not flee Him through caution or fear for our person, however much it might cost us, so that God might be served by us through the good will that we had to serve Him. Wherefore we asked the king that it should please him, because our honour would be his. And if God was to give us much to gain, he (who had many sons), would be able to trust in having his own part in the gains that we would make: "And it seems that God wills it; and since God wills it, we cannot receive harm."

[478] When these discussions between him and us were over, the next day we left Toledo and went to a village that has the name Illescas.[30] And the king of Castile went to another village. All the other nobles, the master of Uclés[31] and the master of the Hospital, who was master in all Spain, spoke of this enterprise of ours, and the greater part of the conversations that there were between them about what they had heard related to our departure.

And the master of the Hospital, who was called Brother Gonsalvo Pereiro and was from Portugal, came up to us and said that he wished to speak with us. So we left the road and we withdrew with him to one side. He said to us that we had a good heart and will, since we wished to serve God. And he added that

---

[29]Engels suggests Alfonso was probably unamused by James's alliance with the Mongol ruler, Abaqa Khān, son-in-law of Michael VIII Palaeologus, the mortal enemy of Charles of Anjou, with whom Alfonso did not wish to sour relations. James was desirous to limit Charles's intervention in the eastern Mediterranean in benefit of his own commercial politics (Engels, 'Rey Jaime I', p. 238).

[30]Between Toledo and Madrid and 35 kilometres from the modern capital.

[31]Gonzalvo Ibañez.

he had a great will to serve us with all that he could obtain from the Hospital in the five kingdoms of Spain.[32] Moreover, he said that we should say this to the king of Castile, so that he would allow him to go with us, and that the king would allow him to take from his land whatever was necessary of what the Hospital had there.

We said that we thanked him very much for the offer he had made to us, especially because he praised the enterprise that we wished to fulfil in the service of God. Furthermore, we said to him that we would speak with the king of Castile, and that immediately afterwards we would call for him; and that he should remain near at hand, that we might have his help when we asked for it.

[479][33] After that we sent word to the king, who was hunting ahead of us, that he should wait; and he waited. And when we were with him, we drew him to one side and we said to him: "King, the commander has offered us his help in this enterprise, if you order it and say that the help that he gives us will please you."

And immediately the king of Castile had him summoned and the commander came. Then the king said in our presence: "Commander, the help and the service that you give to the king of Aragon pleases us much, as much or more than if you did it for us. And we ask you and we order you to do this."

And we said to the commander: "It seems to us that it shall not remain undone because of the king."

And he said: "So I see, for the king orders me to do it."

Upon that we left that council, and we greatly thanked the king, since we saw that he wished to help as much as he could.

[480] The next morning, the king of Castile came out from one village and we from another. And as we were going to Ademús,[34] we saw his banner there where we had to pass. And the king was there, and we greeted him, and he said that he wished to speak with us, and he asked that Don Manuel, Don Gil Garcés,[35] and Don Juan García might be there.

And he said: "King, referring to this journey that you wish to make, God knows that it grieves us on the one hand, and pleases us on the other hand. It grieves us that you wish to risk your person in so great an enterprise, and with such terrible people, and so far away. Yet it pleases us if you can make so great a gain for the Christians as you think you will, and may it please God that it be

---

[32]Referring to Aragon, Castile, León, Navarre, and Portugal.

[33]In this chapter and ch. 480, James switches between Castilian and Catalan, like a true bilingual. The use of Castilian is not limited to the king of Castile and his men, but appears in the narrative, too.

[34]Ademús in the kingdom of Valencia, but halfway between Cuenca and Teruel.

[35]Gil Garcés de Azagra, also mentioned by *Desclot* (ch. 65) as participating in the Murcian campaign, was a relative of James's common law wife, Teresa Gil de Vidaure (*S*, p. 374).

so. As we cannot prevent it, for you have so much set your heart on it, I would not wish you to go without my help, as you did the same for me when I needed you to help me. And to help you I give one hundred thousand gold *morabetins* and one hundred horses."

And we said to him that we would not take help from anybody in the world except the Church, but that we were so bound to him that we did not wish to refuse his help. And we thanked him for it very much.

[481] The next day we passed through Uclés,[36] because the master had invited us. And on the day we left there, the master offered to go with us with one hundred knights. And we said to him that we thanked him very much. And the next day Don Gil Garcés said to us that he would go with us with all that he could raise. But afterwards neither the one nor the other fulfilled this. When the time came that we had to part from the king of Castile, he said to us: "Take sixty thousand *bezants* that the king of Granada has sent us, and we give this to begin with and the rest will follow later."

And we took them, and we left Brother Perellonet[37] and Pere Guilabert for the rest. And he gave them to us. And that day we went to Moya,[38] and from there we went to Valencia.

[482] While we were in Valencia, Jaume Alaric came to us, with the Tartars, and another messenger from Greece who was there.[39] And they said to us on behalf of the Great Khan,[40] who was the king of the Tartars, that he had the intention and the will to help us. Moreover, if we went to Alaya,[41] or to another place, he would come out to us and in his land we would find what we needed. Thus, jointly with them, we would be able to win back the Sepulchre. And he said that he would provide us with war-machines and provisions. And the other

---

[36] In the province of Cuenca.

[37] He is probably the Pere Peronet who was a commander of the Templars at Borriana in 1273 and certainly until 1277 (*M*, p. 488; Forey, *Templars*, app. 2).

[38] Moya lies to the south of Ademús, but in the kingdom of Castile. These events are of January 1269 and James had arrived at Valencia city by 18 January (*M*, p. 419).

[39] The messenger from the Emperor Michael VIII Palaeologus (1258–82). After the Murcia campaign, James had expressed to the pope his interest in conducting a campaign to help the Holy Land, where the Christian position had significantly deteriorated in the previous years. Pope Clement IV was reluctant to accede to this request while James continued his illicit union with Berenguera (*Documentos de Clemente IV*, no. 120), but in January 1268 found it necessary to seek the king's help (*Documentos de Clemente IV*, no. 171). James's support for the venture depended on a firm alliance with both the Mongol Khān and Constantinople. Michael VIII was ready to accept the Union of the churches in return for Western support (more in the attempt to halt Charles of Anjou's ambitions to restore the Latin kingdom than for any other reason). The Khān had expressed a desire to convert to Christianity.

[40] Not, in fact, the Great Khan, Qubilai, but rather his nephew, Abaqa (the second Īlkhān).

[41] In Asiatic Turkey.

messenger, that of Palaeologus, Emperor of the Greeks, said to us that he would send supplies by sea.

[483] At that we hurried to prepare and organize our voyage, in such a way that after seven months we were in Barcelona[42] ready to cross the sea. And then the queen of Castile sent a message saying that we should meet with her, and she came to Huerta with her sons.[43] Thus, our sons, Prince Peter, Prince James, and the archbishop of Toledo, our son, were there, and for two whole days, weeping and calling on our mercy, they besought us to stay, but they could in no way persuade us to remain. And we returned to Barcelona[44] to undertake our voyage. When we arrived at Barcelona, there were, what with knights and horsemen, a good eight hundred or more.

[484] Before we undertook the voyage, we went to Majorca to see if there were any ships there, and to ask the men of the town to help us in our expedition.[45] We crossed there in one galley and a cutter, and when we arrived, we asked them to help us. And they said that they would do what we wished and what we said. Seeing then the good will that they had, instead of the seventy thousand sous that we wanted to ask them for, we only asked them for fifty thousand, which they gave to us very willingly and happily. And with what they gave us we hired three ships. And from the *almoixerif* of Menorca we received, what with oxen and cows, one thousand.[46] Then we went home, so that by the first day of August we had already reached Barcelona.[47] Three or four days before Our Lady of September,[48] we set sail and we spent all that night beating to windward, and were more than forty miles out. And when it was morning, Ramon Marquet[49] said: "Lord, it seems to me that you will have

---

[42]In August 1269. But James had already been in Barcelona in the spring (*M*, pp. 421, 423).

[43]The visit to Violante and family at Santa María de Huerta probably took place in early June 1269 (*M*, p. 426).

[44]James had returned to Barcelona by 31 July 1269, but in the meantime he had visited Daroca, Teruel, Valencia, Amposta, and Majorca (*M*, pp. 426–9).

[45]James was at Majorca by 21 July 1269 (*M*, p. 428; Santamaria, 'Expansión político-militar', p. 135). On 23 and 24 July, James granted them many privileges in return for their support (Martínez, *Tragica storia*, p. 44).

[46]The Menorcans appear to have paid the tribute to Majorca, agreed in the 1231 treaty, with great regularity in this period (Abulafia, *Mediterranean Emporium*, p. 67).

[47]On 31 July 1269, James was at Barcelona (*M*, p. 429).

[48]The fleet, according to Pere Marsili (*Crónica latina,* IV, ch. 24, p. 377), left on 4 September, though he probably deduced this from James's account. The Feast of the Nativity of the Blessed Virgin Mary is on 8 September.

[49]A very distinguished citizen of Barcelona from a family of merchants and naval outfitters, he served under both James and Peter III and became admiral of Catalonia. He had been royal ambassador to the sultan of Egypt in 1261. Alongside Berenguer Mallol, he was in charge of the Catalonian fleet that defended Barcelona from the French fleet in 1285. The success of the Marquet family as real estate developers in Barcelona and as merchants at a time of great maritime expansion aroused the jealousy of their competitors. In 1257, Ramon's brother,

to return to land, so that all the fleet will draw together and see us. If you do not do that, they will lose us in the sea, and they will not be able to find us."

And we saw that he was right, and did what he said.

[485] When we had returned, we found but one galley, because the rest of the fleet had gone towards the waters of Sitges. And with that galley, we returned to the sea, and the other vessels went to Menorca.

In the morning,[50] we saw the sails some twenty-five miles away towards Menorca. And there were perhaps some seventeen sails. And we sailed all that day and all that night, and the next day, at the hour of vespers, we arrived and a terrible storm arose from the east; and a blue and red arc appeared, one of those that they call of Saint Martin,[51] and a squall stirred up the sea, which turned from white to pitch black. Then an easterly wind arose, and it began to blow when the sun set and it continued to rage all through the night, so that, as soon as the weather had changed, we had to strike sails, and we did not see any vessel or any ship. And that was on Saturday in the night-time, on the eve of Our Lady of September.[52]

[486] When Sunday came the wind changed to a south-easterly, which lasted all that day until midnight, and at midnight it changed to a warm south-west wind. And on Monday[53] the weather was fiercer than it had been on Saturday or Sunday, as all four winds met and all four fought with one another. And this lasted all day Tuesday and through the night into Wednesday, without that bad weather abating for a moment, so that the sailors who had been twenty-five or twenty-six times to Outremer said that they had never seen such bad weather as that.

[487] When it was day we saw the ship of the Temple close upon ours, and it sent a message to us saying that it had broken its rudder, and they asked us that we should give one to them. We wanted to give it to them, but Ramon Marquet said to us that we should not do so, because our ship could not go forward without a rudder in reserve. And then their ship separated from us and we lost sight of them in the night. Towards vespers the ship of the sacristan of Lleida, who was afterwards bishop of Huesca,[54] came and passed us by the stern, as

---

Bernat, had been stoned to death in a riot instigated by their enemies (Bensch, *Barcelona and its Rulers*, pp. 329–32, 336–41).

[50] 6 September 1269.

[51] A rainbow.

[52] 7 September 1269.

[53] 9 September 1269.

[54] Jaume Sarroca was elected bishop of Huesca in 1273, so this section of the text must have been written down after then. Jaume was the king's secretary, confidant, treasurer, and unofficial chancellor during his last years. He appears to have been either the king's son or

did the ship of the commander of Alcañiz, who was of the brothers of Calatrava. And we called for Ramon Marquet and Galceran de Pinós,[55] who were with us in the ship, and some knights who were there, and we said that they should listen to the words that we wished to say to them. And we said: "Ramon Marquet, it seems to us that Our Lord does not will us to cross to Outremer. For once before we were prepared to cross to there, and the bad weather lasted seventeen days and seventeen nights before we could go back. And the feast of Saint Michael was already eight days gone."[56]

[488] Then the bishop of Barcelona, the master of the Temple[57] and the master of the Hospital, who were of our land, with all the notables of Barcelona, and the masters of the ships and the sailors, came to us, and they called on our mercy, for God and Our Lady, that we should not wish to make that voyage, because they were afraid to miss the land because of the thick fogs there were in Acre at the beginning of winter. And if they missed it, they feared that they would not arrive there and would "place you in peril of death." So they did not dare advise us "that you should make this voyage."

Because of the entreaties that they made of us, and because we understood that they spoke the truth, we had to remain there. And we had delayed the crossing, which we should not have delayed so long, for the space of a good two months. "And since we could not cross the other time, that now for all time God should make us stay, pleases me, because it appears that our voyage does not please Him. For we could well endure the cruel sea if we had the wind behind us."

Moreover, since He did not give us the wind to go where we were supposed to go, it seemed to us that it did not please Him, and we ought not to go.[58] And

---

perhaps his nephew, perhaps son of Pere del Rei, the sacristan of Lleida, who was James's half-brother. Jaume is mentioned many times in this last section of the *Llibre* and it is very possible that he aided the king in the construction of the final part of the text.

[55]Marsili (*Crónica latina*, IV, ch. 25, p. 378) here substitutes Pere de Queralt in place of Galceran, who was to arrive at the Holy Land (Carreras, 'Creuada', 1, p. 134), something which he could not have done on James's ship.

[56]In 1245, Innocent IV had sought to persuade James to aid the Holy Land though James, disinclined to join forces with Louis IX of France, showed himself more interested in lending help to Constantinople. Here too he won papal support but nothing came of either venture (Goñi, *Historia de la Bula*, pp. 178–83). James is probably referring to events of Autumn 1260, when, perhaps hoping to combine with a fierce Mongol offensive against the Islamic world, and no doubt encouraged by a strongly worded letter of Alfonso X advising him against the venture, he laid plans for a campaign to the Holy Land (Goñi, pp. 206–7). Valencia city had made James a loan of 48,000 sous for the planned crusade (*Diplomatarium*, 2, no. 360a). James again had his sights set on the Holy Land at the time of the Murcian revolt (Carreras, 'Creuada', 1, pp. 107–8).

[57]Arnau de Castellnou, provincial master 1267–78 (Miret, *Cases*, p. 515; Forey, *Templars*, app. 2).

[58]There is a poignant contrast between the king's reasoning here and his bold approach to the Majorca crossing forty years before when he had trusted that God and Our Lady would be

we said that we would see if the wind improved that night and that if it improved, we would go there, but if not, we could not force the will of Our Lord.

And that night, with the warm south-westerly wind that we had, we managed as best we could, sailing until dawn. But when the sun rose, the east wind came straight at us and we could not go forward.

[489] When we saw that it was thus, and that God did not wish to improve the weather, we made a signal to the ship of the sacristan of Lleida, who was later the bishop of Huesca, to that of Calatrava, and to that of Pere de Queralt, that we were turning back. And they turned at the same time as we did. And the point of the shaft of the ship of the sacristan broke, and the antenna fell on the deck.

And if by chance somebody asked why our ship and those that turned with us did not continue forward, while the others did, this is the reason. They received so much of the warm south-westerly wind, that they were able to use it to continue the voyage,[59] while we, on the other hand, could not overcome the wind as we were lower in the water than they were.[60]

Meanwhile, when we were in that storm, a full three days and nights, whenever we could retreat to the place where we slept, (which in ships they call paradise), we prayed to Our Lady Saint Mary of Valencia that she should pray to her beloved Son that, if He considered our voyage to be a good deed, He should allow us to complete it, since neither death nor harm to us would prevent us from doing so. And if He held that it was not profitable to us or Christendom, then he should return us before the altar of Our Lady Santa Maria de Valencia.

---

on his side against the weather. In 1269, the king was over sixty years old. There were many rumours that he abandoned the trip because he could not bear to be parted from his beloved Berenguera (Dufourq, 'Vers la Méditerranée', pp. 8–9). The number of the concessions of castles, towns and goods made to Berenguera around this time would suggest she was very much in his thoughts (*Alicante*, nos. 455, 465–6, 471, 482, 488, 503, 506–7). It should perhaps also be noted that James travelled more in 1269 (approximately 4380km) than in any other year in his reign and changed residence some forty-seven times (Gual Lopez, 'Nuevas aportaciones', pp. 86–7).

[59]Certainly eleven ships (and probably a few more) arrived at Acre in the second half of October, including those of the king's illegitimate sons, Fernando Sánchez and Pedro Fernández. (Indeed, part of the reason for the expedition, as well as the religious motivation and the opening up of commercial routes in the East, may have been a quest to find land for James's children.) Perhaps some three to four hundred knights also arrived there. Diplomatic contacts were established with the Emperor Michael and the Mongol ruler both of whom continued to give support to the venture but, militarily, little was achieved. The remains of the Aragonese fleet returned home in February 1270 (Goñi, *Historia de la bula*, pp. 214–15; Carreras, 'Creuada', pp. 119–20).

[60]Perhaps meaning that James's ship and others were sailing some distance to the south of the rest of the fleet and therefore could not benefit from the wind or perhaps referring to the type of vessel in which James sailed.

And it pleased her that we should return, in a manner that we were able to arrive at the port of Aigüesmortes. And when we were about two miles away, a wind came out to us from the mouth of the harbour, and it made us shift sail by force, and blew all that evening and night, so that we arrived at Agde.[61] And we again prayed to the mother of God that our landing would not be in any remote part of our land nor in any place except where we would be found near to her church, so that we could adore her and thank her for the mercy she had done us, in delivering us from that danger and allowing us to worship at her altar.

[490] When the next day came we had a gentle and friendly west wind, which took us to that port. And the following morning we went to the church of Notre-Dame de Vauvert[62] to thank her for the mercy and the good that she had done us in rescuing us from the peril in which we had been.

And while we were at that port, our head cook said to us that outside in a boat were Fra Pere Cenra[63] and Fra Ramon Martí,[64] who had arrived from Tunis. And they asked what ship it was and they said to them that it was the ship of the king, who had returned because of the bad weather. And we thought that they would wait there for us, but they went from there to Montpellier.

And we, the next morning, went to Vauvert to again give thanks to Our Lady Saint Mary for the mercy she had done us. And the bishop of Maguelonne and the son of Raymond Gaucelm[65] came out to us, and they said to us that as soon as we arrived, if we wished it, they would return with us to sea and that there we could renew the provisions, since our company would become very discouraged if they did not find us there.

[491] And we said to them: "You, what help will you give, if we return there?"

And the son of Raymond Gaucelm said: "I will follow you with ten knights."

And then the bishop of Maguelonne said that he would follow us with twenty. For they added people would talk a lot if we did not return to sea.

---

[61]On the Languedocian coast.

[62]In the region of Montpellier. It was perhaps 17 September 1269 (*S*, p. 378).

[63]A Dominican from the house at Barcelona.

[64]Born at Subirats (c. 1230), he was a notable Dominican scholar who studied under Albert the Great. He was closely associated with Saint Ramon de Penyafort and was one of the members of the order set the task of learning oriental languages. His earlier work influenced Aquinas, while it was during a trip by Ramon Martí to Paris in 1269–70 that Penyafort's suggestion to Aquinas of the little handbook that became the *Contra Gentiles* was passed on. Ramon, in 1278, himself composed an apology for Christianity, the *Pugio fidei adversus mauros et judaeos*. An Arabic vocabulary is also attributed to him. He died in 1285 (Bréhier, 'Maître orientaliste'; Burns, 'Christian-Islamic confrontation', pp. 1408–11; Fort i Cogul, *Catalunya i la Inquisició*, p. 68).

[65]The lord of Lunel who undertook many important missions for the king (S, 379; Benoit, *Recueil*, no. 335).

And we responded to them: "We do not know what people will say, but Our Lord knows that we were forced here in this matter and that nothing in the world has ever grieved us as much or more. So I greatly marvel that you can say such a thing, because in my ship alone there are some fifteen horses lost or destroyed, and I believe that in the other ships there are some hundred lost or destroyed. And it will not be very profitable for us to return to sea with thirty more knights. For we have just come from the sea, and are all damaged by the sea, so that we would not return to it for anything, nor do we think that such a thing could be done. But I would like you to tell me with whom you have agreed that."

And they said with Raymond Marc[66] "and with others who speak of it."

And we said: "When will Raymond Marc come here?"

And they said: "Tomorrow."

And we said: " We will see Raymond Marc and we will speak with him in your presence. And we will see what he will advise and what not."

[492] The next day while we were at Vauvert,[67] Raymond Marc arrived and we sent for the Bishop of Maguelonne and Raymond Gaucelm. And we said to him: "Raymond Marc, listen to what the Bishop and Raymond Gaucelm have said to me, as they say it seems good to you, and I wish to know from you if you are in this agreement that I should return to Outremer."

"Lord," he said, "On other matters I know well how to advise you, but in deeds-of-arms you know more than I do, and you know what is best, since whatever you do not know, neither I nor the others will ever know."

And the Bishop and Raymond Gaucelm, who had said that to me, held themselves to be reproved for what they had said. And so I ignored what they had said to me; and afterwards we entered Montpellier.

And the next day we sent for the consuls and the best men of the town, (some fifty, or sixty), that they might come before us. And they came and we explained how the expedition across the sea had gone, saying that it seemed that Our Lord did not wish that we should go to Outremer, for we had already attempted it once before. Because when previously we were in Barcelona in order to go there, we travelled seventeen days and seventeen nights without the ships being able to take land because of the rough sea that there was, from the south-easterly and the Provençal winds, and we could not enter there.

(And if it were not for the fact that it would lengthen this book too much, we would explain many other things that happened; but we will limit ourselves to the most important words.)

Then we said that the enterprise had cost us a great deal, but that we trusted a great deal in them, and in that they would help us in a manner that we would

---

[66]Lord of Boutonnet (Baumel, *Histoire d'une seigneurie*, 2, p. 126).

[67]Perhaps 18 September 1269 (*S*, p. 379).

be satisfied. And by means of the Friars Minor of Montpellier they had it said to us that they would do so, as long as we gave them a guarantee. So, we did it according to their will, since they intended to help us in that expedition which we made in the service of God. And as God had brought us to the town of Montpellier, we besought most insistently that they would help us. And they said that they would deliberate on that, and they would return the next day with their answer.

[493] The next day they came to our presence, and the response that he gave us was this: that they well understood we were grieved and saddened at having not crossed to Outremer, and that it was true that we had asked for help from them. And they did not deny having said to the Friars Minor that they would help us, but their offer was that when we crossed to Outremer, they would help us with sixty thousand sous tournois.

And we said to them: "Worthy men, you have given me the most novel response that any man has ever given to his lord and that you could have made to a lord such as I. And I marvel at the wisdom of Montpellier, that you think to satisfy me with such a response, and that you would give me more to go from you than you would for me to remain in the land. Because my men of Aragon and Catalonia would give me a thousand thousand sous to remain in the land,[68] so that we should not go to another land. And I marvel how you can offer me money to part from you and to go to Outremer where I could be killed or captured."

[494] After that we left there and we returned to Catalonia,[69] and later we entered Aragon and we went to Zaragoza.[70] And when we arrived there, messengers came to us from the king of Castile, who asked us, since God had returned us to our land, to go to the wedding of our grandson Don Ferdinand.[71] And he besought us most insistently. We recognized that it would be fitting to do it, and we agreed to it. And we said to him that we would be there the day that he indicated to us in his petition. And we went to Tarazona, and the king of Castile was at Agreda.

Then we left Tarazona and we went towards Agreda, and we met the king of Castile, who had come out to receive us, halfway there. And he was very happy

---

[68]In fact, Barcelona, thinking on lucrative trading posts in the East, had offered James substantial amounts of money (including 80,000 sous in 1269) to undertake the crusade (Bensch, 'Early Catalan contacts', pp. 137–8).

[69]James left Montpellier on 7 October (Baumel, *Histoire d'une seigneurie,* 2, p. 127) and was at Perpignan on 9 October 1269 (*M*, p. 431).

[70]The king goes to Girona, Barcelona, and then Lleida, where he is on 29 October 1269 (*M*, p. 433). This visit to Zaragoza would probably have been in early November 1269.

[71]The first-born of Alfonso X, Fernando de la Cerda was about to marry Blanche of France, daughter of Louis IX.

to see us, and he embraced us three times and we cried. And then we entered Agreda.

Afterwards we went through Soria towards Burgos in manageable stages. And one day, while we were on the road, we spoke of his affairs and ours. And we said to him that we asked him that the things that he wished to do he would do with our advice, and that if he made mistakes, he should come to us, and we would put it right. And he thanked us very much and said that he would do so.

[495] Then we went to Burgos.[72] And his nobles went with us too, that is to say, his uncle Don Alfonso de Molina,[73] and his brother Don Felipe, Don Nuño González de Lara, and all the other bishops and nobles of Castile.[74] And the daughter of the king of France was there. And the Comte d'Eu,[75] brother of John of Acre, and a bishop, and other honoured men came with her.

And there, Don Ferdinand took the daughter of the king of France as his wife.[76] And the king of Castile made him a knight, and Don Ferdinand made his brothers knights but not Don Sancho, because we asked him that he would make his other brothers knights but not him.

And the king of Castile said to us that he and the other brothers wanted that, and that if they wanted it, he ought to be able to make them knights. And we said, before Don Felipe and Don Nuño and his nobles, that he who had advised Don Ferdinand to make his brothers knights had given him bad advice.

But he said to us that he wished that, and as they wished it, he might well make them knights. And we said that it would sow discord and anger amongst them, and that forever more, when they did not act well, he would reproach them saying that he had made them knights, and the others would feel annoyance and anger.

And we asked them if they wanted that, and they said that they did. And Don Sancho[77] was near us, and we whispered into his ear that he should do no such thing. And he said that he would do what we advised him. Then we asked Don Sancho in front of everybody: "Do you wish to be made a knight by Don Ferdinand?"

And he said: "Grandfather, what you want, I want."

And we said: "Then we want this: that you receive knighthood from your father and from no other man."

---

[72]27 November 1269.

[73]The son of Alfonso IX of León.

[74]Once again, James mimics Castilian words, here referring to 'so tío, e so ermano'. In the exchange between James and Sancho below, both grandfather and grandson use Castilian.

[75]'Comte Dodo' in the manuscript of Poblet appears to refer to Alphonse, the brother of John of Brienne and of Marie de Brienne, who was in Spain in 1269 seeking help from her Castilian relations for her husband, the deposed Latin Emperor of Constantinople, Baldwin II.

[76]30 November 1269 (*S*, p. 380).

[77]Later Sancho IV of Castile (1284–95).

And he said: "Lord, it pleases me, and I will do as you want and as you advise."

And the king made Don Ferdinand a knight, and Don Ferdinand made his brothers knights, except for Don Sancho. And he also made Lope Díaz de Vizcaya and other sons of nobles, and others, knights. And we remained there fifteen days, or not much less.

[496] And while we were there, one day Don Alfonso de Molina sent word to us that he was not well, and we went to see him. And when we returned from the Hospital of Burgos, where we were staying, we were with Don Nuño González de Lara, who came to me. And we went aside with him and we ordered the others to ride forward, through the gully of Burgos, and we spoke with him as we returned to our lodgings.

And he offered to serve us, saying that it was his intention to give service to us more than to any other man in the world, except the king of Castile, and that in certain matters he would serve us above him. Moreover, he said that if we sent him but one letter, he would come to us with one hundred or two hundred knights. And we said that we thanked him very much for the offer he had made us, and that when we needed it, we would accept it from him.

Then we said something to him, as it seemed to us that it was to the point and fitting to say it: "Don Nuño, I know that the king of Castile does not love you, and complains of you and of other nobles of Castile. And I also know that you complain of him, and that, whether through your fault or his, you and the others do not desire him the good that you should desire him. And now would be a better time to resolve that than at any other time in the world, because I have more reason to involve myself in his affairs than any man. And what the others do not dare say to him I would say to him as forthrightly as to a knight. And you may believe in truth that if he has wronged you, I will say so to him, and I will make him repair it. And if he does not wish to do so, I will show myself so dissatisfied with him that you will see that in the end he will do it; or if not, I will be so dissatisfied with him, that you would thank me for what I would do."

And another day we found him satisfied with the king, and he said that he had endowed him with lands, and married him off, and had done him all the duties that a lord could do his vassal. And it seemed to us that it was not necessary for us to interfere, since he had told us such good things.

[497] Afterwards we went to Tarazona,[78] and the king of Castile followed us, because he did not want to be separated from us while we were in his land. And we asked him to celebrate the coming festivities with us, which must have

---

[78]The king probably left Burgos between 10 and 12 December 1269 (*M*, p. 234).

been Christmas, and he made some excuses, but in the end he had to bow to our entreaties and came with us to Tarazona. And we had it all prepared so that he and all those who came with him had all that they needed. And we arranged it in such a manner that every noble who came with him had bread, wine, wax, salt meat, fruit, and all that he required in his tent, so that one need not bother another for the things that he needed. And we arranged it just in the manner mentioned above, and we believe there was not one to whom we did not give a ration of partridges or dried grapes and all the things that he asked for.

[498] He remained there with us for seven days, and in those seven days we gave him seven pieces of advice that he should follow in his affairs. The first was that if he had ever given his word to anybody that he must in all ways fulfil it. For it was better to bear the shame of saying no to someone who asked for something than to feel heartfelt pain for not having fulfilled what he might have promised.

The other advice was that, if he had made a charter to someone, he should abide by it, but that first he should consider whether he ought to grant it or not. The third piece of advice was that he should retain all his people under his lordship, for it was necessary for all kings to know how to retain the people God had commended to them, willingly and gladly. The fourth was that if he was to retain any, he should at least retain two parts, if he could not retain all. They were the Church, the poor and the towns of the country, because God loves these people more than the knights, because the knights rise up more readily against lordship than the others. And if he could retain all parts, that would be better, but if not, then he should retain these two, for with them he could destroy the others.

The fifth piece of advice was that God had given him Murcia, and we, with the Lord, had helped to take it and win it. And the charters we had drawn up with the settlers of Murcia, and those that he had drawn up afterwards, were not being fulfilled but had been infringed. And inheritances had been taken from them, and they had given them twenty or thirty tafulles, and to those who got most, fifty tafulles. But fifty tafulles were no more than two Valencian jovates, which only made twelve *cafizes* of seed corn. And we said that the fact that people should say that neither he nor his men knew how to divide Murcia, when it was the best town in Andalusia after Seville, was a very grave error.

For Murcia would never again be prosperous unless he did one thing, and that is: "That you place one hundred men of worth there, who, when you come to the city, know how to receive you, and that you should do it in a manner that they have good inheritances (for a man of value will not be properly endowed with one hundred or two hundred tafulles). And as for the others, let them be menestrals, and so you will have a good town. And if you have given inheritances to men who do not live there, make agreements with them and give them to the men who are going to live there."

Another piece of advice was that he should not do justice in secret, since it was not for a king to make judgements in his own house or secretly.

[499] Then he left Tarazona and went to Fitero;[79] and a message came to us from there saying that he was very ill from a blow that a horse had given him in the leg at Burgos. And we went there immediately. And some four or five knights went with us, as well as our household, and we saw him and comforted him. And we brought one of our surgeons with us, called Master Joan,[80] and we brought all that was needed with us. And we remained there with him for some four or five days. Then he earnestly besought us to go back, since he was cured. And he went to Castile, and we went to Calatayud,[81] where we remained for at least a month.

[500] After a month, we entered into the kingdom of Valencia[82] and we found that there had been a dispute between the man who represented us and another official, named Guillem Escrivà.[83] And we gave them our judgement. Later Guillem Escrivà and others of the town brought charges against our bailiff and we heard the case and we gave our judgement, and we punished them, so that the city remained in peace and good order.

[501] Then news came to us that the king of Castile wished to meet us between Requena and Bunyol,[84] and we replied that that pleased us. And we went out to receive him with the intention of showing him the kingdom of Valencia.

And we went out to him at Bunyol, and afterwards on the road of Requena, and we received him well and fittingly, both him and the queen, for since the time that we had married her to the king of Castile she had not entered our lands.

And before he arrived, we arranged for him to be well received by the bishop,[85] the knights, and the good men of the city. And they prepared many games, marvellous and diverse, and the town was well adorned and there were beds through the squares of the town.

And he entered the city and was received well and joyfully, in such a manner that had he gone to a town settled for one hundred years he could not

---

[79] A town of the province of Soria, a day's journey from Tarazona.

[80] Joan Jaume (*S*, p. 381; *M*, p. 516).

[81] James was there on 1 February 1270 (*M*, p. 435).

[82] James was at Valencia on 10 February 1270 (*M*, p. 435).

[83] A creditor of James (*S*, p. 382) and perhaps the same who died fighting against the crusade of Philip the Bold in 1285 according to *Desclot* (ch. 149).

[84] In the province of Valencia.

[85] Andreu Albalat.

have been better received or better provided with all that he needed. And he remained happy and satisfied, because while he was with us he lacked for nothing, neither in his lodgings nor in other things.

[502] Afterwards he left Valencia, and we went with him as far as Villena.[86] And he asked us to remain with him for three days and we did so. And after that we took our leave of him, and he went towards Murcia, and we went to Xàtiva from where we passed to Dénia.[87] And there we established a town called Orimboi, and another in the valley of Albaida, called Montaverner.[88]

[503] Then one day we were at leisure near Biar, and when we arrived at Ontinyent[89] some men from Zuera[90] came to us, and they said to us that in an ambush and raid that Artal de Luna had made with knights and footmen, he had killed twenty-seven of their men. After that we returned to Valencia, and then we entered Aragon.[91]

As we were coming to Torrijas, which is near Camarena, a village of Teruel, Prince Don James, our son, came to us, and with him came the abbot of Poblet.[92] And there, at Torrijas, he told us that the king[93] and the queen of France had proposed to him a marriage with the Comtesse de Nevers, and that they had promised it to him and had fixed a date. Therefore, he besought us and called on our love and our mercy, as his father and lord, that we should help him that he might bring that business to fulfilment to our honour and to his.

And we, the next day, entered Camarena, and from there, we went to Teruel. And there we gave him forty thousand sous in gold to help him with the aforementioned expenses.[94]

[504] Afterwards, from there we went to Zaragoza, where we sent for Don Artal de Luna to come to us on the evening of the Assumption.[95] And the next

---

[86]It appears to be May 1271 (*S*, p. 382).

[87]James was in Dénia on 20 May 1271 (*M*, pp. 448–9).

[88]The Vall d'Albaida in the province of Valencia. James was in the valley on 26 and 28 May 1271 (*M*, pp. 447–8) and indeed he was founding new settlements.

[89]Ontinyent, a town of Valencia to the south-west of Albaida. The king was at Valencia from 29 May to 3 June, at Albaida on 5 June and at Ontinyent 6 June 1271 (*M*, pp. 449–50).

[90]In the province of Zaragoza at the side of the River Gallego.

[91]James was at Valencia on 18 June, was still there on 1 August and then on 8 August 1271 was at the Aragonese town of Cella (*M*, pp. 450–2).

[92]Arnau Duliola who was abbot of Poblet until 1275 (*S*, p. 383).

[93]King Philip III (1270–85) and presumably the queen is Margaret of Provence, widow of Louis IX.

[94]The projected marriage, like an attempt previously to marry James to Beatrice, the daughter of the count of Savoy (*H*, 5, nos. 1503–4), was not realized and James married, in 1274, Esclarmonde, sister of Count Roger Bernard III of Foix (1265–1302).

[95]14 August 1271. James had arrived at Zaragoza the previous day (*M*, p. 452).

day we summoned him. And Don Artal came at the third citation that we made, and those of Zuera brought forward their charge and their plaint about the men whom he had killed in that ambush. And Don Artal asked us that we should give him as his defence Don Juan Gil Tarín,[96] and we gave him to him. So began the suit between him and them; and this is how it ended. One day we were at Ejea,[97] and Don Pedro Cornel and his friends came to us and they asked that we might show mercy to Don Artal. And we deliberated, and we granted him mercy in this manner. We ordered him to repair the evil that his men had done to the men of Zuera, and that he should give twenty thousand sous and that he should go from our kingdom for five years, with the knights who had participated in that with him. Furthermore, we ordered that the men of Erla should be exiled for three years, and that a scribe of his, who had done great evil, should be banished forever. We gave ten thousand sous to the orphans and the widows for the husbands they had lost there, and then we went to Zaragoza.[98]

[505] While we were at Zaragoza an urgent message arrived from the king of Castile, asking that we might meet with him on very important business that he needed to resolve, pertaining both to our affairs and his. So we sent to him Don Jaume Sarroca, the sacristan of Lleida, who was our notary. We sent him to say that we were very busy, and that what he wished to tell us, he could tell him, because we would act by his letter just as we would if we saw him ourselves. Yet he sent word to us that he did not want that, rather he begged us in all manners that we should meet with him, as there were things that he would say to nobody in the world but to us.

[506] After that we left Zaragoza and, just as he had sent word to us to do, we went towards Alicante, which was where he was.[99] And when we met him, he told us that he knew for certain that our nobles had made agreements with the nobles of Castile and with the Moors to go against us. In addition, he asked our advice upon what he should do in the business of the king of Granada and the *raises*, telling us that the king of Granada offered him help against the *raises*,

---

[96]A prominent Zaragozan lawyer. He was justiciar of Zaragoza (*M*, pp. 510, 521).

[97]This seems to be another small leap since the king was not at Ejea until March 1272 (*M*, p. 459).

[98]The king passed the sentence at Ejea on 12 March 1272 (Zurita, *Anales*, 3, ch. 80) and on 15 March he went to Luna and published the decree of exile against Artal de Luna and his followers Lope Ortiz, Diego García and others (*M*, p. 460; *S*, p. 383).

[99]But James does not appear to have been in Zaragoza for some time (*M*, pp. 457–60) and was at Valencia on 14 February 1272 (*Alicante*, no. 562). The repeated mention of Zaragoza may simply be James giving us the impression that he had been made to travel a long way to Alicante to see Alfonso, such was the desperate position of the Castilian king.

and that the *raises* offered him help against the king of Granada. And he asked that we should advise him on what he ought to do and whom he ought to help.

[507] We advised him to help the one with whom he had first made agreements to help. And we asked him who that was, and he said to us that it was the king of Granada. Then we said to him that if the king of Granada had made an agreement with him and had not broken it, it was necessary that he observed it. But if the king of Granada had broken the agreement, he need not observe it, but could side with the other *raises* and make an agreement with them without his word being of less value for that. And it pleased us greatly that he had divided them in this way, as it was much better that they were two parties rather than one. He replied that we had advised him well, and that he would do it as we had said.

[508] After that we left him and we went into the lands of Valencia. And when we left Valencia, and went to Morvedre, Fernando Sánchez de Castro sent us a letter together with one of his men. And he told us in the letter that Prince Don Peter had gone to Borriana to kill him and that they had looked for him under the bed with their swords and under some hemp that was in his house. And that if he had not learnt of it before, and had not left with his wife, they would have taken him. When we heard that, we were greatly saddened, and we said that we would give one thousand silver marks that nobody might know of the matter except we, the prince, and Fernando Sánchez.

[509] Then we left there and went to Aragon, where we convoked the prince and the nobles to the *Corts* at Lleida[100] so that they should all attend there in mid-Lent. And we were there, and the prince, and the nobles of Catalonia and Aragon. And we asked him in private, in front of some confidants of ours and his, why he had surprised Fernando Sánchez at night in order to attack him and kill him. And he replied that he had not gone there with the intention of killing him. But we said to him that it seemed likely that he had gone there intending to kill him, because he had entered into the chamber where he and his wife were accustomed to sleep, and with their swords drawn they had looked for him under the bed and under some hemp there was there. And we and the others who were with us considered that the defence that he had made was insufficient. Therefore we took away the procuration that he held from us.[101]

---

[100]The *Cort* at Lleida took place on 20 March 1272 (Kagay, 'Emergence', p. 241). The nobles in attendance included Ramon de Cardona, Guillem de Castellnou, Ramon de Montcada, Pere de Berga, Bernat Guillem d'Entença, Blasco de Alagón, Guillem Ramon de Montcada, Berenguer d'Anglesola, Galceran de Pinós; the bishops of Lleida and Vic were also there (*M*, pp. 462–3).

[101]Prince Peter had held the office of general procurator in Catalonia from 1257 and general procurator of Aragon from 1262.

[510] When that was done we went into the lands of Valencia, and before we got there the prince had already arrived.[102] And he came out to receive us near Borriana, as we were entering there. And he came to us, and we entered the town hunting. And with great joy we went to Morvedre, and afterwards to Valencia.[103]

[511] When we had been at Valencia for some fifteen days,[104] the bishop of Valencia, Brother Pere de Genoa[105] and Tomàs de Jonqueres, who were learned men in law, and Jaume Sarroca, who was sacristan of Lleida and afterwards bishop of Huesca, came to us.

In front of them, we told and besought the prince that he should not wish to commit such great cruelty in the business of Fernando Sánchez, who, as he was his brother, would give him satisfaction, through us, for any complaint that he had of him. Wherefore we asked him and we ordered him that he should accept this, since when a man wished to submit himself to justice in the power of an earthly king, it was right that he should receive it, and especially because there was such great kinship between them. Moreover, if he did not wish that, we made it known to him that we would defend Fernando Sánchez from him, since the latter was prepared to give him satisfaction. But if that was not sufficient for him, and he did harm to Fernando Sánchez, he would have to contend with us, as well as with him.

[512] He said that he would deliberate and respond to us. And we asked him when, and he said that he would respond to us the next day. Then we said to him that he spoke well, as the better he deliberated the better he would know what he had to do. (And he did not give us his response when we expected him to, the next day.) And on the third or fourth day they told us that the prince had gone outside the town, with two or three knights, and that he had left wearing his purpoint and his mail shirt, and with his iron cap on his head, and riding his horse.

When we heard that, we wondered greatly for two reasons: one, because he did not wish to obtain justice from them with our power, and the other, because he left by night from Valencia, which was unnecessary, since even if he had

---

[102]James was at Lleida certainly until 25 April 1272 and then went to Carcassonne, Montpellier, and Agde. He did not return to Valencia until May 1273 (*M*, pp. 463–81). Prince Peter, after the *Cort* at Lleida, went directly to Valencia and probably remained there all the time until his father arrived.

[103]James was at Valencia on 15 May 1273 (*M*, p. 481).

[104]End of May 1273.

[105]Fra Pere de Genoa was a Dominican who took part in many of the disputes that occurred between the Dominicans and the Jews in the 1260s. He was encharged by James to investigate possible Jewish blasphemies against Christ and His mother (*S*, p. 585).

said no to us, we would not have thought badly of him, provided he did no harm to Fernando Sánchez or to his things.

[513] A few days after Peter had left the town, Fernando Sánchez came to us from Valencia, and he thanked us very much for the favour we had done him, in speaking to our son on his behalf. And after he had been with us for a good eight days, he went on his way and returned to his own land. And while we were at Valencia, with Jimeno de Urrea, father-in-law of Fernando Sánchez,[106] Don Ferriz de Lizana,[107] Don Pedro Martínez de Luna and many others, the prince sent us his messengers, named Don Roís Eiximenis[108] and Tomàs de Jonqueres; and a letter of credence was brought to us, saying that they wished to speak with us in the presence of our nobles, knights and the men of the town. So we had them assembled.

When they were assembled, Tomàs de Jonqueres got up and said, on behalf of the prince :

[514] "Lord, the prince has sent both Roís Eiximenis and myself to you, and we have come to you. And he says to you that his departure from Valencia was not intended to do you any harm or any affront, but because he did not wish to answer no to what you had asked of him. And he says one thing to you that he has kept secret until now, because you guarded so much against it. He says to you that Fernando Sánchez has done such things against you that you ought not to intercede on his behalf nor ought you to wish that he should pardon him. For he is someone who has said that you ought not to reign, and he attempted to have the prince poisoned, and he has wished to raise your whole land against you, jointly with the nobles and the principal men of the town. And at the fitting place and time he will prove this, and show that nobles and others have been involved in this plot. And most of them are from Aragon."

[515] We replied to him that it would greatly please us if he wished to disclose it, since he spoke ill of many persons, and that if he were able to prove it, we would not be able to avoid doing what we ought to do. And we said that we would deliberate upon the matter. Then we withdrew to take counsel, since our palace at Valencia was full of people in front of whom he had spoken. And Don Bernat Guillem d'Entença, Don Jimeno de Urrea, Don Ferriz de Lizana and Don Pedro Martínez de Luna came out with us to deliberate. And when we

---

[106]Fernando was married to Aldonza de Urrea, daughter of Don Jimeno.

[107]Probably the half-brother of Fernando, sharing the same mother, Blanca de Antillón. Ferriz was certainly with James from June to August 1273 and witnessed many royal documents. On 22 August, James pardoned Ferriz for all the damage caused in the war he had sustained against James. Perhaps the events here related are of August 1273.

[108]He was often found in the following of Prince Peter and received land and castles both from the prince and James (*S*, p. 386; *M*, pp. 457, 517, 532).

were outside, I said to them: "He has said terrible things about you, Aragonese, and it is necessary that someone responds to this."

And Don Jimeno de Urrea said that he would respond, but since that cleric was a lowly person, he would delegate to another who was of the same ilk to reply to him. And he said that he would give a knight and he would respond to it. And so we left that council, with neither he nor the knight responding or saying anything on the matter.

[516] Then we responded to Roís Eiximenis and Tomàs de Jonqueres that the prince had spoken some very strong words and had challenged many in what he said, but still they should fix a day for Fernando Sánchez, and, if the prince were to give him safe-conduct, then he would come. And if Fernando wished to answer to it, all would be well; but, if not, we would give him the punishment he deserved for that deed. But they said that they had no authorization to fix another day, and they left.

[517] Afterwards, we convoked the *Corts* at Alzira,[109] including the archbishop, and four of each of the bishops, the nobles, and the good men of the towns. Then Fernando Sánchez came to us at Valencia, and we told him the words that they had said about him, and that not even Don Jimeno de Urrea, who was his father-in-law, had wished to respond when we told him that he should respond for himself and the others, since the honour of all was offended by something that questioned their loyalty, if it was true. But none of them had wished to respond.

After that we decided to go to Alzira, which was held by the prince, and to place ourselves at the river-crossing, so that we were better able to resist him if he wished to come against us. While we were there hunting, we listened out for what the prince would do or not do. And when we least expected it, they told us that the prince had crossed by a ford, further down from Seguereny, and that he had gone to Corbera, and that some twenty-five or thirty horsemen went with him.

Now, we had already convoked the *Corts* at Alzira, and they were attended by Prince Don James, the archbishop, the bishops (of Barcelona, Lleida, and Valencia),[110] and García Ortiz,[111] Don Artal de Luna, and men of the cities of

---

[109]James was at Alzira from 10 to 20 September 1273 when he may have convoked the *Cort* (*S*, p. 387).

[110]The king was at Alzira from 6 November to 16 December 1273 (*M*, pp. 487–8). This *Cort* appears to have been held around 12 November 1273, when all the major characters here were present as witnesses to a sentence given by James in a dispute between the Templars and the Hospitallers (*M*, p. 488). The archbishop of Tarragona was Bernat d'Olivella, and we have Arnau de Gurb of Barcelona, Andreu d'Albalat of Valencia, and Guillem de Montcada of Lleida all present.

Lleida, Zaragoza, Teruel, and Calatayud, and other places. Reflecting on the offence that the prince had done us, in not wishing to settle his disputes with Fernando Sánchez according to the law, although we had proposed that to him, and still further in having the castles he held from us fortified, we asked the *Corts* to be aggrieved at what he had done to us. And they said that, since he had gone to Corbera, they too would go there and attempt to reconcile him with us. And we, when we saw that he was doing all this against us, took back all that he held from us in Aragon and Catalonia.

[518] Then the said nobles went to the prince at Corbera, except for Don Artal,[112] who did not go there. And they found him very fierce and very adverse to what they said to him, so that they parted from one another on bad terms. When they returned to us at Alzira, they said that each would go to his own land. And we then took a decision upon what we should do and what we should not do.

And the archbishop explained to us the discussion that he had held with him. But we said to them that they should not have proceeded in that way, between us and him, rather that he, who was an archbishop, and the bishops and the nobles, and the citizens who were there, ought to say to him: "Why have you fallen out with your father? For he says to you that if he has wronged you, he will repair that, to your satisfaction. And if you do not wish to do so, we must inform you that you will lose us and all the kingdom and we will go against you, as one who is a rebel against his father.

"And if you had said that, he would not dare to have departed without abandoning his opposition to me. And how could you leave here, where you are gathered together, without making any progress against so great an evil as there is between him and us? When you meet anybody on the road, and he asks you how it is that you have left the king and his son at war and in conflict, you will have to turn away as miserable wretches."

Then they said that they would go back there and tell that to him. And they asked that Don Artal should go with them, so we sent him there.

[519] When they arrived there, they said to the archbishop that he should explain the matter on behalf of them all, and he said that he would not do so. And they said to the bishop of Barcelona and to the other nobles that they should say it, and nobody wished to do it. Then they said to Juan Gil that he should speak on behalf of them all. And Juan Gil said: "And how should I

---

[111]The son of Pedro Fernández de Azagra, he was a notable figure late in James's reign. He was ambassador to Manfred of Sicily in 1263 and to Navarre in 1274, on the Murcian frontier with James in 1273, and in 1276 opposed al-Azraq (Martínez, 'Turolenses', pp. 112–13).

[112]Most probably referring to Artal de Luna who was presumably supposed to begin his period of exile.

explain this business, when an archbishop, bishops, and the nobles are here? How should I do it?"

And all said that they wished him to explain it. Then he raised his hands towards Our Lord and said: "I thank God that they have entrusted me to explain the business; and may God will that I might explain it in such a manner that may be to the honour of the king and the profit of the prince."

And he explained the matter, but neither as fully nor as forthrightly as we had told them to. And afterwards they returned to us and told us that they could not resolve it. And they told us what the prince wished to do, and that he would do something to our injury, but we did not wish to believe it. Then the nobles said that as they were unable to resolve anything and had already spent what they had, they would go from there. And we said: "Now go, and bad luck go with you, as we will finish what we had asked well enough without you." And so they left.

[520] And then, on the third or fourth day, the prince sent us a message saying that we should send to him the bishop of Valencia[113] and two knights in whom we trusted. And we did so. Then we left for Xàtiva,[114] leaving Alzira with a garrison established. And when we were at Xàtiva, the bishop of Valencia came to us and said to us in private and with great secrecy: "The prince wishes to place himself unconditionally in your power and wants to come into your mercy, and he will do as you wish, and will come to Xàtiva."

And that pleased us greatly; and it was the Wednesday before Christmas.[115] And he came that very day with all his company, coming to us in our houses at Xàtiva. We rose to greet him, and we received him well and joyfully when we saw that he had come so humbly before us. We said to him that he should go and rest, and that he should speak with us in the morning. And he said that he would not go to rest or to any place in the world, but rather he besought us, and called on our mercy that we should send for our knights and the good men of the town. And we did so.

When they had all come, he got to his feet and said: "My lord, what I have done greatly grieves me, and I feel great sorrow in my heart if I have done anything to grieve you. And I come here to your mercy, and you may do with me and my things and mine whatever you will. And you may give what you want and you may take what you want."[116]

Then he threw himself at our feet and he kissed them, and he asked God that we might pardon him. We were very moved, and we took pity on him, and we

---

[113] Andreu Albalat was very much the king's man and, on 10 December 1273, James placed the goods and revenues of the bishop and chapter of Valencia under his special protection.

[114] James was at Alzira on 16 December and at Xàtiva on 17 December 1273 (*M*, p. 490).

[115] 20 December 1273.

[116] Peter speaks Aragonese here.

could not stop tears from coming into our eyes. And seeing his great devotion, we pardoned him.

[521] The next day, in the morning, we made him come to our presence at the church of Sant Feliu, and we drew him to one side, with the master of the Temple[117] and the bishop of Valencia. And the master of the Hospital,[118] whom he was holding prisoner, came with him. And he brought him there and delivered him to us. And we told him that we would abandon those claims we made of him, which came to a good fifty to sixty thousand sous.[119] Then we said that we would discharge him of all his debts, that is, all he owed in the kingdom of Valencia; and that amounted to some two hundred thousand sous. And so we remained satisfied and content. And he said that he had no intention of ever falling out with us again, but rather he was prepared always to do what we commanded. Then he besought us that we should allow him to go to Valencia, because he had much to do there. And we gave him permission and he went.

Afterwards he came to us at Dénia.[120] And he came with the sacristan of Lleida, who was already then bishop-elect of Huesca. And there he asked us that, if it pleased us, he would go to Catalonia for he had much business there. And we said that it pleased us, since he wished it. Then he went to Catalonia for the business that he had there, attending the consecration of the sacristan of Lleida at Tarragona, who at that time became bishop of Huesca.[121]

[522] And we went towards Murcia,[122] and beforehand we let it be known to the notables that we would go there. And if anyone ever took pains to receive a king well, these men did so with us. All those who were there came out to receive us, some on foot, others on horseback, and they made a parade before us. And they said that they thanked God and His blessed mother for seeing us,

---

[117]Guillem de Beaujeu (1273–91) who died at Acre.

[118]The master of the Hospital and castellan of Amposta was Berenguer de Almenara. On 15 December at Alzira James had written a letter to the archbishop of Tarragona and all the prelates in his kingdom concerning the troubles between him and Prince Peter in which he mentions that Peter had seized Berenguer and imprisoned him in the castle of Bairén without deference to the Hospital, Amposta, God or James (Fondevilla, 'Nobleza catalano-aragonesa', p. 1110).

[119]The matter of the payment of the prince's debt has been dealt with in some detail by Soldevila (*Pere El Gran*, 1, pp. 340–8).

[120]James was at Dénia from 4 to 9 January 1274 (*M*, p. 491). Many of the most important documents concerning the liquidation of Prince Peter's debts were dated at Dénia on 7 and 8 January 1274 (Soldevila, *Pere El Gran*, 1, pp. 340–6).

[121]Another reference to Jaume Sarroca, who perhaps helped the king with the later stages of his text.

[122]The king was at Murcia on 16 January 1274 (*M*, p. 492).

because whatever good they had in that place they had through us and they had never had so great a joy as at our coming.

We went to rest at the palace of the queen, and we dined at that of Don Ferdinand.[123] Then, in the evening the good men of the town came to us. And a notable of the town, named Andreu d'Òdena, got to his feet and said that they thanked God for our coming, as they well knew and recognized that all the good that they had they held through us. For they understood how we had helped them at Burgos when we were there and had spoken personally to the king on their behalf.[124] Thus, they besought us and they called on our mercy that we would remain there with them for two or three days or more.

And we did not wish to agree to remain with them but for one day. Nevertheless, they called on our mercy that we might hold them in honour, both on our own behalf and with the king of Castile. So we conceded that to them. And we remained there nineteen days, hunting and at sport.[125] Now, we had gone there to see how the town was populated,[126] and we were as greatly pleased at their well-being as if they were our own men.

[523] Then we returned to Valencia, and when we were at Alzira,[127] a messenger, named Fra Pere d'Alcanar, came to us from the pope, Gregory X,[128] with a letter, in which he asked that we might give him help and advice on the matter of the Holy Land of Outremer. This greatly pleased us and we were very happy. And we sent word to him that we would be there on the day he had said.

Then we prepared to go to the Council of Lyons[129] just as he had said and requested. And because of the time we would spend there we sent for our lodgings to be prepared for us, having sent all that we would need for two months or more.

---

[123]That is, the residences of James's daughter, Queen Violante of Castile, and his grandson Ferdinand (Fernando de la Cerda).

[124]James seems to be referring back to his stay in Burgos in November 1269 (ch. 496).

[125]The last reference to the king's stay at Murcia is of 28 January 1274 (*M*, p. 492) but we do not have further notice of him until 5 February 1274, when he is found at Biar (*M*, p. 493).

[126]The king was also preparing to give help, if it was needed, to Alfonso X against Granada but James's hunting tour and his keen interest in the repopulation of the town and district, while allowing him to see if there was any chance of a Moorish uprising that might threaten the kingdom of Valencia as well, also might suggest that his original motives in helping Castile against the Murcian revolt of 1264–6 were less altruistic than he would have us believe.

[127]10–19 February 1274 (*M*, p. 493).

[128]Pope Gregory X (1271–6), a tireless promoter of the crusade. In fact, Gregory had announced to James that he had chosen Lyons as the place for the council and had asked him to attend in a letter of 13 April 1273 (*Documentos de Gregorio X*, no. 75).

[129]From 20 February, James was occupied with raising the necessary resources for his trip to the council (Tourtoulon, 2, p. 385).

In the middle of Lent we set out from Valencia,[130] leaving for Lyons. And when we arrived at Girona, Prince Peter, our son, invited us to spend Easter Day at Torroella.[131] And we were there with him. Then we left there and went towards Perpignan,[132] and he followed us as far as there and then we ordered him to turn back.[133] Then we left for Montpellier, and we remained there for eight days before setting out on the road again.[134]

[524] When we arrived at Vienne, the pope sent us his official messengers, asking us that we should wait a day at Sant Soferí,[135] so that he would better be able to receive us. And we did so. And this place was three leagues from Lyons. Then, on the next day, we got up at dawn and entered into Lyons, and it was the first day of the month of May. And the Cardinals, the master of the Temple of Outremer,[136] Jean de Grailly,[137] Gerard de Roussillon (who held the city for the pope), and many other bishops and nobles came out to receive us, a league or so outside the town. And it took us from the morning until midday to travel the space of a league to the palace of the pope, so great was the multitude of people who had come out to receive us.

The pope ordered the gatekeepers that they should not guard the gate, but that whoever our men might command to enter there should enter there. Thus, when we entered, all our men entered with us, along with all those who wished to enter there.

[525] The pope was in his chamber, and when they told him we had arrived he came out in his full robes. And we saw him pass in front of us, and he went to sit in his chair. And we did him the reverence that kings do and have been accustomed to do to a pope. And they had a chair set out for us to sit on, near his and on his right. We said to him that we had come on the day that he had said to us, which was the first day. And then we said that we ought not speak to him of any business on that day, but rather on the following day. The following

---

[130]On 27 February 1274, James was still at Valencia and on 4 March 1274, he was at Ulldecona. Ash Wednesday fell on 14 February and Easter on 1 April (*S*, p. 390).

[131]The stay of the king and the prince in the area is confirmed by various documents (*M*, p. 498; Soldevila, *Pere El Gran*, 1, p. 350).

[132]The king was certainly at Perpignan from 6 to 9 April 1274 (*M*, p. 498) and Princes Peter and James were with him.

[133]Prince Peter then took charge of the battle against the viscount of Cardona and the other rebel nobles (Soldevila, *Pere El Gran*, 1, p. 353).

[134]15–22 April 1274 (*M*, p. 499). James was borrowing heavily in this period to pay for his voyage to Lyons and the planned coronation (Baumel, *Histoire d'une seigneurie*, 2, pp. 139–40).

[135]Saint-Symphorien-d'Ozon, between Vienne and Lyons.

[136]Guillem de Beaujeu (1273–91).

[137]Seneschal at Bordeaux for Edward I of England.

day we would come before him and we would listen to what he said to us, and we would respond to him in such a manner that he would be content with us.

[526] The next day in the morning we went before him and we found him in his chamber with his cardinals. And the archbishop of Tarragona, and the bishops of Barcelona, Valencia, Majorca, and Huesca entered with us.[138] We sat down, and when we were seated, the pope immediately began to speak of the matter of the Holy Land of Outremer, and said that he had come for that reason, and that Our Lord had brought them there to resolve that business. He said that he felt great joy at our coming, and hoped God, by means of us and the others, would give him such counsel as would profit the Holy Land, and through which it would be won.

[527] Then we got to our feet and went to take our hat from our head. And the pope said we should not do that, but that we should sit down and put our hat back on our head. And the cardinals, all with one voice, said the same thing.

When we had sat down, we said to him that he had sent us a message asking us to come there on the day of the council. And that later he had sent us a preacher by the name of Fra Pere d'Alcanar, who had brought us a letter saying that we should believe what he would say on his behalf. And we said to him that we would recall some words that Our Lord spoke in the Gospel: *Gloriam meam alteri non dabo.*[139]

"Now, I say these words for this reason. Because I wanted to come to you and since you had sent me a message, I did not wish to disclose my intention to anyone but you. Moreover, it was not fitting that I should show my good intentions to your messenger, but rather it was necessary to show that to you personally and before whomsoever you might wish. We find in the Prophets, that is, in Isaiah, that on the feast of Our Lady Saint Mary, when she brought Our Lord to offer at the Temple, she said: *Lumen ad revelationem gentium,*[140] which means to say 'The Light is revealed to all peoples'. And so it is true. For, when He was born and Our Lady Saint Mary offered Him to the Temple, the Son of God was revealed to the peoples. For which reason, we can refer these words regarding this, your council, which will be good and holy, in likeness to those.

"Let what the other popes could not do nor accomplish in recovering the Holy Land of Outremer, in which land God wished to die for us and be buried, now be accomplished through your words and your works, which you

---

[138]Bernat d'Olivella of Tarragona, Arnau de Gurb of Barcelona, Andreu d'Albalat of Valencia, Pere de Morella of Majorca, and Jaume Sarroca of Huesca.

[139]Rather Isaiah 42:8 ("My glory I give to no other").

[140]Luke 2:32 (fulfilling prophecy of Isaiah 42:6). The words in the Gospel are spoken not by Our Lady but rather St. Simeon.

undertake with the clergy and the nobles. And let that light which could not shine fully until now, shine in your times, and be lit by you. Now, I have come here for the two things about which you sent to ask me, and a third of my own. The first is that you sent for me to give you counsel; and the second, to give you help. I have come here to give you the best advice I can and know how to and that God will place in my thoughts; as well as to help you. The third reason is my own: because I will encourage those who have no desire to serve our Lord by taking part in this, and I will have so much to say and will do so much to achieve this, that they will be persuaded."

On hearing these words, the pope and the cardinals began to laugh because we had spoken so well.[141] And we left them very content with us, and they thanked us very much for the words that we had spoken to them. And then we returned to our lodgings.

[528] Afterwards the pope sent word to us that he greatly besought that we should attend the council that he would celebrate in the church the following Friday.[142] We told him that it would please us very much, and that we would attend the council since he had sent to ask us to do so. And on that Friday we were there. The archbishops, the bishops and others were already there from dawn. And we went at sunrise, but the pope did not wish to begin his speech until we had arrived.

When we entered the church, we saw marvels, because among archbishops, bishops and abbots we saw some five hundred or more, along with the pope who was on the rostrum, higher up than the others, and the cardinals and the patriarchs who were on two benches, in front of the pope. And he had us called so that we would be near him; making us sit on his right, very near to him, so that nobody could come between us and him. And his chair was not a palm higher than ours was.

[529] Then the pope began to speak, in Latin, saying that he had come, with the cardinals, despite the bad weather and storms, and Our Lord had guided them and led them there because of this good enterprise, and neither illness nor storms could prevent all from assembling.

For he said that we knew God created us and had given us the goods that we possessed, and all the things he had granted us for our service. And that, just as He had given them to us, it was certainly right that we should give to Him not all but a share of what was ours, in order to redeem that Holy Place held by His

---

[141] James appears to have been the the first ruler of Aragon to 'preach' sermons and in spite of his efforts in the *Llibre* to portray himself as a warrior he was to receive a reputation as a scholar (Cawsey, *Kingship and Propaganda*, ch. 4).

[142] 7 May 1274.

enemies, who did not believe in Him. Wherefore we had to make this exchange with Our Lord, since He had died so lovingly and suffered passion for us.

"And who would it be who would fail Him at this time and at this hour? Because it would be impossible that, being able to serve Him who created us and would save us, any man should rather serve the devil than Him."

He expounded these arguments and others for our benefit and for the salvation of all our souls. Then, at the end of his sermon, he conceded that all the sins that those who served God in that enterprise had committed in this world would be pardoned; except for robbery, usury, and theft, because these are sins that involve a wrong that one man has done to another, and he could not pardon them without restitution. But those sins by which somebody had offended Our Lord, because they were between God and man, these he pardoned. For he had the power that Our Lord had given to Saint Peter on earth so that he might bind and loose, and thus such a pardon would be well received. In addition, he conceded the pardon to those who through old age or sickness could not go, yet who would give him as much as they could spend on the voyage.

[530] Then the council rose, and the pope asked us to come to see him the next day, because he wished to speak with us as there were messengers who had come from the kings and princes of Outremer. We went there in the morning,[143] and the others were already there, each for his lord, or king or prince. And we were there, before the pope, and the cardinals, and the master of the Temple and Fra Joan d'Escarcella (who was the oldest brother there and represented the master from beyond the sea).[144] And there were many others who were there.

Then the pope began his speech, and spoke in this manner: that Our Lord created man and all other creatures, placing them all at the service of man, and that He had given so much honour to man, as He had made him in His image and His likeness. Thus, as He had given so much honour to us and had wished to die for mankind, it was certainly right that we should do so much for Him as to go to His aid in that place where they held Him captive. And he said that we should make our love correspond to His love, which had cost Him so dear that He wished to die for it: "So then, who will he be who does not wish to help and place his person at His service?"

And if anyone could not go there in person, he should at least offer what God had given him: "Because this world is like fire and tow, in that when one has a portion of earthly goods, whoever has more has more pride. And in this image we find this world. For, as with tow, which once lit is burned and

---

[143]8 May 1274.
[144]Rather Guillem de Corcelles represented the Master of the Hospital, Hugh de Revel (1258–77).

consumed rapidly, so is the glory of this world which one has in earthly goods; when the hour of one's death comes, all passes away and is as nothing. Hence, each of you ought to consider that, as God has given you His goods, you should give Him a share, and each of you should give to Him in such a way that you can receive the glory of Paradise. So that all that we have and our own persons, we have to give to Him since He has done so much for us. And we should place ourselves in His service, in our persons and in our goods, in such a way that with the service that we offer Him the land of Outremer may be won."

[531] After he had finished his speech, we got to our feet, and he made us sit down, since he did not wish us to be standing. And we said to him: "Holy Father, we wish to speak on this matter before anybody else, as there is no other king here except us. And we give you as our advice, in the first place, that you send five hundred knights to the Holy Land and two thousand footmen. And you should immediately send your letters to the masters of the Temple and the Hospital, the king of Cyprus[145] and the city of Acre to let them know that you have called this council for the business of Outremer, and that you will send these forces at once. For in August they will set out to cross there. Tell them that they should not go to fight but to garrison the castles and the places that need to be garrisoned and that they should busy themselves with that until the expedition crosses. And that this should take place two years after the next feast of St John;[146] and you should hurry, because if the Moors know that you wished to send forces there, they would look to them, and the Christians would be unable to withstand them. As regards the help, we reply to you that we will help you, and just as you have the tithes of your bishops, we will give you those of our land. And you may trust that we will be more rather than less generous in this. Regarding the other matters, we say to you that if as you have said you will go to Outremer, we will go there with you with one thousand knights on the condition that you help us with the tithe from our land. And this is the advice that we give to you and the help that we will offer you."

[532] When we had finished speaking, everybody was silent, and nobody spoke. And when we saw that they were all silent, we turned to the pope and we said to him: "Holy Father, now it is necessary that those who are here respond, since they will promise you more, for fear of being shamed by us."

And the cardinals said that we spoke the truth. Then the pope said: "Now you speak, Alart de Valery, and the others."

But they were silent. Then he said to the master of the Temple and Joan d'Escarcella that they should speak. And the master of the Temple said: "Sire,

---

[145]Hugh III of Cyprus and I of Jerusalem (1267/9–1284).
[146]24 June 1276.

let Misser Joan d'Escarcella speak, as he has been a brother for some sixty years."

And Brother Joan responded and said: "Master, do not concern yourself about my years."

Then the pope said to the master that he should speak. And the master, in place of saying that the pope ought to thank us for the words that we had spoken upon the enterprise of Outremer, did not recognize at all that he and the others should thank us for it. Instead he said that there was great need for help in the land of Outremer. And when he asked him what help, he said of every kind – arms, provisions, and still more, of troops, for there were not any there. And also people, as there were not so many there as were needed. Furthermore, he advised that at that time some two hundred and fifty to three hundred knights were needed, and five hundred footmen.

And we were unable to refrain from replying and we said to him: "Master, if the pope wishes to send five hundred there, what do you have to say to that?"

[533] After that, the pope asked how many ships the sultan[147] was able to have. And the master said: "Sire, if God helps me, I have heard that he was trying to arm his vessels and wished to besiege Acre, and he could not arm more than seventeen vessels, among galleys and other craft."

Then the pope said: "We would need as many again or twenty."

And we said to him: "Holy Father, that is not necessary for you; for if you wish to arm ten from our land,[148] I assure you that they will not flee before seventeen or eighteen or twenty, but rather they will take them by the throat."

[534] Then, at that, Alart de Valery[149] got to his feet and said: "Sire, this matter is a great matter and though many men have gone there over such a long time, they have never been able to take it. Now, if kings and many great men have crossed to Outremer, and they have not been able to obtain it, so I hold for good advice what the Master of the Temple has said."[150]

After that they were all silent. And we turned to the pope and we said to him: "Holy Father, since nobody else wishes to say anything, we will leave."

---

[147]The Mamlūk Sultan al-Ẓāhir Baybars (1260–77). Baybars I was an exceptional warrior who halted the Mongol advance, consolidated the position of his dynasty, and inflicted severe defeats on the Western crusaders. He was also an able administrator and established an efficient postal service (pigeons being the electronic mail of the Mamlūk world).

[148]The king's confidence here is a testimony to the dramatic advance of Catalonian naval power since the beginning of his reign.

[149]The constable of Champagne (a practised crusader) was the representative of Philip III of France.

[150]Here James indicates that Alart de Valery is speaking French: 'Sire, cesta xosa, sí és gran xosa.' Mimic-French words also appear in the speech of Jean de Grailly in the next chapter.

And the pope said: "Go, with the benedixio de Dominidio."[151]

[535] So we got up and we went outside with our company, and we said to them: "Worthy men, we can go now, for today all Spain is honoured."

And we went outside and we mounted our horse. And John Grailly was there. And having spurred the horse on, we made a display of our horsemanship, and the French said: "The king is not as old as people said, since he can still give a great lance-thrust to a Turk."

And with that we went to our lodgings.

[536] The next day,[152] we sent for Ramon March and Bernat de Castanyet, who are our subjects and close confidants of the pope. And we told them privately that, if the pope was agreed, we wished to be crowned by him,[153] since God had brought us to his council. And it would be a great honour for us and for him if we could receive the crown at that council rather than having to go to Rome.

Moreover, we said that we had the crown that he might place on our head, and that in all Lyons nobody would find another as fine as that, since it was made of gold and precious stones and was worth more than one hundred thousand sous tournois. And they said that they would say that to him, and that what we had said to them greatly pleased them, and that they would return to us with a full response.

[537] In the morning they came to us, and they responded to us on behalf of the pope, saying that it would please him greatly and that he would give the crown willingly. However, we should confirm a tribute that our father had given to Rome upon the kingdom of Aragon, when he was crowned at Rome, which amounted to two hundred and fifty thousand jussiphies;[154] and we should pay the arrears, and afterwards we could do just what our father had done.

We responded to them in this manner: that we found it very strange that he demanded a tribute of us from the time of our father, and because that tribute should not now amount to more than forty thousand *mazmudins*. But if he

---

[151]'The blessing of the Lord God'. The pope addresses the king in Italian (Pujol, 'Cultura eclesiàstica', p. 152).

[152]9 May 1274.

[153]James had previously expressed a desire to be crowned and an Aragonese embassy went to Pope Gregory IX in 1229 but nothing came of it (Fried, *Päpstliche Schutz*, p. 242).

[154]On 11 November 1204, Peter II had been crowned by Pope Innocent III in the basilica of San Pancrazio, and agreed to pay a tribute of 250 *mazmudins* each year. The exact reasons for Peter's actions are not known (he was not predictable) but he certainly needed to increase his authority within his own kingdom and wished to increase his renown in Christendom (Palacios, *Coronación*).

wished so much to have it from us we would give it to him. Nevertheless, since we had readily given him our advice and offered our help it was not seemly that he demanded this of us, but rather he ought to waive three times that amount. Moreover, we would not make a new charter which imposed a tribute on us, because we had served God and the Church of Rome so well, that we did not think it fitting that he and we should discuss these trivialities.[155]

[538] They said that they would return to the pope and they would tell him that, and that they would explain it to him in the same manner in which we had said it to them. So they went there and they told him that. And he replied to them that if it only depended on him and the cardinals who were with him, they would happily waive that demand. But Richard[156] and John Gaetano,[157] who were two of the most important and influential cardinals, were in Rome, and without them he could not do so.

Then they replied to us in that manner on his behalf. And we said that we had not come to his court to place ourselves under tribute, but rather so he could concede us freedoms. And, since he did not wish to do that, we would prefer to return without a crown than with a crown. And so it came about that we did not wish to have ourselves crowned.

[539] Later on he celebrated another general council of the prelates of the Church who were there, and we attended it.[158] And as he came to the end of his sermon, he greatly praised us, as well as the offerings we had made to him. Moreover, he ordered that throughout Christendom a special prayer should be said for us at the Sung Masses, and that they should say the Mass of the Holy Spirit for us. And he ordered those who could not celebrate masses that they should say the Psalter for us, and that they should thank Our Lord for the good will that we had shown in the deed of the Holy Land. Furthermore, he asked that they should ask God to give us life and health so that we could fulfil these and other things to the honour of God, and in the service of the Church. Then he finished his sermon, and we left there.

---

[155]The matter was neither trivial to James nor to his successors who were usually careful to distance themselves from Peter II's actions and never allowed the coronation to be performed in the manner that Pope Innocent III had set down (Palacios, 'Bula de Inocencio').

[156]Cardinal-deacon of San Angelo. He was of the powerful Annibaldi family.

[157]Cardinal-deacon of St. Nicholas in Carcere Tulliano. John Gaetano Orsini, an able diplomat, became Pope Nicholas III (1277–80). He had played a key role in Gregory's election as pope.

[158]18 May 1274. On this day Gregory declared the crusade and to pay for it imposed the tenth on the Church for a period of six years (Goñi, *Historia de la bula*, p. 223).

[540] The next day in the morning we went to see him and we asked him about the matter of Henry of Castile,[159] in order that, if he thought it fitting, he might be released from prison. For through that business the Church was brought into disrepute, because King Charles of Naples had imprisoned him on behalf of the Church, according to what people said, and so King Charles himself said. We said that Henry was not a man to be ransomed, nevertheless we and the king of Castile would guarantee to him that neither the church of Rome nor King Charles would ever come to harm through him.

[541] Then he replied and said that, saving our honour, those who said that were wrong, because he was not imprisoned because of the Church, rather he himself had already asked Charles to release him. Nonetheless, he exonerated himself from having done him harm in word and deed, and from having wronged him.

"Now, it greatly pleases us," we said, "since you have proved yourself guiltless, and we shall prove you guiltless in many places."

Then we asked him that he should nevertheless, for love of us, not omit to beseech Charles about that. And he granted us that he would beseech him, and that he would seek for him to be released.

[542] We had already been there for twenty days, and on the twenty-first day,[160] having arranged our affairs in order to leave, we went to him, at vespers, in order to take our leave. And we went to one side with him, and we said to him: "Holy Father, we wish to go, but we do not wish to do so in the manner that the proverb says – 'He who goes to Rome a fool leaves a fool.' It will not happen thus with us, because we have never seen a pope before you, wherefore we wish to receive confession from you."

He was very happy and satisfied, and he said that he would give it to us. And we told him our sins and likewise of the good that we had done which we remembered. And he did not give us any other penance but that we should guard ourselves from evil and persevere in good.[161] On that we bent our knees

---

[159]Prince Henry, brother of Alfonso X of Castile, had fought alongside Conrad, the grandson of Emperor Frederick II, at the battle of Tagliacozzo and afterwards was taken prisoner by Charles of Anjou and imprisoned at Canossa. (*Desclot* (ch. 62) relates how Henry had fled to a convent but the nuns had given him away.) In spite of the insistence of many princes, including Alfonso X, Charles refused to set Henry free.

[160]21 May 1274.

[161]Unfortunately, James failed to persevere in good and, while Gregory X was amenable to allowing the case of the annulment of the king's marriage to Teresa Gil de Vidaure to be treated at Rome (Tourtoulon, 2, pp. 453–4), after the king had procured an annulment from the amenable bishop of Valencia, James took the wife of one of his nobles as his concubine. (It appears to be Sibília de Saga.) On 25 July 1275, the pope admonished the king, recalled James's proposals to aid the Holy Land, and pointed out to him the bad example he set his subjects (*Documentos de Gregorio X*, no. 192). On 22 September 1275, the pope again

before him, and he placed his hand upon our head and gave us his blessing five times. And we kissed his hand and we took our leave. And the next day we went from the town and returned to Catalonia.[162]

[543] When we arrived at Girona,[163] they told us that the prince had demanded from Bernat d'Orriols a fief that he held for Ponç Guillem de Torroella, which the prince had said Bernat could not leave to his daughter.[164] On hearing that, we said that we would make the prince leave that path, because it was unreasonable that a man could not leave what was his to his daughter just as to his son or any other relation.

Then we sent Bernat de Sant Vicenç[165] to Solsona, where the nobles of Catalonia, wishing to put pressure on us, had assembled. And he found Arnau de Torrelles[166] there, whom the prince had already sent from another part. And he told them our message on our behalf: that it was not necessary for them to swear against the prince or against us, because we would have that declaration, which they said the prince had made, revoked. And they responded that they had not sworn against us, but rather only to maintain and conserve the customs and usages which their ancestors and they had observed. And he said: "Then, why have you assembled here? For as the king has sent word to you that that will not be done, but rather will be revoked, you ought not to do this, since the king has not the heart to do you wrong by infringing your usages and customs or any other thing."

And they did not wish to do anything, and they held to the agreement between them. And so the messenger left them and he returned to us.

[544] Then we entered Barcelona.[167] And Ramon Cardona and the nobles sent Guillem de Castellolí and Guillem de Rajadell to us, and they said to us that they wished to speak with us before our court.[168] And that pleased us very much.

---

instructed James to abandon this adulterous relationship (*Documentos de Gregorio X,* no. 199), but to no avail.

[162]James was at Montpellier certainly from 29 May to 8 June 1274 (*M,* p. 501) and at Perpignan from 15 June to 7 July (*M,* pp. 502–4).

[163]8 July 1274 (*M,* p. 505).

[164]In fact, James had heard the case at Perpignan (*S,* p. 393).

[165]Bernat appears sometimes in the following of the king and sometimes in that of Prince Peter. He certainly acted as the king's envoy in this matter (Fondevilla, 'Nobleza catalano-aragonesa', p. 1126).

[166]Arnau figures a number of times in the following of the prince and his intervention before the barons in this matter is confrmed by the surviving documents (Fondevilla, 'Nobleza catalano-aragonesa', pp. 1123–4).

[167]James was at Barcelona on 16 July 1274 (*M,* p. 505).

[168]July 1274. Guillem de Castellolí, who had already taken part in the Murcian campaign, was a confidant of Ramon Folc de Cardona, and had already appeared before the king in

And they asked us and called on our mercy that we would not do them wrong, since we were doing them wrong in seizing their fiefs and their *honors*, without having had a judgement in a court. And they said that as we had seized these without a judgement, we should return them to them, and that they were ready to give us satisfaction according to our court.

And we replied to them that we did not deny them the justice of our court, but that we wished that they would fulfil what the usage said, and that they should look to what it said and did not say, since we would follow it. And that for that reason a judgement was unnecessary, since the matter had already been determined by their ancestors and ours.

And they insisted that it was not justified by law or usage, nor did it seem lawful that the lord turn out the vassal from his possession without the recognition of the law; and that upon that matter we should have a trial.

And we said to them that the matter was clear: that they held their fiefs through us, and that we had ordered them to serve us but they had not wished to do so, and for that reason we had taken the fiefs.[169] And since it had already been judged, another judgement was unnecessary nor could they gain anything else from us.

[545] When they saw that they could not gain anything more, they renounced allegiance to us and Prince Peter. And before the days of grace were over, they went to Figueres,[170] which belonged to Prince Peter, and despite the offer to accept the law, they burned the town and destroyed it totally, in a manner that, when we were going to help and got to Girona,[171] we already knew they had destroyed it. And we returned to Barcelona to reach an agreement about that evil action and to proceed against them as it was right to do according to law. There we organized our frontiers for the defence of our towns. And as we did this, the bishop of Barcelona and Gonzalvo, Master of Uclés, came before us and asked that we should permit them to go to talk with the nobles to part them from that evil path which they well knew they were going down. And we responded to them that that pleased us very much.[172]

March 1274 in defence of Cardona's rights (*M*, pp. 496–7). Guillem de Rajadell was one of the barons who had revolted against the king alongside Ramon Folc de Cardona.

[169]James set down his argument from the usages to Ramon Folc and Pere de Berga in a letter from Barcelona of 29 July 1274 (Fondevilla, 'Nobleza catalano-aragonesa', pp. 1131–2; Soldevila, *Pere El Gran*, 1, p. 360).

[170]Figueres had been founded before 21 June 1267 when James granted its town charter. *Desclot*, also comments on this matter, saying Prince Peter had not founded the town long before when the count of Empúries took it and demolished it (ch. 69). Peter was away pressing his claim to the throne of Navarre and fighting against his half-brother, Fernando Sánchez.

[171]These events are of November 1274. On 5 January 1275, the king's accounts make reference to the expenses he had recently undertaken while going to Girona (*M*, p. 509).

[172]We know that on 19 November 1274 James empowered the commander of Montalbán and the archdeacon of Urgell to establish a truce of ten days with Ramon Folc, Pere de Berga,

[546] Immediately afterwards, that very day, a letter arrived to us from the bailiff of Tortosa in which it was stated that the king of Castile, and the queen, with their children, would enter Tortosa on the following Thursday.[173] Having heard this letter, we arranged to go to the king of Castile, to receive him and honour him. And the next day we left Barcelona and we went to Vilafranca.[174] And the bishop of Barcelona, Ramon Cardona,[175] Berenguer de Puigvert and many other nobles of Catalonia came to us, and called on our mercy that we should pardon them if they had erred in anything against us. Furthermore, they begged us that we should give them judges who would judge if we had done them any wrong or if they were debtors in anything to us.

Then we, wishing to cede to those entreaties that they and many others had made, gave them as judges the archbishop of Tarragona, the bishop of Barcelona, the bishop of Girona, the abbot of Fontfroide, Ramon de Montcada, Pere Berga, Jofre de Rocabertí and Pere de Queralt. Afterwards they entered with us to Tarragona,[176] where, in agreement with the said judges, we fixed a day for them in mid-Lent.[177] And we ordered all the nobles of Catalonia and Aragon that that day they should go to Lleida, and we and Prince Peter, our son, would also be there that day, and the abovementioned judges would judge on the matters that were in dispute between them and us. And a letter was drawn up to that effect. And while this was going on, the king of Castile and the queen his wife and all their children, except Don Ferdinand, arrived at Tarragona. And we left there, and he spent the Feast of Christmas with us.[178]

[547] After the Feast had been celebrated, the king of Castile asked for our advice, and he told us that he wished to visit the pope about the wrong the said pope had done him in the matter of the Empire[179] and concerning many other

---

and their supporters. On the same day, James also convoked the *Cort* (Fondevilla, 'Nobleza catalano-aragonesa', pp. 1141–2).

[173]December 1274. It appears to be this trip which *Muntaner* (ch. 23) describes in great detail (since the king and queen of Castile lodged at one of his father's residences) though he places it prior to the council of Lyons.

[174]On 25 December 1274, James recognized a debt of 2500 sous to Jaume Coll for expenses and duties undertaken on his recent visit to Vilafranca with the king and queen of Castile (*M*, p. 510).

[175]The same document of 25 December 1274 mentions the actions undertaken by Jaume Coll for the king when Ramon de Cardona and other nobles of his party and his family had come to Vilafranca to call for mercy (*M*, p. 510).

[176]In December 1274 (*M*, p. 509). *Muntaner* (ch. 23) says the rulers of Castile passed eight days at Tarragona.

[177]Letters convoking the *Corts*, dated at Barcelona on 26 January 1275, fixed the date for Shrove Tuesday (Fondevilla, 'Nobleza catalano-aragonesa', p. 1146).

[178]At Barcelona (*M*, p. 510).

[179]Alfonso, through the rights of his mother, Beatrice, hoped to claim the German empire, an ambition he had long nurtured (as had many others, James included). The papacy had

wrongs that he had done him. And we advised him that he should by no means go, because it was not fitting for him to go to a land so far away and, moreover, because he would have to cross the land of the king of France, whom he feared. And he did not wish to follow the advice that we had given him, and he went to see the pope.[180]

As soon as he had left Barcelona,[181] we went towards Lleida, because of the day of the *Corts* which we had arranged with the nobles. And we arrived there,[182] and Prince Peter was with us, and lodged in the castle with us. And Ramon de Cardona, the count of Empúries, the count of Pallars and the other nobles of Aragon and Catalonia were all assembled at Corbins,[183] and they did not wish to enter Lleida. And Fernando Sánchez de Castro, Artal de Luna, Pedro Cornel and many others were there. And they would not enter Lleida because they said they feared for their lives. And we sent word to them that we would protect them from everybody. But, despite that, they did not wish to enter there, but sent Guillem de Castellolí and Guillem de Rajadell as their procurators. And they asked us that we should give them advocates. And we assigned to them Ramon de Valls, canon of Lleida, and Ramon Gili.

[548] Meanwhile, we presented the plaint that we had against them. And they said they were not obliged to respond until we had made restitution to Fernando Sánchez of all that Prince Peter had taken from him. And we replied to them that we were in no way obliged to make restitution to Fernando Sánchez of what they demanded, as he, Jimeno de Urrea, Artal de Luna, and Pedro Cornel, despite the offer of justice, had broken with the said Prince Peter and had done him evil. Therefore we were not obliged to deliver anything to him, above all because Fernando Sánchez had taken the castles of Alquézar

---

initially encouraged Castilian and Aragonese involvement in Germany in order to harass Frederick II but, although Alfonso's claim was reasonable, the pursuit was expensive and the chances of success unlikely. He had never had James's support in this matter. In 1259, James had instructed Alfonso that he was not subject to any emperor. James had approved the marriage of Prince Peter to Constance of Hohenstaufen, daughter of Manfred, and had supported the latter's pretensions to the inheritance of Frederick II against his Castilian son-in-law (Engels, 'Rey Jaime I', p. 237), something Alfonso did not appreciate. In 1274, at the council of Lyons, Gregory X declared Rudolf of Hapsburg as king of the Romans, making Alfonso's chances more remote than ever.

[180]Alfonso was to meet the pope at Beaucaire in May 1275 concerning this matter. But news of the African invasion of the Iberian Peninsula had just broken and Alfonso was forced to abandon his dream (Linehan, *Spanish Church*, pp. 212–13).

[181]James certainly remained in Barcelona until 4 February 1275(*M*, p. 512).

[182]James went from Barcelona to Cervera, then to Tàrrega, Agramunt, and Almenar and was at Lleida by 24 February 1275 (*M*, p. 512). Peter had been with James at Barcelona, then went to Aragon, and after a spell at Huesca, where he was on 10 February, he went to Lleida where he was certainly on 10 March 1275 (Soldevila, *Pere El Gran*, 1, p. 370).

[183]Ten kilometres from Lleida, at the right side of the Noguera Ribagorçana.

and Naval[184] from us by force, and did not wish to deliver them to us, and he held them when he ought not to.

[549] Then the judges gave a ruling that those procurators ought not place the abovesaid exception, and that they were obliged to respond. And so those judges took up the measure and gave it to the procurators. Yet they did not wish to take it and threw it on the ground. In this manner the *Cort* broke up, without having decided anything. And we paid ten thousand sous to the judges for the expenses they had made, but the others did not wish to pay anything that they owed.[185] And when we offered them justice before those judges, they did not wish to take it and they went away.

After that was done, we ordered Prince Peter to enter Aragon to defend our land and to do evil to our enemies.[186] And we left for Barcelona[187], and we summoned our armies. And, when the forces were assembled, we went against the count of Empúries. And when we arrived at l'Empordà,[188] we found out that Prince James, our son, had besieged La Roca, a castle belonging to the count of Empúries. And we went there, and we made him raise the siege. And, in the meantime we entered into Perpignan to see the queen of Castile, our daughter, who had been there since the king of Castile had left our land and gone to see the pope.

[550] Before we left there, news reached us of how Prince Peter, while besieging a castle of Fernando Sánchez, had taken him prisoner and had had him drowned.[189] And this greatly pleased us when we heard of it,[190] because it

---

[184]In the province of Huesca. The capture of these castles is confirmed by the surviving documents (Fondevilla, 'Nobleza catalano-aragonesa', pp. 1138, 1145, 1148).

[185]According to a letter of the king to Prince Peter written on 29 March 1275, the judges considered that the barons had greatly prolonged the case and therefore they sought the expenses for the case to be covered. Yet while the king said he had paid ten thousand sous and would continue to pay, he wrote that the barons refused to pay anything until judgement had been given (Fondevilla, 'Nobleza catalano-aragonesa', pp. 1149–50; Soldevila, *Pere El Gran*, 1, p. 370).

[186]In the letter of 29 March 1275, James specifically instructs Peter to do evil to Fernando Sánchez, Jimeno de Urrea and Lope Ferrench de Luna (Fondevilla, 'Nobleza catalano-aragonesa', pp. 1149–50). In the last chapters the text is at times very close to the documentary sources, which suggests that they were consulted during its construction to a greater extent than in some earlier parts.

[187]James was at Lleida certainly until 8 May, and on 13 May 1275 he was at Barcelona (*M*, p. 518).

[188]The king certainly remained at Barcelona until 2 June 1275 and then was at Perpignan on 8 June 1275 (*M*, p. 519).

[189]Fernando had fled in disguise while Peter was besieging Pomar but he was unable to swim across the Cinca and was captured and executed on Peter's orders (*Desclot*, ch. 70; Soldevila, *Pere*, 1, pp. 374–5).

[190]There is no real reason to doubt that this is what James said and intended to say (Soldevila, *Pere*, 1, pp. 376–7). It reveals that streak of cruelty in his character, which we have

was a very serious thing that he, being our son, had risen against us, after we had done him so much good and given him so noble an inheritance.

When we had left Perpignan,[191] we went to receive a part of the army of Barcelona that came by land. And we found it at la Bisbal. Then we left there, and we passed by a castle of Dalmau de Rocabertí named Calabuig,[192] and we took it and we had it demolished. And afterwards we went to receive the other part of the army of Barcelona, which came by sea. And so, with all that army, and with that which we had, we besieged Roses,[193] a castle of the count of Empúries. And Ramon de Cardona, Pere de Berga and some other nobles of Catalonia learned of that and they entered Castelló, where the count of Empúries was; and they were there a few days.[194]

[551] Then they came to us, at the said siege of Roses,[195] and they brought the said count to us and they placed him in our power to do with him just as we wanted, and, furthermore, that he might be subject to our judgement in the matter of Figueres, which he had burned and demolished to the harm of the prince.

Then, seeing that the fact that he had placed himself in our power was sufficient for the fulfilment of our will, we lifted the siege and entered Girona. And there we brought many charges against the said count. And he appeared before us, together with Pere de Berga, and they begged that we should convoke the *Corts* at Lleida, at which the Catalans and Aragonese should attend, and that he would then respond to the charges and would do all that we would demand of him. And they said that those *Corts* would give us the opportunity to restore order throughout Catalonia and Aragon.

When we had heard their supplication, we granted it to them, and we told them that we would arrange matters so that Prince Peter, our son, should attend there. And we convoked the *Corts* for All Saints.[196]

[552] While we were at Girona, we received news that Ferdinand, the first-born son of the king of Castile, and our grandson, had died.[197] And we received

---

already seen at work elsewhere. *Desclot* (ch. 70) tries to redeem James by saying that he grieved greatly as well as being relieved at the news.

[191]James was still at Perpignan on 25 June 1275 (*M*, p. 520).

[192]In the province of Girona, two kilometres from Bàscara. The Dalmau in question would appear to be the brother of Viscount Jofre III de Rocabertí, rather than his father, Dalmau II (1212–29), or his son, Dalmau III (1282–1304).

[193]The king was already at the siege on 11 July 1275 (*M*, p. 521).

[194]Ramon de Cardona was already at Castelló d'Empúries from 8 July 1275 (*S*, p. 397).

[195]The last date we possess at the siege of Roses is of 22 July 1275 (*M*, pp. 521–2).

[196]On 6 September 1275, James, at Barcelona, sent letters convoking the prelates, barons, and townsmen for a *Cort* fifteen days after the Feast of Saint Michael (Fondevilla, 'Nobleza catalano-aragonesa', pp. 1161–2).

this news with great anguish. And afterwards we arranged to go to the *Corts* that we had convoked at Lleida, which we and our son Prince Peter attended.[198] And from the other side, Ramon de Cardona, the count of Pallars, the count of Empúries and other nobles of Catalonia and Aragon attended there. And also Bernat Guillem d'Entença, García Ortiz and other nobles with them.

And before our son, Prince Peter, had arrived and entered Lleida, the said nobles of Catalonia spoke with us, and they besought us, among other things, that we should confirm to the count of Pallars the fief of Berga and those of other places that Pere de Berga, who had recently died, held through us and had left to him.[199] And that if we did that and fulfilled it, they would do all that we wished and we ordered. And all that we wished to do in Catalonia to put the land in order would be pleasing to them.

We replied to them that when the prince arrived we would speak to him of it, and that, with him, we would resolve the matter in a manner that, if he had done them any wrong, we would make him repair it completely.

[553] When the said prince, our son, arrived, we spoke with him. And he responded to us that if, by chance, we considered that he was in any way obliged to the nobles of Catalonia and Aragon, and had done them wrong in anything, he would very willingly make amends for that wrong to them, to our satisfaction. And we had the said nobles informed of the response which our son had given to us. And when we wished to speak with those nobles, in the presence of the notables of Lleida, they left the town without a word of farewell, so that in the said *Corts* nothing more could be decided on that matter which we had treated and resolved with them.

[554] After the *Corts*, while we were at Lleida, a messenger arrived to us from Valencia saying that all the people of Valencia, generally, had conspired against our lordship, and had destroyed many houses belonging to some of the notables of the town, and had done many other evil deeds.[200] Furthermore, we

---

[197] Abū Yūsuf Ya'qūb of Morocco had put himself at the head of all his forces and crossed to Spain in mid-1275. In August 1275, Fernando died at Ciudad Real, awaiting reinforcements for the war against Abū Yūsuf. James's son, Archbishop Sancho of Toledo, died in October 1275, executed after having been captured in battle. Don Nuño González de Lara had been defeated and killed in the previous month near Écija. Alfonso again called upon James to help. While the war was mainly directed against Castile, Valencia was to become a second major theatre of war.

[198] Peter was at Lleida on 31 October 1275, then went to Huesca, and then returned to Lleida, where he was on 19 November 1275 (Soldevila, *Pere El Gran*, 1, p. 385).

[199] On 20 October 1275, Ramon de Cardona and other executors of Pere de Berga transmitted to the count of Pallars the palace of Berga and other goods (Soldevila, *Pere El Gran*, 1, p. 385, n. 45).

[200] The uprising is confirmed by contemporary documents. On 13 December 1275, the king, addressing Ponç de Materó and others, wrote to them of the many Christians and Saracens who

had news that Miguel Pérez, with a great company of footmen, was attempting to sack some places belonging to the Saracens of the said kingdom of Valencia.[201]

And for the two reasons we have mentioned, once we had resolved some business that we had to deal with in Lleida,[202] we prepared to go to Valencia in order to exact punishment and set the abovementioned things in order. And when we arrived at the said city of Valencia, we sent our son Pedro Fernández de Híjar with a company of knights and footmen, against the said Miguel Pérez and all his company. And when they heard of the displeasure we felt against them, they hurried to leave the kingdom of Valencia out of fear of us. And we had the others who remained there taken and executed according to the manner of the law.

[555] When that was done,[203] we had an inquisition conducted against those who had demolished the houses of some of the notables of Valencia, as we have said, and we punished them and condemned them to pay one hundred thousand sous.

And when we wished to proceed against some men of the city who because of the reason mentioned above had made themselves liable to corporal justice, news arrived to us that the *Alcaid* Abrahim had risen up,[204] and that he had fortified a castle called Serra de Finestrat,[205] which we had demolished some time before. And, on learning that, we left to one side the business we had at Valencia, and we hurried to help, towards that part where the castle was.

---

had risen up in the kingdom of Valencia and done evil to his land and, on the same day, addressing the men of Gandia and other towns spoke to them of certain Christian malefactors of the kingdom of Valencia who had risen up and did all the evil that they could to the land (*M*, p. 526; *S*, p. 397).

[201]The king treats this general Valencian uprising (which involves both Christians and Muslims) and the raids (probably supported by those gathering for the new crusade against the sultan of Morocco) as two unconnected events and this may well be correct. The identity of Miguel Pérez is uncertain. Possibly he is the same who appeared in a lawsuit against Doña Teresa (ch. 393) and is a vassal of Violante of Castile, or perhaps a knight of the household of Prince Peter, or even of the king himself (*S*, p. 397). He may be the squire who knew Arabic (ch. 189) who was involved in the ransoming of captives at Almassora, but that was forty years previously.

[202]The king was certainly at Lleida until 26 November 1275 and, on 9 December, he was already in Valencia (*M*, p. 526).

[203]December 1275–January 1276 (Burns, 'Social riots', p. 398).

[204]James now had to redirect his attentions from civil unrest to the larger problem of a widespread Muslim revolt, a problem he had anticipated since early 1275 (*Alicante*, nos. 707, 709). In November 1275, he had commissioned Prince Peter to go to the aid of the king of Castile (*Alicante*, nos. 736–8).

[205]Finestrat in the province of Alicante.

And when we arrived at Alzira,[206] we had news that the Saracens of Tous[207] had risen up at the castle, and we immediately sent a message to them saying that they should deliver it to us. And they gave us the reply that we should give them ten days and that, after that, they would deliver it to us. However, they did not wish to do this, but fortified it even more, because the rumour circulated that a company of light horse was coming to their aid. And we, knowing their intention, went towards Xàtiva.

[556] While we were in Xàtiva,[208] we received news of those horsemen who had entered into our land, and we decided to send some forty horsemen to reinforce the town of Alcoi, and to place a garrison at the castle of Cocentaina, through where the horsemen must pass. And when some two hundred and fifty of those light horsemen arrived at Alcoi to fight, they suffered great losses in the battle, and, moreover they lost their leader al-Azraq,[209] who once before had risen with some castles of the said kingdom, which he was forced to abandon and had to leave from all that land for ever.

Afterwards, the same forty horsemen we have mentioned, without any agreement between the one and the other, went to pursue the light horse, and fell into an ambush which the latter had prepared, and the greater part of those Christians were killed or captured. And the Moors of the country, when they knew what had happened to the Christians, and thanks to the reinforcements and the help of the light horse, went to attack some castles that we had not strengthened since we had not been informed that they had that plan to rise up against us who was their lord. And through the power they had and the efforts they made, they took some of the castles.[210]

[557] Seeing the plan that the said traitors had against us, we sent for our nobles and our knights, and the first to come were García Ortiz and the master of the Temple. And when they arrived at Valencia, some thousand Moorish footmen came to ravage Llíria. And our men consisted of some one hundred and twenty horsemen. And they overtook those footmen and they overcame them all, and they killed some two hundred and fifty of them there without suffering any losses except for five horses and a squire.

---

[206]James was still in Valencia on 4 February but was then at Alzira on 9 February 1276 (*M*, p. 528).

[207]In the province of Valencia and the region of Alzira, at the left side of the Xúquer.

[208]11–18 February 1276 (*M*, pp. 528–9). On 13 March 1276 James convoked an army to assemble a month after Easter (5 April) because the rebels had conquered three castles and were expecting African and Granadan support. A week later he was aware that many castles had fallen (Burns, *Islam under the Crusaders*, pp. 42–3).

[209]Late April 1276. al-Azraq had returned from exile at the head of a Granadan force.

[210]By mid-June some forty castles were in Muslim hands (Burns, *Islam under the Crusaders*, pp. 42–3).

[558] When they returned to Valencia they undertook to come to us at Xàtiva. And when they arrived, news came to us that the light horse had crossed through the Vall d'Albaida and that they were going to help the Moors of Beniopa,[211] who, on our command, our son Pedro Fernández de Híjar besieged and later captured. And there were more than two thousand of them.

When the light horse knew that the Moors of Beniopa had been captured, they sacked la Pobla de Llutxent.[212] And when we learned that they had sacked Llutxent, we wished to go out before them, and we left from Xàtiva with our company of horse and foot.[213] And when we were already outside the town, the master of the Temple, García Ortiz, the bishop of Huesca and many others besought us that we should not go there, nor should we make the expedition that we proposed to make against the light horse, because it was very hot and it could do us great harm, since we had been in bad health. And we, seeing that they were troubled because we had such an intention, wished to appease them and we returned to Xàtiva.

[559] Then García Ortiz, the master and his company, with a company of footmen, went to Llutxent and because of the journey they had made and the great heat there was that day they were all exhausted, through thirst and tiredness, which both the men and the horses had suffered. And on arriving in the district of Llutxent, they saw the light horse, and they were some four hundred or five hundred knights and more than three thousand footmen. And they fought with those Moors, whereby García Ortiz de Azagra, and the son of Bernat Guillem d'Entença,[214] and many others both of horse and foot died there.[215] And the master of the Temple and some other brothers were taken prisoner, who, after some days, when they had been imprisoned in the castle of Biar, escaped with a Moorish captain who was guarding them.[216]

[560] On hearing this news that the Christians were defeated, we were distraught and we felt great sorrow. And some days later Prince Peter, our son,

---

[211]A town of l'Horta de Gandia, in the province of Valencia.

[212]A town of the Vall d'Albaida.

[213]James finally left Xàtiva, after a stay of three months, on 28 June 1276 (*M*, p. 534). This brief sortie was before that date.

[214]Bernat Guillem II was with the king in March 1276 at Valencia but Miret suggests he long survived these events and therefore it would treat of another son (*M*, p. 575; *S*, p. 399).

[215]*Desclot* (ch. 67) and *Muntaner* (ch. 26) also mention the incident. García's death would have been between 16 June, when he witnessed a diploma of the king, and 28 June 1276, when James leaves Xàtiva (*M*, p. 534).

[216]The master of the Temple in question was Pere de Montcada according to *Desclot* (ch. 67) but the provincial master at this stage was still Arnau de Castellnou. Pere was provincial master 1279–82 and lieutenant of the provincial master in this period (Forey, *Templars*, app. 2). The name of the Moorish captain is given by Soldevila as Abdalà Bloch (*S*, p. 399).

arrived in Xàtiva, with nobles, knights and a great company.[217] We had sent an order to him that he should come and remain at Xàtiva, with all his company, to defend the frontier against the Moors.

Meanwhile, through the troubles we had suffered, and because it was pleasing to God, a sickness befell us. So we left Xàtiva and went to Alzira to send provisions to the prince and his company.[218] And there our illness increased and worsened, so much so that, thanks to Our Lord Jesus Christ, in our good and full memory, we confessed many times to the bishops, the Preachers, and to the Friars Minor, with great contrition for our sins and with many tears.[219] And then, purged of our worldly sins in virtue of the aforementioned confession, we received the body of Our Lord Jesus Christ with great contentment.

[561] Having done all that, and seeing ourselves weakened by reason of the said malady, we sent a message to Prince Peter, our son, saying that he should come personally to us at Alzira. And he, having asked what state we were in, came rapidly to Xàtiva to fulfil our will.[220] He came to us, and on the evening he arrived, he came immediately to our presence. And we received him, and he gave reverence to us, as a good son ought to do towards his father.

[562] When the next day came, this very son remained with us, and we heard our Mass. And having heard Mass, we, in his presence and that of the nobles, the knights and the citizens, said the following words. Firstly we spoke of the manner in which Our Lord had honoured us in this world, especially over our enemies. Then we spoke of how Our Lord had made us reign in His service for more than sixty years, more than any other king who had loved the Church had reigned in the memory of man from the time of David and Solomon to these times. And we told how we had been the general object of love and devotion on the part of all our people, and how we were honoured by that.

We recognized that all these things had come from Our Lord Jesus Christ, and because we, on the whole, had tried to follow His path and His commandments. Then we told him that he ought to follow our example in that, as it was the way of good; and that the same good would befall him, if he fulfilled and did that.

---

[217]By 27 June 1276 (Soldevila, *Pere El Gran,* 1, p. 410). Peter would spend the first fourteen months of his reign in a grim struggle to retain Valencia against the rebels. The chronicler *Muntaner* (ch. 10) commented that it could certainly be said that Peter had conquered part of the kingdom of Valencia a second time.

[218]James left Xàtiva on 28 June 1276 and on the same day he was at Alzira (*M,* p. 534).

[219]With the king in his last days were Bishop Jaume Sarroca, Archdeacon Hug de Mataplana of Urgell, the sacristan of Lleida Pere Sarroca, Albert de Lavànya, and the king's chaplain Arnau Caynot (Tourtoulon, 2, pp. 462–3).

[220]Peter was with his father at Alzira on 20 July 1276 (Tourtoulon, 2, p. 459).

[563] After that we ordered him and we besought him that he should love and honour Prince James, our son, who was his brother on both the father's and the mother's side, and to whom we had given a guaranteed inheritance, so that he would have no motive to contend with him. And since we were giving to him the greater inheritance and all the honour, he should be satisfied.[221] And he might well be so, because this would be easier for him to do. Equally, Prince James, our son, should love him and obey him in what he ought, as one should an elder brother.

Moreover, having said all that in the presence of the entire council, we commended him to the bishop of Huesca, (whom we had raised and had had raised from childhood until then, who was elevated to the honoured benefice of the episcopate through us, and who had been chancellor of our court until that day), whom he ought to love and honour, out of honour and respect for us.[222] And after that we commended him to the sacristan of Lleida,[223] brother of the said bishop of Huesca, and to the archdeacon of Urgell, and all the other wise men of our court and to all our household generally, to all of whom he was indebted, as were we to this present day, and we said that they should fulfil their duty to him as they had done to us.

Giving him our blessing, just as a father ought to give his son, we said many other words to him (concerning the good conduct of his person) which would take a long time to tell.

[564] Having said all that, we said to him and we besought him that he should leave there, and that he should have provisions and other things established in the castles of the kingdom of Valencia, and that he should direct the war well

---

[221]For much of James's reign, there were many contentions concerning the partition of the kingdoms. Initially, all was to fall to Prince Alfonso, the son of Eleanor of Castile. But after James's marriage to Yolanda in 1235, a new division was made. While Alfonso would receive Aragon and Catalonia, the son of Yolanda, Peter, was to receive the kingdom of Majorca, Roussillon, Cerdagne, Conflent, Vallespir, Montpellier and the conquests that were to be made in Valencia. The births of two more sons, James and Ferdinand, complicated the picture further until the matter was placed before the arbitration of the Aragonese and Catalan *Cortes* in 1250: Aragon fell to Alfonso, Catalonia to Peter, the kingdom of Majorca to James, and the ultrapyrenean lands to Ferdinand. The deaths of Ferdinand (1251) and Alfonso (1261) simplified matters. By the definitive agreement of 1262, Peter was to have Aragon, Catalonia, and Valencia, while Prince James was left with the Balearic islands, and the Pyrenean and southern French holdings. The agreement pleased nobody (Peter, least of all) and led to many problems after James's death, first between the two brothers and then between their successors.

[222]In James's will of 20 July, only Prince James and Sibília de Saga (the king's final lover) are commended to Prince Peter before the bishop of Huesca is commended (Tourtoulon, 2, p. 458).

[223]Pere del Rei was, indeed, the brother of Bishop Jaume and is not to be confused with the former sacristan of Lleida of the same name who was son of Peter II and half-brother of James I. He had died in 1254. They could well be father and son (Burns, *Crusader Kingdom*, 1, p. 297).

and forcefully, and especially that he should expel all the Moors from the kingdom of Valencia,[224] as they were all traitors, and they had proved it to us many times, for, though we had done good to them, they always looked to do us harm and to trick us if they could; and they would do the same to him if they remained in the land.

And furthermore we besought him that if we were to die from this illness while he was occupied in providing for the castles, he should not move our body from the kingdom at that time because the land, in the absence of the said Prince Peter, might be lost. And that if we died in the midst of all this at Alzira, the Bishop of Huesca and the others of my household who were there with us should bury us at Santa Maria d'Alzira or at Santa Maria of Valencia, just as we had already ordered. And we besought the said Prince Peter that, when the war had ended, if we had died, he should have us taken to Santa Maria de Poblet,[225] to which we were already bequeathed.

[565] When we had said all these words, the abovementioned prince, as an obedient son to his father, received our commands and our requests as good and true, and promised to fulfil all that has been said above. And before he parted from us, in his presence and that of all those who had assisted at the discussions mentioned above, in honour of God and of His blessed mother, who in this world had given us so much honour and help, and in penance for our sins, and in the presence of all the nobles, knights, and citizens, we abdicated in favour of our said son, Prince Peter, whom we left as heir of all our kingdoms and all our land.[226] And we vested in the habit of the Cistercians and we made ourselves a monk of that order. And our said son, to fulfil the order that we had made to him, took his leave of us, along with all the nobles and the knights, amidst great tears and lamentations. And he returned to Xàtiva to strengthen the frontier.

[566] And some days afterwards, when we intended to go to Poblet and to serve the mother of God in that place, and we had already left Alzira,[227] and were in Valencia, our illness became worse. And it pleased Our Lord that we should not complete the said journey that we wished to make.

---

[224]On 20 July 1276, in a codicil to his final will (Tourtoulon, 2, pp. 458–9), James required of Prince Peter that he should fulfil the promise James had made, both to the pope and the Virgin Mary, that the Saracens would be altogether expelled from his lands. But on 1 April 1276, James had ordered that only rebel Moors be attacked and not those who had remained loyal to the king (*Alicante*, no. 793). The king's ambivalent attitude towards the Moors had been lifelong.

[225]James had already expressed a desire to be buried at Poblet in his second will of 1241 and repeats this in the codicil of 20 July 1276 (Tourtoulon, 2, pp. 425, 456).

[226]20–21 July 1276 (Soldevila, *Pere El Gran*, 1, pp. 421–2; Tourtoulon, 2, p. 403).

[227]James was still at Alzira on 23 July 1276 (Tourtoulon, 2, pp. 460–3).

[And here in Valencia, in the year 1276, on the sixth of the kalends of August,[228] the noble James, by the grace of God, King of Aragon, and of Majorca, and of Valencia, Count of Barcelona and of Urgell, passed from this world: *Cuius anima, per misericordiam Dei, sine fine requiescat in pace.*

Amen.]

[This book was commissioned by the honourable Ponç de Copons,[229] by the grace of God abbot of the monastery of Santa Maria de Poblet, in which monastery lies the most high King James. And this book speaks of the deeds that he did and what happened to him in his life. And it was written in the said monastery of Poblet by the hand of Celestí Destorrens[230] and was finished on the day of Saint Lambert, on the seventeenth day of the month of September in the year 1343.]

---

[228] 27 July 1276.
[229] Abbot of Poblet 1316–48.
[230] The scribe who copied James's book was probably a Majorcan and not a monk of Poblet (Mateu, 'El manuscrito', p. 528).

Bibliography

Abulafia, David, *A Mediterranean Emporium: The Catalan Kingdom of Majorca*, Cambridge 1994.
- *The Western Mediterranean Kingdoms 1200–1500*, Longman, 1997.
Alcover, Antoni and Moll, Francesc de B., *Diccionari català-valencià-balear*, 10 vols., Palma de Mallorca, 1926–68.
Adroer, Anna, and Català, Pere, *Càtars i Catarisme a Catalunya*, Barcelona: Rafael Dalmau, 1996.
Alicante y su territorio en la época de Jaime I de Aragón, ed. José Martínez Ortiz, Alicante 1993.
Alvira, Martín, *Guerra e ideología en la España Medieval: cultura e actitudes históricas ante el giro de principios del siglo XIII: Las batallas de Las Navas de Tolosa y Muret*, PhD thesis: Universidad Complutense de Madrid, 2000.
- 'La cruzada albigense y la intervención de la corona de Aragón en Occitania. El recuerdo de las crónicas hispánicas del siglo XIII', *Hispania*, 60 (2000), pp. 947–76.
- *El Jueves de Muret: 12 de septiembre de 1213*, Barcelona: Universitat de Barcelona, 2002.
Annales Pisani, of Bernardo Maragone, *Rerum Italicarum Scriptores*, VI, pt. 2, Bologna 1936.
Arroyo, F., 'Blasco de Alagón y el comienzo de la reconquista valenciana', *Estudios de Edad Media de la Corona de Aragón*, 9 (1973), pp. 71–99.
Asperti, Stefano, 'Indagini sull' "Libre dels Feyts" di Jaime I: dall'originale all'archetipo', *Romanistisches Jahrbuch*, 33 (1982), pp. 269–85.
- 'Il re e la storia. Proposte per una nuova lettura del Libre dels Feyts di Jaume I', *Romanistische Zeitschrift für Literaturgeschichte*, 3/4 (1983), pp. 275–97.
- 'La tradizione manoscritta del Libre dels Feyts', *Romanica Vulgaria*, 7 (1984), pp. 107–67.
Aurell, Martí, *Les Noces del Comte: Matrimoni i Poder a Catalunya (785–1213)*, Barcelona: Omega, 1998.
Auvray, L., ed., *Les registres de Gregoire IX*, 2 vols., Paris 1896–1910.
Badia, Antoni, *Coherència i arbitrarietat de la substitució lingüística dins la crònica de Jaume I*, Barcelona: Institut d'Estudis Catalans, 1987.
Badia, Lola, 'Llegir el Llibre del Rei Jaume', *Serra d'Or*, 385 (1992), pp. 53–6.
Bagué, Enric, 'Pere el Catòlic' in *Els primers comtes-reis: Ramon Berenguer IV, Alfons el Cast, Pere el Catòlic*, ed. Percy Schramm, Barcelona: Vicens Vives, 1960.
Ballesteros, A, *Alfonso X el Sabio*, Barcelona 1963.
Barceló, Miquel, 'El tractat de Capdepera de 17 de juny de 1231 entre Jaume I i Abū 'Abd Allāh b. Muḥammad de Manūrqa: sobre la funció social i política dels fuqahā", *Bolletí de la Societat arqueológica lul·liana*, 38 (1981), pp. 233–49. (Repr. in his *Sobre Mayūrqa*, Palma de Mallorca: Imagen, 1984.)
- 'Expedicións militars i projects d'atac contra les Illes Orientals d'Al-Andalus', in his *Sobre Mayūrqa*, Palma de Mallorca: Imagen, 1984, pp. 144–64.

Baró y Comas, J., 'Relaciones entre Aragón y Navarra en la época de Jaime I el conquistador', *Anales del Centro de Cultura Valenciana*, 12 (1944), pp. 159–93.

Batlle, Carme, *L'expansió baixmedieval [segles XIII–XV]*, Barcelona: Edicions 62, 1999.

Baumel, Jean, *Histoire d'une Seigneurie du Midi de la France, tome II: Montpellier sous la Seigneurie de Jacques Le Conquérant et des Rois de Majorque. Rattachement de Montpelliéret, 1293, et de Montpellier, 1349, à La France,* Montpellier: Editions Causse, 1971.

Belenguer, Ernest, *Jaume I a través de la història*, 2 vols., Valencia 1984.

Benoit, Fernand, *Recueil des Actes des Comtes de Provence appartenant à la maison de Barcelone. Alphonse II et Raimond Bérenguer V (1196–1245),* 2 vols., Monaco 1925.

Bensch, Stephen, *Barcelona and Its Rulers 1096–1291*, Cambridge 1995.

- 'Early Catalan contacts with Byzantium', *Iberia and the Mediterranean World*, 1, pp. 133–60.

Bisson, Thomas, *The Medieval Crown of Aragon*, Oxford 1986.

- 'The Finances of the Young James I (1213–1228)', in *his Medieval France and her Pyrenean Neighbours: Studies in Early Institutional History*, Hambledon Press, 1989 (originally in *X CHCA*, 2 (1980), pp. 161–208).

- 'Unheroed Pasts: History and Commemoration in South Frankland before the Albigensian Crusades', *Speculum* 65 (1990), pp. 281–308.

- 'La época de los grandes condes reyes (1137–1276)', *Historia de Cataluña*, eds. Joaquim Nadal and Philippe Wolff, Barcelona: OikosTau, 1992, pp. 239–73.

Bonet, Maria, *La Orden del Hospital en la Corona de Aragón. Poder y gobierno en la castellanía de Amposta (siglos XII–XV)*, Madrid: CSIC, 1994.

Bréhier, André, 'Un maitre orientaliste du Xiiie siècle: Raymond Martin O.P.', *Archivum Fratrum Praedicatorum*, 6 (1936), pp. 267–311.

Brodman, James, *Ransoming Captives in Crusader Spain: The Order of Merced on the Christian-Islamic Frontier*, Philadelphia: University of Pennsylvania Press, 1986.

Bruguera, Jordi, *El vocabulari del Llibre dels fets del Rei en Jaume*, Valencia/Barcelona: Publicacions de l'Abadia de Montserrat, 1999.

Burns, Robert I., 'Journey from Islam: Incipient Cultural Transition in the Conquered Kingdom of Valencia (1240–1280)', *Speculum* 35 (1960), pp. 337–56 (repr. *Moors and Crusaders*, XII).

- 'Social Riots on the Christian-Moslem Frontier (Thirteenth-Century Valencia)', *American Historical Review* 66 (1961), pp. 378–400 (repr. *Moors and Crusaders*, III).

- *The Crusader Kingdom of Valencia: Reconstruction of a Thirteenth-Century Frontier*, 2 vols., Cambridge, Mass.: Harvard University Press, 1967.

- 'Christian-Islamic confrontation in the West: The Thirteenth-Century Dream of Conversion', *American Historical Review*, 76 (1971), pp.1386–434.

- 'The Medieval Crossbow as a Surgical Instrument: an Illustrated Case History', *Bulletin of the New York Academy of Medicine*, 48 (1972), pp. 983–9 (repr. *Moors and Crusaders*, VII).

- *Islam under the Crusaders: Colonial Survival in the Thirteenth-Century Kingdom of Valencia*, Princeton 1973.

- 'Immigrants from Islam: The Crusaders' Use of Muslims as Settlers in Thirteenth-Century Spain', *American Historical Review*, 80 (1975), pp. 21–42 (repr. *Moors and Crusaders*, II).

- *Medieval Colonialism: Postcrusade Exploitation of Islamic Valencia*, Princeton 1975.

- 'Spanish Islam in Transition: Acculturative Survival and its Price in the Christian Kingdom of Valencia, 1240–1280', in *Islam and Cultural Change in the Middle*

Ages, ed. Speros Vryonis Jr, Wiesbaden, 1975, pp. 87–105 (repr. *Moors and Crusaders*, XIII).

- 'The Spiritual Life of James the Conqueror, King of Arago-Catalonia, 1208–1276: Portrait and Self-Portrait', *Catholic Historical Review* 62 (1976), pp. 1–35 (repr. *X CHCA*, 2, pp. 323–57; *Moors and Crusaders*, I).

- 'The Realms of Aragon: New Directions in Medieval History', *The Midwest Quarterly*, 18 (1977), pp. 225–39 (*Moors and Crusaders*, XIV).

- *Moors and Crusaders in Mediterranean Spain*, London: Variorum 1978.

- 'Jaume I and the Jews of the Kingdom of Valencia', *X CHCA*, 2 (1980), pp. 245–322.

- 'A Lost Crusade: Unpublished Bulls of Innocent IV on al-Azraq's Revolt in ThirteenthCentury Spain', *Catholic Historical Review*, 74 (1988), pp. 440–9.

- 'The Many Crusades of Valencia's Conquest (1225–80): An Historiographical Labyrinth', *On the Social Origins of Medieval Institutions*, pp. 167–77.

- 'The Crusade against al-Azraq: A Thirteenth-Century Mudejar revolt in International Perspective', *American Historical Review*, 93 (1988), pp.80–106.

- 'El rei Jaume i València: perfil d'un conqueridor', *Història del país valencià*, 2, pp. 43–56.

- 'The Many Crusades of Valencia's Conquest (1225–80): An Historiographical Labyrinth', *On the Social Origins of Medieval Institutions*, pp.167–77.

Burns, Robert I., and Paul Chevedden, *Negotiating Cultures: Bilingual Surrender Treaties in Muslim-Crusader Spain under James the Conqueror*, Leiden: Brill, 1999.

Canellas López, Ángel, *Aragon en su historia*, Zaragoza: Caja de Ahorros de la Inmaculada, 1980.

Carreras, Francesch, 'La creuada a Terra Santa (1269–1270)', *I CHCA*, 1, pp. 106–138.

Cawsey, Suzanne, *Kingship and Propaganda in the Medieval Crown of Aragon*, Oxford 2002.

Cateura, Pablo, 'Sobre la aportación Aragonesa a la conquista de Mallorca (1229–1232)', *X CHCA*, 2 (1980), pp. 17–40.

Chabás, Roque, 'Sección de documentos', *El archivo*, 4 (1890), pp. 288–408.

Chamberlin, Cynthia, 'The "Sainted Queen" and the "sin of Berenguela": Teresa Gil de Vidaure and Bereguela Alfonso in documents of the Crown of Aragon, 1255–1272', *Iberia and the Mediterranean World*, 1, pp. 303–21.

Chanson de la Croisade, ed. Eugène Martin-Chabot, 2 vols., Paris 1931.

Chevedden, Paul, 'The Artillery of King James I the Conqueror', *Iberia and the Mediterranean World*, 2, pp. 47–94.

- 'The Hybrid Trebuchet: The Halfway Step to the Counterweight Trebuchet', *On the Social Origins of Medieval Institutions*, pp. 179–222.

Chevedden Paul, Zvi Shiller, Samule Gilbert, and Donald Kagay, 'The Traction Trebuchet: A Triumph of Four Civilizations', *Viator* (2000), pp. 433–51.

The Chronicle of James I, King of Aragon, surnamed the Conqueror, translated by John Forster, with an historical introduction, notes, appendix, glossary, and general index by Pascual de Gayangos, 2 vols., London: Chapman and Hall, 1883.

The Chronicle of San Juan de la Peña, trans. Lynn Nelson, Philadelphia: University of Pennsylvania Press, 1991.

Còdex Català del Llibre del Repartiment de Mallorca, ed. Ricard Soto Company, Mallorca: Conselleria d'Educació, 1984.

Colección diplomática del Concejo de Zaragoza I. 1119–1276; II, 1276–1285, ed. Ángel Canellas López, Zaragoza 1972–5.

Colección diplomática del rey Don Sancho VII (el fuerte) de Navarra, ed. Carlos Marichalar, Pamplona 1934.

Colección de documentos inéditos del archivo general de la Corona de Aragón, ed. P. de Bofarull y Mascaró et al., 42 vols., Barcelona 1847–1973.

Coll i Alentorn, Miquel, 'Llibre dels Feits', *Gran Enciclopèdia Catalana*, 14 (1987), p. 71.

'Nuno I de Rosselló-Cerdanya', *Gran Enciclopèdia Catalana*, 16 (1988), p. 259.

Cortes de los Antiguos Reinos de Aragón y de Valencia y Principado de Cataluña (1064–1237). Cortes de Cataluña, 1, Madrid 1896.

Costa i Robert, Xacbert, *Xacbert de Barberà, Lleó de Combat, 1185–1275*, Perpignan 1989.

Crònica de Bernat Desclot, ed. Miquel Coll i Alentorn, Barcelona: Edicions 62, 1999.

Crònica de Jaume I, ed. and trans. Josep Maria Casacuberta, 2 vols., Barcelona: Barcino, 1926–64.

La Crónica latina de Jaime I: edición crítica, estudio preliminar e índices, ed. Maria Martínez San Pedro, Almería, Gráficas Ortiz: 1984.

Crònica de Ramon Muntaner, ed. Vicent Josep Escartí, 2 vols., Valencia: Institució Alfons el Magnànim, 1999.

Danús, Micaela, 'Conquista y repoblación de Mallorca: Notas sobre Nicolau Bovet', *X CHCA*, 2, pp. 41–63.

Diago, Francisco, *Historia de la Provincia de Aragón de la Ordén de Predicadores*, Barcelona 1599.

Diplomatarium of the Crusader-Kingdom of Valencia: The Registered Charters of Its Conqueror, Jaume I, 1257–1276, ed. Robert Burns, 2 vols. to date, Princeton: Princeton University Press, 1985.

La documentación pontificia de Honorio III (1216–1227), ed. Demetrio Mansilla, Rome 1965.

La documentación pontificia hasta Inocencio III (965–1216), ed. Demetrio Mansilla, Rome 1955.

La documentación pontificia de Inocencio IV (1243–1254), ed. A. Quintana Prieto, 2 vols., Rome 1987.

La documentación pontificia de Urbano IV (1261–1264), ed. I. Rodriguez de Lama, Rome 1981.

Documentos de Clemente IV (1265–1268) referentes a España, ed. Santiago Domínguez Sánchez, León: Universidad de León, 1996.

Documentos de Gregorio X (1272–1276) referentes a España, ed. Santiago Domínguez Sánchez, León: Universidad de León, 1997.

Documentos de Jaime I de Aragón, ed. Ambrosio Huici and Maria Cabanes, 5 vols., ValenciaZaragoza 1976–82.

Dufourcq, Charles, 'Vers la Méditerranée orientale et l'Afrique', *X CHCA*, 1 (1979), pp. 7–90.

Engels, Odilo, 'El rey Jaime I y la política internacional del siglo XIII', *X CHCA*, 1 (1979), pp. 213–40.

Fiscal Accounts of Catalonia under the Early Count-Kings (1151–1213), ed. Thomas Bisson, 2 vols., Berkeley 1984.

Fondevilla, Fernando, 'La nobleza catalanoaragonesa capitaneada por Ferrán Sánxez de Castro en 1274', *I CHCA*, pp. 1061–1168.

Font Rius, Josep, 'La Conquesta: Un Procés Històric', *En torn al 750 aniversario: Antecedentes y consecuencias de la conquesta de Valencia*, Valencia: Consell Valencià de Cultura, 1, 1989, pp. 237–78.

Forey, Alan, *The Templars in the Corona de Aragón*, London 1973.

Fort i Cogul, Eufemià, *Catalunya i la Inquisició*, Barcelona: Aedos, 1973.

Freedman, Paul, *The Diocese of Vic*, New Jersey: Rutgers University Press, 1983.

- 'Cowardice, heroism and the legendary origins of Catalonia', *Past and Present*, 121 (1988), pp. 3–29.

Fried, Johannes, *Der Päpstliche Schutz für Laienfürsten: Die politische Geschichte des päpstlichen Schutzprivilegs für Laien (11–13. Jh)*, Heidelberg 1980.

García Edo, Vicente, 'Blasco de Alagón', *Boletín de la Sociedad Castellonense de Cultura*, 62 (1986), pp. 415–6.

Garrido, Josep-David, *Jaume I i el regne de Múrcia*, Barcelona: Rafael Dalamu, 1997.

Gesta Comitum Barcinonensium, eds. L. Barrau Dihigo and J. Massó Torrents, Barcelona 1925.

Goñi Gaztambide, J, *Historia de la Bula de la Cruzada en España*, Vitoria, 1958.

González, Eduard, 'Recull de documents inèdits del rei En Jaume I', *I CHCA*, 2 (1913), pp. 1181–1253.

González, Julio, 'Reclamaciones de Alfonso VIII a Sancho el Fuerte y tratado del reparto de Navarra en 1198', *Hispania*, 3 (1943), pp. 545–68.

- *Alfonso IX*, 2 vols., Madrid 1944.

González Anton, Luis, *Las Uniones aragonesas y las cortes del reino (1283–1301)*, 2 vols., Zaragoza 1975.

- 'La revuelta de la nobleza aragonesa contra Jaime I en 1224–1227', *Estudios Medievales*, 2 (1977), pp. 143–63.

- 'Notas acerca de la evolución preparlamentaria en Aragón en el reinado de Jaime I', *X CHCA*, 2 (1980), pp. 415–29.

Gonzalvo, Gener, ed., *Les Constitucions de pau i treva de Catalunya (segles XI–XIII)*, Barcelona 1994.

Gonzalvo, Gener, and Salas, Manuel, 'Guillem IV de Cervera, cavaller i monjo de Poblet', *Anuario de Estudios Medievales*, 28 (1998), pp. 405–18.

Gual, José, and Zafra, Juan, 'Nuevas aportaciones al Itinerario de Jaime I el Conquistador', *X CHCA*, 2 (1980), pp. 81–8.

Gual, Miquel, 'Reconquista de la zona castellonense', *Boletín de la Sociedad Castellonense de Cultura*, 25 (1949), pp. 417–41.

- *Precedentes de la Reconquista valenciana*, Valencia 1952.

Gudiol, Josep, 'Les bregues sobre lo senyoríu de Vich en temps del Rey En Jaume I', *I CHCA*, 1, pp. 194–218.

Guichard, Pierre, *Les Musulmans de Valence et la reconquête (XIe–XIIIe siècles)*, 2 vols., Damascus: Institut Français de Damas, 1990–1.

Guinot, Enric, *Els fundadors del regne de València*, 2 vols., Valencia: Biblioteca d'Estudis i Investigacions, 1999.

Higounet, Charles, *Le Comté de Comminges*, Paris 1949.

Hillgarth, Jocelyn, *The Problem of a Catalan Mediterranean Empire, 1229–1327*, London 1975.

Història del país valencià, ed. Ernest Belenguer, 5 vols, Barcelona: Edicions 62, 1989–90.

Huici, Ambrosio, *Las Grandes Batallas de la Reconquista durante las Invasiones Africanas*, Madrid 1956 (facsimile edition Granada 2000).

Iberia and the Mediterranean World of the Middle Ages, eds. Paul Chevedden, Donald Kagay and Paul Padilla, Leiden 1995–6, 2 vols.

Ibn alAbbār, 'Un traité inédit d'Ibn alAbbār à tendance chiite', trans. A. Ghedira, Al-Andalus, 22 (1957), pp. 31–54.

Ibn Khaldūn, *The Muqaddimah: An Introduction to History*, transl. Franz Rosenthal, 3 vols, Princeton: Princeton University Press, 1967.

Junyent, Eduard, *Jurisdiccions i Privilegis de la Ciutat de Vich*, Vich 1969.

Kagay, Donald, 'The line between memoir and history: James I of Aragon and the Llibre del Feyts', *Mediterranean Historical Review*, 11 (1996), pp. 165–76.

- 'Army Mobilization, Royal Administration, and the Realm in the Thirteenth Century Crown of Aragon', *Iberia and the Mediterranean World*, 2, pp. 95–115.

- 'The Emergence of "Parliament" in the Thirteenth-Century Crown of Aragon: A View from the Gallery', *On the Social Origins of Medieval Institutions*, pp. 223–41.
Kosto, Adam, *Making Agreements in Medieval Catalonia: Power, Order, and the Written Word, 1000–1200*, Cambridge 2001.
Leroy, Beatrice, 'La Ribera Navarraise entre les royaumes de Navarre et d'Aragon dans la premiére moitie du XIIIe siècle', *X CHCA*, 2 (1980), pp. 431–47.
Lladonosa, Josep, 'Jaime I el Conquistador y la ciudad de Lérida', *X CHCA*, 2 (1980), pp. 449–59.
Liber Feudorum Maior, ed. Francisco Miquel Rosell, 2 vols., Barcelona, 1945–7.
Libre del Repartiment del Regne de Valencia, ed. Maria Cabanes and Ramon Ferrer, Zaragoza: Anubar 1979–80, 3 vols.
Llibre dels Fets, trans. Josep Pujol, Barcelona: Teide, 1994.
Llibre dels Fets de Jaume I, trans. Antoni Ferrando and Vicent Josep Escartí, Barcelona 1995.
Llibre dels Fets del rei en Jaume, ed. Jordi Bruguera, Barcelona 1991, 2 vols.
Llibre del repartiment de València, ed. Antoni Ferrando, 4 vols, Valencia: Vicent Garcia Editores, 1978.
Linehan, Peter, *The Spanish Church and the Papacy in the Thirteenth Century*, Cambridge 1971.
Lomax, Derek, *La Orden de Santiago (1170–1275)*, Madrid 1965.
- 'El Padre de Don Juan Manuel', *Don Juan Manuel VII Centenario*, Murcia: Universidad de Murcia, Academia Alfonso X el Sabio, 1982, pp. 163–76.
López Elum, Pedro, *La Conquista y repoblación Valenciana durante el reinado de Jaime I*, Valencia, 1995.
- 'La Conquesta', *Història del País Valencià* 2, pp. 57–85.
McCrank, Lawrence, 'Documenting reconquest and reform: the growth of archives in the Medieval Crown of Aragon', *The American Archivist*, 56 (1993), pp. 256–328 (repr. *Medieval Frontier History in New Catalonia*, London: Variorum 1996).
Macabich, Isidor, 'Es Feudalisme a Ivissa', *I CHCA*, 1, pp. 457–82.
Maleczek, Werner, *Papst und Kardinalskolleg von 1191 bis 1216*, Vienna 1984.
Marquès, Josep, ed., *Pergamins de la Mitra (891–1687): Arxiu Diocesà de Girona*, Girona 1984.
Martín Duque, Ángel, and Pérez, Luis, 'Relaciones financieras entre Sancho el Fuerte de Navarra y los monarcas de la Corona de Aragón', *X CHCA*, 3 (1982), pp. 171–81.
Martínez, José, 'Turolenses en la conquista e integración de Valencia y su reino', *X CHCA*, 2 (1980), pp. 101–117.
Martínez Ferrando, J., *La tragica storia dei re di Maiorca*, Cagliari 1993.
Mateu, Felipe, 'El manuscrito del "Llibre dels Feyts" (a. 1343). Algunas observaciones paleográficas', *X CHCA*, 3 (1982), pp. 527–43.
Miravall, Ramon, *Ponç de Torrella, bisbe dels tortosins*, Barcelona: Rafael Dalamu, 1972.
Miret, Joaquim, *Investigación histórica sobre el Vizcondado de Castellbó*, Barcelona, 1900.
- 'Itinerario del Rey Pedro I de Cataluña, II en Aragón', *Boletín de la Real Academia de Buenas Letras de Barcelona*, 3 (1905–6), pp. 79–88, 238–49, 265–84, 365–88, 435–50; 4 (1907–8), pp. 15–36, 91–114.
- *Les cases de templers y hospitalers en Catalunya*, Barcelona 1910.
- *Itinerari de Jaume I "El Conqueridor"*, Barcelona 1918.
Molas, Joaquim, *Diccionari de la literatura catalana*, Barcelona: Edicions 62, 1979.
Montoliu, Manuel de, *Les Quatre Grans Cròniques*, Barcelona: Alpha, 1959.
Ollich, Inmaculada, 'Vigatans a la conquesta de Mallorca i València', *X CHCA*, 2 (1980), pp. 131–48.

On the Social Origins of Medieval Institutions: Essays in Honor of Joseph F. O'Callaghan, eds. Donald Kagay and Theresa Vann, Leiden: Brill, 1999.

Palacios, Bonifacio, 'La bula de Inocencio III y la coronación de los reyes de Aragón', *Hispania*, 29 (1969), pp. 485–504.

‐ *Los actos de coronación de los reyes de Aragón, 1204–1410*, Valencia 1975.

Pallarés, Matías, 'Don Blasco de Alagón, señor de Morella', *I CHCA*, 1, pp. 219–31.

Peal, A, 'Oliver de Termes and the Occitan nobility in the thirteenth century', *Reading Medieval Studies*, 12 (1986), pp. 109–130.

Pladevall, Antoni, *Guillem de Mont-rodon: Mestre del Temple i Tutor de Jaume I*, Lleida 1993.

Puig, Joan, 'Conquista d' Ares i Morella', *Boletín de la Sociedad Castellonense de Cultura*, 14 (1933), pp. 126–42.

Pujol, Josep, *Sens i conjuntures del Llibre del Rei en Jaume*, PHD thesis: University of Barcelona, Divisió dels Centres Universitaris del Camp de Tarragona, 1991.

‐ 'The *Llibre del rei En Jaume*: A matter of style', *Historical Literature in Medieval Iberia*, ed. Alan Deyermond, London: Department of Hispanic studies, Queen Mary and Westfield college, 1996, pp. 35–65.

‐ 'Cultura eclesiàstica o competència retòrica? El Llatí, La Bíblia i El Rei En Jaume', *Estudis Romànics*, 23 (2001), pp. 147–72.

Les quatre grans cròniques, ed. Ferran Soldevila, Barcelona: Editorial Selecta, 1971.

Recueil des historiens des Gaules et de la France, ed. M. Bouquet and L. Delisle, 25 vols., Paris 1869–1904.

Repartiment de València: edición fotocópia, ed. J. Ribera y Tarragó, Valencia: Centro de Cultura Valenciana, 1939.

Ribas de Pina, Miquel, *La Conquista de Mallorca pel Rei en Jaume I: Estudi Tecnic Militar*, Mallorca 1934.

Riera, Jaume, 'La personalitat eclesiàstica del redactor del "Llibre dels feits"', *X CHCA*, 3 (1982), pp. 575–89.

Riquer, Martí de, *Història de la Literatura Catalana*, 3 vols., Barcelona: Ariel, 1964.

Rodrigo of Toledo, *Historia de rebus Hispanie sive Historia Gothica*, ed. J. Fernández Valverde, Corpus Chistianorum Continuatio Mediaevalis, 72, Turnhout: Brepols, 1987.

Roquebert, Michel, *L'Épopée Cathare*, 5 vols., Toulouse 1970–87.

Rubio García, Luis, *La Corona de Aragón en la Reconquista de Murcia*, Murcia: Universidad de Murcia, 1989.

Rubiés, Joan Pau and Salrach, Josep, 'Entorn de la mentalitat i la ideologia del bloc de poder feudal a través de la historiografia medieval fins a les quatre grans cròniques', *La formació i expansió del feudalisme català. Actes del col·loqui organitzat pel Col·legi Universitari de Girona (8–11 de gener de 1985)*, ed. Jaume Portella, Girona: Estudi General, 1985–86, pp. 467–510.

Salrach, Josep, *El procés de feudalització [segles III–XII]*, Barcelona: Aedos, 1998.

Salvat, Juan, *Tarragona y el Gran Rey Jaime I de Aragón (Estudio histórico crítico literario) 1228–1229*, Tarragona 1957.

Sanpere, Salvador, 'Minoría de Jaime I: vindicación del Procurador Conde Sancho: Años 1214–1219', *I CHCA*, 2, pp. 580–694.

Santamaria, Àlvar, 'La expansión políticomilitar de la Corona de Aragón bajo la dirección de Jaime I', *X CHCA* (1979), 1, pp. 91–146.

‐ 'Comunidades Occitanas en la conquista y repoblación de Mallorca', *Jornades d'Estudis Històrics Locals*, 4 (1986), pp. 9–19.

Shideler, John, *A Medieval Noble Catalan Family: The Montcadas, 1000–1230*, Berkeley 1983.

Sobrequés, Santiago, *Els Barons de Catalunya*, Barcelona: Vicens Vives, 1989.

Soldevila, Ferran, *Ramon Berenguer IV el Sant*, Barcelona: Barcino, 1955.

‐ *Els Primers Temps de Jaume I*, Barcelona: Institut d'Estudis Catalans, 1968.

- *Vida de Jaume I el Conqueridor*, Barcelona: Aedos, 1969.
- *Jaume I, Pere el Gran*, Barcelona: Vicens Vives, 1985.
- *Pere el Gran*, 2 vols., Barcelona: Institut d'Estudis Catalans, 1995.

Soto i Company, Ricard, 'La porció de Nunó Sanç: repartiment i repoblació de les terres, del sudest de Mallorca', *Afers*, 18 (1994), pp. 347–65.

Suárez Fernández, Luis, 'Historiografía y Fuentes del reinado de Jaime I, desde 1909 hasta 1975', *X CHCA*, 1 (1979), pp. 313–40.

Swift, F. Darwin, *The Life and Times of James the First, the Conqueror, King of Aragon, Valencia and Majorca, Count of Barcelona and Urgel, Lord of Montpellier*, Oxford 1894.

Torres, Juan, *La reconquista de Murcia en 1266 por Jaime I de Aragón*, Murcia: Academia Alfonso X el Sabio, 1987.

Tourtoulon, Charles de, *Don Jaime I el Conquistador, rey de Aragón*, Valencia 1874 (re-ed. Valencia 1980).

Ubieto, Antonio, 'Navarra-Aragón y la idea imperial de Alfonso VII de Castilla', *Estudios de Edad Media de la Corona de Aragón*, 6 (1956), pp. 41–82.
- *Orígenes del Reino de Valencia. Cuestiones cronológicas sobre su reconquista*, Valencia: Anubar, 1975.
- 'La reconquista de Valencia y Murcia', *X CHCA*, 1 (1979), pp. 147–65.
- *Listas Episcopales Medievales*, 2 vols., Zaragoza 1989.

Vajay, Szabolcs de, 'Eudoquía Cómnena, abuela bizantina de Jaime el Conquistador', *X CHCA*, 2 (1980), pp. 611–31.

VauxdeCernay, Pierre des, *Histoire Albigeoise*, trans. P. Guebin and H. Maissonneuve, Paris 1951.

Ventura, Jordi, *Pere el Catòlic i Simó de Montfort*, Barcelona: Aedos, 1960.
- *Alfons el cast, el primer comterei*, Barcelona: Aedos, 1961.

Villanueva, Jaime, *Viage literario a las iglesias de España*, 22 vols., Madrid 1803–52.

Vincke, Johannes, *Staat und Kirche in Katalonien und Aragon während des Mittelalters*, Münster, 1931.
- 'Der Eheprozess Peters II. von Aragon (1206–1213)', *Spanische Forschungen der Görresgesellschaft*, 5 (1935), pp. 108–189.

Zurita, Jerónimo, *Anales de la Corona de Aragon*, 9 vols., ed. Ángel Canellas López, Zaragoza: Institución Fernando el Católico, 1975–80.

Glossary

Albacar – (Arabic Baqqār) Walled space adjoining a fort, tower, city, or castle either to corral and protect livestock or to serve as refuge during an attack.

Alcaid – (Arabic Qā'id) A military administrator, commander or governor.

Alfaquim – (Arabic Ḥakīm) Savant-physician, master of knowledge.

Algarrada – (Arabic 'arrādah) The light pole-framed traction trebuchet. A rotating-beam siege engine.

Aljama – Each local community of Muslims or Jews subject to the Christians in Spain, in its juridical personality as a semiautonomous corporation. Not the physical location (Burns-Chevedden, *Negotiating Cultures*, p.233).

Almajanech – It is synonymous of fenèvol in the text. It was perhaps of Islamic design.

Almogàvers – A formidable group of ferocious light-armed warriors. Mercenaries who formed a significant part of James's armies.

Almoixerif (Arabic Mushrif) – A treasurer or collector of taxes.

Bezants – In Valencia, the silver bezant equalled just a little more than three solidi. Approximately 370 seventy solidi made up a knight's annual revenue.

Bovatge – The tax to secure the peace in Catalonia, levied by James to fund his military campaigns.

Brigola – A large pole-framed, easily manoeuvrable, counterweight trebuchet.

Cafiz – A measure of grain.

Corts – (in Castilian, Cortes) Parliamentary assemblies. At James's time they were at their earliest stage of development.

Fenèvol – Neither a traction trebuchet (powered by teams pulling on ropes) nor the counterweight trebuchet (powered by the descent of a large pivoting mass) but an intermediate form, the hybrid trebuchet, utilizing both gravity and human power (Chevedden, 'Hybrid trebuchet', pp. 179–222).

Fueros – Laws, customs, or privileges of Aragon or other non-Catalan regions; or charters containing them.

Herbatge – A tax on the pasture of animals.

Honors – Baronial tenure in Aragon.

Jovate – A land measurement. The most common measurement was a fanecate (eight hundred and thirty-one square metres), six of which made a cafiz, and six cafizes made a jovate (Burns, *Islam under the Crusaders*, p. xxiv).

Manganel – Most probably a type of traction trebuchet (powered by people pulling ropes).

Mazmudin – Almohad gold coin originally worth one gold dinar.

Monedatge – (Castilian, Monedaje) A tax to secure the stability of coinage in Catalonia or in Aragon (where it is called monedaje).

Morabetin – Almoravid gold coin often valued at seven Barcelonan sous.

Paria – A tribute paid by the Saracens in return for protection.

Rais – (Arabic Ra'īs) Meaning a chief, the word applied to holders of a wide range of public offices, but James uses it in the sense of a Muslim governor.

Repartiment – The division and distribution of the lands after the conquest of Islamic cities, generally supervised by a corps of surveyors and distributors. The distributions were enregistered in a codex.

Tarida – Cargo ship which transported both men and horses.

Trebuchet – Here used for a large trestle-framed trebuchet that may have had either a fixed or a hinged counterweight attached to the short end of the rotating beam (Chevedden, 'Artillery', p.71).

Wālī – A Muslim governor.

Index